# IN SEARCH OF HUMAN NATURE

What is wrong with the West's 'scientific' picture of what and who we are? Was Thomas Hobbes right to sum up human life as 'solitary, poor, nasty, brutish, and short'? In this magisterial new work, biologist Mary Clark delves deep into the roots of human nature, offering a timely re-evaluation of the basic attributes all humans share.

*In Search of Human Nature* offers a wide-ranging and holistic view of human nature from all perspectives: biological, historical and sociological. Clark takes the most recent data from disparate fields – paleontology, primatology, ethology, genetics, neurosciences, physiology, anthropology, linguistics, ecological psychology, archaeology, mythology, fine arts, history and conflict resolution – and weaves them together with clarifying anecdotes and thought-provoking images to challenge outmoded Western beliefs with hopeful new insights. Beginning with the distortions intrinsic to analogizing human behaviour with that of 'intelligent' machines, Clark tackles an astonishing array of problems, from how environment and experience shape the brain to the ways we think about identity, meaning and conflict, to peaceful processes for healing and adaptive social change.

Ending with modern-day examples of successfully changing communities, *In Search of Human Nature* offers a firmly grounded reason to be optimistic about humankind's future.

**Mary E. Clark** was formerly Drucie French Cumbie Chair in Conflict Resolution at George Mason University. Her previous books include *Contemporary Biology* and *Ariadne's Thread: The Search for New Modes of Thinking*.

# IN SEARCH OF HUMAN NATURE

*Mary E. Clark*

Routledge
Taylor & Francis Group

LONDON AND NEW YORK

First published 2002
by Routledge
11 New Fetter Lane, London EC4P 4EE

Simultaneously published in the USA and Canada
by Routledge
29 West 35th Street, New York, NY 10001

*Routledge is an imprint of the Taylor & Francis Group*

©2002 Mary E. Clark

Typeset in Galliard by Taylor & Francis Books Ltd
Printed and bound in Great Britain by TJ International Ltd, Padstow, Cornwall

*British Library Cataloguing in Publication Data*
A catalogue record for this book is available from the British Library

*Library of Congress Cataloging in Publication Data*
A catalog record for this book has been requested

ISBN 0–415–28659–X (hbk)
ISBN 0–415–28660–3 (pbk)

This book is fondly dedicated to John W. Burton, an Australian curmudgeon and brilliant pioneer theorist – and practitioner – of conflict resolution. John, you have been the beacon that focused my efforts, told me where to search and what to look for. Your intuitive guidance has been incredibly valuable. Thank you enormously!

# CONTENTS

CONTENTS

# ILLUSTRATIONS

## Tables

## Figures

# ACKNOWLEDGMENTS

To paraphrase John Donne, "No author is an Iland, intire of its selfe; every author is a peece of the Continent, a part of the maine." And so it is with this author. This book is my attempt to put into a meaningful story the ideas and work of countless people, some no longer with us, many still very much so. They are not to blame for how I have interpreted their efforts.

During the decade of this book's gestation dozens of people have provided helpful inputs, responded to queries, clarified obscure points, and read various drafts of a huge, complicated text. They have been a diverse and constructive group of friends and colleagues. Dedicated critics of the whole book in its various stages include Shari Anker (Biologist-Educator), Jean Maria Arrigo (Military Ethicist), Estelle Bern (Psychological Counselor), Elise Boulding (Peace Activist and Author), Harry Heft (Ecological Psychologist), Linda Holler (Scholar of Religion and Mind), Michelle LeBaron (Scholar of Intercultural Conflict), Michael Nagler (Mythologist and Gandhian Scholar), Bill Nichols (Professor of Literature), Kathleen Shepherd (International Conflict Resolution Practitioner), Greg Smith (Sustainability Educator), Anita Taylor (Professor of Communication and Women's Studies), Mary Taylor (Mammologist and Museum Director), and Ted Warren (Classical Philosopher).

In addition, the following have provided valuable comments on one or more chapters: Hans Guggenheim (Humanist, Artist), Mary Midgley (Moral Philosopher), Alec Panchen (Evolutionary Biologist), Hal Saunders (Diplomat and Peace-Maker), and Mary Jane Warren (Social Psychologist).

Enthusiastic supporters who are familiar with the manuscript include: Carolyne Ashton (Researcher in Post-trauma Education in Healing Countries), John Baldwin (Researcher in International Development), George Besch (Activist and Film-maker), John Burling (Psychologist/Educator), Rose Carruthers (Illustrator), Trina Cleland (Social Researcher), Darci Collins (Nurse), Jayne Docherty (Researcher in Intercultural Conflict Resolution), Gail Hoelzle (Bookstore Owner and Local Activist), Bonnie McCay (Researcher of Common Property Regimes), Evelyn Pinkerton (Researcher of Common Property Regimes), Diane Rocheleau (Researcher in International

Development), Paul Rothkrug (Activist), Mary Evelyn Tucker and John Grim (Researchers in Environmental Ethics and Religion), Hugo van der Merwe (Researcher in Peace and Reconciliation in South Africa), and Sandra A. Wawrytko (Asian Philosopher).

The following are some of the many people with whom I have shared and discussed my ideas over many years: Peter Alpert (Ecologist and Science Philosopher), Chet Bowers (Environmental Educator), Constance Brown (Quaker Activist), William Caspary (Deweyite Expert), Clifford Cobb (Generator of Alternative Economic Indicators), Herman Daly (Ecological Economist), Ellen Dissanayake (Researcher in Origins and Meaning of Art), John Goldthorpe (Broadcaster), Henry Janssen (Political Scientist), Albert Johnson (Ecologist), Dick Jacobs (Educator and Politician), Saul Lemkowitz (Dutch Engineering Professor), Doug McKenzie-Mohr (Social Psychologist), John McDonald (Multi-Track Diplomatist), Dick Norgaard (Ecological Economist), Glenn Northcutt (Brain Evolutionist), David Orr (Environmental Educator), Steve Roeder (Concerned Physicist), Lionel Rothkrug (Religious Historian), S.A. Shah (Indian Forester and Philosopher), Peter Söderbaum (Swedish Economics Ethicist), and John Todd (Ecological Inventor).

In addition to the above, I would like to thank the following persons whose contributions they will readily perceive: my sister and brother-in-law; my nephews and their families; and my many friends in the delightful town of Cottage Grove, Oregon, where I live. I especially thank my nephew, Bill McConnell, a human geographer, for his enduring interest in and support of his aunt's developing ideas. He has been a central blessing in the writing of this book. I am also deeply grateful to Peter Barnes for his generous support of the Common Counsel Foundation and its writing retreat at the idyllic Mesa Refuge in northern California where I spent two peaceful month-long sojourns processing my ideas.

Finally, I want to thank those who turned my efforts into a final product: my artist, Ms. Michele Lukowski, who converted crude sketches into delightful illustrations; the Reference Staff at the University of Oregon Library, for much intricate searching; my neighbors Jacki and Jim Lukowski for patiently sending and receiving my e-mail messages; my friend, Fran Ross, who rescued me on my computer, often and always cheerfully; and Tony Bruce and his associates at Routledge, especially Carol Baker, for the tender care needed to bring an enormously complex book to the light of day.

I thank all of you, from the bottom of my heart. None of you is responsible for either the interpretations presented or any errors that remain; those belong entirely to me.

# A WORD TO THE READER

This book came to be written because my students, along with many others, were searching for answers to the seemingly overwhelming problems that we human beings have created on our planet. The psychological exhaustion they experienced at the enormity of these problems was followed by despair at their seeming inevitability. Students enrolled in a course called Our Global Future at San Diego State, which dealt in depth with those problems, regularly would say at the end, "Well, you've shown us all the problems, but none of the solutions." My quip in reply was usually, "Now you know the problems, you've become part of the solution." It was a lame answer, a cop-out, and I knew it.

Another frequent comment that expressed their feelings of hopelessness was, "You just can't change human nature." They really believed human history was being inexorably driven by a set of biologically grounded, rather nasty behavioral traits. Their belief was grounded in the whole Western world view that most had been immersed in since birth. History focussed on powerful men constantly engaged in violent struggles with each other. It never mentioned peaceful societies, nor the lives of women. Economics painted a world of perpetual scarcity where competition was inevitable – and was also the only route to more efficient utilization of resources. It never explored successful societies that had managed their resources in common, without undue competition.

In science, Darwin's innocuous phrase "survival of the fittest" was turned into a biological war of all-against-all, an idea made concrete by the invention of the concept of the "selfish gene." Psychology and political science, both obedient to Enlightenment philosophy, mistook emotions as unfortunate left-over animal traits in need of being tightly controlled by a stern, paternalistic Reason. And the whole of science, for 200 years or more, has been grounded in a linear view of causes-and-effects analogous to those found in machines. All entities, even human nature, and all events, from the evolution of the universe to the behavior of modern societies, could ultimately be understood by dissecting them into smaller and smaller pieces.

Though the cracks in all these assumptions are now evident and growing wider daily, the institutions based on them – especially their view of an individualistic, self-centered, naturally aggressive and competitive human nature – reinforce these beliefs in people's everyday lives. Western society begins its indoctrination early, in school. Kids are surrounded by competition; they see it in the classroom, on TV, in sports. They are taught early to *want* and *consume* for status, that income "counts." And every textbook they use incorporates and reinforces these assumptions. Politicians tacitly assume them in arguing public policy. In fact, the whole political process is couched in a "win/lose" framework. Conflicts are settled by votes, not violence, but though the tools are different, the logic of the process is the same.

My professional life has spanned two supposedly disparate disciplines: biology and conflict resolution. I was forced to bring them together, to look long and hard at how Western assumptions about human nature had affected *both* disciplines. I began twelve years ago to explore the growing cracks being opened up by maverick thinkers in many disciplines while teaching a course I called Mind and Conflict in a graduate program at George Mason University. It was to be the beginning of this book, of building a new "theory of human nature."

It has proved to be a hugely difficult task, far harder than I had supposed. I already knew most of the central ideas I wanted to address. One problem was that there was just too much information on each topic, much of it pertinent but specialized and complex. But even more problematic was the sequence of chapters. Each piece of the story only made sense in relation to the whole picture of human nature that was forming in my head. How could the reader be helped to make sense of all the pieces as they were presented separately?

This book is, like every book of its kind, a compromise between detailed arguments and an overall gestalt, a coherent whole story. The many years it took to write were needed to arrive at the best compromise I could manage. Imagine a huge table onto which someone has dumped a million-piece jigsaw puzzle, and your task is to sort them out, to put them into seemingly likely categories, then try to fit each group together without losing sight of the connections among all the groups. Meantime, as you are working, people keep creating (in the form of new books and articles) *more* pieces to be slotted in. You also realize that some pieces do not belong at all – or worse, that there are two or more alternative pieces for one spot in the puzzle, supposedly only one of which can be correct, though they all make sense.

The pieces represent the ideas, hypotheses, facts, data, arguments, and interpretations generated about human nature by thousands of scholars and philosophers and other creative thinkers. Some pieces are historical, others scientific. Some are logical arguments, others are hunches, insights, myths, and personal stories. The one thing they have in common is they all say something, some opinion or observation or parable, about the nature of "human nature."

In a single book, I could not possibly consider every piece, nor discuss every point of disagreement. I had to make choices. I had to start, tentatively, with my own broad outline of what was my "best guess" about human nature, based on over seventy years of lived experience, much reading, and some thirty years of teaching in two disciplines in several universities in three countries. The more I have read since, the more convinced I've become that my "best guess" is pretty close to who we really are, certainly much closer than the rather unpleasant Hobbesian view on which so much of Western society's self-image is based.

I make no claims as to the picture of human nature I present being the complete story. Very likely, that will forever be beyond our species' capability. No one mind can grasp and organize all there is to know and say about human nature – which is what makes us such an endlessly fascinating subject. Rather, what I offer here is a more optimistic working model of "Who We Think We Are", or perhaps I should say, "Who *I* Think We Are". It is one that, while certainly incomplete and imperfect, I believe opens up many new approaches to solving the multiple crises that beset us as the new millennium gets underway.

With regard to the style of this work, I have tried to avoid the specialized jargon largely understood only by experts in particular disciplines. For the sake of readability, I have not presented every side of controversial topics. The side (or sides) I do present I have consciously selected. My goal has been to produce a single coherent picture that makes sense as a whole, not to argue over details of every point along the way. This of course means my picture is biased. But to think usefully about anything at all necessitates that kind of selecting. For the evidence I do present, there are bibliographic citations and, from time to time in the notes, a brief discussion of alternative viewpoints. To humanize the text I have also incorporated concrete examples about real people, as well as personal anecdotal information, to give flesh-and-blood to my story.

I trust my readers will find themselves stimulated to reflect further on their own ideas about human nature. I believe that the social adjustments needed to correct some of the worst of our self-inflicted threats can only come about through a big change in the gestalt with which we view ourselves and the world. It will only happen successfully through participatory dialogue among a consciously aware citizenry – in every part of the globe – where we mutually discover new ways of "seeing" ourselves that, in turn, open up new directions and goals for human society to pursue in the future. To entice you into this huge tome, I will tell you now that I believe our true natures are far more lovable and positive than we in the West currently believe them to be. There is indeed great hope for us after all. Overleaf I offer quotations from two very different, both highly eminent, contemporary thinkers who share my optimism. Their words set the stage for what is to follow.

It is still my firm conviction that human nature is essentially compassionate, gentle. That is the predominant feature of human nature.... I believe that our underlying or fundamental nature is gentleness, and intelligence is a later development. And I think that if human ability, that human intelligence, develops in an unbalanced way, without being properly counterbalanced with compassion, then it can become destructive. It can lead to disaster.

But, I think it's important to recognize that if human conflicts are created by misuse of human intelligence, we can also utilize our intelligence to find ways and means to overcome these conflicts. When human intelligence and human goodness or affection are used together, all human actions become constructive.

His Holiness, The Dalai Lama (1988: 54, 55)

Modernism has cultivated a widespread belief that humans are by nature greedy, individualistic, and aggressive, and that progress depends on a competitive process by which the strong displace and destroy the weak. Conversely, this belief system suggests that cooperation is not in our nature and if it were, it would be a barrier to progress.

Fortunately, we don't have to look very hard to realize that compassion, cooperation, even love, are the foundation of most human relationships and indeed, are an essential underpinning of civilization. It seems self-evident, therefore, that these capacities are at least as inherent in our nature as is our well-demonstrated capacity for greed, violence, and destruction. It is a matter of which capacities we choose to nurture in ourselves, our children, and the larger society.

David C. Korten (2001: 51)

# INTRODUCTION
## Framing the problem

> If we think of the world as separate from us and constituted of disjointed parts to be manipulated with the aid of calculation we will try to become separate people whose main motivation with regard to each other and to nature is also manipulation and calculation. But if we can obtain an intuitive and imaginative feeling of the whole world as constituting an implicate order that is also enfolded in us, we will sense ourselves to be one with this world. We will no longer be satisfied merely to manipulate it technically to our supposed advantage, but we will feel genuine love for it. We will want to care for it, as we would for anyone who is close to us and therefore enfolded in us as inseparable part.
>
> David Bohm *

Who do we think we are? What is human nature really like? That first question actually embodies several queries, depending where one puts the emphasis. "*Who* do we think we are?" implies a question of our general identity: what sort of beings are we? "Who do *we* think *we* are?" implies a select group that has a special interest in itself. "Who do we *think* we are?" suggests that we are curious about our own self-constructed image of ourselves, realizing it is more an assumption than a complete picture of whoever we "really" are.

Each of these three phrasings of our original question is important for our project, the goal of which is to inquire into our self-understanding and explore the role it plays in our behavior. The answer to the first phrasing seems easy. We are human beings, *Homo sapiens*. But what exactly does that mean? What defines the nature of our species? The second phrasing suggests it is important to know who is asking the question, because not all people who call themselves "human" would give the same answer. It depends on which group is doing the thinking. And that leads directly to what is implied in the third phrasing, namely that we do not absolutely know who or what we are; we can only have theories about ourselves.

---

* The source of this quote escapes both me and several knowledgable colleagues. We all agree that it is definitely David Bohm, but where exactly he said it remains a mystery. Important works that develop this concept include Bohm (1980 and 1999).

1

Every society, every culture has its own theory of human nature, which it takes as *the* truth. And to complicate our lives even more, every person within a given culture has a slightly different "take" on what she or he thinks people are like. Aspects of our individual theories of human nature turn up in most of our conversations, our books, our myths, and our opinions. We are constantly explaining ourselves to each other, comparing views on what human beings are like and why they act as they do.

Why is understanding ourselves so important to us that it consumes this much of our attention? Why do we need a "theory" of who we are anyway? And why can't we all agree on it? Why are there such big differences among groups of humans in their self-perceptions? If we're all really one species, why don't we see eye-to-eye about it?

This book seeks answers to these questions, especially the last two. It addresses how we think and what we feel. It explores the limits of our minds to comprehend reality and the extent of our control over our feelings. It shows why it is so hard to "change one's mind," to see the world from someone else's point of view. As the twenty-first century begins, gaining this level of self-understanding about our nature as human beings seems critical to our species' continued survival. My hope is to persuade people to see that there are other sets of spectacles with which to view the world than the ones they have been taught to see through, and that sometimes these other aids to vision can solve problems in ways they otherwise might never have thought of.

Two fundamental ideas – two premises – underlie the arguments that are to follow. The first is that how we humans "see" reality, what we comprehend, is always constructed. Our world view – the working "truth" we use as a map for living – is always culturally created, and it is always a selected and partial understanding. Yet however imperfect, some kind of map is essential for a society's survival. Nevertheless, as circumstances change over time, that map must be revised if a society is to continue to exist. That is how the human species adapts.

The second premise is that today a single world view is becoming increasingly dominant around the planet – that of the West (Figure 0.1). Such a premise makes certain deep assumptions about how the world should be viewed that profoundly affect both our understanding of human nature and the way we treat the world that supports us. I believe, along with many others, that these assumptions are leading to dangerous, indeed pathological, consequences for all humans. There is therefore a need at the outset to grasp what a world view is and to perceive what is entailed in adapting it to meet new, changing conditions.[1]

## World views: constructed gestalts

The empirical basis of objective science has thus nothing "absolute" about it. Science does not rest upon rock-bottom. The bold structure of its theories rise, as it were, above a swamp. It is like a building

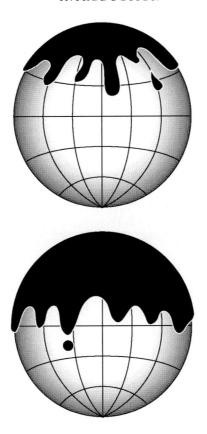

*Figure 0.1* Spreading of the Western world view
The spreading of the Western world view over the past 200 years is pictured here using the advertising image of a paint company, whose neon signs show a red blob of paint spreading down over the globe, with the motto: "Sherwin-Williams covers the Earth."
*Source*: Original art rendered from author's sketch by Michele Lukowski

> erected on piles. The piles are driven from above into the swamp, but not to any natural or "given" base; and when we cease our attempts to drive piles into a deeper layer, it is not because we have reached firm ground. We simply stop when we are satisfied that they are firm enough to carry the structure, at least for the time being.[2]

In this description of objective science (which grew out of the Western world view), philosopher Karl Popper visually describes for us the structure of a world view – in fact, of *any* world view. All human thought, all our knowledge, ultimately is grounded in certain "givens" – certain inescapable beliefs and assumptions. On them we construct our model of reality or "truth" that allows us to function with confidence, more or less automatically.

3

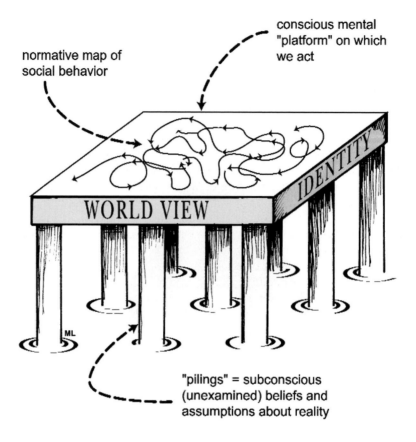

*Figure 0.2* How we frame our world perception
A model for how we frame our understanding of the world. Our conscious norms, institutions, and expectations are based on the underlying beliefs and assumptions we make about the nature of reality.

*Source*: Original figure by author appeared in Clark (1995: 65); redrawn by Michele Lukowski. Used with kind permission of Blackwell Publishers

The English essayist, William Hazlitt, once observed, "Without the aid of prejudice and custom I should not be able to find my way across the room."[3] Walking across the room was Hazlitt's metaphor for living through the events of everyday life. We each make a working model of the universe, which is based on "prejudice." This is inescapable. People selectively see, take in, and interpret what they need to know, ignoring the huge amount of extraneous information that constantly bombards them. And it is "custom," provided by the culture we live in, that tells us what to pay attention to, and how to interpret it. We are all biased in this way; we are all inevitably "ethnocentric."

This conceptualization of a world view is shown in Figure 0.2. The beliefs and assumptions by which an individual makes sense of experience are hidden deep within the language and traditions of the surrounding society. They are the gestalt – the pilings, the vision of reality – on which rest the customs, the norms, and the institutions of a given culture. They are tacitly communicated through origin myths, narrative stories, linguistic metaphors, and cautionary tales. They set the ground rules for shared cultural meaning.

These subconscious beliefs are sacred, a kind of religion or faith. One's place in society, indeed often one's very survival, depends on accepting them. On top of those subconscious pilings are conscious traditions and institutions that form the normative map of behavior which makes complex social living possible. Is it any wonder that we have such a powerful tendency to cling to them, to defend them, to find it painful in the extreme when they are threatened and we are forced to give them up and adopt new ones? Social change is not easy, especially when the changes are not superficial changes in our institutions, but profound ones touching on our deepest beliefs.

A couple of examples of differences that can exist between cultures will help. One that may seem trivial, yet which can cause profound misunderstandings, is the difference in assumptions made about eye contact. In Western societies, we assume a person who fails to "look me in the eye" is untrustworthy, hiding something, feels guilty or ashamed. In some other societies, however, it is taken as a sign of rudeness, of intrusion, to stare directly into another's eyes. It is a threat, an invasion of their personal space. (When Westerners ride packed together in elevators, they unconsciously avoid eye contact with strangers as a way of increasing the feeling of space around them.) During cross-cultural encounters, especially during conflict negotiations, such social "errors" can cause serious misunderstandings.

A completely different kind of cultural difference occurs in the area of oceanic navigation, where it is the mental representation of the physical world that varies. What is happening as the ship sails from one place to another can be envisioned very differently. In the West, sailors have an image of the ship moving between two fixed points; a knowledge of direction (by observing celestial bodies and using a compass) and of the speed of the ship are critical for finding their destination. Among Micronesians, however, sailors travel without maps or compasses across long stretches of open ocean, from island to island. Their perception of what is happening is quite different. For them, their ship and the stars are stationary and it is the islands that move. They navigate by lines of stars, all rising or setting over the island of their destination, using an imaginary island to triangulate on.[4]

Even when Westerners grasp the trigonometric principles involved in Micronesian navigation, it is still almost impossible for them to envision intuitively how the Micronesians "see" what is going on physically. The fundamental preconceptions about the world held by different cultures provide very different understandings of "reality" – and it often takes an enormous gestalt shift to move from one set of preconceptions to another.

This book critically examines the gestalt underlying the increasingly dominant Western world view. Both its science and its beliefs about human nature are grounded in its tacitly held understanding of reality. An alternative gestalt, another way of picturing reality, is presented alongside one that I believe permits a healthier, more humane conceptualization of "who we are," as well as a better way of thinking about Nature overall. I introduce them in metaphoric form here, as basis for discussion in later chapters.

### The "Billiard Ball" Gestalt

One of the most basic images of reality on which the Western world view rests is that all entities in the universe are isolated, discrete objects that have distinct boundaries, much like we imagine atoms to be. Indeed, the "atomistic universe" would be a good label. The Western view of human or animal societies is that they are simply aggregations of "social atoms." Yet for most of us except physicists it is hard to mentally envision atoms interacting. So I have chosen the metaphor of billiard balls, a highly Newtonian model, because so much of Western thought is in fact based on this way of "seeing" the universe. They are masses in vectored motion, exchanging energy with each other at every collision, some of which is dissipated into the air creating the familiar "crack!" sounds of the billiard parlor and pool hall. The effect of the impact of each moving ball can be calculated from Newton's laws of motion. The balls are discrete, bounded objects; they have no permanent relationships; theirs is an individualistic, "atomistic" universe. (Figure 0.3).

One can think of many sports for which the same physical rules are evident. Bowling comes to mind. So does archery, where bowstring tautness, air resistance, and wind speed combine to determine the flight pattern of an arrow. These are all examples of interactions taking place among a set of "independent" objects. Of course, few billiard players or bowlers or archers think consciously about the laws of motion. But they do intuitively come to understand the relationships between objects in general Newtonian terms as they acquire skill in their sport.

What happened in the West was that this same understanding of events as interactions between independent objects – so appropriate for a game of billiards – was extrapolated to all events, everywhere in the universe. From the physicists' atoms to the astronomers' heavenly bodies, events could be understood as interactions taking place between discrete, separate objects. Force and mass explained everything, and once you knew the position and momentum of every particle in the universe, you could, in theory, run history forward (or backward) in a predictable manner.

Though this idea, now known as the Laplacean fallacy,[5] is no longer believed by physicists, whose more recent theories of quantum mechanics and chaos have made events in the universe seem much less deterministic, it is by-and-large still the way Westerners frame their everyday views of the world. Objects

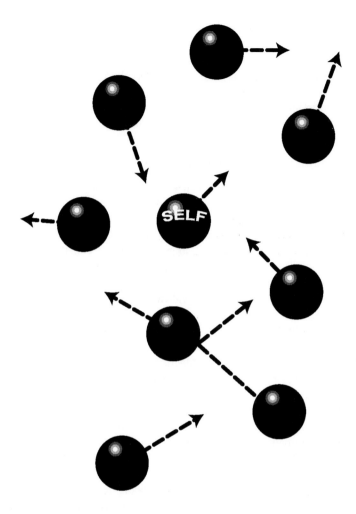

*Figure 0.3* The "Billiard Ball" Gestalt: an individualistic universe

The Billiard Ball Gestalt of the universe depicts isolated objects moving independently and colliding randomly with each other. It models the cause-and-effect, linear events of an atomistic or individualistic world view. The "Self" is discrete and separate from the whole.

*Source*: Original art rendered from author's sketch by Michele Lukowski

have boundaries. We think of "a tree" as separate from the soil and air in which it grows, ignoring the unbroken chain of molecules it is constantly exchanging with both. We think of a river as an "object," but it is in fact untold millions of water molecules in motion, some evaporating, some running into the ground, perhaps to re-enter the river later.

The objects in the world around us, both animate and inanimate, are not discretely bounded. They change. They have histories that are not independent of the histories of other objects around them. Yet Western thinking – while acknowledging this – tends in everyday life to prefer the precision of argument offered by a "Billiard Ball" universe. It is relatively easy to frame an event in mathematical models if only one or two objects (or conditions) are varying. It makes the science of "controlled experiments" possible.

So pervasive is this way of thinking, it has become *de rigueur* for those who study human societies and human nature. Economics, psychology, ethnology, and all the other disciplines that attempt to explain human behavior are now lumped together as the "social sciences." And in the standard tradition of the Billiard Ball (or "atomistic" or "individualistic") universe, human beings are imagined very much like independent, isolated, bounded objects having a variety of cause-and-effect "collisions" with each other. Friendly collisions, amorous collisions, deceitful collisions, angry collisions, collaborative collisions.

It is largely based on this image that theories of a self-centered human nature have been constructed. Unlike billiard balls, however, we are viewed as living in a world of scarcity, and must compete during our collisions. We thus are envisioned as "rational objects," game theorists, calculating contract makers, each out for herself. Our pro-social feelings are merely a form of self-deception to cover up the fact that our selfish genes are really driving each of us to serve what is in our own best interests. We "exploit" others for our own individual benefit; that's how we survive.

I have put this rather bluntly, yet a surprising number of Western societies are grounded on just such beliefs, with the United States as the most extreme case. Its view of human society demands that people compete (for jobs, status) to survive; it also expects they will try to be free riders (go on welfare), or cheat (lie, steal); and so it protects itself by threats of severe punishment (homelessness, punitive fines, harsh jail sentences) for those who don't "measure up."

The Billiard Ball Gestalt of the universe thus closes off many useful ways of thinking about ourselves and solving many of our seemingly intractable problems that an alternative gestalt might open up. I now offer such an alternative.

### The "Indra's Net" Gestalt

When one moves away from Western-dominated parts of the world one discovers people who perceive very different "realities." In one common variant, everything in the universe is seen to belong to a single, interconnected whole. Each culture has its own myth or symbolic image for expressing the essence of this gestalt. The one I have chosen as metaphor is Indra's Net. The image comes from Mahayana Buddhist tradition, from around 2000 ya (years ago).

8

Indra was the chief god of the Aryans who overran the Indian subcontinent beginning around 5000 ya and wove their own myths with those of the local Dravidians, giving rise to the earliest, Vedic form of Hinduism. Indra remained part of the south Asian pantheon ever after, but his net seems to be an embellishment by the followers of Buddha, the Awakened One. In Figure 0.4, I present my remembered image of what I believe was a symbolic representation of Indra's Net.[6] I take the figure to be Indra, seated on the universe over which he has cast his jeweled net. A description of its meaning follows:

> The principle of all things reflecting or "containing" one another is … symbolized by the so-called "Net of Indra," which is an imaginary net of jewels that reflect each other with the reflections of each jewel containing reflections of all the jewels, each of which reflections also contains the reflections of all the jewels, ad infinitum.[7]

As Thomas Cleary, the translator of *The Flower Ornament Scripture*, from which the above quote is taken, explains, the whole belief of Buddhism is a philosophy of the universal interdependence of all that exists as parts of a sacred whole, often referred to as Buddha's "teaching body," or *Dharmakaya*. "All things, all beings, mind and space itself are bodies of Buddha."[8] No thing (object, entity, concept, phenomenon) exists in reality because the cosmos is an interdependent whole. He explains this interdependence of all phenomena further.

> Their interdependent existence and emptiness of own being are two sides of the same coin…. The noumenal nature, or emptiness, of our phenomenon, being the same as that of all phenomena, is said to at once pervade and contain all phenomena; and as this is true of one, so is it true of all. Furthermore, the interdependence of phenomena means that ultimately one depends on all and all on one, whether immediately or remotely; therefore, the existence of all is considered an intrinsic part of the existence of one, and vice versa.[9]

Indra's Net is therefore a metaphor for a world of connectedness, of interacting, interdependent entities, whether they be human bodies, an economy or other social arrangement, an ecosystem, or a galaxy. Within each entity, the parts are likewise interdependent, and it is their reciprocal interactions that keep the whole universe functioning. Indeed, each part, each entity *contains* the whole, *is* the whole, and nothing can survive apart from the whole. No entity is unconnected to, unaffected by, all the others. There are no discrete "billiard balls."

Writes David Standlea, a student of the applications of Buddhist thinking to the modern Western world:

*Figure 0.4* The "Indra's Net" Gestalt: a connected universe

The "Indra's Net" Gestalt of the universe, depicted by a jeweled net where each jewel is connected to and hence reflects upon all the others. No one entity can be its discrete, autonomous "Self" independent of its connectedness with the whole of reality.

*Source*: Original art rendered from author's sketch by Michele Lukowski

Indra's net is not merely a quaint poetic image derived from an ancient Buddhist *Sūtra*; it is a symbol for a heightened consciousness of the world and interlocking life force we abide within. It implies a world view prompting an open-ended compassion toward mutually dependent life forms.[10]

Buddhist teaching, as captured in the Gestalt of Indra's Net, leads to a very different theory of human nature. It rejects notions of competition, of "self," and of dominance over, while embracing the need for constantly seeking harmonious relations with all-that-is. "Winning" is an alien concept in Buddhist thinking, where the purpose of life is to discover meaning, not to achieve power. The conquest, if it can be called that, is directed inward, over oneself.

### *A summary comparison*

These two gestalts are distinct, in the extreme; essentially they are mutually exclusive. The universe appears either as a single, interlocking net of mutually dependent phenomena, or as a mixed assemblage of discrete objects colliding with each other as they follow their independent trajectories. Certainly neither one can be an accurate picture of the whole of reality, though each metaphoric image is recognizable in certain aspects of the universe. Competitive struggles are observed in nature, as well as within and between groups of human actors. Equally, we see examples of harmonious interdependence among planetary bodies in space, and the more we understand about the complex interactions among ecosystems, the more they resemble an exquisitely complex set of multiple feedback interactions, a good approximation to Indra's Net. But how well does each describe human nature?

In Table 0.1, I summarize succinctly the consequences of each gestalt, especially when applied to our expectations about human nature. The sequence in the Table roughly follows the path to be taken in later chapters, as indicated in parentheses. We begin with (A) the overall universe and its impact on scientific theories. Next comes (B) Darwinian evolution, especially as it applies to primates. This is followed by (C) expectations of the human psyche. And finally comes (D) the kinds of social beliefs and organizations that each gestalt promotes. Three broad observations emerge.

First, the beliefs a society holds about the universe and about human nature in particular tend to *create* the very behavior they *predict*. How we see the world *does* shape who we are. World views tend to be self-fulfilling prophecies when it comes to human nature. This raises a cautionary warning about the validity of scientific studies on human behavior conducted by Western scientists on Western subjects. The scientists' cherished hypotheses will predict the behaviors they do in fact find, "proving them correct." No matter how "objective" the study, it cannot overcome the biases of the entire milieu in which it is conducted.

*Table 0.1*    Contrasting two different world-view gestalts. How the Billiard Ball and Indra's Net Gestalts frame the world at four different levels of "seeing"

| | *A*<br>*Universal perspective (see Chs. I, II)* | *B*<br>*Evolutionary perspective (see Chs. I, II, III, IV)* | *C*<br>*Psychological perspective (see Chs. V, VI, VII)* | *D*<br>*Consequences for social perspectives (see Chs. VII, VIII, IX, X, XI)* |
|---|---|---|---|---|
| Billiard Ball Gestalt | Discrete, bounded objects | Competition for survival among isolated individuals | Self-centered, me-first | Power-based struggle; hierarchy natural |
| | Atomistic; individualistic | "Winning matters" | Based on cognitive intelligence and deception<br>Identity insecure, self-created | Need for social controls to suppress violence<br>Rule of law; retributive justice |
| Indra's Net Gestalt | Blurred, fuzzy objects, in a continuous universe | Interrelations with surroundings essential for survival | Belonging and attachment are first priority | Order of custom; contextual justice aimed at reconciliation |
| | Everything interconnected | "Fitting-in matters" | Emphasis on feelings, compassion<br>Identity through social relationships | |

The second observation is in the form of a rhetorical question and its answer. If neither of these gestalts is a truly accurate picture of reality, why should we bother with them at all? The answer, briefly, is because the whole of reality is far too vast and complex for us to get a mental grasp of all of it, and so we must create a selected, partial image, some metaphoric gestalt, in order to think about it. We weave an *Ideenkleid*, a tissue of ideas (*Ideenkleider* are what Einstein once called "thought experiments"). We construct a working model of reality, an "hypothesis," inevitably simplified and full of "prejudice" and "custom," that allows us to "walk across the room" of life. Yet no matter how often we modify our image of reality, according to experience and more thought, it still remains a theory, forever partial and incomplete.

I chose two distinctly different gestalts in order to demonstrate both the obvious incompleteness of either one as an *absolute* or *final* picture of reality, and to show how powerfully whatever metaphor or gestalt is chosen influences the actual behavior of people. As Mary Catherine Bateson once said, when complaining that others spoke of the Gaia hypothesis as "merely a metaphor": "Metaphors are *never* 'merely'."[11] They *are* how we think, and especially how we communicate what we think.

The third observation is how mentally difficult it is for the human mind to flip back and forth from one view of reality to another, from one set of beliefs about human nature to another. As the standard textbook example of shifting gestalts shows, once you've fixed the old hag's face in your mind it is terribly hard to see in the same physical image the entirely different side view of a young woman's head (see Figure 0.5). Changing our deepest beliefs, those "pilings driven into the swamp" that underlie our world view require us to shake up the kaleidoscope of our collective mind and rearrange the facts – the pieces of colored glass out of which we construct reality – into a new, more adaptive pattern.

*Figure 0.5* Shifting gestalts: "young or old?"
This picture, conceived by E.G. Boring, an American psychologist, is on display at the San Francisco Exploratorium. It is a typical example of how the same image can be interpreted in two quite different ways. Hint: locate the eye in each of the two gestalts.

*Source*: Redrawn by Michele Lukowski, with kind permission, © 1999, Exploratorium, www.exploratorium.edu

As suggested at the beginning of this Introduction, the human species faces enormous crises, both environmental and societal, that demand some changes in the ways we do things and especially in how we relate to each other. Such change in our world view, in our "way of seeing the world," is how we human beings adapt. Being able to change in this way brought our ancestors through the Pleistocene. Yet as just demonstrated, changing our fundamental assumptions, our basic "take" on the world, is not easy. Those groups of people in the past who remained blind to coming crises – despite obvious signs – became extinct. They refused to "see." It remains the same today. Once we have a "map of the world" fixed in our heads we find it enormously hard to take it apart and reconstruct it. As Murray Gell-Mann has said: "When thinking, we tend to cling tenaciously to our schemata and even twist new information to conform to them." The story he tells goes like this:

> Many years ago, two physicists associated with the Aspen Center for Physics were climbing in the Maroon Bells Wilderness near Aspen, Colorado. While descending, they lost their bearings and came down on the south side of the mountains, instead of the north side near Aspen. They looked below them and saw what they identified as Crater Lake, which they would have spotted from the trail leading home. One of them remarked, however, that there was a dock on the lake, which Crater Lake does not possess. The other physicist replied, "They must have built it since we left this morning".... It took them a couple of days to get home.[12]

If it is so easy for supposedly open-minded scientists to ignore what they have seen with their own eyes, how much easier is it for the rest of us to refuse "to see the obvious," to doubt, to distort, or to simply dismiss. Yet the magnitude of the crises (and probable crises) that are building up before our eyes, and the degree of change they require from us if catastrophes are to be avoided, demand that we understand how human beings can peaceably create the necessary change. This, in turn, requires a deeper understanding of human nature and human behavior than most of us possess. The purpose of this book is to offer insights that I believe can increase greatly our understanding and open up paths to the needed adaptive change process. But first, a list of some of the critical crises that are clearly on the horizon may persuade us to begin thinking and acting *now*, before one or more of them is upon us.

## Crises in the making

Earth today increasingly is showing the impact of a burgeoning *Homo sapiens* community. During the past half century, our global population doubled, the air over the world's cities became polluted, and toxic substances seeped into more and more underground aquifers, poisoning streams. Fossil fuel consumption increased enormously; so did extinctions of various species, and the destruction of forests. Mostly unknown, or unnoticed, in 1950, these environmental problems are now commonplace. Despite some modest attempts to slow these trends, however, not a single one has been stopped or reversed. The response has been half-hearted, at best.[13]

Meanwhile, many old social problems have continued to worsen and new ones have emerged. Most evident globally is the ever-widening gap between the minority of wealthy and the majority of those struggling at the bottom. Despite the end of the so-called Cold War, there has been no decline in military spending globally, nor any significant increase in non-military assistance to most post-colonial peoples or those who have suffered from wars or oppression. (This is in strong contrast to exploitative investments for profit which have grown rapidly, to the benefit of the relatively few rich consumers and even richer share-holders.)

Another global stress factor is the growing pace of technological change that is increasing tensions among the populations of industrialized nations, while displacing people from the land, and even from their countries, in less developed areas. Such people contribute to the growing flood of migrants from poor to rich countries. All these are destabilizing factors, and they are not being ameliorated by the necessary top-level efforts, either within or between nations. Indeed, the rapid dispersal to even the most remote places by modern communication technologies of information about growing inequalities and exploitation simply adds to the instability.

There follow several examples of crises in the making. Because crises resulting from social psychological stress vary from culture to culture, I have used the American situation as exemplar. The fact that the world's remaining superpower is not immune from such occurrences should be a salutary warning to all others who would mimic its self-proclaimed "success," and strengthen the will to resist of those being forced to follow in its footsteps, to "globalize" the American way. Crises brought on by environmental collapse will be considered in a more global setting.

### *America's social crises*

> O would the Lord some giftie gie us
> To see ourselves as others see us.

This couplet of Robert Burns ought to become the national prayer of Americans. While observers abroad increasingly note obvious flaws in contemporary America, most citizens remain steadfastly oblivious. The virtual absence from our dialogue of the human need for real community, our enormous emphasis on *individual* rights and *individual* guilt, and the overriding demands placed on us for ever-more social efficiency, measured in purely economic terms, are all intensifying our feelings of insecurity, alienation, powerlessness,

15

and meaninglessness. Yet given our assumptions about human nature as selfish, individualistic, and materially motivated, we do not see these stresses as stemming from social problems, but from the inability of individuals to conform. And so we punish and shame those who are not "well-adapted." Yet in the long run, this is not a solution; it only postpones inevitable crises. It will take new ways of organizing society to correct the problem.

Over the past half century, huge changes in the physical and social nature of the home, school, workplace, and community have been taking place under the driving force of "modernity." The push for "progress," narrowly defined as constant growth in production and consumption, has turned social life into a largely commoditized, paid-for experience. Unpaid human activity, such as parenting or volunteering, or simply passing along gossip over the backyard fence – all essential to stable human communities – falls outside the social accounting system. It does not contribute to the accountants' assessment of "societal efficiency" and so can be eliminated – until, of course, the social fabric begins to collapse. It is mainly unpaid social interactions that bring us the most psychic satisfaction, and it is those that we are destroying![14]

The patterns of behavior being imposed on almost every life-setting in American society all have similar negative impacts: separation from others, excessive competition, increasing stress to "succeed," and impossible demands on the time and effort needed to do so. All this denies one a sense of personal identity and of deep attachment to meaningful groups. These new patterns are causing significant losses of personal control over the context of one's own life, regardless of the ballyhoo in America about individual freedom and rights.[15] Moreover, these negative impacts permeate all our behavior settings – home, school, workplace, community – so there is no respite from the psychological stress they bring.

### The shrinking family

For most of human existence, children grew up not just in their parents' household, but in the midst of their local band or village, most of whose members were real or adoptive relatives. "The family" extended even further – to other villages and, for Polynesians, even to distant islands. By blood, marriage, custom and trade, people felt personally related, and had multiple rights and obligations toward each other.

In modern America, such extended families – if they exist at all – are anachronisms, relics from the past. By the beginning of the twentieth century, "the family" consisted of a married couple and their minor children: the "nuclear family." At first, grown children stayed in close touch with the "grandparents," but by the end of the century "the family" could mean as few as one person living alone, or a single mother living in a trailer – or perhaps on the street – with her children.

As the family shrank, so too did its social support network. Grandparents, aunts and uncles often became unavailable as mobility grew.[16] Even so, through the first two-thirds or so of the twentieth century, bonds between grandparents and their grown children remained strong, so the grandchildren had a sense of continuity. But as divorce rates climbed and adult children moved ever farther away, extended family bonds waned in social importance. Today couples, and especially single parents, are very much on their own.

This shrinking of the village-wide and extended family down to the single-generation nuclear family has effectively privatized the intimate relationships among family members. Closeted within the four walls of the family castle, tensions are hidden away from public gaze. Unable to seek help or find relief outside, family members experience a build-up of stress to high levels. This is due in part to increasing stress in society as a whole, which has had its most overt effect on the psychic security of men.[17]

Since Victorian times, perhaps before, there has been growing physical and psychological abuse in the home, committed especially but not exclusively by fathers. Today, battered women and battered children are a standard part of the daily scene in America's hospital emergency rooms, and the problem is accepted as real and increasing.[18] For much of the last century, however, there was a long period of social silence, during which time the problem went unrecognized and victims' stories were not believed. With the women's movement, this long silence has been broken, and social psychologists have come to realize that amnesia regarding such trauma is a real phenomenon – as is amnesia following other severe psychological traumas. Recovered memories are being listened to and corroborated by workers such as Catherine Cameron (see Cameron 2000). Though some recovered memories may indeed be false recollections, it is clear that the problem of sexual abuse in the home is real and prevalent.[19]

So high are societal stress levels that the use of drugs and alcohol by one or both parents is common across all social classes.[20] According to the *California Journal* (2000), fire-arms are found in 40 percent of American homes. Though some are used for recreation, the right of citizens to keep them – a right enshrined in the American Constitution – is vocally defended by all owners. More than in any other industrialized nation, children in American families are growing up surrounded by both the idea of violence (guns and television) and (too often) the direct experience of violence, whether as witnesses or recipients, in their own homes and neighborhoods. The homicide rate in America is higher than anywhere in Europe outside the remnants of the old Soviet Union. Yet it is not only gun ownership that is responsible, but the accepting attitude within American culture itself toward violence that is to blame.[21]

Amazingly, in America, society may even put in jail children who run away from domestic violence, whilst allowing the perpetrator to remain free.[22] It also tries to solve the epidemic of drugs by outlawing them, instituting "zero toler-ance" of use, and building ever more prisons at great public expense to put away users as "felons" for incredibly long sentences. It never asks, Why do these people seek drugs? As a result, America now incarcerates over two million persons, most of them minority males and many of them for victimless "crimes." This is a far higher rate than that of any other country, industrialized or not, with but one or two exceptions.[23] It is one of the many kinds of temporary or "band-aid" treatments American politicians apply to "fix" deep-seated social ills. Remove the symptomatic people *after* they have fallen prey to the system and assume you have fixed the problem. As psychologist Aaron Kipnis points out, government resources spent on anti-drug propaganda and long-term incarceration of users could have far more positive results if spent on social support programs and vocational and college educations for problematic youths.[24]

Another factor affecting family social integrity has been modern communications technology. The super-interdependence of family members for social interaction began to wane with the introduction of the radio, though at first it unified families as they all shared the *same* new novelties it presented. Television, in my experience, put an end to family conversation, as dinner was eaten in a silent semi-circle while we watched … well, whatever was "on": the Huntley/Brinkly evening report or that night's boxing match. Once the set went off, we did not discuss what we'd seen. Sometimes, though, we shifted to old family things – a game of cribbage or chess, perhaps.

The electronic age has eaten even further into family life. A middle-aged friend told me about visiting the home of a single mother and her two teenagers. Each child had a private bedroom equipped with a personal telephone, TV, and computer system. While my friend was visiting, the mother heated the instant dinner in the microwave, then informed each child *by telephone* that it was ready. When the son appeared in the kitchen, he stayed only long enough to pick up his tray before returning to the electronic world of his bedroom. This is not atypical. In America, 65 percent of America's children, ages 8 to 18, have TV sets, 45 percent have video game players, and 21 percent have computers, usually in their own rooms. According to John Murray, a developmental psychologist, this separation in the home contributes to a "fracturing of family life." "The whole pattern of use of mass media works to isolate children from adults," according to William Damon from Stanford University's Center on Adolescence.[25]

The powerful impact of the electronic world on direct personal relationships between flesh-and-blood human beings cannot be overstated. More than two decades ago, people such as Herb Schiller, Jerry Mander, and Michael Nagler were warning us about the social and psychological impacts of television, especially on young children.[26] Because human social life is so complex, however, it has seldom been possible to "scientifically prove" that TV causes specific social pathologies. This of course has allowed politicians and mainstream media to brush aside serious dialogue about it. By now, though, there is an avalanche of literature concerned with these issues: the extreme violence, both physical and sexual, of much of the subject matter; the power of the media, especially of the advertisers, to shape social mores along with consumer appetites; and the impact on the way young minds develop. To maintain attention, the images on a TV screen must change frequently (now up to two or three times a second during commercials), which may be establishing a different pattern of information processing in the brain to that of ordinary human experience. Though there has been no research to date on this topic, one wonders if it might be contributing (along with artificial food additives and other contemporary environmental factors) to the high and growing incidence of ADHD (Attention Deficit Hyperactivity Disorder) that is now occurring, even among pre-school children. One in twenty such children is being diagnosed in the United States, and many of them are being treated with Ritalin and other psychoactive drugs, even though no tests as to their safety for toddlers have ever been carried out.[27] Once again, America is applying band-aid solutions to serious social problems.

Another criticism of TV is its passive nature, which some claim is now being "corrected" by interactive electronics such as Nintendo and the Internet. But these children still suffer from excessive mental stimulation on the one hand and lack of social controls on the other.[28] Finally, as pointed out by Linda Holler in her new book on the importance of touch for human psychic health, the virtual world offers only visual and auditory stimuli, and is bereft of any of the deep psychological comforts that we receive through physical contact in all its many forms.[29]

One social function that American conservatives preach loudly in favor of is a return to the transmission of "family values," including sexual mores, civic responsibility, self-control, and other so-called "Christian" ideals. (Christianity of course has no exclusive claim to these values, which are important in virtually every known society, though how they are defined can vary considerably.) What neither liberals nor conservatives are willing to tackle, however, is the extent to which the media, advertising, the corporate culture, and the competitive nature of American social life together transmit to the younger generation value perceptions that differ hugely from what mainstream society claims it has in mind. Here, I consider only sexuality, perhaps the most problematic of them all.

American cultural emphasis on individual freedom and its idealization of romantic love have been appropriated by the market-based economy as a source of huge profits. The insecurity of personal identity in a competitive society and the hope of fulfillment of one's need to "belong" through sexual attractiveness drive the sale to increasingly younger children of such diverse products as cigarettes, "sexy" or violent toys, status-conferring sneakers, and fast cars. Sexual innuendoes accompany the sales pitch of every possible product. The importance of sexuality for success in life is further stressed in violent films, and on TV sitcoms, not to mention on plenty of Internet sites to which youngsters have access.

Thus we should not be surprised that the incidence of teenage pregnancies is still increasing and that sexual activity is now widespread, even among 11- and 12-year-olds. America's biggest increase in AIDS and other sexually transmitted diseases is among the age group 12 to 24. In particular, oral sex is increasingly common, and at ever earlier ages. Girls have quickly learned to ask for cash in return for service, since they've discovered doing "it" for free does not ensure them the steady boyfriend they'd hoped for.

According to researcher Lucinda Franks, parents and school administrators react in disbelief to her data, while the kids say "You got it right!," or even, "You've only told half of what's out there." With both parents out at work, unsupervised kids use their own homes for their liaisons. The parents, it seems, ignore telltale signs: the smell of weed and disappearance of liquor. Many feel powerless to confront their own children, who simply laugh at them. And the schools, too, seem powerless; old-fashioned sex education, with a condom on a plastic penis, is a joke to today's youths, says Franks.[30]

*Schools vs. children*

Compulsory education has been in force in most Western nations for well over a century, with its original goal to achieve a literate citizenry, necessary for a democratic society. But increasingly it became a tool for supplying a skilled workforce for the national economy.[31] During the twentieth century, the extension of compulsory education through high school has meant separating not only young children from the community at large, but adolescents and young adults as well. Schools resemble prisons in the way they keep the next generation isolated from meaningful participation and engagement with society around them. Instead of being part of, they are apart from, the world they are preparing to enter. Though they peer at it through the windows and fences that separate them, they experience it second-hand, through formal textbooks and rote exercises, all designed to produce increasingly high "academic" standards – for twelve long years.

In recent years, as budgets have declined and demands for more "information-rich" and "academic" learning have become ever-louder, non-academic "frills" have been stripped from the curriculum: not only art, drama, and music, but also practical skills such as driver training, shop and sewing classes, health education and citizenship. Politically, education has become a one-size-fits-all proposition.[32] Teaching to tests and "ratcheting up" academic performance are filtering down from middle school (where it was located in the 1930s and 1940s) to pre-school. By age 5, children are expected to count, do simple addition, tell the time, and read – all as preparation for kindergarten! There is increasingly less space in the curriculum at all ages for learning physical skills, such as handling tools, drawing and penmanship, or playing an instrument, or for acquiring social skills such as cooperative learning, conflict resolution, and making group decisions.

Children are always tacitly aware of how society views them, and the present generation is no exception. At increasingly younger ages, a sophisticated cynicism replaces the enthusiasm with which youngsters first begin school. They quickly perceive the public's apathy toward them, as well as the extremes of competitiveness they are being forced into. As social psychologist Elliot Aronson points out, "This is a school atmosphere that most of the student body finds unpleasant, distasteful, difficult, and even humiliating." Social life in school lacks empathy and becomes "competitive, cliquish, and exclusionary," full of taunting and rejection, "a living hell" for those in out-groups who feel insecure, unpopular, put-down, picked on.[33] It is no surprise when particularly vulnerable kids commit mass murders, as they did in several American high schools during the 1990s. To Aronson, "[t]heir behavior was the pathological tip of a very large iceberg."[34]

The typical American response is not to go to the root cause, but once again to apply band-aids aimed at repressing the behavioral symptoms: ask kids to report on "suspicious" peers; put up metal detectors; hire security guards; do away with lockers in which weapons or drugs could be stashed. The onus is placed upon the children, not upon the hierarchical social setting that makes for anger, insecurity, and bullying. The impact of the larger society that promotes guns, finds violence entertaining, and teaches boys, in particular, to act tough and demand "respect," are all ignored. As Aronson points out, it takes more than bribes or punishments to change kids' feelings and attitudes; it takes more than enforcing rules for superficial behaviors, such as dress codes or saying "Yes, ma'am," or "No, sir," to teachers; it takes more than moralizing lectures from visiting police officers.[35] (What it *does* take comes at the end of the book, once the needs of human nature are understood.)

America, of course, is not the only society facing issues concerning youth at school. It is an issue faced by all industrializing societies and those trying to compete in the global marketplace now flowing out over the planet (Figure 0.1). Excessive competition, an elitist approach to education, and an atmosphere of "winners" and "losers" – adopted for the same reasons – produce similar consequences everywhere, only without the bloody massacres since guns are far less accessible.[36] As Swiss psychologist Alice Miller demonstrated over twenty years ago, emotionally scarred children in any society too often grow up into unfeeling, violent adults. The industrial societies are actively "nurturing" their own social time-bombs![37]

### Anger in the workplace

On the surface, a lot has changed in the world of work since 1906, when Upton Sinclair's muckraking novel *The Jungle* first appeared. An exposé of capitalism's worst side – the intolerable lives of immigrant workers in Chicago's slaughterhouses and surrounding slums – this book launched decades of social and political reforms. Yet for all the new laws governing working conditions and despite the role of overseer now played by OSHA (the Occupational Safety and Health Administration), employees today feel increasing distress at work. A century later, the dissatisfactions engendered by a strictly profit-oriented capitalism are even more powerful, since physical dangers, albeit now less blatant, are compounded by increasingly virulent psychological stress.[38]

Two decades ago, social psychologist Paul Wachtel coined the term the "portable self" to describe the status of the individual in American society.

> Our view of the self is that it is "portable," it can be carried around from place to place, fully intact, and then plugged in whenever necessary.[39]

At the beginning of the new millennium, this mercenary status of the "self" has reached a new high. It has become a free agent, out to work for the highest bidder, without allegiance or loyalty on either side – employee or employer. Mutual human feelings are outside the contract. A worker may leave for a better job, or he can equally be fired (or "downsized") with only minimum notice on either side. The meaning of a "social contract" has been pushed to its furthest limit. Says sociologist Richard Sennett:

> Today a young American with at least two years of college can expect to change jobs at least eleven times in the course of working, and change his or her skill base at least three times during those forty years of labor.[40]

The lives of America's workers are being yanked about in much the same way as their minds are yanked by TV commercials: change, *change*, **CHANGE!** It is as the Red Queen says to Alice in Lewis Carroll's *Through the Looking Glass*: "Faster! Faster!" When Alice complains that "[I]n *our* country, you'd generally get to somewhere else – if you ran very fast for a long time as we've been doing," the Queen replies, "A slow sort of Country! Now, here, you see, it takes all the running you can do, to keep in the same place. If you want to get somewhere else, you must run at least twice as fast as that."[41]

Modern psychologists read this problem of escalating stress in the workplace in two opposing ways. Those seeking to treat the anger or depression of their downsized clients try to erase their pain with such unsympathetic approaches as: The corporation is not your mother, nor is it an emotional day-care center; its job is not to provide you with a secure identity, but shareholders with profits. So your anger and hurt feelings don't do anyone any good. They just make it harder for you to get a new job. No one wants to hire someone who's angry at the world. To ease some of the workers' psychic distress at their peremptory dismissal, some socially minded firms offer support counseling and follow-ups for the workers they let go. But in the end, it is each worker's job to accept "modern reality."[42]

Yet many social psychologists see anger and dissatisfaction at work not as the worker's problem, but as the sign of a seriously pathological society. Tom Brown points out that past attempts to solve workplace complaints among middle- and upper-level white-collar workers have failed. Fixing the physical environment didn't help; nor did stock options, "employee involvement" programs, or vision statements posted on the walls. None of these changed the fact that most people at work felt little creative pride, little meaning, little sense of contributing to the social good. This, combined with ever-increasing pressure on the worker to produce more and more, to have his or her work regularly scrutinized by an often equally stressed and embittered supervisor in the corporate hierarchy, left too many employees within a firm with nowhere to ventilate their anger – except at home. In some notorious cases, workers have brought weapons to work. The United States Postal Service is widely known for multiple shootings. The feelings build, they turn to rage, and finally they turn to violence.[43]

In actual fact, outright violence in the workplace is merely the tip of the iceberg. For all the hype about the "healthy American economy," stockmarkets do not measure the health, mental or physical, of ordinary people. Brown predicts an implosion – a meltdown of corporations grown far too large to serve the psychological needs of their workers and too blind to see that their ultimate social purpose is to produce not for the sake of shareholders' profits, but for the overall social good. That is the only legitimate purpose of *any* economic system, capitalist or otherwise.[44]

Among the "social goods," perhaps the most important is the opportunity for every person to feel that he or she, through personal skills and dedication, is creatively contributing to the good of the whole. Each person's contribution has intrinsic worth by which society benefits and which therefore gives each worker's life significant meaning. Modern capitalism, in its new and extreme forms, effectively denies this basic psychological need to the vast majority of working men and women. Meanwhile, the economists argue that "this is the wave of the future," to which all humans must adapt. People, they say, have always managed before; they can adapt to anything. These spokespersons are ignorant of the many past societies that failed because they could not or would not adapt to fundamental human needs. Our most recent example, of course, is the social and economic chaos now taking place in the former Soviet Union, especially Russia.[45]

I believe more and more Americans today are not adapting to societal demands because they *cannot*. Sociologist Alan Briskin points out that when emotions are ignored, souls rebel. More than one in four American workers feel anger some or all of the time. The American Medical Association reports that 70 percent of complaints seen by primary care providers are either caused or aggravated by psychological stress.[46]

Nor are the promises of a "growing economy" being met. When economists argue that a "rising tide lifts all boats" they seem blind to the fact that economic growth does much better at floating yachts and cruise-liners than row-boats and rafts. The developmental psychologist Urie Bronfenbrenner has joined with a group of colleagues to assess how Americans today are actually faring. They report that between two-thirds and three-quarters of parents surveyed in 1995 thought the American dream – of equal opportunity, personal freedom, and social mobility – has become and will continue to become harder to achieve than it was ten years earlier. The increasing disparity between the incomes of the rich and the poor is widely perceived, especially by those near the bottom of the pyramid. Inflation adjusted figures show weekly wage earners (blue-collar workers) *lost* 20 percent of their incomes during the period when those with hourly compensation (doctors, lawyers, consultants) *gained* 8 percent. Median family incomes have stayed level since 1970. The modest gains made by two-income families have been offset by the number of single mothers with few skills whose wages have fallen sharply.[47]

While psychological stress is sending more and more people to their doctors, health care coverage in America remains abominable, where four in ten are uninsured or grossly under-insured.[48] Other stress symptoms include the school violence already discussed, and drug and alcohol abuse, especially in poorer inner city neighborhoods – though these have been spreading out across the whole of society. Bronfenbrenner and his colleagues note that despite "economic growth" in the United States since 1960, the growth in violent crime increased even faster, far outstripping that of all other industrialized countries. Even more serious, the age group in which violence is growing fastest is among youths under 18. (The slight fall in violent crime in the 1990s was probably due as much to the declining proportion of young men, always the most violent group, in the overall population, as to police crackdowns or economic growth.)[49] In the same four decades, jail and prison populations have also grown, the American national rate of incarceration having tripled since 1960. The rate for black males is seven times higher than that for whites,[50] but increasingly offenders of whatever race are being locked up for longer periods and for nonviolent crimes, especially for drug use.[51]

Much of the "economic growth," as reflected by the stock markets, is actually the result of having to pay for social pathologies. By the late 1990s, California was spending more taxes on building new prisons than on new higher education facilities.[52] Tellingly, the United States Department of Labor predicts that future job growth will be greatest in the following sectors: cashiers, janitors (neither highly paid), and in prison-building and the treatment of depression – hardly an "uplifting" vision of America's future.[53] The outlook for the mental health of the average American worker is not bright. What happens, you may well ask, as the "dream" diverges ever further from the social reality?

### Diagnosis: a "socially toxic environment"

This term, coined by the outspoken child development expert James Garbarino, cogently summarizes the state of American life at the turn of a new century. Ordinary, decent human beings are trying to live dignified lives against a cultural backdrop of media spewing violence, sex, and material consumption; of uncontrolled technological change and personal uncertainty over which ordinary people feel no control; of unbridled competition for a place in the economic hierarchy that spawns envy and greed; of increasing society-wide personal stress; and of the disappearance of caring communities.[54] Though Garbarino argues rightly that children are most at risk in such an inhumane environment, its existence affects everyone, in a self-reinforcing cultural cycle.

In particular, individual alienation and stress have been eating away at Americans' sense of community, of being active participants in a meaningful society. In a supposed "democracy" that is held up as the model for all the world, barely 50 percent of eligible voters bother to participate, even in a major election. Curtis Gans, Director of the Committee for Study of the American Electorate, blames this political apathy on three things.

First, a decreasing public trust in the integrity of America's leaders, starting when Lyndon Johnson reneged on his promise not to send American boys to Vietnam, and continuing all the way to Clinton's impeachment. Beyond this disillusionment, however, Gans points to citizens' feelings of being "disconnected" from a distant government; they see themselves as helpless, passive observers of the world, not as active participants. There is little civic education in schools; the confrontational political "dialogues" staged on the TV shows are, at best, passive entertainment. Only a few read newspapers. In short, there is a sense of having lost any control over the nation's life. A lack of personal power, of "ownership," of real autonomy, is widely experienced.

Finally, Gans notes the subliminal sense of alienation, of the "decommunitizing" and "depersonalizing" of society. There is no longer a feeling of "community life," as people find themselves increasingly separated by TV, by malls and shopping centers that replace local neighborhoods, and by freeways that cut across cities and towns alike. Without any feeling of a community to belong to, there is no longer the possibility of a shared meaningfulness, not even a sense of truly belonging.[55]

Americans and Europeans, too, are desperately seeking out default meanings in life (see Figure 0.6), while remaining blind to the causes of their own social ennui. They are trapped in a way of "seeing reality" that prevents their searching for more satisfying ways of "seeing" – and therefore of "being." As the pathologies and the costs of the ineffective band-aid solutions grow ever greater, a point will come when the whole system collapses of its own overheads (Figure 0.7). What once was a beneficial world view becomes a liability. As Joseph Tainter has shown, this is a characteristic of giant civilizations throughout history.[56] Being too cumbersome to adapt when the breaking point comes, they predictably undergo a sudden collapse. Already, I suggest, the signs of breakdown are readily visible.

Meantime, Americans are ignoring the growing global crises that are steadily building and which will certainly affect them. Any one crisis could tilt the scales of the tenuous stability that temporarily exists on Earth.

*Figure 0.6* The search for default meanings
Humor is often the best tutor when we must address puzzling or unpleasant realities about ourselves. Here a cartoonist underscores the unreality of "virtual reality" in an electronic age.

*Source*: From "Stan at Ease," by Stan Eales, *The Ecologist*, July/August, 2000

### The global outlook

My earlier book, *Ariadne's Thread*, laid out in considerable detail the global trends now in progress: explosive population growth; over-utilization of non-renewable resources; and planet-wide environmental destruction. At that time I observed that our species was building up a growing debt to Mother Nature and sooner or later we would have to "pay back" what we owed. The future from which we were borrowing would one day become the present.

Already, our "environmental credit-card account" is coming due on several fronts, some of which no one foresaw clearly. Here I address only briefly the ramifications of three apparently inevitable global crises that are already underway: energy shortages, global warming, and epidemic diseases. Like everything else, they are interrelated.

### Energy shortages

Before 1800, virtually all the energy humans used globally came from Earth's annual allotment received from the sun: biomass (burned directly or fed to working horses and bullocks) and hydro or wind power (waterwheels

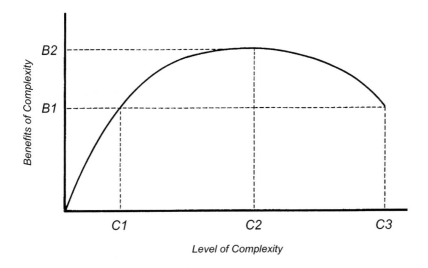

*Figure 0.7* The diminishing benefits of complexity

Tainter's curve for the social costs and benefits of increasingly complex civilizations reveals that complexity requires effort to construct and maintain the necessary institutions and infrastructure. At first, small investments in complexity (costs) C1, bring big returns (benefits) B1, but gradually the returns per added cost fall off and eventually turn negative, B2. At some level of complexity, C3, the excessive costs cause the society to begin to fail, after which point it collapses.

*Source*: Reprinted with the permission of Cambridge University Press from Joseph Tainter, *The Collapse of Complex Societies*, Figure 19, p. 119

and windmills). Only a tiny amount of coal was burned. By 1900, more than half the world's energy came from coal, used mainly in the industrializing nations. By 2000, fossil fuels supplied fully three-quarters of the world's energy consumption, which was growing exponentially for two reasons: more people plus more energy used per person. We all know fossil fuels are finite resources, representing millions of years of stored sunlight that we are now consuming in a little over two centuries, the twentieth and the twenty-first.

At the turn of this millennium, oil and natural gas production are reaching their peak of global production. Their consumption patterns are closely following the curves originally predicted for them by geophysicist M. King Hubbert back in 1956 in a report to the American Petroleum Institute[57] (see Figure 0.8). Despite these early warnings and the fact that new "big finds," such as the Alaskan North Slope, would only meet America's needs for a few years at most, the corporations that supplied both energy and the things that consume it turned their backs on the coming crisis. So did the politicians. The concerns of some scientists and solutions offered by maverick inventors designing an alternative, sustainable future through novel energy-collecting devices and more efficient energy-consuming products were largely ignored.[58] Most industrialized nations during the early 1990s instead tried to solve the growing problem of energy supply (which until then had been considered a public good in need of oversight) by deregulating it, letting "the magic of the market" do its work. In Europe, where energy has never been as available as in the United States, taxes on petrol and other forms of energy have always put a damper on extremes of consumption. Not so in the United States, where average per capita consumption is twice what it is in Europe.

Today, the whole of the industrialized world is physically and institutionally structured around the consumption of large quantities of fossil fuels: the cities, the communication and transportation systems, and the production sector. In addition, all countries trying to industrialize are following suit. Nor are the newer, modern technologies being introduced globally any more energy efficient or any less polluting. The old, extractive and smelting industries were energy-costly, water-consuming, and heavily polluting. Yet today's highly touted "information technology" hardware is based on the water- and energy-intensive and highly polluting manufacture of silicon chips.

In terms of cheap energy, then, it looks like our environmental credit-card account is in fact coming due. California's energy crisis in early 2001, brought about when the price of deregulated supplies of power soared and the utility companies were prohibited by law from passing on the full costs to consumers, was a wake-up call to its thirty million inhabitants. Households saw their energy bills double and triple (to the amounts allowed) while the state took on billions of dollars in debt to buy the energy the nearly bankrupt utilities could not afford.[59] For many weeks, Californians were subjected to continuous energy alerts and rolling power black-outs during peak hours.

So far, the "answer" to this relatively small crisis has been "we must build more generating plants to meet growing needs." Given that the world is entering on the downward slope of available fossil fuels, as shown in Figure 0.8, and that people everywhere on the planet are seeking more and more energy, this answer seems disingenuous. Especially since it is predicted that the global supplies of oil and gas will both be well into the steep descent by 2030, barely a generation away. There is a real global crisis looming on the horizon. The further we go down the curve, the higher will be the cost of energy.

One further caveat remains. To restore much of the planetary support system that modernization has devastated – our forests, wetlands, fisheries, and croplands, all of which provide "free services" when they are functioning well – requires that some of the energy still available to us must be used for these purposes. Paying back this part of our debt to Mother Nature will leave

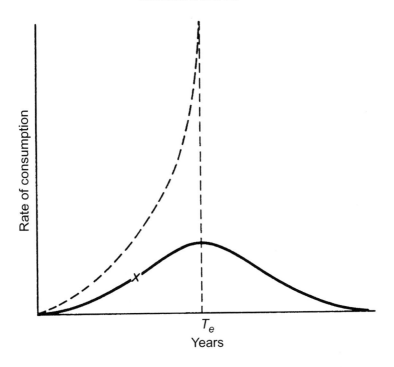

*Figure 0.8* The limits to fossil fuel availability

Back in 1956, geophysicist M. King Hubbert predicted the total usage pattern over the entire lifetime of a finite resource, shown as a solid curve. At first, consumption increases logarithmically, but with time, as it becomes harder to find and extract the resource, the rate of consumption tapers off (at point "X", the slope grows smaller, not larger with time). Even though total annual consumption continues to grow for a while, eventually it, too, will begin to decrease. Today, the world is very near the maximum, after which production and consumption will both begin to fall off. (The dashed line shows why continued exponential growth is impossible: one day there is maximum consumption; the next, total depletion at time $T_e$.) Despite new "discoveries," we are very much following Hubbert's curve globally.

*Source:* Author's drawing, Figure 2.6 from *Ariadne's Thread: The Search for New Modes of Thinking* (1989), used by kind permission of Palgrave Macmillan

even less energy for personal and industrial consumption. At some point, too, the top energy consumers of the industrialized world will need to face up to the growing demands for sharing the world's energy and other resources. Social justice is another credit-card account with a very big debt accumulated, that is now coming due!

## Global warming

As Ross Gelbspan has said, "the heat is on." With the early 2001 report from an international group of scientists, there is no longer any doubt that the global climate is changing, even faster than had been predicted previously. Whether it is due to human actions or not may still be a matter of vigorous debate.[60] Gelbspan, along with many climatologists, argues that not only is global warming real, it is driven by the human emission of greenhouse gases. Geographer Harm J. de Blij, on the other hand, suggests that though human activities contribute to this warming, their effect is minuscule. The planet, he believes, is entering one more of the rapid swings in climate that have periodically punctuated the last Ice Age – sudden warming that lasts a few centuries, and then just as sudden cooling with a return of the glaciers. It was not unique in human pre-history, he says, for whole continents to become unlivable within just one or two generations.[61] Whatever its cause, warming is real and inescapable. No matter what steps we take to try to ameliorate it, there *are going to be serious consequences*, soon, and people will have to adapt. Nature's "progress" is of a sort that we humans really cannot stop!

Among the coming crises are increasingly frequent and more powerful storms. Record floods have been occurring in river valleys from Bangladesh, to China, to Great Britain. As the oceans continue to warm, their waters will expand, inundating low-lying areas such as Florida and the Netherlands, and totally swamping many tiny island nations such as Mauritius and the Seychelles. Meanwhile, other areas, from Texas and Mexico to parts of Africa, have been plagued by severe, prolonged droughts. In both Mexico and Brazil, protracted dry spells have led to wildfires in the rainforests. In populated areas of industrialized countries, climate-related disasters have threatened many insurance companies with bankruptcy; many saw their annual losses grow six times during the decade of the 1990s.[62]

Plants and animals often cannot tolerate significant changes in climate. In the oceans, recent warming destroyed in a single year (1997–8) more of the world's coral reefs (16 percent) than all prior human pollution had damaged (11 percent). Since reefs are among the world's most productive ecosystems, their loss will gravely affect fish catches.[63] Other fisheries, such as salmon, will be shifted northward as oceans become warmer, dislocating local economies.[64] Similar effects are likely in many parts of the globe, destroying the livelihoods of local artisan fishermen, like those in Kerala, India, with their small boats and selective nets, who depend on near-shore catches. Such people are already being threatened by the invasions of mechanized commercial trawlers from distant ports.[65]

On land, the distributions and total populations of animals are already being affected by climate change, and the predicted rate of change will far exceed the capacity of whole ecosystems to migrate. For humans dependent on particular sensitive crops, this could mean massive economic dislocations. Warming locally can increase pests while simultaneously lowering yields of such crops as rice and wheat.[66] Farmers, as they track climate changes, are likely to find themselves crossing political borders.

Meantime, shifts in precipitation will create new problems over humankind's most precious resource – fresh water. Areas of the world already prone to dryness will become drier, and vice versa. Since water scarcity has been the reason for most of the giant water-management schemes of the world – which now barely meet current demands – even less precipitation will force millions to migrate, adding greatly to the present stream of economic refugees and those fleeing war and ethnic violence. As water tables fall and groundwater sources dry up, and elaborate irrigation systems run low, water scarcity will mean food scarcity. South African Education Minister, Kader Asmal, predicts that by 2025, one-third of the world's population "will struggle just to find water to drink and bathe, much less grow food."[67] At the same time, the pollution of freshwater systems continues in many developed countries. Especially in the United States, increasingly strong hurricanes are causing more and more run-off of pesticides and animal waste pollutants into local surface and groundwaters in the southeast. Thus, those already with enough or too much water are also finding water management ever more difficult as a result of climate change.[68]

Geography and climate have always shaped human societies. Swings in climate – and their concomitant ecological impacts – played an important role in human pre-history, as well as during the last millennium. During and after Roman times, global climate was relatively mild, so that vineyards flourished in northern Europe and Britain and the Vikings could regularly sail to their settlement in Greenland and visit Canada and the northeast American coast. But around AD 1200, the climate turned cold, ice sheets crept further south and there began a "Little Ice Age" that lasted, with some ameliorations, until around the mid-1800s.[69] During the entire brief period of the Industrial Revolution, the world's climate has been relatively moderate and stable. It is to this momentary climate that modern industrial civilization is adapted.

What is critically different about the impact of climate change today from that in 1200 or even in the mid-1700s is that, then, people could migrate, taking their livestock, tools, and seeds with them. Now the world's population is eight times greater and most people live in giant cities that are highly dependent on a complex infrastructure that cannot be moved for their survival. The capital investment of peoples is no longer portable, but securely anchored to one geographic spot. Climate change, whether warmer or cooler (the latter is very likely to follow once current global warming subsides several generations hence), has not been factored into either Industrial Age or "post-industrial" thinking and planning. Somehow we human beings are going to need to make up for this deficiency – and quickly! Within a generation or two, the impacts will be fully upon us – that is, in about the same length of time as from the end of the Second World War until now.

*Epidemic diseases*

We tend to think of epidemics as something caused by infectious agents spread from one person to another (though other things can spread too, such as fear or panic). But whole communities can also be afflicted by debilitating diseases that are not transmitted from one person to another, but are caused by factors in the environment that can affect everyone. Both sorts of epidemics are increasing globally. I start with the first kind, those caused by pathogenic organisms.

No other large host, prior to humans, provided such ready access to virulent parasites. We stand today exposed to our own numbers and our own mobility, the only species readily susceptible to pandemics. The sudden 1999 appearance of West Nile virus in New York City attests to the leaps of distance now possible. No doubt local climate aberrations favorable to the reproduction of the vector mosquitoes aided its spread. As epidemiologist Paul Epstein observes, bigger swings in the weather favor population explosions of insect vectors that transmit diseases from host to host. And general warming trends further expand their ranges to both higher elevations and higher latitudes. By 2020, humans living in the highlands of Africa, New Guinea, Central and South America, and India, and in southern England and Sweden, all of Finland, and much of northern Siberia, will be newly at risk not only for malaria, but for other mosquito-borne diseases such as dengue fever and yellow fever. Meantime, the frequency of these diseases in areas where they already occur will increase even further.[69]

Malaria, along with tuberculosis, remains one of the world's deadliest killers. Not unlike resistant bacteria, the various strains of *Plasmodium*, the protozoan that causes malaria, are 80 percent resistant to chloroquine, once the standard drug used to prevent or control an infection. They are even becoming resistant to the latest replacements. One possible new drug comes from China, where extracts of the qinghao plant (*Artemisia annua*) have been used to treat "fevers" for over two thousand years. Unfortunately, despite successful tests in Thailand, Western medicine has been slow to test and approve it.[70]

Other diseases which are transmitted directly from person to person are increasing because of local crowding. Among these is leprosy, now common in urban parts of India, Bangladesh, and Brazil. Fear of the disease prevents effective treatment, which is dependent on the treatment of all possible contacts of someone with lesions, since those in latent stages of the disease are also infectious. The extreme social ostracism of lepers prevents those without symptoms from coming forward.[71]

Another combined result of crowding and climate change is an increase in cholera and other water-borne diseases. During severe floods, drinking water often is contaminated with sewage. In poor areas, neither an alternative water source nor the fuel to boil local water is always available. Infant deaths from dehydration following a bout of infectious diarrhea remain extremely high in some areas.

Finally, the current HIV/AIDS epidemic perhaps originated as an outcome of population growth. No one is certain how the human immunodeficiency virus (HIV) came into being, though Africa is surely the place. It is also the one continent where expanding human populations have increasingly come into close contact with our very near cousins, the great apes. Several of their viruses may have jumped the relatively low species barrier and been transmitted to humans, including SIV (or simian immunodeficiency virus), a close though less virulent relative of HIV.

HIV/AIDS is widely feared, especially in Africa where drugs for treatment are expensive, scarce, or non-existent. A few countries which have mounted widespread multi-sectorial responses and strong government and community commitments have begun to reduce infection rates: Uganda, Zambia, Senegal, and in Asia, Thailand and Cambodia. Elsewhere, in just a decade, the incidence of adult infection has zoomed: from 1 percent in 1990 to 20 percent in 2000 in South Africa, and in Russia, from 100 persons in 1993 to over 15,000 in 1999. Throughout much of sub-Saharan Africa, the impact on the demographics is bleak. By 2020, in Botswana, a much-reduced young adult population will have grown up, many as orphans deprived of a normal childhood. The next younger cohort will be even more diminished through the deaths or infertility of infected potential mothers, or through the death of their HIV-infected offspring (see Figure 0.9). Geographer Harm de Blij notes that in just five years, from 1995 to 2000, the average life expectancy at birth in Botswana declined from 61 years to 39 years, and continues to decrease.[72] The cultural impact is almost unimaginable. It is like the Pied Piper of Hamelin turned upside down, with the parents spirited away and the children left behind to fend for themselves.

Added to these infectious diseases are all those non-infectious diseases that humans face, those belonging to the second group mentioned at the start of this section. They may be caused by natural disasters, human activities, or some combination of these. One that is surely epidemic is malnutrition. Over one billion human beings today are seriously underweight, an equal number are seriously overweight, and many hundreds of millions more are malnourished because they are deficient in critical nutrients such as iodine, iron, or Vitamin A. Causes of malnutrition range from droughts, to wars, to poverty and economic dislocations, to governmental and/or corporate misbehaviors. Though obesity is growing while hunger is decreasing, the total fraction of the nutritionally deficient in the global population remains constant – as do the health effects. "Indeed," say Worldwatch Institute researchers, "poorly nourished people are a sign of 'progress' gone awry: prosperity has either by-passed them and left them hungry, or saturated them to the point of overindulgence."[73]

Meantime, as the globe heats up, the incidence of "sunstroke" and heat prostration will rise, with deaths from heatwaves doubling by 2020. And when temperatures rise, so do the effects of air pollution, including asthma and other respiratory diseases as well as allergies.[74] Other manmade contaminants in

## Projected population structure of Botswana 2020

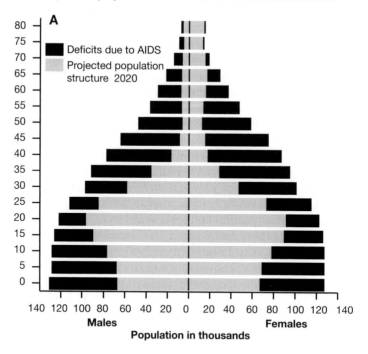

*Figure 0.9* The impact of AIDS in Africa

Population age structure in Botswana in 2000 and 2020. The normal "pyramid" of age structure seen in 2000 will be greatly distorted in less than a generation. The people aged today between 20 and 40 years old will almost all be dead by 2020. The youngest of them will have had very few children, creating a highly abnormal population age structure in the next generation, and a shrunken total population.

*Source*: Redrawn by Michele Lukowski from B. Schwartländer *et al.*, "AIDS in a New Millennium," *Science* 289, Figure 3A, p. 66; ©2000 by American Association for the Advancement of Science; used with permission

urban air are the extra small particulates now associated with increasing deaths from lung and heart disease.[75] Airborne toxins such as dioxin, released by sources in the central United States and carried aloft into the jet stream, are now contaminating the lands of the Inuits (Eskimos) in the farthest reaches of northern Canada.[76]

This brings us to perhaps the most dangerous and widespread of the non-infectious diseases. In fact, it is not one disease but a whole host of illnesses caused by releases throughout the environment of manmade chemicals. Urban smog, lead in gasoline, and nitrates in drinking water that kill babies are familiar examples from the past. So too are pesticides such as DDT and malathion. But in addition to these old culprits there is now a whole host of new ones, found in food additives, plastics, farm chemicals, building materials, wastewater – an alphabet soup of PAHs, PCBs, HAAs* and on and on. They occur at very low levels in the environment, levels so low they are hard to detect. Yet they are becoming ubiquitous. Most of them seem to have an effect on the hormonal systems of humans and animals.

Known as "endocrine disrupters" or "hormonally active agents," these chemicals have been identified as causes of developmental abnormalities, infertility, cancers, and even behavioral problems.[77] An article in *Time* magazine suggested they could be the causes of premature puberty in American girls, some of whom have started developing breasts and pubic hair before age 10.[78] The precise connection between the suspect chemicals and the symptoms observed is still tenuous, however. An investigative committee of the National Research Council, America's most prestigious, respected, and independent scientific organization, reported that while the symptoms are troubling, their causes are less clear. Like all environmental toxicology, the number of potential factors influencing the appearance of a given symptom is overwhelming; it is almost impossible to say *this* chemical alone caused *this* symptom. One of the committee members explained his views to me in this way. "The pathologies being observed are real and troubling. The chemicals are out there, and very likely are involved. But I am not sure they are acting in the specific ways [as endocrine disrupters] that are being claimed."[79] Nevertheless, in whatever ways the chemicals may be acting, they *are* having an impact, and once released they cannot be recalled!

## To change or be changed?

If even only a few of these crises develops fully in coming years, it is clear that the West's rosy expectations for the twenty-first century, of an economically globalizing planet developing smoothly by the simple extrapolation of its own ideology and institutions, will not come about. The West's world view, its "Billiard Ball" Gestalt, when pushed to its logical limits of extreme competition fails to meet the deepest needs of human nature; indeed, it becomes pathological to the human psyche. Moreover, its need for unending economic growth in order to maintain social harmony totally ignores the already stretched limits of the planetary support system. Nor does this gestalt, especially as exemplified by the United States, the world's remaining superpower and self-proclaimed world leader, offer within its logic any way to address either the inner psychological crises or the external environmental crises that are so obviously imminent.[80] To date, its response to early symptoms of these crises is to blame individuals for not being able to adapt to the inevitable future being laid out for them, and to count on new, ever-more sophisticated band-aid technologies to surmount the environmental crises and suppress the psychological ones.

It is already clear that stress is increasing around the world – it is not unique to American society. But much of it is due to attempts to follow "moderniza-

*polyaromatic hydrocarbons; polychlorinated biphenyls; hormonally active agents

tion" along Western lines of social organization. Today, no matter where people live, they are feeling increasingly stressed. The psychological symptoms apparent in American society are already paralleled in most industrialized nations, albeit with culturally distinct differences in how the symptoms are displayed. In France, a recent editorial in the newspaper, *Le Monde*, blamed the increasing deaths on French motorways on

> ... a loss of the sense of belonging to a community; a money-driven society; the ethos of "every man for himself"; fanatical individualism; a disregard for other people that sometimes amounts to contempt; and sheer aggression.
>
> *Those faults are cloaked with respectability by an extreme neoliberal ideology that is all too often used to justify a rejection of such notions as civic solidarity....*
>
> The only watchwords on the road [said a French racing champion] should be "love one another" and "share the road."[81]

In India, too, social life is likewise deteriorating. An Indian friend, well into his seventies, who lives half of each year in India and half in the United States, told me how his impressions of India are changing in recent years. On returning to his home in Vadodara, Gujarat, he senses a growing loss in civility as the impact of this same, extreme neoliberal ideology takes hold in his native land. He bemoans the "eroding [of] the long cherished values ... [the] perceptible absence of humanness, compassion and tolerance."[82]

In Japan, many over-stressed workers, instead of becoming angry and violent, are dying from stress directly, whether from strokes and heart attacks, or by suicide. In modernizing communist China, well-paid government computer programmers find the pressure of ever-longer hours without leisure time for themselves that is now demanded by their jobs to be increasingly unbearable. Many are seeking to emigrate, legally or otherwise, in the belief it would be better elsewhere.[83]

Stresses in developing countries arise from many different causes: economic and social disruptions, often from outside; unresolved ethnic disputes; droughts, floods and other natural disasters (including devastating earthquakes that take extraordinary tolls in poor, densely populated areas where buildings are not well enough constructed to withstand them); and, as noted above, uncontrolled diseases. By 2020, the World Health Organization predicts stress-related depression will be the planet's second most disabling disorder.[84]

Change – of some sort – is going to occur. The question is, will it be a change that human beings have worked out for themselves, or will it be a change they are subjected to and feel helpless to direct? I believe there are two prerequisites to achieving, as nearly completely as possible, the first. One is to understand that we have the power to change direction, to take control. We are *not* destined to continue as we are doing; there is nothing about human nature that forces us to continue, nothing inevitable about the path we are now on, no genetic force driving us to compete, to strive for maximum economic efficiency at the expense of all else. There is no such thing as a predestined direction of "progress" that we are helpless to stop.

The other prerequisite for change is to understand what it takes to bring it about, the processes necessary by which human societies evolve their meaning systems and adapt their world views to new situations. Both these prerequisites, I believe, can be found by a close look at human nature itself. In particular, we need to get rid of some Western-generated assumptions about ourselves as necessarily selfish and highly individualistic, and thus driven to behave in self-centered ways. We simply are *not* biologically constructed in that way. And once we begin to perceive under what conditions we feel most comfortable in our being, thinking, and acting, we can also begin to see by what processes we can constructively and peaceably undertake the necessary adaptation that we all face. We will discover how to become creatively flexible in the face of crises.

Yes, we have a lot to learn about ourselves – who we are and how we came to be that way. We have a lot of revising to do of some odd and often highly destructive beliefs. However, it is a pleasant undertaking because the bottom line about ourselves is that we are potentially a lot nicer than most of us ever dreamed. Having a more optimistic image to work with (even if it turns out not to be perfectly correct) allows us to develop a more adaptive way of thinking. As we come to recognize how our feelings and our thinking are tightly woven together, we can devise ways of communicating with each other that allow for a compassionate mutual understanding to be established that gives everyone the freedom to accept change without feeling coerced. Curiously enough, the West has a word for it – it is called "democracy." But what I am talking about is not the distant, non-engaged sort where one simply votes in elections and writes a few letters, and may even attend a few meetings. What I am talking about is real, strong democracy that begins at the grassroots and in which everyone actively participates and feels ownership of the decisions that shape the world around them.

But of course, you cannot possibly do this without a better understanding of human nature itself, of who we "really" are! As the Dalai Lama put it:

> So no matter how much violence or how many bad things we have to go through, I believe that the ultimate solution to our conflicts, both internal and external, lies in returning to our basic or underlying human nature, which is gentle and compassionate.[85]

Chapter I will serve as an introduction to the rest of this work. It opens with a critique of attempts to apply the methodology of science to our understanding of human nature, taking note of the public backlashes against some of the claims being made about Who We Are. After a brief explication of my own philosophy of "knowledge" and "truth" (that underlies the narrative forthcoming in later chapters) I contrast the two gestalts from this Introduction in greater detail.

The chapter then continues with a framing of our basic human propensities, hinting at their probable evolutionary significance, and noting how they can easily come into conflict with one another – a key to making sense of many of the tensions that develop both within an individual psyche and between individuals or groups. At the end, I offer a map of how the book unfolds.

# I

# QUESTIONING THE "SCIENTIZED" IMAGE

The most fanciful idea of all is the notion that the world can be described, inscribed, or specified independently of our involvement with it and experience of it. Without us there is no game in town ... Naked reality, alas, is in eternal purdah; she can never let herself be seen. It is dressed up, in style, that she appears in public, clothed in those preconceptions we left for her outside the bedroom door.

Richard Shweder (1991: 358)

Each of us has the waves of every other organism entangled within our own make-up ... We are not isolated atoms, each jostling and competing against the rest in a Darwinian struggle for survival of the fittest. Instead each of us is supported and constituted, ultimately, by all there is in the universe.

Mae-Wan Ho (2000: 23)

The opening quote from anthropologist Richard Shweder sets the frame for this chapter. His premise that ultimate reality is always hidden from us and that we can only construct a tissue of ideas as a working image of truth is one I accept in this book. But it goes against the grain of an absolutist Western science, some exponents of which firmly believe their methods of inquiry will ultimately reveal all that exists in the universe. One of the world's most respected biologists, Edward O. Wilson, is among them. His recent book *Consilience* lays out in elaborate detail his own vision of how science will ultimately explain all aspects of human nature, pulling all the disciplines into a single, scientifically-based explanation.[1] Over fifty years ago, when training as a scientist, I too held this grand belief as an article of faith. It all seemed so reasonable, so satisfying. Much hard thinking has led me to be more circumspect; some of those thoughts are incorporated in this chapter.

Not only does Western science have great faith in the power of its methods, however. It also "sees" the universe as comprising discrete objects (the Billiard Ball Gestalt) that interact in linear, cause-and-effect fashion. Moreover, it takes the everyday world as essentially "static," near equilibrium, and one in which

39

predictable "laws" govern events. Such assumptions work well for limited kinds of events having to do with physical and chemical and thermodynamic systems that are near equilibrium. But when we try to use them to study the biosphere, that thin layer of atmosphere, oceans, and land in which climate occurs and all known life exists, the gestalt of discrete objects interacting in predictable ways begins to fail. A different set of premises, a different gestalt, is needed to understand complex systems that exist far from an equilibrium state and are subject to sudden change.

Physicists, recognizing decades ago the explanatory limits of linear thinking, discarded the idea of a deterministic universe (the Laplacean fallacy) and came up with new theories, new models, of reality, including relativity, quantum mechanics and, more recently, chaos theory. The latter, it is hoped, will help model, among other things, the vagaries of weather, so notoriously unpredictable. Yet even chaos theory has some significant problems of its own.[2]

Meanwhile, the life sciences, and especially the social sciences, adopted the old physical assumptions about the universe in creating their theories of living organisms, including human beings, treating them as discrete objects in a "billiard-ball" world. The old methods of physicists would reveal new truths about the forces of natural selection and hence about human nature. Darwinian evolution could be explained scientifically by making the *initial assumption* that competition for survival in a world of scarcity was its primary driving force. And, as a product of evolution, human nature could be explained in these terms. By "human nature" they meant literally the whole spectrum of human behavior. This model has, of course, the great scientifically prized attribute of being readily amenable to mathematical modeling!

This model has led to the development by a fairly large group of evolutionary biologists, neoclassical economists, and behavioral psychologists, of a rather unpleasant picture of human nature. It is this image that the molecular biophysicist Mae-Wan Ho so strenuously objects to in her quote at the start of this chapter. Her work in liquid crystallinity has led her toward an Indra's Net Gestalt of the universe. Increasingly more academics are speaking up in opposition to the old picture, which by now is widely disseminated in the popular mind: namely, that we are individualistic, self-centered, and competitive creatures, *by nature*. A few pithy comments from a handful of them will serve to give the reader a sense of the kind of objections raised against these widely advertised ideas.

Barry Schwartz, a psychology professor, points to the scientists' cultural biases:

> The disciplines in question have mistakenly treated the particular social conditions in which we live as representative of the universal human condition. As a result, they have mistaken local cultural and historical truths about people for natural laws. As a further result they have helped contribute to the perpetuation of these conditions by appealing to their natural inevitability.[3]

Jerome Kagan, a rigorous experimental psychologist, bemoaned the over-simplification of the concepts involved, calling them popular fallacies. Regarding hedonism he stated: "Today, evolutionary arguments are used to cleanse greed, promiscuity, and the abuse of stepchildren of moral taint." These are claimed by the scientists in question to be "natural, part of a genetically-driven selfishness." Regarding abstractionism: "Psychological traits are not stable structures hidden deep in the person's core." There are no law-like causes of behaviors that hold for all cultures, all epochs, indeed (as some scientists claim) for all species.[4]

The outspoken humanist-psychologist, Sigmund Koch, decried

> ... the tendency for psychology to "enact" science rather than to seek knowledge, and to subordinate inquiry to superficially assessed but reassuringly "fail-safe" methodologies borrowed from extrinsic sources.[5]

Finally, in reviewing Karl E. Sheibe's book, *The Drama of Everyday Life*, his fellow psychologist, Rom Harré, points to the contrast between Scheibe and the mainstream evolutionary psychologists.

> Are the relations between the sexes, formal and informal, best treated by an analogy to cost–benefit analysis, or do we get a better grasp by looking at them as if they were lived out in accordance with the narrative conventions of a local culture? ... Much psychology seems unrealistic because it freezes the moment in an attempt to extract some universal principle that, it is assumed, must underlie the phenomena in question.[6]

To sum up, I add the comments of Charles Taylor, a Canadian philosopher:

> There is a constant temptation to take natural science theory as a model for social theory: that is, to see theory as offering an account of underlying processes and mechanisms of society, and as providing the basis of a more effective planning of social life. But for all the superficial analogies, social theory can never really occupy this role. It is part of a significantly different activity.[7]

To illustrate the problem, I offer one of these "scientific" explanations of how our genes supposedly drive our behavior. It has to do with sex – a central concern of both evolutionists and Western culture, hence the great popular interest in what scientists have to say on the topic.

## Sex and survival: a caution about "just-so" stories

Rudyard Kipling invented his "just-so" stories to explain how leopards got their spots and elephants their trunks. In the modern story of human evolution preferred by evolutionary psychologists, there is a plethora of "just-so" stories parading under the guise of scientific explanations of human behavior. The images of both men and women are being reduced to simplistic, gene-driven automata. That, they argue, is what evolutionary theory dictates. They claim males are naturally aggressive, competitive, deceitful, and especially that they are sexually promiscuous because it is to their evolutionary advantage to have a large number of offspring. After all, they argue, men invest little in the survival of any offspring, and so the smart thing is to inseminate as many females as possible, thus ensuring *their* genes dominate in the next generation. Reproduction is the central goal of the evolutionary game. Even rape is explained as a natural result of this male mating strategy.[8] That all males in all societies do not exhibit these tendencies scarcely troubles our theorists.

Females, on the other hand, are said to invest much more in pregnancy, lactation, and nurturing of these joint offspring, and are therefore naturally coy and choosy about a mate. They select (depending on who's telling the story) the guy with the biggest muscles, the best hunter–provider, or the most attentive, committed chap who is more likely to stick around and help with the kids. In fact, only after women primatologists in the 1970s and 1980s had reported repeatedly that female monkeys and apes actively choose the males they mate with was even this degree of female choice admitted into theories of primate reproduction. Before that, the male-dominated discipline had argued that males, being stronger, naturally dominated females sexually. This was believed despite Darwin's argument for the importance of female choice a century before.[9] This is but one of innumerable examples of how scientists' preconceptions can affect their observational powers. Yet most scientists – both men and women – persist in claiming they could not be biased, that they are truly objective.

The theory of evolutionary psychology, then, claims that men and women ought to have very disparate biological life goals. Males to make as many babies as possible. Females to mate only with helpful, responsible, genetically fit males. It is a law of life encoded in their genes. Or so the story goes. But how does this supposed reproductive disparity between the sexes, this supposed universal Law of Life, accommodate the lifelong, monogamous mating that occurs in other species, such as grebes (and some other birds) or gibbons (and some other primates)? In both cases, females still invest more than males, yet the males aren't driven to promiscuity. So why should this be the case for human males?

We seem to need an expanded explanation. How about: baby grebes and baby gibbons apparently need both parents in order to survive, so the male has to hang around if his genes are not to become extinct. But isn't the helpless human baby at least as needful? It is time to modify the story. Suppose the genes of our earliest ancestors evolved a compromise agreement between promiscuous males and coy females. They formed, at the very origin of *Homo sapiens*, lifelong pair bonds, or "marriages." The male (even if occasionally guilty of cheating), devoted most of his time to his mate's offspring, while making pretty sure all of them were actually his! Thus is marriage endowed with biological meaning (which should make devout religious leaders happy). The nuclear family arose as a genetically encoded human institution from the very beginning.

But what was it that attracted a male and kept him around? Continuous female sexual receptivity seems a pretty good bet, and I can go along with that idea. But evolutionary psychology wants to make *sure* that they're attracted, so it concludes that as soon as our ancestors walked upright, females evolved large, alluring breasts. But how do we know the human breast evolved its shape in order to attract males? The fat has nothing to do with milk production, so it does not signal fitness for motherhood. When and why breasts developed is a biological mystery. Sure, they attract males. Just as the swollen red bottoms on baboons signal "fertile female" to male baboons, so enlarged breasts on women signal "mature, receptive female" to human males.

But was that the original adaptive purpose of an enlarged breast? Just watch a mother suckling her babe. The shape of the breast allows for eye contact between a human mother and the infant she is cradling in her arms (Figure I.1). Other primate infants, when nursing, have their faces buried in their mother's fur. It seems extremely plausible to me that large breasts evolved in step with the evolution of the facial muscles of human beings. Elaborate facial expressions were surely an early stage in the development of human symbolic communication: the conveying of feelings by means of smiles, frowns, pouts, the lifting of eyebrows (surprise or doubt). Larger breasts would permit this earliest form of language communication between mother and infant, the first step in a baby's cultural learning.[10]

That breasts evolved for the biological purpose of attracting males is also a "just-so" story, or, in scientific language, a hypothesis. Like Kipling's "just-so" stories in *The Jungle Book*, it sounds plausible. Yet the alternative I have suggested is an equally adaptive biological explanation for this trait. To my mind it is far more likely. Males have plenty of clues about who is a male or a female without the signal of big breasts. Curved hips, for one; higher pitched voices for another; distinct ways of walking for a third. But helpless human infants in need of learning to live in a human society if they are to survive require all the practice they can get, and mom's face is a great place to begin. Indeed, babies just a few months old begin to mimic adult facial expressions; by age 2 or 3, they not only use facial signals, they repeat every adult phrase they hear. Other primates do make eye contact with their offspring, but while holding them at a distance and not during nursing. They also have fewer facial muscles and a much smaller repertoire of facial signals.

The evolutionary psychologists' story of males as genetically promiscuous and females as coy also seems highly "iffy." Cultures seem to have much to say about who gets to be promiscuous and why, as that great student and defender of the world's indigenous peoples, David Maybury-Lewis, has so comprehensively documented.[11] I am convinced that Western cultural assumptions

*Figure I.1* The evolution of the human breast

The fatty tissue that gives shape to the human breast is not necessary for milk production. It is likely that it was adaptive in helping nursing human infants make eye-to-eye contact with their mothers and so discover the meaning of various human facial communications. "[W]hen the infant is at the breast, its mother's face is at about the distance at which it can focus most clearly." The cooptation of human sexuality for social cohesion naturally led to stimulation of the breast as a pleasurable contribution to both sexes during sexual arousal.

*Source*: Redrawn by Michele Lukowski from Robert A. Hinde (1974), cover illustration; quote is taken from p. 181.

routinely affect the hypotheses (or "just-so" stories) constructed by evolutionary psychologists, or by any other scientist for that matter.

Likewise, we can ask, was long-term pair bonding central to human evolution, or is this also another "just-so" story, a plausible-sounding hypothesis? Again, Maybury-Lewis offers so many cultural variants on the concept of "marriage" and its relationship (or lack thereof) to biological parenting as to cast serious doubt on such bonding as a genetically driven, universal human trait. He offers instead what seems to me a much more plausible explanation, namely: a universal *cultural* need to codify human sexual behavior so as to limit conflict and promote social harmony. This throws the institutions all gathered under the rubric "marriage" back onto a much broader, more general, and hence more likely, genetically driven human need for survival – the need for membership in a functioning, coherent social group.

Despite their highly speculative nature, however, these simple "just-so" stories of the evolutionary psychologists not only persist, but are growing in number. They are being elevated in the popular mind from hypotheses to "facts."[12] Illustrations in "the origin of man" books and dioramas in museums showing Australopithecine couples (Lucy and her "husband") with the male's arm slung protectively over the female's shoulders and her hairy but enlarged breasts prominently in view, as if in some R-rated movie, reinforce these mental images of ourselves (Figure I.2).[13] An unaware public now takes those images as scientifically proven representations of our ancestors: human social life really began with nuclear families (albeit with faithless husbands), with couples who bonded for life (or at least while the kids were small), and who had two or three children.

Sex and breasts are good subjects with which to open a book on human nature written for a Western audience. Both loom large in our cultural self-image and grab everyone's attention, as Madison Avenue well knows. But neither trait has left any substantial evolutionary clues. Neither behaviors nor soft tissues leave behind any physical evidence as to when and why they evolved, and we can only guess what adaptive functions they might originally have had. Particularly when it comes to behavior, which is so variable from culture to culture, we are on thin ice when we look for strictly Darwinian answers: traits coded in our genes that are universally present in our species. Ethnologist George Barlow once complained that "[f]or all but the most general principles [of human behavior] ... you can always find some obscure human society that negates the generality." [14]

The current popular picture of human nature, then, is based mostly on purely imagined claims about how our behavior "must have evolved." But because modern science has such popular authority, its current working theories are easily elevated to well-founded "laws of nature," especially when a vocal group of scientists actively promotes them, and the popular press, aware of our deep interest in ourselves, reports them widely. This elevation of unproved hypotheses to the status of hard facts or truths about reality has been called "scientism."[15] In a book that attempts to reconstruct our image of human nature, it is necessary to be aware of the dangers of scientism, and to set a few ground rules about what are "facts" and what are "stories," and even more importantly, how well do the stories (hypotheses) actually fit the whole of human nature, rather than explain isolated, specifically selected aspects.

For the philosophers amongst my readers, I offer the following ground rules employed in making the arguments in this book. For those less interested in the rules and more interested in getting straight to the story, I invite you to skip ahead.

*Figure I.2* The "Lucy" diorama at the American Museum of Natural History
This Australopithecine couple ("Lucy" and her "husband") are seen walking across the ash-covered African savanna some two to three million years ago. Note the presumption of pair-bonding and of enlarged breasts on the female. There is no evidence that either of these traits was present then. That they are portrayed here is evidence of unfounded presumptions about selective forces during early hominid evolution.

*Source*: Used by permission: Neg.No338 315, Photo by: W.D. Finnan/C.Chesek/J.Beckett, courtesy Department of Library Services, American Museum of Natural History

## Evolution, scientism, and the battle over truth

The methods of science have indeed proved powerful over the past few centuries. They have put the sun in its proper place at the center of the solar system. They have explained what happens during the combustion of wood or coal. And more recently, they have unleashed the power of atoms to make bombs or to produce energy.

In the nineteenth century, the careful observations and creative thinking of Charles Darwin and Alfred Russel Wallace led to a detailed explanatory outline of the theory of evolution, the origin of one species from another and of modern humans from ape-like ancestors. Today, the overall concept of evolution has so much solid evidence supporting it – from fossils, to morphologically

46

related species, to similarities in DNA – that not only do all scientists accept it as true; so do all but a handful of religions.

What remains less certain, however, are the details of the process. What traits are "adaptive" and which merely serendipitous? Indeed, what even counts as a "trait"? When it comes to human behavioral traits – how and why we think, feel, and act as we do – science has almost no direct information about how our genes might be involved. Yet the general public remains largely unaware of the highly speculative nature surrounding the details of the evolution of human behavior. Most people also know little of the broader philosophical disputes among academics over what counts as scientific truth. The obvious successes of twentieth-century science and technology have accorded the pronouncements of modern science a status once reserved for religious doctrine. The public shows little skepticism about the accuracy of scientific "facts," unless, because of political or economic repercussions, a dispute arises that is picked up by the media: for example, arguments over the facts of global warming, where much is at stake. But mostly, any uncertainties go unnoticed by the public. Moreover, few learn in school or elsewhere of past incorrect scientific "truths," of which there is a long list.[16]

Sometimes those incorrect claims have had terrible social repercussions. We need only recall the science-based eugenics movement of the early twentieth century, when tens of thousands of supposedly mentally defective women were forcibly sterilized, with a level of sanctimonious fervor reminiscent of the religious witch-hunts in Massachusetts three centuries earlier. There is a tendency among today's evolutionary psychologists to similarly impose their theories about human nature on the world, while dismissing their critics as still clinging to superstitious religious explanations. The latter are labeled "sky-hooks" by the philosopher Daniel Dennett, who claims some people use them as "psychic crutches." Those who differ with him, he says, simply cannot accept the "truth" that is being uncovered by science.[17]

## "Science wars": excessive hubris and its backlashes

In the past fifty years there has been a growing tendency for promoters of absolutist science to make extravagant claims for the truth of their hypotheses. Evolutionary psychologists are not just finding out interesting things and offering some new insights into reality; they claim they are uncovering the "true answers" to human nature.

Not surprisingly, such hubris has generated anti-science backlashes in several quarters, which in turn has raised the hackles of some in the scientific community. Labeled the "science wars," enough of this angry dialogue has been taking place around the halls of academe to cause the prestigious New York Academy of Sciences to fight back in a special symposium called "The Flight from Science and Reason." Far from being a multi-sided discussion, the meeting featured only the points of view of the evolutionary psychologists and their colleagues.

Though the published proceedings are more a collection of personal beliefs than a thoughtful philosophical debate, the book that emerged drew public attention by its title alone.[18] Implied throughout is the view that critics of science are, at best, benighted and, at worst, outright charlatans. In either case, criticism of science amounts to the Heresy of Unreason, and is not to be tolerated!

The backlashes against scientific hubris fall roughly into three categories: (I) philosophical questioning about the possibility of absolute knowledge; (II) philosophical questions about application of scientific methods to highly complex subject matters such as human nature; and (III) popular dissatisfaction, often intuited rather than articulated, with the meaninglessness of a purely material, mathematically defined universe.

### *Backlash I: The impossibility of absolute knowledge*

Reductionist forms of science are patterned on the "billiard ball" conceptualization of the universe described in the Introduction. Reality is constructed of discrete objects that interact with each other. Science's task is to unravel those relationships. Even if today's science is "still in process," still self-correcting, it always claims to know more than anyone else and to possess the best answers available.

On the other hand, those who believe that reality is always hidden from view, known only approximately, revealed in bits and pieces but never completely, are sometimes called constructionists because they are aware that culture can, and often does, construct what we see in the world and how we interpret it. They are also called relativists because they suspect that scientific understandings are only shadows of reality, not reality itself. Their beliefs stem from a sense of the enormous complexity of the universe, similar to the alternative Gestalt of Indra's Net described in the Introduction.

This dispute is hardly new. For the West, it began in classical Greece. Plato said we can only know our world from the shadows it throws on the walls of the darkened cave of our mental existence. His pupil, Aristotle, challenged this skeptical view of our knowledge of Nature, claiming the possibility of a certain degree of scientific achievement: the human mind could comprehend some aspects of the universe it experienced. But the hubristic claim that humans could ultimately know all there is to know seems to be recent, perhaps a logical extension of Descartes' simplification of the world through the abstraction of its parts from the whole. There has long been, and continues to be, a philosophical dispute about the nature of that huge word, TRUTH, and of how we know when we have found it.

What can human beings *really* know? As Canadian philosopher Ian Hacking observes, it is an impossible question. Scientists, being themselves human beings, cannot *know* what human beings can and cannot know. In his book on the subject, he wisely refrains from taking sides. Says Hacking, what the critics of the absolutist view, many of them excellent scientists themselves, are reacting against is the tendency to elevate scientific theories, even successful ones, into ideologies, into claims of absolute knowledge.

> Their target is not the truth of propositions received in the sciences, but *an exalted image of what science is up to, or the authority claimed by scientists for the work they do* ... The received wisdom [of the absolutists] is that scientists must not be challenged, because they are the deep probers of the inner constitution of things.[19]

On the whole, I am much more inclined toward the constructionists' caution than the absolutists' hubris, especially when it comes to claims about the "truth" of human nature. If the complexity of Indra's Net is a better model of the universe than is the sharply defined Billiard Ball model, then indeed the constructionists' view seems a more sensible choice.

### Backlash II: The distortion of complex subjects

The criticisms of the preceding paragraphs have been shown to apply even to simple objects such as subatomic particles like quarks and the structure of small molecules such as water.[20] If truth is elusive in such seemingly straightforward cases, how much more elusive is it when the subject matter is ourselves?

One does not have to be a Creationist, or even religious, to doubt the "truths" about human nature propounded by evolutionary psychologists and described earlier in this chapter. One can believe firmly in the well-grounded theory of evolution (as I do) and still disagree strongly with the claims being made by this group of scientists as to Who We Are. When it comes to being scientific about ourselves, the British philosopher Mary Midgley wields a powerful pen. She has no patience with philosophical short-cuts by those who would lop off huge chunks of our humanness in order to create a simplified, scientifically manageable "human nature." You cannot turn human emotions into left-over animal drives, nor artificially sever feelings from reason.[21]

Most recently Midgley has decried the attempt to understand cultural evolution by reducing the whole human psyche into arbitrary units of thought – called "memes" by the theory's inventors – which, analogous to genes, supposedly move independently from one society to the next.[22] This latest application by the absolutists of the methodologies of reductionist science, Midgley argues, systematically eliminates from our inquiries any subjective, personal insights. But these are the most important, indeed the *only* clues we can really have about what questions to ask about human nature.[23] By discrediting *meaning* and *value* as appropriate aspects of human nature to be studied, the methods of natural science effectively reduce human beings to meaning-free objects. A half-century ago, Michael Polanyi pointed out the consequences:

Admittedly, the pursuits of biology, medicine, psychology and the social sciences may rectify our everyday conceptions of plants and animals, and even of man and society; but we must set against any such modification its effect on the interest by which the study of the original subject matter had been prompted and justified. *If the scientific virtues of exact observation and strict correlation of data are given absolute preference for the treatment of a subject matter which disintegrates when represented in such terms, the result will be irrelevant to the subject matter and probably of no interest at all.*[24]

I submit that Polanyi is right. Arbitrarily objectifying human nature has the effect of disintegrating the subject matter by removing that which is "human" from the "nature" being described. The reductionist Billiard Ball model destroys our ability to seek self-understanding. Once again, Indra's Net seems the more useful model for a complex reality.

### Backlash III: Popular rejection of meaninglessness

A central need of human beings is for meaning. Our need for meaning is our greatest need, superseding all others. People voluntarily give up food, sex, companionship, even life itself in search of and in defense of what they value – what means something to them. The Holy Grail, the Trance State, the Vision Quest, the search for Shangri-La, Nirvana, or Paradise: all embody the same need for transcendent understanding.

Ideally, science, too, is engaged in this pursuit. But modern science seems to deny the very need for what it aims to help us find. It claims the facts it uncovers are neither good nor bad; they are value-free. It is what people – other people, not scientists – *do* with the facts that gives them value, whether positive or negative. But where do people's values come from? Are they part of reality, or are they somehow outside it? Can we be inside and outside at the same time?

If all facts about the universe are value-free, this seems to imply a meaningless universe – amazingly vast and complex, wondrous, esthetic even, but meaningless. Evolution has no purpose. Life has no purpose. Human existence has no purpose. And, coming full circle, the work of scientists themselves has no purpose. Now that's an idea most hard-working, dedicated scientists, who are usually pretty decent men and women, find hard to take (or would do, if they stopped to reflect upon it). Clearly, there are human reasons for science, reasons based on feelings, biases, cultural purposes and a whole lot of value-laden causes. Where does this need for meaning come from?

Do you remember Data, the emotion-free android in television's *Star Trek* series? He found thinking without feeling was impossible. In episode after episode, he demands *reasons* for doing things, and the reasons always turn out to be grounded in feelings. These preceded logic. There can be no reason without purposeful values, and purpose demands motives, and motives are the product of feelings.

When scientists forget to acknowledge this and claim their work is "value-free," ordinary people begin to take fright. The scientists remind us too much of HAL, the disembodied computer in Stanley Kubrick's film *2001: A Space Odyssey*, or his other scary character, the mad scientist, Dr. Strangelove, who believed in the logic of nuclear annihilation.

Modern science, which after World War II seemed to promise a brave new world of material wealth and security, has lost much of its drawing power. People still look to it for solving practical problems. But failure of the promise of unlimited, cheap nuclear power, the toxicity of pesticides and other chemicals, and fears over the unknown consequences of the genetic manipulation of plants and animals have cast doubt on the value of the "value-free" knowledge that science has provided. As the gloss fades from the hope of "ever-better living through chemistry" (and now, silicon chips and genetically modified organisms) and current technological miracles no longer seem "miraculous," people are becoming more disenchanted with modern materialism in a universe increasingly devoid of meaning. Is life only about food, water, and sex, as the "hard facts" of evolution seem to argue our genes are bent on?

Fewer people today look to science for answers in their lives. They search elsewhere: in encounter groups, through alternative healing, and via familiar or strange religions. In America, religious fundamentalism is making a resurgence. (Witness the banning by the State of Kansas of the teaching of evolution in its schools in fall 1999, rescinded in 2001 after much public outcry. Though reversed in this instance, the backlash is not over.) The image of the universe, and particularly of ourselves, being offered to us by mainstream science, based as it is on the Billiard Ball model of reality, offers no wisdom, no guidance, no existential answers whatsoever. Yet some of its practitioners claim their science is the only legitimate way of knowing.

I conclude this discussion of the popular backlash with several observations by that outstanding twentieth-century thinker, Fritz Schumacher. Economist by training, humanist by nature, Schumacher was among the most insightful and eclectic philosophers of our age – yet one with his feet well-anchored in the soil, wise in the ways of Nature, and sensitive to the needs of common people. The quotes are taken from his last work, *A Guide for the Perplexed*, which opens with a critique of modern science and the world view it offers. The quotes also include thoughts from Viktor Frankl.

The maps produced by modern materialistic Scientism leave all the questions that really matter unanswered; more than that, they deny the validity of the questions.

It is being loudly proclaimed *in the name of scientific objectivity* that "values and meanings are nothing but defence mechanisms and reaction formations"; that man is "nothing but a complex biochemical mechanism powered by a combustion system which energizes computers with prodigious storage facilities for retaining encoded information."

"What we have to deplore ... is not so much the fact that *scientists are specializing*, but rather the fact that *specialists are generalizing*." ... "The true nihilism of today ... is reductionism ... Contemporary nihilism no longer brandishes the word nothingness; today nihilism is camouflaged as *nothing-but-ness*. Human phenomena are thus turned into mere epiphenomena."[25]

## My philosophy of truth

What people need, Schumacher was suggesting, is a new map, a new way of looking at the world, a new gestalt. In this book, I offer the beginning of such a map, one that identifies within its overall framework a place for such crucial human experiences as complexity, feelings, meanings, and relatedness. In a word, it offers as replacement for the narrow, limiting vision of a Billiard Ball universe, the more complex, less rigidly specified, and far more inclusive vision of Indra's Net, an interconnected vision of the universe in which human beings are integrally embedded.

The new map incorporates evolutionary theory along with innumerable pieces of information from many fields of inquiry, while at the same time disallowing the elevation of their propositions and hypotheses to the status of absolute truths into which all observations must be squeezed (or, as Schumacher noted, ignored if they do not fit the Procrustean bed). What is different about this map is its 180 degree shift in how reality is to be construed, from atomistic to interconnected. It incorporates descriptions of small, seemingly isolated pieces of the whole, that are based on local, direct causes and effects. But it refuses to extrapolate such narrow findings into sweeping generalizations about the whole. Rather, it seeks to see where they complement the whole, making sense of its connectedness.

My overall "big picture" of an interconnected universe within which human nature is embedded is thus a tentative one, with few sharply defined boundaries or hard-and-fast laws such as exist in the Billiard Ball model of reductionist science. It is more intuitive and flexible, less precise, rule-bound and rigid. Yet it has coherent meaning despite its looser structure. And, in my view, it explains more satisfactorily what is known about human nature, gathered from disciplines ranging from physics to religion and everything in between. Of course, at the end of the book, it is up to each reader to concur, or not.

### What counts as knowledge?

I believe there is no such thing as perfect truth in our personal knowledge of reality. The best we can hope for are adaptive working hypotheses. Everyone's understanding is always an approximation. Even an expert whom we seek out for the special knowledge he or she has gives us facts that are *selected, simplified,* and *interpreted.* A brief example from the field of ecology (a *bona fide* science that parallels human nature in its level of complexity) provides an insight into this obvious limit.

The example comes from a colleague, a plant ecologist who set out to learn how mosses, supposedly confined to moist environments, could occur in semi-desert habitats where they were subject to drying out for varying lengths of time. What was their microhabitat like? How much did they dry out? For how long? These were the questions he asked.

The microhabitat, it turned out, was the shaded undersides of huge boulders strewn across the slopes of southern California. In the course of his study, my friend, Peter Alpert, realized that he was making many simplifying assumptions as he went along. In the field, with his data sheets awaiting numerical positions of mosses on boulders to be written into the empty columns, he realized that non-spherical, unevenly shaped boulders had to be converted into something mathematically amenable: namely, round spheres which conveniently have a latitude and longitude, and lie at a precise angle to the slope of the hillside. He took Galileo's comment to heart: "Nature is a book and the characters in which it is written are triangles, circles and squares." Only, as Peter realized, triangles (or in his case, spheres) "twinkle only in our eyes."

Peter describes how he made numerous other selections and simplifications in his work. One was the accuracy (or lack of it) in his measurement of the water content of the desiccated mosses. It varied slightly with the time of day and the humidity, and hence was only a statistical approximation. Other assumptions were that the boulders were all much alike in surface texture, that there was no competition for sites, that no predators were affecting distribution of the mosses, and so on. As he says: "An assumption is a hypothesis one is not prepared to test." In his article about his work, aptly titled "The Boulder and the Sphere," he summarizes his thoughts thus:

> Facts never speak for themselves. Like the distribution of moss on boulders, they are constructed from a variety of sources, including philosophical disposition [of the scientist]. When science involves politically sensitive issues, scientific results tend to correlate with the political views of the scientist.[26]

All knowledge, even that of modern science (which often claims itself to be objectively free from such interpretive constraints), is thus selected from the totality of reality, and *interpreted* in the conceptual language of a particular time and place. Science is just one, often very effective, way of making a highly messy, unique world understandable by constructing generalizations that approximate to apparent recurring patterns. As Alpert says, "scientific results should be used as judgments, not facts." In particular, he cautions against

53

investing too much faith in the assumptions and simplifications already used in the past. Too often these take on a reality of their own, one that substitutes for the inconveniently complex world of Nature. In this same paper, he notes Herbert Marcuse and Aron Gurwitsch's description of this extreme sort of fallacy as an *Ideenkleid*, or "tissue of ideas ... cast upon the life world so as to conceal it to the point of being substituted for it." It resembles in its opacity the clothes with which we always must dress up reality, as described by Richard Shweder in the opening quote to this chapter.

Yet, as Shweder implies, we have to work with such "tissues of ideas," since they comprise the beliefs and assumptions on which our conscious perceptions of reality are based. (These, of course, are the pilings that underlie our thought-world, as shown in the Introduction, Figure 0.2.) I believe that over the past several centuries, the tissue of beliefs that has been cast over the real "us," not only by science but by history and political and social theories as well, has hugely distorted our understanding of human nature by making us out to be much more dislikable creatures than we really are. By ignoring or distorting some of our biologically grounded good human traits and tendencies, we are creating institutions that are increasingly self-destructive. Over half a century ago, the philosopher Alfred North Whitehead warned us that we need to constantly review our simplifying assumptions, our *abstractions*:

> You cannot think without abstractions; accordingly, it is of the utmost importance to be vigilant in critically revising your *modes* of abstraction. It is here that philosophy finds its niche as essential to the healthy progress of society. It is the critic of abstractions. *A civilisation which cannot burst through its current abstraction is doomed to sterility after a very limited period of progress.*[27]

In this book I attempt to do what Whitehead urged – to burst through our current "tissue of ideas" or abstractions about human nature by creating a new, alternative set of assumptions, a new gestalt, if you will, that offers possible answers and explanations for many of our most pressing queries about ourselves. Yet because, like our current Billiard Ball Gestalt, it is supported by interpreted facts, it cannot and should not be considered as a final answer to the question "Who Are We?" All that I shall argue is that my theory seems likely to be more adaptive in the new millennium than that of our present image of ourselves. We human beings, after all, evolve and adapt mainly by changing the ways we think – by quite literally *changing our minds*!

## Contrasting views of "human-nature-in-the-universe"

When the Billiard Ball model of the universe is applied to evolutionary theory, its assumptions go like this: "The planet has limited resources, and since all species produce more offspring than can be supported, the better adapted will likely survive." That is more or less what Darwin said, and so far there is no problem. But then the argument continues: "Being better adapted means winning out over others in a direct competition for survival." That is the part that is not necessarily so. Being better adapted can mean a whole lot of things: hiding better; running away faster; tasting bad; being more efficient; learning to use different resources; creating new resources; even cooperating better.

Almost all the latter forms of adaptation are virtually ignored, however, by modern evolutionary theorists, especially when it comes to the evolution of behavior. It's a zero-sum game. Everybody is directly competing with everyone else. Spontaneous cooperation (unless through a binding contract) is a waste of time. Sacrifice for others is foolhardy. "Selfish genes" do not allow for love, for empathy, for being virtuous. Those are evolutionary no-no's; they just aren't efficient. They decrease one's fitness to survive. Natural selection long ago eliminated any such tendencies. The living world is a war zone, whether overt or covert.

When it comes to human nature, the Billiard Ball view says that evil is an evolutionary good, and virtue is an evolutionary dead-end. So even when we do good, it has somehow ultimately got to be a selfish act. Either we consciously deceive and cheat others or we manage to deceive ourselves into not seeing how selfish we really are. According to the evolutionary psychologists, even those warm feelings we have when we help a stranger are merely self-deception. Life is nothing but a competitive game; behavior, nothing but a strategy for winning the survival contest.

Oversimplified though I have made it, this sketch sums up the frightening image of human nature we are told we must accept by the proponents of the Billiard Ball Gestalt, which underlies the "selfish-gene" theory of evolution. To my mind what is left unexplained or glossed over by this theory is insurmountable. I cannot see how we could ever have evolved at all if we were constructed in this way. Indeed, I cannot see how any social mammals – the other primates, dolphins, elephants – ever came into being following such rules of natural selection for behavior. Too much fast-talking and distortion is needed to make experience fit this model. Too much of ourselves is missing, ignored, dismissed.

Indra's Net, the alternative gestalt of the universe introduced in the Introduction, replaces "individual-competition-in-a-world-of-scarcity" with "fitting-in-better-with-the-ever-changing-whole" as the basis of evolutionary thinking. This view, which I develop step-by-step here, does not eliminate competition as a factor in evolution (and hence in human behavior); but it demotes it from its privileged position as the *only* factor. Immediately, a great many human traits and behavioral tendencies become plausible as being adaptive in the universe. Our desire to live in groups, our empathy, our feelings of love and grief – they all make sense. Virtue and evil both have a role to play, but the role of evil is changed from being hopelessly engraved in our genes to being amenable to amelioration by the changing of cultural beliefs and institutions.

A pivotal difference between these two gestalts is that the Billiard Ball vision utilizes Rational Game Theory, a form of reasoning that comes out of the Enlightenment and excludes feelings from any role in the universe, while Indra's Net, being all-encompassing, allows feelings to exist and play a role. We might well ask, how does Nature herself work? And I would answer, she works by means of attractions and repulsions, by feelings, not by reason. Thus, the behaviorist, B.F. Skinner, was himself completely wrong when he said it was wrong to ask what an animal or human "feels" when it responds to a stimulus because no physicist ever would ask a falling body what it "feels" as it falls towards the ground.[28]

Yet that is exactly what physicists do ask: what are the feelings, the forces, that guide a falling body? What attracts? What repels? An inanimate body has no brain with which to reason. But still it acts. The same holds for electrons, for everything.

At every level, the universe works in this way, juggling attractions and repulsions back and forth in a constant dance of force and matter that forms patterns of enormously varying dimensions and durations: from the millionth fraction of a picosecond in sub-atomic particles to the billions of years of the stars in the galaxies. But even the longest-lasting patterns are only semi-stable, undergoing continuous chaotic fluxes, little wobbles, large swings, sometimes disappearing altogether. Almost all the "laws of Nature" that we identify – daily and seasonal cycles, behaviors of prey and predators – are repeating patterns of sufficient duration to allow us humans (and many other forms of life) to make predictions and to adapt accordingly. Yet they are not necessarily fixed patterns; ultimately, the "laws of Nature" may themselves evolve.

Life's adaptations may be in the form of the selected survival of randomly varying genetic traits (Darwinian adaptation) or of behaviors made in direct response to the environment (experiential adaptation). Even one-celled amoebas respond to attractive or repulsive stimuli. A fallen, but still-living tree turns old lateral branches into upward-growing tree trunks in response to gravitational force. Corn plants actually move their genes around in response to certain environmental patterns, thus changing what those genes do and so improving the plant's chances of survival.[29] And any number of species of animals can be trained to change behavior, from worms to mammals, through the process of learning, which involves non-heritable physical changes in the structure of the organism's nervous system.

All life is thus constantly responding – as is the rest of Nature – by way of attractions and repulsions – or "feelings" – to the patterns around it. Does the universe have its own, internal "reasons" or "purposes"? No one knows. But Nature in some sense does "feel" at every level. Everything is interconnected.

Now what is really interesting to me about modern science is that it argues in the following way: the events in the universe that science sets out to uncover have no discernible purpose or meaning of their own that we can detect. Scientifically speaking, the world is a meaningless place and human existence as part of that world has neither meaning nor purpose. It just "*is.*" Yet out of the other corner of its collective mouth, science claims to rely on reason (which is said not to exist in the universe, except, of course, in ourselves) rather than feelings (which in some form or other apparently *do* exist) to justify the legitimacy of its claims to truth about Nature. Human feelings, human emotions, are biases that science claims get in the way of knowledge and truth. What modern evolutionary science has done by excluding feelings from its understanding of life is to close its eyes to the most important clues there are. It fails to ask what feelings in humans and other species has natural selection actually selected *for*?

The feelings that drive behaviors are pieces of *actual* information. They are hard to interpret, certainly. But they are far more likely to help our understanding than are logical laws of behavior constructed by the imaginings of that most recent evolutionary adaptation, the human cortex. Reason and logic are not built into Nature. They are simply new tools we humans use to better perceive fuzzy patterns in a fluctuating universe by simplifying and encoding them. Reason and logic are abstracters of the whole – what Whitehead warned us about. They are Peter Alpert's "circles and triangles of Nature that twinkle only in our own eyes." Logic and reason are simply extensions of a very human need, the need for explanatory stories that help us adapt. They are not a path to final truth – and never can be.

When it comes to understanding human nature we are particularly foolish to rely on logical abstractions as descriptions of Who We Are, while ignoring the feelings and emotions that guide us, along with the subconscious insights and understandings our mental equipment spontaneously comes up with. Together, feelings, intuition, and conscious thought or reasoning all contribute to what we call human nature. Nor can their contributions be disentangled, one from the other, as recent studies of brain function now tell us. By forcing human feelings and intuition to fit uncomfortably into a purely logical/mathematical description of evolution, with its obvious oversimplifications, some modern evolutionists are distorting our self-understanding in ways I believe to be dangerous. It is time to take a new look at the meaning of feelings and of intuition – where they come from and what they tell us about our psychological needs as a living species.

## Human nature, with feelings

The picture of human nature I propose downplays the majesty of our conscious intelligence as the centerpiece of Who We Are. Thinking is definitely powerful stuff, but it can go nowhere without guidance from the deep emotions built into us during our evolutionary past. People writing about human nature usually make a long list of the emotionally driven needs of our species, often coming up with a dozen or so: food, water, sex, security, acceptance, protection, status, power, independence, identity, etc. And they make equally long lists of our guiding emotions: happiness, grief, despair, hate, love, anger, depression, fury, passion, joy, sorrow, contentment, etc. Each is then analyzed separately as a circumscribed condition.

In this book I propose that there are but three basic drives or needs that specifically constitute *human* nature, as distinct from the nature of animals in general. Most animals seek out food, water and mates, and so do humans, but for us these are subsumed by even more powerful needs that arise by virtue of our being wholly and imperatively social. I label these three needs "propensities" rather than "instincts" or "drives" (the more common terms for genetically programmed emotions) because while propensity still implies a powerful innate tendency, it suggests far more flexibility in the behavioral responses by which it can be satisfied. The three propensities are for *bonding*, for *autonomy*, and for *meaning*.

Bonding within a social group is the *sine qua non* of primate and, hence, of human survival. One may shift from one group to another, but acceptance within some group is essential; evolutionarily, total exclusion is tantamount to a death sentence for human beings. The existence of a functional group *precedes* the possibility of individual survival. *The ability of the individual to reproduce is secondary to the ability of the group to maintain itself.* Thus, remaining attached to a group is the primary survival *and* reproductive goal of individual primates.

Unlike the social attachments of honeybees or schooling fishes or flocks of birds, the attachments of primates evolved in concert with the development of intelligence: the ability to modify complex behaviors through learning. The relative increase in cognitive capacity of the primate brain that makes highly adaptive, intelligent *group* life possible also demands autonomy of *individual behavior*. Big, relatively unprogrammed, adaptive brains must learn *through experience* how to survive. And learning demands spontaneous engagement by the developing infant and juvenile with its world. The absolute necessity for independent, self-generated behavior begins at birth and continues throughout a primate's life.

Bonding and autonomy are propensities humans share with other primates. It is our further propensity or need for meaning that makes us unique.[30] During our evolution, the developing cortex acquired the capacity for symbol-formation and abstract thought. Language – first mime, then speech – made the communication of ideas possible by the telling of "stories." Not only outright events ("I just saw a lion across the ravine") but suppositions ("She may have a cub") and proposals ("We should move out of her way") could be communicated. It is but a short step to *valuing* choices about what to do, to providing *reasons* for those choices, and to justifying them with causal explanations. For the first time, internal perceptions of the significance of experience can be communicated with others and valued by a group. Conceptual meanings come into existence, are shared, and ultimately become the structural basis of culture. The resulting cultural meaning or cultural narrative becomes what connects the individual with the group she or he depends on for survival.[31]

It is my thesis that these three psychic propensities – for bonding, for autonomy, and for meaning – frame virtually all human social behavior. Of the three, meaning has subsumed the other two, as cultural narratives have generated institutions for prescribing bonding patterns and for limiting autonomy (about which more in a moment). But all three persist throughout life and are defended by powerful emotions. We seek bonds and resist their rupture. Broken bonds may lead to anger or to grief. We strive for independence and resist constraint, especially physical coercion. And we seek meaning, not only as individuals within a group, but especially collectively, as *whole groups*. Threats either to our individual identity within the group or to the integrity and the identity of the entire group are powerfully resisted. And all of these emotional responses are the result of the importance, during our evolutionary history, of each of these propensities for our successful survival.

### Ongoing complications due to our human propensities

It is a mistake to assume that the processes of evolution produce perfectly adapted creatures. Most species are effective compromises, unfinished agglomerations of traits that sometimes are out-of-synch with each other. And nowhere is this more evident than for primates, especially humans. Our powerful propensities for bonding and autonomy, both important adaptive functions, come into constant conflict. There is always the potential for disruption of the group on which everyone depends when the autonomous behaviors of two individuals clash. As pointed out, especially by primatologist Frans de Waal, all primates have developed ways of reconciling, or "making up," of restoring group harmony.[32] Among humans, the development of language greatly facilitates the ease with which reconciliation can potentially occur. Yet too often in history, our meaning systems have added an insurmountable complication, creating deep barriers to understanding between individuals or groups. And sometimes language even exacerbates rather than ameliorates the problem.

During human evolution, cultural meaning systems became such an incredibly powerful adaptive force for coordinating social action and adaptation to new environments that they acquired the extremes of emotional protection that we experience today. Danger, even death, are willingly faced on behalf of one's ethnic group, one's religion, one's fatherland. Our meaning systems have been the source of the amazing productions of humankind: the arts, the sciences, the monuments, the wisdom; and also of its most terrible acts, the horrors of brutality and destruction wreaked on other humans and on Earth itself.

In a culture with an ideal meaning system, both the need for bonding and for individual autonomy are equally well accommodated, the human psyche thrives and conflict within the society is minimized. But though our need for meaning is surely genetically driven, the *particular* meaning system, the *particular* cultural vision in which a person grows up and on which his or her survival depends, is a human construct. Our cultural narratives too often imperfectly resolve the tensions within each of us between the bonding that leads to social harmony and the autonomy that is necessary for our personal development. Each narrative meaning system, with its own history of human choices, thoughts, innovations, and beliefs, may or may not meet the needs of the human psyche well enough to produce widespread satisfaction and social stability. Culture, just like genes, can run a population into an evolutionary cul-de-sac.

Thus it is that, over time, cultures come and go – much faster than genes do. Some cultures fail as their meaning systems (and sometimes all their members along with them) become extinct. Sometimes a culture fails, but its members survive, subsumed into another, momentarily more stable, cultural system. In general, those that prevail are the ones that are able to adapt to new circumstances.

### The good news and the bad news

Adaptation through cultural change is the hallmark of humankind. Since almost all of our behavior is culturally honed, we are freer than any other species from the grip of genetic determinism. The "good news," then, is that we have it in our power to change our cultural narratives. In the past, when the rate of change required was relatively slow, as when climates changed gradually (not always the case) or population increased slowly, adjustments to beliefs, customs, and social relationships could be made almost imperceptibly over several generations. New ways did not threaten social stability; meaning systems could be subtly modified. Myths and customs were reshaped to adapt to new circumstances.[33]

The "bad news" is that, whenever rapid change becomes necessary, whether due to environmental collapse or social pressures, successful adaptation may fail to occur. Our genes, bless them, encourage us to cling to and defend old meaning systems because, evolutionarily, that has been essential for social survival. Threats from external meaning systems (the "infidels") are met with fierce resistance: and (as the astute reader has surely anticipated) threats from within a society are labeled heretical or subversive. Even the high emotions, inflammatory rhetoric, and negative campaigning that characterize modern "civilized" politics can be symptoms of the same problem. Changing meaning systems is not simply an intellectual problem; it is profoundly emotional.

It is part of my thesis that the organized violence and mayhem that pepper human history have almost always been the result of clashes between meaning systems (or between power groups whose identities are at stake, which is a corollary of problematic meaning systems). Only seldom have they been struggles over resources *per se*, necessary for simple survival. Such battles are of relatively recent origin in terms of the whole of human history.

Thus, the so-called "dark side" of human nature is not due to some gene-driven inner selfishness based on competition for material resources, or for women, or for any other "scarce" commodity. The primary problem lies in our need to belong to a meaningful society. In human life, it is not the food and reproduction that really matter, it is the meaning that underlies everything else. How else do we account for celibate monks, for soldiers joining up against hopeless odds in battle, for Gandhi and other political leaders undertaking life-threatening fasts? History needs to be understood in a new way, as the multiple unfoldings of our innate need for shared meaning, and our ability, or lack thereof, to change and adapt it. As the anthropologists Signe Howell and Roy Willis have put it:

> [I]nnate sociality supposes a predisposition in human beings towards the continual absorption of existing meanings and the creation of new meanings in local universes of thought that are constantly being discovered, destroyed, and negotiated anew in the process of social interaction.[34]

Once we see ourselves in this light – in a gestalt of meaningful connectedness to other human beings because that is how humans must live to survive – we can comprehend the emotional forces that are built into us and begin creating institutions that satisfy our deepest longings, rather than ones that try to override and suppress them in a misguided attempt to impose a rigidly prescribed social order. Such insights into human nature have the power to open up new approaches for resolving our conflicts and achieving non-destructive, adaptive social change.

## A map of the book

My task in this book is to stimulate people to see that there are other sets of spectacles with which to view themselves and their relationship with the world than those that they have been taught to see through. We need to shake the kaleidoscope of our vision, to reorganize our observations and experiences into new patterns of understanding, into new schemata.

My message is optimistic despite daily reports of violence and destruction over the instantaneous global news network. Yes, much is wrong, as humans stress each other and the planet, and stressed people and a stressed planet reciprocate. The danger from impending crises, both social and environmental, is high. Yet given the levels of stress, it is amazing that the mayhem and suffering are not far worse. For each horror story there are dozens of others, under-reported, of enormous caring and self-sacrifice. Human beings, it seems, are capable of amazing moral extremes of both evil and virtue. This book argues that both extremes make evolutionary sense. They were, and still are, explain-able as evolutionary adaptations, but not in the way suggested by the evolutionary psychologists.

In the book I further argue that cultural contexts affect greatly the balance between the two behavioral extremes. Societies promote prosocial and antisocial behaviors in very different ratios, often having to correct coercively the consequences of their own unsuspected misreadings of human nature. I dismiss the notion that violence and aggression are behaviors forced on us by "selfish genes." Rather, they are the extreme forms of communication that humans use when social conditions necessary for their individual or collective survival are not being fulfilled. When violent and senseless behaviors happen it is because there are virtually always either personal or cultural causes in the life experiences of those who commit them.[35] Not all cultures are equally adaptive; not all meaning systems accommodate equally well the needs human nature demands. None is "ideal," but some really do succeed in satisfying all our human inner propensities better than others. It behooves all peoples to try to learn from each other what "works" and why.

We begin our exploration of the nature of human nature with our cousins, the primates, often used as models for our early ancestors. The question is: What preconceived model of the evolutionary process itself should we be using to interpret primate nature? If we discard the old, individualistic model and replace it with a connected one, known as "group selection," then cooperative social life, promoted by innate feelings of empathy and affection, becomes evolutionarily credible (see Chapter II).

This new interpretation offers a gestalt shift in how we reconstruct our own evolutionary history over the past few million years. The old "killer ape," selected for hunting animals and violently defending territory and competing with others, is plainly incorrect. Our ancestors lived in small, closely bonded, wandering bands that were selected for their group's adaptability, particularly in the face of repeated sudden and dramatic climate changes. Communication and meaning systems, so necessary for survival of groups with helpless infants, played a far more critical role in our ancestors' survival than did "winning" competitions against other groups (see Chapter III).

Selection for group survival is reflected in the structure of the modern human brain. The once popular belief that emotions are a "problem" still lurking in an ancient "animal" part of our brains, and that the real, human part of us is our big cerebral hemispheres, is not borne out by what is now known about how the brain works. Feelings and thoughts are profoundly linked, in a brain that does most of its work without our conscious selves ever noticing (see Chapter IV).

As it turns out, the human brain is primarily a meaning-making organ, exactly what is needed for successful group living. And it makes meaning out of direct experience with its environment. Mind is the entity that emerges from the interactions among brain, body, and the socio-environmental milieu in which the self exists. Meaning, or the interpretation of experience, is shared through that marvelous abstracting tool called language. The meaningful sharing of minds-in-context is what creates the opportunity for coordinated cultural action. Such complex cooperative behaviors as net-hunting and navigation become possible (see Chapter V).

The cultural embeddedness of the human mind is possible only because at birth the brain is largely unprogrammed, open to being shaped by experience. The brain of the human infant requires two critical conditions for optimal development: security (or bonding) for positive emotional development, and appropriate opportunities for experience (or autonomy). Excessive trauma, whether physical or psychological, actually alters brain structure, adapting it at the cost of its more sophisticated functions to survive under otherwise unbearable circumstances. If healing of such brains does not occur once the stress is past, persons may be unable to live comfortably in more normal social settings (see Chapter VI).

Every culture has the task of providing psychic identity to its members. "Self" exists only in context of the meaning system of one's culture. Sexual identity is a universal question, with as many answers as there are cultures. The meaning of "male," for obvious biological reasons, can be the most tricky to construct satisfactorily. What *is* the purpose of men? Fitting different identities into a single cultural narrative is another complex problem for meaning systems. What is gained, and what lost, by ranking? Hierarchies can be efficient, but because they maintain stability by repressing the fundamental psychic needs of some of their members, they become rigid, unable to change for fear of social unrest (see Chapter VII).

This leads to a reinterpretation of human prehistory and history. Conventional explanations in Western history texts of the rise and fall of cultures and civilizations rest on a sequence of leap-frogging technological advances and the supposition of constant conflict between societies for control of material resources. The old social-Darwinist theory of humans as engaged in a constant war-for-survival has badly distorted our view of human nature. Vendettas of revenge may well have been present always, but reconciliation was present also. Organized war arose, I suggest, out of clashes over meaning systems. Explanations of human history must include not only favorable ecosystems and technical advances,[36] but also the interactions, whether peaceful or violent, constructive or destructive, between disparate meaning systems. Threats to cultural beliefs and ethnic identities, religious fervor, and national shame and anger, all have wreaked more havoc in human history than battles over water-holes, river valleys, and grazing lands (see Chapter VIII).

Moving to today's world, I undertake an analysis of the trauma to the human psyche being inflicted by the dominant Western world view. This extreme version of the Billiard Ball Gestalt promotes an unrelenting competitive capitalism that seriously began metastasizing around the globe at the start of the twentieth century. It led, among other things, to social resistance in the form of Marxist ideas, and to feelings of national rejection from the global scene by both Germany and Japan that led to terrible slaughter in World War II. It spread via colonialism and then post-colonialism, destabilizing cultures almost everywhere else. It invites competition not only between individuals but between nations with world views that hold different cultural values. It has become a religion as powerful as any in the past, making it difficult to unseat. It is top-heavy with self-created social and environmental overheads. And it suffers from such a high degree of technological dependency as to make it rigid and unadaptive (see Chapter IX).

The difficult process of cultural adaptation, not by technological invention but by modification of meaning systems, is the basis of most of the intractable conflicts that occupy our world. The fervent desire for local group autonomy exists almost everywhere: from Native Americans, to Palestinians, to Kurds, Kosovars, and the East Timorese. Such demands meet emotion-laden resistance from those whose own power, and therefore identities, are at stake: political leaders in Canada and the United States, in Israel, in Serbia, in Turkey, in Indonesia, in China. Unlike struggles over material resources, these conflicts cannot be settled by negotiated contracts. By using our insight about the human propensity to defend meaning systems, we can develop new, psychologically more valid approaches to resolving human conflict that avoids the out-dated, Machiavellian use of economic, diplomatic, and military threats. When violence ceases, however, it is only the beginning of resolution, as the example of contemporary South Africa shows. We in the West are barely at the beginning of understanding what some human cultures already know how to do – active reconciliation (see Chapter X).

Finally, I make some tentative suggestions for the future that a better appreciation of human nature might offer. Included are ways of raising new generations to be more empathetic and to discover more significant meaning in their lives by changing our approach to schooling. This is followed by several examples of societies that are already creating more rewarding, just, and meaningful lives for their members. They offer concrete hope to us all for the hidden potential that lies in every human being and in every human group, which requires only an appropriately accommodating shared meaning system in order to flourish. Once a society learns how to practice participatory social change through dialogue, which all members then "own," they have a powerful opportunity for creating a more satisfying, meaningful cultural life (see Chapter XI).

# II

# WHY WE PRIMATES ARE NOT "GAME THEORISTS"

Behavior is not "just like" morphology in relation to evolution. Unlike a bone or feather that remain the same physical entities through repeated measurement, a behavioral pattern is an abstract conception of many occurrences, each of which is different. Furthermore, behavior can be transmitted to offspring by cultural tradition, whereas extra-genetic inheritance of morphology is severely limited. Finally, behavior itself does not fossilize, and the record of its results in footprints, nests, and the like is scanty.

Jack Hailman (1982: 250)

If there is an essence of being a primate, it is the progressive evolution of intelligence as a way of life.

Alison Jolly (1985: 250)

[B]y 1980, it [was] about as difficult to find a truly natural primate as a truly natural "savage."

Donna Haraway (1988: 92)

When two naturalists adopted three orphaned grizzly bear cubs in the Kamchatka wilderness with the intent of returning them to the wild after their first summer, they wondered whether the cubs would be able to discover for themselves how to survive. Aside from protecting them from potentially molesting adult male bears, leaving out food for them to find for a few weeks, and walking the cubs out and about in their wilderness home, the naturalists showed them but one thing: that fish live under water. As they watched, the three cubs automatically knew which plants to eat, how to catch the fish, how to climb trees and rocky slopes and slide down snowbanks – even to seek out a den. It takes considerable intelligence to be a bear, and plenty of practice to become a skilled bear. But evidently much of the skill simply unfolds, through exploration and practice; it does not have to be learned from another bear. Most of the knowledge about how to be a bear is somehow innate.[1]

No primate infant can do this! There are a few recorded instances of human infants being nursed and raised by wolves, but they ran on all fours, ate raw meat, and had no human attributes at all. Their brains and bodies had acquired the skills for living as wolves, not as people.[2] Unlike grizzly bear cubs, human babies do not automatically know how to become like their own kind. That only occurs when they have interacted with other human beings who are attentive and responsive, from whom they learn to become human. The normal development of body and brain of a newborn requires intimate, protracted contact with a social group. Without such contact, brain and body do not mature, as the following sad case attests.

> Genie, a girl who had been locked away by her parents all her life, was discovered at age thirteen by Los Angeles authorities, some years ago; she was mute and incontinent, crawled on all fours, and understood nothing that was said to her, a primitive creature without any evidence of mind. But it was not because of gross brain defectiveness; within four years, in foster care, she had developed some language ability, many social skills, and the mental capacity of an eight-year old.[3]

This absolute need of human infants for an environment that includes other human beings, not just for protection from danger and for nourishment, but to *complete the process of normal development*, is shared by other primate infants. In the 1950s and 1960s, H.F. Harlow and his colleagues deprived baby rhesus monkeys of all social contacts, creating in them a desperate and permanent autism. Such babies sat huddled in a corner, hugging and rocking themselves, and ultimately wasting away. Infants provided with a furry surrogate cloth mother fared somewhat better, as did two or more infants placed together.[4] These heartless experiments provided scientific proof, if such were needed, that primates have a biological need for physical and emotional contact with their own kind. Social life is essential for normal primate development to a degree not seen in other social species, with the possible exception of cetaceans and elephants, and now, it appears, condors.[5]

The eventual evolution of the human mind, with its enormous powers of adaptation – of thought, inventiveness, and capacity to control the environment – depended on the coupling of two trends in primate evolution: close-knit social groups and premature birth of helpless infants with incompletely developed brains and bodies. Primate intelligence was a *co-evolution* between: (1) increasingly plastic infants that completed their development less in response to genetically specified guidelines than in response to patterns of behavior learned from the living community around them; and (2) increasingly coherent groups capable of forming and maintaining shared patterns of behavior. What primate behavior is *not*, is behavior programmed in highly detailed ways, that follows particular, internally coded rules.

Yet the idea that human behavior (indeed the behavior of all organisms) can be explained in terms of a few simple evolutionary rules that must be genetically encoded has suffused the whole new discipline of evolutionary psychology. Laying claim to their own version of neo-Darwinian thinking, evolutionary psychologists have constructed what they consider an airtight theory: each individual organism's behavior is genetically designed to promote only its *own* survival and the reproduction of its *own* genes. Obviously behavior of some sort is essential for survival; absence of behavior signifies death. But these theorists imply that virtually all behavior is designed to promote survival and reproduction and, further, that it must have been genetically selected and encoded.

So widely promoted has been this adaptationist theory that it now appears in the popular press, as in a Valentine's Day article entitled "Jealousy Genes" that appeared in my local weekly. The real (i.e. biological) reason we feel jealous if our significant other has an affair with someone else is because infidelity interferes with our reproductive security – at the genetic level! A man is afraid his wife's baby (which he will help support) may not be his; and she is afraid her husband won't be as supportive of her child if he has another somewhere else. Or so says the article:

> Infidelity [thanks to contraceptives] no longer necessarily endangers paternity and women [thanks to women's liberation] are perfectly capable of providing for themselves and their children. The tragedy – and comedy – of evolutionary psychology, however, is that our social evolution has vastly outpaced biological evolution; we continue to try to negotiate our way through a space age world using stone-age minds. Today, a jealous response is, logically speaking, antiquated; a reaction to a threat that is no longer genetic life-or-death.[6]

Later on it will be evident that human sexual jealousy has little to do with biological parenting and a great deal to do with the stability of social groups. Yet the theories of evolutionary psychologists, who tell us our behavior "is all in our stone-age genes," are no longer restricted to their corner of the academic world. The belief that an ever-increasing number of specific human behaviors are genetically dictated is becoming ever-more widely promoted.[7] Before addressing what primate behaviors actually might have been selected because they favored our survival, I need to deal with the game theory approach to evolution that now dominates so much current evolutionary theorizing. It illustrates how overly simplified some scholars are trying to make the complex phenomenon of natural selection.

## Game theory and genetic determinism

The door of the neo-Darwinian age opened wide when the nature and structure of genes were discovered. They were lengths of double-helical DNA, able not only to code for the synthesis of proteins, the working molecules of life, but also to reproduce themselves, as the theory of inheritance demanded. Now, it seemed, evolution could be explained in satisfyingly scientific, molecular terms. Or could it? Of course, genes do code for proteins, and increasingly we know which proteins. We also know something about what some of the proteins do at the molecular level. But we are only now discovering the genes that bring about the formation of a whole organ, such as a limb or a heart. And, with but one or two exceptions, we know almost nothing at all about how genes might code for particular behaviors.[8]

These limits to our present knowledge, however, have not caused a group of theorists to shrink from proposing that once the information encoded in an organism's genes is known then virtually everything else about that organism can be deduced, the genes being the source of all else about the organism. The foremost spokesperson for this group, Richard Dawkins, recently suggested that by the year 2003, when the human genome has been completely sequenced, all the information necessary to make a human being could be put onto a couple of standard CD-ROM discs.

> These [discs] could then be sent into outer space, and the human race could go extinct secure [sic] in the knowledge that [perhaps one day] a sufficiently advanced civilization would be able to reconstitute a human being.[9]

But as biologist Richard Strohman points out, "The theory of the gene has mistakenly evolved into a theory and a paradigm of life ... into a revived and thoroughly molecular form of genetic determinism."[10] One set of molecules has been taken as the beginning and the end of the explanation of all life processes, from cells to ecosystems.

Before discussing how this paradigm of genetic determinism, which arises directly out of the linear thinking of the Billiard Ball Gestalt, has been used by a subset of neo-Darwinist proponents to explain the entire evolutionary process, let's look at what Darwin himself proposed, using excerpts from his own writings to see how circumspect he really was in his thoughts about the meanings of key ideas such as adaptation, fitness, and natural selection.

### What Darwin said

Darwin's theory begins by noting that all forms of life regularly produce more offspring than can survive (a species would soon become extinct if it did not). Second, the offspring are not identical; they vary in heritable (genetic) ways. Third, the chances of being a survivor are increased for the best-adapted or "fittest" offspring of each generation. This latter process, of being "chosen" to survive by virtue of better traits, Darwin called "natural selection." It is a problematic term, for it seems to imply the active agency of a reified Nature that chooses some individuals as winners and the rest as losers in the game of life. In addition, there has been a tendency to assume that every survivor is, *ipso facto*, fitter, ignoring that most often survival is a matter of sheer chance. Finally, trying to identify what trait actually makes one offspring more fit than another is often impossible. Darwin himself was extremely cautious in trying to predict which individuals within any generation would survive, and why.

Here is one of his observations on this puzzle, made during his five-year voyage on *HMS Beagle*:

> Every animal in a state of nature regularly breeds; yet in a species long established, any *great* increase in numbers is obviously impossible, and must be checked by some means. We are, nevertheless, seldom able with certainty to tell in any given species, at what period of life, or at what period of the year, or whether only at long intervals, the check falls; or, again, what is the precise nature of the check. Hence probably it is, that we feel so little surprise at one, of two species closely allied in habits, being rare and the other abundant in the same district; or, again, that one should be abundant in one district, and another, filling the same place in the economy of nature, should be abundant in a neighbouring district, differing very little in its conditions. If asked how this is, one immediately replies that it is determined by some slight difference in climate, food, or the number of enemies: yet how rarely, if ever, we can point out the precise cause and manner of action of the check! We are, therefore, driven to the conclusion, that causes generally quite inappreciable by us, determine whether a given species shall be abundant or scanty in numbers.[11]

Here Darwin attributes the observed difference in abundance (or "success") of two competing species as due to differences in their adaptive fitness that are far from obvious to us. How difficult it is, he says, to identify what traits are being selected for or against. As in all his writing, Darwin is very cautious. Even extinctions, he argues, need not have violent (competitive) causes, but may simply result from failure to maintain a large enough population to reproduce. Sometimes species just fade away. Instead of physical competition, Darwin's words imply something much broader, namely the notion of adaptation as "fitting-in" with the environment. Instead of the Billiard Ball model of independent entities, we can imagine the connectedness model of Indra's Net.

Though the above quote by Darwin refers to the differential survival of two similar species through the "check" of natural selection, the same principle applies to the differential survival of members of the same species who vary in some trait. Not all siblings survive; those that do, at least sometimes, are better adapted, or fitter. Even if their advantage boosts their chances of survival by only a tiny percentage over their siblings, after many generations that inherited trait will eventually come to dominate in the population.

Once genes were discovered, and the existence of alternative genes for the same character (flower color, hemoglobin type, etc.) was recognized, genes were seen as the causal agents of the differences that natural selection acted upon. From there it was but a short step to a theory of competing genes, each selfishly trying to win in the struggle for survival. Even if these pieces of DNA could not possibly have goals or purposes, it was easier to think about their role in evolution by pretending that they did. However, metaphors do matter, and can too easily lead us astray.

### *Game theory takes over behavioral evolution*

Once evolution was defined as a competition for survival between genes in theoretical conflict, and each organism was seen as driven by its genes to survive and reproduce, it was easy to extrapolate further and assume that cooperation between organisms was a very unlikely proposition. If their genes were selfish, so must their behavior be. By rights, social life should not exist. This unjustified, indeed fallacious, extrapolation has become the dogma accepted as a correct explanation of evolution by the evolutionary psychologists. The obvious fact that there actually are social organisms had to be explained somehow. How could cooperation with a supposed competitor ever be adaptive?

The theory developed by some evolutionists was based on the idea of life-as-information. It fitted well with the image of a universe of competitively individualistic entities, the Billiard Ball Gestalt described in the Introduction to this book. Invented in the 1940s to predict the behavior of rational actors (such as modern human beings) in continual conflict in such a universe, it was applied to politics (wars) and economics (haggling over prices in the marketplace).[12] And, just like (Western) people, all living organisms were playing games whereby they each optimize their behavioral choices, taking all information into account. This theory of optimal strategies, which became known as game theory, was then applied to the problem of evolution. Genes became mindless players in the evolutionary game, whereby natural selection automatically optimized various strategies. Nature, herself, ensured that rational choices were indeed being made, both by individuals in their behavioral choices and in the course of natural selection for survival of those anatomically or physiologically better endowed. Nature was "rationally" selecting the most adaptive traits, as supplied by alternative genes.

Based on these assumptions the following explanation of social evolution was deduced. Any genes that would promote cooperation with (or, even worse, sacrifice for) another individual would naturally be eliminated as against one's best interest. Only if, the theorists argued, those I help are either (1) closely related (and hence share most of my genes) or (2) they help me exactly as much as I help them (and so my costs equal my benefits) then – and only then –- could social life have evolved. These two conditions, labeled respectively "kin selection" (or inclusive fitness) and "reciprocal altruism" (or tit-for-tat), have been searched for as scientists observe and interpret the behaviors of social animals.[13]

Mathematically based game theories have been applied with some success to the evolution of social organisms with highly stereotypical behaviors. In particular, kin selection accounts very well for the extreme reproductive altruism, or genetic sacrifice, among social insects such as bees and termites. Though only a few members of the group actually reproduce, all the others that assist them are sibling relatives, essentially helping their own genes survive into the next generation. But when it comes to mammals, and especially primates with their highly flexible behaviors, the assumptions needed for game theory break down. Only some individuals in these fluid social groups are near relatives, as there is much movement of one or other sex among groups. Among baboons it is the males that move from troop to troop; among chimpanzees, it is the females. Yet social interactions are strong among both males and females in both species.[14] Kinship, while a factor in primate societies, by no means explains the breadth of their social behaviors.

The problem becomes even more difficult if we try to apply reciprocity to the acts of nonhuman primates. When apparently cooperative acts were observed among vervet monkeys in Africa, the scientists made the following comments:

> Are the monkeys really calculating the costs and benefits of a grooming bout or alliances and then computing the difference between them?

> It is difficult to determine whether monkeys possess a concept of reciprocity *like our own*, because it is difficult for us ... to determine precisely what costs and benefits the monkeys attach to different sorts of interaction.[15]

When reciprocity in social behavior moves from the domain of rigid, genetically stereotyped behaviors effected through the blind process of natural selection, and becomes a conscious choice in a flexible behavioral repertoire, then we are forced to assume that genes are bestowing an ability on the organism to calculate the appropriate costs and benefits. Not even humans, let alone other primates, are genetically wired to think like accountants, keeping track of reciprocal acts with all our fellow beings, as the above quote implies. Whether or not humans act like accountants is a cultural trait, one common to Western societies whose world views are framed on the notion of social contracts. This is not universal in all cultures.[16] To their credit, the scientists studying vervets admit difficulties with the theory: "[W]e must be aware that theories of reciprocity ... are slippery concepts – difficult to state precisely and difficult to translate into rigorously testable predictions."[17] I suggest that any theory of genetically-based reciprocity is misleading, even dangerous, because it limits our self-image of our biologically constructed selves to one of calculated selfishness, implanted in us by our genes.

## *Why game theory is inappropriate*

None of the assumptions noted above as necessary for the application of mathematical cost/benefit analyses to genetically controlled behaviors is met when we come to complex, flexible, learning-modified behaviors: (1) genes are not the sole cause of the development of any behavior; (2) to the extent complex behavior has any genetic basis, it will involve a whole panoply of interactive genes, all working together; and (3) prosocial behaviors are not necessarily a potential sacrifice. Such an assumption is arbitrary, dependent on the observer's interpretation of the whole context of the behavior. In fact, the very idea of sacrifice in social life becomes quite unnecessary if all possible levels of natural selection are taken into account (as Darwin was trying to do when considering the relative abundance of species).

## *Who's in control here?*

One underlying assumption of game theory when applied to the evolution of social behavior is that genes are controlling that behavior. That is, there are identifiable genes that code for specific social behaviors beneficial for the individual who has those genes. Thus they are actually "selfish genes," because they promote their own survival in the next generation.[18] The theory further assumes "one-gene, one-behavior," with alternative, competing genes for prosocial and antisocial behaviors.

While it is obviously true that genes influence an organism's survival, the mere possession of a gene by no means guarantees it will be maximally expressed. Genes are working molecules, not rigid blueprints. Their effects in an organism are known to be contingent on their environment. Richard Strohman, mentioned earlier, has pointed out that far from being the linear causes of any traits (let alone behaviors), genes simply carry the outlines of information needed to construct an organism. Their ability to influence the actual traits, the phenotype, of an organism is strongly affected by their surroundings: other genes, the local chemistry of the cell, even the environment in which the whole organism finds itself. The same gene, under different circumstances, may create a very different trait.[19]

Try, if you will, to picture a mindless gene, sitting inside a living cell. When will it be activated? If it is activated, will it be coordinated with other genes to produce a functional metabolic sequence or a functional organ, such as a brain, or a wing, or a liver? Like all other entities in the universe, genes do not function in isolation but *in context*, in an environment that influences what they actually can accomplish. Genes are not self-activating, nor do they control what happens during final production of the proteins they code for.

Recently, early in 2001, the human genome project dropped a scientific bombshell into our entire understanding of how genes code for inherited traits. For a half century it had been supposed that each protein is coded by a separate gene, assisted by other nearby genes turning on and off the signals to this working gene. It was generally estimated there would be some 300,000 or so genes needed to create a human being. In fact, the number is only around 30,000, not many more than are found in an earthworm (so much for human genetic superiority). Indeed, the same gene may turn up repeatedly in the genome, producing rather different proteins depending upon the rest of the DNA that surrounds it in each different location. Thus the almighty gene – supposedly the controlling blueprint of all life – is in fact as affected as any other entity in the universe by all of the entities that interact with it: a true example of Indra's Net in action. In the controlling forces of life, there is no "top dog" – only larger or smaller networks of interdependent entities.[20]

To sum up, genes by themselves are not "in control." The final appearance and behavior of a whole organism, its phenotype, is the non-linear outcome of a whole host of developmental events, including thousands of genes, acting in a coordinated fashion. Genes in turn require pre-existing living cells in which to do their stuff. The DNA that created the cloned sheep, Dolly, had to be inoculated into a denucleated sheep egg-cell, which is a giant (from the gene's perspective) habitat of extremely complex, highly organized, dynamically interacting non-genetic molecules. Those same genes could not have worked inside a different kind of egg-cell, let alone built a cell, all by themselves, from scratch in an artificial medium. Genes on their own are helpless. (Which likely makes Dawkins's CD-ROMs in outer space quite useless, unless those who found them happened to have egg-cells that could provide the appropriate human environment.)

During development, the immediate environment within and around each cell sequentially turns on some of that cell's gene clusters and turns off others. While a gene is turned on, it effects changes in the local environment of that cell, and even in neighboring or distant cells. These in turn signal new genes to come online and others to shut down. An ongoing, nonlinear feedback network exists among all the cells in a developing organism, including those affected by the exterior environment. There is thus continuous cross-talk between the activated genes and their constantly changing local environments; the latter are only partly controlled by the organism's genes. Development is thus never precisely determined. Even identical twins are not absolutely identical.

Genes, then, are not the managers of life; they act only in response to their surroundings, and that environment can extend even outside the organism. Barbara McClintock, who discovered "jumping genes" that move from one place in chromosomes to another in environmentally stressed maize plants, thus producing very different consequences, has stated:

> We know about the components of genomes ... We know nothing, however, about how the cell senses danger and initiates responses to it that are often truly remarkable.[21]

And here is how Strohman sums up the question, "Who's in control?"

We cannot assume, as genetic determinism does, that constraints and developmental rules are all in the form of genetic programs.

The illegitimate extension of a genetic paradigm from a relatively simple level of genetic coding and decoding to a complex level of cellular behavior represents an epistemological error of the first order.

*We are trying to fit dynamic nonlinear change into a linear theory of the gene, and it will not fit there.*[22]

It is not just our genes that create us and influence how we behave. It is the entire environment in which we develop: the complex, multiple, nonlinear interactions among thousands of genes, the chemistry inside cells, the physiology of the whole organism, *and the interactive dynamic of the living ecosystem.* The boundaries are fuzzy: the whole biosphere is interconnected in a huge continuum, like Indra's Net. We set up arbitrary "edges" for our convenience in thinking about the whole, because that is the way our minds tend to work.

### One gene, one behavior? Not so!

Are single genes programming for particular traits? Evolutionary game theory, as it is modeled, sets up two opposing traits vying against one other as if they were alternative (competing) genes for the same position in the genome.[23] When it comes to social behavior, supposedly a single gene for "altruism" is pitted against one for "selfishness," and one for "cooperation" against one for "competition."[24] And so on for other pairs of behaviors. An individual may have one or the other, but not both. In a given environment, one or other competing gene of each pair is selected as better adapted (the winner) and the other as less fit (the loser). This one-gene, one-behavior model offers a simple way of turning behavioral evolution into a strategic game, but is it realistic?

There are three problems with the model. It assumes that a gene known to affect behavior has no other function – perhaps a far more critical function – that makes it essential. It also assumes that only a single gene is necessary for the appearance of such complex behaviors as aggressivity or altruism or competitiveness.[25] And third, it assumes that organisms can get by with one or the other of these complex behaviors, but that they never need both.

Take the assumption that a gene affecting behavior has no other significant survival functions, so its being replaced would affect only the behavioral trait in question. For this, let's look at the gene for prolactin, a hormone that occurs throughout the vertebrates and is directly implicated in parental behavior. It is certainly a prosocial gene, though it should not be considered altruistic since a parent tending an offspring shares half its genes and thus is not really sacrificing from the game theorist's point of view.

Prolactin is a protein hormone found in a wide range of species from fish to humans, and it promotes a wide range of very different parental behaviors, each species-specific and species-appropriate. In some fish, it promotes the aeration by an attentive father of a nest of developing eggs; in other fish, the brooding of babies in parental mouths is prolactin-dependent. In birds, the hormone promotes the brooding of eggs and feeding of young; in mammals, nest building and the retrieval of young. Among primates, maternal instincts seem to be prolactin-facilitated.[26]

But prolactin (a molecule closely related to growth hormone and coded by a similar gene) plays numerous other critical functions, not only behavioral and social, but in embryonic skeletal development, in the adaptation to freshwater habitats of some fish and amphibians, and for milk production in the crops of pigeons and the mammary glands of mammals. A gene that clearly influences social and reproductive behavior (albeit in highly diverse ways) has other critical adaptive functions as well. Who is to say that the parenting behaviors were the *most* important factor in the evolution of prolactin via natural selection? As Darwin said, we can seldom know on what particular trait natural selection is acting, and this is especially difficult at the level of genes that act on many diverse traits in the same individual.

What holds for prolactin is true for the products of many other single genes: they perform multiple functions that affect diverse phenotypic traits – behavioral, reproductive, physiological, developmental. We must also assume that many other, quite separate, genes are implicated in the development of each of the traits that, say, prolactin is involved with. Thus, with respect to our second criticism of game theory, it is the exception rather than the rule that a single gene causes a single trait. And in the case of such complex behaviors as those we have been considering here, surely we will be hard put to find such a simple relationship. Though this area has not been studied in detail, we can suppose that the so-called trait of aggression is scarcely caused by one gene acting alone. Any number of hormones, coded for by different genes, are likely involved, for example, adrenalin, testosterone, cortical hormones, thyroxin, and their near relatives. In addition, there likely are other clusters of genes that influence sensitivity of various parts of the brain, such as the amygdala and the hypothalamus, that are known to increase response to threats.[27] Most behaviors are likely to have multigenic causes.

Indeed, there are very few cases where a single mutation seems to significantly change behavior, and most of those that do, such as the gene for Huntington's chorea, cause extremely dysfunctional behaviors. There is at least one well-studied example, however, where single-gene mutants do result in the appearance of a particular behavior. The trait for emitting warning calls on sighting a predator that turns up in some species of songbirds seems to be inherited this way. In any flock, those with this "altruistic" trait warn the others of danger while putting themselves at considerable risk by attracting a predator's attention. It seems to be a case of true altruism, of self-sacrifice. If we assume that natural selection acts only in individuals, it is difficult to see how such a gene could ever have evolved. I turn now to this puzzling question. Its solution demands thinking of natural selection as occurring at multiple levels: within the genome; within the cell; within the organism; within the group; within the ecosystem.

### Why social life is not a "sacrifice"

So far I have argued that genes, alone, are almost never linear causes of behavior. Observed behaviors are variable, being joint outcomes of complex, reciprocal interactions among genetic instructions, current environments and remembered experiences (learning). Natural selection can act at any level in this complex inter-action of gene-plus-environment-plus-experience. Moreover, a single gene may affect multiple phenotypic characters in an organism and not just a single behavior. Since some of these may be more important to survival than others, exactly where is Darwin's "check" falling? Since complex behaviors are likely to be influenced by multiple genes, each with its own nonbehavioral contributions to survival, on which aspect of a gene is selection acting? To picture competition and cooperation as single-gene, alternative behaviors is clearly a meaningless simplification. Finally, how can we imagine animals like us primates, with our flex-ible, nonstereotypic behavioral repertoires, as not having a wide range of complex behaviors, some competitive, some cooperative, some prosocial, others antisocial – all dependent upon the context of the moment and past experience?

If we change our gestalt view of evolution from a vision of bits of informa-tion (genes) surviving *vis-à-vis* the environment (natural selection) – a distinctly Billiard Ball way of thinking – to a more realistic view of genes-interacting-and-fitting-in-with the multiple levels of a complex ecosystem, we come up with a different understanding of how evolution occurs. Again, it is Indra's Net that serves our thinking best. Each alternative gene must fit in first with its co-workers, the other genes in the genome, then with the living cell wherein it functions. This is the first level of natural selection – one that may seldom be observed by scientists if the developing early embryo in which a misfit gene occurs dies long before birth. (Most early miscarriages, those "extra-late" menstrual periods, are usually the expulsion of non-viable embryos.) As two creative thinkers in the field of evolutionary theory, Elliott Sober and David Sloan Wilson, have stated:

> With only a few exceptions, the only way for a gene to increase its fitness is to increase the fitness of the entire genome ... Genomes that managed [in the past] to limit internal conflict [between their own genes] presumably were more fit than other genomes.[28]

(As a brief aside, I note here an important point to be taken up later regarding the evolution of human nature: namely, there is always the likelihood of conflict within the genome of any species. Pieces of information often fit uneasily together, and may force compromises in an organism's development or behavior. Natural selection can reduce such inner conflicts, but probably it can never altogether eliminate them. Each new adaptation to a changing environment can disturb the internal harmony of the genome. As Stephen J. Gould repeatedly states, living species are never perfectly adapted; rather they are jerry-built compromises. Modern humans, whose humanity has only recently and so very rapidly evolved, surely possess more internal genomic conflict than most older species, in which selection may have had time to eliminate more of it. This applies particularly in the case of conflicting behavioral tendencies, such as our needs for bonding and belonging on the one hand and for autonomy and freedom of action on the other. We humans are still "unfinished" evolutionary products.)

Having accounted for how genes must fit in with each other in the genome, I turn to the second level of selection, that of the individual organism. "With what must an individual organism 'fit-in'?" If it is a sexually reproducing organism, it clearly needs members of its own kind near enough to mate with. If it is a terrestrial organism, as are primates, it cannot rely on water currents to mix spawned eggs and sperm; it must physically meet up with a partner. Reproductive success, then, first and foremost means being an integral member of a population of one's own kind. Some sort of social life is essential, however infrequent. For primates, physical mating is an evolutionary necessity.

We should not be surprised therefore that for some sexually reproducing species, aggregations of reproductive individuals into cooperating groups proved adaptive. Actually, the formation of initially adaptive, and eventually indispensably integrated, communities of reproducing organisms has an ancient history, having occurred repeatedly almost since the beginning of the origins of life. Primordial reproducing molecules, once existing independently, clustered together to form primitive cells, the procaryotes, similar to modern bacteria. Later, different species of procaryotes fused into larger communities called eucaryotes, such as the single-celled amoebas. The nuclei, mitochondria, flagella and other "organs" of those new cells were all derived from once autonomous ancient bacterial species. Later, some of these single-celled organisms clustered together into permanent communities at a more complex level, forming modern multicellular organisms, from the simple slimemolds whose loosely aggregated cells are all very similar, to familiar plants and animals with highly specialized cells, organs, and tissues. Among some of these multicellular organisms, even more complex levels of organization have come about, such as the social organisms that form reproductive groups of closely associated individuals. Examples range from coral colonies in oceanic reefs and clusters of sea anemones on intertidal rocky shorelines, to flocks of songbirds singing the same song "dialect," to groups of elephants, troops of primates, and the extreme example, the social insects we have already mentioned (see Figure II.1).

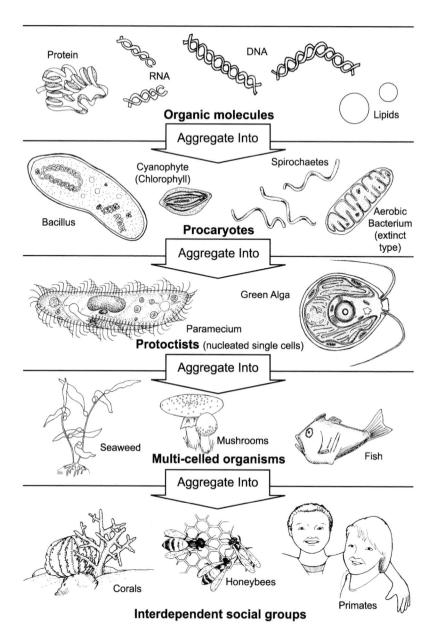

*Figure II.1* Sequential evolution of levels of interdependence

There is now good evidence that life has evolved through increasing levels of interdependence: first among organic molecules aggregating to form simple, non-nucleated cells, some of which in turn aggregated to form complex single cells, some with, others without, chlorophyll. Some of these further aggregated into multicelled organisms, and many of these aggregated, however loosely, into obligatory interdependent social groups, sometimes (as with lichens and some corals) incorporating two very different species. (Original art by Michele Lukowski.)

Each of these evolutionary stages represents a new level of natural selection into which any particular genetic variant that enters must fit. They offer a vision of a living world much more interconnected than that of the "selfish gene." Again, the model is closer to Indra's Net than the old Billiard Ball universe. Genes still mutate, and natural selection still occurs, but the criteria for success look very different. The fitness of a particular gene can be measured along a whole continuum of surroundings which it must fit into, from the chromosome and the genome, to the cell, to the organism as a whole, to the group in which the organism lives and reproduces, to the entire population, to the ecosystem as a whole. Selection occurs at multiple levels. Darwin's "checks" on the reproduction of a particular trait may occur at the level of any one of these interactions. For an organism such as a primate, where individuals depend on a functioning group in order to successfully reproduce, if the group fails to adapt to a changing environment, then its individual members will not reproduce; the whole group may become extinct. Selection can, and does, occur at many levels. Indeed, multilevel selection is the norm.

Multi-level selection offers an explanation of how even something as altruistic as a gene for warning calls in birds could come about. If birds that live in semi-permanent flocks have in their midst one or two callers that warn of predators, then the whole flock will be more likely to escape predators than one without such callers. They will tend to produce more offspring. Over time, birds with the calling gene will increase to some level such that most flocks will have several callers and will produce better than before. Presumably the gene will not become ubiquitous because those that have it are still more likely to be taken by predators. Some balance between callers and non-callers will be established.[29] What is significant here is that selection is acting not at the level of the individual, but at the level of the group: *flocks with callers do better as a group at reproducing themselves*. Known as "group selection," this phenomenon is the key to understanding primate social evolution and the emergence of human nature.

Once we understand how selection can occur at the level of reproducing groups for such a totally self-sacrificing trait as sounding warning calls, then all other group-promoting traits clearly could arise in the same way. All that matters from an evolutionary standpoint is that the group as a whole be more successful at surviving and reproducing than groups without the trait. In fact, the evolutionary possibility of group selection, long claimed as impossible, has actually been demonstrated recently under controlled circumstances, namely that of chickens crowded together in modern, automated henhouses. More "efficient" from the human labor standpoint, these automated rearing conditions proved inefficient biologically. The hens became stressed; they fought each other violently; and they laid fewer eggs. However, when offspring from whichever group of hens was most productive *as a group* were selected for each new generation (rather than selecting offspring from individual, high-laying hens, as is usually done), within just six generations, egg-laying from the selected groups went up by 160 percent, and stress and aggression were virtually eliminated. This is but one example of how selection can occur at a level higher than that of the individual organism.[30]

Indeed, it has been possible, under laboratory conditions, to demonstrate the process of evolutionary selection in whole ecosystems comprised of thousands of species (millions of individuals) of soil organisms. By selecting for a desired "trait" among a series of soil samples from the forests, the researchers were able to increase the level of the trait in succeeding generations of soil samples in the lab, using as "parents" the soil samples showing the most of the trait. As the biologist John N. Thompson says:

> Living organisms have evolved in ways that absolutely require them to use a combination of their own genetic machinery and that of one or more other species if they are to survive and reproduce.[31]

Once we accept that group selection can occur, the explanation of primate social evolution shifts radically away from having to find selfish reasons for every behavior and having to assume that competition, cheating, and deception are universal traits. Empathy, love, fellow-feelings, caring, sharing, cooperation, and all the other "virtues" are no longer mere self-deceptions. They really exist and are necessary for group survival.[32] This does not mean competition and selfish behavior do not also occur, but they do not underlie all social action. Reciprocity (tit-for-tat) behavior also surely happens, but it, too, is not critical for social existence. Game theory is not needed to explain primate behavior. The horizons of our imagination are greatly expanded.

## What, then, is "primate nature"?

The first place we turn in a scientific search for human nature is to our nearest living relatives, the great apes, with whom we share more than 98 percent of our genes, along with certain similarities of appearance and behavior (see Figure II.2 for the proposed evolutionary tree). What sort of social life do they have? How did it evolve?

Evolution, according to the fossil record, occurs in fits and starts. For millions of years, species, even whole ecosystems, may remain almost unchanged. Then, through some catastrophe – a climate change (through continental drift or the ice ages), an earthquake (such as the one that closed the Straits of Gibraltar five million years ago, causing the Mediterranean to dry up), or a meteorite (such as the one near the Yucatan Peninsula in Mexico 65 million years ago that coincided with the disappearance of the dinosaurs) – there are mass extinctions and a rapid explosion (geologically speaking) of new species.[33]

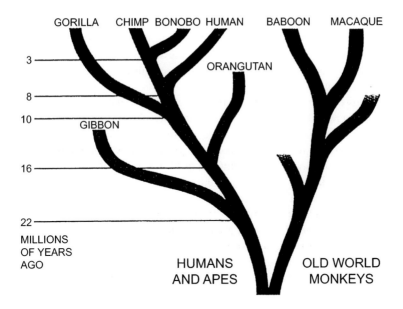

*Figure II.2* Evolutionary tree of primates
Based on DNA analysis, this evolutionary tree of primates shows that humans diverged from bonobos and chimpanzees a mere eight million years ago. The three species share more than 98 percent of their genetic makeup.

*Source*: After F. de Waal (1995: 84). Used by kind permission of Ms. Laurie Grace, illustrator

Ancestral primates branched from small, shrew-like animals, the stem placental mammals, before 70 mya (million years ago), while the dinosaurs were still around and the future continents were still more or less connected. The continents soon began drifting apart, however, and early primates in the future North America died out due to the cold, while those in South America survived in the warmer forests to give rise to new world monkeys. The sudden global extinction of the dinosaurs that coincided with the meteorite mentioned above allowed an explosion of mammals, including the primates.[34]

The new primate niche was the upper canopy of the tropical and subtropical forests, with their patchy but abundant year-round supplies of food and few other competing consumers. This arboreal paradise selected for a variety of traits. Locomotion in the forest canopy was facilitated by stereoscopic vision, necessary for judging distances between branches; prehensile hands, feet and tails for grasping firmly onto limbs; and extraordinary physical coordination. Primates are gymnasts, par excellence. The development of these traits was favored by increasingly larger brains. Discovering the location of patchy food sources in this complex environment also benefited from sharing knowledge among a social group through evolution of communication skills. Whoever located a fruiting fig tree called to the others; there was more than enough for all. To repeat the opening quote from primatologist Alison Jolly: "If there is an essence of being a primate, it is the progressive evolution of intelligence as a way of life."

The obvious benefit of social life based on a shared intelligence about food resources was increased food security. But it also permitted simple learned skills to be shared and transmitted to future generations without the necessity of genetic coding, greatly increasing the behavioral repertoire of primates and the storing and transmission of learned information. This, in turn, expanded the opportunities for adapting to changing circumstances. Yet these evolving big brains also became a constraint on their owners.

The female primate's birth canal could not significantly enlarge to accommodate a larger-headed infant, for that would have affected her agility. Nature's answer was the birthing of increasingly premature infants that arrived in an ever-more helpless state. This greatly endangered the infant's chances of survival, demanding continuous maternal care and a period of physical dependency lasting up to several years in some species. The biological cost of rearing offspring went way up, and losing infants was a serious threat to the reproductive success of the whole social group. Instead of producing lots of offspring, only a few of which survive, as do most other living species, primates were locked into producing only a few, and then taking very good care of them.

I would also argue that this hyperdependence of helpless young was a further stimulus toward mutually supportive group behavior. Not only the lactating mother, but other adults and juveniles, males included, were biologically attracted by and attentive toward new infants. This situation reinforced the tendency to form highly bonded social groups, leading to the tightly linked co-evolution of social life with expanding intelligence.

"Premature" birth also meant that much more of the development of the brain occurred after birth, in an interactive social environment. Genetic programs for behavior could be less rigid, less instinctive, and more open-ended, directed by broadly based propensities rather than rigid instincts. We now begin to see why baby grizzlies are able to survive with a minimum of care, while baby primates cannot.

I shall return at the end of this chapter to a consideration of these propensities. First, though, what are the stories about primate, and hence human, nature that scientists have proposed? I begin with the image that came out of the selfish-gene branch of evolutionary thinking and gave rise to the game theory model just discussed.

### The ultra-Darwinians' primate psyche

Several decades ago, a cover of *Time* magazine showed a pair of human marionettes attached by strings to long double-helices of DNA, the genetic molecules. The male and female danced to the tunes imparted by the DNA that controlled them. It was a terrific image of the genes-control-all evolutionary model that is still so popular today in the public mind (as indicated by the Valentine's Day quote above). Niles Eldredge, a paleontologist at the American Museum of Natural History, sums up that model in a nutshell:

> Natural selection, to a modern ultra-Darwinian, is the competition among organisms (or even among their genes... ) for reproductive success – an active race to leave more copies of one's own genes to the next generation.[35]

As Eldredge says, they have factored history out of the equation, reified natural selection into an active agent, and turned behavior into a single-minded effort to reproduce. On the part of males, this means inseminating as many females as possible with little regard as to whether *any* of their offspring ultimately survive. When it comes to helpless primate infants, this strategy makes even less sense, even from a gene's point of view.

This we-are-all-in-a-big-competition way of thinking about natural selection leads to a rather peculiar explanation of the benefits of intelligence. Instead of being beneficial as an aid to survival of the group as a whole in cooperating to find food and in supporting each other, intelligence is argued to have evolved because it was advantageous to an individual who happens to live in a society, which it can now manipulate to its benefit. Intelligence, in short, is Machiavellian. If it pays to cooperate, then do so; otherwise use deceit, trickery or force for personal gain.[36]

If you do not admit the possibility that whole groups can be selected for because their members act *as a group*, then it is difficult to explain intelligence in any way other than Machiavellian. Social skills, which among primates surely do require considerable intelligence, are "adaptive" only because being in the group is somehow necessary for individual reproductive success. The critical question boils down to: what is there about group life that promotes individual success? The evolution of intelligence merely to get along in a group does not answer this key question. In fact, the next several chapters are devoted to answering it, and the central finding is that *shared group intelligence*, independent of genetically determined behaviors, promotes the survival of groups, and hence of all their members.

Unfortunately, ultra-Darwinism as a gestalt for thinking about primate evolution has had a distorting effect on the interpretations of observed behaviors. (Recall from Chapter I scientists' tendency both to choose what sort of data to look for and then to interpret it in accordance with a preheld theory.) Among the generalizations about primate social behaviors long promoted by ultra-Darwinians are that they are structured in dominance hierarchies; that males dominate females; that males compete for access to females, and this is the basis of male aggression; that males are naturally promiscuous, while females carefully select the supposedly fittest male, often the most aggressive, to father their offspring.[37] Furthermore, acts of sharing or grooming are means for currying favors, thus creating allies in some sort of social power struggle. Among primates, deceit and cheating are naturally commonplace, given their Machiavellian intelligence. Indeed, according to some, intelligence and communication supposedly arose as a means of detecting and socially controlling cheaters and free-loaders.[38] (Sometimes one realizes just how much this theory seems to reflect modern Western society, a possible reason for suspecting its objectivity.)

This Hobbesian view of primate nature was reinforced by the early studies on primates, mostly conducted in zoos or on other captive colonies. Only in the past few decades, when observers (mostly women) began unobtrusively watching groups of wild primates close-up for months at a time, did a different image of primate social life emerge. (Even they, as we shall see, sometimes unwittingly influenced their subject animals' behaviors.) In the absence of stress, primates behave very differently, shattering many of the ultra-selfish preconceptions. Only when crowded, constrained, or continuously threatened do they exhibit extreme dominance, excessive aggression, and other Hobbesian tendencies. Such observations of course are useful for understanding why we humans behave as we do under stress, but they fall far short of providing a complete picture of human nature. It turns out that context *matters greatly.*

A brief recounting of the study of baboons will make the point. Though monkeys, baboons have long been an important model for human social evolution because they are the one primate that lives on the open savanna grasslands where the earliest hominids have been thought to live, rather than in dense forests.

### History of the baboon model: a cautionary tale

In the late 1920s, British primatologist Solly Zuckerman assembled a large number of captive hamadryas baboons from various places around the world and put them all into a 100 by 60 foot enclosure at London zoo. Despite the presence of adequate food and water, a violent free-for-all broke out that lasted several days. Of the original 130 animals, 94 were killed, and high levels of violence continued over the entire three years of Zuckerman's observations. The structure of baboon social life he deduced from this was a rigidly hierarchical society organized through male aggression into harems of females, each controlled by a dominant male.[39]

Zuckerman's model was to dominate primate research for four decades. Such was his standing among scientists that later influential primatologists such as Sherwood Washburn, Irven DeVore, and Ronald Hall adopted his paradigm to interpret their own field observations. Three quotes from later baboon observers Shirley Strum and William Mitchell summarize the enormous impact of Zuckerman's ideas, not only for science, but for society as a whole:

The themes that emerged directly from the baboon model included: the adaptive nature of aggression, its use and control through a male dominance hierarchy, the differences in rules between males and females, and the relationship between aggression, dominance and reproductive success.

[O]ur concepts about *primate* society were, for many years, actually generalizations about *baboon* society. This then became the basis for our reconstructions of the social life of early hominids.

Ironically, just as specialists were abandoning the baboon model, the popular press and nonspecialists interested in interpreting human evolution adopted and championed that view of primate society.[40]

How powerful, indeed, are scientific paradigms that – even when abandoned by science – become the accepted "truth," part of a culture's beliefs about human nature. But that abandonment is still not wholly accepted by all primatologists.

In 1972, when Strum, a graduate student of Washburn, first approached the "Pumphouse Gang" (her name for a troop of olive baboons in Kenya that she has continued to study ever since) she was warned by her fellow (male) students not to leave the van, but to observe from the inside, using binoculars. Otherwise she would frighten the animals, whom they viewed as highly dangerous.

Strum realized she would never see detailed interactions among all members of the troop; mostly only the larger males were visible through the tall grass. Finally left on her own, she moved outside the van and very gradually habituated the animals to her presence. Taking her cues from a nearby young male baboon trying to enter the troop, she – and he – sat almost motionless in sight of the troop day after day, very slowly moving a little closer. After a few months, the young male had befriended an adult female and finally was allowed to groom her. Gradually, through her, he was accepted by others: first, her offspring, then closest friends, and finally, without fuss, by other males. Gradually, he was able to groom various members of the troop and be groomed by them, and he mated with several females. At the same time, Strum, too, was accepted by the troop but by turning her back and refusing to look them in the eye, she gently but firmly rebuffed their efforts to touch her. Once accepted into their midst, she was able to distinguish each one of the sixty or more individuals, and as she watched, she became increasingly puzzled:

Each day I spent with the troop it became clearer: sooner or later I would have to confront the fact that I was seeing things I was not supposed to be seeing, finding patterns that were not supposed to exist. Worse still, I was *not* finding patterns that everyone else said did exist. The intellectual framework I had brought with me from Berkeley had become unrecognizable.[41]

A short list of Strum's findings summarizes how differently olive baboons in fact do behave when compared to the generalized primate model. (Page references are to Strum, 1987.)

- Males (who as adolescents leave their natal troop to join another) do not gain acceptance by aggressively defeating dominant males, but by gradually habituating the troop to themselves (p. 27ff).
- Though adult males enter into aggressive fights, they seldom seriously harm each other; more surprisingly, neither the winner nor the loser acquires the prize; the estrus female slips off to mate with another, uninvolved male (pp. 78, 91, 121); meanwhile, the disputed meat or other resource is left behind as the winner chases after the retreating loser (p. 111).
- Male dominance is ephemeral (pp. 77, 78), and newcomers dominate males who have been longest in the troop, regardless of size or strength (pp. 117–18).
- The most successful males at mating were the lowest-ranking, longest-resident of the troop (p. 118).
- Though males are physically able to dominate females, this does not ensure copulation; females avoid, run away from (p. 120) or simply sit down in the presence of an unwanted male (lecture at University of California at San Diego, 1989); long-time familiarity and friendship that includes much reciprocal grooming are much more successful than coercion (p. 121).
- Adult females are the core of the troop, and have a much clearer dominance hierarchy than exists among males (p. 79); offspring of a dominant female outrank others, and the youngest sibling takes precedence over older brothers and sisters (p. 39).
- Female/female bonding and reciprocal grooming are far stronger than male/male bonding; females maintain peace within and between families, and defend members of the troop from bullies or outside threats (p. 79).
- Baboons seek each other's company; proximity to others is the foremost goal (p. 51); friendship, "peaceful sociality," is more in evidence than dominance and aggression (pp. 52–3); grooming is essential for bonding, and is used during reconciliation after a row (p. 52).
- Males make stronger bonds with females and infants than with other males, by grooming them (pp. 81, 114, 152); males may hold befriended infants as shields to protect themselves from aggression by other males, especially newcomers, since if an infant is attacked the whole troop will come to its assistance (p. 125); holding an infant also has a calming effect on an agitated male (p. 126).

- Infants are befriended by as many members of the troop as the mother allows (pp. 42, 43), and there is troop-wide protection of infants and mothers (p. 125).
- Neither males nor females are leaders; females know their home range in great detail, while males know a wider area, which is of possible use in times of drought (p. 80); dynamic males and conservative females complement each other in baboon society (p. 81); real power lies with the wise rather than the strong (p. 151).

Admittedly, the olive baboons that Strum observed are not as aggressive as the hamadryas variety Zuckerman and others studied, which even in the wild tend to be more hierarchical than olive baboons. Yet the old rigid picture that had been widely accepted as the model for *all* primates was still so strongly held in 1978, when Strum first presented her main results at a conference of baboon researchers, that they were rejected outright by all but two of the eighteen participants.[42] It was a classic instance of supposedly objective scientists refusing to hear something that disagreed with their current paradigm: for mid-twentieth-century primatologists, *male dominance must exist!* (Later I will show why it is not only scientists, but people in general, who cling with such tenacity to their beliefs.)

### Of course genes matter – but context matters more

It is surely true that closely related primate species can and do differ biologically in their behavioral patterns. Even in the wild, the hamadryas baboons of the highlands of the Horn of Africa tend to form hierarchical societies more readily than do their lowland cousins, the olive baboons.[43] Among macaque monkeys, Frans de Waal has observed contrasting social behaviors between two species, the feisty rhesus and the more placid stumptails. The former are prone to violent aggression at the least provocation, and the lines between dominants and subordinates are sharply drawn. Because threat by a dominant means a severe bite for the other, the usual response is to run away. Not so for the more relaxed, egalitarian stumptails, who tend to ignore many dominance threats. Often they will try to out-stare each other, and one may even offer an extremity for a ritual bite, that never causes harm but serves to end the confrontation.[44]

As for chimpanzees, the two species, *Pan troglodytes*, the common chimp, and *Pan paniscus*, the pygmy chimpanzee or bonobo, are quite different in their social habits. Ordinarily chimpanzee females only mate during estrus, while bonobos are receptive much more of the time. Bonobos are also the only primates besides humans to copulate frontally – in the so-called "missionary position." Unlike chimpanzees, both male and female bonobos routinely use genital rubbing with members of either sex to reconcile after spats and to calm one another, especially in the presence of food, something they often share. Among bonobos, female groups surpass the male groups in organizing social life. As de Waal has pointed out: "[C]himpanzee males are more dominance oriented and 'political' than their bonobo counterparts."[45]

It is clear that though all primates are social, their social habits vary considerably from species to species for biologically determined reasons. Yet even within a single species, social behaviors can vary surprisingly owing to past history or present conditions. Context can strongly influence social structure, often in parallel ways from one species to the next. The influence of context on intrinsic behavioral tendencies is indeed powerful.

However, before tackling the most powerful contextual factor of all, *stress*, I want to relate a brief anecdote about the two macaque species that illustrates just how flexible primate behavior can be when the context changes. Primatologist Frans de Waal wanted to see how the rhesus monkeys' feisty behavior might be affected by the presence of the more placid stumptails, so he placed several juveniles of each species together in the same enclosure for five months. At first the rhesus monkeys were scared of their slightly larger cousins; then they were puzzled by their own inability to get the stumptails to respond to threats – they neither fought back nor ran away. Gradually, the rhesus stopped their threats and learned to use the stumptails' methods of reconciliation. The two groups then became friendly, with lots of cross-grooming. Even after the stumptails were removed, the rhesus retained their newly acquired pacifism and reconciliation skills. As de Waal puts it: "Like chemists altering the properties of a solution, we had infused a group of monkeys of one species with the 'social culture' of another."[46] Context clearly had a big influence on behavior.

### Stress and social structure

In order to discover what primates are like biologically, one must appreciate that their behavior (and ours) varies with context. Under low stress (i.e. "ideal") conditions, primates are free to wander in groups over large areas. Food, though patchy, is usually plentiful and can be shared by a whole group. When disputes arise, or if food becomes scarce, larger groups break into smaller ones, a process known as fissioning. Such small groups will tend to fuse again later on, often with noisy reunions. This fission–fusion process, that in some species also includes the frequent movement of individuals from group to group, has the effect of lowering stress levels, and hence the intensity of conflict.

To what extent such "ideal" conditions persisted during the long period of monkey and ape evolution is not clear. What is clear is that most wild primates today are stressed in some degree by humans, who have encroached on and often destroyed their habitat, and even hunted them for trophies or zoos. Even observers going as unobtrusively as possible to watch them can have some impact, and they most certainly do so when they provide food for the animals in order to view them better. Finally, animals observed in captivity, even in large enclosures such as the chimpanzee colony at Arnhem zoo and the bonobo colony at San Diego zoo, are obviously unable to fission and thus are under a mild yet irreversible stress.

These comments are not intended as criticisms of the observers, whose patient work, after all, reveals to us how primates behave under stress. Such information is essential if we are to understand our *own* behavior under similar conditions. The examples that follow are presented rather to show how stress changes social behavior in somewhat predictable ways.

### *Unconstrained vs. constrained "wild" populations*

Since 1950, the human population has more than doubled, from two and a half to over six billion, and the highest growth rates have occurred in Africa, South Asia, and Latin America, the native habitats of most primates. Human encroachment on the freedom of movement of primates (including remaining nomadic human tribes) has been enormous. Yet it was during this period that systematic observation of wild primates began.

One of the first to notice the impact of human pressure on the social structure of our nonhuman relatives was Phyllis Jay. The langurs, or Hanuman monkeys, are familiar inhabitants of India. In the uncrowded north they live in small, egalitarian troops with little hierarchy or internal strife. (I should note that "egalitarian" does not mean all are "equal" in popularity or behavior in the group, but that there are no obvious dominance situations in which one or a few individuals physically control others in the group. By the same token, "hierarchical" means there is a coerced ranking of individuals in social relationships which is enforced by frequent antagonistic encounters.)

This same species of langur in the south, where the human population is much more dense, lives in large, strongly hierarchical groups surrounded on all sides by humans. There is incessant squabbling and a high level of social tension. Jay has also recorded similar responses to crowding and constraint in other primates.[47]

As for chimpanzees, the primate most thoroughly studied in its native habitat, the first reports from the early 1960s by Vernon and Frances Reynolds described relatively loosely constructed groups that were slightly more organized in open savanna habitats than in dense forests. There seemed to be no territorial behavior, and when groups happened to meet, adult males (who are the core of chimpanzee groups) sometimes displayed excitedly, other times touched and embraced. In the forests, particularly, no antagonism was seen.[48]

It was in 1960 that Jane Goodall first went to study chimpanzees at the wildlife area known as the Gombe Stream Reserve, a narrow strip of land some 17 km long and 3 to 4 km wide, bounded on the west by Lake Tanganyika and on the east by the rift escarpment that rises to 1500 meters. Her description of the change in the area surrounding the Reserve between 1960 and 1986 is telling:

In 1960 rather large tracts of undisturbed forest stretched to the east of the rift escarpment, forming part of the extensive miombo woodlands of the Kigoma region, and chimpanzees were reported to the east and south of the park. To the north, pockets and strips of forest almost certainly linked the Gombe chimpanzees with the chimpanzee population of Burundi. Today, however, the picture is different. The land to the east of the rift 'scarp' has been quite extensively cultivated, and the same is true north and south of the park boundaries. While chimpanzees still exist in patches of forest outside the park, the number and size of these refuges are gradually diminishing as human cultivation spreads. It seems likely that in the not-too-distant future the Gombe chimpanzees will be virtually isolated.[49]

What happens, one may ask, to the behavior of an ape population accustomed to fissioning and fusing over a large territory, when the available forest area shrinks so drastically in just two decades (one ape-generation), leaving about 160 animals to live severely constrained? The first thing recorded in Goodall's data was an increase in tension among individuals *within* a group. (This may have been exacerbated by provisioning the animals with bananas, as discussed below.) When two groups met to share a particularly rich food supply, where once the occasion would be marked by noisy, convivial "carnivals," the males now began to treat each other more aggressively. They also began to attack strange females that entered the group, often viciously killing or maiming their young.[50] By 1972, part of the original large colony fissioned off to the south, attempting to separate itself, though living still within the boundaries of the old shared range. The two groups became enemies, with many violent encounters. Eventually, gangs of males from the larger northern group deliberately tracked down and killed or drove off all members of the southern group, which ceased to exist by the end of 1977. The winners reoccupied their full range, but found it necessary to patrol the edges, presumably from incursion by other, outside groups. By 1981, the group's southern border again had been pushed northwards by an even larger new group entering the Reserve.[51]

Another well-studied wild ape that has experienced increasing stress as a result of human activities in recent decades is the mountain gorilla population at the junction of Uganda, Rwanda, and the Congo, all of them unstable countries with burgeoning human populations. Poachers setting traps to capture infant specimens for zoos have created horrendous stress as animals of all ages are often maimed or killed in the process. Normal gorilla societies are organized with a single dominant silverback male overseeing a small group of females, but younger males are frequently observed joining such groups and even mating with the females. Dian Fossey, who spent many years observing wild gorillas until she was murdered, presumably by poachers, believed that the infanticide that sometimes occurred when silverbacks took over a group of females with offspring was not a natural behavior. (Such behavior is what game theory strategy predicts, of course, because the females soon come into heat and will then bear the incoming male's offspring.) Rather, Fossey saw it as a result of stress on the population. This was certainly the case when she witnessed the killing and eating of an infant gorilla by a nonrelated female and her daughter.[52] Even in captivity – certainly an abnormal situation – male gorillas are restrained in their aggression against females and youngsters. As Frans de Waal reports:

> An adult male gorilla is the most formidable fighting machine of the primate world, undoubtedly physically capable of holding off, even killing, a number of the much smaller females of his species. Psychologically, however, he appears incapable of fully exploiting this advantage. It is quite spectacular to see an alliance of barking females chase – even best – the gargantuan male, whose hands seem tied behind his back by the neurons in his brain.[53]

In the wild then, it would appear that it is not crowding *per se* that causes increased violence and hierarchy among apes, but rather the consequent stress of shortages of resources and, as with the gorillas, constant threats from violent humans. The latter two factors are clearly direct threats to survival, creating stress and increasing hierarchic ordering and potential violence within and between groups. This interpretation is borne out by recent studies of crowding in captive chimpanzees; crowding, it seems, though somewhat stressful (increased cortisol output, a sign of inner stress, has been noted), does not increase aggression within the group as long as there is sufficient food. Rather, though crowding may increase tensions, these can be suppressed by increased conciliatory behaviors such as touching and grooming.[54]

### Artificial feeding

Another possible human-induced stress for wild chimpanzees has been artificial provisioning in order to allow observation for longer periods. At two long-term study sites, observers made abundant food available from time to time. At Gombe, Goodall supplied bananas; at nearby Mahale, Toshisada Nishida and his colleagues provided sugar cane. (Neither are locally available foods, but the animals quickly learned to utilize them.) The results of both strategies were analyzed by Margaret Power, who concluded that artificial feeding created a novel conflict situation. The artificially supplied food became a "scarce commodity." In the wild, chimpanzees forage alone or in small groups. Only when a truly abundant source is discovered – such as a giant fig tree laden with fruits – do they call others to join their find. But the banana and sugar cane supplies were always at a particular site, yet available at *uncertain intervals*. It was never a secure supply, as is the food given to animals in permanent captivity. The animals learned to come looking for a big feed, only to face competition or meet up with strangers. Such mutual frustration led to aggression, that spilled over from the feeding site into social life in general. Power suggested that direct frustration over food supplies is abnormal for chimpanzees (except in the rare cases of a small-game kill). "Wild chimpanzees do not, in nature, experience this loss of autonomy in regard to a food supply."[55]

### Stress in captivity

Much of our insight into primate behavior comes from captive animals, far removed from the natural habitats to which they were biologically adapted. I already noted the mayhem at the London zoo when strange baboons were suddenly thrown together in a small enclosure. Similarly assembled groups of humans react in the same way. (The social tensions in modern prisons, where mutual cooperation is scarcely possible, are all too evident. Stress is high; fission impossible.) In almost all closely caged groups of primates, where opportunities for separation are minimal and frequent social encounters inescapable, the behavior of both sexes tends to become hierarchical, sometimes aggressive. At one research center, the killing of others, by females as well as males, was not uncommon, especially if the population in the enclosure grew or new outsiders were introduced. At another center, however, there was a high level of stress, but little aggression.[56]

Modern zoos, fortunately, are providing increasingly spacious, well-vegetated enclosures that help reduce social stress, as does the provision of plentiful food. The inability to escape contact with each other, however, still affects behavior. On the one hand, it increases hierarchical organization. But it also increases the efforts to repair ruptures when they occur. An example of both is a particularly bloody conflict that occurred in the chimpanzee colony at the Arnhem zoo in Holland. Two subdominant males ganged up on the alpha male, Luit, one night in their sleeping cage (males and females are separated at night). They attacked him, bit off some of his fingers and toes, and ripped out his testicles. By morning, Luit was mortally wounded. When the keepers arrived, however, Luit and his two attackers were locked in a three-way embrace. Loser and winners were trying to "make-up." They were not to know that Luit would soon die of his wounds, despite the best human efforts to save him.[57]

This violent tragedy, though used by some as an example of our evolution from "killer apes,"[58] offers instead a very important insight into primate nature, one that has been easier to observe in captivity. We have Frans de Waal to thank for a new awareness of the extraordinary propensity among virtually all primates to reconcile after conflicts. The tendency to repair ruptured bonds is so critical to primate survival that it deserves a few words on its own.

### The power of reconciliation

All social primates constantly signal their feelings toward each other, and despite their lack of spoken language nonhuman primates are adept communicators, able to send and receive a wide variety of signals. *Facial expression*: eye contact, grimaces (of fear/submission or of open-mouthed threats), pouting, lip-smacking (a kind of non-contact kissing); *body language*: posture upright with hair-raised or shrunken/bowed; out-stretched hand; chest-pounding; exposure of genitals (a sign of submission or threat, depending on species); *sounds*: screams (of anger or empathy), whimpers (begging), various pants (sexual, warnings, advertisements, "laughs"), grunts (reassurances); *contact*: touching, patting, hugging, grooming, kissing, grabbing, pushing, biting. These are but a few of the signals in the primate repertoire. Different species, of course, use them to varying degrees and in somewhat different ways.

The point is, that like humans, other primates have a complete spectrum of feelings they communicate as they negotiate social life. When angry, they scold, threaten or attack; when frustrated, they pout or throw tantrums; when excited, they holler and rush around; and when fearful, they cringe or flee. But most of all they spend a great deal of time touching and grooming each other, reaffirming affection and trust. When bonds are ruptured, or even threatened, there is a strong desire to repair them, not only on the part of the parties in conflict, but also by other members of the group. Frans de Waal cites numerous instances where a third party intervened to stop a conflict in progress, or to repair a rupture between two former friends.[59] Primates, it seems, are uncomfortable with ongoing conflict (see Figure II.3).

The techniques used in reconciliation by various primates are varied, and are summarized briefly in Table II.1. Note the frequent use not only of touching, hugging and grooming, but also of sexually related behaviors, something humans sometimes also use in a similar way. Among apes, it is the bonobos, the only primates, other than humans, in which the females (at least in captivity) are almost continuously receptive and often copulate face-to-face, that are among the most peaceable of our nonhuman relatives (again, at least in captivity). Genital rubbing between any two animals (male or female) is used not just for reproduction, but for calming a stressful situation, as after a spat or when a food supply is discovered. This high level of sexuality greatly reduces aggression (as it also appears to do in the highly sexual, yet placid, stumptail macaques), lowering competitive tensions and establishing interpersonal bonds, much the way hugging and grooming do in chimpanzees. It also lowers male aggression toward females and their offspring, allowing them the advantages of continuous male protection and food sharing. As de Waal concludes: "Bonobos thus substitute sexual activities for rivalries. Sex keeps competition down at feeding time and facilitates rapprochement in the aftermath of fights."[60]

*Figure II.3* Primate reconciliation
A group of female rhesus macaques, with their offspring reconciling after a serious fight between the two sisters (left and right). Note the absence of direct eye contact as they huddle together, lipsmack, and look at each other's offspring, prior to grooming.

*Source*: Drawn by Michele Lukowski from original photograph by F. de Waal (1989: 111). Used with his kind permission.

### Other prosocial behaviors

> Had bonobos been known earlier, reconstructions of human evolution might have emphasized sexual relations, equality between males and females, and the origin of the family, instead of war, hunting, tool technology, and other masculine fortes.[61]

This observation of de Waal's reminds us how much emphasis is still placed by Western cultures on the antisocial rather than prosocial aspects of human nature. The prosocial behaviors of other primates have generally been over-looked or played down. Like the topics in our daily newscasts, stories about primate dominance, aggression, and competition attract our attention more than the less showy acts of cooperation and mutual support that characterize most of their social life. At the close of this chapter, it is thus fitting to make a short list of examples of such prosocial behaviors.

Befriending and protecting infants belonging to the group is widespread among primates. Typically, when a new infant is born, not only its older

*Table II.1* Primate reconciliation behaviors

| | |
|---|---|
| Vervet monkeys: | Rows are commonest among females. They reconcile by grooming the opponent and her offspring. |
| Rhesus monkeys: | After a row, they avoid eye contact to initiate reconciliation. Approach; "accidentally" bump; touch; lipsmacking, followed by grooming. |
| Stumptail monkeys: | Subordinate presents bottom for dominant to hold ("hold bottom" behavior). Dominant may "mock-bite" to demonstrate punishment. |
| Baboons: | Present bottom, tail raised, for dominant or opponent to sniff. Females use this to invite copulation by males and also to appease them. Both sexes use it as a way to reconcile or to initiate a friendship. Accompanied by lowered chin, narrowed eyes and lipsmacking. Followed by grooming. |
| Chimpanzees: | Opponents actively seek each other out after a row, make eye contact, reach out, touch, embrace, kiss. Two males may jointly display first. Females may act as mediators (in captive colonies). One party offers backside to other, with genital fondling or mounting (even between males). Grooming often commences in anal region. |
| Bonobos: | Females almost continuously sexually receptive. Bonobos use sex as a substitute for competitive conflict and to calm each other, as when food is suddenly located or males have fought over the same female. Sexual contact, either mounting or frontal rubbing, occurs in all combinations: male/male, female/female, male/female, and among all ages except young infants. Either partner may elicit. Females beg food by offering sex. Ejaculation or orgasm is not critical; at least three-fourths of the encounters could not result in pregnancy. |

*Sources include*: Cheney and Seyfarth (1990); de Waal (1989); de Waal and Lanting (1997); Goodall (1986); Strum (1987)

siblings, but unrelated animals make attempts to touch it. Protective mothers often relent after an inquisitive individual reassures her by grooming her first. Among many monkeys, it is other females who are most attracted, but with baboons (as we saw) as well as with chimpanzees and bonobos, males also may befriend new infants, tolerate them, even play with them.[62]

Another surprise observation (unexpected according to game theory) was that on occasion male primates will serially copulate with a willing female in estrus. This noncompetitive sharing of reproductive access to females has been reported in chimpanzees, where "there is usually a striking lack of overt aggression on the part of the males present,"[63] while the easy promiscuity among bonobos makes impossible either sexual "jealousy" or concern about paternity (whether conscious or unconscious).[64]

Social structures are often stabilized through group cooperation in enforcing accepted behaviors. As already noted, peacemaker adults will intervene to stop disruptive conflict from escalating, and a troop of baboons will cooperate in attacking any threat to one of its infants. Likewise, a group of primates may punish "rule-breakers." At the Arnhem zoo, de Waal reports a case in which two juvenile chimpanzees obstinately refused to enter the night cages for two hours, forcing all the others to wait for their dinner, which only came when all were in their sleeping quarters. That night, the pair were caged separately because of the obvious anger of the others. Next morning, however, when all were free again, the two were chased and beaten (though not seriously injured) by the entire colony.[65]

Finally, there is evidence among primates generally of sensitivity toward others: of physical attachments to others (even after they have died); of sharing of emotional feelings (comforting the fearful or sad, becoming excited or angry when others are); even of insightfully helping others in distress (throwing a chain to a bonobo friend in a moat; bringing a water-containing tire to a chimpanzee "aunt" who had been unable to obtain water for herself). The latter two incidents suggest strongly both *conscious awareness of the need of a specific other*, akin to insightful human empathic behavior, and a surprising level of *problem-solving capability*.[66] Bonobos, in particular, exhibit an extraordinary level of sensitivity to each other. Much eye contact occurs, between adults and offspring as well as when frontally mating – both moments of intense attachment. Children are played with by nonrelated adults. And bonobos' sensitivity to the moods of others and ability to share experiences is almost uncanny.[67]

In summary, then, for all primates, social life in one form or another is their most critical survival need. Other members of the group are not merely utilitarian objects to be manipulated for the selfish benefit of the individual. Without a cohesive group, there *is* no individual. No observation attests better to this than the following from de Waal:

> [Among almost all primates studied] there is a systematic increase in friendly interactions following aggressive ones. Quite a few studies have been made and have concluded that former opponents are *selectively attracted*, that is, they tend to come together more often than usual, and more often with each other than with individuals who had nothing to do with the fight. The phenomenon seems widespread in the primate order: we now have systematic evidence for chimpanzees, bonobos, mountain gorillas, golden monkeys, capuchin monkeys, red-fronted lemurs, patas monkeys, vervet monkeys, baboons, and a variety [eight species] of macaques.[68]

The preservation of social life is the *sine qua non* of primate existence, and as de Waal and his colleagues have most recently shown, under the stressful conditions of crowding, as long as food and water are plentiful, they redouble their efforts to avoid conflict and maintain positive bonds.

> Our research leads us to conclude that we come from a long lineage of social animals capable of flexibly adjusting to all kinds of conditions, including unnatural ones such as crowded pens and city streets. The adjustment may not be without cost [i.e. internal stress], but it is certainly preferable to the frightening alternative [of unrelieved mayhem] predicted on the basis of rodent studies.[69]

To sum up the story so far: There have been at least three camps in the thinking about the nature of primates and the origins of human nature. One, that of the game theorists, I have spent a great deal of time over, and trust I have shown it to be overly simple as well as misleading. The other two camps are more subtle and thoughtful, and I have only hinted at their distinctions so far. One is that primates, or at least the living great apes, are "naturally egalitarian," not given to forming hierarchies, and are essentially peaceable – the Rousseauian model, promoted by Margaret Power (cited above) and others. They argue that early human bands were like that. *Bondedness* dominates primate behavior.

The other camp, that based on the Hobbesian model, holds that primates have always possessed hierarchical tendencies, but since they *also* dislike being bossed about, they engage in a kind of primitive democratic politics where the more numerous, but less powerful, members gang up to control would-be tyrants. Christopher Boehm, the main proponent of this view, calls it a "reverse dominance hierarchy interpretation" of egalitarian primate societies. *Individual autonomy* dominates primate behavior.[70]

In this chapter I have tried to introduce the notion that neither the Rousseauian nor the Hobbesian extreme is an accurate picture of primate nature, and therefore of human nature. They are not mutually exclusive as all too many would argue, but rather are two aspects of primate social organization that depend on the *context* in which a group finds itself: low stress tends to lead to egalitarianism, high stress to hierarchy with the possibility of more aggressive behaviors. In my view, both are "natural" outcomes of our universal primate propensities for bonding on the one hand and autonomy on the other, which under ideal conditions are readily modulated. Stressful conditions tend to restrict individual autonomy, which in turn creates potential frustration and tends to increase frictions which strain social bonds. Excessive stress leads to coercive hierarchies and, ultimately, to violent conflict. How this plays out in human societies I shall try to show in the following chapters.

# III

# THE SELECTING OF *HOMO SAPIENS*

Creatures have diversified to fit different evolutionary niches –
and this is all that we humans have done, like any other life-form.
In that context, the hypertrophy of the human cerebral cortex can
be examined as an evolutionary trait on the same terms as the
expansion of ... the albatross's wings: very useful for some
purposes, a great nuisance for others.

Mary Midgley (1990: 47)

What images come to mind when someone says "human evolution"? Is it
perhaps a series of gradually evolving males stretching across a page, from a
knuckle-walking ape on the left to a fully upright-walking modern specimen on
the right? The first crouching hominid carries a stone, the next a club, and
finally, a briefcase or a gun, depending on the artist's politics. Perhaps it's the
image of the Australopithecine "Lucy" and her mate, described in Chapter I?
Or an African desert scene, such as in the opening of Stanley Kubrick's film,
*2001: A Space Odyssey*, in which two bands of agitated apemen battle over a
waterhole and suddenly discover that a bone can be a weapon: Voila!
Intelligence is born! Or is it a more idyllic picture outside a cave where fur-clad
men with clubs are dragging home an outsized deer carcass as women suckle
babes, tend fires, and scrape skins? Maybe it's a cave painting of stick-figure
males, supposedly at war, or else hunting gorgeously portrayed exotic animals.

Whatever the images, they all imply that humans were selected for hunting
and provisioning by the male, and that weapon-making was the technology that
gave our ancestors an edge; scarcity and war are implied. Period. No signs of
women and children gathering most of the food, though they certainly did this.
No signs of people signaling or grooming each other, or laughing together,
though they certainly did these things. No signs of the *group* acting together to
defend its children against attacking carnivores, though they surely did this. No
signs of larger groups sometimes gathering to harvest abundant fish or fruits,
though this probably happened. Finally, the habitats shown are mainly semi-arid
grasslands, or dank northern forests, almost never the tropical and temperate
wooded riverways or the ice-free, food-rich coastlines that surely attracted our
ancestors as they evolved in Africa and later migrated across continents.

If we want to understand the brains – and the behaviors – that were being shaped during the whole six million years of hominid evolution, we need to know what the environments then were like, the "environments of evolutionary adaptation," or EEAs, as evolutionists call them. (Note that I use the plural here.) Though evolutionary psychologists tend to speak of *the* EEA as if that whole period, or even just the last million years of the Pleistocene, was but one continuous set of environmental conditions, it was in fact the exact opposite. It was one of the most unstable periods in Earth's long climatic history. Our ancestors were being honed by ongoing environmental instability, which selected *against* rigid genetic control over behavior and *for* indeterminacy and flexibility. While many other genera of mammals that could not adapt were becoming extinct, and new ones were appearing all around them, once our ancestors of the genus *Homo* emerged around 2.5 mya, some of them managed, by luck and wit, to squeak through because they never did become "naturally (i.e. genetically) adapted" to any one environment.

The overly simplified and unrealistic pictures of hominid life before and during the Pleistocene that are commonly presented are, I believe, highly misleading. Not only do they distort our interpretations of modern human nature; they leave far too much unexplained. What were women doing? What held societies together? What aspects of "intelligence" were actually adaptive? What made humans so much more emotional than any other primates? What, as Midgley's introductory quote suggests, was the evolutionary niche for which we were being selected? Is it not the case, as J.R.R. Tolkien implied, that for humankind, "The rule of no realm is mine"? Humans have no specific niche of their own; wherever they are is "home." In whatever place they find themselves, they have had to learn and invent ways of living and surviving. Flexibility is the ultimate hominid adaptation, and it took a great many failed experiments by our ancestors along the way before the emergence of *Homo sapiens*, and many more cultural failures after that, even to the present day, for us "moderns" to emerge.

This chapter offers an overview of our evolutionary history rather different from those with which most readers will be familiar. Its emphasis is not on the "triumph" of an increasingly clever species evolving to succeed and advance on a straightforward path leading inevitably to modern humans. Rather, it is on the unrelenting selection by a fickle environment of a few cohesive social groups of increasingly less specialized, more flexibly behaving individuals who somehow managed to survive one catastrophe after another, groups of individuals whose behaviors came to be guided by increasingly powerful emotions rather than by genetically programmed patterns. For our ancestors, driven to migrate long distances by relatively sudden global climate swings, quick learning, problem-solving, and the creative *sharing of knowledge* superseded all other adaptive qualities. Resources were not so much scarce as obscure. Between- or within-group competition was mostly meaningless. Overcrowding was seldom a problem, and when it was, migration to somewhere less populated often took place. Yet most migrations were surely climate-driven, not population-driven. In all cases, survival of the group was imperative, and the possibility of its extinction was an almost constant threat. Outside a group, no one survived. Throughout its long evolution, our whole species faced the possibility of near extinction many times.

There is not very much direct physical evidence to provide any detailed picture of hominid behavior. Fossil bone fragments from a few hundred ancestors, collected from three continents and covering 4.5 million years of history, give but a limited amount of information about soft tissues. Assorted chipped stones, animal bones and other associated artifacts tell a little about how they made a living, but not much. Most of the evidence decayed long ago. Yet even a few bones can tell us some things. The sizes of various muscle attachments indicate which muscles were used most. A cranium can reveal not only the size of its owner's brain, but what bumps were on its cortex – bumps indicating the beginnings of new skills, such as speech. The wearing down of teeth gives a clue to diet. Sometimes the bones even suggest the cause of an individual's death, whether from accident, predation, or disease. There are other important clues, also. Contemporary fossilized remains of animals and especially of plants, when they exist, give an idea of probable foods and of the habitats and climates existing at different places and times. From this knowledge, possible migratory pathways can be deduced. Yet even all these together are sparse data from which to erect grand theories about the evolution of human nature.

More recently, evidence from the global distribution of genes in different modern populations has suggested that there were at least two waves of hominids spreading out of Africa to the north and east. This seems to have occurred, but the further assumption, widely made, that the second wave totally replaced the first, raising the possibility of direct competition between these two sets of ancestors, is, I believe, suspect. My belief is grounded in good scientific reasons, to be taken up shortly. Still, this image of a Pleistocene takeover of earlier "bumbling" ancestors by high I.Q. moderns persists in the popular mind.

I begin this chapter with a summary presentation of the fossil finds, their locations, dates, and possible genealogies. This is followed by a short history of the various evolutionary interpretations put on the data as they have accumulated during the twentieth century. Then I present the two competing ideas about the origins of modern humans: (1) the second migration out of Africa either *replaced* the first, or (2) *fused* with its remnants in a continuous evolutionary process. This leads to consideration of the role of genetic "bottlenecks" in evolution, and finally to a pattern of probable dispersal routes across the world during the most recent glaciation. The chapter concludes with an inquiry into what behavioral traits *must* have been selected, and what kind of complex human nature they created? Like previous theories, mine, too, is a "just-so" story. It cannot be otherwise. The story presented here sets the stage for the rest of the book, which will connect the Pleistocene to the present – and perhaps even to a different vision of the future. Surely we can learn from the past something about ourselves that will help us in the millennia ahead.[1]

## Skeletons in the family bushes

"Hominids" is the name given to all the prehuman-like species after they branched off from our common ancestor with modern apes. The first of them emerged in Africa around six million years ago, perhaps even earlier, when the climate at the end of the Pliocene began undergoing frequent fluctuations. Dry, cold periods alternated with the formerly continuous warm, wet ones, causing the borders between lush forests and dry savannas to move back and forth. This climatic instability has persisted to the present, and was particularly severe during the four recent glaciations that began about one million years ago. As now seems clear from fossil records everywhere, it is during such periods of rapid (geologically speaking) environmental change that most evolutionary spurts have taken place.[2]

During this period, there occurred in Africa a great burst of new primate species after our shared ancestor with modern chimpanzees had branched into two evolutionary lines. One of these branches led to our modern cousins, the common chimpanzee and the bonobo, both mentioned in Chapter II. Neither one of them evolved an increasingly large brain, nor strayed far from the remaining wet tropical forests in which they had always lived. They remained confined to a specific niche. The other branch, that led zig-zag to modern humans, produced two sequential "bushes" (rather than linear "ladders") of hominid species – the *Australopithecus* bush, followed by the *Homo* bush. This great explosion of species is sketched out later in Figure III.2.

One notices first that though several species were contemporaneous in Africa over most of this time (some even for a million years or more), all save modern humans eventually became extinct.[3] So far as the evidence goes, there is no indication that any of these species was a direct or indirect cause of the extinction of any other. Rather, they seem all to have failed to adapt to the ongoing climatic stresses. The fact that of so many hominid species, only one has survived has given rise to considerable speculation about what special traits characterized those ancestors who did survive at each stage. What attributes made them more successful than other sister-species that became extinct?

Two quite different theories have been put forward. The first, and still most prevalent, is that the primary evolutionary problem to be solved was one of food scarcity and that early hominids began to utilize meat much more than their tree-living ape cousins, as they moved out onto the open savannas of a cooler, drier Africa. Big brains, it is argued, evolved early (or so the story used to go), along with an upright gait, for the intelligence needed for tool and weapon-making skills and cooperative hunting strategies by males. Selection was not only for hunting prowess but also for winning, in direct, often warlike confrontations with competing bands of hunters: the *2001: A Space Odyssey* imagery. The origins of human society revolved around the bonding of relatively aggressive males for the tasks of hunting and fighting. It is an image that fits the individualistic, Billiard Ball model of the universe. Hence, the evolutionary sequence pictured in Figure III.1.

*Figure III.1* "The evolution of man"
The male evolutionary ladder. This is how most textbooks illustrate the steps in human evolution, based entirely on males and their weapons.

*Source*: Original art by Michele Lukowski from author's sketch

This popularized image, however, leaves out the most significant part of the evolutionary problem that our earliest ancestors faced. Becoming smarter (for whatever purposes) meant birthing ever-more helpless, premature infants, and investing a great deal of extra time and effort in nursing them, teaching them, and protecting them. Females (who incidentally gather well over half the group's calories in extant foraging societies) required increasing assistance from other adults in watching over and protecting their helpless young from predators, and for providing additional food to the group's cohort of mothers, especially during lactation, which eventually came to last four or five years. The adaptational requirements already placed on earlier primates were increasingly critical for evolving hominids.[4]

Success at reproduction was no longer a matter of just a mother, or even of two parents (such as many species of birds manage with). It became necessary that there be a whole, collaborating, functional group. Without such cooperating, sharing groups of ancestors, the intellect of modern humans could never have evolved. In fact, fossils show that upright gaits and living in small nomadic bands had developed early, and that brain size, though somewhat large by general primate standards, grew mainly in proportion to body size among the Australopithecines, and remained like that for about three million years. It only began to increase significantly *relative to body size* when *Homo* emerged. Even then, it really took off around the onset of the ice ages and the migrations out of Africa. That marked the beginning of the enormous selection pressures expe-

102

rienced by our ancestors. But the necessary evolutionary step of strongly bonded groups had already been set long before.

This second, or revised, theory of hominid evolution is far more inclusive and complex. It deals with the problems being faced by all the individuals in the group, not just adult males. It is an image that fits well with the Indra's Net model of the universe, one that emphasizes multiple connections. Groups – human cultures – really can be selected for, as reproductive entities.

I now turn to the actual data on which either theory must rest. How have they been interpreted? How *might* they be interpreted?

## The fossil data and their interpretations

Back in 1924, when Raymond Dart found the first fossils of one of our earliest ancestors in a cave at Sterkfontaine in South Africa – the skull of a child – he believed he had discovered a young "killer ape." The bones he found, to which he gave the name *Australopithecus africanus*, or southern African ape, were not only mixed with those of other animals, but themselves showed signs of severe injuries. Given the beliefs about human nature and human evolution held at the time, Dart presumed that his humanlike apes had inflicted those injuries on one another as well as on the animals they had supposedly killed. Not only were they hunters, they were also murderers.

This interpretation persisted for decades, and became a kind of working truth. Writers such as Desmond Morris and Robert Ardrey wrote popular books describing our killer ancestors and their territorial and other competitive behaviors. Says anthropologist Rick Potts about those days:

> In *African Genesis* (1960), Robert Ardrey introduced to the world at large the hypothesis that hunting and a murderous life-style played the leading role in the origin of the human lineage.[5]

But as Bruce Winterhalder has further noted:

> The direct evidence for this killer-ape reconstruction has always been flimsy. *Nonetheless it was eagerly embraced by key authorities* ... "Hunting is the master behavior pattern of the human species" ... "Men enjoy hunting and killing ... [T]he evolutionary success of hunting exerted a profound effect on human psychology".[6]

More recently, sophisticated new methods for studying the history of old bones (known as taphonomy, which analyzes the scars incised into bones) revealed how completely wrong Dart and everyone else had been. The remains of his tiny ape-people (they stood only about four feet tall) as well as those of the other animals in the cave had been scarred not by apes' teeth nor by sharp stone tools, but by the teeth of large carnivores.[7] These early hominid ancestors were not the predators, but the prey of other species. Dart had discovered the lair of some ancient South African carnivore. Thus the "killer ape" hypothesis was laid to rest, once and for all.

### *"Man the Hunter"*

Nevertheless, the image of humans having evolved primarily through male skills in hunting persists. Because among most of the few still-existing foraging peoples it is mainly men who hunt meat (sometimes, but not always, in small groups), the assumption was made that male bonding for the purpose of bringing down large game was the driving force in human evolution (see Figure III.1). In 1965, anthropologists studying these foraging peoples held a convention entitled "Man the Hunter," where this idea dominated.[8] The upright gait of our earliest ancestors was supposedly an adaptation to tracking game across the expanding savanna grasslands of Africa. When the climate began to cool, some of the forest apes came down from the trees, began to walk bipedally, and developed large brains to coordinate their game-tracking efforts. The whole evolutionary argument was based on the presumed critical activities of males. It turns out that almost all of the story is wrong, or at best, misleading.

The first assumption to go was that large brains, supposedly evolving to coordinate group hunting, appeared at the same time as bipedalism. But they did not evolve together. Upright walking appeared early, and seems to have evolved independently among different branches of Australopithecines.[9] Yet the brains of all these early hominids were about the same size as those of modern chimpanzees, around 450 cc (about one US pint, in volume). The slightly larger Australopithecines that appeared over a million years later had proportionately larger brains (600 cc), appropriate to their larger size. It was only with the emergence of the bigger-headed *Homo* species that the brain case began to enlarge, suggesting newly acquired intellectual capacities. It is not surprising that the great migrations out of Africa did not occur until bigger brains had developed. Flexible intelligence probably only then became available.

A second assumption associated with the hunting hypothesis was that large brains evolved for the purpose of cooperating during the hunting of big game. Yet though the brain of *Homo erectus* had nearly doubled in size compared to that of the Australopithecines, and they had migrated across the Eurasian land mass, there is no clear evidence that they ever hunted big game. That occurred only after modern *Homo sapiens*, with their modern-sized brain, appeared on the scene.[10]

An alternative hypothesis to coordinated hunting has been advanced for how our earliest ancestors probably made their living. They were scavengers, feeding on the kills left by the large predators of the African savanna. It is likely both males and females participated almost equally in this, as well as in gathering edible plants, birds' eggs, small animals and insects.[11] Later on, even among *Homo sapiens*, new evidence suggests that the main source of protein for many groups was not the hunting of big game by males but the use by the whole group of nets for trapping small birds and mammals and for catching fish.

The ability to knot strands of fibers into strong nets is now known from several archeological sites around the world where, by good luck, either the plant material itself was preserved, or the knots left clear imprints in the clays in which they became buried.[12] Such communal food collecting could be participated in by everyone, even children, with some holding the net and others noisily driving the animals into it. Unlike tracking game, it was relatively safe and produced high yields of quality food. And of course food collected in this way belonged to and was shared by all. It is a food-gathering technique especially appropriate to open woodlands. Once common natural habitats, most such areas have long been coopted for agriculture. Hence, net-hunting is not common among extant foragers who have been pushed into such extreme habitats as deserts, rain forests, or arctic regions, but net-fishing, of course, is still widespread.

Finally, among some living peoples who continue to practice hunting and for whom it is mainly a male small-group activity, there is low correlation between prowess in hunting and status in society, and males are not particularly singled out for their skills.[13]

Neither is there correlation between hunting and warlikeness. In those instances where they are correlated, or where males seem to dominate females, Paul Shepard has suggested that it is because the societies have come under external stress, leading to the development of internal tensions, similar to those described in Chapter II for recently stressed populations of wild primates. As Shepard says, "More value is placed on men than women only as the hunt is perverted by sexism and training for war."[14] All this suggests that, while hunting has been important in later human evolution, it is not "in our genes" as a naturally aggressive sort of pursuit. Our attitudes toward it are shaped not by biology, but by cultural meaning systems.

### *"Man the Warrior"*

In the modern world, hunting and war-making often seem closely related, even though they serve quite different purposes and occur in different contexts. Today both are viewed as male occupations; both can require physical endurance and psychic courage; and hunting weapons have often been modified for killing people, from axes, to spears, to guns.[15] In many modern societies, both activities, when successful, bring admiration. Thus the obvious link was assumed: if humans (specifically male humans) evolved as hunters, they must also have evolved to be aggressive warriors. There must be a natural propensity to pursue both activities. Nor did Raymond Dart's "killer ape" proving not to be a killer, either of game or of other apes, dampen the search for proof that an aggressive drive for both hunting and war-making is intrinsic to (male) human nature.

But what is the paleontological evidence that warlikeness is a natural human proclivity? Yes, there is occasional evidence of arrow points embedded in a skeleton of some of our ancient ancestors. There are some instances of dismemberment of bodies, of removal of flesh, and even of possible cannibalism. But these instances do not, in themselves, prove that human beings have an instinct, a drive, toward killing each other as Konrad Lorenz proposed.[16] Furthermore, the evidence in the fossil record is impossible to interpret, since as we know from historically recorded societies, war and other forms of aggression are not the only causes of violent death. Accidents are one possibility, especially during hunting. (Accidental homicides among modern, gun-toting hunters, are all too frequent.) Killing someone as punishment (as we Americans regularly do, to the horror of many other societies) is another. Sacrifice for religious purposes is a third. And some mutilations may be carried out ceremonially *after* death. For example, until recently, the women and children of the Fore tribe in New Guinea ritually removed and ate the brains of departed relatives as a sign of respect.[17] Eating of slain enemies could also be ceremonial. Finally, during periods of extreme stress, women often commit infanticide, being unable to take care of one more offspring (usually it is female infants that are killed) and at such times people may also resort to cannibalizing dead or highly dependent members of the group as a survival strategy.[18]

To assume that any of these is evidence of innate homicidal tendencies is simply not justified. How can one account in the same breath for contemporary America's unwillingness to sanction assisted, voluntary euthanasia for dying patients while blandly justifying state-sanctioned executions? It cannot be genetic. It must be cultural.

And to conclude: so far as I have been able to discover there is no good paleontological evidence for any of the contemporaneous species of hominids in Pleistocene Africa attacking or causing the extinction of one another, despite their living contiguously in many cases. Members of *Paranthropus robustus* and several early *Homo* species, for example, seem to have coexisted without conflict over a long period (see Figure III.2). The idea that any of our ancestors succeeded because they directly eliminated closely related, competing species is without evidence. This is especially important when we consider that *Homo erectus* had spread to every continent except the Americas (and perhaps Australia) long before the advent of the first modern humans, *Homo sapiens*.

Thus, when anthropologist Robert Edgerton, in his book entitled *Sick Societies: Challenging the Myth of Primitive Harmony*, argues that peaceful, harmonious societies never have existed, he is extrapolating from a troubled present into the past. As Paul Shepard points out, all Edgerton's examples of violence among still extant tribals, be it rape, homicide, genital mutilation, wife beating and more, are "limited to habitat fringe groups: the Inuit [in the arctic], the Papuans [in deep rain forests], and the Siriono of Bolivia, for example."[19] This is not to say that there never was organized violence in the long history of human evolution; only that it was not a built-in part of human nature, a "drive", an inevitable tendency encoded in our genes. Certain kinds of stress can, predictably, lead to violence (as I will argue in later chapters). That war-making was a survival strategy that was being genetically selected for during our long Pleistocene evolution is, however, totally unsubstantiated. The repeated die-offs of human populations during that epoch that were being caused by sudden climate swings would have made further killings in wars suicidal for our emerging species.

For what was actually going on then, let us now turn to events during that last million years of the Pleistocene.

## Imagining the Pleistocene

For the past 10,000 years, all of human written history, our planet has been in a moderate warm spell, with relatively stable weather conditions. So accustomed are we to this stability, that we tend to think of it as permanent, something that will continue forever. We think of the ice ages as a prehistoric time, consigned to the past. The last glaciation, for most of us, means the last *ever* glaciation in Earth's history, as though the ice ages were forever behind us.

Unfortunately, we have been spoiled. Climate change is not forever over. We at last are realizing we are entering another period of global warming, to which we are definitely contributing, but probably not altogether causing – a very presumptuous thought.[20] Its magnitude and rate of onset are not unlike those of the past, and it could well be followed, in a few centuries, by a renewed glaciation, which can likewise come into being in the span of a generation or two. It seems likely that we modern *Homo sapiens* are about to experience what life was like for our Pleistocene ancestors.

Indeed, to the extent that Mother Nature has shaped human nature, that natural selection has made us what we are biologically, most of that shaping took place in a very short period of time, evolutionarily speaking. The whole of the Pleistocene, as already noted, was a period of repeated major climate swings during which many extinctions occurred and, at the peak of each of the four past glaciations, huge areas of the planet were uninhabitable.

We begin, then, with a look at those climate changes, at what was really going on. Then we turn to the dispersals of our human ancestors around the globe during that time, stopping along the way to interpret how we remained one species, despite such seemingly great isolation of populations. Finally, we examine the period at the end of the Pleistocene, when the glaciers finally began to recede, and what that meant for human survival and population growth.

### A brief history of climate change

Earth seems to have had four prior periods of off-and-on glaciations or ice ages: one about 2.3 bya (billion years ago) that lasted a couple of hundred million years; one that lasted from 915 to 600 mya; one at 450 mya in the Ordovician,

*Figure III. 2* The fossil record of
human evolution

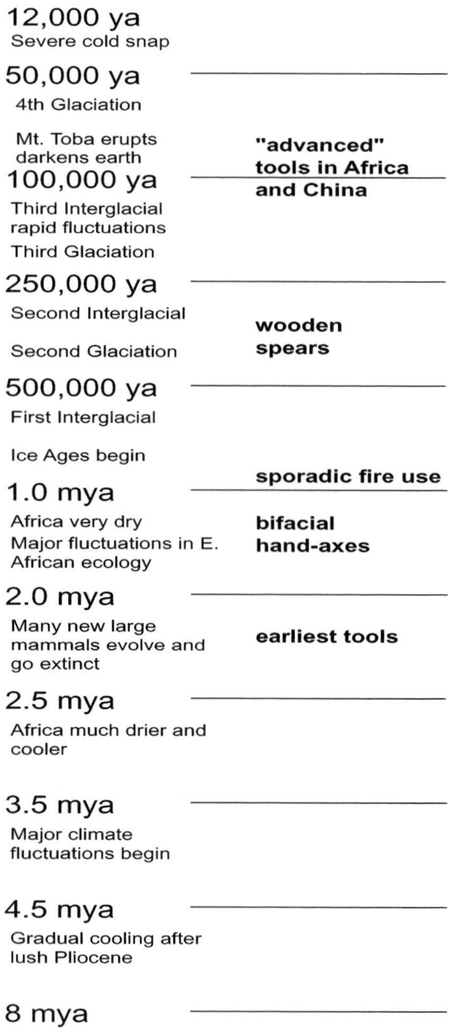

**12,000 ya**
Severe cold snap

**50,000 ya**
4th Glaciation

Mt. Toba erupts
darkens earth
**100,000 ya**
Third Interglacial
rapid fluctuations
Third Glaciation

**250,000 ya**
Second Interglacial

Second Glaciation

**500,000 ya**
First Interglacial

Ice Ages begin
**1.0 mya**
Africa very dry
Major fluctuations in E.
African ecology

**2.0 mya**
Many new large
mammals evolve and
go extinct

**2.5 mya**
Africa much drier and
cooler

**3.5 mya**
Major climate
fluctuations begin

**4.5 mya**
Gradual cooling after
lush Pliocene

**8 mya**

**"advanced"
tools in Africa
and China**

**wooden
spears**

**sporadic fire use**

**bifacial
hand-axes**

**earliest tools**

This composite summary synthesizes many sources, not all in agreement with respect to names or lineages (arrows). Note that the timeline is not linear: ya = years ago; mya = million years ago.

There are two main, branched lineages or "bushes": the Australopithecine bush and the Homo bush, the former containing two species, *Australopithecus* and *Paranthropus*, the latter only *Homo*. These are designated by *A. P.* and *H.*, respectively, followed by species names. Each species is located at the date of its earliest fossil. Underneath are given location of find and cranial capacity (in cc = cubic centimeters) where known. Note that several species overlapped in time on these bushes. All of the Australopithecines became extinct long ago (indicated by an arrow ending in three lines). Lineage arrows are solid where agreement regarding continuity exists; interrupted arrows indicate uncertainty of descent or possible "missing" intermediates not yet found.

As indicated in the text, a hotly disputed point is whether *H. erectus* was totally replaced by later *H. sapiens*, or interbred with the latter, contributing some of its genes to modern humans. Thus, I have indicated two possible

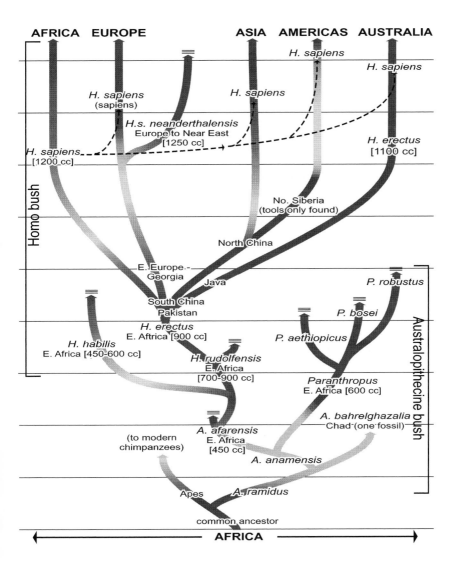

AFRICA   EUROPE                    ASIA   AMERICAS   AUSTRALIA

*H. sapiens*

*H. sapiens*

*H. sapiens*
(sapiens)

*H. sapiens*

*H.s. neanderthalensis*
Europe to Near East
[1250 cc]

*H. sapiens*
[1200 cc]

*H. erectus*
[1100 cc]

**Homo bush**

No. Siberia
(tools only found)

North China

E. Europe -
Georgia

Java

*P. robustus*

South China
Pakistan

*P. bosei*

*H. erectus*
E. Africa [900 cc]

*P. aethiopicus*

*H. habilis*
E. Africa [450-600 cc]

*H. rudolfensis*
E. Africa
[700-900 cc]

*Paranthropus*
E. Africa [600 cc]

**Australopithecine bush**

*A. bahrelghazalia*
Chad (one fossil)

(to modern
chimpanzees)

*A. afarensis*
E. Africa
[450 cc]

*A. anamensis*

Apes    *A. ramidus*

common ancestor

← ————————————————— **AFRICA** ————————————— →

lineages for modern *Homo*: one a continuation of *H. erectus* in continents where it occurred, and another (dotted lineage lines) showing *H. sapiens* traveling out of Africa to reach all continents. Both probably occurred, though genes from the later migrations dominate today.

Finally, note the major climatic fluctuations on the timeline in relation to extinctions and to migrations, and, just to the right, the earliest appearance of successive technologies. Climate rather than competition seems to have been the main selection force in human evolution.

*Source*: Author's summary of data, illustrated by Michele Lukowski. Main Sources: C. Wills (1993); P.B. deMenocal (1995); R. Potts (1996a, 1996b; and S. Stanley (1996). Other Sources: (1) evidence *A. anamensis* walked upright: M. Leakey and Alan Walker (1997); (2) *H. antecessor* as common ancestor for Neanderthals and modern humans: Ann Gibbons (1997a) and J.M.B. de Castro *et al.* (1997); (3) *Homo* in Australia 200,000 ya: M. Wolpoff *et al.* (1993); and *H. sapiens* in Australia 60,000 ya: Alan Thorne *et al.* (1999); (4) age of Java Man at 1.7 mya: R. Lewin *et al.* (2000)

which affected north Africa; and one in the Permian 280 mya, that affected most of the southern hemisphere. After that ran its course, the Earth became warmer by 10°C than it is now for at least 150 million years. In each of those past glaciations, especially the last two, there is fossil evidence of major extinctions, followed by new evolutionary branchings. The most recent, Pleistocene ice age, that followed a long, slow period of gradual cooling, began, as noted earlier, about one million years ago, and presumably is still in progress.

No one knows for sure what triggers the onset of a major ice age: sunspots, Earth's wobbles and orbital shifts, or perhaps continental drift. When large masses of land move to the poles, their surfaces become cooler and ice begins to accumulate. Once glaciers form, they reflect the sun's energy, augmenting the cooling effect. Drifting continents can also change the shape of the oceans, and hence the circulation patterns of the deep waters that help warm the icy polar waters. Another likely factor is phytoplankton, the one-celled plants that thrive in colder regions where upwelling waters bring needed nutrients to the surface. When these plankton populations take off, they can sequester enough carbon dioxide in their bodies to lower the concentration of this greenhouse gas in the atmosphere, thus hastening cooling. Finally, as oceans cool, they dissolve even more of the atmospheric $CO_2$, causing even more cooling.

How to evaluate all these possible causes of climate change is still an ongoing task as scientists around the world try to make predictive global models. But as Thomas Levenson says, in his very readable book on this subject, *Ice Time*, "some climate changes, either those discovered in the past, or those we might yet experience, will always come as surprises. Predictable unpredictability."[21]

It is characteristic of ice ages that, though they last for millions, even hundreds of millions of years, they go through internal cyclic periods of warming and cooling. Like the major ice ages, it is not clear what triggers these less severe climate swings, though the same causes (except maybe continental drift) may be at work. During the present ice age, with its sequence of four glaciations (so far), the cold periods, with large ice sheets growing and shrinking and growing and shrinking, last some 90,000 or more years. Each is then followed by a warmer period of around 10,000 years when most of the ice recedes. Even during these warm periods, though, there may be periods of much cooler, dry weather ("Little Ice Ages") between more balmy, wetter periods.

There are two other important characteristics of these climate changes to note. First, while the major periods of cold develop on a millennial time scale (incredibly slow from the point of view of a human life-span), the internal swings from heavily glaciated to warmer periods and back again, have mostly occurred rapidly, especially in the northern hemisphere during the current ice age.[22] Rapid warming of up to 10°C occurred repeatedly in Greenland during the last ice age, each time taking just one or two decades.[23] And, as geographer Harm de Blij points out, severe cooling, even the onset of a new glaciation, can occur almost equally as fast.[24]

110

The other important thing to know about these secondary climate changes is that they don't necessarily occur all at once over a wide area. While some regions may begin to start warming rapidly, others on the same continent may remain in the grip of bitter cold. Nor are these patterns predictable. Thus, the warming that occurred in the Middle East beginning somewhat before 12,000 ya was not experienced in northern Europe and North America until nearly a thousand years later.

Yet as de Blij points out, when the ice left North America, it did so at an almost cataclysmic speed. Twelve thousand years ago, a thick layer of glacial ice covered Canada, the Great Lakes and extended down to the Ohio River. Two thousand years later, it was completely gone, even from most of Canada. Sea levels rose by the day; coastlines disappeared, wiping out our ancestors' earlier migration routes along exposed continental shelves.[25] Finally, the last large mass of ice sitting over Canada slid off into the Atlantic, precipitously cooled its surface waters and brought on a sharp period of cooling for much of the surrounding northern hemisphere around 10,000 ya. As de Blij says, people living then had to adapt or die; they (or at least some of them) did adapt, by developing irrigation and agriculture. But I am getting ahead of the story.

### The Pleistocene dispersals

Of all the various hominid species that evolved in Africa over the past seven million years only two types, both of the genus *Homo*, seem to have ventured beyond that continent, expanding into the Middle East, Europe and across Asia to the southwest Pacific. All the rest became extinct in Africa. The first of these was *Homo erectus*, whose oldest fossils in Africa date to around 2 mya. Capable of making simple stone tools, these people were sufficiently adaptable to venture into unknown lands very early. As East Africa became drier and less habitable, they traversed long distances relatively rapidly, arriving in Java, Pakistan and south China around 1.7 mya, some 200,000 years after they first evolved in Africa. Their fossils also recently turned up in Eastern Europe from about this same time, and slightly later ones have been found in Italy, Nice and Jordan. (These latter fossils have been assigned to a different species by some paleontologists, who find minor differences in skull shapes.) By the time the ice ages began, *Homo erectus*, or its near cousins, were dispersed across the still habitable parts of Europe and the Near and Far East – and later fossils continue to be found sporadically in these areas.

What routes did they use? Were there one or many waves of *Homo erectus* migrations? No one knows the answer to either question. What is clear is that they were amazingly successful, learned to make more sophisticated tools, including wooden spears for hunting, and seem to have used fire more than 500,000 years ago, which would make available new food resources requiring heat to make them palatable, as well as offering a way to survive in colder climates. They, or their near relatives or evolutionary descendants, seem to have survived in Africa, Europe and across Asia for well over 1.5 million years.[26]

Among paleoanthropologists there is, of course, much debate as to how many *species* of *Homo* there actually were in Africa and migrating outward. And also, how many waves of migration there were. Were there many or few? Did each new advance in tool-making imply a new wave from Africa, or was there exchange of information over long distances, or was there independent, yet convergent, evolution of new technologies?[27]

There tend to be two camps: the splitters and the unifiers. For the splitters, slight cranial difference or tool improvement means a new species, genetically different and reproductively isolated from the earlier species in the same location that it supposedly replaced. For the unifiers, once *Homo erectus* evolved in Africa there was but one global species that, by back and forth exchanges of mating partners along migration routes, evolved as a single species, albeit with modest regional differences in anatomy and tools, not unlike modern "races". This is known as the multiregional evolution of *Homo sapiens*, or modern humans.[28]

I believe that parts of both stories are probably correct. There surely was some replacement, especially in areas where earlier migrants had become extinct, which must surely have happened all too often during the ice ages. But there is also good evidence for regional retention in modern humans of very ancient anatomical differences already visible in *Homo erectus* fossils, despite their all carrying modern genes as well. In such cases, newcomers would have interbred with older populations, leading us to infer that early humans really were all one species, and never became totally reproductively isolated (as did, for example, sheep and goats).

Before I turn to the genetic arguments regarding this dispute, however, it is necessary to ask why our ancestors left Africa and how they managed to get to their destinations?

### Conditions of the dispersals

The earliest wave of *Homo erectus* migrations occurred between two and one million years ago, during the slow final cooling of the planet before the ice ages began in earnest. Their movements were surely a response to the drying of eastern Africa and the resultant migrations of evolving species of animals north, and then east, into more temperate latitudes. By that time, according to Pat Shipman, *Homo* had become thoroughly omnivorous, utilizing a diet that included considerable amounts of meat. Its tools and its more powerful build suggest it might have been the earliest true human hunter, though it surely had already been a scavenger. As Shipman points out, a high-protein diet would enable females to care for increasingly helpless, "premature" offspring, making possible the further evolution of enlarging brains that occurred between 2 million and 200,000 ya. Since population densities for predators (or high-level scavengers) tend to be lower than for total vegetarians, they would have had to forage over larger areas, living in small, mobile groups.[29]

The late Pliocene cooling, before the ice ages began, would have affected whole ecosystems, causing some species of prehuman hominids to migrate toward the equator and others to become extinct. It seems likely that the large Australopithecines in eastern and southern Africa, who all had massive jaws, indicative of dependence on one sort of vegetation, became extinct when their normal food supply began to disappear (see Figure III.2). Animals that are utilized for food by today's humans can, of course, actively migrate to more favorable habitats, and it is likely that our *Homo erectus* ancestors simply followed along after them, perhaps increasing the proportion of animal calories in their diets as they entered areas of unknown vegetation.

How many waves of *Homo erectus* issued out of Africa is unknown, though we may suppose there were several during periods when climate changes promoted migrations. Sometime between 100,000 and 80,000 ya, however, new migrations began, again out of northern East Africa, of humans whom we call *Homo sapiens*, people sharing characteristics with all modern peoples. Exactly who they were and where they lived is not clear. Long before, about 500,000 ya, some say, early *Homo sapiens* arose, most likely also in Africa. They, in turn, gave rise to a branch known as the Neanderthals, whether in Africa or perhaps in western Asia or Europe, where their only fossils have been found. Though presumably without full capability of complex language, these near cousins of ours nevertheless managed to survive from around 300,000 to about 35,000 ya, a longer time than we fully modern humans (*Homo sapiens sapiens*) have so far managed, and under much more severe climatic conditions to boot!

Meantime, back in Africa and quite likely the Middle East, genetically modern people were evolving. The trail of fossil intermediates suggests Africa as the main locus. At this time, toward the end of the third interglacial and onset of the fourth Ice Age, there were especially severe climate swings. By then, a new, slightly larger-brained and language-competent population was thriving, and perhaps came under population pressure. By at least 100,000 years ago, during periods favorable to migration (of animals as well as humans) they had spread to the southern tip of Africa and into the Middle East.[30] The latter population, however, seems either to have become extinct, or to have migrated back into Africa or south and east, moving along the coastlines of central Asia, perhaps across the Indus and Ganges valleys of north India, and into southeast Asia. From there, they could have gone south to New Guinea and Australia and north to China and Japan.

Whether it was this population or several later waves of migrants out of Africa (or quite possibly both), within a very short time in evolutionary terms, modern humans had reached Australia (60,000 ya) and Europe and even the Americas (around 43,000 ya). Evidence of a significant site as ancient as 18,000 years has been found in Virginia; and in the Amazon, archaeologist Anna Roosevelt has demonstrated the existence of highly complex, centralized cultures as ancient as 12,000 years.[31] Surely the first entry into the New World, whether by way of a Bering land bridge or some other route, had to have preceded these established, larger sites by several millennia.[32]

How did these people manage to migrate so fast? The answer to this question probably is the same one as "What was driving them?" The solution seems to lie in the repeated glacial comings and goings during the fourth Ice Age. There would be long periods when a thick layer of ice covered much of the northern hemisphere and the southern end of South America. The extent of land where humans now live that was either under ice or so cold that only tundra existed, with few edible plants, was enormous. Really habitable areas were restricted to an equatorial belt that was greatly extended along the continental coastlines, where oceans ameliorated climates.

A map of the world then would look very different from now. Especially, one would not recognize the coastlines. The sea level being much, much lower at the height of each glacial advance (with so much water stored in ice), the continental shelves were exposed, creating the Bering land bridge, and also a probable near-land bridge between the southeast Asian islands and Australia. In addition, it opened up a relatively flat, coastal pathway along which humans could travel without serious obstruction and with constant access to the rich supplies of intertidal invertebrates and inshore fish that most coastlines offer. These coastlines, long ignored when drawing maps of our ancestors' probable migration routes, are now being considered seriously.

Not only could people have walked and camped along the shorelines. They could also have used boats to travel short distances. As archeologist Margaret Jodrey of the Smithsonian Institution points out, humans very likely had watercraft at least 40,000 years ago, made of animal skins or wood (neither of which is likely to be preserved, of course). But at a 14,700-year-old site in southern Chile, anthropologist Tom Dillehay has uncovered all kinds of hand-crafted artifacts from a bog where they were preserved, including knotted cords and tent remnants. These people could fish, gather the edible berries, weave plant fibers into clothes, baskets, and nets for fishing and hunting, and build boats. As archeologist James Adovasio, who has excavated a 13,000 year-old site in Pennsylvania, puts it: "By focusing only on stones, we are ignoring 95 percent of what these people made and what they did."[33]

So much, then, for the standard image of the ice age hunter going across the continent killing off big game. Though this may have been the case for some migrations, it is by no means the only explanation of how our ancestors spread around the globe in record-breaking time (archaeologically speaking). These new insights open up a multitude of possible migration routes for our ancestors. The Americas, for example, may have been peopled by groups traveling (on foot) across the Bering land bridge, or (with or without boats) along the north Pacific coastline, or even, with the aid of short ocean voyages, from northwest Africa, along the Atlantic coasts of Europe, Iceland, Greenland and Canada –

though that is less likely. It could also have facilitated the peopling of the Japanese islands, temporarily connected to the Asian mainland, as well as other now-offshore archipelagoes. Another great advantage of coastal migrations, of course, would have been the opportunities to utilize and develop local populations inland, along the valleys of the many streams and rivers they would have come across. Tidal estuaries are among the richest biological sites known, and their resources are relatively easily harvested by men, women, and children.

The fourth glaciation, however, was not climatically consistent. Between the maxima of ice advances, there were sudden periods of thawing when the glaciers receded a bit, sea levels rose rapidly, and temperatures rose somewhat. Then, after a few generations or centuries, the climate would reverse itself, as the ice reformed and sea levels fell. Recall that most often these changes were very rapid, occurring in just a few decades. Such unpredictable swings must have caught many migrating populations off guard, with many local groups dying off, unable to move or adapt in time. After each catastrophe, populations would rebound, as the survivors adapted to new conditions. But the need to stay in closely supportive, cooperating bands without too much internal strife must have been imperative. Both culturally and perhaps genetically, there must have been natural selection for highly bonded and coordinated social groups.

The Pleistocene was thus a time of constant catastrophe and rebound for our immediate ancestors, with the global population climbing, and then being sharply cut back. One of the worst catastrophes, one that surely must have wiped out a very large proportion of the humans (and other species) alive at the time, was the gigantic eruption of Mount Toba, an Indonesian island that blew up and disappeared 73,500 ya. The ash it spewed into the atmosphere turned the whole planet dark for some seventeen years; only in the northern equatorial zone was there much light.[34] It is important to realize just how severe population cutbacks could have been during our evolution, since these produced what are often called "genetic bottlenecks," an idea I will take up in the next section.

First, however, there is one more concept to consider about our ancestors' migrations. This has to do with the fact that migrations were by no means unidirectional, radiating out like ripples from a stone cast into a lake. Rather, there was much back and forth contact among bands of peoples along the migratory routes. In all social primates, one or the other sex moves from its birth group to another group and, as for chimpanzees, among humans it is the female who leaves "home" to join up with and reproduce in another band. In fact, when we look at the rates of migration of male genes and female genes historically (and prehistorically), it is the female genes that move fastest. On the whole, male offspring, generation after generation, stay in one spot, only a few venturing into new territories as population or resource pressures grow. But females move back and forth along migration routes, mixing up the genes of the larger population, even over long distances.[35]

Add to this the fact that both die-offs and local climate reversals would have caused whole bands to move backwards as well as forwards along those linear-looking arrows on migration maps and you get a picture of a global population in a giant, albeit sparse, network. Today, we humans are a single species, capable of interbreeding globally. One thing I have not addressed yet is what happened when new waves of migrants came upon peoples already living in an area? Surely the later, "modern" humans would have come across remnant populations of earlier migrating *Homo erectus*, and also of Neanderthals. Did they dispose of them in battle? There is no direct evidence for that, for either case. Did they simply cause their extinction through more successful resource use, not unlike what humans are doing to the great apes in Africa today? Possibly, sometimes. Or did they perhaps also interbreed with them, absorbing some of their genes into what would become today's modern humans? Some scientists (the "unifiers") argue forcefully that this is what did happen, and others, equally vehemently, say there never was genetic mixing because these were truly separate species, incapable of interbreeding (the "splitters").

This point would be mainly academic if it did not imply that the demise of our more ancient predecessors was probably the result of the supposedly innate violence of modern humans. Almost every textbook, despite the absence of any direct evidence, suggests that, if they did not become extinct by themselves, "we must have killed them. Look at how violent we can be." But "can" and "must" are two different things. And if interbreeding were indeed possible, why should it not have happened? The appearance of "extinction" in the fossil record would be much the same.

### What genes can – and cannot – tell us

A few years ago a great breakthrough in human evolutionary history was announced: an original "Adam" and "Eve," just as in the Bible, had been identified as the genetic founders of all modern humans. They had lived in Africa, about 200,000 ya, and were the ancestors of everyone alive today. Of course, the story made a great splash in the popular press, becoming known as the "out-of-Africa" theory for the origin of all modern humans.

This claim was made possible by new techniques developed in recent decades for studying differences in DNA, the genetic material passed from generation to generation. By making assumptions about the amount of time it takes to accumulate random mutations in our genes, scientists used the number of differences in DNA among modern human populations to calculate how long ago we all shared a common ancestor.

The determination of "Eve's" age and location was made on the small pieces of DNA in the mitochondria, those tiny organelles within our cells that we acquire only from our mother's egg. (The sperm's mitochondria supposedly never enter the egg during fertilization, but this is now disputed.) Counting backwards from present variants of this mitochondrial DNA (known as mtDNA) now existing around the world, the researchers claim to have pinpointed a single population in Africa that existed around 143,000 ya.[36]

A few years later, a similar genetic tracking study was done on the Y-chromosome of humans, which defines maleness and is passed only from fathers to their sons. (There are no related genes on the two X-chromosomes that women carry.) This research identified an "Adam," also in Africa (apparently in Ethiopia or Sudan), the putative father of all modern humans, who luckily enough lived at the same time as "Eve" – about 143,000 ya.[37] Presumably "Adam" and "Eve" would have had to be members of the same African population if they were to be the founding couple.

This story, of an apparent single pair (or perhaps very small, homogeneous population) being the original parents of all modern humans, is highly oversimplified, however. We tend to picture one, highly successful, perhaps even aggressive group of Africans that succeeded in pushing their way across continents, replacing whatever predecessors might still be living there. (It is all too reminiscent of the Europeans' aggressive colonizations of "backward" people starting in the sixteenth century. How convenient to find this tendency seemingly coded in our genes.)

But as the well respected population geneticist Luigi Luca Cavalli-Sforza states, this was misleading:

> While calling this woman Eve attracted a good deal of publicity, it was wrong and gave rise to much misinterpretation. Many scientists believed – and perhaps some continue to believe – that genetic data suggest there was only a single woman at that time, whom it was natural to name Eve.
>
> Because these mitochondrial data, like all other genetic data, indicated an African origin for modern humans, it was possible to call her African Eve. But it is clear that many women lived throughout that period. Their mitochondria, however, did not survive. "African Eve" is simply the woman whose mitochondria were the last common ancestors of all surviving mitochondria today.[38]

What Cavalli-Sforza is talking about is the normal loss of some genes from a population by what is called "genetic drift." Simply by chance (not natural selection), such genes are not reproduced in a whole generation. This is very common in small populations. During the Pleistocene, this sort of thing took place regularly owing to the repeated catastrophic population die-offs. These produced what are known as "genetic bottlenecks," when a great many genes simply were lost through chance owing to enormous shrinkage of the population. The chance of one or more variants of a particular gene (whether in mtDNA, on the Y-chromosome, or elsewhere) being completely eliminated is, in fact, quite high if the surviving population is small.

An analogous situation that helps explain how a bottleneck would work is to take a jar with one hundred marbles, of which one-fourth are red, one-fourth blue, one-fourth green, and one-fourth yellow. These are the frequencies of different kinds of mtDNA in the population in the jar – the kinds of females in the population. Now there is a huge die-off, an evolutionary "bottleneck." I randomly withdraw only 10 marbles, the surviving women. Once in awhile, only red marbles will "survive." From then on, these red marbles pass their mtDNA on to their offspring. Even if only five are red, but the other five women have only sons who survive, the result is the same. That one gene becomes the ancestor for all future generations, until new mutations begin to accumulate.

Another well-known population geneticist, Francisco Ayala, made use of computer simulations to determine just how small the global population would have to become if it were to create bottlenecks that would eliminate some of its genes (giving the appearance of a "founder" population) without losing most of the diversity present among all the rest of its genetic sites. He estimated that it would require a decline to 100,000 reproductive females (or a total population of around 400,000, since males, post-reproductive females, and girls that died before reproducing would not be included in the calculation) for a "mitochondrial Eve" to emerge, for a single type of mtDNA to survive. Given that the global population during the Pleistocene never exceeded eight million and probably had more common maxima around four million, this meant a die-off of some 90 percent (less if the global population were smaller at the time of the catastrophe). It is probable that such severe population reductions occurred repeatedly during both the *Homo erectus* and the *Homo sapiens* stages of evolution. Alternative genes at particular sites in the genome could easily have been eliminated on many occasions; there would be nothing special about such an event. (Note that the same gene could be eliminated from a whole bunch of smaller reproducing groups simultaneously just as easily as in a single population of 400,000; the probabilities remain the same.)[39]

Thus, while a single founding couple, or even population, is by no means demonstrated, the evidence is certainly convincing that most of the genes present in modern humans came "out of Africa," though precisely how and when is not clear. One or more waves, over a few hundreds or a few thousands of years, or more, are quite possible. As Cavalli-Sforza points out:

> The origin of a mutant gene that is the last common ancestor of a gene or of a DNA segment and the separation of populations are different events. The second event, the actual division of populations (e.g., the leaving of Africa by parties of modern humans settling in Asia) is later, possibly even much later.[40]

Further, the times when "Adam" and "Eve" lived are statistically uncertain by at least 10,000 years.[41]

What these gene studies cannot tell is exactly where alternative genes were lost, and when subpopulations migrated away from a parent population. Nor can they say how new genes came in to populations. New mutations are of course one answer. But they could also come from earlier populations already inhabiting an area. Here I refer to the theory of "multiregional evolution," an alternative process that some believe was going on both before and after later populations carrying modern genes arrived. In other words, not all modern genes came from the second sweep out of Africa, or were later mutations of the same. Some were introduced *locally* by interbreeding with extant populations of originally more ancient humans.

The main evidence for this theory comes from relatively recent fossils, particularly in east Asia and Australia, that form an unbroken sequence from ancient *Homo erectus* fossils to recent modern humans in their anatomical similarities. The main proponents of this theory, American paleontologist Milford Wolpoff and Australian anthropologist Alan Thorne, argue for a multifocal evolution throughout the Pleistocene of geographically distant but not genetically isolated populations of *Homo erectus*. During all that time, there was but one species, they argue, that spread from Africa to Asia and parts of Europe, that kept in genetic touch by constant back and forth migrations of individuals, presumably mainly females. The obvious anatomical continuities among Wolpoff and Thorne's specimens are hard to dismiss.[42] Indeed, the similarities of some ancient specimens in southeast Asia to the skull structure of early and even modern Australian Aborigines is remarkable.[43]

Most recently, Wolpoff and his colleagues have presented anatomical data linking a modern (15,000 year-old) Aboriginal skull more closely with a 100,000 year-old, late-surviving *Homo erectus* skull from nearby Java than with early modern *Homo sapiens* skulls from the Middle East or Africa. Similarly, they found skulls of early modern humans from the Czech Republic more nearly resembled late Neanderthals than earlier *Homo sapiens* from both the Middle East and Africa. Both these results refute Africa and the Middle East as the *only* source of genes in peripheral populations of modern humans, which the "out-of-Africa" theory demands.[44]

Meantime, mtDNA analyses on the oldest modern human ever, a 60,000 year-old fossil in Australia, show that it had mtDNA more primitive than that of any living modern human. (Its mtDNA contains short pieces of DNA that long ago [long before "Eve"] inserted themselves into one of the regular, nuclear human chromosomes of modern people.) How could this specimen have got to Australia if all modern mtDNA came only from moderns in Africa, who lack this piece? Alan Thorne, one of the investigators in this study, says there had to be genetic breeding with ancient local populations in which this DNA jump never occurred![45] (For the reader who is confused by all this, it simply means that there is no linearity of DNA inheritance among various recent human fossils; all modern genes did *not* all originate from just one ancient population.)

How are all these seemingly conflicting genetic theories to be accommodated in a single, plausible working hypothesis of human evolution? Francisco Ayala, to my mind, sums up our probable history as a species well:

[T]here seems to be no definitive reason to exclude the possibility that different genes may have different populational origins [the multiregional theory]. The average [genetic] distance would then reflect the relative genomic contribution of various ancestral populations. The results would thus be compatible with a model in which a modern African replacement was concomitant with some regional continuity.[46]

Ayala goes on to make it clear that a total replacement of *Homo erectus* by a new population from Africa was not necessary to produce globally interbreeding, cross-fertile populations of modern human beings. Both theories are possible simultaneously.

What useful insights are to be had from this lengthy survey of what genes and fossils tell us about our past history (aside from the usual fact that scientists cannot all agree)? There are several. (1) During most of the Pleistocene, the human population was globally sparse, growing during climatically stable times, and shrinking, even crashing precipitously, during periods of catastrophic climate change. This surely was critical in the shaping of the human brain and the development of human culture. (2) Rates of migration could frequently be rapid, two or more kilometers a year, which is twice as fast as the first agriculturalists would migrate many years later across Europe. (If this sounds slow, imagine your entire community picking up and moving 35 to 40 miles away at every generation, generation after generation.) Such rapid migration suggests that cultural evolution was directed less toward the accumulation of tools and other capital goods that are hard to carry from place to place, and more toward the creative skills needed to replace these things from a different set of resources in a location. Powers of natural observation must have been honed to a peak as new habitats were explored and adapted to. (3) Migrations were not always "outward," radiating away from Africa and across the continents. Rather, they were back and forth, with people moving long distances in both directions along established migratory routes. Not only would genes be mixed by this process; so, too, would accumulated knowledge.

But what can these insights suggest to us about how human nature was being honed, about the probable ways our behavioral propensities as social beings were being shaped? What possible imprints did the Pleistocene leave on human nature?

## Possible imprints of the Pleistocene

I move now, of course, to the realm of speculation. The picture to be drawn here is surely tentative, an imaginative filling in of large gaps between a sparse handful of difficult-to-interpret facts. What is not in doubt is that the Pleistocene itself was a period of repeated uncertainty, with sudden, dramatic changes in environment that are hard for us moderns, with over 10,000 years of relatively stable and propitious weather in our cultural memories, to conceptualize. (It is hard enough for us in the West to imagine a time without electricity, or automobiles, or even toilet paper!) People were forced to migrate or adapt. Many failed to do so. Populations fluctuated hugely between stable periods and stressed periods. Whole bands died out; group selection was in force. The one thing that was definitely *not* being selected for among our ancestors was specialization for a particular niche, for one sort of habitat. Utilize all possible foods, shelters, habitats, skills, social inventions. The paleontologist Richard Potts has called this "variability selection":

> Variability selection requires a long sequence of large-scale habitat oscillations such that individuals of a lineage living at different times experience different adaptive conditions. Over a span of recurrent extremes, some gene combinations and complex behaviors may be favored that enable resilient and novel responses to new conditions.[47]

The ancient hominid habit of living in socially bonded yet readily fissioning and fusing groups was perhaps the initial critical trait for our ancestors' survival. Small groups would grow in size during stable periods, fissioning to relieve pressure on local resources, occasionally fusing across greater distances to exchange mates (and thus genes) and, significantly, to exchange newly learned skills such as the crafting and use of tools or preparations of new foods. Among the earliest tools that we have evidence of are chipped stones which, as Potts says, were simply "extensions of their digestive tracts,"[48] used to split open bones, coconuts and other hard seeds, to cut off strips of scavenged meat, and to grind tough seeds and leaves to make them digestible. Even simple stones can open up a much wider survival niche.

Given the extent to which our ancestors spread across three gigantic continents, populations must always have been spread relatively thinly, and the potential for extinction of both local bands, and even the entire species, was repeatedly present. Competition for resources was unlikely, given the extraordinary mobility, but competence in utilizing them was probably critical. That some of those ancestors did survive each crisis is likely due to selection for two classes of traits. One was the strong tendency to care for each other *and* each other's offspring, thus maintaining reproductive capacity, so that surviving populations could bounce back after periods of decimation (the "bottlenecks"). *Group selection* was thus key to our ancestors' continuing survival. The other was *selection for intelligence*, the broad capacity to innovate, problem-solve, and communicate information. (It has almost nothing to do, however, with scoring high on modern I.Q. tests.)

### Selection for bonded groups

The propensity for living in groups, already strongly present in primates, became even more compelling for humans during the Pleistocene. Groups were selected for their ability to survive as reproductive units during highly stressful environmental periods. As noted in Chapter II, the relatively bigger brains of primates required birth of ever-more premature infants, with increasingly longer periods of dependence on parental care – up to five years or more for apes and hominids. Not only were these increasingly helpless infants more likely to succumb to disease, accidental exposure, or predation. Their mothers could produce only a limited number of offspring during their reproductive years. Moreover, the birth process itself became increasingly risky. Modern mothers (and presumably their Pleistocene ancestors) are at the edge of the size of the head that can traverse the birth canal. The human infant must rotate along the way, and unlike other primate babies, it emerges facing away from the mother. As anthropologist Wenda Trevathan says, "Human birth is so painful and risky that mothers need help from others to deliver a baby successfully."[49]

During the Pleistocene, failure to reproduce enough surviving offspring to replace itself may have been a major cause of group extinction. Thus any propensity that strengthened group ties, especially in support of females with infants, would increase survival chances of the whole. Babies became highly attractive to all group members, not just mothers; they were given attention and protected by all, and food was shared with their mothers and later with them. Assistance at birth was one more instance of this empathic instinct at work.

The successful protection of helpless infants would also require a high degree of harmony among group members. This suggests a suppression of competition and of extreme hierarchical behaviors as well. In those social animals prone to forming aggressive dominance hierarchies, the reproductive capacity of dominant members is actually *reduced*; they have a shorter life-expectancy, and females have higher rates of miscarriage.[50] Hierarchical stress also tends to reduce the capacity for learning and memory, which also would have jeopardized survival during the Pleistocene.[51] (The effect of stress on brain structure and behavior, and the short-term selective advantages of the brain's responses, are both discussed further in Chapter VI.)

Prosocial behaviors that promoted group survival would thus have been strongly selected for. As noted in Chapter II, among primates there seems to be a universal tendency to reconcile after a fight, and surely this behavior would have been reinforced among our surviving ancestors. Another important trait that evolved at some point among those ancestors was for continuous sexual receptivity of females, and their loss of external signals of ovulation – such as the obviously swollen vulvas of female chimpanzees and baboons. This surely had the adaptive effect of keeping males in the vicinity of the females and their offspring, further ensuring the safety of the young and facilitating the sharing of food. Whether such non-reproductive sexuality also promoted group harmony by reducing societal tensions, as is the case among bonobos (or at least those in captivity), is not clear. The role played by the emergence of human cultural systems in regulating sexual behavior obscures other possible adaptive purposes of our "excessive" sexuality. (This is discussed in depth in Chapter VII.)

Finally, given the highly disperse nature of small bands of hominids during much of the Pleistocene, it is unlikely that intergroup competition played a major role in shaping human nature. Perhaps, when local populations grew overly large during a stretch of clement climate, there was competition for resources. But the old migratory pathways must still have been familiar through occasional large gatherings and exchanges of women among bands over large distances. Under such conditions, or particularly when the climate changed, stressed groups made the normal primate response – they split. Migration was a common event. Likewise, when groups became dangerously small through inability to reproduce and support their offspring, they would fuse with neighbors if possible, migrating with them in search of new resources. Optimum group size was a compromise between local resource availability and the need to have a large enough group to successfully replace itself over time.

For these reasons I agree with Margaret Power, who claims it is constraints on the ability to fission and fuse, to freely migrate, that causes intergroup violence among primates.[52] Those bands of Pleistocene hominids who undertook violence toward other bands would surely have endangered their own precarious survival. Perhaps, during the stress of sudden climate change and large populations, such violence did occur, hastening the population decline that was coming anyway. But such violence was of dubious benefit in terms of adaptation, in my opinion. In good times, the energy of the group would go toward rebuilding population density, and in stressful times, energy would be directed toward migrating in search of more abundant resources. Under *either* condition, to allow population stress to develop into violence would not, I believe, have secured future survival of that particular group, but more likely sealed its extinction. Any genetic propensity for warlikeness would have been selected against.

This argument, I further believe, militates equally well against the likelihood of *Homo sapiens* populations having competed directly in a warlike way with local *Homo erectus* bands in a Pleistocene "takeover," and supports the multifocal, continuum theory of Wolpoff and Thorne as at least a part of the human evolutionary story. It would not, however, preclude the destruction of some *H. erectus* or early *H. sapiens* populations through diseases introduced by later waves of migrating bands, similar to what happened to Native Americans when Europeans first came to the New World.[53]

I thus envision throughout the Pleistocene multiple small, nomadic bands, striving not to become extinct. In environmentally difficult times, their reproductive rates would drop perilously low. Each female would produce only four or five offspring, of whom only two or three were likely to reach maturity. Local populations comprising several small bands were in constant danger of dying out. In more favorable times, when food was truly plentiful and populations could be semi-sedentary (when they lived, perhaps, in rich estuarine or riparian habitats with plentiful fish and small game), the reproductive capacity of females would nearly double, with as many as seven or eight pregnancies per female, shorter lactation times, and average survival of four or five offspring to adulthood.[54] This flexibility of human reproductive capacity must have been critical for our species' ability to bounce back from near extinction many times during the Pleistocene.

### Selection for multiple intelligences

The chance of surviving the vagaries of the Pleistocene was greatly enhanced by randomly occurring and quickly selected increments in the brain's capacities to innovate, solve problems, and communicate information. Though often lumped together under the general term "intelligence," they in fact comprise a broad range of independent abilities, including learning, remembering, spatial, temporal, and symbolic conceptualizations, and much more. (Recently, psychologist Jerome Kagan specifically warned against lumping all cognitive talents under the control of a single gene for "intelligence." Intellectual abilities are not "a unitary characteristic."[55]) These multiple intelligences were no doubt heavily selected for, because they not only raised the chances of individual survival, they also enhanced the critically important survival of groups.

It cannot be emphasized too strongly that a large brain *co-evolved* with an increasingly interdependent social life. The environment to which each individual had to adapt in an absolute, uncompromising way was, in fact, one's social group; it was the focal point. It was the group, *as a whole*, that adapted to the commonly shared surroundings – the natural habitat. It was human *groups* that adapted to changing environments, and they did this not via genetic selection of specialized anatomical traits but by the acquisition, sharing, and transmission of accumulated and coordinated *group* knowledge and skills. This was the cradle of cultural evolution, though signs of cultural learning were apparently already present among other primates.[56]

The emergence of culture as *the* critical survival adaptation among our Pleistocene ancestors required considerable modifications in brain structure and function. These obviously included the well-advertised advances in cognitive skills, loosely called "intelligence." But even more important was the development of what can only be called a "social mind" – the ability to see the world sufficiently similarly so as to be able to think and act *as a group* in highly coordinated ways. This ability has two underlying psychological components: the well-recognized capacity to communicate complex information, and the less acknowledged but equally important propensities to belong to a group and to share meaningful understandings about the world and the nature of group life in that world. These latter two very broad propensities, I believe, became critical to Pleistocene survival, and are biologically grounded in the powerful physical connections in the human brain between the emotional centers of the limbic system and the various cognitive centers in the expanding human cortex. It was this evolving of the whole brain that permitted our successful cultural evolution during the Pleistocene, and that needs to be understood today if we are to deal more wisely with the psychic equipment we have inherited.

We can conclude with a statement about this central role of group selection in the evolution of *Homo sapiens*, made by David Sloan Wilson and Elliott Sober at the end of their excellent book on the subject:

> According to biologists, group-level adaptations can evolve only by a process of natural selection at the group level ... [The] social structures [created by humans] and the cognitive abilities that produce them allow group selection to be important even among large groups of unrelated individuals.[57]

Once selection began to focus more on adaptive *cultural groups* than on *individuals*, the evolutionary advantages of unrelated individuals, from many different subpopulations, intermigrating and interbreeding with each other, could spread among the entire species, giving rise to functional communities of genetically highly diverse individuals able to live in large cohesive groups. (This is discussed in Chapter VIII, which reveals the last 10,000 years of human history to be a history of meaning systems first, and genes second, not the other way around. For humans *meaning* matters more than *genes*.)

As the opening quote from Mary Midgley suggests, like most of the adaptive traits of organisms, the human brain that evolved during the Pleistocene was (and is) something of a compromise. It was very good at getting us through that harrowing period, but in some ways it is an imperfect organ, with built-in problems that are more evident perhaps in recent times than they were then. The stresses we face today are different, but our emotional wiring remains the same. Just as the albatross's huge wings are beautifully designed for flying great distances over oceans, but are a great nuisance when the birds have to waddle about on land when nesting, so human brains are terrific for adapting to new demands by means of the fission and fusion of small, wandering groups able to move as they will, creating new solutions as they go, changing their shared social beliefs and traditions slowly over several generations. Those same brains are not nearly so good at the kinds of constraints our species has faced increasingly for several thousand years – and especially the rapidity of change it is facing today, driven not by the climate (yet!) but by human-made stresses we are placing on ourselves.

The next three chapters examine this brain we inherited from our Pleistocene forbears: its structure, how it creates cultural meaning, and finally, how its functions are altered by severe stress. In particular, I focus upon the role that cultural meaning systems play in our lives, and the powerful emotions brought into play when they are threatened or are unable to satisfy our other psychological propensities for bonding and autonomy.

# IV

# BRAIN MATTERS

The neurological evidence ... suggests that selective absence of emotion is a problem. Well-targeted and well-deployed emotion seems to be a support system without which the edifice of reason cannot operate properly. These results and their interpretation called into question the idea of dismissing emotion as a luxury or a nuisance or a mere evolutionary vestige. They also made it possible to view emotion as an embodiment of the logic of survival.

Antonio Damasio (1999: 42)

Any book on human nature must inquire into that amazing organ, the human brain, and the behaviors it orchestrates. The difficulty is, as with all seriously studied aspects of "us," the academic disciplines have each constructed their own narrow view of what brains are all about. (That, after all, is what disciplines do; they break the world down into small pieces.) So we have psychology, with its emphasis on cognition and reason, and on "controlling" our emotions. The United States alone must have tens of thousands of classes in anger management for its disruptive citizens, yet no one asks "Why? Why are so many in need of these special classes?" Emotions, or at least some emotions, are seen as problems, not part of mature being.

Then there are the ethologists or social psychologists (depending on whether they are watching groups of monkeys and apes or groups of humans). In recent years, those watching other primates (which were long believed to be lacking self-awareness) have reported evidence of sophisticated knowledge of complex social relationships as well as prolonged memories of past encounters with others.[1] Both are indicative of a certain level of self-awareness and autobiographical perception. Also frequently reported among our primate relatives are clear abilities to creatively solve problems. Such skills suggest sophisticated levels of abstract thinking that for long were believed to be restricted to humans.[2]

Next there are the ideas about human nature proposed by neuroscientists. Until very recently, those studying brain anatomy and physiology, the connections and functions of its various parts, gave great emphasis to human cognitive

126

capacities. How were internal images of the external world processed and stored? As this chapter will show, great strides have been made in this field. Yet, aside from neuropharmacology to control or ameliorate mental illnesses, less attention has been paid to the role of emotions and feelings from the neuro-anatomical point of view, let alone from the evolutionary point of view. In his book *The Mind's Past*, well-respected cognitive neuroscientist Michael Gazzaniga devotes only three pages of an entire book to emotions, and these deal only with subliminal emotional influences in situations of risk-taking. While interesting, they are still only a tiny part of the role emotions play in daily behaviors. As pointed out by neuroscientist Antonio Damasio, emotions and the feelings they give rise to are essential for effective thought and decision-making. Understanding them is critical to a thorough appreciation of human nature.[3]

The behavioral scientists, in an attempt to imitate the physical sciences, have focussed their studies on those aspects of the brain–behavior story that are amenable to reductionist analysis. Most tend to ignore or gloss over the less tidy problems, such as the role of emotions in evolution, and the multiple levels of consciousness and self-awareness: those "inner sensations" which organisms experience but which are essentially invisible to an outside observer. (Lie detectors are but one, not very successful, attempt to surmount this enormous barrier to a more comprehensive understanding of human behavior.) The ecological psychologist Harry Heft has stated the problem very well when it comes to identifying what behavioral scientists believe their subject is about.

> [I]n psychology, it is [the] very core presuppositions that are usually being contested. We continue to struggle among ourselves as to the best way to think about the subject matter of psychology.
>
> With a few exceptions, the field of psychology has attempted to develop a science of animate beings on the back of concepts borrowed from the sciences of the inanimate. For this reason, when we step back and view it from a distance, the picture of psychological functioning that emerges from our science often violates our sense of everyday life. Moreover, it engenders unresolvable conceptual conflict in our theories.[4]

This dilemma is one more example of the tendency of modern science to fragment the world in order to understand how it works. When it comes to human nature, however, such fragmentation is particularly dangerous, especially when the omissions lead to skewed descriptions of the human mind that, when held as true by a whole society, can lead to disastrous social institutions. Once again, there is a need to move away from the reductionist Billiard Ball Gestalt toward a more integrated, Indra's Net image of who we are.

In this and the two following chapters, I shall try to show that the brain evolved as a connected whole; that brain and body are a connected whole; and finally, that brain, body, and environment are a connected whole – and this latter connectedness creates the interactive information system we call "the mind." To do this, I shall, perforce, have to draw on anecdote and personal knowledge to infer those parts of the story that are part of the "inner experience" of each individual and thus are difficult to be scientific about, in the narrow sense of the word. Yet that should not stop us. After all, one cannot be "scientific" about music, nor about art or sacred myths, but that does not mean one ignores them when trying to understanding human nature.

Brains evolve to handle information about both the inner state of the body and the state of the outer world in which an animal lives. First, they must recognize information that is important for survival; this they then interpret and weigh; and finally they decide how to respond. How did the Pleistocene shape the human brain? What kind of "tool" did natural selection bequeath to us? Some imagine the brain as a sort of combination camera and tape-recorder, storing experiences that are then "remembered" and used to decide on present actions. The experienced world seems to be a true representation of "reality out there." Brains, however, are far more interesting and versatile than slavelike machines. Evolution has produced a specialized organ that selects what information we take in, then alters some of it, emphasizes some, discards some, forgets some, and even invents some. It is not nearly as rational and straightforward as is often presumed.

These rather surprising facts are known thanks to the enormous efforts of cognitive neuroscientists over the past few decades, and they do help us understand some aspects of human nature. But as just noted, cognitive functions are by no means all that our brains are engaged in. There is increasing evidence from medicine and developmental biology for the profound role of emotions not only in human health, but in the very development of the brain itself. Furthermore, brains function as emotional signalers, guiding our actions in ways that, at least most of the time, are adaptive. It will become clear that the brain, though constructed of many specialized regions, functions as a whole, with rational and emotional aspects inseparably woven together. Nor is the brain isolated from the rest of the body; people function as whole beings, not as puppets run by a computer in their heads.

I begin with a brief overview of the trends in brain evolution that led to our present condition, the functions that have evolved over time. I turn then to the anatomy of the brain itself, its various regions, and compare the two ways in which its present structure has been interpreted from an evolutionary point of view. In particular, I contrast the conventional description of how intelligence and emotions are related with an alternative one that emphasizes the adaptive significance of their interrelationship. Next I consider how the brain actually processes information, how it works, followed by a consideration of consciousness, memory, thoughts, feelings, and actions – how the brain attempts to meet our inner survival needs in relation to the external world. By the end of the chapter I hope to have convinced the reader that the great advantage of the hominid brain has been the increasing opportunity for flexibility in behavior. This, in turn, has enabled humans not only to adapt to many environments through creative inventions culturally passed along to offspring (chimpanzees already are rather good at that); it also has enabled highly complex group-coordinated activities that require multiple knowledges of different individuals to function together to achieve a common purpose. The process of group selection reached its greatest level of development with the appearance of modern humankind.

## Evolving propensities of the hominid brain

What were the mental qualities that evolved in the course of our species' evolution that make us human? Our amazing mental capacities and the powerful technologies they have spawned invite delusions of superiority and uniqueness. Animals, despite their similar brains, surely cannot be consciously aware, experience feelings or meaning, let alone communicate them. Yet if we are careful observers, we see that some animals do all these things. In his columns on animals, published in the *Guardian Weekly*, Ralph Whitlock regularly reported such stories. These included accounts of birds, such as swans and Australian galahs, grieving for lost mates; neighborhood cats howling over the backyard grave of a dead companion; and various animals, from pet cats to wild grizzly bears, traversing more than 200 miles of strange terrain to return to a former homesite.[5] He also recounts the story of an unknown dog helping out a family pet that was lost. And one of my most trusted friends told me a similar story he heard from a pet owner. For two days in a row his dog's dish was missing from the porch; next day he watched to see what happened. His dog picked up the plastic plate in his jaws and trotted to the edge of the woods where another dog was caught in a wild animal trap, thus sharing his meal.[6]

Let me also add a brief personal story. One bitterly cold but sunny day, while walking around the Houses of Parliament in Ottawa, my friends' dog, Pepper, was suffering greatly. Salt water from puddles the sun had formed on the gravel path was instantly freezing into painful balls of ice between her pads. Every few seconds she whimpered, lifting one paw after another, to have the balls removed. When her owner, in an ordinary voice, said to the rest of us, "Let's head for the car," Pepper leaped three times straight up in the air to shoulder height! Evidently some kinds of animals do have conscious awareness, they do have empathy, and they do communicate.[7] The point is that the hominid brain shares many capacities potentially present in the brains of at least some other mammals. It was the exaggerated expansion of certain aspects of that generalized brain that led to the particular cluster of qualities that gave rise to the human brain and the distinct attributes we call "human."

No one needs to be reminded of the remarkable increase in the size of the cerebral cortex, the locus of cognitive intelligence that makes complex thought and problem-solving possible. Without it, *Homo erectus* could not have spread so widely into such varied habitats. Yet as noted earlier, that smartness came at a price – premature helpless infants that required even stronger group bonding and cooperation to ensure their survival. And those infants also required plenty of scope for freedom to experiment, to learn, to try to do things – they needed ever more autonomy. Anyone who has ever parented a child through the "terrible twos" is only too aware of what autonomy means! Self-initiated action is a hallmark of human nature that surely is essential for full development of both the mental capacities and motor skills of a brain that is born only half-formed.

These simultaneously increasing propensities to bond on the one hand and have autonomy on the other became part of genetically ingrained "drives" embedded in the motivational centers of the evolving brain, as are our "drives" for water, food, shelter, and mating. Obviously the pair of them exacerbated the opportunities for inner psychic tensions as well as social stress when bonds came into conflict with independent behaviors. Fortunately, the evolution of an enlarging intelligence enabled the emergence of better means for communicating both our thoughts and feelings, in particular the use of the audible symbols we call language.

Spoken language had two great benefits. First, it made clarification of emotional states easier, thus facilitating processes of conflict resolution and reconciliation – tendencies already well ingrained among other primates. In addition to touching, grooming, kissing, and hugging, one could also express contrition: "I'm sorry. Please forgive me." Second, language allowed the construction of a shared view of the world – a "social mind" – that greatly increased the ability of a group to act together and thus do things that individuals alone could not do. Organized scavenging, organized building of shared nests or shelters, organized net-hunting, and organized big game hunting. This shared social mind also allowed groups to accumulate and pass along new information.

An emergent human need, arising (perhaps around the same time as our earliest language) out of the increasing mental and emotional capacities of the growing brain, was a need for meaning. *How* do things happen and *why* do they happen – including the miraculous aspects of birth and death? This emerging holistic, consciously shared aspect of human existence became absolutely vital to the survival of the group, and hence of the individual. There developed within our ancestors a third ingrained propensity – a need for shared sacred meaning to give conscious purpose to the life of the group and identity to the individual. Like bonding and autonomy, it became essential for a group to function as a coordinated whole. All three propensities have become the guiding frame for modern human action. They are embedded in our brains and propel us to belong and be accepted, to seek freedom and independence, and to generate and live by sacred stories. And when any of these propensities is hindered or threatened, our brains automatically resist, and we tend to behave in ways that correct the situation. It is this automatic resistance to the frustration of one or more of these three internal propensities that gives rise to what is most problematic in human nature.

But again, I am leaping ahead of my story. First comes a look at the brain and its functions. Language and meaning will be considered in Chapter V; here I consider the brain itself, beginning with its anatomy.

## Anatomy of the evolved brain

The human nervous system consists of the sense organs – eyes, ears, nose, tastebuds, and diffuse pressure and temperature detectors in the skin; the central brain and spinal cord, the processors of sensations and initiators of actions; and the motor nerves from the central system that excite muscles to contract. In addition, there are nerves running in both directions connecting the brain with our viscera: heart, lungs, digestive tract and its associated glands, and our kidneys and reproductive organs, as well as receptors in our muscles that send signals about positions and states of tension. The brain also communicates with the rest of the body via its blood supply, receiving both nutrients and chemical signals, and also releasing its own wastes as well as chemical signals into the circulation. Indeed, the brain plays a critical role in almost all our body's activities; in addition to its obvious control of our behavior, it also affects our endocrine states and our immune responses, along with aspects of digestion. With, or more often without, our conscious knowledge, the brain keeps all our survival functions in hand, constantly monitoring and modulating them. Its overall task is not just to observe and respond to the external world, but to coordinate those responses with the immediate survival needs of the internal system.[8]

Figure IV.1 gives a midline view of the modern human brain showing its main regions. Its physical architecture and chemical functioning are presumably the source of all our thoughts, feelings and actions. The regions shown are also present, though in very different proportions, in all vertebrates, and generally speaking they serve similar functions.

The part of the brain connected directly to the spinal cord is known as the brainstem and comprises both upward, incoming and downward, outgoing neural pathways. All incoming nerves except the olfactory (smell) and optic (vision) pass through the brainstem on their way to the upper reaches of the brain. Its subparts are known as the medulla, pons, midbrain, and tectum. The main neural pathways end or begin in the thalamus.

The medulla, at the base of the brain, contains the centers that control vital functions such as heart rate and breathing. Incoming nerve fibers continue upward, via the pons and midbrain, where some of them pass through an area known as the reticular formation, that subconsciously monitors them, passing through only those of "importance" to the higher, conscious areas of the brain. This region also plays a role in awake/sleep cycles. During the dreaming stages of sleep, virtually no incoming sensory signals are allowed through. The reticular

131

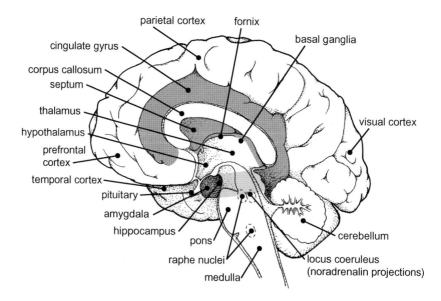

*Figure IV.1* The human brain

This mid-sagittal section, which cuts the brain into right and left halves, shows the brain-stem, surrounded by the cortex. The five major regions are as follows:

CEREBRAL HEMISPHERES (paired): the *corpus callosum* consists of fibers connecting right and left sides. The *pallium* (or neocortex or isocortex) has four areas: *visual, parietal, temporal,* and *frontal + prefrontal* parts.

The *subpallium* (or archecortex) has six areas: *cingulate gyrus, basal ganglia, fornix, septum, hippocampus,* and *amygdala.*

DIENCEPHELON (upper end of brainstem), which has two areas: the *thalamus,* a relay center, sending signals up and down between the extremities and the cortex; and the *hypothalamus* which monitors emotions and controls the *pituitary gland,* the hormonal control center.

MIDBRAIN (continuation of the brainstem), whose main areas are the *cerebellum,* a backward-bulging swelling that coordinates muscle movements, and the *pons* (or "bridge") that carries direct and indirect fibers upwards and downwards. Indirect fibers pass through a special area (the Reticular Activating System) that controls sleep–awake cycles and our states of "calm" vs. "arousal." Its *locus coeruleus* stimulates arousal by releasing adrenalin into the thalamus; the *raphe nuclei* calm the brain by releasing serotonin into the thalamus.

MEDULLA (or hindbrain) connects the brainstem with the spinal cord and regulates heart-rate, breathing and other basic tasks.

The areas of the brain in *italics* are connected by reverberating circuits, and constitute the *limbic system* that links emotions with conscious actions. (See Figure IV.3 for more details.)

*Source*: Drawn from many sources; art by Michele Lukowski

132

formation also assists in blocking pain sensations during emergencies. And when conscious awareness is needed, it "arouses" the cortex as well.

To the rear of the pons bulges the cerebellum, the locus of motor coordination and possibly some sensory and cognitive functions as well.[9] Just above the base of the cerebellum lies the tectum, which plays a role in consciousness. Meanwhile, the fibers running upward through the brainstem, just beneath the cerebellum and tectum, enter the thalamus, where they terminate. The thalamus is the brain's major relay center, its Grand Central Station or major airport hub. It sends, by way of neuronal connections known as synapses, incoming signals into both cerebral hemispheres; some end in their inner areas, others extend into parts of the cortex. The thalamus also receives outgoing signals from these areas, commands going out to the body's muscles and glands. As will be shown, it is extremely important in multiple ways and plays a large part in consciousness.

Under the thalamus, on the floor of the brain, lies the all-important hypothalamus, which signals the state of physiological "needs," such as our appetites for food, water, and sex. It is also closely associated with the pituitary gland, the master endocrine organ of the body, to which it sends chemical signals, creating a major interface between brain activity and body chemistry. Moreover, hormones from other glands in the body bind at selected sites in the hypothalamus where they promote such behaviors as sexual libido and maternal care.

Above and all around the thalamus and hypothalamus lies the huge forebrain, which comprises paired swellings, the right and left cerebral hemispheres. These are connected with each other by a thick layer of nerve fibers, the corpus callosum. When partially cut (as is done in severe cases of epilepsy to stop the spread of seizures throughout the brain), both hemispheres still function, but they no longer can signal each other. The many studies carried out on such "split-brain" patients reveal the specialization of the two hemispheres, often known as the "left brain" and the "right brain." The roof, or pallium, of each hemisphere is highly convoluted, and various regions carry out a variety of tasks, as described below.

The floor, or subpallium, of each hemisphere is not convoluted, and comprises a cluster of swellings. Among these are the paired basal ganglia that fine-tune our conscious motor control (and fail to function normally in Parkinson's disease). Nearby is a looped complex, the limbic system, which encircles the thalamus and hypothalamus and has multiple connections with both. Various parts of the limbic system have to do with emotional states, and together with the hypothalamus, are often called "the seat of the emotions." When selected regions are stimulated in experimental animals, they exhibit various affective states interpreted as aggression, fear, or pleasure.

Other areas of the limbic system are involved in memory recall (hippocampus), in pleasurable sensations, including sexual (septal area), and in unpleasant or "nasty" feelings (the amygdala). Once signals enter the limbic system, they appear to reverberate around for a considerable time, perhaps coordinating the whole mixture of emotional stimuli into an appropriate affect state. As is shown later, there are important connections between the cerebral cortex and the limbic system, suggesting a reciprocal role. (In Chapter VI, evidence is presented for how that relationship can be significantly altered during periods of profound stress.)

How are we to understand the workings of this brain we have? Is it some monstrosity inherited from our animal past, overlaid but not completely controlled by the "intellectual" cortex? Or is it in fact a pretty well integrated organ that can, when presented with the right social environment, deal successfully with the primate paradox of striving toward two opposites: bonding and autonomy?

### The "layer theory" of brain functions

Ernest Haeckel, a famous nineteenth-century German zoologist, after observing the evolutionary sequence among fossil vertebrates from fishes to mammals, claimed that developing human embryos progressed through all the evolutionary stages of their ancestors while in the womb: early gill slits were reminiscent of fishes; the early vertebral column appeared to have a tail; and so forth. This notion, that "ontogeny recapitulates phylogeny" – or development repeats the steps of a linear evolutionary sequence – has now been discredited scientifically, but it has left its mark on popular ideas about human origins, especially about the brain.

Many of Freud's theories about the presumed psychosexual basis of all human behavior can be traced to his belief in Haeckel's idea: modern people relived, during infancy and childhood, various sexual fears supposedly rampant among adults in some evolutionary past.[10] More recently Carl Sagan, popularizer of modern astronomy, wrote a widely read book called *The Dragons of Eden*, wherein he imaginatively invents a story of how human brains evolved from those of our lizardlike ancestors. (Mammals, as a class, developed from a group of reptiles when dinosaurs were still flourishing – hence the title.) It was not pure fantasy, however, being based on a comparative study of the cerebral hemispheres of vertebrate brains by the neuro-anatomist, Paul MacLean. According to MacLean, the cerebral hemispheres of humans comprise three evolutionary "layers": (1) an ancient reptilian layer, the equivalent of our basal ganglia, dedicated to what he called animal-like behaviors such as aggression and stereotypical patterns of courtship and mating; (2) a primitive mammalian layer, comprising mainly the functions of today's limbic system; and (3) an advanced layer congruent with the deeply folded outer cortex of the primate brain. For MacLean, very little modification of layers (1) or (2) occurred during the development of our enormous cerebral hemispheres. Rather, he believed modern humans carry around, in the subconscious parts of their brains, unmodified reptilian behaviors and equally

134

unmodified early mammalian behaviors, over which ancient layers a veneer of self-conscious human behavior has been added in the form of a huge "neocortex." These three layers, he claimed, functioned virtually independently, and one should therefore expect residual reptilian and early mammalian behaviors to turn up little changed in the human repertoire, especially after damage to parts of the cortex.[11]

MacLean's ideas, promoted by Sagan, fit well into popular assumptions about the inferior, "animal nature" of our emotions and the superior, uniquely human qualities of cognition and reason believed to reside in the giant outer cortex. They also supported prevalent beliefs in supposed gender differences in intelligence and emotions. As Stephen Jay Gould reminds us, millions of human lives have been influenced by scientific theories promoting such ideas of evolutionary recapitulation in modern species.[12]

### Doubts about layered brains

By 1990, when the second edition of MacLean's book on his theory appeared, it was no longer possible to entertain its scientific claims; there was just too much evidence disproving his assumptions. The basal ganglia were much more ancient than reptiles, and the limbic system was present long before the earliest mammals. And interpreting the uncontrolled movements during an epileptic seizure as a display of reptilian emotions was never very good evidence for his theory. MacLean's model, however, suited those who wanted to blame human problems on our animal ancestors: competitive selfishness was reptilian, and emotions, even good ones, were typical of "lower" mammals. Only rationality was truly human. Furthermore, his image implied that brains became linearly larger and more complex during the evolution of all the vertebrates, from fish to humans, which fitted beautifully with the anthropocentric viewpoint of evolution: we are at the top of a very tall evolutionary ladder!

I address this last assumption first. MacLean was not the only one to assume, from study of the gross anatomy of vertebrate brains, that the forebrain had undergone progressive evolutionary changes, grounded in *scala naturae* assumptions "which held that vertebrates form one linear series and reflect increasing complexity." The earliest are the "lowest" and we, the most recent, are the "highest."

The recent work of Glenn Northcutt, a comparative neurobiologist from whom the above brief quote is taken, has invalidated this simple idea of a single evolutionary progression in the vertebrate forebrain. In fact, at each major branch-point in vertebrate evolution, both branches have continued to evolve. There has been an evolutionary sequence of sharks, another of bony fishes, and a third of reptiles, birds and mammals – each a product of long, but separate evolutionary radiations. Among each group there are some living species with quite small, supposedly primitive forebrains and others with very advanced forebrains that resemble the complexity of those of primates. Of course, larger animals tend to have larger brains than do smaller animals. But in some cases, the scaling is disproportionate. The great white sharks have very large cerebral cortices, shaped similarly to our own. Likewise for the largest bony fish such as tuna, except that their cerebral cortices curve outward (like iris petals) rather than inwards (like suncups). But in both instances, the patterns of nerve pathways are parallel to ours. Though the brains are obviously adapted to perform different behaviors, their homologous regions appear to serve similar general functions in all three evolutionary series. The same basic vertebrate brain plan is common to all vertebrates. Nothing uniquely new has been added.[13]

Northcutt has also pointed out that within a single group, such as frogs or birds, animals of the same body size may have forebrains (cerebral hemispheres) four or five times greater than others. Among birds, turkeys and pigeons have tiny forebrains relative to parrots and crows (birds of respectively similar body sizes). Turkeys, like chickens, have remarkably simple abilities whereas parrots are well known for their verbal and thought skills. Similarly, crows can use tools and count, but pigeons have been the species most studied by comparative psychologists, badly biasing our views on the intellectual possibilities of birds in general! Likewise with mammals, the brain of the squirrel monkey is twice the size of that of the galago (a lemur) and seven times that of a more distant relative, the hedgehog, though all have a similar body size.[14]

"Braininess" has evolved several times. What selective factors drove cortical enlargements in the brains of sharks, bony fishes, reptiles and birds, as well as in mammals, is not clear, and we can only guess at what kinds of intelligences many of these animals possess. Yet the basic brain plan is evolutionarily homologous in all vertebrate groups. In fact, it is already seen in simple form in the living pre-vertebrate "ancestor" the lancelet *Amphioxus*. The same genes are being expressed in the swollen front end, or "brain," of its developing embryos as are acting during the embryogenesis of vertebrate brains.[15] There have thus been several independent evolutions of very large, highly complex forebrains, parts of which, in all instances, are homologous with the misnamed "neocortex" of mammals. The mammalian cortex is not "new" at all. It is just different in its details. I conclude this section with several quotes from Northcutt, who emphasizes three main points:

> [V]ertebrate phylogeny cannot be viewed as a linear scale, characterized by increasing anatomical or functional complexity... [O]ne cannot speak of "lower" and "higher" vertebrates... [T]here are no living primitive animals. Rather, all living animals are characterized by both primitive and derived features.

> Major changes in almost any brain character ... have not occurred in a linear manner... For this reason, the designation of any brain character as paleo-, archi-, or neo- has no validity.

Nor do recent data on relative brain size support the idea that brains become larger and that the most complex functions in these brains occur more rostrally [toward the front of the brain] ... Instead, these data indicate that relative brain size has increased in every vertebrate radiation, and when such an increase has occurred, most parts of the brain, not just the most rostral part, appear to have increased in size

and he concludes:

[I]t appears that vertebrate brains, once they arose, retained a basic pattern of organization.[16]

Not only has the vertebrate forebrain been enlarged and differentiated in a variety of ways; so too have the connections between the thalamus and the fore-brain which seem to vary among groups, suggesting another point where evolutionary variation, acting during embryogenesis, has been possible. All this gives support to the notion of remarkable plasticity in brain structure that has been continuously available to the forces of natural selection during the whole of vertebrate evolution. The human brain is not a layered piece of work; it evolved as-a-whole, along the lines of the entire primate radiation.

### The holistic alternative

For far too long our self-understanding has suffered from the old psychic dualism, the presumption that our brains comprise two warring factions: unruly and rather beastly animal emotions kept in check by a rational intelligence. Instead of understanding our emotions we have tried to deny or suppress them. They receive much attention in their pathological states. Psychiatrists are seldom sought to resolve our intellectual problems; rather it is our emotional problems that many of us need help with. But emotions, because they are so difficult to evaluate, are largely ignored by behaviorists and neuroscientists alike, who hope to get "hard data" on how our minds work. Thus an alternative theory, to be developed in the rest of this chapter, of how our emotional and intellectual selves evolved side-by-side, producing an integrated, pretty well adapted brain for surviving during the Pleistocene, must rest on less evidence than one would like to have. I shall just have to make do with what there is.

The overall argument goes something like this. The primate propensities for bonding and autonomy that produced successful group behavior and allowed hominid intelligence to further evolve depended on a genetically based emotional guidance system. Primates *want* to belong and they *want* independence. They are motivated to form attachments; they are motivated to reconcile; they are motivated to explore strange objects; they are motivated to practice leaping, jumping, throwing – to play, to practice social and physical skills. These motives are not conscious; they are not calculated. Like the search

137

for food when hungry or water when thirsty, these motives exist to fill ongoing psychological and, in most cases, physiological needs. (Grooming has calming effects on the endocrine system as well as the benefit of removing irritating parasites; spontaneous physical play develops muscle coordination and heart–lung capacity, as well as social negotiating skills.)

And as with our other biological needs, we experience positive feelings when the conditions of our lives fulfill such needs and negative feelings when they do not. These propensities, as I suggested before, are so vital to our survival that the emotions by which they are guided and defended – that drive us to seek to fulfill them and to resist their frustration – are powerful indeed. We long for contact, for acceptance, for secure belonging. We fear denial; we resent threats to our bonds; we grieve over the loss of them. It is the same with autonomy. We willingly give spontaneously to others, but resent being coerced; we seek freedom from parental (or other) controls, but hope not to lose our bonds of affection thereby. Though these dilemmas of daily human life are a central concern of social psychologists,[17] they get only the briefest mention in current texts on brain evolution and brain function.[18]

In contrast, it is my central premise in this book that it is our psychic needs, and the feelings that accompany them, that are at the root of human nature. They have been the keys to our survival. Our much touted intelligence evolved, at least in part, to service these more elemental, survival-determining aspects of ourselves. Brains of a purely intellectual sort have little use in the absence of goals and needs (expressed as motives or propensities) to direct that intelligence, and of feelings and emotions to tell us whether or not we are "on track" in pursuing those needs. For most of us, it is easier to see humanity in an intellectually deficient Down's syndrome person or one who suffers from fetal alcohol syndrome (both have poorly developed cerebral cortices), than in one suffering from Capgras's syndrome where feelings of bondedness are unrecognized and family and friends are treated as dangerous imposters. We tolerate deficiencies of intellect far better than deficiencies of emotions.

### Why such a big brain?

It is not clear whether the initial selective force for the significant cortical enlargement that marks the evolution of the human brain was for a single function located perhaps in a particular area of the cortex (maybe for increased visual processing) or for a generalized intelligence. As Barbara Finlay and Richard Darlington have pointed out, the genetic modulation of brain development could well be the same in either case. If, say, increased visual processing were being selected for, it could well have resulted from mutations in genes controlling the relative size of the entire cerebral cortex. It is much easier, they argue, for genetic "modifications [to be] made only to total duration of development [of a whole region of the brain, than for] a coordinated enlargement of many independent components of one functional system without enlargement of the rest of the brain."[19]

This sort of argument fits well with the still respected ideas on the evolutionary role of allometric growth, first postulated by D'Arcy Wentworth Thompson in 1917.[20] He suggested that much anatomical modification during the stages of evolution of a sequence of organisms could be explained by differences in the relative rates of growth of developing body parts. This theory fits well with recent identification of genetic mechanisms involved in the modification of limbs and other organs among various vertebrates, where variations in a small number of genes can result in limbs as different as reptilian legs, birds' wings, and primate forearms simply by exaggerating differences in growth rates along three axes of development.[21]

As Finlay and Darlington suggest, it is possible to account for the general enlargement of the cortex as having been triggered by any one of numerous potentially adaptive traits.

> For human evolution ... theories that start from [one] primary behavioral trait appear to account for human evolution many times over. Dexterity and tool use, language, group hunting, various aspects of social structure, and the ability to plan for the future have all been proposed as primary in the cascade of changes leading to the constellation of traits we now possess ... [T]he highly conserved sequence of events in neurogenesis provides a reason why selection for any one ability might cause, in parallel, greater processing capacity for all the others. This observation strengthens the case for the [cerebral cortex] as a general purpose integrator that allows the organism to take advantage of the extra brain structure in ways not directly selected for during evolution.[22]

It is impossible to guess what kind of intelligence was being specifically selected for during the Pleistocene when the hominid brain was doubling in size. One possibility is technical. The quality of tools definitely improved from early *Homo erectus* to later *H. erectus*.[23] Another assumption that I believe is justified is that the increasing cortical capacities themselves made social bonding and social interaction even more important, since the ability to share with others the benefits of increasing individual intelligence (however that may have expressed itself) greatly enhanced the survival expectations of the entire group. This was the beginning of the shared "social mind," that was to lead to the emergence of highly coordinated human societies.

Thus it seems that whatever the adaptive feature(s) was (were) that selected for an enlarged cortex, there also emerged the possibility for much else to evolve, making use of underutilized neurons for newly emergent purposes. This sort of evolutionary process was what Stephen Jay Gould and Richard Lewontin were discussing in a controversial 1979 paper when they argued that some evolutionary opportunities arise not because they were initially "adaptive" at all, but as the serendipitous spin-off from some other adaptation that *was* being

139

selected for.[24] There seems no reason to suppose that this has not been a common occurrence during the whole of evolution.

I turn next to a consideration of how modern brains seem to function.

## How the brain works

*The "entire brain-process" is not a physical fact at all.* It is the appearance to an onlooking mind of a multitude of physical facts. "Entire brain" is nothing but our name for the way in which a million of molecules arranged in certain positions may affect our sense.[25]

What the famous psychologist William James was arguing many years ago is that our subjective sense about the world and of who we are – our "consciousness," if you will – has ultimately to be based on the collective behaviors of real objects, the molecules in the millions of cells in our brains. One had to discard, once and for all, the idea that "spirit" was distinct from one's physical body. So far, however, experimentally convincing explanations of how consciousness comes about have yet to appear, though increasing numbers of theories are being proposed.[26] Even if we still cannot precisely explain consciousness, however, we now have a much better understanding of how the brain functions than when James was writing. We know some of the regions involved in thinking and feeling and how they interact.

My task, though, is not to catalog the mountains of detailed facts about various brain functions but to develop an overview of our mental processes that may aid in our self-understanding. As noted, emphasis will be given to the integration of feelings and thoughts.

### Processing an experience: the automatic brain

Our sense organs are constantly bombarded by energy: light waves, sound waves, stimulating chemicals, pressure, heat. Even so, we detect only small bands of all the oceans of energy that surround us. Bees and many other insects see ultraviolet colors that are not visible to us. Bats sense sound frequencies much higher than we can hear. The worlds they perceive appear physically different from ours. Moreover, most energy that we can perceive we ignore: virtually all of it, when asleep, which is why smoke alarms must emit such awful noises. Even when awake we are not conscious of much of the energy impinging on us. The unconscious parts of our brains, however, receive continuous, low-grade signals from the world. It is usually sudden changes in those signals that elicit a response, and more often than not, we are not even aware that our brains have registered the change and our bodies have done something. One of the first lessons about experience is that much of it is not consciously felt.

This is a good thing. Our conscious selves, our minds, would otherwise be constantly flitting from one minimal change in our world to the next, unable to distinguish important experience from the trivial. We have all habituated (grown accustomed) to background noise. Noise is a common experience in a modern urban setting. (Urbanites, however, tend to be very aware of the silence of a rural setting, the absence of the accustomed background city sounds.) But our unconscious selves are doing more than just monitoring background noises. It is necessary to understand the degree to which our brains actively work without our ever "knowing" what they are up to, without our consciously experiencing what is going on.

When we are babies still in the course of forming our first permanent memories, we learn through conscious, attentive effort how to perform a great many skills, such as crawling, standing, walking, making sounds, speaking first words, and then sentences. I shall say more about the circumstances of this period of learning in Chapter VI. For now it is enough to point out that the capacity to perform these skills, while gained through painstaking, conscious effort in infancy, ultimately becomes a part of our unconscious knowledge. Later in life, we learn to play the piano, or to play a game of tennis, or to drive a car in ways similar to those of learning to walk and talk: through initial conscious effort that, after repeated practice, becomes automatic and can be carried on without detailed conscious thought.

In the course of this sort of skill-learning, the conscious memory centers of the mind in the prefrontal cortex transfer the directions for performing the task elsewhere in the cortex and to the cerebellum.[27] Eventually the behavior becomes automatic, no longer requiring consciously focussed attention. We see pianists in hotels and bars playing mood music flawlessly while carrying on conversations with the customers. During a concert performance, an accomplished virtuoso pianist attends not to what each finger is doing, but to the total emotional content of the whole piece as it is played. We drive a car home from work without noticing how we did it. (After moving house in San Diego, I found myself on several occasions driving to my old address after work before I had "automated" the new route into my subconscious memory!)

Whether we know it or not, however, it is not just consciously learned skills that influence the structures of our brains and hence our consequent behaviors. We, who pride ourselves on our consciousness, assume that of all the animals, we are in total control of our actions, have conscious will power, and choose what we will attend to and how to interpret it. Yet in recent decades it has become widely accepted among psychologists that our conscious minds are not in control of very much. By far, most of the information our brains take in is processed, even remembered, without our knowing it – without, if you like, our "permission." Known as subliminal learning, it has long been used by advertisers to persuade us to act in ways their clients want us to. Whether or not we are consciously aware, the awake brain is processing much of the sensory incoming information. This is not "repressed information" of the sort proposed by Sigmund Freud that can be recovered to consciousness through psychoanalysis. Rather it goes on all the time and is almost never subject to conscious retrieval. Its presence can only be detected after one has unconsciously acted upon it without being able to explain why.

What is the brain secretly doing? For a long time cognitive psychologists were looking for a central processing unit like the one in modern computers. Eventually, they realized that brains are not analogous to linear computers, just as they are not analogous to TV cameras; instead, there are dedicated regions and each one records a different aspect of a particular experience. For example, take a visual experience such as "seeing a yellow pencil." Reflected light from the pencil falls on the retina, which then sends a barrage of electrical impulses to the visual cortex at the back of the brain (see Figure IV.2). From there several discrete electrical signals are sent out. Some project forward and down to the temporal lobe, one to a region that specifically records the color (yellow) and another that notes the size and shape (small, long, rounded object). Another signal goes forward and up into the parietal lobe, which notes the relationship of the object to the self: What is it to me? How can I use this? The whole of the

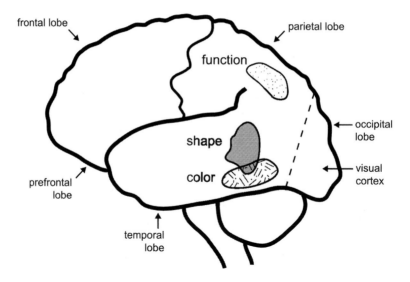

*Figure IV.2* Parallel distributed processing of information
In this illustration, visual images of objects from the retina pass via the optic nerve and "project" onto the visual cortex which, however, does not store the information. Instead, it sends different aspects of it to several locations in the rear half of the cerebral cortex, especially in the left hemisphere, shown above.

*Source*: Original art prepared from author's sketch by Michele Lukowski

*Note*: ▨ = area for recording color; ▦ = area for shape; ▨ = area for the function or meaning of object.

original pencil is not located anywhere. Rather, bits of specific information are spread about over the cortical brain. This all happens simultaneously and very rapidly. It is known as "parallel distributed processing," or PDP.[28]

When we realize how, every waking moment, much more information than just that in a single yellow pencil is reaching the sensory areas of the brain and then is being distributed in a parallel network of fragments throughout the cortex while still retaining (at least for a time) traces of the newly formed neural network, we become astounded at the brain's capacity to perceive and organize details. Much of what we unconsciously experience is never made conscious, though if particular subliminal experiences are encountered often enough they can indeed affect our conscious thoughts, even though we cannot specifically recall them to conscious memory.

One might well ask what is the use of this unconscious cognition? Actually, it is essential. Most of what we do every day depends on it. While our conscious selves (which think and process much more slowly than our unconscious brains) methodically plod along, the mental processes of which we are unaware are simultaneously maintaining posture, keeping us in general contact with our surroundings, permitting us to carry out standard routine acts (like brushing our teeth) with only minimal attention to what we are actually about. The psychoanalyst, Joseph Weiss, has observed:

> It seems that the cognitive capacities of the unconscious mind have been underappreciated and that human beings can unconsciously carry out many intellectual tasks, including developing and executing plans for reaching certain goals.[29]

In addition to these extremely important services of the unconscious parts of our brain, it appears to present us from time to time with conscious thoughts and ideas that break free from the unconscious realm. Often called "hunches" or "insights" or sudden "ahas!," these are moments when our minds seem unexpectedly to come up with answers to puzzles we have been struggling with and consciously cogitating over without success. They are the solutions not available through any form of logical reasoning (those inductive and deductive explanations we are so fond of). Rather, they simply pop into our heads, quite unexpectedly. Often we experience such sudden insights on awakening. The philosopher Charles Sanders Peirce named this process "abduction," and was himself apparently good at turning off his conscious flow of semantic thinking and allowing his mind to fall into a passive state of receptivity. On one occasion he used this technique to identify conclusively a thief aboard a riverboat, even though he could not explain how he knew the man to have been guilty.[30]

So far we have dealt with what the Danish science writer Tor Nørretranders calls the "me" brain: the largest and evolutionarily earlier part of our mind, the subconscious self. It is to the conscious part of our brains, to the "I" brain, that I turn now.

## *Consciousness*

> She took of the fruit ... and did eat, and gave also unto her husband
> with her; and he did eat. And the eyes of them both were opened, and
> they knew that they were naked...
>
> (Genesis 3:6 & 7)

Those ancient and familiar words refer to a universal human feeling that we are aware in ways that other creatures are not, that we are conscious in ways that no other life is. Yet though prevalent and widely accepted, it is hard to make scientifically identifiable definitions of what awareness and consciousness are beyond those that human subjects report to human experimenters. Said Cal Tech neuroscientist J.J. Hopfield, "until an operational definition can be given to 'awareness' independent of the brain of humans, there is no way a science can be made out of consciousness."[31] The boundaries between being in a coma, deeply anesthetized, asleep, awake but not fully conscious, and consciously aware are hard to delimit. Coma and deep anesthesia are not states common to daily living. While they are interesting for medical reasons, they have little to say in terms of evolutionary significance and I shall pass over them to sleep.

Sleep is the easiest state of the brain to explain, but even it occurs at several levels. Sleep under drugs or anesthesia from which instant arousal is difficult or impossible is different from ordinary sleep. But even normal sleep has several stages: the slow, synchronized brain waves of deep sleep contrast amazingly with the awake-looking, chaotic brain waves of dream sleep. During dreaming, the brain takes on a life of its own, while the rest of the body, seemingly severed from its head, goes excessively limp. Only our eyes are busy moving under their lids (from which comes the name, "rapid eye movement" or REM sleep). Dreaming, when the consolidation of much waking experience may be occurring, is essential for healthy brains, and when we awake, we often have sharp, albeit usually ephemeral, memories of our dreamt experiences.[32]

The contents of dreams, once interpreted by Freud as "wish-fulfillment" of suppressed desires, are usually more prosaic, being simulations of the real world played out in diffuse, yet episodic ways: stories that unfold. They often correspond to waking experience and almost always encompass some sort of emotional concerns from our waking life. Most interesting is the finding of both cultural and gender differences in the content of dreams. William Domhoff, a psychologist from the University of California at Santa Cruz, makes this observation:

> [M]en's dreams usually contain a greater percentage of physical aggressions than do those of women, but there are also *large differences from culture to culture in the occurrence of physical aggression in men's dreams.*[33]

144

This observation is particularly significant for our understanding of the underlying causes of male aggression and violence, which are discussed more fully in Chapter VII. (Interestingly, animals also appear to dream, waking themselves suddenly, as we do, if it becomes too terrifying. Do they, too, briefly "remember" their dreams? They certainly have memories of waking events.) Sleep, an activity undertaken by most warm-blooded vertebrates, is a recurring period of true unconsciousness, during which brain cells, particularly in the upper brainstem and cortex, may be recovering from the enormous metabolic activity that occurs during wakefulness.

I return, then, to that difficult concept, "consciousness." It gets used to mean many things: from being awake, not asleep, all the way to being totally self-aware of everything around you and how it relates to you. As I have suggested already, being awake does not mean being aware – "consciously aware" – of things. If you awake briefly at night, you are dimly aware it is not yet daylight, roll over, and go back to sleep. In the morning, you may be aware it is daytime, but not notice whether it's sunny or cloudy. You put on robe and slippers automatically. Nothing focusses your attention. You are not aware of thinking about anything at all. Not until your waking output of adrenalin has been circulating awhile and your blood pressure rises, do you begin to notice the world. Finally, perhaps after a cup of strong coffee, you are totally aroused, alert to what is going on, listening to the news, reading the paper, planning the day's schedule. All systems are activated and "you" – the conscious self – are very much involved in what is happening. You are fully conscious.

These two levels of consciousness are not sharply delimited. The first, the semi-aware state, is what I believe neurologist Antonio Damasio means when he talks about "core consciousness," and the second, the fully involved, self-conscious state is what I believe he means by "extended consciousness." In his excellent book, *The Feeling of What Happens*, Damasio attempts to pinpoint the areas of the brain that are involved in the gradations from simple wakefulness through full extended consciousness; the latter, he says, is limited to human beings.[34]

In general, these centers begin in the brainstem (where sleep–awake cycles are initiated by the raphe nuclei and locus coeruleus among other regions – see Figure IV.1). The pre-conscious, proto-self arises mainly in the brainstem. It "recognizes" incoming signals, whether coming from the body (e.g. pain), from outside (e.g. your dog), or from memory (e.g. some stored past images). However "you" are not aware of these. But if one of the incoming signals has some importance related to oneself, a new set of neural centers, from the midbrain tectum to the thalamus and the cingulate gyrus in the subpallium, begin firing. These create core consciousness: you now become consciously aware of the signals. You attend to them.

This level of arousal, if it persists, causes our attention to focus on the object and we begin to realize its existence and think about it, at least temporarily. At some stage this new information gets contrasted with our past experience – our autobiographical memory. Humans, and perhaps some other primates, utilize parts of the prefrontal cortex at the base of the frontal lobe of the brain to develop a full, extended consciousness, with (at least for human beings) a strong concept of individual identity (the prefrontal cortex is shown in Figure IV.1). Figure IV.3 summarizes Damasio's gradations in the sequence from wakefulness – characteristic of most familiar animals – all the way through core consciousness to the extended consciousness that led to further human developments: language, creativity, and conscience or moral thought.

Damasio pointedly emphasizes how little of our consciousness depends on the huge cortex of our cerebral hemispheres. Only the somatosensory cortex (near the front edge of the parietal lobe, shown in Figure IV.2) plays an important role in our self-awareness. What he is saying is that consciousness, at whatever level, from wakefulness to total self-awareness and engagement, is not a recent evolutionary addition, but has probably been critical to the normal functioning of most vertebrates, and certainly of other primates. The differences between them and us are more in the degree of engagement at the various levels than the result of any new additions to brain structures. (This agrees well with Northcutt's views of brain evolution among vertebrates.) To quote Damasio:

> These structures [that are involved in consciousness] are of old evolutionary vintage, they are present in numerous nonhuman species, and they mature early in individual human development.[35]

Another aspect of consciousness (from the core level on "up" in Figure IV.3) is how much it depends on the storage of nonverbal "stories" or narratives. Damasio emphatically states that the old, commonly held belief that language is necessary for consciousness and thought is simply wrong, as his studies on numerous patients deprived of language capabilities demonstrated. He says:

> The contribution of language to the mind was, to say the least, astounding, but its contribution to core consciousness was nowhere to be found.
> The very nature of language argues against it having a primary role in consciousness. [If it did, n]onlanguaged animals and human babies would be just out of luck, forever unconscious.[36]

Studies of apes in captivity fully demonstrate their abilities to recall, and even to communicate in nonlinguistic ways, simple episodic events. Narrative thought – and for humans, story-telling – is ingrained, a natural aspect of the way our brains work: they are story-making organs! This, as Damasio suggests, explains our love for hearing stories, and accounts for our widespread addiction to movies and especially television; whatever the quality of the story, our attention is easily engaged.[37]

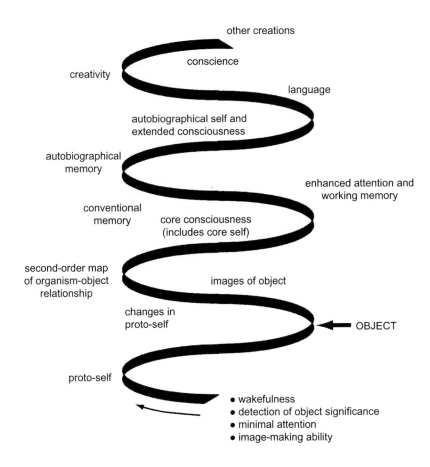

*Figure IV.3* Evolutionary stages in the emergence of consciousness

Damasio's stages in the evolution of various levels of consciousness, from <u>wakefulness</u>, which most warm-blooded animals and perhaps many others, share all the way up the scale to <u>extended consciousness</u> and <u>autobiographical self</u>, which he believes are limited to human beings and are further enhanced by language. The latter gives rise to creativity and conscience, or moral awareness, as well as other attributes. One of his most important points is that there are no sharp divisions along this evolutionary path; we cannot be sure how much is unique to us and how much is shared by other species at various levels along the way.

*Source*: From A. Damasio (1999: 310) Fig.10.1; original art by Dr. Hanna Damasio. Used with kind permission

One last, highly significant point must be made about consciousness, human or otherwise. It is never purely "cerebral." Consciousness, awareness, and the thoughts they engender are not the result of a brain that is manipulating bare facts as a logical calculating machine would. They are always modulated by the emotional responses they simultaneously call forth. These responses, positive or negative, contain the critical message that connects the event with the survival of the self. Most events, most experiences, are in some way either favorable or unfavorable for the continued existence of the organism. An animal need not be consciously aware of past emotions, need not consciously "know" what it feels, in order to remember the lessons in survival it learned in the past. It simply "feels" positively or negatively toward the present occasion.

According to Damasio, for us humans, one more level of awareness has been added on. We can also be *consciously aware* that we have "feelings" of how some event, past, present or imagined, makes us feel. This awareness of our emotions, of how we *feel* about things, is much more than a survival mechanism. It is the very essence of being human. Without the feeling aspect of human consciousness, life would be essentially meaningless: no sorrow, no joy, no suffering, no pleasure – and all the other attributes that promote conscience, compassion and, ultimately, our powerful need for a meaningful purpose to our existence.

### Is consciousness an accident or an adaptation?

It is hard for any human being to perceive life without the extended consciousness we take so much for granted. Was consciousness *per se* what was being selected for as our brains became bigger and bigger? Or was it the general increase in information-processing capacity elsewhere in the cortex (the ability to process and store the images of objects, sounds, smells, and events)? After all, as already noted, 95 percent of the brain's work is totally unknown to us. Perhaps consciousness was not selected at all. Perhaps it just emerged – the result of a cortex that was enlarging for other reasons.

This is the view of several scientists.[38] Neuroscientist Raja Parasuraman summarizes the argument well, accounting for consciousness as an epiphenomenon forced on evolving primates whose large cortices faced sensory overload. Without some sort of focus, they would not be able to produce directed behaviors – only conflicting, disoriented actions:

> The primate brain presumably evolved mechanisms of selective attention to cope with that limitation.
>
> Without such selectivity, organisms would be ill-equipped to act coherently in the face of competing and distracting sources of stimulation in the environment.[39]

One synonym for consciousness, even at the basic core level, is "attentive-ness," the ability to focus on one thing at a time without being distracted, to *select* what "matters." One of the most critical forms of attentiveness, and maybe the oldest, is vigilance, the ability to maintain sustained attention for a long time. A cat waiting for prey to move closer sits motionless for many minutes, ignoring all else, poised to pounce. Similarly, an animal being stalked focusses its entire attention on the predator, ready at an instant to dash off or fly away. Vigilance, already present in so many sentient creatures, must surely have been enhanced by the increased focussing power of the primate brain. (Later, in Chapter VI, I consider how excessive vigilance develops as an adaptive change in brain structure in highly stressed humans.)

The difficulty that I find with this theory of the origin of human conscious-ness is that it addresses mainly core forms of consciousness that are not part of the cortex at all, but of the brainstem and the limbic system. They are attributes we share with many other animals. Furthermore, much of what the cortex processes is hidden from our consciousness, from our awareness; only when the signals have some emotional content relating to survival do they attract our attention. From the standpoint of human nature, the most important function of consciousness lies in our *extended* consciousness, in the ability to select and control a whole sequence of thoughts in a directed way. Like all animals, we efficiently monitor a whole lot of information continuously, without a great deal of attention. But our extended consciousness allows us humans to play around with a whole lot of experiences, present and past, *intentionally*. To take them apart and put them back together in new ways, to recast the story-line: in short, to think creatively. To do that, we also need to be able to selectively retrieve memories of past experiences. While it is certain that other primates share our ability to "attend" to sensory patterns, using the same parts of the brain, it is not clear that they are able intentionally to search for remembered events. In any case, it is the mental mark of humankind that we are highly capable of such tasks if our brains are intact. All of which leads us to a consideration of memory.

### Memory and thought

Much of what our brains "remember" is not acquired consciously at all, and is mostly inaccessible to consciousness except when someone is able to recall a subliminal memory through "blanking their mind," as Charles Peirce did when identifying the thief. Brain patterns are established reflexly, after repeated stimuli; it is unconscious learning. Most of the memory we are able to consciously draw on when thinking, however, has been consciously acquired. Not surprisingly, it passes through the same regions of the brain on its way to being stored as are later used (in reverse) in retrieving it and thinking about it.

The regions of the brain that serve a double duty as memory-formers and thought processors are located in the front part of the brain. They comprise a close association among the inner part of the vertebrate forebrain, the limbic system, and the frontal lobes of the cortex. Each of the large primate hemi-spheres has four regions, of which the visual, temporal, and parietal lobes are largely dedicated to the parallel distributed processing and storing of sensory information, creating the diffusely stored patterns of our experiences – our memories. The fourth region, or frontal lobe, especially its most forward part, the prefrontal cortex, is much less involved with processing and storing and much more involved with sampling information and manipulating it. The frontal lobe occupies one-third of the total cortex. It is where we consciously think; it is active both in conscious learning and in conscious remembering. The Russian neurologist Alexander Luria called this part of the brain the "planning cortex," in contrast to the other three lobes, or the "sensory cortex."[40]

As shown in Figure IV.4, there are multiple connections between regions of the thalamus and hypothalamus, on the one hand, and both the inner parts of the limbic system (the septum, hippocampus, amygdala, and the cingulate gyrus) and the frontal lobe, on the other. These are known as the thalamocortical pathways. They are, not surprisingly, virtually the same pathways active in conscious thinking, with its short-term memory function. The frontal cortex also has multiple connections with the areas of the sensory cortex that are used for the storage and retrieval of long-term memories. Injuries to the hippocampus, part of the subpallium lying beneath the temporal cortex on each side of the brain, severely impair the short-term memory function needed during both thinking and the processing of memories for permanent storage. Lesions in the prefrontal region prevent the focussed attention needed for concentrating on a single stimulus.[41]

In the course of forming a conscious memory, information flows from the sense organs, via the thalamus, thence to the frontal lobes, and finally to the sensory regions where it is stored. These thalamocortical signals must persist for *at least half a second* if transfer is to be successful. (Presumably something similar occurs much more rapidly during nonconscious information storage, which bypasses the frontal lobes.) To achieve permanent memory storage, retrievable in the future, *conscious attention* is required. Usually rehearsal of the information to be stored is also needed, unless the event is so emotionally laden that it is likely to be remembered because it is brought repeatedly to consciousness spontaneously. (Examples would be events on one's wedding day, or the circumstances of a terrifying experience. Most everyone alive at the time remembers where she or he was when news came of President Kennedy's assassination.) We must work very hard to memorize dry facts for final examinations, but we have no trouble at all remembering details of a gripping play. (This underscores once again Damasio's central point about our memories: not only do we store memories of events themselves; we store along with them our feelings at the time. That which matters very, very much stays embedded in our memories virtually for the rest of our lives.)

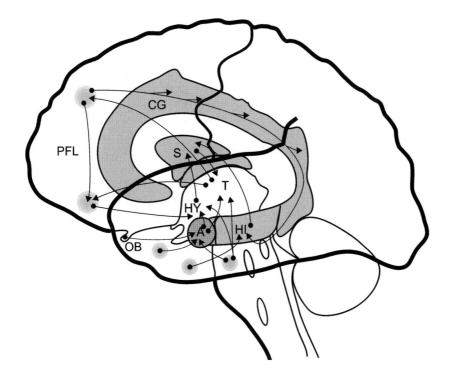

*Figure IV.4* Interactions between the limbic system and the cortex

The cortical hemispheres surround the central areas of the *limbic system* (shaded), with which they make multiple connections. Here are shown those between the "emotional brain" (*thalamus, hypothalamus* and the *inner cortex*) and the "aware" or "thinking brain," (*prefrontal lobes*). These multiple connections (of which only the main ones are shown) create the "integrated self", by coordinating motivation with thought. Note that arrows go in both directions, setting up reverberating circuits that presumably generate our general moods.

*Key.* PFL = prefrontal lobe: sampling and manipulation of information; short-term memory (e.g. thinking)
OB = olfactory bulb, where smells are recorded; odors are highly evocative of memories
CG = cingulate gyrus, part of the inner cortex (subpallium) that forms the *limbic system*
S = septum, part of the subpallium's *limbic system*
T = thalamus: the central relay point for ingoing and outgoing information; critical for transmitting emotions to the PFL
HY = hypothalamus: central relay point between the PFL, *limbic system* and endocrine system (by way of the pituitary gland, as seen in Figure VI.3)
HI = hippocampus, a part of the subpallium, next to the cingulate gyrus responsible for memory and for balanced control of emotions
A = amygdala, also a part of the subpallium; profoundly involved in swinging one's mood away from "placid" to "disturbed" – either violent or depressed (see C.B. Nemeroff, 1998)

*Source*: Composite drawn from several sources. Original art by Michele Lukowski

Conscious thinking takes time. Normally the brain can, unconsciously, react to an emergency well before we are even aware that an emergency exists. When a child runs in front of your car, your foot is on the brake and your tires are screeching before you are even aware of what you are doing. It takes at least a half a second (two spoken syllables) before we become conscious of anything. Even a very short stimulus – such as a flash of light or a pinprick – must set off an ongoing internal excitation in the thalamocortical pathways of the brain that lasts for half a second before we become aware of it. The brain, however, tricks us into shifting time around, so we have the sensation that we are simultaneously aware of such brief events *when they happen*. As Tor Nørretranders writes, *"the conscious experience is projected back in time... What we experience is a lie, for we experience it as if we experienced it before we experienced it."*[42]

As just noted, consciously experienced stimuli can start off a response even before we become aware of them: as when stopping the car in an emergency. But even subliminal stimuli that are too brief or too weak to ever rise to consciousness can also result in actions for which we have no explanation. We do not know what we reacted to. Nørretranders, again:

> It is possible to react without being conscious of why. It is [even] possible to preprogram complicated patterns of action that are sparked off without our knowing why.

> Not only do we not know what the idea of acting is; we have no idea what made us act.[43]

Do these facts mean we are, in truth, without free will after all, that we are not responsible for our actions? Not at all. The seemingly automatic or unconscious self is in fact trained during development to respond "appropriately" under demanding, often stressful situations. We consciously learn to control spontaneous behaviors, so that we come to perform them later quite unconsciously. One of the earliest is the emptying of our bladders. We learned, consciously at first, to go to the bathroom when we felt the urge, but still had to wear diapers at night. Eventually, we trained ourselves to hold our sphincter muscles closed, even when in deep sleep – finally waking up to relieve ourselves, perhaps after several frustrating dreams about searching for an appropriate place to accomplish our biological task!

As we grow up, we are trained in similar kinds of behavioral inhibitions. Even our unconscious selves are not mere stimulus/response machines, genetically programmed to react automatically. The human brain is too unformed at birth for much stereotypic behavior to be present. Among the few computer-like programs, or "algorithms," that we have at birth are specific reflexes, such as involuntary breathing, swallowing, and blinking, and some more complex, yet still involuntary, rhythmic behaviors, such as the cyclic rhythms of sleeping and waking, and of searching for food – as in the suckling response of hungry infants. Other apparently spontaneous behaviors present at birth or shortly after are smiling, crying, laughing, and showing various other emotions. Human babies at about two months automatically smile when shown a mask of a human face, and they also pay characteristic attention to rhythmic sounds of the human voice, such as songs and metered verses. Finally, there are a few universally found adult behaviors in addition to the affect expressions already present from infancy. These include bowing the head and exposing the nape of the neck, and often also averting one's gaze (looking down toward one's feet), as signs of submission; the eyebrow "flash" as a sign of recognition; and covering one's eyes or mouth when embarrassed, thus hiding from the viewer how one is affected.

On the whole, though, there are virtually no specific behaviors that can be said to be probable genetic algorithms. The psychologist George Mandler is particularly dismissive of attempts to argue for inheritance of tendencies to watch TV or to become divorced. Indeed, he argues that while there are certain genetically determined limits to what our brains can do, such as processing only one idea at a time, there are few behaviors beyond those noted above that can be said to be hardwired.[44]

Mandler is also critical of too much reliance being placed on twin studies as indicators of the heritability of behaviors. He cites work on the concordance for schizophrenia in monozygotic (identical) twins. If they share the same placenta (as is usual) then both twins show schizophrenia in 60 percent of cases, but if they happen to have separate placentas, this concordance falls to only 11 percent, the same frequency as for nonidentical twins or ordinary siblings. It was the local environment in the womb, not the fact of sharing the same genes, that made the difference in the appearance or not of a known heritable trait.[45] Thus, "inherited" traits are almost never due to genes alone, but to *genes + environment*, even for those with high potential heritability.

The unfinished brain of a human newborn undergoes a long period of both unconscious and conscious training: the culturally guided, experiential develop-mental processes that create the necessity for our spontaneous, independent behavior and probably our life-long tendencies to playfulness. (We shall say more about these developmental processes and how context affects them in Chapter VI.) Our evolutionarily honed characteristics are not to be found in stereotypic, reflex behaviors at all, but rather in the very broad propensities that are the central argument of this book, propensities that are guided by general feelings emerging from the emotional centers of the brain.

Before moving on to how our thoughts lead to actions, I will note one or two more things about memories. First, memories are not about individual objects or decontextualized actions; they are whole, detailed pictures of a unique experience. They are integrated. We cannot conceive of a scene that is not integrated, that is "not experienced from a single point of view." Imagine the house you grew up in: layout, from floorplans to light switches, events that occurred in various rooms, smells, colors of things, emotions felt, neighbors, the history of those years... It is remembered as a whole entity. Furthermore, conscious memories are remarkable for their extraordinary differentiation or complexity. (You could go on forever about the minute details of your childhood home.) This means that for each memory, an enormous amount of information is diffusely stored throughout the brain's sensory cortex. In order for it to be "consciously remembered," all this detail must be simultaneously linked together in what neuroscientists Giulio Tononi and Gerald Edelman call a "dynamic core" – a sustained link-up of activated neurons lasting for a considerable period of time, of at least half a second.[46]

As you think about your house, however, you begin to "focus" on a particular detail, the color of the dining-room rug, the panels on the doors; but then you can shift to another place and describe it in detail also. Yet only one view at a time is in our consciousness. What this means is that our remembering – indeed, all our conscious thinking – is linear; that is, we go from one view to the next. It is like a story, a sequence. We remember as if we were physically reliving each discrete viewpoint. This sequencing of our conscious attention is brought about by a region in the prefrontal cortex, the "thinking region," that is connected to the nearby cingulate gyrus, that by-now familiar part of the limbic system. Known as the "executive processor," this region directs our attention and inhibits other signals; it organizes the sequence of things we attend to; it plans tasks to think about; it monitors our progress; and finally, it helps us remember where we are in a thought sequence. This is the center of our "working memory" – the locus of our organized thinking.[47]

There is another important place in the brain called the "interpreter." Located in the left cerebral hemisphere only, it has the task of making sense of our thoughts. Our consciousness works with one thought at a time, building a sequence of thoughts. Many stimuli can lead us into a memory cluster, such as the word "childhood," or (for me) mention of "fog" and "foghorns" (as in San Francisco), or the smell of the sweet scent of hills covered with newly grown wild oats maturing in the early summer. (All these were part of my childhood, and each brings on memories.) But once we have a memory, especially a sequence of memories making up an episode, then we depend upon the interpreter to make sense of those memories. Our brains seem to have a "need" to make a reasonable story out of the information they possess.

For example, sometimes with our memories, we are not absolutely sure what happened. At such times, the interpreter will automatically *make up* a reasonable story, which the conscious self, the "I," believes to be actually true. We know this to happen from many sorts of experiments, particularly those on split-brain patients who will make up "explanations" for weird choices of objects on lab tests, in order to make those choices "reasonable." (Their weird choices, of course, come from the fact that their left and right hemispheres cannot communicate – one half does not know what the other is thinking, or has chosen. But when faced with the oddity of their choices, their interpreter concocts a "reasonable" story.[48]) The interpreter, then, is the potential source not only of scientific theories or other grand suppositions about the world. It is also the source of false memories, and tellers of such memories (even persons with normal brains) are unaware they are false. This is an example of how strong is our need to have narrative meaning in our lives. (That is the subject of the entire next chapter.) Clearly, it is a very profound human need, and we have a powerful propensity to seek meaning continuously.

In concluding this brief discussion of memory, it is well to remember that even while an event is taking place, our minds are selecting what to notice, then interpreting it, "making sense" of what is being stored so it can be retrieved as a whole story rather than disconnected snapshots. Thus, our experiences, like a scientist's data, never speak for themselves; they are always interpreted. In the other direction, memories, especially ugly ones, can also be repressed. More often, our memories are incomplete; we remember fragments of an event, and fill in the gaps with a logical story of what "must" have happened. Both repressed and false memories can cause much trouble in courts of law and other "truth-seeking" venues.

### Thoughts, feelings, actions

It is perhaps the quintessential error of the modern Western world view to suppose that thought can occur without feeling. The assumption that thought and feeling are separable; the supposition that they are located in evolutionarily distinct parts of the brain; and the presumption that thoughts are superior and more human than feelings, all are quite mistaken. I have just reviewed the evidence that conscious thinking is the result of close interactions between the prefrontal lobes, evidently devoted to thought, and the limbic system and the thalamus, which are associated with emotions. Conscious thinking, with its requirement for access to stored memories and information, however, depends completely on this connection. The brain surgeon, Wilder Penfield, who has had experience with hundreds of patients, reports on the critical role of the thalamus (or diencephalon) in conscious thought:

> Consciousness continues, regardless of what area of cerebral cortex is removed. On the other hand consciousness is inevitably lost when the function of the higher brain stem (diencephalon) is interrupted by injury, pressure, disease, or local epileptic discharge... [I]t is clear that within the diencephalon there is a system of nerve fibers and gray matter [nerve cells] that communicates directly with the functional units of the two hemispheres. It is on the action of this system that the existence of consciousness depends. By means of it, the action of cortical mechanisms is started and stopped.[49]

It is not the famed cortex that is the *sine qua non* of conscious thought, but the brainstem and limbic system, once thought to be more "ancient."

Moreover, the two supposedly distinct entities – thoughts and feelings – are located in exactly the same parts of the human brain. In fact, it is not possible to separate conscious thought from feelings. The British chemist-philosopher, Graham Cairns-Smith, explains it in this way:

> Conscious thought *includes* feelings. Intellectual feelings we might call them, subtle pleasures, satisfactions, irritations, frustrations… Some of these – feelings of dismay, of recognition, of conviction and so on – we can give names to. Others, like the feelings engendered by listening to music, may be more difficult to describe; yet all such feelings are part and parcel of conscious thought. It seems to me that it is precisely the element of feeling in conscious thought which makes it conscious… [F]eeling, broadly understood, is the essential quality of consciousness.[50]

Indeed, if you stop to think about it, even our strongest emotions – overwhelming love, violent anger, abject fear – are aroused in us by conscious experiences. No matter how bland our conscious thoughts may be, they produce in us some level of feeling. Even the most modest sensation – a particular color, say, or the quality of a sound – elicits in us an opinion about it, either positive or negative. (When we have no opinion, the sensation is likely either puzzling or totally without interest.) Sometimes our feelings may be so mild we scarcely notice them, but they can also grade into increasingly stronger positive (ahhh!) or negative (ughh!) responses. We are attracted or repelled with ever-more force, until we come to full-blown feelings: love, joy, passion, hate, fury, rage, terror, grief.

As they grow in strength, our feelings stimulate release from the brain of both neural signals and chemical hormones that can produce a whole panoply of physical symptoms: tingling, sweat, trembling, nausea, mucus secretion, salivation (or lack of it), accelerated heart rate, and so on. Other times a cluster of nonspecific feelings may persist, giving rise to moods: depression, anxiety, euphoria, contentment, determination…. It is *absence of feelings* that gives rise to boredom.

We are pretty much aware that our strongest emotions tend to affect our behaviors. People who are angry act in angry ways: they scowl, shout, hit, plan revenge. People who are grief-stricken act in sad ways: they are solemn, they weep, perhaps wail; they stand and walk as though weighed down by a burden. People who feel joyful wear a smile, walk with a light step, are often more friendly than usual. But aside from these affective signals (letting others know what to expect from us), our emotions are internal signals, too, that affect our behaviors in less obvious ways. We try to avoid or correct situations that cause negative feelings; we are attracted to and promote situations that cause positive feelings. Feelings, then, are constantly part of our conscious life. (Eavesdrop on a teenage conversation and you will immediately see what I mean.) A set of musical notes, a sweet-scented rose, an elegant mathematical equation – all can produce a sense of aesthetic pleasure, of "ahhh!" or perhaps "aha." A wrong note, a gas leak, and a letter from the Internal Revenue Service, on the other hand, can all produce mild distaste, those "ughh!" feelings.

But the description thus far does not explain why all these feelings came about. Why is it important to have all the emotions we have? Humans have more powerful emotions than any other animal. As Damasio repeatedly points out, of all species, it is we humans who are most consciously aware of how we feel. Not only do we feel more strongly, we also display our feelings more explicitly. No other species laughs, or cries, or jumps for joy, or scowls and curses as vigorously as we do. Why are we so emotional? The answer has to be that our feelings are evolutionarily adaptive. As Cairns-Smith says: "[P]leasures on the whole go with acts that promote our survival and pains with the oppo-site."[51] Feelings are not just *responses to* a situation, they are in fact *guides to* behavior. It is our behaviors that respond to pleasurable situations and avoid painful ones. Our feelings direct us. They establish our goals, our motives. Without feelings, our large, flexible, adaptive brains could not work at all. They would not "know" what to do.

Consider for a moment a honeybee. It does not need conscious feelings in order to survive. Its behaviors are entirely "programmed." Randomly searching scouts locate flowers. They return to the hive using the sun as a guide, aided by a scent trail they leave on the ground. They "teach" other workers how to find the honey source by doing a stereotyped "dance" in the hive that specifies direction and distance. All this, and their other life activities, are programmed into their fairly elaborate brains as "instincts" – patterns of behavior that are narrowly rigid and permit of only one way of living as a honeybee. They are responding reflexively to incoming stimuli.

Animals with less rigidly-patterned brains can lead rather more flexible lives. They are able to adapt to somewhat larger "niches" in the environment, and rely on rather less specified behavioral patterns, often called "drives." Migrating species may be said to have "drives" as they follow certain environmental clues in meeting lifetime (salmon) or annual (birds) "needs." Our primate relatives, with their sophisticated social lives, lead far less programmed lives than, say, an ostrich or a zebra. Their behaviors are much more flexible, and they clearly experience – and display – far more elaborate emotions, approaching our own. In place of rigid patterns found in most species, the inherited "drives" of primates and humans might better be described as *broad propensities* that guide an overall behavior pattern that is learned mainly from experience and from social culture. In Chapter II, I introduced two primary propensities among primates that insure flexibility in their survival behavior: *bonding* and *autonomy*.

We humans – behaviorally the most flexible species we know of – have a brain relatively free of algorithmic patterns laid down genetically. Rather, we depend hugely on learning, on experience, and on culturally accumulated skills. It is this capacity that gives us the flexibility to live in almost every habitat on

Earth, to move to strange places and survive. We saw in the last chapter how the Pleistocene honed the learning skills of our ancestors over and over again. And the reason we could adapt was because we had emotions to guide our behaviors, that led us to explore, create, invent, and most of all, communicate with each other. It was our ability to recognize *consciously* our emotions, to be guided by our feelings, that assured that our human ancestors, when making behavioral decisions, would choose in ways that would help them survive. To maximize the potential for learning that their enlarging brains offered, those ancestors had to use the brain's way of learning efficiently. And the brain's way of learning is by making stories, narrative episodes of memory, of accumulated, organized information. And this requires conscious thought, guided by emotional awareness.

To conclude this chapter, I would like to quote once more from Antonio Damasio, as he summarizes the nature of consciousness.

> Consciousness begins when brains acquire the power, the simple power I must add, of telling a story without words... Consciousness emerges when this primordial story [of an organism trying to survive in its surroundings] can be told using the universal vocabulary of body signals. The apparent self emerges as the feeling of a feeling... I suspect consciousness prevailed in evolution because knowing [i.e. being aware of] the feelings caused by emotions was so indispensable for the art of life.[52]

In other words, being made consciously aware of what one needs to do to survive through an acute awareness of one's own emotional signals is a break-through in evolution. It is knowing how we feel that has made us humans so successful, so able to adapt. Emotions – feelings – need to be listened to and understood, not suppressed as troublesome remnants of our evolutionary past.

I will make two final points. The first has to do with stories. Stories are explanatory; stories carry meaning. Our brains are *story-learning, story-creating* organs. We need stories to live by. We make up stories for ourselves. We share them with each other because we are designed to live in groups. Stories, narra-tives, cultural myths, systems of shared meaning, are the mental food our brains and bodies feed upon, every bit as critical to our lives as the plants and animals that provide physical sustenance. And because *we need stories*, we seek them out. And once we find an explanatory story on which to ground our actions, a story that explains who we are and how we should live, *we cling to it*. The coherence of our group, and hence the survival of our individual selves, depends on being guided by that shared story. And so we find in the world, both past and present, that *human beings protect the sanctity of the overall, big story that structures their lives*. They defend it from threats, whether they come from within the group or without. They resist changing it without careful deliberation. Cultural stories are, in essence, ultimate stories about how to be human – and as such they truly become matters of life and death. Meaning and meaningfulness in life are never trivial; indeed, they are basic to our existence. Not to understand this is not to understand the most profound aspect of human nature.

My second point is really derivative to the first. Given the profound role of feeling in all human behaviors that have significant survival value, we should not be surprised to discover that the other two propensities I have identified as essential aspects of human nature – those for bonding and for autonomy – are equally defended by powerful emotions. They, too, are part of our human survival kit and, I would strongly argue, are also the subjects of intense feelings.[53]

With these words, I turn now to the question of how this "thirst for meaning" was able to evolve and become increasingly fulfilled and shared – how human culture came about.

# V

# A THIRST FOR MEANING

[M]eaning and context are not elements that can be handled separately or derived from adding elements together. Context is not so much a set of stimuli that impinge upon a person as it is a web of relations interwoven to form the fabric of meaning.

Barbara Rogoff (1982: 149)

The individual mind is immanent but not only in the body. It is immanent also in pathways and messages outside the body: and there is a larger Mind of which the individual mind is only a sub-system. This larger mind is comparable to God and is perhaps what some people mean by "God," but it is still immanent in the total interconnected social system and planetary ecology.

Gregory Bateson (1972: 461)

So far as we can perceive with our own five senses, from the point of view of a star, a volcano, a dawn redwood, a salmon, perhaps even a dog, whatever is, simply *is*. But from the point of view of a human being, whatever *is* has *meaning*. Everything that exists, every event that happens, has some sort of cause and some sort of purpose. We are not always able to say what those are, but we believe profoundly that causes and purposes do exist, and much of the time we are actively searching for them. Causes and purposes are what narrative stories are made of and, as shown in Chapter IV, our brains are story-making organs. That interpreter in the left cerebral hemisphere insists on creating stories for us, because they are what consciousness needs to think with. Stories, reasons, purposes – all are part of the behavioral guidance system needed for human survival. Without stories, without meaning, our amazing flexibility of action, our precious freedom and free will, would be incoherent. Our enormous ability to "learn from experience," and hence adapt to widely diverse environments, could not properly be orchestrated. We need context, a story, a frame for thinking.

When did all this conscious mental story-telling come into being? Surely not all at once. It is clear that our ape cousins can remember significant past events and their emotions about them when something triggers such memories, though how they experience those memories is not at all certain. Some of those who try to reconstruct our cultural evolution insist that what Antonio Damasio calls full extended consciousness (see Chapter IV) is a very recent event, occurring somewhere between 12,000 and 3000 ya.

The more recent date comes from Julian Jaynes, who insists that at the time of the Trojan war (around 3300 ya) the right and left halves of the human brain were not fully connected up, and the thoughts generated (supposedly only in the left hemisphere) were experienced by the behavior-motivating right hemisphere as coming from outside, the voices of powerful gods dictating their human actions:

> Thus, Iliadic men have no will of their own and certainly no notion of free will.[1]

Their thoughts were like hallucinatory phenomena, Jaynes argues.

The earlier date is one given by Morris Berman in his book, *Wandering God*. Berman assumes that the first glimmerings of self-conscious awareness did not begin until around 35,000 ya among hunter-gatherers. He cites the increased grave goods dating from that time as evidence of what he calls "a diffuse, peripheral type of awareness" to which he gives the label, "paradox." The "outside" world is simply a given in which "the I" is immersed. There is (in so far as I understand him) no awareness of self-in-relationship, and certainly no need to explain the meaning of existence. Most of all, there is no authoritative explanation about how one, as individual or as member of a group, ought to act. No conscious tradition to be protected. For Berman, only with the advent of the hierarchical nomadic cultures on the Asian steppes some 12,000 ya, where a paternalistic authority dictates the rules of human existence, does full-blown, extended consciousness come into being.[2]

I remain totally unconvinced by either set of arguments. The progression from apelike social knowledge and minimal self-awareness to the fully extended consciousness of modern humans surely began much more than 35,000 ya. I am much more inclined to accept the sequence proposed by Canadian psychologist Merlin Donald, for whom the process of making and communicating symbolic meanings began back in the early Pleistocene. He argues that the human mind began to emerge when our *Homo erectus* ancestors started to mime, to act out events, to "tell" stories.[3] Out of this early beginning a half-million years ago arose music, art, and finally spoken language, the package of symbol-using skills we now have for making and sharing meaning: in brief, out of this long process came human culture.

Large brains need meaningful stories to function, but meaning without symbols is severely limited in what can be thought about, conveyed, and shared. Symbols, especially languages, have the double function of expanding both individual thought and the sharing of thoughts among a whole group. They are what permitted our individual brains to become loosely linked into a "group mind," giving rise to coordinated group behaviors of increasing complexity.

This chapter aims to uncover what this means for our understanding of modern human nature and human behavior. It emphasizes that we are, first and foremost, social creatures absolutely dependent on others for survival, for happiness, for psychic health, for personal identity, in short, for everything!

I begin by redefining what "the mind" is. Then I turn to how symbolic language probably arose and how it continues to evolve. In particular, I note how languages differ in the metaphors they use to describe the world and its events – evidence that languages are specific to cultural world views, the two reciprocally creating each other continuously over time. When two cultures interact, they are often seeing the world from two completely different sets of metaphoric assumptions. Finally, I conclude with an explanation of why culturally shared meaning systems have become the dominant "need" of human beings. Because our meaning systems subsume our propensities for both bonding and autonomy, they become the dominant guideline for our actions and hence are defended by extremely powerful emotions. Cultural narratives define for us "what counts as a bond, as acceptance," and also "what are the approved limits of autonomous action." They create our self-identity as individuals at the same time as they create societal coherence and coordination through shared group meaning.

## What and where is "the mind"?

There is a powerful tendency to think of mind as synonymous with brain. People often use the terms interchangeably. At best, we conceive of brain as a physical object, a tool, and mind as the process the tool carries out for us. "Minds are what brains do."[4] We think of the mind as inside the head, housed within its bony cranium, quite separate from the world out there. The conventional Western concept of the mind/self as something housed inside each person's head, that acts entirely from that one locus as a free and independent agent on an external and quite separate entity, the environment, is part of the Billiard Ball conceptualization of the universe. The very different model presented here falls within the Gestalt of Indra's Net – of a connected universe. It goes something like this:

The mind that determines my actions at any given moment is partly in my brain, but it is also partly out in the world, in the brains and actions of others, indeed, in the whole context that surrounds me just then. My mind extends beyond myself and my body out into my surroundings. Furthermore, that part of my mind that is in my head changes continuously, as synaptic relationships are constantly undergoing adjustments as the result of my ongoing experience, of my interactions with the environment. Mind, then, is something more inclusive than brain, or even brain plus sense organs, though of course they are all intimately related. Mind is what connects my individual brain-plus-body to the universe, gives my actions meaning, and makes them adaptive. My "self," then, extends beyond my individual body, and my mind is my body *plus all its relationships.*

In this conceptualization of mind I am following the lead laid down twenty-five years ago by Gregory Bateson in his (then) revolutionary book of essays, *Steps to an Ecology of Mind*.[5] Even today, only a handful of scholars concern themselves with the contextual, ecological nature of our thoughts and actions. Yet I believe it to be critical for understanding "Who We Are," as thinking beings interacting with the universe. Because the distinction I am making is such a big gestalt shift in trying to imagine ourselves not as self-created and self-directed entities but as intimately engaged with and formed by our surroundings, one of Bateson's examples will surely prove helpful. He asks us to consider a blind man with a stick:

> Suppose I am a blind man, and I use a stick. I go tap, tap, tap. Where do *I* start? Is my mental system bounded at the handle of the stick? Is it bounded by my skin? Does it start halfway up the stick? Does it start at the tip of the stick? But these are nonsense questions. The stick is a pathway along which transforms of differences are being transmitted. The way to delineate the system is to draw the limiting line in such a way that you do not cut any of these pathways in ways which leave things inexplicable.[6]

Just like the vibrations of the blind man's stick reaching his fingers, the energy from my surroundings that impinges upon my body – eyes, ears, nose, skin – becomes a *part* of my self, of my mind, at each instantaneous moment. The perceived environment, or at least those aspects of my surroundings to which I attend, becomes integral with myself.

This is the notion of mind that I want to develop in this chapter. It will be difficult to maintain, owing to my own (as well as the reader's) mental conditioning about what the mind is, and there will be many lapses because I do not yet have all the necessary insights to write easily in such a new way. Yet I hope to convince you that the human self is utterly and integrally connected to and part of both the social and natural worlds around the individual person, worlds that we now conceive as lying outside the edges of ourselves.

### An ecological theory of mind

Much of the research on human cognition, both learning and recall, has been conducted under controlled laboratory conditions. The subjects under study are exposed for short periods of time to an array of stimuli to which they either make a physical (point a finger or push a button) or verbal response; sometimes they are wired with electrodes to measure skin conductance (which increases when we are anxious), or their brains are scanned for signs of local activity. But the settings in which learning takes place are essentially passive (all too reminiscent of life in most of America's classrooms). Such experiments virtually ignore any sort of feelings, of spontaneous motivation or active discovery by the subjects. They are about as inappropriate as it is possible to be for understanding how the human mind functions in the everyday world.

A much needed alternative approach was suggested years ago by America's great social philosopher John Dewey,[7] and later developed by the unconventional perceptual psychologist, James J. Gibson, who put Bateson's metaphor of the blind man's stick into practice in his research and thinking. Gibson developed a theory of *active learning*. The survival of sentient beings (including but not limited to humans) depends, he argued, on their actively exploring their environments by moving through them: moving their eyes, their heads, and their entire bodies. Their task is to learn to navigate in the world, and to do this they inquisitively seek information. (This, of course, is one of the major human propensities stressed in this book – our strong urge to act autonomously, to strive and explore.) Guided by instincts or propensities, as the case might be, and equipped with the accompanying appropriate emotional signals of attraction or repulsion (which are very much fine-tuned by learning), animals *actively* discover the location and nature of significant aspects of their surroundings. The latter Gibson labeled "affordances" – those parts of the whole environment important to the survival of that particular species. The sum of its affordances is synonymous with its ecological niche.

A concrete example or two will help explain what I mean. Take the task of learning to walk from home to school. As we rehearse it (with our mother or older sibling) we learn several turnings and other significant landmarks. "When you get to the bottom of the hill from the house, turn left, past the grocery store. Turn right at the stop sign, and follow the creek until you come to the footbridge. On the far side, over a little rise, you will see the schoolyard."

This is the typical map we use to tell someone how to get from A to B. But it needs no details of distances, or intermediate description, just the critical (i.e. *meaningful*) transition points.[8] (As an example of how little of the detail one may actually store, I discovered with some surprise that, after walking a mile and a half along twisting streets from home to university for several years in the city of Bristol, England, I was quite unable to recognize the name of one of those streets when a stranger asked if I knew where it was. Only the next time I walked home did I consciously notice the street name for that short segment of my journey.)

Likewise, when asked to recall the house where you grew up, you have suddenly dozens of images. Some from the front, the sides, the backyard, others, inside, in this or that room, facing this or that way. The house, however, is not remembered as a map. Even though you know the relations of the rooms, your mental image does not resemble a builder's blueprints. Rather, the house is a mental whole that you assume to be there, built up from many images. As Gibson put it:

> When the vistas have been put in order by exploratory locomotion, the
> invariant structure of the house, the town, or the whole habitat will be

apprehended. The hidden and the unhidden become one environment.... One is oriented to the environment. It is not so much having a bird's-eye view of the terrain as it is being everywhere [in it] at once.[9]

What is interesting about these two commonplace examples is that both are acquired by actively exploring – moving through the environment – and neither requires a graphic map to be recalled. We do not need to be able to read, or write, or even draw, in order to establish useful mental images. We do not even need language to learn these ways of navigating in our environment, though it comes in handy if we want to tell someone else about these places when we are far away from them.

### Events, episodes, and narratives

We are so used to thinking of learning as the acquisition of isolated facts, of disconnected, memorized bits of information, that we fail to appreciate that what we need in order to survive is familiarity with whole happenings, whole episodes, and with what they *mean*. Experiences are not instantaneous snapshots, they are temporal events that have patterns which flow through time and space. Each episode has significant *sequential* aspects, marked by memorable, emotion-laden signals: surprises, rewards, warnings, and so on. These might be called "attention-getters" that stimulate our interest and cause us to remember.

Learning through experience is thus the storing of a sequential pattern that forms an episodic story. It is the only form of learning that animals have (except when being studied by scientists in laboratories, who stimulate them with some isolated signal, and then reward or punish them); and it was the primary kind of learning available to our ancestors prior to symbolic communication. They, like modern chimpanzees, learned patterns through simple repetition of similar events. From these, they learned the *meaning* of certain signals or sequences. When a juvenile male chimpanzee sees a charismatic adult raise the fur on his neck and shoulders, pound his chest and hoot, he knows from past experience of similar episodes that a charge display is likely. Though such episodes do not repeat exactly, if enough signal elements are present, the meaning becomes fairly clear and the outcome fairly predictable.

For the highly social primates, much of what has to be learned about survival is grounded in social relationships, the multiple episodes that occur among various individuals in the course of a day. Since the contexts of these interactions are never identical, much more complex learning processes are needed. Unlike learning a path through the forest, which appears much the same on each occasion, social episodes are constantly varying. The individual needs to learn and sort out the key signals present during each event, and interpret their meaning as the situation unfolds. There is no way that simple stimulus–response behavior could possibly work here. One must have the ability to draw upon many past episodes, more or less similar to the present one, but never identical, in order to guess how one should react.

In the case of the juvenile chimpanzee and the big male, the youngster must assess who else is present, what has just happened, who is the likely target of the coming charge, and whether the big guy is really serious or just bluffing. In other words, on this particular occasion, a whole lot of pieces of past episodes must be drawn upon *as it is unfolding* in order to decide the best thing to do.

This is where the big brain comes in. In the last chapter we noted that information about a single object, such as a "yellow pencil," seems to be stored as diffuse bits in the brain, and is reconstructed when we consciously need to retrieve it. This same process – parallel distributed processing, or PDP – has been suggested as an explanation for how the various bits of information from a cluster of similar but not identical episodes are stored and later drawn upon. In the midst of such an unfolding event, none of the old narratives is being re-enacted exactly; a new one is taking place. As it proceeds, different signals from prior episodes, and their contents, are being retrieved, giving rise to new meanings of the unfolding event.

This theory is by no means agreed upon as an explanation for the complex blending of multiple past episodes to make a new, similar yet unique situation comprehensible.[10] However, though the details of how the brain manages to organize the distinctive details of similar episodic events into clusters of patterns is not clear, what is evident from the research itself is that we recognize *categories* of events. Known as "schemas," they are generalized, though not at all rigid, patterns that typify a set of similar events.[11] "A walk in the woods" generates a schema, as do the phrases "the smell of dinner cooking" and "trick-or-treat." Obviously, the ability to form schemas was essential for the emergence of symbolic communication, where one symbol stands for a general category of object or event.

Before considering the emergence of human language, however, I should note that it is likely that our primate cousins are able to generate schemas of a sort, giving them their high level of social knowledge. What they are not able to do is to explain to one another what is significant, how they each internally interpret a given situation. It is certain that among our ancestors, the internal processing potential, the ability to form schemas, had to be present before the ability to communicate about those schemas could evolve. What were the likely steps?

## From displays to speeches

If we grant that modern apes have the mental capacity to categorize events as to their meanings (or affordances, to use Gibson's term), this would explain their obvious ability to recognize one another individually, to comprehend social relationships, and to remember past encounters, or episodes. This is a much more difficult task than simply learning where the nearest fig tree is located. What apes cannot do very well is communicate their feelings, especially *why* they are feeling as they do. Nor can they explain to each other the knowledge they individually possess about each other and the environment. They do learn much by watching and imitating, by following others, and they learn much socially by testing each other: attempting grooming, or threatening a display, for example. In brief, they have schemas of their own, and surely must contemplate them at some level; but they cannot explain them to each other.[12]

The intelligence of our ape cousins and of our earliest hominid ancestors was essentially an individual intelligence that could not easily be accumulated from one generation to the next. Though there are some minor cultural differences between separated populations of wild chimpanzees, such as one group that uses stones to crack open coula nuts and passes this skill on to the next generation, a skill other groups lack.[13] Chimpanzee cultures are based mainly on individually learned skills acquired by imitating others' discoveries. There is little opportunity for developing coordinated group action that would increase the group's survival chances. As evolutionist H.C. Plotkin has put it:

> The chimpanzee has therefore evolved modules of knowledge gain that extend to the third (learned) level ... but the changes ... are specific to hand use.[14]

In other words, chimpanzees can transmit observable, physical skills, but not abstract ones.

What happened among the hominids was the gradual process of building *group intelligence*, where the information within the entire group is greater than that of any single member. At this point, selection begins to shift in a major way from intelligent individuals to intelligent groups. Selection is no longer for genetically smart individuals, capable of learning, but for culturally knowledgeable groups: communities of individuals able to pool their knowledge and interact successfully *as groups*.[15] This requires being able to share schemas, or categories of experience with each other: in short, to communicate abstract ideas.

According to psychologist Merlin Donald, this probably occurred in two distinct steps: the stage of miming to communicate ideas, and the stage of speech.[16] It is likely that miming accompanied increases in schema formation and categorical detail as brains evolved during the Pleistocene, especially among *Homo erectus*, and that these in turn made the later emergence of spoken symbols for these categories possible. (By categorical detail I mean the grouping of many similar objects or events into one mimed or spoken symbol: for instance, in mime, "bird" might be expressed by waving the forearms in the semblance of flight.)

## *The languages of mime and song*

Many years ago in Union Square, San Francisco, I observed a whole crowd that was spellbound as a famous French mime communicated the following story without aid of speech or props. A sleeping man wakes, stretches, starts to move about, only to discover he is restrained by invisible walls and ceiling. He is first surprised at being enclosed, then grows frantic as he seeks a way out; finding none, he ultimately collapses in total despair. Through movement and expression alone, this artist could move his cross-cultural audience through discovery, terror, and hopelessness because they shared the same *symbolic referents* or preconceived concepts. The primary referent was the virtually universal concept of a "building," but shared knowledge of "transparent glass" helped make the story more realistic as told.

Of course, in this example, both performer and audience were modern human beings with brains full of schemas, or as linguist George Lakoff calls them, *idealized cognitive models*.[17] Though our *Homo erectus* ancestors did not possess quite such capacious brains, they had most of the physical abilities the French mime used to communicate: facial expressiveness, body comportment, gestures and movements of all sorts. We too often forget these communicative tools in our focussed absorption with spoken and written language. It is likely that cognitive perception, schema formation, and signaling skills evolved together, *and always depended upon universal cultural familiarity with the symbolic referents*.

It is hard to overemphasize how critical to our present human nature this point is. The ability to think in concepts depends on capacities in the brain, but also on social interaction. The brain is not genetically programmed to make specific schemas or categories; rather these come to it from the outside, from social interaction as well as individual experience. We quite literally learn to think by being members of a "thinking community." Our ability to think in typical human ways – to imagine, to create, to plan – cannot form without our having been exposed to a set of schemas, of abstract categories, while growing up. The possibility of complex mental life only exists in the presence of a *cultural continuum*, where whole narratives embodying all of the schemas and categories and their meanings form a framework for thinking that is passed along from generation to generation. The brain and body of each one of us are thus shaped into a "mind-connected-into-the-social-environment," the culture, in which one is reared. The attachments one feels for one's own society are tremendously powerful, and make perfect sense from an evolutionary point of view. (I will return to this point several more times in later chapters.)

One can now begin to imagine our Pleistocene ancestors communicating through mime and also perhaps with imitative sounds that mimicked animals with certain traits: "roaring" like a lion to signify fierceness, or "barking" like a hyena as a warning. In such ways, both feelings and information might be conveyed. Grunts, whines, laughs, and other affect-signaling sounds might well have been adopted and come to acquire symbolic meanings such as "OK," or

"No," or "Please." Similarly, facial expression, already present in apes, was surely developing rapidly: smiles, pouts, eyebrow movements, staring, lip-smacking, and so on (try them in the mirror). Mostly conveying inner emotional states, they could also have been used to give encouragement, to raise doubt, or to invite attention. (Modern films are full of facial expressions, and often sparse on dialogue, unlike both theater and radio, where facial expressions are less or not at all visible.)

It is likely that the extensive human facial muscles necessary to communicate expressions evolved early on. Apes are capable of some facial grimaces, but modern humans possess a far bigger repertoire that is understood cross-cultur-ally around the globe.[18] In addition to variously nuanced smiles, frowns, and pouts, there are more subtle signals, such as constricted pupils (negative affect) or dilated (positive affect), by which we involuntarily communicate our internal states (blushing is another example). Moreover, the voluntary facial expressions, such as smiles, pouts, and surprise, are mimicked by infants only a few weeks old. Clearly, in modern humans, non-linguistic facial signals are complex and readily learned, and many surely were present in *Homo erectus* also. Such signals quickly come to have symbolic meaning. The pouting face of a child being weaned conveys unhappiness to the mother, who then compensates with extra physical attention. As adults, we use the same look to elicit acquiescence to our wishes from others. Surely, early "conversations" were of this sort, dialogues based on spontaneous exchange of affect signals that were being used in ever-more symbolic ways.

Likewise, other facial signals become metaphors for more general situations. Sweet tastes elicit smile/lick/suck movements; sour ones result in lips pushed forward, wrinkled nose and closed eyes. And bitter tastes cause the corners of the mouth to lower, eyes to close, and tongue to extend, as we reject the item. As Irenäus Eibl-Eibesfeldt, the well-known human ethologist, observes, these occur in all societies as well as among the deaf and blind, and make excellent symbolic referents of approval and rejection in a whole host of social situations. This situation is "sweet" (we lick our lips), and that one is "sour" (we screw up our faces). And how many times as kids didn't we stick out our tongues, eyes closed, in strong rejection of someone else, as if ridding ourselves of a bitter-tasting substance?

We also use body motions and attitudes as referent symbols in more abstract social ways. The message, "I am really displeased with you," might be expressed either by the bitterness rejection or, with a more dominant approach, by hunching the shoulders upward, with hands on hips, making us look as big and ferocious as possible. (The same effect is achieved by epaulets on military offi-cers' uniforms and by shoulder pads in men's and women's clothes!)[19]

Such symbolic forms of communication were surely part of *Homo erectus* culture, probably becoming ever more abstractly applied during the 1.5 million years of its existence. Of course, different local populations (cultures) might have co-opted the original facial and body signals to stand for somewhat different metaphoric derivatives, but because the referents were so obvious to *all* members of the species in their general meanings, slightly different symbolic uses might still have been cross-culturally understood or quickly learned.

But mime alone could not have led to the emergence of speech. Prior to that event, conscious control of breathing was necessary, and the voice box had to evolve enough to create the necessary sounds, or linguistic phonemes. Not only did the brain need to be able to process abstract symbols, but the muscles of voice box, mouth, and tongue had to be coordinated, and their anatomy adapted for the generation of complex sounds. Grammatical language did not simply burst forth, replete with parts of speech, full inflections, tenses, voices, moods and all the rest. Thought had to precede words; and anatomy had to precede language.

One of the first prerequisites of speech is the ability to interrupt inhalations, and especially exhalations, in the course of emitting sounds. Among the sounds most meaningful to chimpanzees is their "laughter." I use quotes, because the panting "ha-ha-ha" sounds of chimpanzees are made as a sequence of brief exhale–inhale–exhale breaths. (Students hearing such recordings for the first time said they sounded like a dog rapidly panting, or someone having acute breathing problems.[20]) As psychologist and neuroscientist Robert Provine explains in his book *Laughter*, our ape cousins do not have the ability to interrupt a flow of air. Furthermore, he argues, this capacity is limited to bipedal animals and to diving mammals. In most animals, breathing is coordinated with locomotory movements: the chest moves in and out in time with their strides. Quadrupedal locomotion causes pressure on the thorax which inevitably links the two movements. Provine believes "bipedalism was necessary for the evolution of speech" through control over the rates of breathing, a control arrived at in a parallel fashion by bipedal birds and diving mammals.[21] All these species are capable of intentionally interrupting breathing *and* of changing the pitch of sounds emitted during a single exhalation. (For diving mammals, locomotion does not compress the thorax as it does for land animals, and they also are capable of controlling their breathing during long dives, allowing slow, continuous exhalations for sound emission.) The interruption of exhalation was a trait that made possible, in humans, first laughter, then song and speech.

Before turning to the development of song and speech, I should say a bit more about the role of laughter in primate, and particularly human, socialization. As Provine notes, among both chimpanzees and humans the tickling of sensitive (vulnerable) places by someone else elicits laughter. "Physical contact or threat of such contact is a common denominator of chimp laughter," says Provine.[22] In particular, it is part of the mother–infant relationship; a baby seeks attention by biting the mother, who tickles it back. In humans, it is more often the mother or other adult who initiates the tickling, and the baby who breaks into smiles and usually outright laughter. The excitement of physical touch and the role of laughter when engaging in it are central to the cementing of social bonds. (Too much tickling, of course, is annoying, even dangerous. Thus, regulating it is part of the social learning process by both participants.[23]) We see play dependent on touch not only among young children (games of tag, for instance), but even among adult humans. Nevertheless, laughter is present.

Provine further observes the contagiousness of laughter in groups of humans. Not only does it cement mother– (or adult–)infant bonds; it also cements relations in groups, and synchronizes a group's mood.[24] Indeed, laughter has a great many social uses (such as derisive laughter, a form of shaming; embarrassed laughter, when we feel insecure; forgiving laughter, after an unintended error, etc.). It was surely present in our preverbal ancestors.

It was Charles Darwin who first suggested that *prosody*, the ability to control volume, pitch, tone of voice and emphasis of the sounds we emit, must have been the initial step toward spoken language. As Merlin Donald observes, prosody is "logically more fundamental than, and prior to, phonetic control; it is much closer to the capabilities of apes than [is] phonology."[25] The ability to regulate the pitch or frequency of a sound is of course fundamental to song, as is rhythm. Some sort of rudimentary, poetry-like "song-making" may well have been the first way that invented sounds were used to convey meaning – reminiscent of chanting, where sounds are iterated over and over. Perhaps this was accompanied by drumming, on the body or on hollow objects.

Evolutionarily, human music is very old, probably preceding spoken language. The oldest instruments so far discovered are bone flutes made by Neanderthals, the oldest dating to 53,000 ya. But a group of scientists has said "it is quite possible humans have been making music for several hundred thousand years."[26] Music has several adaptive functions. One is its effect on emotions. Various combinations of notes, rhythms, and tempos communicate specific moods in those who hear them. An individual's brain waves become synchronized into a particular pattern, according to the nature of the music being heard. From the serenity of lullabies to the aggressiveness of martial music, to the coordinating rhythms of work songs such as sea shanties, music serves to establish a particular shared affect throughout an entire group. Words are not necessary for this. Even today, the Sami people of northern Scandinavia sing "yoiks," songs with nonsense syllables that, nevertheless, convey episodic information about a person, or a place, or some aspect of nature.[27] This resembles Gaelic mouth-music (nonsense syllable songs) taught by Scottish folk-singers to school children in the inner cities in the twentieth century.[28]

By coordinating group moods, music must have become a major contributor to other significant cultural activities, such as the earliest religious ceremonies, rites of passage for adolescents, occasions of grieving, and celebrations of the seasons. None of these required words, only the episodic meaning captured in the musical sounds themselves. Furthermore, the spontaneous motor responses humans make to rhythmic sounds, which are apparent in the first years of life (how often have we not been entertained by a toddler spontaneously moving in time to the local band at a picnic) suggests that group dancing accompanied the communal singing of shared songs. Add the sounds of drums (surely very ancient) and the stage is set for acting out episodes in a culture's history. By miming the actions and mimicking the sounds of people, animals, the wind, thunder, running water and other elements, stories could be told, over and over, without any words at all.

This capacity for music fortuitously had another adaptive advantage, which is also correlated with group survival, namely its ability to stimulate associated memories. A piece of music, even one without any words at all, can sometimes recall vividly the time and place when it was heard before, especially if it was a highly significant occasion. We remember with great nostalgia the favorite lullaby our mother sang when we were small, or the stirring notes of *Pomp and Circumstance* when we marched at our high-school graduation. Like smells, music can remind us of people and places that matter to us. The music of one's own culture, of one's own generation, causes a welling up of memories often full of emotions. In this respect, music, even more than the language that came after it, has helped to preserve and transmit cultural knowledge over thousands of years. In fact, before writing, music and rhymed verse were the means for preserving oral history over many, many generations. Both music and rhyme are powerful aids to memory. Even today, if you want to remember something, set it to music.

One stunning example of the adaptive function of musical memory comes to us from the Aborigines of Australia. Even today, they still know the *Songlines*, the long mythic narratives their legendary ancestors sang when they first created the terrain of the continent, by which a traveler can even today find his or her way from one sacred landmark to the next.

> The Aboriginals ... were a people who trod lightly over the earth.[...]
> [E]ach totemic ancestor, while traveling through the country, was thought to have scattered a trail of words and musical notes along the line of his footprints.... "A song...was both map and direction-finder. Providing you knew the song, you could always find your way across country".[29]

Thus wrote the inveterate observer of nomadic peoples, Bruce Chatwin, about the original Australians. The sagas told by the Celtic peoples of Wales and Ireland, and the Vikings of Iceland, some of which took days to recite completely, were likewise set to music. We can imagine that Homer's epic poems were meant to be sung, as well. (It is no accident that modern advertisers create catchy "jingles" to ensure that you and I will remember their product.)

Finally, I would note that memory for music and the ability to appreciate it are far less affected, if at all, in many patients with Alzheimer's disease, whose ability to use ordinary language is defective or, in my own mother's case toward the last, completely absent. It was a great shock to me to visit her a few months before she died, when, not knowing what else to do, I took her hand and began singing old hymns and Girl Scout songs she had taught us, keeping time with her to the music. Though she had shown no sign of knowing me, or of understanding anything that was said to her for several years, that day she gently cried; something was still there that "remembered." Apparently, the ability to remember and respond to music is much more widely spread through both hemispheres of the brain, with the hearing and feeling aspects quite separately placed. Only some aspects (perfect pitch, for example) overlap with spoken speech and the recognition of "phonemes," or speech sounds.[30]

Another aspect of communication prior to the emergence of speech that is almost always overlooked in most histories of human cognitive evolution is art, which surely complemented music and mime. Here I am not referring to the elaborate cave paintings, some of them known to be at least 30,000 years old (about which we shall say more later), but to the likelihood that art in the form of body-painting and other sorts of self-decoration was present much earlier. There is at least one record, dated at 300,000 ya, of pieces of yellow, red, brown and purple ochre at a site in southern France, along with well-crafted wooden bowls and stone tools.[31] One senses that a mind able to chant musical sounds and mime significant information must surely have had an early aesthetic sense as well. The "making special" of important places and of one's own or others' bodies is a likely undertaking, even among *Homo erectus*. It would be a natural part of the emotional guidance system that was being selected for.

An appreciation of the human propensity for "making special" – for "making meaningful" – significant aspects of cultural life has been marvelously developed by Ellen Dissanayake, philosopher and theorist of the role of art in human evolution. She sees the esthetic sense of human nature as being profoundly important in the survival of our hominid ancestors: "*a core behavioral tendency on which natural selection could act ...* [one] that could have been possessed by protohumans, the early hominids who existed one to four million years ago." Long before spoken language, art could give form to feelings, allowing them to be shared and made significant. "[T]he arts ... are containers for, molders of feeling." If, as suggested in the previous chapter, feelings made consciousness possible, then the arts, far from being frivolous entertainments for the well-to-do, as modern society treats them, were, and still are, absolutely basic and necessary to our natures.[32]

Even though primordial mime, prosody and art have left few physical signs of their existence during the time of *Homo erectus*, I think it is reasonable to construct an imaginary tale (otherwise known as an hypothesis) about how these various forms of communication were evolving and creating a sense of shared meaning that was an essential, strongly selected foundation for the final emergence of language. Together with mime and vocalizations in imitation of natural sounds, the adornment of the human body with paints, feathers, shells, and other natural objects further enhanced the significance of what was being communicated. By "making special" in dramatic ways the self-in-the-world, people in groups could symbolically express and come to share abstract values and beliefs about things important to their common survival. Art and music, mime and dance, thus became the earliest means of establishing extended communal consciousness. We can imagine that when diffusely spread Pleistocene peoples came together in gatherings (similar to the "carnivals" described among modern chimpanzees by Margaret Power[33]), they were able to renew bonds with those in scattered neighboring groups and keep the larger community "in touch." And these gatherings, as with both bonobos and chimpanzees, would be occasions of enormous social activity. Only, the early humans would have added primitive music, dance and sharing of food to the celebrations, no doubt decorating themselves for the occasion much as chimpanzee males use tree branches to enhance their charging displays. What Megan Biesele has written about the significance of group trance dances of the recent San peoples in southern Africa I suspect applies also to the celebrations of more ancient beings:

> [P]eople become a unit acting together for mutual benefit, undivided by words. The dance thus embodies the values of egalitarianism and tolerance, and reinforces the idea of mutual effort against misfortune.[34]

While Pleistocene humans would not have had words for egalitarianism and tolerance, neither do the modern San, who live in southern Africa; but they do have institutions that promote these outcomes.[35] One does not need spoken words to share a feeling of needing one another, of enjoying the company of others, of rejoicing in a coming together. Once again, I reiterate that emotional propensities had to be in place long before our conscious awareness of them, and certainly before those feelings were given symbolic names.

Finally, before leaving our ancient friends, we should note a feature of their universe that was to disappear when groups of *Homo sapiens* began to construct symbolic languages through which they interpreted the world and communicated about it to each other. I refer to the fact that there could not have been large differences in cultural identities in the mimetic world of *Homo erectus*, or even the earliest *Homo sapiens*, and hence no reason for warfare with strangers whose symbolic communications in fact differed little from one's own. Given the low population density and the obvious mobility of our *Homo erectus* and early *Homo sapiens* ancestors, it seems more likely that old-fashioned dispersion was the commonest answer to frictions within groups – the familiar fission/fusion pattern of other primates. It would have been relatively easy for individuals or small groups to break away and later join up with another group, which would naturally find them compatible as long as the still-universal friendly approaches were maintained. (Recall the ready acceptance of a new member within a baboon troop when he moved in slowly enough so that the others habituated to him and he was able to make friends appropriately.)

I turn now to symbolic language, when the Tower of Babel was erected.

## The floodgates of speech

Body language, mime, and melodic utterances have only a limited capacity to communicate complex ideas, as anyone who has played charades knows. (And charade players often use linguistic knowledge in their silent communications, such as symbolic signs for spoken syllables.) When our ancestors acquired the ability to make a string of abstract sounds stand for a complex sequence of events, the necessary thought processes were already in place. According to George Mandler, two areas on the surface of the left hemisphere necessary for modern speech have been detected in cranial endocasts of our most ancient ancestors: Broca's area, necessary for the fine motor control needed in speech, seems to have been developing among Australopithecines, and Wernicke's area, which deals with the symbolic aspects of language, shows up in *Homo habilis*.[36] It was the anatomy of the larynx, or voice box, that may have been the last piece of equipment to evolve.

Speech, the assembling of words to recount events, obviously facilitated communication of daily events and thus the spread of general knowledge. It also made planning cooperative undertakings far easier. These are the immediate, practical results for group survival, the "efficient" consequences of speech that evolutionists (who often think much like economists) assume were being selected for. But speech has had more far-reaching impacts on the social life of human beings, impacts which have had enormous consequences during our long history. I refer to the gradual expansion of human thought through the construction of abstract concepts: the use of *simile* and *metaphor* to expand the meanings of symbols from a concrete world of direct personal experience to a world of invented ideas, of things that never could be experienced directly. Language has allowed the building up of mental conceptualizations of the most extraordinary sorts.

Shortly I shall examine how language gave rise to distinctly different cultures and explore a couple of significant examples of how these cultures can create quite different, yet entirely functional, mental pictures of the universe. But first a few words are needed about the evolution of the structure of language, keeping in mind that a unique cultural history underlies the structure of each particular language.

## Categories, metaphor, and meaning

Because modern linguists who develop theories about the origin and structure of language grew up in literate societies, possessing dictionaries that explain the meaning of words and give their pronunciations, and most had to parse sentences and identify the tasks of words in a sentence (the parts of speech), it was natural to theorize, as Noam Chomsky has, that all grammars are basically similar and that children are born with an instinct for thinking in this "universal grammar." All they need is to learn the symbols appropriate to their native language in order to communicate. It is the "pieces" of language, the sounds or *phonemes*, and the words, or *symbols*, that make languages different, not the patterns of meaning behind those symbols.[37]

But other linguists, studying language acquisition by young infants, argue that cognition and the conceptualization of events come first.[38] Even before they understand speech, children make sense of what people are doing and how it relates to them. They also communicate this knowledge nonverbally. Only later do they learn what others are saying about those actions, and finally they themselves begin to talk. And when they do begin, they may even start with short sentences. "Don't do that!" were the first words of my great nephew at age 2. In this respect, developing infants resemble our ancestors in being able to form thoughts prior to being able to speak. The idea exists *prior* to the words.

In fact, we apparently do not need words in order to think, even about abstract concepts such as "heaven," or "national government," or "time." Besides the babies already mentioned, who clearly can think about some things before they know the words for them, there are the instances of persons deprived of the use of language. Merlin Donald recounts the case of Brother John, a priest who suffered moderate epileptic seizures during which he lost the ability to speak, read, write, or understand spoken words, yet remained conscious. Once, on a journey, he had a seizure on the way to a hotel. With sign language, he managed to get a room. At dinner he pointed randomly at the menu and got something he disliked, but ate it anyway. After a good night's sleep he recovered, and went to the desk to explain what happened. The point is, Brother John knew all that he needed to do in the situations he was in *without any access to language*. Donald also points out that prior to modern sign language and special reading classes, most deaf-mutes lived out their lives using only mime, but they were certainly capable of thought. Recently in Nicaragua children in a deaf-mute school have spontaneously evolved their own sign language, without any adult input![39] As long as we experience directly some sort of human society, we can learn to think, at least in concrete terms, without spoken language. But without special assistance, we would be unable to conceptualize more sophisticated abstract ideas. For that we need exchangeable symbols, and analogous situations – better known as words and metaphors, respectively.

## Categories

Returning again to early cultures and the evolution of language, the first thing one notes about symbols, or words, is that one word covers a whole lot of objects. "Bird," for example, is not a particular sort of bird, but everything from a baby chick, to an ostrich, to a robin, to a condor – to the extinct dodo. They have some things in common, but not everything. When native peoples first see an airplane they often call it "big bird." It has no beak or feathers, but it does have wings and tail, and it flies.

The name for almost every object, or action, or event, is like that. It refers to a general class of items, but it has fuzzy boundaries. Each language has different primary examples or *prototypes* in mind as the most common representatives for each word. Children in America and Britain learn the meaning of the English word "bird" mostly from the pictures of robins and chickens in their first books. (Interestingly, American and English "robins" are quite different species; they just have similar red breasts and are very common.) My guess would be that the ubiquitous and noisy parakeet is a prototype for "bird" in the languages of children living in rural India. Already we see that categories described by certain symbolic names will vary from language to language in the images they most frequently elicit in people's minds.

Thus categories, or generalized terms, do not directly reference a universal reality; rather they reference a contextualized, culture-based meaning of what the category stands for, and that meaning is captured by a reference prototype (or prototypes) that most people think of first. As linguist George Lakoff emphasizes in his description of how languages come into being, the concepts that the word-symbols stand for embody the preconceptions about the universe that a culture already has. And those symbols, in turn, reinforce the groundedness of the whole cultural way-of-seeing, the common world view. *Language embodies a culture's framework of reality. Culture precedes categories, it precedes language.* The whole unified world view creates the semantic content of a language.[40]

These contrasting theories of the nature of language are profoundly different. As Lakoff explains it, Chomsky and other "mainstream" linguists, having divided the human mind into disciplinary compartments (in accordance with the standard Western Billiard Ball framework), implicitly assume that language and grammar are "a separate 'modular' system, *independent* of the rest of cognition," and "that categories are classical (and hence can be characterized by [universal] distinctive features)."[41] From this view, language is a mechanism, to be understood by mathematical examination of its parts: phonemes, words, and syntax. "Meaning" already exists in external reality; language is merely the tool for transferring information about that reality from the head of one individual to the next.

By contrast, the Indra's Net Gestalt, which Lakoff's model fits better with, sees meaning as coming from everywhere: from reality, from the interpreted past and present experiences of individuals, and from the developing language they share. All three are interacting. Thus, language both constructs and reflects the interpreted reality that is held in common. Ideas and meanings are embedded in the very symbols and syntax (see Figure V.1). This second view, I believe, helps explain the extreme emotional attachments members of ethnic groups have for their native tongue, and the cultural destructiveness that is wrought when oppressors forbid them from speaking it. (I return to this point in a later chapter.) It also helps explain how different cultures build different abstract ways of thinking by the metaphoric extrapolation of concrete experience, to which I now turn.

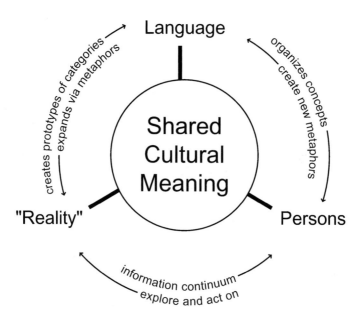

*Figure V.1* The reciprocal interactions that generate meaning systems

Cultural meaning is generated from the three-way reciprocal interactions among the experienced external world, or "reality," the persons who are members of the society, and the language the people use to make sense of and communicate about their experiences. The whole meaning system undergoes constant flux; it evolves, as patterns of understanding shift along the directions of the arrows.

Note that "reality" includes not only the original natural environment, but also the physical and abstract "constructed" environments that people create over time. (In the modern world, roads, taxes, and the United Nations are part of "reality.")

*Source*: Original art by Michelle Lukowski, after author's sketch

## Metaphor

Once a proto-language acquired a number of words and phrases that stand for categories of common concrete ideas, such as "seek water," "give food," "hold baby," and so forth, we may suppose that the already present capacity for thought began to discover analogies between combinations of symbols and new, as yet unverbalized, concepts. This, according to numerous linguists (and especially George Lakoff and his collaborator Mark Johnson), led to the gradual construction of metaphoric meanings about more complex concepts which could not be expressed easily before. A possible example from the above phrases might be to invent from the symbols "food" and "hold" a symbol "foodhold" that meant any sort of container. And from there, the term might have become used for any bounded collecting place, such as a corral, or a meeting place.

This metaphoric development of words can be seen, for instance, in the evolution of the English word "window," which comes from Old Norse, *vindauga*, or "eye-of-the-wind," the name for the hole in the roof through which the rising smoke (visible "wind") escapes – already a metaphor in Old Norse! Today, window stands not only for openings for light and air in the walls of buildings, but for other more abstract kinds of openings – a "window of opportunity," "window upon the world" or a "window into his mind," and most recently, "windows" as access sites in a computer program.

Linguists George Lakoff and Mark Johnson provide a whole host of metaphors in modern English. Almost all are derived from recognizable physical referents. A few examples will make the point.

*any process gone awry may be said to be:*

> a bumpy road (auto)
> off the tracks (train)
> on the rocks (boat)

*names for parts of the human body may be used for other objects:*

> foot and shoulder of mountain
> head and heart of cabbage
> leg and foot of table

*spatial relations may shift from physical to abstract:*

Harry is –
> *in* the kitchen (place)
> *in* the Elks (social situation)
> *in* love (emotional state)

A particularly informative example produced by Lakoff and Johnson are the multiple metaphors around the word "argument."

ARGUMENT AS WAR  win, lose, strategy, attack, defend
ARGUMENT AS JOURNEY  proceed smoothly, hit a snag, be on the right path
ARGUMENT AS CONTAINER  holds water, is full of holes
ARGUMENT AS BUILDING  constructed carefully, easily torn down.[42]

Their point is that we create, through the accumulation of metaphor upon metaphor, a means for discussing concepts that, in themselves, have no immediate physical referents, but are given such referents through analogy with more concrete, sensible events. In this way, language permits each culture to create verbal expressions for abstract mental images that could not have been expressed through mime or other physically grounded means of communicating. Through metaphoric transformations into more and more abstract symbolic constructs, human beings became able to mutually create and share ever more complex and abstract concepts. (How might you do a charade of "window of opportunity"?)

This is where the Tower of Babel comes into effect. Each ethnic or linguistic group historically has built up its own metaphoric conceptualization of the world, its own myths, its own sophisticated understandings about what life is for and how people should live, none of which have direct referents in physical experience. Thus, as a language matures, its idioms and metaphors, and the world view that these are creating, grow increasingly incomprehensible to those speaking other languages. More and more abstract concepts also become increasingly value-laden, carrying sacred explanations and moral understandings that are culturally and historically derived. Thus, it is relatively easy to translate from one language to another ideas that are closely associated with their physical referents: "The boy went home," "This is a big and ancient city." But when one moves into discussions of feelings or philosophies, the idioms and metaphors become increasingly value-laden, filled with historical meanings that are incomprehensible in another culture, and are not readily translatable.

An excellent example of this problem comes from Ted Warren, a classical philosopher and colleague of mine. He relates how certain key terms in ancient Greek regularly were misleadingly translated and interpreted by modern historians. In his teaching, he found he had to "create another model of the world, a set of different cultural meanings" for his students. To do this, he had to become aware, himself, of how "the [Greek] language itself disclosed a different way of seeing the world, and [how] the pictures that they [the ancient Greeks] drew were significantly different than the ones a student would get from reading the histories or, for that matter, the translations. No scholar was trying to mislead; they just did not see the world through the Greeks' conceptual eyes."[43]

### Meaning

And so I come to the tangled connection between language and meaning. The late David Bohm explained that elusive term in the following way:

> According to the dictionary the word *meaning* has three definitions. One of these is significance, the second is value, and the third is purpose ... [N]othing will have high value unless it has a lot of significance ... When you say that life is meaningless, you are really saying that it has no value.[44]

Bohm goes on in this essay to argue that this kind of significant meaning is founded on meaningful relationships with other people, and these, in turn, arise out of shared understandings about the purpose of life. As I have argued in earlier chapters, cultural meaning systems and the languages in which they are couched, both of which are modified and re-created in each generation, have become essential to human survival. They are as important to the human psyche as are land, air, and water to the body. Indeed, in the past it has been the cultural narrative that imbued land, air, and water with sacred meaning. Recall the "Songlines" of the ancient Aborigines in Australia described earlier in this chapter, where the terrain is made sacred in song, and knowledge of it can thus be readily transmitted across generations.

Much argument exists among anthropologists, linguists, cognitive scientists, and evolutionary psychologists as to the different ways in which people from various cultures actually comprehend reality. How disparate are their frames of meaning? How well can anthropologists from one culture really communicate back home the mental world of a distant culture? How much alike *are* all human beings? Can all cultures be judged by the same set of measurements? If so, who sets these and decides what to measure? What is meaningful, and why?

For some, these questions can be answered by rational science, which assumes the infinitely complex components of "meaning" can be subdivided and explained functionally. These absolutists, the taxonomists of human behavior, lump actions into categories of meaning – dominant, submissive, conciliatory, competitive, cooperative, and so forth – without regard to context. Theirs is, in short, a thin description of meaning that tosses aside details of an event which are indeed explanatory "facts" and an integral part of the data. It is hard enough to design a scientifically "controlled" comparison of two fields of corn being tested for responses to different levels of fertilizer. To similarly compare the cultural impact of, say, differing levels of modernization on the stability of two premodern societies is absurd. Too many uncontrolled variables are ignored.

The thick descriptions produced by those who really do try to gain holistic insights into the meanings of "other" peoples are so complex, however, as often to seem useless to bureaucratic aid dispensers, foreign policy-makers, or global corporate heads, who are used to responding only to selected details of a situation. As Clifford Geertz puts it so well, the understanding of cultures (others or one's own) "involves discovering who they think they are, what they think they are doing, and to what end they think they are doing it ... [For this] it is necessary to gain a working familiarity with the frames of meaning within which they enact their lives."[45]

I am convinced that the shared meaning of a culture is not to be discovered simply in the structure of its language, though this may offer clues as to how it categorizes objects and events and builds its abstract conceptual metaphors. The structure of a language does provide some insight into how others frame the world and give meaning to experience. But languages – words – have major limitations, too, as philosopher Huston Smith points out. Though "they are indispensable to our humanity, for without them we would be but yowling

Yahoos," they also concretize our perceived world, thus (1) excluding others and closing us off, (2) inadequately expressing the full richness of our experience, and hence (3) leaving out all experience for which words are unavailable: music, passion, transcendent feelings and more.[46] Indeed, Mahayana Buddhism along with other meditation-based teachings seeks to empty the mind of this habit of "concreteness," of experiencing only word-based thoughts. Though antipathetic to the mindset of the Western Age of Reason, this advice makes good sense. Given the fact (noted in Chapter IV) that most of our brain is functioning outside "consciousness," perhaps the best way to get in touch with the rest of it is to banish language from our minds from time to time. Taoist thought, another Eastern philosophical school, approaches the problem of words in a slightly different way, by insisting on the complementarity of opposites and rejecting absolutist ways of thought.

Suffice it to say, any who have sojourned within another culture for a time soon learn there is a whole other way of seeing and relating, of expectations and habits, another tempo and melody and set of solutions to daily experience. If you stay long enough, some of these new qualities seep, unseen, into your own being. But, as the saying in Bambara (one of the Malian languages) goes: "No matter how long the log lies in the river, it never becomes a crocodile."[47]

And so I turn to my final task in this chapter: a look at the practical aspects of cultural world views, on the one hand, and their sacred aspects, on the other. (The differences between these are more apparent than real.)

## Culture as meaning

Culture is one of those vague words that has been applied to almost everything that has collective properties and is alive: cultures of bacteria growing in test-tubes and oysters being raised in a bay; animal "cultures"; the structure of human societies; and a high, often affected, state of esthetic appreciation: "He has 'culture'." I noted earlier that chimpanzees and other primates may develop local skills that are adopted directly by others through imitative learning, which is a kind of culture. The sort of culture that is of importance here, however, is that characteristic of all human societies, and is not to be confused with the elitist meanings of either high civilization (ancient Greek or Mayan "cultures," which are but one sort of societal culture) or people who passed through finishing school (whose "culture" is merely a snobbish part of a larger societal meaning system). An idea of what culture comprises is shown in Figure V.2. In a way, it resembles Figure V.1 in reciprocally relating the material culture (practical aspects of the environment), the social culture (persons), and the ideological culture (language and the meanings and beliefs that it conveys). Culture, then, is what ties all three components together in a workable pattern of life.

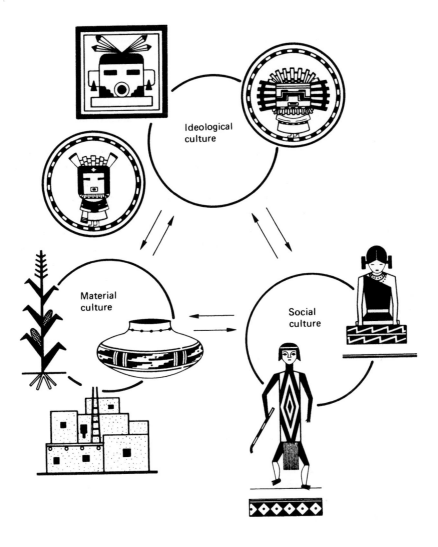

*Figure V.2* The three primary elements of culture

Material culture depends on environmentally available resources; social culture comprises kinship and political patterns; ideological culture embodies the belief system and myths. All three elements interact to create a meaningful world view.

*Source*: Basic idea from A. Pacey (1983: 6), Fig.1; Hopi motifs by Anne-Marie Malotki can be found in E. Malotki (1978), various pages. Used by kind permission of Massachusetts Institute of Technology Press and of E. Malotki, respectively

The ideological culture or meaning system is what holds everything together. It must accommodate both the limitations of the physical and social environment and the psychic needs of human nature for bonding and autonomy if it is to remain viable. It must also evolve over time, adapting to new conditions and correcting its own shortcomings. (In later chapters I present instances where meaning systems have failed – indeed are failing – to adapt adequately to changing conditions.) The enormous practical significance of shared meaning systems, of shared ways of seeing the world, of shared world views, too often goes unappreciated in Western society. (Our Billiard Ball view of the universe heavily accentuates individual autonomy and independence of beliefs and plays down the necessity of a shared meaning system to coordinate the social whole, while covertly imposing just the opposite: limited freedom of individual action in an economic system which demands conformity to a set of economic "truths" invented and imposed undemocratically by an elite group; such a structure interferes with bonding and autonomy and serious meaning.) In later chapters, some social consequences of this Western cultural shortcoming are addressed more fully. First though, we need a clearer understanding of the very practical, adaptive function that a shared meaning system has for a group's survival.

For a concrete example, I turn to the important human task of being able to move about safely on the surface of the Earth. I have already mentioned the role of the Songlines of preliterate Australian Aborigines for moving across uncharted land. I turn now to the case of navigation across open bodies of water.

### Navigation and culture

At the opening of his book, *Cognition in the Wild*, psychologist and anthropologist Edwin Hutchins describes how a naval vessel, the U.S.S. *Palau*, on entering San Diego harbor, suddenly lost power for no apparent reason. The crew had the collective task of steering the still-moving vessel to a safe spot at the edge of the narrow shipping lane without going aground, before dropping anchor. In effect, the ship itself became a single "living entity" moving in the liquid environment between stationary Point Loma on the left and North Island on the right, and the crew were its "brain," a collection of interacting "neurons." (Though Hutchins does not use these metaphors, they may help the reader picture the high degree of communication going on amongst the various crew members.)

The ship could neither accelerate nor slow. When the steam turbines went out, there was a brief period without power even for steering or communication, until the back-up generators came on. The ship nearly hit a buoy, then almost rammed a sailboat. Meantime, orders, calculations, steering directions, warnings, and information on the ship's position were flying back and forth from engine room, to bridge, to chart room, to flight deck. The crew had to use the manual rudder and sound the manual horn. Here are quotes from Hutchins's account:

On the basis of the slowing over the first 15 minutes after the casualty, it became possible to estimate when and where the *Palau* would be moving slowly enough to drop anchor. The navigator conned the ship toward the chosen spot.

Twenty-five minutes after the engineering casualty and more than 2 miles from where the wild ride had begun, the *Palau* was brought to anchor at the intended location in ample water just outside the bounds of the navigation channel.

The safe arrival of the *Palau* at anchor was due in large part to the exceptional seamanship of the bridge crew, especially the navigator. But no single individual on the bridge acting alone – neither the captain nor the navigator nor the quartermaster chief supervising the navigation team – could have kept control of the ship and brought it safely to anchor. Many kinds of thinking were required to perform this task. Some of them were happening in parallel, some in coordination with others, some inside the heads of individuals, *and some quite clearly both inside and outside the heads of the participants.*[48]

This incident is an excellent real-life example of how human cognition – or knowledge – actually functions. (Hutchins called his book *Cognition in the Wild* to distinguish his discoveries about human thinking from those obtained by experimental psychologists under artificially controlled laboratory conditions.) It reveals the *interactive nature* of the human mind that was proposed at the start of this chapter. Each member of the crew had to carry an overall picture of the process in his head, yet at any moment, no one held all the relevant information that was continuously flowing back and forth, and included the ever-changing relationship of the ship to sightings on the shore and soundings in the channel, as well as the multiple facts being passed among members of the crew. We see here the social nature, indeed the ecological nature, of "mind" as it processes an ongoing event through time. Where, exactly, *was* the mind that was making all this happen?

Socially distributed knowledge of the sort used by the crew of the U.S.S. *Palau* is critical for any human society, and the more complex the culture's institutions, the more necessary it is that all the participants share the meaning system that allows them to think together in any given setting. (Indeed, more and more corporations today are beginning to realize this, as will be discussed again in later chapters.)

A corollary to this need for a shared mental understanding of a group task is that people who come from two different cultures, with very different ways of perceiving the world, may accomplish the same task in ways incomprehensible to one another. We can borrow again from Hutchins's insights into navigation. I present only a brief glimpse of what is involved in the two instances he describes: modern Western navigation and that of Micronesians sailing between distant islands in the western Pacific. For a long time, their methods, devoid of instruments or maps, puzzled Westerners. How did they do it?

## Western navigation

Modern ship navigation is based on a physical map of the area to be traversed that is drawn to scale on a chart. Global coordinates are used to locate fixed objects, the land masses outlined on the chart. A course is defined in some direction relative to the reference coordinates. Once the direction is determined, if one knows the distance and the rate of motion, one can calculate how long the voyage will take. All of this information can be measured using instruments, and progress is plotted on the chart aboard the ship. With an accurate timepiece, one can correct for the effects of winds and currents on the ship's position by taking celestial sightings of the sun or stars. These act much like mile-signs along a highway. Obviously, to navigate effectively using this approach, one needs good instruments, an accurate chart, and for convenience, some sort of calculator to work out positions. (Today, satellites and computers are included in the navigator's tool kit.)

The important point here is that the perception of the navigator is that it is *the ship that is moving* between stationary points of land, perhaps two islands.

## Micronesian navigation

Long before Westerners had invented compasses (about AD 1100) or sextants, or accurate timepieces, or even useful maps, the Micronesians were sailing long distances across the open ocean without the aid of instruments or charts of any kind. How did they do it? The answer is, they used an entirely different mental frame for knowing where they were, one that did not require such complicated props. For the Micronesians, it was not the vessel that moved. It remained stationary in their mental model. So did the stars. It was, rather, *the islands that moved past the ship and the stars.* These navigators used lines of stars that all rose, sequentially, at the same point on the horizon. From this line, one had a fixed point on the horizon all night long that was used as a compass – a sign of direction from where one was. The navigators knew the rising (or if they were traveling west, the setting) point of the linear constellation that marked the direction of the island they wished to sail to. And to return home, they knew the setting (or rising) linear constellation that located their home island from the position of each island they visited. (The slight shift in positions on the horizons of linear constellations for north–south journeys were negligible for the distances traveled.) They checked their rate of travel by noting the "movement" of unseen (often imaginary) "etak" islands to right and left of their travel direction, for which they also knew the correct linear constellations along the route (see Figure V.3).

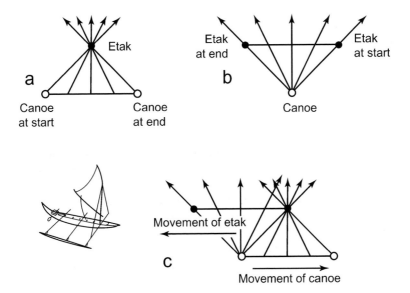

*Figure V.3* Contrasting views of a sea voyage

(a) The Western view is of a canoe starting at one island and moving to another, while passing by an "etak" island out of sight to the left of the canoe. *The canoe moves and the islands are fixed.*

(b) The Micronesian view of the same voyage shows *the canoe standing still and the "etak" island moving* from ahead to-the-left to behind to-the-left. Likewise, the starting island has moved far back behind the canoe, and the island of destination has now "arrived" at the canoe.

(c) Overlapping views show that the movement of the "etak" island under the stars is a different but comparable way of showing the canoe's movement in relation to the same stars. (The arrows in each case represent the horizontal star bearings during the voyage.)

Here is how Hutchins describes their experience in the canoe:

> Back along the wake ... the island you left falls farther behind while the one toward which you are heading is hopefully drawing closer. You can see neither of them, but you know this is happening. You know too that there are islands on either side of you, some near, some far, some ahead, some behind. The ones that are ahead will in due course, fall behind. Everything passes by the little canoe – everything except the stars by night and the sun in the day.[49]

By this process, the sailor roughly estimates his position. He knows, also, the expected length (in time) of the journey, and can make adjustments if he senses winds or currents are not as expected. Near the island he may use the flight of seabirds at nightfall as a final guide to where the island lies, or changes in the ocean swells as the sea bottom contours begin to change. As Hutchins notes, the amount of information about the night sky in these sailors' heads was remarkable. They carry star-maps of the linear constellations for multiple islands, and gain much tacit knowledge about a canoe's speed and position through sailing with more experienced navigators.

If it is difficult to imagine how these people navigate, you should not feel bad. Take it, rather, as proof of how hard it is for a person culturally trained to see and interpret the world from one standpoint to visualize it from the quite different but equally functional standpoint of another culture. And if the shift in gestalt is this difficult for concrete, sensible aspects of the world, how much more difficult is it when one is trying to shift from conceptualizations about abstract social values and moral codes held by one's own culture to those of another. A quote from famed American anthropologist Ruth Benedict makes the point:

> The lenses through which any nation looks at life are not the ones another uses. It is hard to be conscious of the eyes through which one looks. Any country takes them for granted, and the tricks of focussing and of perspective which give to any people its national view of life seem to that people the god-given arrangement of the landscape. In any matter of spectacles, we do not expect the man who wears them to know the formula for the lenses, and neither can we expect nations to analyze their own outlook upon the world.[50]

One begins to appreciate just how profoundly different are those hidden pilings – the tacit beliefs and assumptions – that underlie each cultural narrative and on which its visible world view is constructed. (In anticipation of later chapters, I shall take issue with Benedict's pronouncement that we cannot expect nations to analyze their own outlook upon the world. It may well become necessary for all nations to begin to achieve this capacity, as a part of our species' ongoing cultural evolution.)

### The mythic side of culture

While cultural differences in practical matters such as navigation may raise some confusion, they are unlikely to be overlaid with passionate feelings. We can hardly feel threatened by the Micronesians because they use a different way of thinking to find their way across the ocean. But when it comes to more abstract questions, those that carry meaning and value, such as the purpose of life, what is held sacred, and how people ought to behave, we touch upon those aspects of our world views that raise strong emotional responses. These are the stuff of religions. There has been a strong move in some Western liberal circles to dismantle religions because of the violent acts too often perpetrated throughout history in their name. But, as I hope is becoming evident, this would entail throwing the baby out with the bathwater. To eliminate religious tendencies would mean eliminating the very core of human nature. The sort of meaning that we call religious or sacred, along with art, music, and other esthetic experience, is at the very center of our feeling selves. As well-known British zoologist, J.Z. Young, who has spent his life studying how brains work, has said about these needs of the human brain:

> I believe that these "spiritual" and creative activities are even *more important*, in the literal, practical sense than the more mundane ones that are the concern of politics, business, and industry.... I shall argue that such satisfactions of our emotional needs provide the motivation that keeps us alive and at work. These are the things that together ensure the continuity and survival of human communities, even more than do the provision of food and shelter. The teaching that "man does not live by bread alone" is perhaps needed more than ever today. I believe that a proper study of how the brain operates will enable us to see more clearly the place that so-called cultural and spiritual activities play in human homeostasis.[51]

This statement encapsulates exactly the central point of this book: *unless we understand the basis of our emotional selves, we shall never understand human nature – Who We Are.*

One of the most unnecessary of "problems" for science, it seems to me, is that of human spirituality, which is often treated as something inappropriate or unexplainable (much in the way consciousness had been treated until very recently). I think the real "problem" is that the Western world view that gave rise to modern science finds no adaptive function for the deep human need for meaning and purpose. Science really does not yet fully comprehend the survival role of feelings and the need of the fully conscious human mind (in all its connectedness with the universe) for meaningful stories. The ultimate story, after all, is the answer to the biggest "why?" of all. "Why does anything exist: us, stars, life, death? Why is 'it' – the universe – like it is?"

Why is science so surprised that, in their search for answers to this giant question, people seek extraordinary conscious experiences, sometimes called trances, or religious experiences, or the attainment of Enlightenment? Why does science find it hard to explain people's use of hallucinogenic plants, or fasting, or repetitive rhythms (such as loud drumming), or rapturous dancing, or deep meditation or prayer, as aids to insights into this eternal question? Science, which prizes itself on dealing only with proximate causes ("little stories") seems unable to grasp this evolved need of human beings as a phenomenon to be explained. Only through some sort of sense of "total connectedness with the whole" – whether we call it Nirvana, or experience of God, or simply of deep and overwhelming awe and wonderment – is some kind of answer to the big "Why?" briefly experienced. These are moments of overwhelming emotional experience that are consciously felt. That the "feeling" parts of the brain, the hypothalamus and thalamus, the limbic system and areas of the prefrontal cortex, are all involved seems only natural.[52] As I show in later chapters, all peoples, even those living in purely "secular" societies, seek out some form of substitute meaning system that allows them a kind of similar experience with which their entire beings seem to be engaged: an ideology, nationalism, a corporation, a football team to "live for," even a street gang. People need to feel loyal to some "idea."

To recapitulate, once language emerged, with its huge potential for metaphoric extrapolation, people began to create explanatory stories, or myths, about where people came from, about what causes life and death (usually spirits or divine beings), and about how humans ought to act. A cultural world view, then, incorporates (1) *practical knowledge* useful for such things as finding food or navigating a canoe, along with (2) *social and moral guidelines* on how to treat each other, as well as (3) *transcendent explanations* about the meaning of existence. The latter two, particularly, emerge out of the implicitly held beliefs and assumptions on which the more pragmatic, conscious, everyday institutions of a cultural world view are based (see Fig. 0.2). It is our moral beliefs and our transcendent meanings that lie deepest in the human psyche. They provide our individual and group identities as conscious beings, and without them societies would be unable to function. No wonder they are protected by all our emotional resources. It is they that make sense of consciousness; without them we would lose the capacity for a coherent, meaningful existence.

This uncompromising need for some kind of sacred meaning in life (in whatever way it may be expressed) is perhaps the aspect of the human psyche that is least understood by contemporary Western society. Human nature demands something of transcendent value, which the pragmatic values of wealth and power, for all their vaunted desirability within the contemporary Western world view, are unable to offer. Understanding what kinds of existential meaning we humans require may be one of our species' most pressing needs as we begin this new millennium. One thing we need strongly to resist is the Western assumption that human beings, if only they will exercise enough "will power," can psychologically adapt to conditions of life that utterly ignore their need for a meaning that can be called religious, sacred, mystical, or transcendental. Somehow, the experience of life has to be made worthwhile, made "special," in a way that the conscious self is not able to put into words, but that it nevertheless seeks and appears to recognize by other means. Threats to a person's deepest beliefs can elicit violence in their defense, and denial of them by over-pragmatized (e.g. "efficient") world views can lead to endless social pathologies.

In later chapters of this book we shall be looking at the ways that different cultures have fulfilled this need for significant meaning, and the success they have had in simultaneously meeting peoples' needs for autonomy and bonding. In the next chapter I look at how the social context in which an individual's brain develops influences the quality of the psychic needs that one experiences during later life, and at how traumas experienced (even as an adult) may deeply influence how one's brain functions; finally I shall look at how healing can take place.

# VI

# HOW EXPERIENCE SHAPES THE BRAIN

A century of study of traumatic memories shows that (1) they generally remain unaffected by other life experiences; (2) they may return, triggered by reminders, at any time during a person's life, with the same vividness as if the subject were having the experience all over again; and (3) these memories are primarily sensory and emotional, frequently leaving victims in a state of speechless terror, in which they may be unable to articulate precisely what they are feeling and thinking.

Alexander C. McFarlane and Bessel A. van der Kolk (1996: 565)

Whatever happens to us, as this opening quote underscores, can permanently shape our brains, at any age. Truly traumatic events, ones that threaten our very existence, even though long buried, may be recalled unbidden from the recesses of our brains by some seemingly innocuous stimulus. Our experience, the nature of the environments in which we live, really does matter. This chapter examines in what ways our experiences shape us. Every society has had its own theory about this and establishes child-rearing traditions that it believes will produce its vision of "ideal human beings." Of course, that vision changes with time, as a culture's underlying beliefs shift and it creates new institutions and then tries to shape people to fit them.

We know that in the West ideas about appropriate child-rearing have gone through several major shifts since the mid-nineteenth century. From Victorian children, who should be seen but not heard, and grew up to "reading, and writing, and 'rithmetic, taught to the tune of a hickory stick," to the first "scientific" era, when sterilized formula replaced mother's milk and mothers were told to let infants cry in their cots lest they become spoiled, to the backlash era, when discipline would somehow warp a child's creativity and block his or her spontaneous intellectual unfolding, to the present over-anxious era of bombarding babies with "enriched" experiences so as to maximize their I.Q. test scores, no matter what happens to their other psychological needs. The "experts" have a lot to answer for. Yet despite repeated mistakes, the basic question does not go away and must be dealt with: "What does it take to develop into a well-balanced adult?"

In the previous two chapters, we saw how our brains evolved to simultane-ously process enormous amounts of information and attend to the powerful feelings necessary to give meaning to that information and guide our actions. In this chapter I try to weave our current "best knowledges" (incomplete though they are) on how our modern brains develop together with what the social lives of children must have been like during the long period of the human brain's evolution. What was growing up like for children during all those thousands of years before writing, and job-markets, and TVs? In the course of this discussion I will emphasize that the development of a well-integrated social being requires satisfying our emotional needs for belonging, for autonomy, and for meaning, as well as the overly emphasized cognitive, information-processing aspects of our minds that Western society focusses upon so strongly. Only by taking *both* aspects of human development into account (whether consciously or not) can a society hope to remain healthy and free of violence. I shall try to show how our experiences, not only those in childhood but also as adults, affect the very ways our brains function and the degree of control we can have over our feelings and actions.

Today there are at least four competing theories among the various groups of scientists, and believed in by some segments of Western society, about how babies acquire the brains and behaviors they end up with as adults. First are the evolutionary psychologists, mentioned in earlier chapters, who see "adaptive" behaviors as genetically controlled. Among such behaviors, they count war, rape, and patriarchy as attributable to innate, genetic propensities. Competing individuals and groups are being selected for their "survival behaviors" (though even this group of scientists will agree that, given modern genocidal weapons, societies must somehow control these tendencies). Second are those scientists who see particular "bad" genes as the causes of mental illness, random violence, and sociopathic behaviors. According to them, such people need to be identi-fied and forcibly controlled.

On the other hand, there are some who argue that babies are essentially *tabulae rasae* – little "blank tablets" whose brains are totally shaped by parents and society; as adults, they cannot be held accountable for any harm they do, since it must have been built into them by others. Finally, there are the hard-liners (not many of them scientists) who think each person is totally responsible at virtually all ages for his or her actions, no matter what genes she or he may have inherited or what things each has experienced. The growing child is in moral charge of her- or himself. (This is the faction that wishes to try every juvenile as an adult, and refuses to allow violent child offenders back into society, no matter how many years later or how well rehabilitated they may be.)

In contemporary Western society, the main social concern seems to be "Who is to blame for bad outcomes?" Is it genes, the child, or the parents? (Only occasionally are society and its institutions called into question.) Good outcomes are expected, but seldom is their cause sought. Parents, teachers, and the child's own will power (the same causes as are blamed for bad results) all get credit. But in the West, the causes of "successful" outcomes (however those are defined) are politically far less interesting than those of the "failures."

In this chapter I argue that understanding the *multiple causes of successful integration into society* is critical for insuring that social institutions themselves accommodate the needs of all children, however disparately endowed they may be either genetically or socially. There is no single best developmental track, no "one-size-fits-all" rearing plan. Ultimately, it is the willingness of a society's collective whole to put flexible institutions in place which can socialize children in diverse ways, that will lead to a socially well-adjusted next generation.

The subject matter of this chapter is therefore multifaceted, but every facet counts. I begin with what is now known about how the brain develops. Next, I ask what we know about genes and brains. Then I invite you imaginatively to go back in time and ask, Under what social conditions did our early ancestors develop from babies to adults? And next to ask, What do modern studies on child-rearing practices that try to mimic these conditions tell us? Finally, I come to the questions of how severe stress affects the structure and function of the human brain, and how damaged brains can be healed.

## The amazing plasticity of the developing human brain

At birth, the brain of a chimpanzee has a volume of about 350 cc (cubic centimeters), about the same as that of a human baby; but a baby chimpanzee's brain will grow only to about 450 cc as an adult. It is thus already relatively well formed, with many connections between its nerve cells already in place. After a mere two weeks, a baby chimp can hold its head steady and extend its arms. At birth, a human brain with the same volume is not yet well organized internally. Only the most basic pathways between its various regions are clearly laid out. Though its external appearance resembles that of an adult brain, the organization of its nerve cells, or neurons, is far from complete. It's rather like having a national motorway system in place, connecting major centers of population, but with no rural roads or city streets. Not until a baby is twenty weeks old are sufficient neurons well-enough organized and muscles well-enough developed for the baby to hold its head steady and extend its arms. A human being at birth is thus called "atricial," meaning that it is a long way from being independent – able to walk, or even crawl. It cannot even seek out its mother's nipple without her help. Without constant attention, it would die, and its brain is "aware" of this fact, even at birth.

Unlike the brain of a chimpanzee, however, that of a human will grow to around 1400 cc or so, about four times as big as at birth. In fact, it reaches 90 percent of its adult size by age 3! But that does not mean new brain cells are being formed during that time. (We now know that the brain, once thought to have all its cells at birth and to be incapable of making new ones, is able to generate new cells, at least in some areas, throughout life, but this power is limited.) We are born with about 100 billion nerve cells (or, as some scientists remind us, about the same as the number of stars in the Milky Way). And we will have about that many neurons throughout life. So what is it that is growing between birth and age 3 that causes the brain to more than triple in size?

The answer is a combination of (1) an increase in the *connections* or *synapses* between the nerve cells (the number and pattern of contacts that they make with each other), and (2) an increase in the special "nurturing" cells that are necessary for neurons to thrive. Imagine our road system suddenly acquiring hundreds of country roads, and in cities, a veritable rabbit-warren of streets, alleys, and paths all connecting with as many others as possible. The cross-wiring among neurons increases phenomenally. Cells can now link up in literally multi-trillions of ways. The patterns by which cells come to link up more or less permanently are determined by experience, by the signals the sense organs and the body itself send to the brain and the signals the brain sends back out in response. The more often a particular pathway is called into action, the greater the number of connections made along it. What is happening is that the brain of a newborn is practicing learning. Every stimulus is "learned" – at least temporarily, until a more reliable pathway replaces it.

By age 3, each neuron in a toddler's brain has about 15,000 synapses with other cells, six times as many as at birth, and many more than are present in an adult brain. As a group of neuroscientists puts it:

> Preschool children have brains that are literally more active, more connected, and much more flexible than ours. From the point of view of neurology, they really are alien geniuses.[1]

During this time, children are instant learners, busy absorbing masses of information, some useful, some not. So the interconnections their neurons form are only temporary. The detailed wiring pattern of the entire brain, and especially in the cerebral cortices, is being made and remade on a daily basis. Eventually some patterns will be retained, where the pathways have been stimulated repeatedly, while others will be lost, sooner or later. This superactive learner's brain survives in this highly plastic state until around age 10, when a rigorous pruning of cell-to-cell connections begins that continues through puberty. These same scientists describe the whole process this way:

> Brains don't just steadily make more and more connections [as needed]. Instead, they grow many more connections than they need and then get rid of lots of them.[2]

That explains why it is so much easier to learn complex patterns of information, such as languages, when one is young and has lots of extra, flexible synapses at one's disposal. For instance, it is easy for a small child to learn several languages without confusing them. After age 10, new languages become increasingly hard to acquire.

Thus human babies are born with very few "programmed" brain patterns and a huge overabundance of potential pathways that can be connected up in different ways. This is what makes human behavior so flexible; experience creates our brains, *not* our genes (or at least not in the way genes do for many other animals). Says neuroscientist Gerald Edelman:

> The genetic code does not provide a specific wiring diagram for this [final selection of nerve-cell pathways]. Rather, it imposes a set of constraints on the selectional process. Even with such constraints, genetically identical individuals are unlikely to have identical wiring, for selection is epigenic [acting after the genes have laid down their modest constraints].[3]

Modern science has too often made public pronouncements about brain development that send parents and educators into tizzies of anxiety. Some have identified "critical stages" when, if something doesn't happen, it is lost forever. Some parents became anxious when they learned of the pruning of connections in children's brains, believing it meant a loss of intellectual potential. Rather than such hyperanxious adults, however, what developing children need is people who appreciate all that is going on in those developing heads so they can care for and guide them with reasonable expectations and appropriate forms of assistance.

From infancy to age 18, the human brain is in constant flux and makes huge emotional demands on its owner. And the ages of heaviest "recasting" of the brain, up to age 3, and later in adolescence, are the times of greatest stress. The juggling of neuronal connections requires a good deal of sleep, since that is the time when consolidation of new connections occurs and, for teenagers, when the heaviest pruning occurs. Adults are used to babies needing lots of sleep. Yet few parents realize how exhausted teenage brains become, how much extra sleep they need, and how their sleep–awake cycles can be shifted. In Western culture particularly, society seems to put excessive demands of extra homework and extracurricular activities onto minds already struggling to stay alert.[4]

Another commonly overlooked aspect of brain development is how young-sters, from about age 2 onward, have the double task of not just learning physical skills and cultural facts, but also of understanding all the nuances of social relationships *as they are understood by those around them*. First-time parents can be caught off-guard by the "terrible-twos." The cuddly, gurgling, adorable child they have so lovingly tended is suddenly rebellious, tempera-mental, assertive, constantly testing relationships with Mom, Dad and everyone else. This child needs to learn the cultural rules.

But far from being signs of innate stubbornness that could become intractable, a toddler's "No!" or "Won't!" are a normal part of the active devel-opment of self-understanding. Johnnie is becoming a self-motivated, active learner; he is developing a conscious awareness of himself as an independent autonomous person. Already powerfully bonded beings, toddlers are simply expressing that other deep inner propensity all primates have – that for autonomous behavior. The only way the child will learn about social relationships is by exploring them, testing them, experiencing all their facets. Such independence is critical for all future development. Every human being learns the most important things in life by doing them. We can imitate, but we need to practice whatever we are imitating. And along the way, we make mistakes – whether in speaking a language, playing an instrument, or becoming a socially accepted member of a community. (And imitation, of course, means parents cannot successfully use dual behavioral standards, i.e. one for themselves and one for their children, when it comes to politeness, anger-control, and apologizing for mistakes.)

A brief comment about infant memories seems appropriate here. There is a common belief that children cannot form permanent memories until around age 3 or 4, or even older; thus, early events, even traumatic ones, are not significant later on. Given that brain pathways are constantly being made in one's earliest years, such an assumption is not unreasonable. Yet as with all memories, those associated with powerful emotions are the ones we recall in detail. (Almost everyone old enough to remember Kennedy's assassination remembers the details of where and when they first heard about it.) Emotionally charged events, even in very young children, can affect them.

Two factors seem to be involved. One is how often and for how long a particular experience is repeated during infancy. As children grow older during this so-called "amnesic" period, they find it increasingly easy to recall a past experience when given a trigger clue. Carolyn Rovee-Collier, a child psychologist at Rutgers, reports that:

> [E]ven very young infants can remember an event over the entire infantile amnesia period if they are periodically reminded.[5]

The other factor is the emotional content of the memory. There is no doubt that memories are indeed formed during the early years, especially for highly emotional events. As another developmental psychologist, Madeline Eacott, explains, children cannot *recall* them until their conscious sense of self begins to develop at about age 2½, with their language-based narrative skills.[6] It thus appears that trauma in early childhood, even though not able to be recalled, can still leave permanent emotional traces in the brain of a very young child. More direct evidence of this comes from studies of infant rats. The nongenetic transmission of "inattentive mothering" by a nursing female was transmitted to her female pups who themselves became inattentive mothers. But if the pups were instead reared by a nurturing foster mother, they, too, became good mothers. The "bad behavior" was not genetic, but permanently learned in the very first week after birth. The authors of this report, citing evidence from studies on human infants, conclude:

197

In humans, social, emotional, and economic contexts influence the quality of the relationship between parent and child and can show continuity across generations. Our findings in rats may thus be relevant in understanding the importance of early intervention programs in humans.[7]

So what should parents do? Will they over-traumatize their children if they discipline them? Will they deprive them if they don't give them every new learning toy that's promoted? Will playing Mozart to babies still in the womb increase their I.Q.s? The notion of enriching early childhood development arose from studies of rats. When taken from their laboratory cages (1 to 3 rats per cage) and put in large cages with other juvenile rats and lots of objects to play with, the number of connections made between nerve cells in their brains clearly increased (Figure VI.1).[8] But small, bare cages are abnormal for rats or any other animal. So the so-called "enriched" environments resembled more closely what rats "in the wild" (in any major inner city) naturally experience. It was, rather, the rats in small, bare cages that were deprived! (Again, as with the birds mentioned earlier in Chapter IV, psychologists have misunderstood the possible levels of rat intelligence when they studied maze-learning by animals raised in bare cages.) As Alison Gopnik and her colleagues conclude:

> The new scientific research doesn't say that parents should provide special "enriching" experiences to children over and above what they experience in everyday life. It does suggest, though, that a radically deprived environment could cause damage.[9]

(Later in the chapter I deal with the possible negative impact of hyperanxious parents on a child's mental state.)

I conclude this section with the wise words of Paul Shepard:

> The interaction of infant and caregivers emerges as a compelling need – perhaps the most powerful shaping force in individual experience. Oddly enough, bonding's "purpose" is separation, successive steps of coming together and departing, in which the individual emerges in new relationships to humans and nonhumans [i.e. Nature] ... Intense early attachment leads not to prolonged dependency but to a better-functioning nervous system and greater success in the separation process.[10]

Caregivers may want to keep three things in mind. One is that as brains develop, they form both cognitive and emotional pathways. To push one without due attention to the other can be far more destructive than missing some supposedly crucial "learning stage." A second point is that learning never stops. No brain is frozen in time. Brains can reshape themselves throughout life,

*Figure VI.1* "Enriched" environmental conditions used in a study of developing rat
brains

This is an artist's rendition of the large experimental cage containing several rats
provided with multiple "play" objects. Rats raised in such an "enriched" environment showed many more connections between their brain cells than did rats raised
alone or in groups of three in small, bare cages about one-eighth the volume of this
one.

*Source*: Drawing made by Michele Lukowski, from a text description of an "enriched" environment,
in Marion Cleeves Diamond (1988)

albeit with increasing difficulty. Even severe psychological or physical traumas
often can be compensated for, as will be discussed at the end of this chapter. A
bad beginning is not a life-sentence; but the healing of distorted or maladaptive
cognitive or emotional patterns requires much more than personal will power
on the part of an affected individual. It requires the provision of social
nurturing and experiential opportunities that were denied earlier.

The third thing caregivers may want to keep in mind is that brains are not all
alike in their strengths and weaknesses. Some are especially "good" at distinguishing visual images, others at solving three-dimensional spatial problems,
others at fine coordination of movements, and still others at hearing and remembering complex combinations of sounds. Likewise, the emotional/feeling
connections do not come in a "one-size-fits-all" mold either. Every mother

knows her children are born with different personalities: easy babies, active babies, cuddly babies, fussy babies, short-tempered babies. Both the emotional-learning pathway and the skills-learning pathway for each child will be unique. There is no standardized form of personhood that can be coaxed out of every newborn, no matter how much pressure parents and society may exert.

And with that observation, I turn to the question of what genes may bequeath us in the way of multiple intelligences.

## Genes, behavior, and intelligence

Long before Darwin provided a scientific explanation for the survival of some traits rather than others, most societies already valued particular qualities over others, believing them to be superior. Conquerors claimed their "superior qualities" as justification for their dominant status. What is interesting is how different the traits can be that diverse cultures nurture, and the uses cultures make of people who strongly exhibit them. Traits range from a strong sense of humor, to asceticism, to aggressiveness, to mature wisdom, to scheming, to a tendency to trance-like behaviors. Some societies view homosexuals as unique people with mystical gifts, able to bridge across two worlds of knowing; others see them as dangerous monstrosities, a threat to social stability. What is a good omen in one place is feared somewhere else.

Western science claims to be able to tell us what problem traits are caused by genes and what might be done one day about repairing such "bad" genes. Never mind that a giant gap still exists between identifying a particular genetic mutation and knowing how it causes problem behavior. Never mind that identifying a genetic potential for a behavioral problem absolves society from asking how its demands, its institutions, its social inequities may be contributing – indeed, may be the triggering factor – in turning a mere genetic disposition into a full-blown antisocial pathology. The gene (and its unfortunate owner) are at fault. *She* lacks sufficient will power, or *he* is a genetic defective.

Let me give an example. Those most likely to either use drugs, develop attention deficit disorder, or even post-traumatic stress disorder after a gruesome experience, are now candidates for genetic cures, or at least for pharmacological treatment to "fix" their problem. They are being diagnosed with a genetic ailment, "reward deficiency syndrome," caused by "the A1 allele [a mutant gene] for the dopamine [a brain chemical] D2 receptor." Translated, they have a minor genetic defect in one kind of neuronal junction in the brain. By identifying people with this gene *before* they get into social trouble and putting them into treatment programs, society and they can be spared the cost of a possible illness. Or so the argument goes. No one ever suggests that the "environmental factors [involved], which are not yet fully understood," might be a better target for ameliorating the problem. For instance, a society less stingy with its social rewards might turn out to make *everyone* feel a great deal better rewarded, while simultaneously preventing many at-risk people from becoming dysfunctional![11] A better diagnosis might well be one of a *society* exhibiting "reward stinginess syndrome," unwilling to extend its approval to a broader range of personal qualities.

This is but one example of the tendency to seek genetic deficiencies as causes of ill-defined mental "abnormalities," without looking for triggering social stresses. The familiar search for genes promoting intelligence is another case. "Intelligence" is an abstraction, a culturally defined quality. In the West it means the ability to rise to the top economically in a literate, competitive, analytically programmed, hierarchical society. Children are tested *for this capacity* and I.Q. tests do predict outcomes fairly well. But they do not work well in other cultures, where other forms of intelligence matter much more. The West's definition of "intelligence" is not universally applicable.

Howard Gardner of the Harvard Graduate School of Education argues that there is not just one "intelligence," but multiple intelligences. He notes that besides verbal and reasoning skills, there are emotional intelligences: capacities for empathy, control of emotions, postponement of gratification. There is also, he says, "a naturalist intelligence," namely, the ability to observe and appreciate other forms of life.[12] In India, for example, it is common for an illiterate peasant to know the names, locations and human uses of over 100 wild plant species. How many American Ph.D. holders have equivalent knowledge? Professor S.A. Shah, a leading Indian forester, repeatedly found uneducated tribal people – men, women, children – could identify *all* the plants in a random quadrat of moist tropical forest, whereas his university-trained colleagues knew only 15 per cent.[13]

Finally (but by no means exhausting the list of diverse intelligences), I will mention musical intelligence. Many well-known and gifted composers, including Schumann, Handel, Mahler, and Rachmaninov were manic-depressives whose creativity seems to have come during their manic phases. The capacity for creating and remembering music appears to be separate from other forms of intelligence such as literacy and mathematics.

There exists a group of "mentally deficient" persons, who all share a pixie-like appearance: short stature and elfin faces, with pug noses, oval ears, wide mouths and small chins. Called Williams' Syndrome, this condition is caused by a deletion of a small segment on chromosome 7. Hence it definitely is genetic, and involves several physical problems (heart murmurs, blood chemistry changes) and great difficulty with visual–spatial representations. In short, while they can understand pictures and tell wonderful stories about them, these people cannot draw things, nor read or write. Though sociable and loving, they score poorly on standard intelligence tests, around I.Q. 50. Yet they often have amazing musical skills, singing or playing instruments. Moreover, they can remember complex music, including the songs and lyrics of long ballads, for years. Before histories were written, when they were kept in oral memory as long ballads or sagas, this special skill would have been prized socially. Such "wee folk" are still sung about in Irish folk songs.[14]

Certain serious mental diseases do have clear genetic causes, including some forms of autism,[15] manic depression, and schizophrenia. Yet even with the latter, the genes predisposing for this serious illness may or may not be expressed, depending among other things on the environment in the mother's womb.[16] While it is important to treat those afflicted with these diseases humanely, and to refrain from blaming their parents for causing them, it is equally important to recognize limits to the usefulness of genetic intervention. And as the cognitive psychologist George Mandler argues, it is meaningless to look for specific genetic causes of such poorly defined behaviors as "male aggression" or "patriarchal dominance" (as some evolutionary psychologists are wont to do), and downright ridiculous to follow the current fashion of seeking a genetic basis for divorce or TV viewing. "Postulating single [genetic] modules for each bit of behavior and rejecting general principles of mental functioning have a distinctly postmodern flavor."[17]

Instead of trying to identify and fix our genes, we would be far better off recognizing that human beings have a rich diversity in their genetic make-up, and every group or category we might conceive has valuable strengths in some behavioral areas and vulnerabilities in others. Weeding out or "fixing" all potentially "bad" genes would mean eliminating or repairing everyone. Instead, I suggest, we strive toward cultivating a social milieu that better accommodates our inherent diversity by harmonizing our universal needs for acceptance, independence, and meaningfulness in ways that satisfy all persons, not just one "kind" of human being.[18]

## Child-rearing in the Pleistocene – and after

The two overarching psychological needs of all primates, I have argued, are for bonding within a group, and for autonomy of behavior. These are "needs" because they are central to survival, and given the utter helplessness of human infants and the huge amount of postnatal development their brains must undergo, they are highly critical. Let me translate these needs into the perspective of a newborn.

(1) "I cannot move myself. I cannot see very far. I am cold. I am hungry. I am afraid."

The need for bonding translates initially into a need for *physical reassurance*: for warmth, touch, rocking, nipple, soft human sounds. In a word: for *security*.

(2) "I must try to learn for myself. I must find the breast. I must grab this person's hair, or finger, or the spoon he holds out to me. I must learn to watch things, touch things, taste things, hear things. I must learn to crawl, to walk, to climb. I must play with things to know what they are. I know

people's sounds, but I must try to make them myself so they will know what I think and feel and need."

The need for autonomy at every moment during development is a need for *experience*, for *learning through spontaneous interaction with the world*.

Of course babies do not consciously talk to themselves in these ways. I have translated innate psychological propensities into the language of adults. An infant communicates its needs in other ways: by crying, to get attention; by red-faced screaming, to register angry frustration, either with adults or itself; by smiles and gurgles, to say "thanks"; by flailing arms, head-turning, and frowns, to say "no, take it away. Don't do that."

My point is that babies have fundamental needs for security and for experience. When both these needs are appropriately met they develop into well-socialized adults, able to interact confidently in stable, trusting ways with others, *because that is how their brains develop*. They feel *secure* in their surroundings and at the same time *free* to be themselves. When these needs are not met, however, babies' brains develop differently. They are constantly on guard, full of suspicion and doubt, insecure, unsure of self as well as others. Failure to acquire independent skills only exacerbates the sense of insecurity and psychic abandonment.

Though the evolutionary force selecting these needs was likely acting mainly to promote the survival of the helpless human infant, so strong is the emotional drive underlying both of them that they persist throughout adult life, where they help to maintain social coherence through strong bonds on the one hand, and social adaptiveness through ongoing exploratory experiences on the other.

The need for psychic security – to be attached to and appreciated by others – never leaves us. Nor does the need for independence of action. As we grow up, how we express and satisfy those needs changes, yet even as adults we retain the propensity for seeking physical and emotional contacts with others as well as for exercising personal freedom to act creatively. We ache for the solace of embraces and bodily contacts in whatever ways they are "permitted" by social custom, at the same time as we strive for behavioral independence. (In some ways, meeting both these inner desires is more often culturally possible for women than men, for reasons I will explore in the next chapter.)

Much evolutionary emphasis has been placed on the fact that human females are not only continuously sexually receptive throughout ovulatory cycles during their reproductive years, but continue to be so throughout their entire adult lifetime. Moreover, unlike the quick, reassuring genital rubbing of bonobos (the only other primate that employs sex for more than simply impregnation), human sexual behavior is accompanied by a great deal of physical affection: kissing, cuddling, caressing, rocking. It is written in most textbooks that this continuous receptivity of females evolved to keep males hanging around to protect and help supply food for them and their helpless offspring. No doubt that is part of the story, but it does not explain the feelings of love, of attachment, of emotional security felt by *both* males and females in healthy sexual encounters. These needs, present in us as infants, persist throughout life. As Eibl-Eibesfeldt has pointed out, the roots of human love, for both males and females, lie not in sexuality, but in parental care:

> From what has been said so far, it should be clear that in point of fact, many behavior patterns which are regarded as typically sexual, such as kissing and caressing, are in origin actually actions of parental care. We remind the reader of this because Sigmund Freud, in a strikingly topsy-turvy interpretation, once observed that a mother would certainly be shocked if she realized how she was lavishing sexual behavior patterns on her child. In this case, Freud has got things back to front. A mother looks after her children with the actions of parental care; these she also uses to woo her husband.[19]

What Eibl-Eibesfeldt leaves out, however, is that not only do women woo men, but men also woo women, using these very same acts of parental care. Moreover, males in cultures where tradition does not prevent them, commonly lavish as much physical affection on babies as do females, whenever they have the opportunity. I see this as an extension into adult life in *both sexes* of the general propensity for physical bonding and the giving and receiving of affection that was prerequisite to human cultural evolution and the formation of enduring learning communities. In later chapters, I examine correlations between the overall psychic security of males in a given society and their sexual behavior. Not surprisingly, there is a high incidence of male dominance and abuse of women, including rape, in societies where men are denied other forms of physical affection and contact. As American re-evaluation counselor John Irwin has put it:

> We males become separated from each other and from females so thoroughly that we become desperate about this one activity in which we are allowed to get close physically and emotionally: sex. This activity is supposed to fill all our needs for intimacy, affection, touch etc. With no other approved sources for receiving intimacy and closeness, we understandably become tense and urgent when we see an opportunity for closeness.[20]

In addition to denying physical bonding to males, many contemporary societies also curtail the exercise of individual autonomy for a large fraction of the population: the ability of a person to contribute to society through her or his spontaneous, voluntary acts. Rather, they are expected to fit into predesigned "slots" (called "jobs") in a faceless economic machine. Much paid work in the modern world is like this: it denies the involvement of a person's own imagination in the goals and purposes of the work he or she carries out. I judge that most modern societies seriously deny both children and adults the very propensities sculpted into their ancestors' genes during our long evolution. We are raising our children to "adapt" to cultures they were not designed to live in (as we are not). I suggest that most of the behavioral pathologies characterizing modern history have been caused by poorly designed social institutions, and those pathologies begin in early childhood as we try to force babies to begin to adjust to them. But it has not always been thus; it cannot have been. As you read on, I ask you to "think Pleistocene."

I believe that during the long millennia of the Pleistocene and into fairly recent times, most human beings in most tribal societies were born into, grew up in, and lived as adults in socially secure surroundings that also offered them considerable freedom to experiment and learn. These were the social conditions that predominated during and for many millennia after the emergence of *Homo sapiens*, and they shaped us biologically. Any past cultures that failed to foster both bonding and autonomy ultimately disappeared. How were security and freedom of experience achieved in the past? We cannot rewind the prehistoric newsreel to see. We can only rely on what we can gather from experience with newborns today, and use our imaginations to interpret how things must indeed have been some 20,000 years ago and before.

### *The need for security*

Mother–infant bonding is the evolutionary basis for the psychological framing of all primate social relations, including both males and females. The powerful bond between mother and child extends throughout the community: from mother–infant, to everyone–infant, to everyone–everyone, thus creating a community web of bonds. Earlier it was noted how attentive all members in a primate troop are toward a new infant: attracted to it and ready to defend it against outside harm. As Jean Liedloff, author of a well-known book on "natural" parenting, puts it:

> The attractiveness of babies and children is necessarily a powerful force: without it they would have no advantage to compensate for their many disadvantages as small, weak, slow, defenseless, inexperienced, and dependent individuals among their elders. Their appeal precludes their having to compete and attracts the assistance they require.[21]

She emphasizes that parenting is not exclusively a female task; males do it just as well. The baby does not distinguish (except for suckling, of course). Caring is universal, and universally rewarding.

"There is no such thing as a baby: there is a baby and someone," said pediatrician D.W. Winnicott.[22] In other words, there is always a *relationship*. As already noted, opinions about what that relationship should be vary widely: from "spare the rod, spoil the child," to "don't give in to your baby's crying," to "a child needs its own room, its own bed," on the one hand, to "breast-feeding is essential," and "you should never scold your child," on the other. The first group reflects standard Western assumptions about child-rearing, with its Calvinistic overtones, and the second, the inevitable counter-cultural reaction. How actually were babies treated through most of human prehistory? Some of the answers will come as a shock; others will seem naturally sensible.

Perhaps the most widespread condition of early child-rearing was the almost constant physical contact between a mother and her pre-crawling infant. Babies were held and carried continuously, and at a few months old, passed from adult to adult. They slept beside their parents, often with the whole family. There was no opportunity for the terror of abandonment. Babies today, usually raised without anything like that level of contact, are often left alone to "cry themselves to sleep." They frequently adopt a particular blanket or cuddly teddy bear as default "security."[23]

Feeding was "on demand." Children suckled as often as they wished. Nursing usually lasted for several years, and certainly continued long after the child began to eat solid foods. Children would seldom cry more than a few seconds before the mother responded. Human milk, which is more dilute than cow's milk (hence dilution of the latter for bottle-feeding), is designed for frequent short bouts of nursing. Feeding on demand seems to reduce colic, or excessive fussiness, probably because of the mother's attentiveness and the constant feelings of security. Night-feeding was simple as the child slept beside its mother and always near her breast. In fact, the stages of sleep of mother and child were coordinated; one would wake when the other did. Even when asleep, mothers can sense their baby's breathing. Sudden infant death syndrome, or SIDS, is the commonest form of infant death in modern societies, where babies sleep alone and are not fed "on demand" during the night; newborns sleeping with their parents is virtually unknown. Apparently their undeveloped brains are not yet trained in "how to sleep" – that is, to shift back and forth from light sleep controlled by neocortical breathing, to the automatic, brainstem-controlled breathing of deep sleep, something they mimic if sleeping beside an adult. Putting babies down on their backs seems to help, but the physical presence of an adult may well be important to their developing brain's coordination of the breathing reflex.[24]

As Liedloff concludes, if a baby experiences flexible parenting that is in tune with its own bodily needs, it gains confidence in its surroundings and is ready to learn fearlessly, free of the anxiety that a stressful, insecure infancy can engender.[25] On the other hand, lest well-meaning Western parents feel anxious about their child-rearing practices, child psychologist Jerome Kagan warns against despairing that the first years of life set an infant's future life in concrete, so to speak:

> [A] fearful, quiet, tense two-year-old who has had an uncertain environment remains malleable should benevolent changes occur, and a laughing, securely attached, smart two-year-old is not protected from angst should her life turn harsh.[26]

Turning again to the past, the security gained in infancy is continued in the social structure surrounding the crawling, walking, and increasingly independently exploring toddler and young child. During its whole childhood, a young person is surrounded by others of all ages and both genders. All are caregivers. All interact with and quietly watch over the developing child. (When visiting villages in India, I frequently saw girls aged 7 or 8 carrying an infant sibling about.) The child is familiar with and accepted by all; little Shakuntala is "centered" in her world, but is not *the* center of it.

This absolute acceptance continues even into adulthood. At each stage, the emerging person gains skills and is expected to take on responsibilities – which are seen as milestones of one's "becomingness." There are respected social tasks at every age. Youngsters may gather firewood. Young girls help with childcare and accompany the women gathering food. Boys play, practicing shooting arrows or throwing sticks, and begin to hunt and assist in other male tasks, such as hut-building. Adulthood and "marriage" bring child-rearing, contributions to the shared economy, and performance of ceremonial tasks. And finally, as elders, there is grandparenting (a specifically human function for postreproductives, that surely increases the survival rate among infants). They are also keepers of the lore, becoming story-tellers who each night recount around the fire the ancestral myths of how the world is. And as wisdom holders, they settle disputes and help the group reach decisions when crises arise.[27]

In short, there is a usefulness, an *identity*, at every age, and each person lives always in the midst of the entire social pattern, not isolated into age classes separate from others. Every child as it grows up witnesses births, deaths, and all that happens inbetween. There is little competition, on the one hand, nor any "peer pressure" to conform to one's age group, on the other. In the two and a half years she spent living with the Yequana, a stone age tribe in the rainforest of Venezuela, Jean Liedloff saw no fighting or arguing amongst the children.

> There is no competitiveness, and *leadership is established on the initiative of the followers....* Although I have seen many a party at which every Yequana, man, woman, and child, was drunk, I have never seen even the beginnings of an altercation, which makes one think that they really are as they look – in harmony with one another and happily at home in their own skins.[28]

Finally, she adds, people had *fun*; they were in constant high spirits, finding much to laugh about and enjoy. For the Yequana, "[t]his party atmosphere is the everyday norm."[29] People like to be playful, at every age!

I suggest that a similar high level of psychological security was typical for most successful tribal societies, the ones that could adapt their ways to changing circumstances without losing their ability to satisfy their human psychic needs. This lasted until at least 20,000 ya – maybe even until more recently – for all human societies that survived. Our genes are unlikely to have changed much since then.

## *The need for experience*

To reiterate once more, being psychologically bonded is the passport to independence and personal autonomy. A child who senses she is not trusted, cannot feel secure. If a parent "expects" naughtiness, or incompetence, she senses this and behaves accordingly. Liedloff suggests that both excessive scolding and excessive praise erode children's sense of self-reliance. They come to depend on constant external signals about their state of social acceptance. This Skinnerian "stick-and-carrot" approach to child-rearing destroys one's sense of autonomy. Being made to feel *unusual,* either inferior or superior, creates internal psychic discomfort for someone seeking acceptance within a face-to-face community.

What kind of experience is it that develops a sense of autonomy? In his excellent book *The Necessity of Experience,* the psychologist Edward Reed distinguished between those things that I discover for myself, first-hand, and those things I learn from others, second-hand. Make no mistake: human beings need both sorts of experience. Without the cultural knowledge and accumulated know-how passed on to us from our parents and grandparents, we would be lost. Yet to assume, as Western society increasingly does, that such predigested knowledge is the backbone of learning how to be a human being is a terrible mistake. There is no emotional satisfaction of self-accomplishment in simply memorizing what others know, or living life vicariously by watching others on a television screen. Human beings need personal, hands-on experience, physical contact with reality, the sort of interactions with their environment discussed in Chapter IV.

Recently at a local market I saw a toddler clinging to his mother's finger as he tottered forward on tiptoe, a huge smile of absolute rapture on his face at the wonderful experience of walking. He was *totally engaged in the experience.* Children spontaneously tackle every new task to be learned that will turn them from being dependent into being independent, autonomous actors in the world. This powerful drive is essential for the development of physical skills, of mental insights, and of social knowledge. It is what Reed meant by first-hand or primary experience: learning to walk, talk, run, throw, make things, solve problems, help out, and most important of all, to understand the meaning of things. Human development entails actively becoming an independent yet integrated member of one's own community.[30] This process is essential if the brain is to achieve a healthy balance between thoughts and feelings.

## *Guided participation*

In his seminal book *Acts of Meaning,* research psychologist Jerome Bruner shows how modern psychology has approached the brain as a kind of calculating machine that learns to make "rational decisions" based on cognitive knowledge, and quite ignored the role of affect or feelings in the learning process. He points out what I have stressed in the last two chapters: that one cannot think and act without the meaning provided by one's culture; that meaning involves values; and that values are related to feelings. Rational behavior cannot exist in a vacuum. It requires a cultural narrative to define it. And it is the acquisition of that narrative, or "folk psychology" as Bruner calls it, that is the task of the developing child as he interacts with those around him. This propensity for meaning is part of our genetically determined nature. The brain is, after all, a story-telling, meaning-making organ.

> [W]e come initially equipped, if not with a "theory" of mind, then surely with a set of predispositions to construe the social world in a particular way ... [W]e come into the world already equipped with a primitive form of folk psychology.[31]

It is on this universal grounding that one's own cultural understandings are built. The process of assimilating (or appropriating) one's cultural meaning system was investigated by the Soviet psychologist, Lev S. Vygotsky, who was among the first to theorize that "mind" develops *in a social context*; it does not simply unfold. He proposed that children develop through participation in activities slightly beyond their current level of competence. Under the guidance of more skilled partners in their society, they acquire new knowledge and meanings. The American developmental psychologist Barbara Rogoff has expanded on Vygotsky's ideas, suggesting that the development process occurs at three intersecting levels: the initiative of and assimilation by the autonomous child; the interactions between the child and her older guiding partner(s); and the larger cultural practice into which the particular skill fits.

As an example, Rogoff describes the factors involved when girls learn to sell Girl Scout cookies, a long-standing practice in American Girl Scouting. These girls are autonomously motivated to belong, to be members of and give support to their own troop. They further depend directly on older girls (who know "the ropes") and on adult leaders for guidance as they learn. And the whole process is embedded in the well-received American social institution of Girl Scouting, and thus has cultural meaning.[32] In her example, Rogoff shows how all three of these factors in the social development of a child are reciprocally intertwined. As with the navigation of the ship entering San Diego harbor (discussed in Chapter V), the institutional knowledge about selling cookies is located everywhere: in the society, in the individual heads of the various participants, and in the interactions among the whole troop. The situation follows our metaphor of Indra's Net: total interconnectedness of human cultural life.

The next question is what kind of "navigational system" does a given culture utilize in guiding its young toward full community membership? What are its assumptions about how children learn? About what is important to learn? These assumptions about the circumstances for learning make a huge, yet seldom appreciated, impact on a child's feelings of security *vis-à-vis* society, and hence on his own self-confidence.

*Cultural variants in guiding: "anxious" vs. "relaxed"*

Though each cultural community has its own theory of child-rearing, cultures tend to fall into one of two large classes: "relaxed" and "anxious." Relaxed cultures, I believe, are more likely to produce adults who feel accepted and self-confident – psychologically grounded. They include most of the less-developed peoples of the world, especially many extant tribal societies; it is likely our Pleistocene ancestors belonged in this group.

By contrast, most modern industrialized societies, regardless of past cultural histories, fall into the "anxious" category. This is particularly true where steep economic gradients exist together with economic mobility, creating a societal atmosphere of constant uncertainty, one based on scarcity and competition. Cultures based on such "bottom-line" thinking tend to produce adults for whom full psychological security is always out of reach.[33] Naturally, parents, teachers, and other "guides" unconsciously signal this prevailing cultural atmosphere as they interact with developing youngsters. Two examples will give the reader an insight into how self-identity can be affected.

The first deals with the learning of tasks. Barbara Rogoff and her colleagues contrasted the ways American mothers and mothers in Guatemala, India, and Turkey, interacted with toddlers when asked to explain a new toy to them: either play-dough or wooden nesting dolls. American mothers went to much trouble to attract the child's interest and repeatedly showed how the toy worked, correcting and praising the child, often in a baby-talk voice. Their concern that the child respond appropriately was evident. By contrast, mothers in the other three cultures briefly showed the child the toy and then left him to explore it while they conversed with the visitor. Whenever the child came for attention, a mother would immediately respond and demonstrate the whole process again, then hand the toy back and return to the conversation.[34]

Rogoff and her colleagues suggest that the opportunity for independent exploration afforded a child by the relaxed group of mothers facilitated the child's acquisition of problem-solving skills and a sense of independence. An American mother seemed less willing to trust that her child would learn without constant instruction and encouragement. This cultural anxiety over successful learning, we might add, persists during school years, where grades and rank-ordering are tacit measures of a child's future "worth" in society. Today, parental anxiety is spilling over into the recreational lives of children, with over-stressed parents feeling compelled to chauffeur their offspring everywhere and cheer-on their performances at sports, recitals and other activities.

The other example of relaxed versus anxious child-rearing has to do with safety. In her work, Rogoff has also examined American parental concerns for the safety of their children, which at times seems almost obsessive when compared with that of other, more relaxed cultures. Among the latter, she notes little concern about toddlers handling sharp knives, being burned by cooking fires, being cared for by only slightly older siblings, or getting hurt while playing. In her book, she shows a picture of an 11-month-old baby in the

210

Democratic Republic of Congo wielding a machete while an adult calmly watches (Figure VI.2). A child is expected, is trusted, to learn for herself. If an accident occurs, the child is immediately attended to, held, and allowed to cry freely until comforted. Though different degrees of danger certainly exist in different cultural settings, it is well to reflect on the degree to which "danger" can become a chronic psychic threat in a child's mind.

*Figure VI.2* Child-rearing practices vary with culture
An 11-month-old infant from the Ituri Forest uses a machete to cut a fruit while a relative watches from a distance.

*Source*: From B. Rogoff (1990: 131), Fig. 6.5. Original observations and photo by David Wilkie, who kindly supplied a copy; used with permission

In both examples, it is clear that a better balance is struck in the more relaxed cultures between the innate human needs to have trust in others for assistance and comfort, while experiencing the freedom to explore and gain a sense of independence and self-confidence. In fact, this is the very point that Robert Bly makes about American culture in his book *The Sibling Society*. Adults never lose the anxiety of having to please someone else in order to feel accepted as valued persons; they remain forever insecure in who they are, a culture of "permanent adolescents."[35]

## *The role of "behavior settings"*

It is not only interpersonal relationships that affect our experiences as we grow up. The environment as a whole, through both its social institutions and its physical settings, offers greater or lesser opportunities for us to have experiences leading to a healthy, balanced sense of self. One person investigating this has been the child psychologist Roger G. Barker, co-founder of a field known as "ecological psychology." Unlike mainstream psychology that looked only at the backgrounds of individual children for explanations of behavior, he asked how goal-directed behaviors were affected by the place, or "setting," in which they occurred. His surprising finding was that settings matter much more than such individual differences as age, sex, or social class. The nature of the setting itself determined how people acted: drugstore, football field, music class, city council meeting. Each setting carried cultural expectations affecting everyone's behavior. With regard to the developing individual, whose behavioral patterns are being molded, Barker's most important findings had to do with the conditions of schooling. When do young people feel most empowered (autonomous), most accepted (belonging), and have the greatest sense of social identity (meaning)? Under what sorts of conditions are all three of these basic psychological needs best satisfied?

He and his colleagues compared how the sizes of secondary schools correlated with the feelings of personal accomplishment and self-worth of their students. It turned out that, relative to students in schools with many pupils, students in small schools had much more opportunity to participate in social activities and to be recognized by peers, thus achieving a heightened sense of personal autonomy and personal worth in their own eyes and those of others. They also gained personal satisfaction at having contributed significantly to the local school community. All three basic human propensities were being met.

In larger schools, where the number of tasks to be performed relative to the size of the student body was much reduced (each school needs only one football team and one band, for example), most students were only passive observers in the social life of the school. They participated only marginally in sports teams, the band, plays, or as class leaders, and received no sense of having made any significant contribution to the life of the school. Their sense of community was largely vicarious, as an admiring audience for the small group of leaders. Barker concluded that in big societies, opportunities for developing autonomy are much reduced. Furthermore, for the majority of students, feelings of belonging and of shared meaning, while still present, were less emotionally satisfying. He suggested that, in societies generally, the psychologically healthiest behavior settings are what he called "underpopulated" environments, where every individual's contribution is necessary for the overall success of the whole group.[36] (This condition, I believe, would have held consistently throughout the Pleistocene, when everyone was "needed!")

Barker's work stunningly shows how not only the gigantic schools that so many children attend in Western societies, but also the gigantic institutions in which later, as adults, they spend their working lives (corporations, the military, public bureaucracies), work against satisfaction of human beings' deepest psychic needs for autonomy, for engaged belonging, and for significant meaning within a community.

To briefly summarize, some of the conditions for the development of the human brain that prevailed during the Pleistocene and that are still likely to be important for fostering healthy minds include: (1) psychic security, or the constant and unconditional access to caring and attentive adults who provide predictable physical and psychological nurturing. This in turn makes possible (2), the space for autonomous development, or the freedom of the individual to explore freely, learn about, and, finally, voluntarily contribute to the life of the community. This latter process is facilitated by (3), guidance from adults in the exploration process, which in turn also imparts cultural meaning to the skills and knowledge being acquired.

These three conditions are greatly affected by two psychologically significant qualities in the social environment. The first is the state of tension involved in the learning process. Over-anxious adults create insecure learners who have difficulty acquiring a mature confidence in their own value. The second is the size of the community in which a learner is acquiring her or his personal identity. If that community is "over-populated" so that only a few are significant actors and the rest are an applauding audience, the sense of personal fulfillment and social meaningfulness will be denied to the great majority. Only in the presence of a powerful cultural mythology that somehow justifies this impoverished emotional status can such a society remain stable; societies in which the majority sense they are "failures" and have no meaningful role will ultimately become unstable.

## Brains under stress

Having outlined the conditions that promote development of healthy brains and psychically well-balanced persons, I turn now to environmental factors that can interfere with how a child's brain develops, and even with how an adult brain functions. Almost all such factors act as *stressors* of brain and body, that in turn affect behavior. A 1996 study by the World Health Organization reports that stress-related psychiatric disorders are rapidly becoming major causes of human disability globally. By 2020, depression is expected to be the number two cause, with HIV infection (AIDS) back at number ten. Yet stress is receiving far less attention than is obviously necessary. Stress comes in multiple forms, and its resulting behavioral problems are all too familiar: alcoholism, drug dependence, suicide, schizophrenia, and uncontrollable violence.[37]

Though genes are major contributors to a few severe behavioral disabilities, such as autism and manic-depressive disorder (bipolar illness), for the most part, genetic variation means simply that some people are more vulnerable to various environmental stresses than are others, and thus have a higher risk for developing what are called "abnormal" symptoms. Furthermore, everyone succumbing to a given stress does not develop identical symptoms. The stress of social rejection, for instance, causes some to become resentful bullies, prone to violence, while others quietly withdraw from society. (The first, of course, garners much more social attention than the second.) The more stressful the environment overall, however, the greater will be the total number who prove vulnerable in one way or another.

Stressors come in many forms, some acute, others chronic: diseases; traumatic events (car accidents, earthquakes); hunger and malnutrition; persistent exposure to toxic chemicals or loud noises; insecure or dangerous social situations (racism, ethnic cleansing, war); and repeated physical or psychological abuse. All these stressors can affect the body by activating its automatic defense system, a network of reciprocal interactions between the brain, the endocrine glands, and the rest of the body.

### Physical stressors

The commonest physical stressors in the world today are malnutrition (with attendant illnesses), toxic agents, and drugs, particularly alcohol. In almost every instance, the origin of these prevalent stressors is traceable to malfunctioning social institutions, either local or global. Malnutrition affects approximately one-fourth of the world's children under the age of 5, when the brain is most in need of good nutrition. Its effects on brain function are not irreversible if the social environment is otherwise nurturing and stimulating. If not, however, even later concentrated schooling cannot repair the damage unless good nutrition also becomes available. Unfortunately, the poverty that underlies most malnutrition is too often accompanied by illness and other hardships, as well as little social stimulation or opportunity for schooling. Too often, the damage becomes permanent.[38]

In their book, *Our Stolen Future*, Theo Colborn and her colleagues document a whole host of human-made chemicals released into the global environment that threaten human health. Many are hazardous to the developing brain, both before and after birth. Among the worst offenders are PCBs (polychlorinated biphenyls), which, in children of mothers known to be exposed, cause physical and mental impairment, including learning disabilities and attention deficits. Though PCB manufacture is declining globally, problems with it continue because mothers still have PCBs stored in their bodies that affect their babies. Other culprits affecting pregnant women include various insecticides, herbicides, and fungicides, as well as a breakdown product of detergents and a plasticizing agent, both widespread in the environment. As well as these culprits, there is a whole host of other factors – environmental lead; iron and iodine deficiencies; and a long list of other pollutants – that affect the mental functions of people, especially children, around the planet.[39]

Finally there is the increasing global use of alcohol and other drugs as a means of escape from stress and despair. Throughout human history, fermented drinks along with various psychedelic drugs have had beneficial social and health uses. Consider, for example, the ritual use of peyote by Native Americans as a community-strengthening ceremony, and the drinking of dilute (and bacteria-free) wine and beer instead of contaminated water during most of "civilized" history. The mild intoxicating effects of these uses may well have relieved stress and promoted longevity, just as alcohol today is sometimes prescribed in modest amounts for those with potential heart problems.

Yet in almost every society in history, those that came under excessive stress took to over-use of alcohol (or other drugs) for psychic relief, with untoward social and medical consequences. Today disinherited indigenous peoples of every continent and the "outcasts" of inner cities are primary over-consumers of these drugs of escape, though more and more, overly stressed well-to-do people are following the same route.[40] Alcohol's effects on the adult brain are less than those of many "hard" drugs, but it can have disastrous effects on the developing brain *in utero*. Known as fetal alcohol syndrome, the disability is tragic, as the outer layers of the cerebral cortex are grossly reduced in size.[41] Such children, though loving, have serious learning disabilities that cannot be "treated." Children of mothers using cocaine and opiates, besides being born with addictions, may continue to exhibit attention deficit disorder and compulsive behaviors long after birth.[42]

Another, quite different sort of drug increasingly consumed by children is caffeine, now added in maximum-allowed doses to so-called "soft drinks." Besides impairing the calcification of bones and teeth, these high doses of caffeine promote nervousness, anxiety, short-temper, and the symptoms of attention deficit hyperactivity disorder (ADHD).[43] It looks as though some of the behavioral symptoms once attributed to either "bad genes" or psychological stressors have one or more physical causes as well.

I turn now to the behaviorally even more significant effects of psychological stressors, which so often turn people on the path toward using addictive chemicals.

### Psychological stressors

The picture painted by the descriptions and statistics in the report [of children made homeless by World War II] is one of horrendous personal agonies, multiplied beyond the power of the mind to conceive, to tens, hundreds, thousands, and chronicles the empty lives that follow the deprivations, the "affectionless characters" of the most grossly deprived; those who have lost the ability to form attachments, which is to say, to know the value of life itself, ever.[44]

Thus does Jean Liedloff describe the contents of a study conducted by the World Health Organization on the condition of tens of thousands of young children deprived through war of parental nurturing.[45]

Assaults on the brain by physical stressors are bad enough in the harm they can do to the developing brain, but seldom do they affect the balance between emotional and cognitive development to the degree that psychological stressors can. The human brain develops and adapts through experience. It *needs* care, security, warmth, and affection in order to create a healthy working relationship between the feelings that guide it and the knowledge it is accumulating, between the cognitive and emotional aspects of mind which, as we have seen, are inextricably linked.

When it does not receive reassuring inputs, the brain of an infant reacts; it develops in ways designed to adapt to a temporary bad situation, to help it survive. When it feels insecure, or in danger, at first a child will cry, desperately calling attention to itself, to its need for help. But if help and comfort do not come, or if the caregiver withholds affection, or, worst of all, is abusive, the developing brain responds adaptively by shutting down its demands for bonding. Its crying only brings pain, not solace. It withdraws, and eventually it can lose its ability to trust at all; it fails to develop the capacity to "feel," to love back, to have empathy. In the absence of intervention and a major shift to a stable, predictable, caring environment, early neglect and abuse can result in what are essentially permanent changes in the brain. As neuropsychiatrist Dr. Bruce Perry points out, what begins as an initial adaptive *state* elicited in response to severe stress can, over time, become a permanent behavioral *trait*. The malleable child's brain adapts to a permanent expectation of stress.[46] This may manifest itself either in extremes of violence (more common among abused male children) or in extremes of withdrawal (more common among abused female children). Perry points out that the lucky ones are those who can suppress their traumatic memories and recover a more balanced behavior pattern if and when they encounter a safer, saner environment.

### Some physiological and psychological changes after prolonged stress

Stress is far too often treated as a "mental problem," something that counselors and psychiatrists can "fix," when in fact it is as much a symptom of a pathology in the environment (just as lack of adequate nutrition is to hunger), than of something wrong "inside" the person. Over the past fifty years it has become evident that the brain (in both its cognitive and emotional aspects) *and* the endocrine system that controls so much of the body's chemistry, *and* the immune system that defends against both external invaders and internal cancers, are all tied closely together in an Indra's Net type of arrangement. A change here or there in this internal system can affect the rest of it. Stress, therefore, affects the whole person, not just one's conscious behavior.

The effects of stress are not yet fully known. The multiple chemical and neuronal pathways linking the whole network together are necessarily complex, and most of them are still not fully understood. In fact, research is constantly turning up new connections and new effects. Though the picture is far from complete, it is still possible to get an idea of how the body tries to adapt to external stress, and what kinds of major behavioral and physiological consequences can occur if the stress is extremely severe or persists for a long time.

I begin with the central endocrine network involved, the so-called *HPA*-axis, which is shown in Figure VI.3. Recall from the earlier description of the brain how closely associated the *h*ypothalamus is with the *p*ituitary, the body's primary endocrine gland. These two structures are linked, by way of the blood-stream, to another endocrine gland, the *a*drenal (actually there is a pair of them, one above each kidney). Together, these three structures form the HPA-axis, a triangular system of interacting stimuli and feedbacks. When a stressful situation arises, your brain sends a nerve signal to the inner adrenal medulla which instantly releases a "rush of adrenalin" into the bloodstream. This "fight-or-flight" hormone causes your eyes to dilate, heart and breathing rates to increase, and blood pressure to soar. Your system is on full alert. Suddenly you are superwoman or superman. In such a hormonal state, petite mothers have shifted heavy objects to free a trapped child. A great flood of natural painkillers, known as endorphins, are simultaneously released in the brain. You stop feeling pain.

The adrenalin rush also affects the hypothalamus, which releases a hormone, *CRF* (*c*orticotropin-*r*eleasing *f*actor) that flows to the pituitary. There it causes release of *ACTH* (*a*dreno*c*orti*c*o*t*rophic *h*ormone) which flows to the adrenal cortex and stimulates release of cortisol and related cortical steroid hormones. These help the body to mobilize fats and carbohydrates into blood sugar to meet the emergency. In less than half an hour, blood cortisol levels can increase 40-fold. Meantime, however, if the stress is short-lived, the corticosteroids will exert a negative feedback upon the hypothalamus, shutting down its release of CRF, which is what started the whole process. Within 60–90 minutes, cortisol levels in the blood drop back to normal. Until then, you may continue to feel shaky.

For most emergency situations, that is all that happens. There are no permanent effects except the unpleasant memories. But if the stress is extreme – one is truly terrorized, or the stress persists for weeks or months – then long-lasting changes take place in the brain and in the immune system. Though my main interest in this chapter is the brain, note that prolonged high blood levels of corticosteroids lead to a suppression of the immune system. Though there is

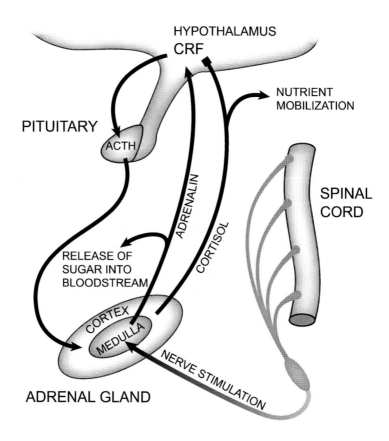

*Figure VI.3* The "HPA-axis" and stress

This schematic diagram shows the main hormonal interconnections via the bloodstream between the Hypothalamus, the Pituitary and the Adrenal glands. This axis has two main functions: maintaining daily sleep–awake cycles, and responding to stress. Only the latter is considered here.

*Note*: arrows indicate an activation; lines ending in a square, an inhibition

***Acute stress***: When the nervous system perceives a sudden stress, it signals the adrenal medulla to release adrenalin into the bloodstream. This triggers release of CRF (corticotrophin-releasing factor, a small hormone) by the hypothalamus, which in turn stimulates ACTH (adrenocorticotrophic hormone) release by the pituitary, that signals the adrenal cortex to release the hormone cortisol into the blood, where levels peak (up to 40-fold) in 15–30 minutes.

The cortisol acts to mobilize more nutrients into the bloodstream. It also acts back on the brain to inhibit the further release of CRF, and the system returns to normal in 60–90 minutes after the stress is discontinued.

***Prolonged stress***: Continued stress overrides this inhibitory feedback. Constant high levels of cortisol are maintained that cause changes in the brain and the immune system (see also Figure VI.4.).

*Source*: Original art by Michele Lukowski from author's sketch

still dispute as to how this anti-inflammatory effect might be adaptive during a stress situation, its existence has been coopted by the medical world for treating severe allergies and life-threatening auto-immune diseases, and for preventing the rejection of foreign organ transplants. But a person with a compromised immune system due to prolonged stress (or to HIV/AIDS) faces increased medical risks: for example, a higher susceptibility to infectious organisms and a decreased ability to suppress precancerous cells (present in all of us) from becoming malignant. (Children born with highly deficient immune systems, even when raised in "space-suits" and germ-free "bubbles," inevitably become riddled with cancer and die after a few years.[47])

As stated earlier, however, prolonged stress not only compromises the immune system; it also results in changes in the brain. It is not clear if the stress itself causes these changes (by altering the sensitivity of brain cells to corticosteroids) or if they are due directly to the high levels of the hormones themselves (see Figure VI.4, arrows 1 – the same sequence as in Fig VI.3). But several areas of the brain are affected, and some of this is reflected in behaviors. The hypothalamus is one such area; corticosteroids increase its release of the hormone *AVP* (or *a*rginine *v*aso*p*ressin) which raises blood pressure and also promotes aggressive behaviors (arrow 2). Both responses, of course, could be essential in an emergency, but are potentially dangerous if they persist.

Another area of the brain critically affected is the hippocampus, important in short-term learning and memory. (Your hippocampus is actively engaged when you are reading a book such as this, for instance.) Under prolonged stress, the hippocampus shrinks in size, its nerve cells lose their connections and eventually die (arrow 3). Not only is cognitive learning grossly impaired; there is also the loss of its normal output of serotonin, a calming brain chemical, into the neighboring parts of the limbic system (the hypothalamus, septum, and thalamus). These areas interact with the prefrontal lobes to modulate our emotions during decision-making (arrows 4). Thus when the hippocampus shrinks, all these normal calming modulations will also be suppressed.[48]

A third area of the brain that is strongly inhibited during stress, especially by occasions of extreme fear or terror (bad accidents, battlefields, rape or torture) are the prefrontal lobes themselves. The ability for considered decision-making is weakened or even temporarily eliminated, as in "blind rage." Conscious controls are closed down in favor of "autopilot," the automatic reactions needed during a crisis, as described in Chapter IV (arrow 5).

At the same time, extreme fear-inducing stressors activate the paired amygdala that lie just in front of the hippocampus on each side of the brain (arrow 6). These almond-shaped bodies have the task of assigning meaning to incoming sensory information. If there is great emotional significance, such as overwhelming fear, attached to an event it is unconsciously stored in memory. Unlike ordinary learning, no conscious concentration nor rehearsal of information is needed to form these memories. They are in a very different category from the ones we form through normal, conscious attentiveness. Traumatic

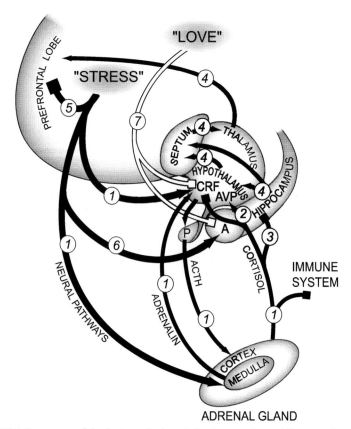

*Figure VI.4* Responses of the brain and adrenal glands to prolonged Stress and to Love
   Above: forebrain and midbrain areas + pituitary gland. Below: adrenal gland (one over
   each kidney)

*Note*: See text for numbered sequence of interactions during "stress" or "love". A pointed arrow
indicates an activation; lines ending in a square, an inhibition.

*Part of outer cortex*: prefrontal lobe of brain; modulates thinking and directs conscious action;
left side develops most strongly in *unstressed* persons, right side in *stressed* persons
*Parts of limbic system*: septum = relay center; hippocampus = conscious memory formation; A
(amygdala) = unconscious memory formation
*Parts of upper brainstem*: thalamus, relays to cortex, especially prefrontal lobe; hypothalamus,
controls pituitary gland and releases CRF
*Parts of endocrine system (hormonal system)*: P (pituitary gland), the "master gland" that
controls adrenals, gonads, etc.; releases ACTH; stimulates adrenal cortex.
Adrenal gland: medulla, produces adrenalin and other "fight-or-flight" hormones; cortex,
produces corticosteroids, such as cortisol and cortisone
*Parts of immune system*: white blood cells, antibodies, lymph nodes, spleen, tissue
macrophages, bone marrow

"Stress" and "Love" are signaled to the prefrontal lobes both by conscious pathways in the
brain's cortex as well as by the midbrain regions of the Reticular Activating System (see Figure
IV.1), and from diffusely stored memory centers throughout the brain

*Source*: Original art by Michele Lukowski from author's sketch

memories often cannot be consciously recalled, but if a "trigger experience" suddenly sets them off, they may flash into consciousness more as purely emotional episodes rather than as narrative experiences capable of being put into words. As Bessel van der Kolk, an expert on trauma, puts it:

> The person may feel, see, or hear the sensory elements of the traumatic experience. He or she may also be physiologically prevented from translating this experience into communicable language.[49]

Stress, then, particularly severe or prolonged psychological stress, has widespread impacts on brain structure and function. Before leaving Figure VI.4, I need to note one more thing, namely that "love," the security produced by experiencing nurturing acceptance and guidance toward autonomous development, has reverse effects on the brain. It inhibits both the destructive HPA-axis response to stress and its triggering of the amygdala's cryptic memory-recording system (arrow 7).

Behaviorally, even mild stress can temporarily impair the brain's cognitive processing in the prefrontal cortex. One finds it difficult to sustain attention, and comes to rely on habitual or automatic responses. Prolonged or severe stress pushes this adaptive behavior even further. As already noted, this may take two quite different directions. One, most common to females or those experiencing chronic depression as the result of stress, is to move inward, to withdraw from social interaction. A child who is repeatedly raped or tortured learns to fall silent, to dissociate from the present traumatic reality, even to become a "different person" or, sometimes, several other persons. Known as multiple personality disorder, it is, as psychiatrist Frank Putnam puts it, "[a] normal defense against stressful or traumatic experiences: one seeks refuge in a more hospitable state of consciousness."[50] In less severe cases, a person may simply seem autistic, unable to make physical or emotional contact with others.

Or the brain may move in the opposite direction, which is more common among males. For the male, the automatic response to stress is to be constantly at-the-ready. Such an individual finds it hard to focus attention, is restless, hypervigilant, and easily roused to anger and aggressive outbursts. Even the most innocent "stares" or "tones of voice" are perceived as threats.[51] Surprisingly, the typical bully can exhibit both kinds of responses, depending on whether or not the momentary situation seems hopeless. In general, the swaggering aggressiveness of bullies is a male-typical behavior, whether one is dealing with humans or experimental lab animals such as hamsters or rats. Young males (of whatever species) who have been mistreated in infancy (or injected with hormones to mimic the same effects) will avoid larger males, trying to withdraw. This is a "hopeless" situation. When they meet up with smaller, less aggressive males, however, they beat them up. Though they retain the same hormonal state, their displays in "hopeless" and "non-hopeless" situations are very different.[52] (Such biological studies have yet to be done on the more infamous of the world's human bullies, but data on animals and some humans suggest that high cortisol levels in the blood, signaling chronic inner stress, are likely present in them, as well.[53])

In conclusion, our brains were designed to adapt to acute stress, and such automatic responses did – and still do – have survival value. But when stress is prolonged and becomes widespread throughout a society, causing more profound changes in the brains of many of its members, then violence combined with apathy permeates daily life and threatens the survival of all. I believe many modern societies are heading toward this very condition.

### On being "sane" in insane places

This leads to the question, Can a whole society be "sick"? Can institutions that profoundly stress the brains of virtually every member of society actually exist? By the end of the last century we had enough data on the pervasive traumas of wars that exposed civilians as well as soldiers to the horrors of battle that I think there is no answer but "Yes!" A particularly horrible example that Russian historian Richard Hellie researched covers a period of nearly 200 years (1558 to 1721) in Muscovy, from Ivan the Terrible to Peter the Great. During that time there were continuous civil wars, invasions by Tartars who took thousands as slaves, and slavery existed within the society as well. Gruesome atrocities were committed on all sides: by authorities, criminals, and the Church. Hunger and disease were rampant. Men and women (with their children) went into voluntary slavery, trading freedom for protection and subsistence.[54]

Hellie felt he had found a biological answer to the question he had been asking – Why would such a state of affairs continue over so many generations? – when he came across Bruce Perry's work with traumatized children (outlined above).[55] The human brain tries to adapt. It learns to live in a world of constant terror. It tries to survive in an insane place. Survival under such conditions comes at a high price. The brain gives up many of the spontaneous qualities we call "human"; it loses the capacity to feel empathy, or to reflect on the consequences of actions ahead of time. It is like the brain of a soldier caught in crossfire during battle, whose only instinct is to stay alive. One is on constant "trigger-alert". Reflections on the meaning of what one is doing, on any possible compassion for others, are not permitted. They could result in death.

When Hellie and Perry appeared together on a nationwide talk show, they agreed that the whole of Russian society had become "chronically violent" as a result of all-pervasive stress. As Perry put it:

> Everybody impacted in that culture had manifestations of impulsivity, of difficulty with abstract cognition, with a certain style of problem-solving that in our current society we would label as post-traumatic stress disorder, and maybe learning disorder, and maybe attention deficit disorder. But in *that* society, it was the 'norm.'[56]

222

*Not* to be hypervigilant and constantly on the alert for danger in that society would have been abnormal – and probably fatal!

That a given cultural environment can be a primary cause of widespread mental stress is still not part of theory-building in modern psychology. Until recently, mainstream American psychiatry refused to admit the impact on the human brain of severe trauma. The cultural assumptions, backed by Freud's dictums, explained deviant behaviors of war veterans and traumatized children alike as either "inherited illness" (schizophrenia was a common diagnosis of Vietnam vets) or as a "problem" of early potty-training or some other equally unhelpful diagnosis. What we now call post-traumatic stress disorder, or PTSD, was prevalent among veterans of World War I. It was dubbed "shell shock." When I was a child, one of our neighbors suffered from it. Poor gentle, kindly Mr. Johnson was said to awaken at night screaming. It was a hush-hush topic.

Not until 1979, half a decade *after* the Vietnam War ended, did the United States government fully recognize the special needs of its war-traumatized veterans. It established the "store front" Vet Centers where for the first time troubled young men and women who had experienced incredible horrors could safely convene, share terrible experiences, and support each other under the guidance of sympathetic counselors.

In his moving book about his experiences with these vets, first as a chaplain in Vietnam and later on the streets of Los Angeles, the Reverend Bill Mahedy, my friend and colleague at San Diego State University, describes their common despair in finding no meaning to their having to kill unknown people and suffer seeing their buddies blown apart. There was no God in Vietnam. Many men went believing in John Wayne and Jesus Christ, and returned believing in neither one, feeling betrayed both by their country and by their superior officers. Once home, many suffered not only hostility and rejection from much of the public, but also sudden onsets of horrendous flashbacks to which they reacted uncontrollably. Their lives were utterly bereft of meaning; nothing they had been taught made sense any more.[57]

This loss of meaning, accompanied by the terror of flashbacks which engender a whole host of unbidden behaviors, has been ascribed by Veterans' Administration psychiatrist Jonathan Shay to the "berserk state," a condition in which the rational self dissolves under the double stress of feelings of "betrayal" by trusted superiors and the violent death in battle of close companions. In this total absence of moral/social grounding, a soldier may suddenly lose all capacity for psychic restraints. As Shay says, "I believe that once a person has entered the berserk state, he or she is changed *forever*."[58] If some stimulus happens to trigger a flashback, one may lose all conscious control of behavior.

Flashbacks, of course, are by no means limited to war veterans: anyone, child or adult, who suffers from PTSD may experience them. This potential raises enormous problems for societies that hold a person legally responsible for each and every act regardless of prior experience. Pleas of "self-defense" or "temporary insanity" may sometimes be allowed, but the public remains skeptical, especially of the latter. In our increasingly stressful modern societies, where unexplained violence is on the rise, it is far more convenient to target, and punish, the individual disruptive child or suddenly violent adult than to examine the overall social environment.

Also unacknowledged as a *collective social problem* are the increases in severe depression, at all ages, and in ADHD among children and adolescents. Both dissociation (depression) and hyperarousal (ADHD) are states of constant, often unconscious, fearfulness that remain present throughout life and can be triggered into conscious awareness by painful stimuli.[59]

Globally, the number of psychically stressed children and adults is growing. Ten years after the Union Carbide poisoning disaster in Bhopal, India, thousands of survivors were still suffering severe PTSD symptoms.[60] In many unstable countries, children as young as age 10 or 12, both boys and girls, are being coopted into child armies and trained to kill, to assassinate, even to cannibalize the dead enemy. An estimated 250,000 to 300,000 under-18-year-olds are serving in armed conflicts globally. Often, their brains permanently lose any capacity for empathy.[61]

Torture and rape are a form of "invisible brutality" used for political control in many authoritarian societies; and they are highly visible during episodes of ethnic cleansing as occurred in Bosnia, Kosovo, and Rwanda.[62] And in the United States, where over eight million children suffer from trauma-related disorders (mainly from domestic abuse), many will develop PTSD as adults. But the largest single group of adults in that country who suffer from PTSD are women survivors of rape and domestic violence.[63]

Societies thus do bear responsibility for the sorts of behaviors that exist within them. On the whole, Western societies have politically resisted the necessary self-inspection that could identify *society as a whole* as the primary perpetrator, intentional or not, of the high incidence of psychological traumas and often consequent crimes of violence among their own populations. Two psychiatrists, the Australian Alexander McFarlane and American Bessel van der Kolk, draw attention to this cultural deficiency:

> This intolerance of victims of trauma, rather than of the circumstances that lead to those traumas, is a function of a willingness to accept the seemingly inevitable conditions that lead to traumatization: crime, wars, poverty, and family violence.[64]

And, as Bruce Perry comments, the turning of stressed individuals toward violence rather than toward dissociative withdrawal (the other, less socially disruptive form of adapting) is itself culturally directed:

> [T]he majority of traumatized and neglected children do not become remorselessly violent. *Belief systems*, in the final analysis, *are the major contributors to violence*. Racism, sexism, misogyny, children as property,

224

idealization of violent "heroes," cultural tolerance of child maltreatment, tribalism, jingoism, and nationalism all unleash, facilitate, encourage, and nurture violent individuals. Without these facilitating belief systems and modeling, neglected and abused children would carry their pain forward in less violent ways, as silent, scarred, adult members of the vast army one commentator has termed the 'Children of the Secret'.[65]

This critical relationship between cultural narratives and the psychic health of human beings is pursued further in the following chapters. First, though, a brief look is needed at what can be done to help heal traumatized minds.

## Healing

Experience so far suggests that deep traumas can never be wholly erased, yet much can be done to reduce the intensity of flashbacks and restore personal control and psychic security to those who are suffering either from dissociation and depression or from excessive arousal and impulsive violence. Since traumatic experiences disrupt the normal integration between motivational and cognitive regions of the brain, between the thalamus and limbic system on the one hand and the prefrontal lobes of the cortex on the other, the task of healing is to restore that balance, to restructure past traumatic memories so they no longer unleash such an overwhelming flood of emotion. The old expression "time heals" only works in a supportive environment, and it may take considerable time and effort on the part of both healers and patients.

There is a powerful tendency in Western medicine to prescribe a drug to ameliorate the symptoms of a depressed patient (usually Prozac) or a disruptive child (usually Ritalin) and then neglect the necessary inter-human work that must follow if healing is to occur.[66] Bruce Perry, whose research has helped illuminate the changes in the traumatized developing brain, takes a multifaceted approach to treating childhood trauma. He combines mild antihypertensive drugs with a process for "restructuring" the brain through building an emotional bonding of trust, a full openness between child and therapist. Finally, the daily environment of the child is evaluated to correct any dysfunctional relations, thus providing stability and predictability in the child's life.[67]

Less conventional, yet still mainstream approaches to healing have been proposed by Herbert Benson at the Harvard Medical School. Among end-of-the-millennium physicians, Benson is somewhere "out in left field." Unlike many, he believes strongly in the body's power to heal itself, *provided that the patient is surrounded by a supportive community*. In the course of practicing old-fashioned medicine, where the physician "orders" medications and life changes (stop smoking, exercise daily, eat fiber and lots of vegetables...), Benson would add such "new-fangled" concepts as actually listening and talking to, indeed even befriending, a patient. Benson argues that instead of being aloof as the "high priests" of medical wisdom, doctors should be friends, counselors, partners with their patients in their healing.

In his book *Timeless Healing*, Benson acknowledges the critical role emotions play in our lives, and also the critical need for meaning, and hence some kind of transcendent story or religion that makes "sense" of existence. He suggests one role of the physician may be to help each person understand their enormous capacity for controlling their reactions to stress and pain. It is not to be accomplished by consuming drugs (prescription or otherwise), but by knowing how our conscious selves can take significant control over what we experience. In many ways, Benson reiterates the prescriptions of Buddhism: change what you can change, and accept what you cannot. Yet he also offers a third way: seek succor from your fellow human companions, for they have healing power.[68]

In his work, Benson stresses the "placebo effect," the potent effect on one's psyche that happens when you or I *believe* that someone else has the power and knowledge to help us. We may be given a sugar pill (the placebo) but because we think it will help, we feel better. Often, just a trip to the doctor makes our symptoms diminish, even go away. Under the stress of modern society, all that many of us need is a sign of human concern, of human reassurance. Our minds, Benson argues, affect our health profoundly. While every disease, of course, cannot be cured only by physician care, or bland prescriptions to exercise and diet, much of our physical health, he argues, does very much depend on how supported we each feel by those around us.

Benson notes that belief can be *enormously* powerful. He cites how the dread fear of evil spirits that exists in some tribal societies can be so internalized that when, say, a voodoo witch doctor casts a death spell on a believer, that person in fact *does* die.[69] His primary message is that our psychological relationships with our fellow beings are enormously powerful, far more than we realize. Just as the internal fear and distrust engendered by other-inflicted trauma (whether in the cradle or the battlefield) can damage our brains, so can other-offered succor and unconditional love heal them. What Benson is actually describing is the enormous health-giving power of acceptance of the self within a fellowship of other human beings: in short, our deep-felt need for secure bonding and shared meaning.

The health-promoting effects of developing positive social relationships, whether personal friends, support groups, or professional healers, have been identified by numerous workers. Not only do stress symptoms go down and patients become less depressed or less angry, their body chemistry improves, as indicated by lower blood levels of adrenalin and cortisol. This in turn benefits the immune system's ability to resist or conquer diseases, from the common cold to cancer. Chances of heart attacks are lower and life expectancy goes up.[70] The benefit to patients in nursing homes of children visiting them has been reported (with benefit to the children as well!), as has the healing power of pets for those living alone. Even a view of Nature (rather than of brick walls) outside one's hospital room can reduce the days needed to recover from major surgery.[71]

Another nonmedical, nondrug approach to illnesses is being applied in the treatment of the vague constellation of symptoms called "Gulf War Syndrome," reported by thousands of American veterans of that encounter. Even though its doctors have no idea what may cause these symptoms, the United States Army has begun taking treatment of them seriously. It consists, however, not of treating the symptoms *per se*, but of helping patients to stop dwelling on those symptoms and whatever it is that they think may have caused them. Patients go to centers where they evaluate all the factors *besides* the disease itself that make them feel better or worse, and then start changing the ratio of these variables in their lives. The more difficult cases get a thorough work-up for any possible physical causes at a medical center. While there, they get daily physical programs and lots of "cognitive therapy" designed to help them change how they think about things. The theory is that "how I think affects how I feel."[72] This is reminiscent of Buddhist teachings that urge one to temper deleterious "natural" feelings of anger and resentment because not only do they not solve the initiating problem, they also are debilitating psychologically and physiologically.[73]

There is some disagreement on the use of crying as catharsis for restructuring the brain following a severe traumatic experience. By some, it is considered essential; by others, it's believed unnecessary. Harvey Jackins, founder of Re-evaluation Counseling, stumbled on the process of letting a traumatized person repeatedly tell his or her story to a trained (but nonprofessional) friend. At first, the story-teller would break down in tears, and was then physically held by the listener-friend until the sobbing stopped. But after several tellings, the sobbing episodes grew shorter, were then replaced by laughter (albeit seemingly inappropriate), and finally the telling of the story brought on no uncontrolled emotions.[74] (The organization he founded now exists in many countries and its literature appears in twenty-nine languages.)

Another program, developed by Roger Mills and his daughter Ami Chin Mills, takes a similar one-on-one approach of listener to client, but in this case the listeners are practitioners formally trained in how to help their patients, and they do not engage in physical contact nor encourage episodes of crying.[75] They are, however, sympathetic and creative listeners, who help clients reconstruct their understanding of past traumatic events without feelings of guilt or rage.

Other approaches also exist. In war-ravaged Cambodia, for example, there is an extremely high level of PTSD, especially among women who experienced terrible events, including the murder of loved ones and repeated rape and torture. Much work is now being done to help these totally non-functional persons heal and return to a constructive social life. The stages include: (1) encourage them to talk about their experiences repeatedly *and* follow this each time with new memories, recalled aloud; this gradually helps establish positive new memories in place of the traumatic old ones; (2) begin to engage them in some socially significant activity, no matter how simple – gather firewood, sweep the floor, weed the garden, and so forth – in order to make life mean-ingful again; (3) teach them income-producing skills with social content, such as manicuring, where they learn to touch other people in a safe, public situa-tion, even people who might once have been considered "enemies" – that is, as belonging to the "other side" in bygone days. The role of *touch* here is to estab-lish trust, while earning an income offers a sense of autonomy as well as social purpose.[76]

Finally, I draw attention briefly to the healing aspects of art, music, and reli-gious contemplation or other deeply engaging pursuits in treating troubled affect states, an approach still overly neglected by mainstream science. In Chapter V, I spoke about the connections of music to memory, even in Alzheimer's patients and others who have lost the ability to recognize or use speech. The deep emotional role of music and of the visual arts is surely impor-tant in reaching areas of the brain that language cannot access, areas where unconscious memories are stored.

Recent studies by Andrew Newberg and the late Eugene d'Aquili of the ways human brains respond to repetitive rhythms, chanting, or the ecstatic dancing of Sufi mystics, as well as to meditation and prayer, show a marked excitation of the hypothalamus, while the self-conscious, "orientation" areas are suppressed, leaving a person with a conscious, transcendent experience.[77] In a recent paper on the subject of music as healing, philosopher Bruce Wilshire has this to say: "[Music] is momentous emotion – emotion as momentum – that can drive us through the shocks and disappointments, the black holes of time. It is universal therapy."[78] How Benson's placebos, or Buddhists' meditation, or music, act to enhance well-being remain obscure. I suspect the entry opportunities into the complex pathways of interaction between the brain, the endocrine system, and the immune system – indeed, into the whole inner person – are almost endless.

All of these psychological healing efforts, by the individual, by therapists, and by society as a whole, work only because the human brain *can* heal. Not only can connections be remade and old regions co-opted to replace damaged areas, but new nerve cells can be recruited for some tasks – something long thought impossible. Neuropsychologist Herman Blumenthal, who specializes in geriatric changes in the brain, summarizes this healing process as

> the capacity of the brain to remodel its neural circuitry over the life span, and to repair damaged circuitry by recapitulating processes similar to those involved in embryogenesis.[79]

In every instance, these disparate approaches to healing share one thing in common: they work because they meet the all-powerful need of all human beings to feel securely accepted into a caring community. It is time now to explore the social contexts in which human beings actually live. How well do our societies in fact accommodate our basic psychological needs?

# VII

# "WHO AM I?" – WHERE BIOLOGY AND CULTURE MEET

One of the fundamental needs of men, as basic as those for food, shelter, procreation, security and communication, is to belong to identifiable communal groups, each possessing its own unique language, traditions, historical memories, style and outlook. Only if a man truly *belongs* to such a community, naturally and unself-consciously, can he enter into the living stream and lead a full, creative, spontaneous life, at home in the world and at one with himself and his fellow men.

Roger Hausheer (1980: xxxvi–vii; emphasis in original)

It is often claimed that the problems of human violence and war are insoluble because they are "part of our make-up" or "in our genes." There is no scientific foundation for this view. Humans are certainly capable of aggression, but it is not inevitable that they should be [violently] aggressive. In the course of evolution, natural selection has ensured that individuals are born with the potential to behave not only aggressively, but also cooperatively, acquisitively, assertively, altruistically and in many other ways. But the extent to which individuals actually behave in any of these ways, and the short-term goals to which their behavior is directed, are *strongly influenced by social experience.*

Robert Hinde (1990: 172; emphasis added)

The above quote from Roger Hausheer so completely encapsulates the theme of this chapter that I chose it despite its outdated sexist language. In two sentences, it expresses the central problem for every human being: to be an unconditionally accepted member of a meaningful community. A community whose shared narrative guarantees that one's biologically grounded needs for bonding, for autonomy, and for meaning are met. Indeed, there have been cultures where these needs are so effortlessly met that the question "Who am I?" cannot be asked; there is no word for "I" because it is not needed. The identity of "myself" is never in question. It is subliminal, taken for granted.

Such a state of "self" – or perhaps I should say "unself" – cannot be imagined by most Western people. Wherever the ideas of the European

229

Enlightenment have penetrated cultural narratives, there is a firm belief in "the self-constructed person." I am in charge of me; I am the one who creates myself. Like most beliefs that humans have held, there is, of course, a kernel of truth here. By our self-initiated, autonomous acts, we do create who we are. We do make choices. We are to *some extent* free of both our genes and our culture, and of our personal experiences, since we can learn to reflect on and change how we feel about our cultures, and our experiences. But genes, culture, and experience also constrain us; they limit our freedom. The trick is to feel "free" while still feeling "accepted," and to achieve this in a welcoming positive environment of shared values and purposes, rather than a defensive, negative one of fear and coercion. People who feel "at home" in their communities because the social milieu meets their biologically innate needs do not require coercion in order to conform to the needs of the whole group; the shared narrative makes such cooperative behavior spontaneous.

This nexus between our biologically innate propensities, or needs, and the cultural narrative or meaning system that we are born into, is the subject matter of this chapter. How well do cultures, past and present, solve the problem posed by our inborn dilemma of simultaneously desiring to belong and to be free? Probably no society in history has ever perfectly resolved this paradox of human nature. Perfect solutions are always out of reach, in some utopia of our imaginations. The social task is to constantly correct the worst imbalances of the shared narrative, modifying it over time. This ongoing process requires some form of social dialogue; today, we call it "politics."

In this chapter, I tackle some of the common problems faced by human societies over time, paying particular attention to how they deal with issues of individual identity, of each person's place in the community according to age, task, and gender. How a cultural narrative deals with this will determine whether a society must use fear and coercion to maintain internal order, and how, in turn, peoples' feelings of freedom and purpose are affected. As I proceed, I shall keep asking: how well does this society create for each person what I call "autonomy within community"? (The meaning of this phrase will emerge as the chapter progresses.)

I begin with a brief inquiry into that important but elusive concept, "culture."

## Culture: a living non-thing

Culture, as I understand it, is not a thing. It is neither a set of encoded rules nor a fixed patterning of behavior. Culture does not stand above individuals like a super self that knows all and sees all. Culture is created through communication.

Culture is the set of stable consensual frames in a social system. Cultural frames may appear fixed and rule-like because they coalesce into products like pottery, languages and writing systems, because their change is slow and distributed across time, space and social networks wider than the one in which we typically live our lives. Pots, languages and writing systems are living things, however. They change to accommodate individuals and their collective actions.[1]

With these words, psychologist Alan Fogel presents us with a view of culture not unlike that described by Edwin Hutchins when he spoke about a crew's navigation of a large ship (see Chapter V). It is a system of *meanings* that exist in people's heads and by which they hold dialogues – with themselves, or directly with each other, or when they read the paper, go to a movie or ball-game, or watch television, shop, or attend church. "Culture is alive in its process and in its products and it lives through its *use* by individuals."[2]

Initially, meanings are learned through direct experience. At age 3 months a baby learns that he has feet and hands as he grasps one with the other and looks at them. We learn the names of things from older people, who guide us by means of their interactions with us. We also learn via stories that explain why the world is as it is and how people should live in it. As anthropologist Paul Bohannan notes, "story is a basic unit in cultural behavior."[3] Gossip, reports, parables, myths, descriptions, testimony – all these are kinds of stories that people share. Embedded in them, along with our recollections, are our feelings and interpretations. We are sharing *meanings* (recall from Chapters V and VI that the human brain is a story-telling, meaning-making organ).

Now this sharing of meanings, by which we enter into a cultural stream, has a paradoxical result. We feel bonded, accepted by the other people in our lives. Yet at the same time, by *accepting* those shared meanings and the behaviors they imply we simultaneously *give up* many of our freedoms of action. We become "socialized." We learn to be regulated by the society around us because we want to belong to it. As Fogel says, this is not because we perceive we must obey hard-and-fast rules, but because the repetition of learned patterns of behavior with others is a reaffirmation of our relationships.

He adds, however, that while some of the patterns imposed on us within the group may make us feel good, others can make us feel miserable, "depending on the nature of the discourse [read, relationship]."[4] A small child may hate brushing her teeth, but accepts the task because she hates even more a loss of parental affection. I may dislike the habits of, say, a brother-in-law, but tolerate him as amicably as possible in order to avoid disappointing my spouse. Any individual living in a group is constantly faced with constraints on her or his freedom of behavior, not because of generalized laws or rules, but because group life, with its net of interpersonal interactions, demands it. People are all connected, one to the next, in affiliative patterns that form an over-arching "group pattern" or set of institutions, which still differs somewhat from group to group even within the same homogeneous society. One is born into a group; one learns the patterns of the group; and one either accepts the constraints, tries to change them (by youthful rebellion, perhaps, or later by mature persuasion), or goes in search of another group (the "fission response" at an individual level). If none of the above is possible, violence may result.

The patterning process described in the two preceding paragraphs would apply equally to packs of wolves and troops of monkeys, as well as to bands of humans. Individuals in all these societies learn the "meaning" of the existing group patterns through repeated interactive experiences. What sets human societies apart is the enormous flexibility in the behavioral patterns they can develop. Unlike packs of wolves or troops of monkeys, whose communication systems are rather limited, human cultures, through language and other symbolic signals, can create an enormous range of group behavioral patterns. What is more, we can imagine *alternative* patterns and dialogue about them; we can envision *alternative* futures. Culture allows for the evolution of complex behavioral patterns incorporating consciously held and elaborately expanded meaning systems, otherwise known as "cultural narratives" or "world views."

It is no surprise that the cultural stories people share differ so hugely from one society to the next in their perceptions of human nature and human needs. It is almost as if they were from alien planets. As Fogel notes:

> Cultures differ in the perception of the individual's control in relation
> to others, in whether they view the self as relational or as autonomous
> and individualized.[5]

What he is referring to are those unconscious assumptions, the "pilings" underlying cultural belief systems, often known as "indigenous psychologies," or "folk psychologies" (see Figure 0.2.). They are the underlying, tacit beliefs about how human beings are constructed. Just as Western cultures tend to apply an individualistic, Billiard Ball metaphor in thinking about the structure of societies, where the autonomous self is the basic unit of social life, other cultures picture people only through their relations with others, akin to the metaphor of Indra's Net. Eskimo cultures, having no word for self-reference (i.e., no "I"), use phrases such as "his making of a sound ... to me" (for "I hear him") and "the being-here mine" (for "I am"). They only think (and thus construct language) from the point of view of *relationships*, not of themselves as separate individuals. And the language of the Ica in Colombia has no pronouns at all![6]

To sum up, cultures are shared social patterns of interaction which are accumulated, and modified, over generations; they are maintained by people living in groups through stories and customs. Embedded in the language itself, as well as in the stories and customs, are the basic perceptions of a people about human nature, human relationships, and the place of humans in the universe. These basic beliefs justify the social institutions of a society, through being woven into its myths, into its "sacred meaning" or "religion," which also confers an identity on each individual. The meaning or purpose of life for every human being thus comes out of her or his relationships with others. (Even a wildly individualistic American, or a retiring Tibetan Buddhist whose "ultimate goal is to understand that the world is created entirely in our imaginations," as Fogel says, can make personal meaning only by working very hard to consciously reject such experienced relationships.[7])

## Identity: the core cultural task

Cultural narratives, if they are to produce stable, cohesive societies, must somehow fulfill, first and foremost, our innate psychic needs. Only when all three are reasonably satisfied can a society thrive without employing fear and coercion. Successful cultural stories create institutions that balance the potential tension between bonding and autonomy. (In this discussion, I am reifying "culture" for convenience, treating it as an independent entity. The reader is asked to keep in mind that "culture" is nowhere and everywhere; it has fuzzy edges; and it is under constant revision over time by the people in whose heads it is distributed. This scarcely makes it insignificant, however. As anthropologist Paul Bohannan makes clear, our shared stories, particularly our myths and origin stories, "can explain whole reaches of cultural tradition that are not susceptible to any other kind of explanation."[8] Indeed, Chapter VIII is devoted to the violent clashes that cultural differences have generated throughout history.)

My identity, my conscious understanding of who and what I am, is a socially dependent self-image. It is formed by the ongoing sum of my experiences as they take on meaning in terms of the cultural narrative shared by those around me. I am born to certain parents, in a particular neighborhood, in a country that speaks a certain language and has its own history, rules, and customs. What I am allowed to become, and how I am expected to act, are implicit in the lives of those I meet. The meaning of what I know, do, and am exists in relation to my social world. If I lose meaningful contact with others, I lose my sense of self. I become empty, dispirited, purposeless, depressed. (Hyperindividualistic Americans often suffer this way. The sad case of the industrialist millionaire, Howard Hughes, who died alone in a darkened room, terrified of catching a disease from his fellow humans, comes to mind as an extreme case.) As anthropologist Richard Shweder puts it, one has lost one's soul.[9]

### *Necessity for bonding*

Our utter dependence on others in infancy creates this lifelong need to belong, to be accepted and appreciated. It is not, however, merely an immature carryover into adulthood. Bonding by adults in stable communities is essential for the successful rearing of each new generation of helpless infants. Though it is common in many societies for males, in particular, to play down this need for attachment to others, such suppression leads to a whole host of potential pathologies. Thus, an "ideal" narrative would embody unconditional accep-tance for all members. Rejection, or rupture of a bond, whether actual or threatened, is a profound cause of psychic distress. And with good reason. Abandonment of an infant results in death. Even expulsion of an adult from a community, at least during the Pleistocene when our psychological needs were evolving, could be nearly as serious, and generally is employed only for unfor-givable acts.[10]

Feelings of rejection can create either depression or aggression, the two responses of the limbic–prefrontal axis to excessive stress. As noted in Chapter VI, on the whole stressed males tend toward aggression and females toward depression, but the difference is by no means absolute. One who is depressed, however much she or he personally suffers, is less socially disruptive than one who is aggressive. Schoolyard bullies rejected by their peers, jealous ex-husbands, and members of socially oppressed groups are frequent "violent offenders"; the others tend to suicide.

Cultural narratives differ greatly in how they meet this need for belonging; some provide for lifelong acceptance, others promote feelings of rejection or oppression, whose violent consequences within the society are suppressed by various forms of psychic and physical coercion. These are typically hierarchical empires. A third category, also hierarchic, possesses morally "corrective" narra-tives that replace the old justifications for keeping some types of people forever at the bottom of the social heap with new opportunities for all to "compete" for places higher up on the social ladder. As shown below, such "liberal" societies are generally riddled with internal conflict that is often forcefully held in check.

### Necessity for autonomy

Frustration of one's freedom of action is perhaps the thing Westerners, espe-cially Americans, fear most. It is embodied in their mantras about human rights and free speech, in the right to carry guns and the right to private ownership of unlimited property, and in their bridling at social constraints ("get government off our backs" – as though government were an evil, alien entity, not a duly elected group of compatriots). As already noted, however, *every* social relation-ship constrains individual action to some degree. One cannot be a member of a social community and not experience some restrictions on one's behavior. The magic of "successful" cultural narratives is the balancing of social constraints with a sense of spontaneity of personal action. They possess two qualities: child-rearing practices that generate secure self-identity and reciprocal trust in and respect for others; and a cultural meaning system that attracts spontaneous support from all its members.

It is not surprising, if one stops to think about it, that these qualities are most likely to be found in egalitarian societies. Here, equality does not mean equal in all capabilities; rather, it means *equally valued for the capabilities one has*. Each social contribution, be it mothering, hunting, or as a growing child, is necessary to the future of the whole – analogous to the mutually necessary tasks of navigating a large ship. One function of the ideal cultural narrative is to show how all the various contributions to social life made during the several stages in the human life cycle have equal significance, and are to be respected and valued equally in their particularities. No one expects a 10-year-old child to possess the wisdom of an elder, nor a gifted shaman and healer to contribute an equal share of food to that of the skilled tiller; rather, all "work" is valued for itself.

Just as respect creates equality, so trust generates spontaneous prosocial activity, without need for threat or coercion. As emphasized in Chapter VI, the natural propensities to belong and to be independent, if carefully nurtured, create in the developing person a strong urge to help the whole group by whom one feels accepted; to contribute to the good of the whole. In cultures with beliefs about attentive child-rearing and trust in the individual's ability to become self-reliant, there is little need to chastise, to threaten, or to coerce; nor is there need to bribe, to promise, to reward. The satisfaction lies in the quality of being unconditionally valued. Life has meaning; one has a profound sense of identity, of being totally accepted, a needed member of the whole.

Though today this may sound utopian, something rather like it occurred in diverse places during our species' long emergence in the Pleistocene, and several dozen examples have been recorded in recent times. The latter, all found to be remarkably non-violent societies, were with but one or two exceptions highly egalitarian. What they all share in common seems to be the belief "that peacefulness is the defining characteristic of humanity." In other words, *how a culture perceives human nature determines the way its people behave!*[11] In general, the narratives of such societies promote equal respect for all contributions, and a balancing of the satisfaction of belonging with the needs for autonomy and independence. This seemingly paradoxical result occurs when a cultural story possesses those two qualities mentioned above: (1) an appreciation that the purpose of attentive nurturing is to develop not obedience, but self-reliance and autonomy (the "trust concept"); and (2) a sacred aspect to the shared social purpose that is embedded in the narrative and lends identity to each individual life and a desire to contribute to the success of the whole. These two together ensure that the uncoerced, autonomous behavior of the individual is naturally directed to the benefit of the whole society. Such societies achieve what I have called "autonomy within community."

All of which brings me to a consideration of the necessity for a meaningful narrative.

### Necessity for meaning

The third need of the human psyche is for a set of beliefs about the purpose of existence. As noted in Chapter IV, an "interpreter" region in the human brain's left hemisphere automatically creates *meaning* out of experience. A satisfying meaning system both explains our function in the universe and tells us how to fulfill that function: what things an individual and a whole society *ought* to do. It justifies a society's social institutions. Hence, an entire group shares the same (or very similar) beliefs. Shared meanings inspire loyalty; they coordinate social activity.

The evolutionarily adaptive function of such a shared meaning system is obvious. It insures effective group behavior *vis-à-vis* the common environment. Not surprisingly, most cultural narratives incorporate an authoritative source for their explanations: an originating spirit, ancient ancestors, one or more powerful deities. They also include rituals of sacrifice to the unseen powers to make sure the sun comes up and the plants and animals flourish, and the universe continues as it should. (These, of course, have the important effect of synchronizing human activities with the local environment, an aspect that the overly objectified, Billiard Ball-type narrative of the West has almost entirely lost.)

All these critical functions are embedded somewhere within the shared cultural stories of every coherent society. And since time immemorial, because successful social life depended on loyalty to the group narrative, it has been defended vigorously. This extreme defense of belief systems (discussed further in Chapter VIII) has often proved problematic throughout history. It may inhibit the changes needed to meet altered contexts, leading to "cultural traps"; and it has been the cause of enormously bloody conflicts between disparate systems. Both of these can be avoided by consciously incorporating into the narrative story processes for *modifying* the belief system over time, and for recognizing that different beliefs held by others are not necessarily threatening to one's own.

Such processes, of course, are supposedly embedded in modern democratic, constitutional governments in which justification for modifying cultural assumptions is sought through the authority of an "objective" science. Yet as suggested in my Introduction, the West still has not found a satisfying solution to our need for sacred meaning. In place of a transcendent myth, an emotionally satisfying narrative that speaks to our humanity, we have created a materialistic religion that leaves us, as a people, empty of an emotionally satisfying, shared purpose (see also Figure 0.6). The purpose of our individual lives is constructed of many partial meanings patched together out of various subcultures to which we each belong. (In my final chapter I offer some new paths for overcoming this vacuum of meaning.)

In the absence of transcendent meanings, people are forced, by that crucial part of our forebrains, to invent what I call "default meanings." These often focus around the idea of a "nation-state," replete with sacred symbols: a flag, a stirring anthem, a founding hero, such as Washington, Ataturk, Lenin, or Mao. (I surprised myself when I personally experienced how profoundly one can be affected by such symbols. During my decade living in Britain, I repeatedly would find tears welling in my eyes at the sight of an American flag or the singing of *The Star-spangled Banner*, something that never happened at home.)

It was Karl Deutsch who pointed out how modern nationalism emerged: people living in societies that were changing too rapidly found it necessary to invent a stable symbolic identity for themselves, based on an arbitrary piece of real estate.[12] One of the most notorious instances was the gradual creation, over several hundred years, of the concept of a single Aryan people. According to historian Lionel Rothkrug, it was in fact a fiction; the German "nation" comprises a mish-mash of ethnic groups that share related Teutonic languages. A terrible result was that this fictitiously "pure" group targeted a people, the Jews, who had a much stronger claim to a continuous history, making them a threat to the German identity. Says Rothkrug:

> In their search for a racial identity, in their struggle to re-create a *Gemeinschaft* – to live again as members of a collective being – the Nazis invoked a "great duty" to exterminate the Jew. For by denying him the right to live, the Nazis thought to transfer and thereby to bury with the Jewish dead their own fears of an ingenerate illegitimacy.[13]

Though the Nazis were an extreme case, the use of an enemy to establish the superiority and legitimacy of one's own cultural narrative, one's own identity group, is still widespread. A people who are truly secure in the identity provided by their own cultural meaning system, however, have no need for such unsavory attitudes, nor even for rules prohibiting flag-burning or for McCarthy-like witch hunts to weed out "deviants." (Later chapters deal with the processes by which societies can overcome such cross-cultural misunderstandings and mistrust.)

In summary, the humane cultural narrative, as Hausheer's opening quote suggests, simultaneously satisfies all three basic psychic needs: for bonding, for autonomy, and for meaning. It is the narrative of the meaning system that tells how bonding and autonomy (and hence, a secure sense of "self") are to be met. It tells what constitutes "belonging" and in what ways individual "freedom" may be satisfyingly exercised.

I turn now to one of the most central aspects of human identity, one that no human society can ignore, namely human sexuality: people are either female or male. What does it *mean* to be a woman? – to be a man? And how are these two distinct kinds of people meant to interact?

## What is sex all about?

Chapter I began with a vigorous critique of the hyper-Darwinian hypothesis of the evolutionary psychologists that men and women are genetically coded to pursue widely different reproductive goals: men strive to mate with as many women as possible, while women carefully choose the responsible father/provider. Male promiscuity, and even rape, are treated as "natural drives" that societies must somehow curb. I likened their story to one of Rudyard

Kipling's *Just-So* stories: a clever explanatory fantasy – nothing more. There are no hard data to support their claims. Other serious Darwinists have been even more outspoken in their criticism:

> [Their] goal ... is a return to the allegedly more rigorous authority of the biological sciences of much that has recently been understood as cultural.
>
> (Lynne Segal, Birkbeck College, London)

> [They keep on] insisting on groping for some adaptationist explanation for everything when all sorts of local or social factors might account for the [behavior] they're trying to study.
>
> (Steven Rose, Open University, UK)[14]

For my purposes in this book, the central problem is that this simplistic pseudo-hypothesis gets widespread popular attention, while serious scientific criticism gathers dust on library shelves. I find the following quote by journalist Natalie Angiers makes this point very well:

> I'm disturbed by the ease with which ... inadequate interpretations of human sexual behavior become engraved in the communal consciousness, to the point where nobody questions the stereotypes any longer, nor offers alternative explanations, nor dares to suggest that change [in current sexual ideas] is possible, nor dares to suggest that love and lust are not the characterological property of either sex.[15]

It might be wise for the public-at-large to remember that the evolutionary psychologists themselves are children of modern Western cultures, within which male aggression is commonplace, and that they seldom are familiar with other societies' beliefs and customs, or with other aspects of human psychology.

### A few facts

What biological facts do we know for sure about human sexual behavior? Not many. We know such things as the location of a handful of genes that determine maleness and femaleness, and about the complex hormonal feedbacks that control sexual development and maintain sexual functions, such as female cycles and pregnancy and lactation, and male production of sperm and accompanying fluids in the ejaculum. We also know there are receptors in the brain that are sensitive to sex hormones, and are closely linked via the pituitary gland to the endocrine system. Sex hormones in the brain also modulate behavior, though, as Angiers notes, we do not know much about the details.

Certainly, interest in sex accompanies the surge of hormones during adolescence; and surely hormones affect our inclination to sexual arousal. For instance,

238

studies suggest that women are most sexually receptive around the period of ovulation, when estrogen levels peak.[16] Men, with their more constant levels of hormones, have a more or less continuous level of "readiness" for sexual arousal. Those *aggressive* males, however, who often exhibit high sex drives along with their elevated testosterone levels, are aggressive first; this is what causes their testosterone levels and their sex drive to soar – not the other way around![17] Heightened sexuality is a consequence, not a cause, of aggression. Moreover, hormones merely alert us toward sexual arousal; we can manage sexual activity without them, given appropriate sensory inputs and mental states.[18] Thus castration is not a particularly useful solution for socially "deviant" behavior.

Along these lines, it has been argued that sex is more important for men than women. Supposedly they think about it all the time, as often as every few minutes, at least in Western cultures. Has no one asked the same question of women? As an adolescent, I thought about sex every time I saw a "handsome guy," and all my girlfriends' conversations turned on dating boys, going steady, and getting married.[19] There is, today, serious doubt that sex drives differ much, if at all, between males and females. We now know that not only do women have plenty of erectile tissue equal to the male penis in sensitivity; they can also experience profoundly satisfying, extended orgasms, during which the cervical lips of the uterus suck up male semen, enhancing the chance of impregnation.[20]

Our genes and hormones also create what is called "sexual dimorphism," a fancy term for the physical differences between men and women, not only in external genitalia, but also in secondary sex characteristics. Shapes of torso and pelvis; general muscularity; amount and distribution of fat and of body hair; tenor of voice. Males tend to be taller than females, and physically stronger, at least in the upper body. Yet there is enormous overlap between men and women in every single such trait, and compared to other primates, the human sexes are very limited in their differences. Today, women sports professionals are coming ever closer to the records held by men (even without steroids), and women drive lorries and fight fires equally alongside men. Likewise, aside from breast-feeding, many modern fathers are becoming nurturers as skilled and effective as the best of mothers. Our biological differences, it seems, are of a minor order. There is no reason to suppose that they have not always been so, that the large exaggerations between the sexes are culturally, not biologically, generated.

Finally, as noted in Chapter VI, stress is the source of most of the violent aggressive behavior in humans, with males more likely to react with aggression (and hence secondarily exhibit heightened sexuality) and females to dissociate and turn away from relationships requiring trust, including sexual intimacy. It seems reasonable that in stressful societies, behavioral patterns of male aggression and sexual dominance and female subservience and self-protection could easily develop, leading to the all-too-common condition of domestic patriarchy, with its frequent concomitants of psychic and physical abuse. Most of written history catalogs a long sequence of stressed societies.

What we know so far about the biological attributes of men and women suggests that both physically and psychologically the sexes are more similar than different. What creates the behavioral extremes in some societies is their cultural expectation that the two genders, masculine and feminine, should be sharply defined as "not the other."

### An alternative "just-so" story

As pointed out in Chapter V, the human brain/mind fills in the blanks in its knowledge of the world by making up explanatory stories. Myths, sagas, and scientific theories help make sense of an otherwise incomprehensible reality. Regarding the biological underpinnings of human sexuality, I contend that evolutionary psychologists have no serious body of data to back up their myth, *their* Just-So Story about our Pleistocene past. So I feel free to offer one I find not only more plausible, but also far more attractive in how it depicts human nature.

The primary selective force during early human evolution was for stable, cooperative *groups*. These provided a secure environment for both the successful rearing of helpless but potentially brainy offspring and the preservation of old skills and new inventions: i.e., accumulated cultural knowledge. Anthropologists call this combination "cultural reproduction." The obvious first requirement was for behavioral adaptations that promoted group cohesiveness and harmony. This was achieved by an extrapolation into adulthood of those same psychological propensities that already assured strong mother–infant (and adult–infant) bonds; there developed a *lifelong need* for close physical affection (already present in some degree in almost all other primates).

In Chapter II, I pointed out the attraction of all adult primates toward a group's newborn infants and their tolerance of rambunctious juveniles. Touching and grooming continue throughout life, contributing to group cohesion. This need for affectionate physical contact surely grew even stronger among early hominids. By extending the period of sexual receptivity of females and eliminating specific advertisements of their fertility (the huge swollen bottoms of most other primate females in heat), males remained constantly near females. In a manner analogous to the bonobos' case, copulation was coopted to a secondary function, beyond reproduction.

Among bonobos, random genito-genital rubbing serves to calm tensions in the group and restore harmony. In humans, the cooptation of sex led to an even more pleasurable sexual experience than that presumably experienced by other primates: prolonged physical contact, called "foreplay," culminated in extended orgasms for both males and, especially, females.[21] We should not be surprised that the nurturing breasts of the female, which offer so much sensual pleasure to her babies as well as herself, became coopted as part of the mutual pleasures of human sex. Nor should we feel surprise that sexual pleasure is not limited to heterosexual contacts. As with the bonobos, male–male and female–female sexual encounters surely occurred among our ancestors, and also helped group cohesion.

240

This enormous craving for physical bonding and affection in adult humans came to be rewarded by what Riane Eisler calls "sacred pleasure" – sexually experienced feelings of transcendent warmth, well-being, and reassurance. Sex is no longer purely for biological reproduction; it is for feeling accepted, wanted, psychically secure. As biologist Humberto Maturana has put it, we humans "depend on love and we get sick when it is denied to us at any point in our lives."[22]

Of course, sex is not the only means for us nonrigidly programmed humans to achieve a sense of secure acceptance. Strong religious feelings, or simply a sense of being valued members of a physically affectionate group, with much touching and hugging and non-sexual contact, can serve as well. Even nontouching signals of affection and acceptance can fulfill this need, though their force is often weaker. It should thus be kept in mind during the next few chapters, that denial of physical affection and/or psychological acceptance may be painful in the extreme, a form of profound, often suppressed stress that can affect brain structure (recall Chapter VI). *This goes a long way, I believe, in explaining the all-too-common acts of male violence in the form of sexual aggression against women.*

This neotenous extension of the physical affection between adults and infants to sexual encounters among adults was part of the social reward system that ensured group cohesion and cooperation. In a way, humans remain "immature" all their lives, enjoying play, laughter, humor, games, and teasing, as well as physical and sexual affection. People prefer harmony to tension. They would rather reconcile and heal than take offense, if the cultural narrative provides a way for this to occur.

That is the end of my "Just-So" story.

### Cultures without "marriage"

Once cultural consciousness came into being, how was this general sexuality woven into the traditions of group life? There being no fossil evidence, we must draw once again on imagination plus whatever is known from the widely varying extant indigenous societies. If a culture in the Pleistocene experienced little internal stress, sex may well have been a somewhat "take-it-or-leave-it" affair in peoples' daily lives, as long as it was frequent enough to meet the reproductive needs of the group. Today's Dani people of West New Guinea, for instance, are apparently so contented socially that sex plays very little role in their lives. They engage in it rarely, abstain, even after marriage, seldom masturbate, and have few homosexuals. None of this is due to repression or disapproval, merely lack of interest.[23]

Such an extremely low-key, nonstressed society must have been unusual, even in the Pleistocene. More likely were societies comprising many small, fissioning and fusing bands of foragers, where exogamy (the migration of adolescents to another band) often occurred during the once or twice yearly

241

larger gatherings. In general, natural selection acted on the extended cultural group. In times of stress, the bands mutually assisted one another. The exchanging of nearly grown offspring between bands cemented kinship bonds, necessary in times of mutual need. (Even today, migrant peoples around the world send money "back home" to help others far separated from them physically. The strength of these long-distance bonds still persists.)

Whether during the Pleistocene it was the adolescent males who migrated most often, leaving permanent bands of older women and their daughters and younger sons as the core group, or whether it was the adolescent females who migrated more often, is not certain. The existence today of both matrilocal and patrilocal native societies supports both possibilities. Studies of gene distributions around the globe marking the early *Homo sapiens* migrations, however, suggest that by that time it was mostly the females who were moving over longer distances, leaving their natal bands to reproduce in a new group. Variants of the male Y-chromosome are geographically more clustered than are the variations in the DNA of mitochondria (a female genetic marker), meaning that "men move very little genetically," according to geneticist L.L. Cavalli-Sforza.[24] No matter which sex was doing the moving, however, the strong kinship bonds between bands due to exogamy surely were critical for survival during the sudden climatic fluctuations of the Ice Ages, when people had to count on help over large areas. (Interestingly, detailed knowledge of complex kinship relations is still highly significant in many cultures today.)

One of the most ancient forms of kinship relations may perhaps still be evident in several recently observed groups of foragers. Among all of them, sexual relations are relatively uninhibited; monogamy (male/female pairing) is not practiced; and the whole group participates in parenting a child. In some cultures, women have many "lovers," and when a child is born, it may have several "fathers" – all those males who have had a significant relationship with the mother. Obviously (to us) only one man is the biological father, but because several males take responsibility, offering gifts and protection, such children have a rather greater chance of surviving than do children with but a single male parent. This kind of multiple male parenting responsibility, called "partible paternity," occurs among the Ache tribe of eastern Paraguay, the Bari peoples of Colombia and Venezuela, and to a lesser extent among the Hadza of Tanzania.[25] Among the Onge people of the Adaman Islands in the Bay of Bengal, a child's "parents" are its birth mother plus all other women who nurse it, and whichever man or woman is credited with finding the food that is believed to have impregnated the mother. Clearly, the Onge do not conceive of male paternity, a concept surely opaque to most prehistoric peoples prior to the practice of animal husbandry.[26]

This pattern of multiple sexual partners, of multiple "fathers" (and sometimes also "mothers"), this sharing of parenting, may well have characterized social kinship relations throughout much of the Pleistocene. Survival of children depended on the survival of a group, and, of course, vice-versa! Without offspring, groups became extinct. The more people taking responsibility for a child, whether their own (biologically) or not, the greater the chances of the child's survival, and hence the future survival of the group. If a man's or woman's biological child were born into such a society, it would far more likely survive with the support of a whole group than with what just the mother, or even a bonded couple, could provide. Reproduction outside a strongly bonded society would be biological suicide. During most of human evolution, the modern idea of a "nuclear family" would have been an evolutionary dead-end.

### Origins of marriage

Given the above, how can one account for the beginnings of the now almost ubiquitous institution of "marriage," usually, but not always, the sexual union of one man and one woman, as the basic unit of human reproduction? No other primates form such permanent one-to-one pair bonds. A few societies are still polygamous, mostly polygynous, with a man having many wives, though the Nyinba tribe of Tibetan Buddhists living in Nepal are polyandrous, with one woman marrying usually two or more brothers. As the insightful anthropologist David Maybury-Lewis has said, marriage customs, of one man and one woman, are recent and diverse, growing out of millennia of the equally diverse customs of kinship grounded not on paternity, but on mothers and their "kin," as that term was defined by custom. Kinship systems were poor predictors of biological relationships. Those who counted as kin were just as likely to be equivalent to modern godparents or honorary aunts and uncles as to be blood relatives.

> Kinship is a kind of mental map, a map that differs sharply from one
> people to another ... [Y]ou have to be able to read those maps in order
> to understand how societies think and live.[27]

Regarding their attitudes toward the upcoming generation, all premodern societies have been more concerned about stable social relations than about parental rights to ownership of a child by its biological mother and father. (In fact, "parental rights" is probably an idea that could only exist in a fluid, multicultural, patchwork society such as modern America, where nuclear families predominate.)

As Maybury-Lewis argues, the widely held institution of marriage was introduced to give a formal parentage to each new offspring. It became a means of identifying the place of the child in the communal group. Children born into a family had both a female and male lineage; they had a place in the social scheme of relationships. And they held this place even if the "father" was not their biological father. The institution of marriage rationalized the freewheeling parenthood of earlier bands, where only maternity was known, and children belonged to the entire group.

The central problem that is addressed by all marriage traditions is how to deal simultaneously with the need for the *permanence* of parental couples that leads to stable social relations (what shares, for example, of access to land, water, and the communal food supply are allocated to each household?), and the notorious *impermanence* of our sexual liaisons. The creative solutions of many traditional societies to coping with sexual passion without disrupting social order put modern Western attempts to legally and morally fuse the two to shame, as distinctly unimaginative, not to mention, unrealistic.

In almost all tribal societies, Maybury-Lewis reports, custom dictates the separation of marriage, a serious matter, from "the passionate whims of imma-ture men and women."

> Most societies ... recognize the power and beauty of [romantic] love, and they are keenly aware that love and sexual attraction are an explo-sive mixture.... So they take care to separate the serious business of marriage from the passionate business of romance. Such societies are amazed by the Western ideal of romantic love as the proper foundation for marriage. They consider it positively weird to allow – no, to insist – that something as important [to society] as marriage be based on noto-riously irrational and volatile passion.[28]

A common solution is to establish a stable marriage ceremony, and to then allow discreet affairs. For example, the Wodaabe of northern Niger have two kinds of marriage: stable marriages arranged in childhood, creating kinship liaisons and a stable family and lineage for children, with the possibility of outside "affairs"; and romantic marriages, where a wife may go to live with another husband, perhaps as a second wife. The jilted husband pretends to give chase, but soon abandons the attempt. The Nyinba, mentioned above for their tradition of polyandry, with several brothers marrying one woman (practiced to keep the males' family lands together in one family), commonly have discreet extramarital affairs, and seek emotional attachments freely, while frowning on rash behaviors such as elopement or divorce and remarriage.

Among the Nayar of south India, at puberty a girl is formally married to a husband, achieving a kinship bond, but is quickly divorced and free to copulate with anyone. Children have no "father"; the mother's brother is the authority figure. Finally, the matrilocal Hopi of the American southwest have a low-key attitude toward sex. Premarital sex is taken for granted, and divorce is easy: a wife (who is owner of the house) simply puts her husband's belongings on the doorstep; any children remain with her, being members of her clan.[29]

A somewhat different approach to marriage vs. romantic attachments is taken by the Dagara people of modern Burkina Faso in West Africa. Among them, marriages are routinely arranged by village elders whose duty it is to bring together two souls with compatible life goals and personalities, who together will contribute to the well-being of the whole community. Such arrangements are not made in haste, but after careful observation. The marriage does not belong to the couple, but to the whole village; it is a festival for village-wide reiteration of mutual support for each other, and for the new couple. With this strong community support they will gradually develop deep and lasting bonds of love and respect. Romantic love is an illusion, a mutual masquerade in which each fantasizes about an idealized other who does not really exist. Says Sobonfu Somé about her tribe's wisdom:

> You cannot start your life together at the top of the mountain. The only place to go from there is down.[30]

These several approaches to marriage Maybury-Lewis contrasts with the modern American "nuclear family," which has no extended kin-network to lend support, and tends to be socially isolated. Extramarital affairs are considered immoral. The destabilizing result has been low commitments to marriage, especially by males, plus widespread family violence, hidden within the privacy of four walls. It leads to the highest level of divorce anywhere in the world, and perhaps to the unhappiest children and adolescents as well.

> These observations might lead to speculation about the purpose of marriage and the family in America. In other societies these institutions are designed both to harness passion in the service of social stability and to provide for children. Americans, on the other hand, idealize passion, isolate the family from society, and insist less on the needs of children.[31]

### Male identity and the problem of aggression

That there are distinct physical differences between males and females, fitting them for different contributions to biological reproduction, is acknowledged in every culture. The unassailable importance of women's bodies as magical givers of life tends to create a need for male identity that exaggerates the otherwise rather modest physical differences, such as in physical strength. After all, conscious reflection suggests that, biologically, males just are not that important. As cultural anthropologist Peggy Reeves Sanday has put it, "Perhaps because women have ways of signaling their womanhood, men must have ways to display their manhood."[32]

Sanday further points out, however, that in relatively unstressed societies where food is abundant and life secure, the tasks of women and men overlap. Among horticultural societies, for example, women and men do about equal amounts of physical labor and both nurture children. Male and female identities are less sharply defined, and tend to be complementary, with males often performing shamanistic tasks. Among the egalitarian Hopi of the American southwest, for example, the males conduct most of the ancestral rites in the sacred subterranean kivas.

In many such societies, something Sanday calls "mythical male dominance" may evolve in the cultural narrative; men have the appearance of superiority over women by being given ritual powers.[33] In such societies, however, instances of outright aggression and violence are rare. These societies are usually matrilocal and matrilineal, *but not matriarchal* (female-dominant). Instead, social power is distributed fairly equally between men and women. Sharing, cooperation and absence of hierarchy are typical.

By contrast, in stressed societies that live nearer "the edge" (whether because obtaining food is more dangerous: hunting, or open-ocean fishing, or nomadic herding; or because of the necessity to defend against other marauding groups), it is the men who are in danger. Males are expendable, biologically speaking; they are the "throw-away" sex. Gender tasks become highly differentiated, and men are often separated from women for extended periods, days, even weeks. Danger increases both stress on males and their tendency to bond together; the society often becomes patrilocal, with related males cooperating to obtain scarce resources; competition among groups of males often arises; hierarchies may develop. Ultimately, if sufficiently stressed, males assume attitudes of physical and psychic dominance over women.[34]

Whatever the particular causes of cultural stress, there is always the tendency, as we saw in Chapter VI, for males to respond to any form of acute threat to survival with increased anxiety, leading to hypervigilance and outbursts of violent anger. In premodern cultures, any unexplained stresses, such as plagues or droughts, were often blamed on some particular person: a witch or sorcerer or evil spirit. Throughout history, as discussed in the next chapter, women have often been targeted as the causes of "evil." In any case, the female tendency to dissociate, to turn psychically inward during stress, would only exacerbate their vulnerability to stress-caused male violence and abuse.

This discussion is, of course, a great over-simplification. What happens when a particular society comes under stress, as Sanday carefully documents, depends largely on its prior cultural configuration. In what ways did the old cultural narrative act to either promote or repress the development of male dominance and aggression?[35] Sanday's observations further underscore the crucial importance of meaning systems in being able to over-ride the biologically grounded tendencies of human nature. When a culture that *promotes competition* and *assumes that male violence is natural* comes under stress it is far more likely to become violent than is a culture that promotes cooperation and assumes violence is abnormal, not just antisocial. The former society controls violence by repression and punishment; the latter, by insuring a meaningful identity for everyone in society. After all, the loss of meaningful purpose in anyone's life is perhaps the worst stress a human being can experience, and may well be responsible for most fatal attacks on others (murders) and on the self (suicides), as well as for the much more frequent instances of lesser violence.

### The "naturalness" of male violence

Finally, I add a few brief words about the "naturalness" of male violence. There is a widespread belief, promoted in the twentieth century by such scientific giants as Sigmund Freud and Konrad Lorenz, that aggression is some kind of genetic "drive" or "need" – the flip side to our innate propensity for acceptance and love. According to this theory, violence is most often expressed in males who, without proper training in controlling it, are naturally liable to such violent antisocial acts as bullying, rape, and murder. Teenage boys, especially those from inner cities, are particularly suspect as potentially violent. The distinguished British anatomist, J.Z. Young, however, is skeptical of this idea:

> The fact that some of the brain areas promoting these [aggressive] responses lie close to those for other appetites lends plausibility to the theory. Nevertheless I think it to be incorrect. Certainly not every individual feels that he has a *need* for aggression, though most are able to be angry when provoked. To show that there is [adaptive] value in such a *fund* of anger we should have to see its biological necessity.[36]

In the course of all the theorizing about the supposed innate nature of male aggression, no one has stopped to ask what possible adaptive function a propensity for violence could serve. For hunting animals is one answer; for competing over females, a "scarce resource," another. But if, as now seems evident, humans evolved through selection of successful, cohesive groups, then a random drive for aggression would be counterproductive. Without "possession" of lifelong mates, there would be no "scarcity" of females, as long as all males were able to mate (whether or not any offspring were their own). And it seems that hunting was never an "aggressive" sport, as it too often is today, but merely one of several means of obtaining food. Random social aggression could only threaten the cohesiveness of the group necessary to its survival. How would that have benefited anyone, including the aggressor?

I conclude that aggression (whether in males or females) is not a psychological "drive" at all. Rather it is a form of communication, a signal of displeasure, of frustration, a desire for a different situation. Our primate relatives use physical force when other signals fail. A mother snow monkey I once watched abruptly thrust away the youngster she was trying to wean. He yelped, returned, jumped on her lap and bit her nipple, whereupon she really walloped him, all amidst much leaping about and screeching by both – clearly a sequence of *physical* communication! A young human child, still unable to explain his needs in words, will also hit or bite in order to convey displeasure, and a mother may slap when the word "no" brings no result. A bully, with his already insecure identity, will, when his status has been threatened, pick a fight. And a man whose wife has been seduced by another may challenge him to a fight. (In fact, females are quite likely to commit any of the above as well, though with perhaps a bit less intensity.) The point is, there is a continuum of "aggression," from nonharmful bites and slaps that help to establish understanding within a social group, to extremes of violence that are socially disruptive. Aggression, then, as Frans de Waal has said, is a well-integrated part of primate relationships; its level of intensity depends on the social context in which it occurs. High levels of social stress invite violent behavior.[37]

The process of socialization in humans – the provision of psychologically secure surroundings together with the training of each new generation in alternative forms of anger communication – allays most violent aggression. This works best where the cultural narrative accommodates each person's needs for bonding, autonomy, and meaningful identity in a balanced, nonviolent way, and provides for alternative avenues of redress when an impasse is reached. In societies lacking such opportunities, or where the institutions are unsatisfactory, the incidence of antisocial behavior tends to skyrocket. Such increases are a red flag: something is fundamentally wrong.

It is well-documented (though not widely appreciated) that most violence is committed against those one knows – spouses, children, fellow employees – those on whom we depend, whom we need to trust, and who establish our identities. They are the ones who are most likely to frustrate or disappoint or otherwise hurt us. It is less easy to act violently toward those one does *not* know, unless we have first converted them into a dangerous "enemy." Yet even with declared but personally unknown enemies, if we actually confront them face-to-face, it is almost impossible to harm them. It is easy to declare hatred for a faceless enemy, someone or some group we can blame for our troubles. But it is much harder for a soldier to hate and kill a stranger in battle than for the women at home to raise their voices and fists in deadly anger. In fact, in both World Wars, only 15 to 20 percent of soldiers in the front lines actually fired their weapons; 80 percent or more could not do it, even under fire. Only those at a distance (cannon teams or air force bombardiers) or in groups (machine gunners) regularly "pulled the trigger" when ordered. As retired Lt. Colonel Dave Grossman reports in his book, *On Killing*:

> [It is] clear that many soldiers do not shoot directly at the enemy. Many reasons are given; one of them – *which, oddly enough is not often discussed* – may be the reluctance of the individual to act in a direct aggressive way.

> [T]he average and healthy individual … has such an inner and usually unrealized resistance towards killing a fellow man that he will not of his own volition take life if it is possible to turn away from that responsibility.[38]

In fact, as Grossman argues throughout his book, soldiers must be thoroughly trained, through repeated drills and simulated battle-field conditions, to act reflexively in combat without conscious awareness, before they are able to shoot at an enemy up close. This was part of the Vietnam soldiers' training, and led to such massacres as that at My Lai. Only when soldiers were both *pretrained to kill* and *given specific commands* on site "to neutralize everything" were they sufficiently desensitized to carry out the slaying of old men, mothers, children and babies.[39]

My point is that human beings, males or females, are not born killers of other people. Aggressive violence is not automatic. It is contextual; it requires meaning, a "justifiable" reason. As Mahatma Gandhi, Martin Luther King, and other advocates of nonviolent action recognized, it is easy to harm or kill face-less strangers at a distance; it is almost impossible to do so (with some significant exceptions to be taken up in later chapters) when face-to-face.[40] It is far easier to hurt someone you trusted, who has broken that trust, or to kill an enemy whom you have seen blow up your buddy. But, as Lt. Col. Grossman says: "Killing comes with a price, and societies must learn that their soldiers will have to spend the rest of their lives living with what they have done."[41] Violent aggression always has a *social cause*. It is *not* a "natural drive."

Finally, there has been much confusion about what is meant by "aggression," by "violence," and by "war." Is the mother snow monkey who wallops the child who just bit her in order to convey displeasure being "violent"? Or is it her means of communicating? She is surely "aggressive." Likewise, when a group of chimpanzees aggressively chastises one of its members when he begs for food from others after refusing himself to share with them on previous occasions, is this "violence," or a way of conveying group rules? When a group of scientists writes, in the *Seville Statement on Violence*, "Violence is neither in our evolu-tionary legacy nor in our genes," they are being, at best, vague, and at worst, dishonest. As primatologist Frans de Waal has pointed out, physical aggression can sometimes be highly adaptive. Preschool aggression, for example, is how small children learn about social relations. But at other times, it is maladaptive: when there is ongoing abuse in the home, or when governments engage in all-out combat. Many "civilized" societies use aggression freely in the punishment of social offenders, even nonviolent ones.[42] Societies that subliminally promote aggressive, competitive behavior as appropriate for adults, while simultaneously expecting all adults to curb any anger they might feel as a result of others' aggressive acts, are inviting escalation of violent behaviors.

In summary, I argue that the human capacity for aggression is innate, being a necessary response to perceived threats against oneself or one's group. It defi-nitely *is* a behavioral tool, but it *is not* an inevitable drive or "need." When, and in what ways, aggression is employed depends on an individual's past experi-ences (level of trust and security) and on a society's cultural narrative (its beliefs about human nature and expectations for human behavior and the need, or lack thereof, for coercive social control). A society that promotes aggression, espe-cially among its males, is likely to experience high levels of violence and to use excessive aggression as a form of social control, triggering off an escalating cycle of violence.

I turn now to a consideration of the diverse ways that cultures provide identities for their members, contrasting particularly egalitarian and hierarchical forms of social ordering.

## Cultures that rank identity and cultures that don't

What a culture thinks about human nature lays the foundation for how its people interact with one another: how they raise their children; how they allocate tasks and resources; and how they meet obligations and deal with conflict. Here I treat the three critical components of personal identity – age, task, and gender – as they are defined in egalitarian and in hierarchical societies, which differ radically in how they address our needs for belonging and autonomy. While no real society fits totally into either of these categories, the frame presented offers a useful reference for later discussions. (Though it is often assumed that egalitarian societies must always be small and personal, and large, impersonal societies must be hierarchical, historical examples exist for hierarchic bands and for egalitarian city-states and nations, but these will not be presented until Chapter VIII.)

In the previous section of this chapter, I briefly introduced the broad range of gender relations found in human cultures, from egalitarian all the way to male-dominant patriarchal societies. It is now time to relate these gender differences to cultural notions of equality or inequality across all aspects of social ordering, where it becomes evident how gaping are the differences in cultural assumptions about human nature.

### *Egalitarian societies*

Earlier I noted that "egalitarian" does not mean equal in everything. It does mean, however, far more than what in, say, America passes for equality: such phrases as "equal before the law," or "equality of opportunity," or "equal at the ballot box." Not only is such equality extremely limited in scope, it has had to be imposed by the force of law and does not represent a deeply held cultural belief that human beings are, by nature, due equal respect and of equal value. True egalitarian societies believe that all persons have equal value and deserve equal respect, regardless of age, task, or gender – or almost any other distinguishing trait. Furthermore, there tends to be an abiding trust that the other is trying to "do the right thing," and that efforts to guide or control another's behavior are a trespass on her or his autonomous self.

With regard to age, for example, egalitarian societies take a positive approach to socialization, assuming at each stage in life that a person is to be trusted – that is, given autonomy with the expectation that she will naturally contribute to the group. Indeed, I think that "trusting" is the essence of unconditional love. An infant acquires trust by constant physical contact with his mother or other adults, and his needs never go unheeded. Nor would an adult presume unnecessarily to impose her will on an infant. As a Native American mother answered when asked why the hair of her 18-month-old son was so long, "He has not asked to have it cut." She awaited *his* signal before presuming to act.[43]

As children grow and become less dependent, they are trusted to explore and learn on their own. In Chapter VI, I noted Barbara Rogoff's comparison between how American mothers and mothers in Central American and South Asian societies interacted with their children when introducing them to new play objects. "Relaxed" non-Western mothers simply showed the child the object – demonstrated it briefly – then left the child to explore it independently, only offering help when requested. "Anxious" American mothers unconsciously pressured their offspring by offering elaborate demonstrations followed by cheering or correcting. The child learns not autonomy but the need for constant, approving feedback. Similar differences also exist in toilet training between "relaxed" cultures and "anxious" ones. In "relaxed" cultures, a mother's close physical contact with her baby sensitizes her to his needs, so she can respond appropriately when he is about to urinate or defecate. Soon the baby learns to signal a request for her assistance. No shame or stress is involved, as can often happen in "anxious" Western societies.[44]

At each age, guidance is available, but motivation comes from the developing child, not from the mother or elders. They will good-naturedly laugh at "mistakes," thus making light of errors and conveying the unpressured expectation of future success in meeting cultural norms.

Later in life, the same mutual trust endures. Adult men and women perform their expected tasks without rules imposed by others because their freedom as children was *rewarded* with increasing responsibilities toward the group. Like young children everywhere, they want very much to be accepted, to "be like adults." They gradually become indispensable members of society. From performing family and household tasks as children; to providing and sharing food and participating in ritual ceremonies as adults; to becoming trusted wise leaders or sages, able to settle disputes and offer counsel to the group: each person has a valued task. No one "stands out," tries to compete, or expects special praise – not even the leaders. As anthropologist Dorothy Lee has put it:

> [T]he authority of the headman or the chief or the leader is in many ways like the authority of the dictionary, or of Einstein. There is no hint of coercion or command here; the people go to the leader with faith, as we go to a reference book, and the leader answers according to his greater knowledge, or clarifies an obscure point, or amplifies according to his greater experience and wisdom.[45]

The leader or elder is thus simply the interpreter of tradition. When there is a grave problem affecting the whole group, everyone meets together to discuss the situation, nonstop, until a decision is agreed upon. Men, women, children – all participate, speaking as they wish, one at a time. A Navajo participant at a meeting I attended once stunned his Euro-Western colleagues by answering our question "How long do your meetings take?" with "Up to nine days." "Well, how long do you go each day?" "Oh, no, nine days and nights without stopping."[46] We gasped! Such a contrast to Congressional decision-making deliberations, where each member is limited to two or three minutes, even on such critical questions as going to war, or impeaching the president, and citizens at large are seldom heard at all in public.

In egalitarian cultures, all tasks are honored, whether they be mothering, carrying out ceremonies, or growing or gathering food, or, for children, growing up. Everyone's contribution is valued as necessary and worthy, however she or he actually carries it out. As Dorothy Lee writes: "[A]n individual can decide to what extent he will fill the responsibility which is his privilege." When a group of Hopi men went to gather turtles for making ceremonial rattles, one offered his car to drive the 600 miles, another paid for the gas, and a third contributed his skill at finding turtles. No one's contribution was better than another. "[R]ather through the variety of individual contributions, the whole could be achieved."[47] (Shades once again of navigating a large ship: the complementary combining of diverse knowledge and skills to achieve a single group task.)

Finally, in egalitarian cultures, men and women have equal power, but different, usually complementary, tasks. In many Native American societies and precolonial African cultures, a senior male is leader or chief, but he holds his position only as long as the senior clan "mothers" approve.[48] Often extant egalitarian societies are matrilineal, with women as heads of clan lines, and often they are matrifocal, where daughters remain with their mothers, while initiated young males move to other bands or villages, thus distributing male kin across numerous groups. This disperses potential male alliances and reduces violent conflict that might ensue in times of stress.[49] (More commonly, from prehistory to the present, however, it has been human females who move to another band, as noted above and in Chapter III.)

To sum up, egalitarian cultures are distinguished by mutual respect and trust for all, implying a culture-wide belief in the intrinsic "goodness" of human beings. This is manifested by minimal ranking and competition among people, as well as essentially unbounded generosity, an unwitting fulfillment of Jesus' pronouncement, "It is more blessed to give than to receive," better translated as, "That person is wealthiest who gives the most." Sharing is expected. All this by no means signifies a society of uniformly identical persons, lacking in diversity of either personality or capabilities. If anything, the secure identity achieved through experiencing unfettered "autonomy within community" gives full opportunity for individual development. Customs and traditions are broad guides, not constraining rules. The numerous rituals and ceremonies to be performed help to keep this sacred meaning vibrant. Far from being viewed as coercive, these are seen as necessary for the very freedom to act that people daily experience. "The intricate set of regulations is like a map which affords freedom to proceed to a man lost in the jungle."[50]

In Chapter VIII, it will become evident that most early human societies were variants based on this generalized theme.

### Hierarchical societies

The Greek-derived word "hierarchy" literally means holy order, a universe not of equals, but of ranked entities, a vertical categorization with the highest, best, most powerful at the top. Often we use the term today to apply to systems of classification with the most *inclusive* on top, as when we classify living species by Kingdom ("top"), through Phylum, Order, Family, Genus, and finally Species ("bottom"). But when applied to human societies, the rank at the top is not the most inclusive, but the most exclusive, and it holds power over every category below. At the top, usually a supernatural power, a god or gods (in the West it is the Judeo-Christian-Muslim male God) ranks over all mortals, even kings and emperors. (Those who happened to watch the television series, *I, Claudius*, will recall the all-consuming anxiety of Augustus Caesar – the first of the Roman Emperors – and of his wife Livia Augusta, that upon dying each should be declared a "god." Indeed, Livia saw to it that Augustus was proclaimed a god, even though she herself had poisoned him.[51])

Heads of powerful modern states seem to be similarly concerned with how they will be remembered by history. This anxiety, first for rank, for climbing up the ladder of power, and then for acquiring immortal status, particularly characterizes the cultural mindset of modern, mobile hierarchies. The very possibility of "upward mobility" means one's position, and hence one's identity, is never secure. Where there is upward mobility, there is also downward mobility! "Being somebody" matters in a ranked society where both up and down are possible. Life is framed by constant competition and insecurity of self-worth. (Indeed, recent American presidents seem unable to free themselves of the fear that their peak identities might not be forever preserved in history.)

It is likely that the earliest hierarchical human societies, like their modern counterparts (and like the societies of other primates under stress described in Chapter II), did not offer secure status to those in power. The ones on top could be toppled fairly easily. For humans, once the cultural idea of a few having power over the rest takes hold, the need to control others becomes acute. Competition, alliances, and the ability to coerce, both physically and psychologically, become critical. And all must be justified, made legitimate by the cultural narrative, if the high costs of constant social unrest are to be avoided. Those in lower ranks must be made to accept their lesser status, their massive loss of autonomy. The myths and stories must explain why God or the king (or whoever is at the top) reigns supreme, why he (or she) is to be obeyed, and why those lower down are less valued, especially the outcasts, serfs, and slaves who have little worth and even less autonomy. Why are these humans to be treated always like immature children, "boys" and "maids," or even as beasts of burden throughout their lives?

In hierarchical societies, then, the task of the cultural narrative is, as far as possible, to say why it is "natural" and "right" for some to have power, wealth, status and control, and others to have very little or none. The story that is told must explain why I must lead a hard life with little freedom, control, or personal choice, while another is waited upon, gives orders to people like me, and may do whatever she or he pleases. Cultural narratives employ two kinds of justification for the existence of a hierarchy: one for "rigid" hierarchies and another for "mobile" hierarchies.

### Rigid hierarchies

The simplest to justify, once it has been established, is a rigid ranking system, such as India's long-standing Hindu caste system, or the former Inca Empire in the Andes, which ranged from the omnipotent Sun-god emperor to the poorest serfs. One is born into a class, and lives and dies within it. There is no culturally perceived possibility of mobility up or down. In such cases, the sacred stories explain the "rightness" of this state of affairs. In Peru, the emperor was considered a direct descendent of the sacred sun-god, Inti, and all peoples were born into various classes to serve him. Low-status girls with beauty or talent might become Chosen Women and serve in the temples, but boys had no hope of such "upward mobility."[52]

Immobility of castes in traditional India is so well-known it scarcely needs reciting. When the peoples of ancient Persia migrated south into India, "the social classes of the Aryans of Iran became the *castes* of the Aryans of India, with theoretically water-tight divisions." The Brahmanic law, or Dharma, outlawed social mobility, and prescribed the "right and duty" of each caste. Imposed identities were fixed from birth to death.[53] Only the hope of reincarnation offered the possibility of a higher status.

Almost every rigid hierarchic society has ranked its members in the order of god/king, priests and warriors, artisans and traders, peasants, and "non-people" – slaves, outcasts, untouchables, and the like. Religious myths, the authority of which was sustained by the priestly class, provided both moral justification for the social structure and the legal power to maintain it. A person, of whatever rank, born into such a society, imbibes from infancy a world view that is permanently internalized. It is one's fate, one's *karma*, to be on the top or bottom. There is no appeal, because that is the way the world is. In such a society religious law specifies the proper social tasks of people in each caste, and children are taught to behave according to their rank, showing deference to those above and expecting the same from those below. Those who fail to accept their status willingly are made to accept it through physical force or psychic terror, such as threats of eternal damnation.

One's passage through life does not change one's place in the overall society. Age confers changing status only within one's own class. And the value placed on one's social task is likewise fixed: supreme and powerful for the priestly and warrior castes, subservient and powerless for those at the bottom. Finally, in every historically known hierarchy, males have had far more status and power than females, for the reasons suggested in the prior discussion of aggressive tendencies. Hierarchies are routinely patriarchies.

In rigid hierarchies, autonomy is under-developed. Even those "on top" have their life task established at birth. (Even a monarch's life is "not her own," as Mary Stuart's mother is said to have cautioned her.) Social identity, in the sense of having a set task, is assured. Social acceptance, in the sense of feeling valued and respected by others, is caste-determined. Like a small child with abusive parents, the Hindu untouchable had nowhere else to turn, no other, more welcoming community. He or she must find psychic meaning even while being despised. Religion may serve here, and help maintain stability, though societies that rely heavily on religious myths for such stability tend to be unable to adapt to changing circumstances; they become rigid.

As an example of how such a rigid belief system can be turned on its head, however, I offer the following observation. While in India in 1992, I witnessed the rapidly growing Swadhyaya movement, with even then many millions of followers in the states around Bombay. This is a newly invented sect, but one that is firmly based on popular Hindu gods and ancient Vedic scripture. Its central tenet is that God is immanent in the being of every person; everyone, even the lowest of the low, is a holy being. The enormous identity this conveys to the outcastes and untouchables who have been the main recipients of the teachings of the group I found truly amazing. Part of each person's worship is giving one day's labor a week in service to God, with the benefits being distributed to children and the needy in the community. Newly achieved feelings of bonding and self-worth have replaced the former need for alcohol and the family abuse that accompanied its use. The ability of this movement to build community and a network of mutual self-help in the poorest of villages and to eliminate violence was remarkable.[54]

Meantime, in much of the rest of India, the priestly Brahman still accepts his veneration as simply his due. Women of any caste are almost always subservient to men. In my limited observations during two visits to the Indian hinterland, lower-caste women were no more likely to suffer than upper-class women. Gender oppression, as well as occasional gender equality, is found at all levels.

In fairly rigid hierarchies, especially where all levels interact in a closed community, as in the Medieval feudal manors or even in mid-twentieth-century rural villages of class-ridden England, social standing among the lower classes came from association with an overlord possessing status. Reciprocal obligations up and down the ladder gave even the lowest members both survival security and vicarious identity. Even in today's more mobile hierarchic societies, "name dropping" is a convenient way for those with less secure status to impress others with their right to respect and social acceptance. (A working-class acquaintance of mine in England, when looking for a village in which to retire, favored those with a well-to-do "squire" in the vicinity. And as a professional woman all-too-often cut short in discussions by male colleagues, I have frequently found myself dropping names of celebrity friends and acquaintances to establish an equal standing. Associations, even slight ones, with "important" persons, are commonly used to establish one's worth in an entrenched hierarchy.)

*Mobile hierarchies*

I turn next to the historically recent mobile hierarchies that emerged from the Enlightenment and have come to characterize today's Western industrial societies. Wherever the cultural narrative makes it legitimate for people to try to improve their status, social stability is obviously harder to maintain. The task of the cultural narrative to justify ranking is no longer god-given, but becomes convoluted, based on a host of myths or social theories about "rights," "fairness," and "merit," that become highly politicized.

There are several interesting, and I believe inevitable, consequences when hierarchies move from "rigid" to "mobile." First, they become increasingly stressful. My identity is never secure, as long as there is anyone who might displace my position on the ladder (see Figure VII.1). Competition is constant; indeed, it is built into the cultural expectations acquired in childhood. Success is never permanent. Thus, the seeming freedom I possess that allows me to constantly try to better myself can easily become a curse. For if I stop striving upward I will sooner or later be displaced. I can never stop worrying that I could fall downwards if I do not keep competing at maximum effort. The past two decades have driven this angst to an almost frenzied pitch in some of the most advanced industrialized nations.[55]

This all-pervasive competition has the effect of decreasing the permanence of bonds of mutual support; alliances are made in terms not of reciprocity over the long-term, but of expedience at that moment in time. Social structure loses its kinship-based, extended-family form of community and becomes impersonal and ephemeral. Individuals with little power tend to band together to acquire more power and status in the hierarchy, often establishing a strongly bonded subculture, usually with a common "enemy." (Today, we call them many things, from "interest groups" to "gangs." History has called them "rebels," "revolutionaries," "heretics," "guilds," "unions," "professional associations," "fraternal lodges," "activist groups," and so on.)

As I will show in detail in Chapter IX, where I address the pathology of modern Western society in relation to the intrinsic psychic needs of human beings, the struggle to constantly compete eliminates much autonomous behavior. For instance, it regiments childhood and adolescence in highly confining ways, all under the guise of "becoming all that you can be" in the competitive *milieu*. It restricts one's unconditional bonds to a very few persons, and puts extraordinary demands on the marital bond to fill the whole of one's lifelong need for secure acceptance and a sense of being valued by others. Furthermore, the meaning system used to justify this emotionally precarious

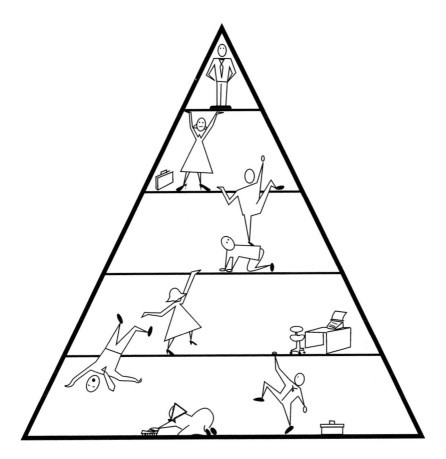

*Figure VII.1* Up – and down – the modern "ladder of success"

Source: Author's original idea rendered by Michele Lukowski

state of affairs is based far more on symbols of "nationality" for its own sake than upon any transcendent or sacred purpose *in relation to other human beings.* Social purpose simply means universal "self-purpose"; bonding and autonomy are made increasingly incompatible, and social meaningfulness is culturally sacrificed, replaced by vaguely defined "rights" and "freedoms." "Meanings" are diffuse, multiple, and private.

### Hierarchy and human nature

[T]he mightiest prince and the greatest statesman or general of civilization may look with envy on the spontaneous and undisputed esteem that was the privilege of the least gentile sachem [tribal chief].

257

The one stands in the middle of society, the other is forced to assume a position outside and above.[56]

The above quote from Friedrich Engels captures exactly the contrast between the holder of authority in an egalitarian society – one who stands in its midst and is but one among many – and in a hierarchy – one who is outside, aloof, above. As sociologist Stanley Diamond has argued, the quality of the social structure of the two is as day to night. The egalitarian society is self-organized by virtue of its shared customs and traditions, from which the power of the chief or headman flows. The result is an order based on shared beliefs acquired from the ancestors and wise elders. If there is a transgression, perhaps a man kills another, then custom says, this-and-such is the proper recourse: not vengeance, but appropriate compensation for the loss; maybe banishment for a time so tempers may cool.[57]

Members of a hierarchical society, however, live under an imposed order. As has been noted, rulers in rigid hierarchies enforce laws and obligations that are dictated either by an authoritarian religion or by themselves. Centralized authority replaces – even erases – individual relationships among kin- and clan-groups. In the case of a transgression, it is the abstract "state" that is harmed, takes vengeance, and punishes the disrupter of "its" order: the King's peace must be kept.[58] (This explains the use of the collective "We" by a royal head of state; he or she claims to speak for everyone.)

Though social historians and anthropologists have argued that hierarchies and the rule of law grew out of a simple expansion of custom as societies gradually increased in size, Diamond argues it was a *discontinuous* process, not a natural sequitur of complexity. The power of kings stamped out earlier cultural traditions, including methods of resolving wrongs between individuals, and replaced them with a set of rules outside the control of ordinary persons. Even the historically recent move from rigid, authoritarian hierarchies to more mobile constitutional ones (so-called democracies) only marginally eliminates the alienation of the individual from a sense of autonomous control over the conditions of his or her life. Hierarchy not only of the state, but of the corporate and bureaucratic worlds of daily life – at work, in school, at the doctor's office, at church – destroys any sense of personal ownership of one's culture, or control over its evolving institutions.

Today, whenever a highly authoritarian society finally frees itself from its militaristic or oppressive regime and becomes a representative democracy with a constitution and elections, the television cameras show us long lines of newly enfranchised voters eagerly lining up to cast votes for their new government. But the hierarchic social order remains: the bureaucracies and the economic institutions. In such mobile hierarchies of longer standing, it is commonly the case that less than half the voters turn out for elections. People soon lose their sense of ownership and regard their still highly controlled lives with resignation, as part of the supposedly "inevitable progress" of human history. As Diamond says: "Pharoahs and presidents alike have always made a public claim to represent the common interest, indeed to incarnate the common good." This "noble lie," he notes, is commended by both Plato and Machiavelli as unfortunate but, in their view, necessary for maintaining order.[59]

> The progressive reduction of society to a series of technical and legal signals, the consequent diminution of culture, i.e., of reciprocal symbolic meanings, are perhaps the primary reasons why our civilization is the one least likely to serve as a guide to "the unshakable basis of human society".[60]

It is unfortunate for our understanding of human nature that the disciplines of both evolutionary psychology and social psychology have modeled their theories of human behavior on subjects born, raised, and living out their lives in hierarchical societies. For dozens of generations, children from infancy onward have been exposed to social ranking, and have submitted to others' power and influence imposed to maintain social control over them. In "democratized" hierarchies, social mobility, with its resultant competitiveness for status, promotes the wielding of aggressive power by everyone. The academic disciplines have legitimized in the popular mind a highly distorted image of human nature. *But because it rather accurately reflects humans behaving in mobile hierarchies, it has become readily accepted as our basic biological nature, and is therefore difficult to question.* Social beliefs about "human nature" regularly become self-fulfilling prophecies.

As already noted, evolutionary psychologists, using an individual competing in a hierarchy as their model, have told us that selfish competition is biologically grounded "in our genes." And the majority of social psychologists, taking the behavior of human subjects in competitive, individualistic hierarchies as their model, claim that people "naturally" use power and influence to manipulate one another. One of the fathers of modern social psychological theory, Bertram Raven, clearly accepts this model:

> *[B]iological evolution* would tend to select for characteristics that help assure biological survival; essentially it would select for tendencies to satisfy selfish interest, for oneself and one's genetic line, without concern for others. *Social evolution* would counter such selfish tendencies, selecting for personal restraint, sympathy, concern for others, and altruism. How many lives were saved when people, motivated by revenge or desire for personal gain, were restrained by religious belief from injuring or killing their neighbors?[61]

But where did these "religious restraints" arise from? Raven imagines that "certain sages, seers, and chieftains" invented over many centuries omnipotent deities and coercive religions that would "counter [biological?] tendencies toward murder, theft, adultery, mayhem, or harmful dietary practices."[62] Nowhere does he acknowledge the human brain's evolved need for either bonding or meaning, for a narrative explanation of the experiences of life. Gods and religions cannot be simple "inventions" of the odd sage or seer. Like the rest of culture, they evolve slowly, through shared group experiences out of which narratives come to be developed that explain how life is to be understood and lived.

Not only psychologists, but also primatologists, tend to ignore this evolved *human need* for meaning in trying to explain human nature. The one who, to my knowledge, comes closest to perceiving this is Christopher Boehm. He at least has a partial explanation for the prevalence of egalitarian societies during most of human evolution. Symbolic communication, he argues, was essential for group coherence during the severe climatic swings of the past few hundred thousand years. Especially during the Pleistocene, there was heavy selection for *groups* (not single individuals) who were cooperative and devised conflict-resolving social behaviors. They learned to make use of "social control," where potentially domi- nant males were quickly suppressed by coalitions of subordinants. As communication improved via language, there developed culturally transmitted moral codes.

At least, unlike most evolutionary psychologists, Boehm acknowledges that group selection was a powerful factor during the Pleistocene, and that intra-group squabbling reduced fitness. But unfortunately he, too, ignores that this evolu- tionary process biologically altered the structure of the human brain, simultaneously increasing its need for meaning (narrative stories) and for an increasingly conscious need for belonging, for committed relationships. It is not a need for a particular meaning, but for *some* meaning; it is much more than a simple symbolic addition to our general primate needs for bonding and autonomy.[63]

What Boehm, Raven, and a great many others seem not to realize is that the balance common to other primates, between the striving for individual autonomy (with its dominance and self-assertiveness behaviors, both important to individual survival) and for bonding (with its affiliative propensities, which are important to survival of one's offspring), *swung greatly toward the latter during human evolution*. The evolution of consciously experienced cultural meaning – a biological, genetically inscribed trait – made human intelligence with its increased group survivability enormously adaptive. Nor are we a "finished" species. No species is. We are still learning, culturally (and perhaps even through genetic selection, though to prove that would take a mountain of careful historical work linked with DNA studies), how to live with our three needs: for autonomy, bonding, and meaning.

Fortunately, almost in spite of themselves, social scientists are beginning to discover that *real* autonomy, equality, and trust, work much better in achieving mutually desired social goals than do such hierarchical behaviors as threats and coercion. You cannot teach people "self-esteem," and to teach them "self-asser- tion" usually offends others and is socially disruptive. Teachers with children,[64] psychiatrists with patients,[65] and even corporate executives with employees[66] are all discovering that they are far more successful if instead of using rewards and punishments or other forms of bureaucratic persuasion/coercion, they treat those with whom they are working with respect, empathy, and trust, as equally valued, albeit not identical, contributing partners in a joint enterprise. Egalitarian societies are not "take-it-or-leave-it" propositions. They are, at this point in human evolution, critical.

I close this chapter with a summary table, Table VII.1, that tries to fuse these two disparate research approaches to the study of human societies: the structure

*Table VII.1* Aspects of cultural meanings

|  | Social Structure<br>"Rational" aspects of culture | Psychological Disposition<br>"Affective" (emotional) aspects of culture |
|---|---|---|
| Factors | **Interest Groups**<br>Marriage/kinship patterns | **Ideology/Beliefs**<br>Assumptions about human nature |
|  | Arrangements for distribution and exchange of goods/trade | Balance between autonomy ("freedom") and bonding ("acceptance") |
|  | Organization of political power | Emphasis on the individual or on the group |
| Considerations | **1 Obligations/Rules**<br>Definitions of fairness and justice | **Source(s) of Authority**<br>Ancestors/traditions/ customs |
|  |  | *or* |
|  | **2 Complexity**<br>Number of cross-cutting networks | **Religious Beliefs**<br>*or* |
|  |  | Legal codes |
| Consequences | **Practical Effectiveness** | **Personal Feelings and Identity** |
|  | Conflict resolution | Attitudes toward child-rearing |
|  | Organizing social action | Attitudes toward gender identity |
|  |  | Level of individual psychic security |
|  |  | Level of group psychic security |

*Note*: These two theoretical parts of a cultural narrative are a useful framework for comparing cultures, devised by Marc Ross (1993a, 1993b). Any given culture has a narrative that unifies both aspects in its overall "story." Paul Bohannan, Jared Diamond, and the evolutionary psychologists all tend to focus more on the social structure of a society than on its psychological disposition, whereas Marc Ross, Rupert Ross, and Peggy Reeves Sanday give more emphasis to the importance of the Psychological Aspect.

of their social institutions, and the psychology of their cultural meanings. Like much else in Western thought, there tends to be a split between the "rational" (hyper-Darwinian, game-theoretical) and the "feeling" (affective, emotional) approaches.[67] As I have been trying to show, this is an artificial dichotomy. Both are biologically and inextricably intertwined in the make-up of human nature and of human societies. Both, in some form or other, are incorporated into the wide variety of cultural narratives that frame our conscious behaviors, and probably many of our unconscious ones as well.

It is now time to look at the diverse ways that cultures have provided meaning and identities for their members throughout history, and how the two extremes of egalitarian and hierarchical forms of social ordering have interacted over the past dozen or so millennia.

# VIII

# HISTORY, THE STORY OF MEANINGS THROUGH TIME

If it is your conviction that people live one short step from hell, that it is more natural to sin than to do good, then your response as a judicial official will be to use terror to prevent the taking of that last step backward.... If, by contrast, it is your conviction that people live one step away from heaven, you will be more likely to respond by coaxing them gently forward, by encouraging them to progress, to realize the goodness within them. The use of coercion, threats or punishment by those who would serve as guides to goodness would seem a denial of the very vision that inspires them.

Rupert Ross (1992: 169)

[R]eligion is more than just a set of beliefs. It is a pattern of practices that gives a certain shape to our social imaginary. Religion – or ... the sense of the sacred – is the way we experience or belong to the larger social whole ... [It is] the very basis of society. Only by studying how society hangs together, and the changing modes of its cohesion in history, will we discover the dynamic of secularization.

Charles Taylor (1998: x)

The first quotation opening this chapter raises a flag about how human nature is commonly interpreted in Western thought. It calls into question the power-based, game-theoretical, Machiavellian ideas underlying the Billiard Ball world view that dictates how past history is currently interpreted. It is the "history" that every schoolchild is taught and shapes the ways our culture thinks. In the last chapter, I noted how the famed ethologist, Robert Hinde, deplored the emphasis on male aggression as the explanatory principle of history; violent behavior is not biologically ingrained. Here, the Canadian judge, Rupert Ross, underscores the crucial role cultural beliefs about human nature play in social institutions. If you treat people as though they are intrinsically greedy, selfish or evil they tend to behave in greedy, selfish or evil ways. Cultures become self-fulfilling prophecies, unintentionally molding people to fit their tacit expectations.[1] The second quotation, from historian/philosopher Charles Taylor, identifies as "sacred" each culture's particular belief about what it means to be human; that *is* its religion.

263

In terms of human nature, I believe history makes better sense as the playing out of diverse cultural beliefs about human purpose than as simply the insatiable search for power that most, mainly male, historians describe. The central task of humankind is not to outcompete others for resources, but to find meaning in one's existence. Mere survival is seldom enough, as demonstrated many times over, from the mass suicide by the Jews at Masada in ancient times to the deaths in the twentieth century of thousands of Iranian and Iraqi boy soldiers persuaded to kill each other in an Islamic holy war over whose ancestors were the "true" ones.[2] Meaning matters. Identity matters, not just for individuals but for whole groups. Yet both evolutionary psychologists and mainstream historians explain history in terms of the so-called "rational" aspects of human behavior, ignoring our innate emotional needs (recall Table VII.1). The visible structures of social institutions are so much easier to "scientifically" quantify and compare than are their underlying beliefs and values. It is the latter, however, that construct meaning and justify a culture's patterns of daily life: its social networks, economic institutions, forms of justice, and processes of group decision-making.

This chapter examines how cultural meaning systems – the "religious ideas" of a people – have changed through time; no society remains forever the same. Complex interactions within even a small band of thirty or so people effect changes in their collective thinking. Almost unconsciously, they modify those underlying beliefs on which their institutions are built, adjusting their myths and customs accordingly. That is how cultures continuously self-correct and adapt to new situations. As anthropologist Paul Bohannan reminds us: "A culture that cannot change is a dead culture. Innovation is a vital part of cultural dynamics."[3]

## The nature of the "sacred"

*If*, as I have argued, the shared cultural narrative – that which gives meaning to life and outlines the rules and values by which it is to be lived – is what keeps a society together, and *if* a coherent society is essential to the survival of the individual, *then* we can expect human beings to have a powerful, innate tendency to defend and protect that shared meaning. Within every cultural world view there is something so important that it becomes "sacred," a "religion." Paul Tillich said it best: "Religion is that to which we give our ultimate attention; it is the object of our ultimate concern."[4]

We are used to thinking of "religion" in its conventional forms: Catholicism, Protestantism, Islam, Buddhism, Hinduism, and so forth, and their myriad splinter groups. Anthropologists would include the hundreds of tribal belief systems, past and present. But these do not exhaust the category of "sacred" beliefs about how humans should live, which includes ideologies such as fascism, Marxism, capitalism, scientism, rationalism, and patriotism.

Note that "democracy," "monarchy," and other forms of social decision-making are not strictly religions or ideologies in themselves, but rather *processes* for agreeing on what the "sacred" should be. They act at the intersection between our need for individual autonomy and our need for shared meaning. Yet because process can affect the nature of what is held sacred, it often takes on the character of a religion; it invites the same emotionally charged behaviors. In fact, in those secular societies that claim to be tolerant of all sacred beliefs, process becomes a kind of default religion: for example, in democracies (like the United States), the election process is held sacred. There is obviously overlap in "process" and "beliefs," but as I will try to show, process *per se* does not really fulfill our intrinsic need for "purpose-in-life," important though it is to facilitating adaptive cultural change.

In order to understand how world views shape human history, it is first necessary to recognize the deep tension that arises within any culture between conserving the "sacred" which holds it together and the need to adapt to new circumstances by modifying those most sacred beliefs.

To explore this crucial tension, I draw upon the work of Martin E. Marty, a highly respected religious historian and social analyst, using familiar contemporary examples to illustrate the nature of our human need for the sacred.[5]

### *The sacred and the profane*

All cultures, from the simplest tribes to multicultural megasocieties, have sacred ideas (or, as Marty calls them, "objects") that are often sequestered in a sacred place: a sacred grove, or a mountain top; a shrine in the jungle; a temple; an ancestral burial site, from ancient tumuli, to Egyptian pyramids, to the Arlington National Cemetery in Virginia. Each sacred site is hallowed ground. It contains the sacred "object," whether bones, or texts, or as in the case of Judaism's Holy of Holies, nothing but the "idea that cannot be spoken." This place is the fanum, the temple, the shrine. The larger area outside the *fanum* is the *profanum*, where the activities of daily life occur (see Figure VIII.1).

In ordinary times, when a society is relatively free from internal or external stress, and hence there is no need to question sacred beliefs, the boundaries between sacred and profane are porous. Often enough, at least in tribal societies, the two are intimately, yet almost unconsciously, intertwined (as for many Native Americans). In daily life, the acts of getting up, preparing food, tilling the soil, are graced with sacred meaning. It is when stress appears (whether internal disputes, famine, disease, or external threats) that the old beliefs come under question. Were they too much ignored? Or were they too much in need of revision? Should we pray harder to the old god, or try out a new one, when the rains don't come and the locusts do? When youthful violence threatens society, is it because we have been too "soft" on the kids, or too "hard" on them?

*Figure VIII.1* Plan of an imaginary early "city"

Author's and artist's conception of an early city focussed around its sacred site, the temple or fanum. Surrounding it is a plaza ringed with buildings, including houses, workshops, and storage rooms; together they constitute the profanum or secular area. (Usually there would also be sacred spaces in homes.) Outside lie fields, an enclosure for animals, and a copse for charcoal.

The fanum holds the ideas and symbols of sacred meaning that ideally flow freely out into the profanum, regulating life there. When they are too separate, there is a tendency for fanaticism to develop.

In contrast to this early city, for foraging peoples the whole world is sacred, and separation of fanum and profanum does not occur, though there may be special sacred places, such as a grove of trees, a well, or a burial tumulus.

*Source*: Author's original idea developed by Michele Lukowski. Concepts inspired by Marija Gimbutas, Martin E. Marty and others

### Aspects of the fanum

To show how the tensions described above can develop, Marty uses the United States to examine the nature of the sacred and what happens when this is threatened.

1  Most human groups, whether a family, a religion, a tribe, or a nation, have (or have had) a sacred object, a fanum. The sacred is often captured in a

potent symbol: a cross, a star, a flag. Take the United States, for example: its Great Seal (printed on the back of a one dollar bill) shows a pyramid under construction, with God's eye poised above: *Annuit coeptis – novus ordo seclorum*, He (God) smiles upon this beginning, the new order of the ages. The seal's other side shows an eagle holding in its beak a banner reading *E pluribus unum*: one out of many.

2   The sacred myth has a history that gives it legitimacy. In the United States, the respected "elders," the Founding Fathers, are the sacred authority. In 1780s' America, it was relatively easy to unify the homogeneous population of male, white, Protestant, English-speaking colonists who held all the political power. Today, "we" (yesterday's powerful men) are losing our cohesiveness, as "we" are forced to accommodate women, other races, other religions, other languages. The old, sacred image is out-of-synch with the new reality. *E pluribus unum* is getting harder to achieve.

3   Evidence accumulates of growing internal threats to the old unity of belief as society diversifies. The old religion is being lost: school prayer was outlawed in 1962; Darwinism is replacing Genesis in children's heads. "We" need to find the villain, the "Other" who is causing these problems.

4   It is "our" sacred duty to strengthen the walls of the temple, to reverse the corrosion.

5   "We" appeal to some supreme power for assistance: God, the Supreme Being; Reason; the Founding Fathers.

6   "We" use whatever means are available to "us": ballot box, persuasion (the media), economic power, outright violence when all else fails.

7   "Our" cause, being right, will *eventually prevail*.

8   *All* is demanded of us: heart, mind, even life itself.

An example of how two major, globally known leaders of the twentieth century communicated points (2) through (8) to their followers is shown in Table VIII.1.

To sum up, every culture has some sort of sacred belief. Under "normal" times this belief carries out its critical function of providing the rhythm and the melody that orchestrate the coordinated acts of the society; it is reassuring, but seldom intrusive. Fanum and profanum interact smoothly.

Under stress, however, fear takes hold, and the boundary between the "true believers" (identified as "we," "us," and "our" above) and the less enthusiastic, and certainly the doubters, becomes sharply defined. Lines are drawn between sides: one inside and the other outside the fanum. Under such stress, *fanaticism* can take hold. Jacob Burckhardt, the nineteenth-century historian, labeled the fanatic as the "terrible simplifier," the one who can cut through everything.

> When you see men renouncing everything for a single object, you have reason to fear troubling them in the passions of what is left to them.[6]

*Table VIII.1* Religious rhetoric of two universally known twentieth-century political leaders

## A Nation under God

A "This is the real task before us: to reassert our commitment as a nation to a law higher than our own, to renew our spiritual strength. Only by building a wall of such spiritual resolve can we, as a free people, hope to protect our own heritage and make it someday that birthright of all men…"

A' "So we go forward with the profoundest faith in God into the future. Would that which we have achieved have been possible if Providence had not helped us? I know that all work of men is difficult and transitory when it is not blessed by this Omnipotence. But if this Omnipotence blesses a work, as it has blessed this work of ours, then men cannot destroy it."

## An Upright, Worthy People

B "There are countless quiet, everyday heroes [in our nation] – parents who sacrifice long and hard so their children will know a better life than they've known; church and civic volunteers who help to feed, clothe, nurse, and teach the needy; millions who've made our nation, and our nation's destiny, so very special…"

B' "When I see, as I so often do, poorly clad girls collecting with such infinite patience in order to care for those who are suffering from the cold while they themselves are shivering with cold, then I have the feeling that they are all apostles of a Christianity – and in truth of a Christianity which can say with greater right than any other: This is the Christianity of an honest confession for behind it stand not words but deeds."

## Renew Belief in Ourselves through God

C "The crisis we are facing today … [requires] our best effort and willingness to believe in ourselves and to believe in our capacity to perform great deeds; to believe that together with God's help we can and will resolve the problems which now confront us."

C' "If we pursue this way, if we are decent, industrious, and honest, if we so loyally and truly fulfil our duty, then it is my conviction that in the future as in the past the Lord God will always help us. In the long run He never leaves decent folk in the lurch. Often He may test them, He may send trials upon them, but in the long run He always lets His sun shine upon them once more and at the end He gives them His blessing."

D "Together let us take up the challenge to reawaken [this nation's] religious and moral heart, recognizing that a deep and abiding faith in God is the rock upon which this great nation was founded."

D' "I believe in Providence and I believe Providence to be just. Therefore I believe that Providence always rewards the strong, the industrious, and the upright."

## An Evil Empire Exists in the World

E    "Yes, let us pray for the salvation of all of those who live in that totalitarian darkness – pray they will discover the joy of knowing God. But until they do, let us be aware that while they preach the supremacy of the state, declare its omnipotence over individual man, and predict its eventual domination of all people on the Earth, they are the focus of evil in the modern world."

E'    "The same foe … still threatens us today. Any lie and any violence are good enough if they help it to gain its end. This is no longer a fight for paltry dynastic interests, a fight to round off the frontiers of States, a struggle for small economic aims: no! this is the battle against a veritable world sickness which threatens to infect the peoples, a plague which devastates whole peoples, whose special characteristic is that it is an international pestilence."

*Key*

A    RRS, p.92
Conservative Political Action Conf., 1981
B    ATFC, p.286
State of the Union Message, 1/26/82
C    RRS, p.145
First Inaugural Address, 1/20/81
D    RRS, p.74
Natl. Day of Prayer Proclamation, 1982
E    RRS, p.164
Natl. Assoc. of Evangelicals, Orlando, FL, 3/8/83

A'    SAH, p.392
Regensburg, 6/6/37
B'    SAH, p.393
Winter Help Campaign, 10/5/37
C'    SAH, p.407
Harvest Festival, Bückeberg, 10/3/37
D'    SAH, p.404
Nuremberg Parteitag, 9/11/36
E'    SAH, p.691
Nuremberg Parteitag, 9/13/37

RRS    *Ronald Reagan Speaks*, Paul D. Erickson, New York: New York University Press, 1985
ATFC    *A Time for Choosing: The Speeches of Ronald Reagan 1961–1982*, Chicago: Regnery Gateway, 1983
SAH    *The Speeches of Adolph Hitler 1922–1939*, N.H. Baynes (ed.), New York: Howard Fertig, 1969, Vol. 1.

Says Erickson, (p.122):

As we gear up for the next presidential campaign, both major parties seem to hope for another great communicator to duplicate Ronald Reagan's power to move voters with words. This trend should distress us, for the use of language requires not only the ability to speak or write, *but also the skill of questioning the words we hear*. We need to listen more suspiciously not simply to avoid being duped by a potential tyrant or an incompetent leader of any political persuasion, but also to keep us from *becoming deaf and blind to our own cultural language.*
*Such scrutiny is the first duty of democracy.*

(All emphases added)

People are most dangerous when they believe totally in one narrowly stated idea – the "sound-bite," the "slogan," the "flag" – and close their eyes and ears to all else about them. They refuse dialogue; refuse ever to admit to another, "Well, yes, you may have a point there." Cut the tiny rug out from under their one idea, their one sacred "object," and you leave them no meaning whatsoever to fall back on. Their identity, their "self," disappears.

### Conditions favoring fanaticism

The fervent, single-minded defense of the sacred myth reaches its peak during times of social unrest, which can lead to various commonly experienced psychological consequences. The common denominator is fear for one's identity.[7] In that sense, all causes of fanaticism are related. As Marty says, a fanatic is one who quite literally fears the loss of everything:

> When identities are at stake; when the question of Who am I? and To what do I belong? and For what will I die? is at stake, is when they are born.[8]

### Reduction of dissonance

The human mind, remarkable though it is, is no match for the overly complex reality in which it is immersed. We must simplify the world around us in order to live in it meaningfully. Language is the main way in which we do this, by categorizing objects, actions and ideas. And that's true for the biggest ideas of all. We are more comfortable with a clear, unambiguous ultimate meaning in our lives than with messy complexity and uncertainty. It was the well-known labor leader and writer, Eric Hoffer, who once said:

> To be in possession of an absolute truth is to have a net of familiarity spread over the whole of eternity. There are then no surprises and no unknowns. All questions have already been answered, all decisions made.[9]

Marty points out, however, that most fundamentalists who are trying to redefine their version of the truth are *not* fanatics. Often, they enter into intense dialogues with others and work hard at thinking through their beliefs. Fanaticism only happens when the portcullis is dropped, closing off the true believers, forming a cult. It is then that the "Other" becomes enemy, is demonized, and made the scapegoat for whatever's wrong. There is no room for compromise, and those who waiver, who have doubts, must be eliminated.

Marty recounts the description by "Mr. Dooley" (the creation of a Chicago journalist in the early twentieth century) of someone who is certain he or she has "the truth":

The fanatic is someone who knows he's doing exactly what the Lord would do if the Lord were also in possession of the facts.[10]

In the United States, politicians who are determined to cut short dialogue, often appeal to "what the Founding Fathers would do," who surely were in possession of "the truth."

Certainty! Fanaticism reduces psychic dissonance. But in its grip, society becomes totally stuck. It cannot change or adapt. It cannot entertain the possibility of a new channel into which it might flow.

### Compensation for self-doubt

Another psychological factor pushing people towards fanaticism is the feeling of inadequacy, or, more understandably, resentment at outright rejection, oppression, and perceived injustice. The man or woman who harbors an inferior sense of identity, or has one imposed on them by others, all too often compensates by becoming a bully. Openly competitive societies (such as those embracing free-market capitalism) that create winners and losers, where losing is a sign of inadequacy, of disgrace, set people up to feel like failures, and too often their psychic discomfort demands someone to blame.

The shame of inadequacy can also afflict an entire community or nation. Examples, to be discussed in Chapter IX, include the Japanese and the Germans prior to World War II. Both, in different ways, experienced what seemed unreasonable rejection by the family of nations, and became, essentially, fanatical in reasserting their right to status. A different kind of shame attended the German people after the atrocities of the Holocaust, and the Afrikaners in South Africa after the horrors of apartheid ended in 1990 (the latter is addressed in Chapter X).

My point is that both individuals and identifiable groups who experience feelings of inadequacy and rejection tend to close themselves off, to find an "Other" to blame, and to seek an absolute, justifying authority for their right to prevail (see the quotes in Table VIII.1). Oftentimes, such feelings of inadequacy already present in a group are heightened by dilution of its strength relative to the larger society around it. An example is the immigration of groups with different identifying traits, who seem to compete for social status. The Protestant laboring classes in America resented the immigration of Catholics from Italy and Ireland at the start of the last century. In Europe today, groups of working-class Germans, French and English openly express hostility toward Muslims and other "foreigners" in their midst. "Our way of life" is being threatened by "those people." It is usually the least secure groups who become most fearful, and thus resentful: "Whatever status we once had is being taken from us."

It is easy to see how militant fanatics arise within such groups. Militias, brown shirts, the Ku Klux Klan. And especially the guerrilla warriors in country after country who follow would-be liberators, from Zapata to Fidel Castro, as they engage in resistance to an oppression far beyond denigrating slurs, one that inflicts life-threatening violence. In some of these contexts, fanaticism makes realistic survival sense: contexts where cultural extinction is imminent, whether inflicted militarily or economically or ideologically.

### *"Rebound" fanaticism*

The notion that you can become a fanatic when on the rebound from something else may at first seem odd. But refer back for a moment to Figure VIII.1. Suppose the profanum, the secular, has come to so dominate the social scene that ultimate meaning and purpose in life have been relegated to an insignificant corner of the larger culture. The most important things in life are "private," not spoken of in daily discourse. By accommodating everybody, a thousand different meanings, the society's admirable tolerance turns into a meaningless, bland social world. There is nothing, as I walk down the street, to engage *with*. There is (except perhaps for an hour on a Sunday or Saturday or Friday morning) nothing sacred about my community, my country. Living here, in this equivalent of an international airport, housing unfamiliar fellow travelers on the planet, I have no sense of identity, of where *I* belong.

I long for something that matters, something I can feel enthusiasm for, where my life will be given uplifting purpose. There is, for me, in this physically safe world of modern technology, advanced medicine, and opportunity for infinite consumption, a huge vacuum of transcendent, significant meaning that I can comfortably share with those around me. Without the fanum, I have no shared ecstatic experience. I am not fully human! I am less oppressed by others than I am depressed by emptiness. Strictly physical needs are met, but human psychological needs are not.

An increasing number of people in the world today are coming to mistrust the notion of "rational progress," of a society devoted purely to "efficient" ways to produce and consume. They rebel at the spread of free-market capitalism, the destruction of both Nature and social relations, the denial of the central place of sacred meaning in human life. They rebel especially when rationality and reason are offered as a *substitute* for sacred meaning, for feeling. They resent deeply the scientist who tells them, with the sort of absolutist authority some in that profession can display, that there is no "purpose" in life, no "meaning" in the universe; there are simply physical laws, and processes that obey those laws.

And so, as Marty would put it, like other fanatics who have been driven too far, people deprived of sacred meaning can "lose it." They, too, can abandon discourse, the slow process of discussion and listening, opting instead for reaction. They invent a new fanum, a new belief, a new absolute truth, a new fundamentalism that serves their very real, human need for an ultimate purpose. Their scapegoats become the too "reasonable," the too "rational," the too "scientific."

272

It is thus very natural that in recent decades popular resentment has increased toward the arrogant authority claimed by some scientists, especially social scientists, "because only our scientific methods can reveal the 'absolute truth' of which we therefore are in sole possession." The exclusivism of *their* tribe is fast becoming its own kind of fanaticism. Stephen J. Gould, when president of the American Association for the Advancement of Science, America's largest scientific organization, castigated some of his colleagues for their

> marches to truth fueled by universal and disembodied weapons of reason and observation ("the scientific method") against antiquated dogmas and social constraints.

Instead, he said of science or any other human search for such absolute truth:

> [N]o inevitability attends our eventual understanding of a real world outside our social construction.[11]

In conclusion, in each form of fanaticism, an "Other" is identified within one's social world as the putative cause of "the trouble." The world is divided into "us" and "them." *We* exclude; *we* are exclusive. As Marty notes, "Somebody once asked the poet, Carl Sandburg, what is the ugliest word in the English language, and he said 'exclusive – exclusivism'."[12]

Yet it is extremely important to realize that many, many societies have existed (and still do) that have managed to provide fully satisfying and meaningful cultural narratives *without becoming exclusive!* The "Other" is *not* ubiquitously present as a threat. When strangers from unknown cultures are encountered, they are tolerated, treated as any traveler is, with hospitality and respect. Thus did most Native American societies first greet the early colonists, assisting them in their precarious survival. They were often curious, ready to trade, to share ideas. Indeed, the more democratic concepts embedded by the Founding Fathers in the United States Constitution are directly traceable to the local Iroquois Confederation, with whom Jefferson, Franklin and others were in contact.[13] (The Constitution, by the way, makes no reference to competing political parties, merely to the will of the people.) Only when trust was broken, when the colonists demanded too much and threatened native customs and livelihoods, did Native Americans earn the reputation of being the dangerous "Other," and invite angry resistance.

Thus a culture may possess its own sacred meaning, be secure in its own dignified identity, *without* being exclusive, *without* finding it necessary to deny or even denigrate the possible truth of others, let alone try to change them. It is entirely feasible to feel wholly secure in one's own sacred beliefs and still remain open to those of others. It is, unfortunately, a feat that has too often escaped human grasp during our long history, to which I now turn.

## Was there ever an Eden?

The information we have from prehistory, the bones of our ancestors and of the animals they ate and odd artifacts such as stone tools or bone fishhooks or remnants of hearths, tell us little about their beliefs, thoughts, or social life. Even cave art or petroglyphs offer endless possible explanations. Most such art depicts gracefully drawn animals, sometimes recognizable, sometimes not, and alongside them are sticklike, stylized humans often carrying what are interpreted as weapons (see Figure VIII.2).

Given the long persistence among archeologists of the "male hunting" theory of human cultural evolution, this art has been interpreted as having a

*Figure VIII.2* Ancient San rock art from southern Africa

This illustration, from an ancient rock painting, depicts a mystical religious ceremony. An animal is being led by people across the parched land, so that its blood may turn to rain. The fallen figure is probably the body of the shaman in trance, his consciousness leaving his body as it creates this hallucinatory event. There is a symbolic line of bees (dots) touching the powerful *n!au* spot on the animal's shoulder, providing it with its rain-giving powers. The honey of the bees gives potency to the trance experience. The painting was probably the work of the shaman himself, explaining to the whole community what only he was able to experience.

*Source*: From J. David Lewis-Williams (1983). Used by kind permission of Professor Lewis-Williams and the Rock Art Research Institute at the Witwatersrand University. Lewis-Williams sees mythic art not as an isolated "discipline" within a fragmented politico-economical-social-psychological-esthetic milieu, but as the embodiment of a holistic vision of oneself in a coherent world, and it has meaning only in terms of that world. As the docents in every art gallery remind us, without knowledge of the myth behind the art, its meaning can only be guessed at.

"functionalist" role as a hunting ritual. But as Lewis-Williams, who has spent a lifetime studying such art, has observed:

> Prehistorians trained in this [hunting ritual] school were plainly ill-equipped to deal with explanations referring to meaning, for "meaning" cannot be inferred from artefacts be they rock paintings or stone tools.... Men's ideas, beliefs and values were... considered epiphenomena of no relevance to the real business of prehistory.[14]

As it happens, this particular rock painting is by the ancient San when their tribe lived over all of southern Africa, and is interpretable even today using extant San religious beliefs and symbols. The animal embodies the power of rain, important in that semi-arid region. It is being led ceremonially across the parched land so that its milk or blood will turn into rain. The whole episode, says Lewis-Williams, is a shaman's "hallucination or intense trance experience rather than an event performed with a real animal."[15]

This painting, and those in southern Europe, thus have nothing to do with hunting and everything to do with the mystical beliefs people held about themselves in the world. Animals, who in most indigenous cultures once were people in the primordial world, still possess important powers over Nature that are crucial to human survival, and the shaman is the interpreter of these powers.[16]

In fact, the role of art in all its many forms is the communication of meaningfulness among members of a culture, what Ellen Dissanayake calls "making special." Painting the body or otherwise decorating it, dancing, singing, embellishing tools with carvings or paintings or feathers, all are ways of emphasizing the special significance of objects in the world. That we take pleasure in the arts is no accident, she suggests; rather, it is evidence of the evolutionary adaptiveness of meaning in human life. Even before language, our ancestors were probably using mime and other forms of art to communicate meaning in their lives: important transitions, special foods, insuring fertility of wild things, marking the seasons, curing illness, and so on.[17]

What is certain is that things which mattered were given special symbolic meaning early on. But what those meanings were, and how well they served the peoples of each culture, is forever beyond our ken. We can only guess, and the range of guesses has run the gamut from the Rousseauian perception of "the noble savage" living in harmony with his fellow beings and their environment, all the way to the Hobbesian view of brutish, competing ancestors given to incessant squabbling until they invented mutual contracts and agreed-upon laws. Even today these extremes seem to persist as either/or images of the past, with some claiming precolonial indigenous people were mostly well adapted, and others, that war and violence have always been universal.[18]

I believe neither extreme is a useful model of the past. The probability that precolonial indigenous peoples were all unstressed seems to me low. Long before the Europeans sallied forth on their global conquests, both natural and socially induced stresses must have affected cultures almost everywhere from time to time. There would be periods of relative peace interrupted by others that were much more violent. And their meaning systems must have changed to accommodate – or perhaps justify – these swings. Cultures that could not change would become extinct. Thus, in answer to the question which heads this section, Was there ever an Eden?, yes, here and there, from time to time there were certainly nearly ideal societies, though never around the whole planet, all at once. Yet that is still one future possibility.

## How small, egalitarian cultures "go wrong"

Since we cannot go back and observe the Pleistocene, the best we can do is to learn from still-existing foraging societies what kinds of fates may have befallen our ancient ancestors before there were permanent agricultural settlements. These were essentially egalitarian societies, without strict rankings or classes. They foraged almost every day. They moved camp regularly, accumulated little material wealth, stored or preserved little. They knew the affordances in their world well, and fissioned and fusioned according to the seasons, exchanging nubile adolescents among bands. The whole of that familiar world *was* their identity, their sacred place, imbued with meaning and spirit.

### *Trapped in time*

Environmentalists daily remind us that we have been destroying our support system, and so we have. Sometimes they seem to imply that past societies never had this problem, which simply is not true, though mostly their numbers were smaller and their technological impacts far less extensive.[19] Here I present two examples of historically recorded societies that ended up in a cultural cul-de-sac, not because of internal violence or external threat, but because they simply could not change their customary way of living. Though not foraging nomads, they model the potential cultural problem for any peoples who too rigidly adhere to old beliefs and customs.

My first example is Easter Island. Prior to the arrival of the Polynesians around AD 400, this uninhabited island paradise was lushly covered with forests, shrubs and grasses. The first settlers had a rich living, harpooning porpoises at sea, catching birds, and harvesting the abundant palm nuts. They cut trees to build houses and canoes, and to make charcoal; they cleared land for gardens. And they instituted a religious competition in building giant statues to their gods. Over time, the statues got bigger and more numerous, while the environment was slowly depleted. By AD 800, the forests were in decline; by 1400, palm trees were extinct; 100 years later, all trees were gone and the land began to erode. There were no more new houses or canoes; no more land birds for food, for pollination, for spreading wild seeds. From a peak population of 7000 or more in AD 1500 the population plummeted by over 75 percent. There were only chickens, rats and other humans(!) for meat, and grass, sedges and sugar cane to supplement the diet. People moved to caves and busied themselves with tearing down each other's statues. And it all happened just slowly enough that they could avoid noticing the disaster they were creating for themselves.[20]

My second example is the curious inability of a twelfth-century Norwegian settlement on the inhospitable western fringe of Greenland to adapt; it lasted about 400 years before simply vanishing. The Norse, it seems, clung rigidly to their old culture, habits of dress, and livestock economy, all the while barely eking out a minimal existence, depending instead on occasional ships from Norway. They failed to utilize any of the rich resources of the sea, though they were clearly in touch with a neighboring Thule settlement (an Inuit group who migrated from Ellesmere Island about AD 1100). The Thule were excellent seal-hunters and fishers, and seldom went hungry or cold. But culture flowed in one direction only, from Norse to Thule. So when the Little Ice Age began, and unusually cool summers reduced the fodder needed for livestock, the Norse began to starve, even eating their cattle and dogs before disappearing. The cold climate kept the ships from home from coming. Says archeologist Tom McGovern, "ethnic purity triumphed at the expense of biological survival ... [I]t seems the Norse in Greenland remained true to the laws and customs of their warmer homeland – and paid the final price for it."[21]

Why is it sometimes so hard for a culture to change, to modify its traditional narrative? Social theorist Ernest Becker, writing about the insights of psychologist Erich Fromm, provides a clue:

> As Fromm so well put it, children are trained to do as the society says they have to do. They have to earn their prestige [identity] in definitely fixed ways. The result is that people willingly propagate whole cultural systems that hold them in bondage, and since everyone plays in the same hero-game, no one can see through the farce.[22]

Becker's words underscore the deep attachment of human beings, both as individuals and as communities, to their shared meaning system. Its integrity is essential if a society is to preserve its communal knowledge base, its institutions, and its wisdom. Any culture that is careless in educating its young or that tries to change too much, too fast, is in danger of losing coherence and dying out (contemporary Russia seems to be threatened by this). It is no wonder that cultural beliefs become sacred and humans have an innate propensity to *defend* and *reproduce* them. Religious values are the most preserved; political values (not unrelated, of course) come next.[23] Religion and politics, after all, frame almost all our institutionalized beliefs about "Who We Are."

This powerful psychological force for *conservation* of a cultural narrative explains past (and present) failures of societies to change even when confronted with clear warning signals. They fall victim to their own "cultural traps."[24] They become "fanatic," suffering from the rigidity of "cultural identity disorder."

## *Theories of causes of violence*

During the past century, biologists and social scientists alike have tended to explain the causes of human violence in simplified Darwinian terms. Whether interpersonal or inter-group, violence emerged, they said, out of competition for scarce resources. Males fought each other for status, and hence for access to both females and food, usually in that order! Supposedly, cooperative hunting created group territorial behavior, the first "armies." Logically, the causes of violence should be sought in the inevitably competitive relations within and between societies (the factors listed on the left side of Table VII.1). "The Territorial Imperative" of the group and "The Selfish Gene" of the individual, each seeking its own survival in a world of scarcity: these were at the root of violence.[25]

As I have already suggested, these factors no doubt contribute to violent human behavior, but seldom, if ever, in such direct ways as have been argued. Meaning systems (the customs, values, and norms embedded in shared cultural narratives) supersede our simple survival urges in the arena of those inner feelings that motivate our behavior. A look at violence, or more often its absence, in small, leaderless bands offers some insights. My argument is that scarcity *per se* is seldom the initiator of violence. It is much more often caused by threats to social stability: unexplained stresses or unjust harms befalling people. In other words, if there is "scarcity" it is more often of a psychological nature than a simple biological one, such as for sex or food. It is the former sort of scarcity that most often rouses people to anger and violence. And failure to prevent that violence often lies less in a society's inability to share food and women than in its failure to resolve conflicts over relationships: hurt feelings, disloyalty, unkindnesses. If there is "competition" it is almost always about status and acceptance and identity: in a word, about meaning.

Throughout the Pleistocene, when our brains were being shaped, small bands of foragers had few ways to deal with "wrongful harm." When a serious act took place (someone was killed, whether in anger or not, or someone fell ill or died unexplainably, which many cultures therefore would attribute to witchcraft) there were few ways to resolve the wrong. There were no jails; there was not even (until much later in the Neolithic) accumulated wealth, such as cattle, to pay as "blood money" to the injured family.[26]

We may suppose however that even in the very earliest societies, cultural narratives tended to emphasize reconciliation, generally under the guidance of elders (recall that this occurs in other primates, as described in Chapter II). The goal was not punishment or "getting even," but "repairing frayed social relationships and [thus] pacifying the ancestral spirits."[27]

If efforts at peace and reconciliation by the elders failed, a band had three options. (1) *Fission*, thus separating the feuding parties. This can occur only in underpopulated areas, which were likely common early on (again from Chapter II, the inability to fission freely among wild chimpanzees and other primates seems correlated with increasing violence). (2) *Banishing the offender*, a potent threat, since being ejected from society could be a death sentence.[28] (3) *Killing the offender.* Of the three, this is the least likely to reduce feelings of anger and restore social harmony; even an offender often has relatives who will take his or her side. In small societies, killing is more likely to lead to prolonged blood feuds than to reconciliation. The natural human anger at the violent death of a loved one too easily becomes institutionalized into an ongoing "war." The Montagus and Capulets, the Hatfields and the McCoys, locked in senseless revenge over generations, all in the name of "restoring family honor." Such prolonged, unchecked conflict would put a small community in danger of extinction.

In the following discussion I examine three of the commonest theories on the "causes" of violence: (1) resource scarcity; (2) cultural stress leading to destabilization; and (3) inability to resolve violent conflicts. A brief comparison of three leaderless societies, all living in similar tropical forest habitats, offers insight into the dominant role played by cultural factors in determining levels of social violence. The societies are: the non-violent Semai Senoi of the Malay peninsula; the (until recently) very violent Waorani of Ecuador; and the Yanomami on the Venezuelan–Brazilian border, reputedly known for their "fierce" behavior. All make their living in similar ways, living in temporary settlements near clearings where they grow the plants that provide most of their food, with supplements of game and fruits from the forest. What has made them so different? Were they always as they are now? How fast can they change?

### Resource scarcity

The first of these cultures to be studied in depth was the Yanomami. In the 1960s, anthropologist Napoleon Chagnon described them as engaged in vendetta killings between villages. During a raid, any Western goods were stolen and young women were abducted to be wives.[29] Chagnon interpreted their violence in terms of males competing for "reproductive success": "Yanomami males are tracking their environment with their own fitness interests at stake."[30] (This forms the basis of the old evolutionary psychology argument: more wives, more reproductive success.) For "proof" he claimed that the fiercest males, that is, those who killed the most, had more wives and children.[31] But Chagnon studied only one area of the Yanomami people; elsewhere neither violence nor female abduction was being practiced. If these actions were due to a universal "urge" to reproduce, why were they so limited?

Another anthropologist, Marvin Harris, argued another form of scarcity, namely game, as the cause of Yanomami competition. He saw warfare as a means of spacing out the villages (a sort of "territorial" behavior), thus increasing available protein through increased hunting territories.[32] Yet Brian Ferguson, a third anthropologist who studied the tribe, found that the most violent villages were not shifting their villages and gardens from site to site as they once did. Instead, they stayed clustered around white outposts, where they acquired such prized trade items as machetes and shotguns.[33] These were what was depleting the game.

In another study that examined the influence of crowding and scarcity on the violent Waorani of Ecuador and the peaceful Semai of Malaya, Clayton and Carole Robarchek found just the opposite of the expected effect. It is the peaceful Semai who have a population density *several times higher* yet live in a far less lush, fertile habitat than that of the warlike Waorani. They conclude the following:

> The comparison of Semai and Waorani, so strikingly similar in terms of their ecological situations and, presumably, their biological propensities, but so different in their behaviors, argues that human behavior is not a determined response to an "objective" reality, either ecological or biological.[34]

Evidently potential scarcity does not automatically create competition nor lead to violent behavior. So what else might trigger it?

### Cultural destabilization

Both Ferguson and the Robarcheks suggest looking at a culture's history for an explanation of violence.[35] There is no information on the recent history of the peaceful Semai, but both the warlike Waorani and Yanomami had had destabilizing encounters with more powerful outside cultures. It is not necessary for a people to be overrun to experience severe stress from outsiders. A few examples include being raided for slaves, or worse, having once friendly neighbors raid your own people and sell them to outsiders.[36] Acquisition of guns and steel implements in exchange for forest products and local "trophies" (e.g. shrunken human heads!) can upset relationships. Diseases of the white man, an invisible danger, killed many and spread suspicion and terror among affected tribes. Such multiple impacts could easily disrupt the customary alliances and local trade patterns, and with them the trust that had existed among kin-groups or neighboring peoples prior to contact with outsiders.[37]

Even as simple a thing as the introduction of steel axes into numerous stone-age cultures had highly destabilizing effects.[38] Among the Yanomami, steel implements and guns created "power" for those bands that first possessed them, and envy and fear in those who did not. Ferguson believes trade in these prized possessions (e.g. swapping guns for women) disrupted old marriage alliances and set off raids with the aim of obtaining both items.[39]

The Waorani in the Ecuadorian rainforest had suffered from raids for slaves from the very beginning of the Spanish era, which may have initiated the first warfare among their villages. Outside pressure later became much more intense when whites tried to infiltrate their lands. Despite the guns of the would-be rubber tappers and oil geologists, the natives' knowledge of the forest and their skill with spears and poisoned blow-guns made their lands impenetrable to outsiders; they ably protected an enormous area. But with their very low densities they formed too few kinship cross-links. As death from foreign diseases, once rare, mysteriously soared, paranoia directed toward neighboring bands took hold, and a cycle of vendettas ensued. Once the killings began in earnest there was no relief from the ongoing vengeance. A mother would patiently wait for her infant son to grow up so he could avenge his father's murder. Sixty percent of deaths among them were from homicides, and their population plummeted to a mere 500 persons. Said one surviving woman, "We were down to almost two people." The tribe nearly died out before the violence was finally stopped.[40]

### Inability to resolve violent conflict

Though the Waorani successfully staved off incursions from whites, once they began killing each other, they had no cultural tools which they could use to stop. Yet only a few years later, a Swiss anthropologist and his wife found these same people living peacefully, with great social equality. How had they managed to end their feuding?

It began when a Protestant missionary, Rachael Saint, befriended a terrified young woman whose family had all been murdered. Dayuma, as she was known, became the go-between, encouraging one group after another to listen to the missionary. In less than a decade almost the entire society had adopted some Christian beliefs and gone "from the most warlike yet described, to one that is essentially peaceful." The new God displaced their old belief in witchcraft and so restored their ability to trust one another.[41] Though most now live at the mission, one-fifth have retained their former way of life. By incorporating an outside explanation for the recently devastating events into their cultural narrative they were able to escape the "trap" of mutual blame and cultural extinction. Not every culture, past or present, is fortunate enough to discover a way to similarly *change* its deepest beliefs about the world; indeed, all too many have not even seen any need to change.

To sum up, it is clear that no one factor can be pinpointed as the cause of a society's becoming violent. Sometimes scarcity results in undue stress; sometimes external factors cause instability, whether disruptive ideas or potent new technologies or virulent diseases.[42] Sometimes their old ways of resolving conflicts, whether fissioning or banishment, fail them. All three may contribute, in different proportions. Yet whether a given culture becomes extinct or successfully adapts depends less on what *causes* the stresses it experiences than on how those stresses are interpreted and responded to. In other words, its *beliefs* are more significant than its *circumstances*. The psychological, or meaning, side of a culture dominates its pragmatic side (see Table VII.1). The three cultures discussed illustrate this point. Human societies do not behave in accordance with supposedly "adaptive" neo-Darwinian principles of competition and self-interest. For better or for worse, culture *is* our primary survival trait today. Darwin, I am certain, would have agreed.

## *Interpreting the power of meaning*

Among the Yanomami, extremely violent groups all share a newly created origin myth "in which the falling blood of a wounded moon [their ancestor, Periborawa] explains their propensity to violence … *The myth is not found in other, more peaceful areas of Yanomami territory.*"[43] It is Periborawa's blood in their veins that makes them "fierce people" – their own name for themselves. Brian Ferguson believes that this new myth is a convenient "story" invented to justify a level of violent behavior with which many still have subliminal psychic unease, yet they cannot resist the Western goods that offer them power and status as a result of the killing. The myth, he thinks, is not yet so culturally entrenched as to be irreversible, but it has catalyzed the emergence of an incipient power hierarchy.[44] Thus it is that a myth can be modified to justify the restructuring of a society, in this case from egalitarian to hierarchical.

The Waorani, so far as I can discover, have a very uncomplicated belief system. Their culturally defined self is one of extreme individual independence: man, woman or child, each is expected to be emotionally self-reliant. Bonds, while important, are not close; personal autonomy dominates self-images. There is little superstitious fear of Nature. On the other hand, the Waorani lack the Yanomamis' mythical belief in their own "fierceness."[45] These traits may help explain both the Waorani's relative lack of enthusiasm for Western technologies and their inability to stop vengeful feuds. The simplicity of their cultural narrative combined with their extreme degree of personal autonomy makes it easy to adopt new cultural ideas. Christianity simply offered convenient relief, providing them with the authority to change a pattern of violence that had become universally objectionable.[46]

By contrast, the peaceful Semai, despite the natural stresses of relative crowding in a much harsher habitat, escaped violence because their cultural understanding is quite the reverse. Nature is dangerous, always ready to strike one down; security lies in humans sticking together to defend each other.

> [T]he Semai world view motivates a powerful affective concern with interdependence and group cohesion. This is evidenced in the extreme reluctance of individuals to become involved in disputes, and in the formal dispute-settlement procedures that are immediately called into action when any conflict emerges into general awareness, a process whose *objective is less the attribution of fault than the restoration of amicable relations between the disputants and within the band as a whole.*[47]

It is evident that internal stress would have to be enormous for the Semai to adopt patterns of regular violence toward each other. (What their present views might have been had they experienced violent threats in the past from outside cultures is a moot point.)

In summary, for small egalitarian societies, violent aggression does not corre-late well with physical stress but does so with the beliefs encoded in the cultural narrative. If you believe humans are dangerous, whether through treachery (Yanomami) or the practice of witchcraft (Waorani), then you are likely to expect the worst and take vengeance for any harm that comes. The number of cross-cutting bonds that stabilize society is low, and readily shifts with changing alliances. If, like the Semai, however, nonhuman forces are where danger lies, you will ensure group security by repressing overt aggressive acts. Bonding is widespread throughout society and social disapproval for disrupting bonds is high. (This does not mean the Semai, or other peaceful societies, are incapable of violent aggression. When coopted in the 1950s by the British army to fight against communist insurgency, the Semai became efficient warriors, *but only after going berserk when they saw their kinsmen slaughtered*. One of them described himself as being "drunk with blood"; all were astonished at their own capacity for violence, returning afterward to their former peaceful ways.[48])

During most of prehistory, then, human societies must have experienced variations on the themes discussed so far: egalitarian societies, sometimes able to adapt to environmental changes or to correct destructive patterns of social behavior, sometimes not. A culture did not have to be over-run in order to die out; it could fail to change its perceptions on "how to live." Those that over-emphasized individual autonomy found it easy to fall into violence and difficult to come together as a community to discuss how to settle conflict, even though everyone was sick of the killing.[49] Those that over-emphasized community agreement suffered a different impediment to change. No one would come forward with a criticism of the current system or suggest an alternative. The peaceful Semai could not even organize themselves to repair a dangerously deteriorating foot-suspension bridge over a chasm. Since they were unwilling to have any person tell them what to do, no one dared to step forward and mobi-lize them.[50] No one must "stand out" or appear to be above others.

Too little, or too much. Cultural world views that over-emphasize either human autonomy or human conformity are equally in danger of failure to adaptively change. That lesson, taken from simple egalitarian societies, so easy for an observer from our age to comprehend, is greatly magnified in impor-tance but made much harder to see clearly in the more complex societies familiar to us. In turning to them, I ask the reader to move into a world becoming more densely populated, with new forms of economic activity, more diverse tasks within society, and new ideas about how communities should be organized, indeed "managed." Equal status and equal respect have eventually given way to layered hierarchies, and the autonomy that everyone once experi-enced has become increasingly reserved for the few at the top. At each step of the way, cultural narratives have been modified, rescripted to justify a "new order." Equality and autonomy are not things human beings readily relinquish; it takes a great deal of social threat and persuasion to accomplish that. In fact, over the past 5000 years, most human societies have short-changed most of their people by failing to satisfy their inborn psychological needs to fully belong, to experience autonomy, and to find meaning in their existence. The historic era recounts humankind's struggles to modify cultural narratives to better meet those needs.

The more humanly populated world of the historic era also introduced another problem: an end to fissioning and easy migration as a solution to conflict. Cultures with quite different beliefs and institutions that once had diverged without significant interaction came increasingly into contact. Not only did each society have to deal with its own internal social conflicts; it also had to preserve its integrity *vis-à-vis* other, potentially incompatible, beliefs. The historic era is essentially a dialogue between belief systems.

## Cities, "meanings," and the origins of patriarchy

Settled agriculture (as distinct from the earlier shifting agriculture in the tropics) was probably forced on our temperate-zone ancestors as the result of two sudden climate swings. Geographer Harm de Blij suggests that rapid warming about 12,000 ya caused edible wild grasses to flourish as never before in several spots around the world. Nomadic foragers living in the Fertile Crescent of the Tigris–Euphrates rivers, for example, found enough wild seeds in one place to feed themselves; they settled down and their numbers soon increased. Then, around 10,000 years ago, the cold rapidly returned for several generations. To get enough food, some groups of these now larger populations had to learn to assist the natural reproduction of their now staple grains through weeding, tilling, and selecting the most productive seeds. Those that did not make this adaptation died out.[51]

Meanwhile, toward the end of this cold spell, nomads on the now grass-covered steppes of Asia began herding sheep, goats, camels, and other hardy grazers. The impacts of these disparate lifestyles on cultural world views would be profoundly different, however, and especially in respect to gender identities and social ordering. In particular, it was the crucial role of male identity that Peggy Reeves Sanday unraveled in her cross-cultural analysis of the correlation between origin myths and the division of labor between men and women. In agricultural societies, in which both food production and child-rearing were shared by all adults, distinctions between male and female were minimal. In such societies origin myths tell of female ancestors or Earth goddesses as the creators of life; men and women, however, had equal status.

In societies where tracking large game or herding separated the men from the women and children for long periods, and life for males became far more dangerous, gender distinctions were emphasized greatly. The cultural myth tells of male creators, either heroic ancestors or sky-gods. The secret powers of women were often feared; they were denied status and influence, and were often abused. Says Sanday:

Thus gender symbolism in origin stories is a joint consequence of sex roles in *childrearing* and *the way the environment is exploited* in the pursuit of food ... Environmentally induced vulnerability (as in the hunting of large game) results in an outer orientation manifested first in the distancing of fathers from infants, and second in beliefs about outer power. On the other hand, the sense of security gained in a lush environment, where food is derived from the earth, results in an inner orientation manifested in nurturing fathers and beliefs about inward power [from the body itself].[52]

Sanday also identifies a third type of myth where both male and female gods participate in the initial creation of life.[53] In such societies, men and women perform separate but complementary social functions. Males hold ceremonial political power (as head men or chiefs), while women, particularly the heads of matrilineal clans, are the ones who in fact enthrone and dethrone the men, or exercise social authority in other powerful ways.[54] In some instances, Sanday claims, the "appearance" of political and ceremonial dominance by men is ceded to them, presumably to support their need for a secure identity (see Chapter VII for a discussion of this occurrence). This state of affairs she calls "mythical" male dominance. When women disagree with men's decisions, they may, for example, withhold their critical contributions to communal ceremonies or, as in some African tribes, even replace the chiefs with new ones.

### The rise and fall of the "Great Mother"

We tend to associate permanent settlements – "cities" – with agriculture. Yet long before food was grown in earnest, people were regularly assembling together in large groups. Year after year they returned to the same favored sites that acquired sacred meaning: the common burial place of their ancestors, or a sacred cave, or well, or grove of trees. Wherever it was, ceremonies would be held there.[55] As agriculture slowly developed, these places became the foci of the earliest permanent settlements. Cities, said the famous historian Lewis Mumford, originated not as utilitarian places but as centers of meaning:

In these ancient paleolithic sanctuaries, as in the first grave mounds and tombs, we have, if anywhere, the first hints of civic life, probably well before any permanent village settlement can even be suspected.[56]

In what follows, I use Europe as an example of how cultural meanings can change over time. But first, a brief account is needed of human and climatic events in Europe from 40,000 to around 4000 ya.

*Events in prehistoric Europe*

Figure VIII.3 shows a map of modern Europe on which I have tried to summarize the climactic events, beginning 40,000 ya, when sea levels were very much lower and the coastlines would in fact have extended out by several miles from those shown. During a period of glacial retreat, modern people, genetically similar to us, began to migrate out in all directions from somewhere in west central Asia. The first wave (40,000 to 35,000 ya) made their way across central Europe, all the way to Spain. They were the painters of the famous cave paintings (arrow #1). A few millennia later, around 25,000 ya, a second wave took a more southerly, Mediterranean route, also reaching Spain. Among other things, they produced the so-called "Venus" or "Mother Goddess" statues (arrow #2). The genes of these first two waves of early migrants are still found in 80 percent of modern European men. (Simultaneous migrations were of course fanning out to India, southeast Asia, and across Siberia, as described in Chapter III.)

The next major event was a return of the ice. The "Last Glacial Maximum" (that peaked about 17,000 ya) covered almost all of Europe: Scandinavia, most of Britain and eastern and central Europe, and even some parts of the Mediterranean countries. Three smallish areas remained habitable (see the circled #3s in Figure VIII.3). These refuges preserved the ancient genes that still exist among modern Europeans. This glaciation lasted from 20,000 to 13,000 ya.

When the ice finally retreated was when the exploitation of wild grains (wheat and barley) began in the Middle East (Figure VIII.3, #4). As already mentioned, the cold blip in this new warming trend was what forced these Neolithic people into serious agriculture. By 10,000 ya, their populations had increased and they very slowly began to radiate outwards once more, into Europe, Siberia, and north India, carrying their goddess figurines, incised ceramics and early, city-like settlements with them (arrows #5). Meantime, however, peoples in the ice age refuges were also beginning to repopulate central and northern Europe. While some of the in-migrating Middle East farmers kept moving along, carrying their genes with them, mostly their impact was cultural. Over thousands of years, local peoples adopted the skills of the newcomers, gradually intermarrying with some of them. On the whole, though, the farmers' cultural innovations moved faster than their genes, though some of the latter did find their way clear across Europe.

As migrations continued and populations grew, new agricultural settlements were formed in the Middle East, in north India, and all around southeastern Europe (the latter region is indicated in Figure VIII.3 by the area bounded by –··–·– ). Mostly these new "first cities" (many were quite substantial) were unfortified, and seem to have been socially nonhierarchical. Their peoples all produced goddess figurines similar to those earlier ones. Known as "Old Europe," this diffuse civilization flourished from 9000 to 5000 ya.

The next critical event was the sudden flooding of the Black Sea around 7500 ya. Originally a large, freshwater lake (indicated by the dashed line in Figure VIII.3) along whose shores agricultural communities flourished, within a few days

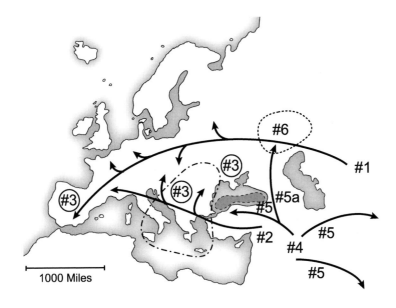

#1 40,000 ya, migrations across central Europe by cave-painting Aurignacians.

#2 25,000 ya, migrations across southern Europe by figure-making Gravettians.

#3 Refuge sites of first Europeans during 7000 years of the Last Glacial Maximum (peaked 17,000 ya).

#4 Site of the first Neolithic farmers ("Fertile Crescent"), 12,000 - 10,000 ya.

#5 Early migration routes of first farmers into Europe, Asia and India.

#5a Some farmers migrated north to the east European Steppe, and became herding nomads.

#6 Area of the sky-god worshiping Kurgan nomads that later made repeated incursions into the first "cities."

—·—·—· Area of "Old Europe," site of the first "cities" in southeast Europe, including the Balkans, Sicily, and Crete.

  Approximate area of the freshwater lake that existed before the Mediterranean flooded into the Black Sea.

*Figure VIII.3* Events in prehistoric Europe

*Source*: Original map by author from several sources and redrawn by Michele Lukowski

or weeks it was suddenly flooded, its level rising to at least 300 feet. The melting glacial ice had raised the sea level, finally breaching the land barriers between the Mediterranean and what we now call the Black Sea. Water thundered in at the rate of 200 Niagara Falls! The former lake's perimeters increased by a kilometer a day. Local residents could only flee, leaving homes and croplands behind. Only now are we finding remnants of wattle and daub buildings, stone tools, and ceramics 300 feet under the Sea. Noah's flood seems to have had a solid historical foundation.

Perhaps the climatically forced migrations of these peoples helped the spread of agriculture across Europe. But another, political, event was likely more important: a series of invasions by nomadic herdsmen into Old Europe's agricultural settlements. These "Kurgans" (so called for the shape of their tombs) had also originated in the Middle East as early farmers, but migrated around 9000 ya (arrow #5a) via Turkey to the steppes of the Eastern European Plain. Though unsuited for agriculture, these grass-covered lands were splendid for herding (Figure VIII.3, #6). The Kurgans tamed the plentiful horses, developed a pastoral economy and by around 5000 ya had developed bronze weapons. They also evolved a new religion, based on a male sky-god.

Around 5500 ya, the climate of the northern hemisphere started becoming drier. The Sahara gradually became more arid; the Eurasian steppe was less green. Nomads everywhere felt the stress. The Kurgans began making sporadic incursions into Old Europe, which were to span several millennia. Genetic evidence for these incursive waves is now emerging. Though few in numbers relative to the settled agriculturalists, they nevertheless managed over time to impose their religion, their language, and their culture on a much larger population. Once unfortified, the old cities became walled and protected. So while these new peoples' genes do not dominate today in Europe, their ideas do – all the way into the twentieth century.[57]

### The meaning of the Goddess

Having outlined the background to events, I return now to the culture of Old Europe, to the "Goddess" cultures of those first agriculturalists. The small carved figurines, mostly of stylized females with pendulous breasts and exaggerated hips and thighs, continue to be found over a wide area, from the Pyrenees to Lake Baikal, and especially around southern Europe, Anatolia, the Middle East, and early Egypt. Incorrectly called "Venuses," they span in time the earliest Pleistocene habitations of modern humans in Eurasia, all the way down to the Bronze Age, just 3000 ya. There are many variations in the forms of these female figures; often she has a bird's head or is incised with elaborate decorative motifs (see Figure VIII.4). Though she preceded agriculture, it is likely she signifies some aspect of the power of a nurturing Mother Earth. Latterly, clay images of animals were also common. It is in the same vicinity as these figurines occurred that the first "cities" were founded, with their craft specializations, religious centers, and permanent civic buildings.

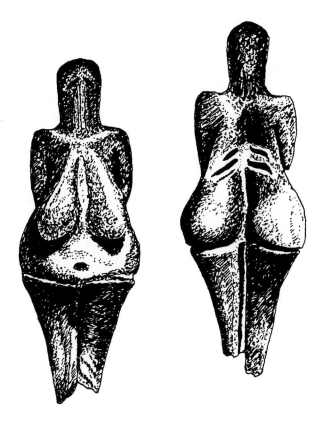

*Figure VIII.4* Example of a Goddess figurine

Front and back of figurine from Dolni Vestonice, Moravia, *c*.26,000 ya. (From James Harrod, 1997, "The Upper Paleolithic 'Double Goddess'; 'Venus' Figurines as Sacred Female Transformation Processes in the Light of a Decipherment of European Upper Paleolithic Language," in Joan Marler, 1997: 487. Original art by Patricia Reis, after A. Marshack. Used by kind permission of Joan Marler and James B. Harrod.)

Most of our understanding of these symbols is due to the work of one woman, Marija Gimbutas. She was fluent in a dozen or more European languages as well as Greek and Latin, and so could read historical writings in the originals. From her Lithuanian childhood she was familiar with not only pre-Christian but even early Indo-European threads in the peasant folklore. This amazing background, coupled with many years spent excavating the earliest settlements in the area she named Old Europe, enabled her to construct a tentative framework for a cosmology of the Goddess. (Friends who knew her tell me she was never dogmatic about her theories of that ancient culture.) In the past decade, however, her theories have gradually attracted attention and are receiving further confirmation.[58]

The myth of the "Great Mother" replaced the earlier animistic universe that comprised a host of natural spirits with a new image focussed more on the cyclical nature of life and death. All that lives must die in order to feed and nurture new life. This grandly integrated process was overseen by a powerful force, symbolized in the exaggerated shape of a woman's body, the most familiar life-giving, nurturing source known to every human being. This Goddess (or goddesses, for there were many parallel cultures spanning the landscape where the figurines were fashioned, each with its own name for Her) was the spirit that regulated these infinite cycles. She brings life; She takes it away. The life-giving power of the human female body became the metaphor for universal power.

Over time the Goddess acquired multiple other symbolic forms besides the female body: the triangle (the shape of the vulva whence birth occurs); the serpent, that sheds its skin in apparent rebirth; the bird goddess; the Tree of Life; the waxing and waning moon; and the butterfly that symbolized regeneration as the adult emerged from the "dead" chrysalis. Early on, She had androgynous qualities. Some statues show Her with a phallus projecting from the top of Her head, and the crescent-shaped horns of the bull, so reminiscent of the moon, were also sacred to Her. (Later on, the bull was to become associated with the sun, as a male fertility symbol.[59]) The Goddess was not simply part of a fertility cult, an ancient pornographic icon. The myths surrounding Her constituted an entire world view, a holistic philosophy of the nature and meaning of life – a cosmology. Enough is known of later Neolithic and Bronze Age mythology to make some sense of what that cosmology was like.

One revealing example of this is seen in the double-bladed ax, a very ancient, later Paleolithic Goddess symbol. On the one hand it stood for death, through sacrifice of the animals needed to sustain human life. On the other hand, for rebirth through cutting down and harvesting the Tree, which stood for the nurturing aspects of the Goddess (trees, in general, produce fruits for people; some trees were symbolically pictured with breasts flowing with maternal milk). Thus, this "ax," a common symbol of the Goddess through the Neolithic, had nothing to do with the later axes used in war – as has been mistakenly supposed.[60] Rather, it was used in rituals re-enacting the cycles of death and rebirth. Indeed, the wings of the regenerating butterfly that resemble the shape of this ax were often combined with it symbolically. As Anne Baring and Jules Cashford argue:

> Since the axe never appears in Crete [a goddess-centered culture] held by a male priest, it does not seem to carry the later Aryan association of the axe with the god of thunder and the battle-cry.[61]

Thus the Goddess, who first appeared long before agriculture arose, came increasingly to symbolize, across Eurasia and North Africa, the eternal continuity of life through unending cycles of birth, death, and rebirth – perhaps an early idea of reincarnation. Mortality was less feared, for She promised rebirth and nurturance. The Milky Way was a sign of the bounty of her breasts; the sacred caves (which were used as early temples) were likened to her womb. Thus did the diverse symbols of the human body and other objects give metaphorical shape to a widely held cosmology that promised a rebirth of life after the sacrifice of death (see Figure VIII.5). Almost all the later religions of the world not only have concern for ancestors, but incorporate some concept of eternal life, of reincarnation, of resurrection.

*Figure VIII.5* Goddess of the Double Ax beside the Tree of Life

In this Mycenaean seal from *c*.3500 ya, the Goddess is seated under the Tree of Life. She welcomes two priestesses (with snakelike headdresses), offering them milk from her breast with one hand and poppy seedpods with the other (the fruit of transformation). Her resurrected daughter emerges from the soil carrying a tiny ax connecting with that of the Mother; new shoots sprout up beneath the daughter as she emerges. On the left, a descending figure points to the skulls of sacrificed animals; on the right, an ascending figure is plucking fruit from the Tree, while overhead monthly and seasonal rebirths are represented in the crescent moon and the sun. It is a secure universe, as short-lived individual life is given meaning through rebirth via the eternal life force. (Note how in this particular seal, the ax is "double-double-bladed," resembling the two pairs of wings of the butterfly that is also sacred to the Goddess.)

*Source*: Redrawn by Michele Lukowski from illustration in Baring and Cashford (1993: 114–15). Original from photograph in Sir Arthur Evans, 1930, *The Palace of Minos*, vol. 2, p. 343, London: Macmillan

## The cities of the Goddess

What was life like for these Goddess-worshiping peoples who lived in Spain, France and Italy in the west, around the Black Sea, in ancient Greece, on Crete, across Anatolia, in North Africa and even in the Indus Valley and further south in India? The best-studied sites are those of Old Europe (see Figure VIII.3), including the later Minoan cultures on Crete and at Mycenae; some of the tels in Anatolia, such as Çatal Hüyük and Haçilar; and the ancient Indus valley cities of Harappa and Mohenjo-daro.[62] Though naturally differing in detail, they share important characteristics.

All were sacred sites devoted to the worship of the Great Goddess in her various forms and under many names, just as Lewis Mumford had predicted. Shrines and rituals were important in daily life, and the bull, with its crescent-shaped horns, was the most common sacred animal. In Çatal Hüyük, the best preserved of these sites, a large proportion of the rooms in the city complex had sacred functions. At other sites, most of the buildings seem to have been temples. All were apparently peaceful societies. Though they traded over long distances and had sailing boats before 7000 ya, *they did not fortify their habitations or their shrines.*[63] Religious historian Mircea Eliade suggests their religious concerns far outweighed their practical interests. In the Indus Valley there were no technological innovations for a thousand years.[64]

Lastly, despite numbering several hundreds of people, these cities did not become hierarchical. Neither females nor males dominated, despite their Goddess-oriented cosmology. While female fertility was sacred, this did not give unusual powers to women over men in daily life. Though the male's role in fertility may not have been understood, the male phallus was celebrated for its "spontaneous life powers" (i.e. its power of erection). Male gods and phallic symbols were incorporated into the general understanding of the power of life. As Gimbutas puts it, "all resources of human nature, feminine and masculine, were utilized to the full as a creative force."[65] Egalitarianism applied not only to gender relations, but to all aspects of life, despite the beginnings of social specialization. There is no indication of the class stratification that characterized the patriarchies that would later overwhelm all these Goddess cultures.[66] Contrary to what is commonly argued, in these cases complexity did not require a hierarchical social structure.

## Downfalls of the Goddess

After several millennia of peaceful life, what happened to these widespread Goddess-based cultures? Why did warlike patriarchies become the dominant cultures that persist today? The answer seems to lie in what was going on in the outlying regions of the west Asian steppe, the less fertile upland grasslands of what is now southern Russia and the Iranian plateau. As noted above, another group of cultures, whom Gimbutas named the Kurgans, were defining meaning in a very different way, one that fit better their nomadic herding life. Their possessions remained few: tents, poles, pots, rugs, a few tools, and their animals. Life was both harsh and full of individual freedom. Survival depended on one's animals, thus one protected them, constantly moving them to new pastures. It was the task of men to oversee the animals and expose themselves to danger, while women remained in the relative safety of the camps with the children. For steppe people, who lived under an open sky, both danger and power resided in forces that came not from the soft, fertile Earth, but from a powerful and threatening Sky. The God that controlled their lives was definitely male and resided up above. Unlike a nurturing mother, He was a powerful and unforgiving father, to be feared rather than loved. He demanded bravery and endurance, and what today is called "rugged individualism."

The Kurgans and other peoples of the steppe who worshiped these powerful and dangerous gods surely valued male strength and control. Whether they conducted wars among themselves is not clear. What is certain is that Eurasian nomads with their mobile mounts began in times of stress to raid undefended settlements of Mother Goddess worshipers everywhere. It was to become the "Indo-European" takeover of Europe, the Middle East and much of south Asia. During the late Neolithic and Bronze Age, one after another of those early goddess-centered civilizations was to be profoundly changed. "War" was no longer an intracultural phenomenon of retributive vendettas among families, but a struggle between distinctly different cultures.

In Europe, the full impact of this struggle was not obvious after any single Kurgan raid. It took multiple attacks over several centuries to replace the cosmology of the Great Mother with their patriarchal cultural narratives, with their languages (now known as Indo-European), and to a lesser extent with their genes. (As noted above, genetic studies show their impact was far more cultural than genetic.[67]) Gimbutas tentatively identified three successive Kurgan waves: 6300–6200 ya, 5400–5200 ya, and 5000–4800 ya. By the third of these, the Kurgans had influence over most of central and southern Europe, and Mesopotamia; in northern India, the final Aryan "takeover" occurred around 3500 ya. From thence forward, cities had walls to defend them. As Baring and Cashford observe about the consequences for Europe:

> [These invasions were to change] the course of European prehistory by imposing a culture that was "stratified, pastoral, mobile and war-oriented" on a culture that was "agricultural and sedentary, egalitarian and peaceful." Their social system was hierarchical and dominated by the most powerful males, with a male priesthood ... What developed after ca. 2500 BC [4500 ya] was "a melange of the two mythic systems, Old European and Indo-European."[68]

The sky-gods of the pastoralists gradually came to dominate the local goddess cosmologies, but only after great mythological struggles for power. The meaning system had to change. As Baring and Cashford show, in almost every region, the

Great Mother became first the mother of the hero Sky-God. Eventually he becomes her lover, and the two are the progenitors of all the people. By the Bronze Age, Innana of Sumer and Babylonian Ishtar, having become goddesses of war, give birth to hybrid mortal/god sons, Dumuzi and Tammuz, respectively, who become hero-kings. The myths began to shift power from the Goddess to her son, who is a mortal figure who rules directly over society. In Egypt it was Isis, the Queen of Heaven, Earth and the Underworld, who gave birth to the first king, Osiris. In ancient Greece, it was the great goddess Gaia, the creator of the universe, who births Ouranos, with whom she then creates all the other gods and goddesses. Another pre-Hellenic goddess, Hera, marries her brother Zeus and together they reign on Olympus. In Roman mythology, it is Aeneas, the half-divine son of Venus, who founds Rome after the Trojan War. And in Christianity, it is Mary, the virgin daughter of the Great Mother, Anne (a surrogate of Innanna), who gives birth to the divine yet mortal Jesus. Later, she herself undergoes re-instatement (by the Catholic See) as Queen of Heaven.[69] More commonly, the fate over time of the Great Goddess was to become the goddess of War, of the Underworld, of Death, and finally, to disappear altogether, as "the feminine" became increasingly associated with evil.[70]

In this way the patriarchic lineages of the invading Kurgans, Aryans, and Semites established in one culture after another the legitimacy of their kings to be rulers over the majority of the original local agricultural peoples. Eventually they achieved the status of "living gods." One of these new sky-gods, the Semitic god, Yahweh, in his later transformations as Jehovah and Allah, has come to dominate the belief systems of several billion of the world's people today as the result of the cultural descendants of those same nomadic tribes having gone on to dominate India, most of southeast Asia, Africa, and the New World; I refer, of course, to the European colonization of the world.[71]

Meantime, similar events were taking place independently in the Far East. Around 8000 ya, ancient China comprised two separate cultures. In the valleys of the rich, warm south, especially the Yangtze, the pre-Taoist Chu peoples became rice farmers. Their animistic religion evolved into a female-centered, fertility culture. In the colder north, along the Hwang Ho (Yellow River), the pre-Confucian Zhou people, perhaps former nomads, were growing millet and forming a patriarchal society. Around 3500 ya, the latter overran the peoples of the south (who genetically are quite different), claiming the "Decree of Heaven" as legitimizing their power. It was their language that became the basis of modern Chinese.[72]

In ancient Japan, with the beginning of agriculture the animistic *kami* spirit world gave rise to a female-based religion whose fundamental tenet was that humans are "good" by nature. Amaterasu, daughter of the primal male and female couple, was the Sun Goddess who rose each morning out of the waters of the eastern ocean. Like the Western Great Goddess, she became mother of human sons, and her great, great grandson became the living embodiment of her lineage, the first sacred Emperor of Japan. Called Jinmu, he ascended the throne around 660 BC. This religion was later referred to as Shinto, "The Way of the Gods," to distinguish it from the godless Buddhism that arrived several generations later.

Initially, the all-powerful shaman in the form of the queen-goddess (and her descendants whether female or male) ruled over both religious and secular matters. But gradually, males displaced priestesses in religious rites and eventually only males could become sacred Emperors. Amaterasu was reduced from supreme goddess to the genderless forbear of the Emperor, sometimes being mistaken for a male god. By the seventh century AD, the social status of women was declining rapidly; it fell even further under the samurai, and was devastated by 1500 under the highly patriarchal Neoconfucian ideology. Women became "unclean" (an idea imported from India), childbirth and menstruation were considered forms of pollution, and until "purified," women were barred from holy places. They lost power in society and at home. Despite frequent "rehabilitations" of Amaterasu for political reasons (to unify the Japanese nation), women in modern Japan still experience significant social repression.[73]

As I conclude this section, I wonder how different today's world might have been if the nomadic societies of Asia had not benefited from the "accident" of the camel and the horse which afforded them political, and hence cosmological, dominance.[74] One can only guess what kind of world an egalitarian, goddess-oriented, socially and environmentally sensitive cosmology might have bequeathed to us.

### The meaning of "civilization"

Was it the sky-gods of the Indo-Europeans who shaped a global history of male-dominant, class-structured hierarchies? Or was it, as Jared Diamond argues, the need for order in ever-larger, more centralized societies made possible by the (supposedly inevitable) accumulation of excess wealth? Diamond calls these large hierarchies "kleptocracies"; political theorists call them "States"; and most historians label them "civilizations." As should be clear by now, causes of social change are seldom obvious, always complex, and can never be pinpointed. But surely meanings played as crucial a role as did the changing material conditions of life in bringing about what social historian Marcel Gauchet describes as a "massive revision of the articulation of the human situation..." – the rise of hierarchical society. Indeed, the two are inseparable.

> This is where our five thousand years of "history-as-growth" really began, a period ridiculously brief and amazingly swift compared to the unimaginably long *duree* from which it arose.[75]

The emergence of the "civilized" State marked an enormous change in the relationships of people with each other as well as with their environments.

Being no longer equal, the vast majority of people lost most of their autonomy. The State, after all, was the first "machine" to be invented, being composed of living human parts. (Cogs, levers, and wheels came later.) People became "pieces" of the new "megamachine."[76] One's sense of identity came from one's position in the hierarchy.

Most people also lost any voice in society. No longer were they heard; no longer did they participate in the social decisions that defined their lives. People lost more and more control as authority became more distant. Where once each person could appeal to and appease local spirits to set things right, now priests and god-kings (and eventually a single omniscient heavenly Father, infinitely far away) sat in judgment and decreed the rules all others must obey. In a seminal paper contrasting the old "order of custom" of traditional societies with the new "rule of law" by centralized States, social scientist Stanley Diamond argues that this shift in the locus of social authority was not a gradual replacement, but a sharp break.[77]

I have tried to summarize the contrasts in these social structures in Table VIII.2. In terms of the innate propensities of human beings for belonging, for autonomy, and for sacred meaning, it is clear that the rise of the State had an enormous constraining impact. The justification for why things are (the "authority" embedded in the cultural narrative) shifts from the individual's direct experience with the immediate world to an ever-more distant, abstract deity, by whom people are controlled. "The State" becomes God's ultimate mouthpiece, his "interpreter." In today's secular state, all authority is subsumed unto itself. Marcel Gauchet summarizes it thus:

> As soon as we enter the sphere of institutionalized domination, we are inside a universe where religion's original and radical core [is] … exposed to the … mechanisms that alter the prospects for life, thought, and action…. The so-called "major religions"…, far from being the quintessential embodiment of religion, are in fact just so many stages of its abatement and disintegration…. When dealing with religion, what appears to be an advance is actually a retreat.[78]

In other words, justification of hierarchical authoritarian States that suppressed fulfillment of our basic human needs for acceptance as fully equal, autonomous beings demanded "religions" that were less engaging, less rewarding, less meaningful than the old primal religions people evolved with. The "march of progress" in terms of human satisfaction was, I would argue, a regression, despite all the artifacts of civilization and modernity. In fact, as Gandhi supposedly once quipped when asked what he thought of civilization, "I think it would be a good idea." When some human beings coerce and dictate to other human beings as part of routine social life, the intrinsic needs of human nature are being thwarted.

*Table VIII.2* Contrasting visions of order

|  | *Custom evokes* | *Law enforces* |
|---|---|---|
| *Basis and form of rules* | Cultural morality: beliefs of community from stories, myths, parables. Flexible | Distant authority (God, King, Dictator, or Majority*), written law; inflexible |
| *Interpreters, arbiters* | Elders of community, before whole group | State judiciary: priests, judges |
| *Nature of "wrongs"* | Personal harm (remediable, payment to victim)<br><br>Harm to community (shame, banishment) | All "crimes" are against the State; restitution is to the State |
| *Enforcement* | Avoidance of social disapproval (desire to belong, be accepted) | Fear of armed authority (military, police) |
| *Goal of justice* | Apology, restitution, reconciliation | Repression and punishment (pay penalty to State: fine, incarceration) |
| *Basis of social relations* | Trust, duty, customary kinship and family bonds (friends may become responsible for each other's actions) | Prescribed by law, or revokable contracts* |
| *Changing of rules* | Group consensus (all participate) | Edicts, or majority rule* (ignorance is no excuse) |

*Source*: Author's summary of Diamond's 1971 contrast between traditional and law-based societies. Diamond emphasizes that, in modern societies, sociologists tend to confuse/conflate "morality" and "legality." The order of customary societies is (ideally) autonomous; that in law-based societies is coerced

*Note*: *Indicates "reforms" of law-based systems in modern republican democracies, which, however, are still deficient compared to customary societies in meeting the needs of human nature in a balanced way

### *Religious correctives to abusive hierarchies*

I thoroughly agree with Gauchet that most of the religions that emerged between 4000 and 1500 ya were less psychologically satisfying than the primal religions, when people had once lived directly immersed in a sacred reality. But I do not think that they survived by convincing ordinary people that oppressive hierarchies were justified; rather, they tried somehow to make up for their misery. Much like the good fairy in the tale of *Sleeping Beauty*, though they could not undo the injustices of hierarchical life, they offered various routes of psychic escape: from Buddha's Nirvana, to the West's Heaven and future resurrection at the end of time, to Hindu and Buddhist notions of reincarnation. The meaning of life is not to be found in the present, but in a future attainable by obedience and faith in a loving Father or an unknowable Essence. This life is but a bad dream from which, on the appointed day you will awake in paradise.

Yet this is not the only solace the major religions espouse. The historian Charles Taylor asks, if meaning is *all* they offer, "why is it that *karuna* or *agape* are so central to these traditions?"[79] "Compassion" and "love" for others are universally found in the world's major religions. The Golden Rule or its equivalent turns up repeatedly in the words of the founding prophets or teachers. Says ethicist Paul Gordon Lauren, a student of the history of human rights:

> All of the major religions of the world seek in one way or another to speak to the issue of human responsibility for others.... This concern is approached through various revelations, narratives, poetry, edicts and commandments, and stories or parables dealing with right and wrong, moral responsibility, ethical principles of justice and fairness, compassion, the essential dignity of each person, and the kinship and common humanity of all.[80]

They seem, in other words, to be trying to rescue for humankind a recognition of those three innate human propensities for bonding, autonomy, and meaning.

In theory, the teachings of these religions held those in power as morally responsible for the welfare of those lower in the hierarchy. The "path of righteousness" was the duty of all. Surely written history (which began about the same time) would have been even more unsavory had these religions not appeared. In terms of human nature, I believe it is this aspect of religion that helped offset the psychic stress civilizations created for such a large proportion of human beings. The feelings of rejection, worthlessness, and injustice that people tended to have (and which we have seen can have highly negative physiological and behavioral impacts) could be psychologically ameliorated by practicing compassion and love for one's neighbors and forgiveness of oppressors. The natural need to be bonded and the powerful health-promoting effects of belonging were as well served as might be possible by the tenets of all these religions, given the inevitable psychic suffering in hierarchical systems.

Written history, which is the history of States, differs from prehistory in two significant ways. Decisions, once made by all, came to be made by a tiny group of the population – the king and his advisors, whether priests or generals. And those decisions were written down, encoded, made rigid. Instead of oral myths and parables that were open to multiple interpretations according to context, the decrees of monarchs were inflexible, carved in stone so-to-speak. Being arbitrarily imposed they required varying amounts of bribery and threat to enforce, and were always liable to be resisted. Says Stanley Diamond, "The absolute reign of law has often been synonymous with the absolute reign of lawlessness."[81] Moreover, the absence of widespread dialogue throughout society during the decision-making process severely limits the amount of collective information and imaginative alternative visions available to hierarchies, all of which traditional societies generally had available. Too few decision-makers means a high risk of major mistakes in judgment.

It is thus no surprise that "law and order" is a central concern in every hierarchy. "The Law" may be legitimized as the Decree of Heaven, the words of God spoken to the prophet, the edicts of an infallible Church, or a Constitution written by a small group of colonists (all well-to-do white Protestant males). Whatever its source, written law takes on the nature of "sacred meaning." The head of State who makes the laws has absolute power, requires tribute or taxes to establish order and maintain his power, and imposes penalties and punishments on those who do not obey. And, as Diamond points out, law makes possible a new idea altogether, that of private property; it protects the rights of land-owners against others, "haves" against "have-nots." The old multiple cross-bonds of kinship, clan, marriage, and tradition that reined in the greedy and selfish through threat of widespread social disapproval gave way in large hierarchies to boundaries of individual ownership contestable in the courts of power. Unlike consensual social approval, dictatorial law could be used to legitimize gross inequalities of both status and wealth.

Not surprisingly, the history of civilizations has been uneven. In Chapter VI, I noted the violently inhumane autocracy of Late Muscovy that began with the terrorist reign of Ivan the Terrible, the effects of which seem not yet to have disappeared from among the Russian people. At the other extreme was the amazing regime of the Indian emperor Asoka, who ruled his kingdom from around 272 to 232 BC. Appalled by the slaughter of innocents in the wars he led, he was deeply moved by the teachings of Buddha, and instituted among his people a period of peace and justice based on compassion. He even strove to spread Buddhist teachings over three continents. His Buddhist wheel-of-law symbol graces India's flag even today, though Buddhism was long ago driven out of most of India by the Moguls.[82]

### The dice of history

At the time when Buddhism, Confucianism and Taoism were evolving as nontheistic, philosophically based religions in the Far East (where the idea of God, if present at all, was as an all-pervasive, immanent life force rather than a distant, authoritarian father-figure), in the West among the sky-god-kings of Egypt, Mesopotamia, Greece and later Rome, there was also Yahweh, the jealous protector of a small sect known as the Israelites: "a tiny band of nomads milling around the upper regions of the Arabian desert ... too inconspicuous even to be noticed."[83] Yet Yahweh, along with his later avatars Jehovah and Allah, today has the allegiance of nearly half of all humankind.

Here I focus on the life and meanings of one of those obscure Jews, Jesus, since the Christian faith that was founded on an interpretation of his teachings was to spread throughout Europe, which in turn became the self-righteous origin of global colonization and exploitation. I am by no means blaming Jesus' teachings for that later history. But the story about which of his teachings and which of his disciples' writings would become sacred text shows how unpredictable the channels are into which human meaning systems, and hence human history, flow. The crucial historical questions were (and are): "Who really has the truth about God's will and God's nature as explicated through the acts and words of Jesus?" "What does it mean to be a Christian?" And, most importantly, "What assumptions about human nature underlie the Christian faith?"

## The Gnostic Gospels

In 1945, a group of brothers stumbled across a clay urn buried in the soft soil of a mountain near the village of Nag Hammadi in Upper Egypt. In it were thirteen leather-bound papyrus books, but it was not until thirty years later that scholars were able to study and decipher them. They turned out to be fifty-two Coptic texts, written around AD 140. (Members of this Egyptian tribe became an early Christian sect.) Some were translations of older Greek texts from AD 50 to 100, written during the lifetime of Jesus' disciples. In one it was written: "These are the secret words which the living Jesus spoke, and which the twin, Judas Thomas, wrote down."[84]

Among them were the Gospel According to Thomas and the Gospel of Philip, in which the disciples included women as well as men, and where Mary Magdalene is described as Jesus' "favorite." Several other Christian texts that do not appear in the Bible were found in the Nag Hammadi urn. None had ever been known by historians directly, only through the writings of the powerful Christian Bishop Irenaeus of Lyons, who in AD 180 wrote a five-volume tract condemning them (and other texts written by some of Jesus' followers) as heresy: *The Destruction and Overthrow of Falsely So-Called Knowledge*. Irenaeus, Hippolytus, and others in the newly established Church of Rome systematically denounced and destroyed all contemporary texts except those few now found in the New Testament. As Elaine Pagels, one of the translators of the Gnostic Gospels, says: "[W]hat we call Christianity ... [is] only a small selection of specific sources, chosen from among dozens of others."[85]

Who decided? On what grounds? Why was what was excluded so "dangerous"? In Table VIII.3, I try to summarize the contrasts between the Orthodox and Gnostic stories, especially their assumptions about human nature.[86] The views of human nature and of humans' relationship with God of these two different stories lie at polar extremes: God as masterful Father and sinful humans as obedient servants in need of love, guidance and redemption, with Jesus Christ as their savior through his personal sacrifice, *versus* God as

300

immanent within all humans who are fundamentally divine and potentially full of grace, if only they will seek this knowledge of divine goodness within themselves by following Jesus' own example. In each story, Jesus has the critical role of redeeming the human spirit, but the path to "truth" differs as night from day.

It is likely that the Gnostics were familiar with the teachings, both Hindu and Buddhist, that were abroad in India. As early as AD 58, St. Thomas, a gnostic himself, established a gnostic form of Christianity on the south coast of India, now modern Kerala. In Hinduism, there is, even today, a sense that something of God is immanent in each person, as embodied in the *Atman* or sacred "breath."[87] (In my own experience with one newly formed religious sect in Bombay, people greeted each other by touching their own breast and saying "*Jai Yogeshwar*," indicating "God is here.") In Buddhism, one is urged to look inward, through meditation, for the sacred space where form and time disappear and this illusory life around us gives way to a blissful Nirvana. Buddha worked hard his whole life to spread his teachings, establishing temples and monasteries as he traveled through India, and offering, as did Jesus, hope for relief from suffering, especially to the poor and oppressed and downtrodden.

It is perhaps this potentially revolutionary aspect of both Buddhism and the gnostic form of Christianity that made them politically dangerous to hierarchical forms of social organization. (One has only to recall how angrily the Chinese government today is stamping out a new, nonpolitical, highly individualized movement, the Falun Gong sect, to see how fearful hierarchies can be of personal independence.) Too much independent thought, too much individualism, are threats to the unity of meaning, and hence to the allegiance needed to hold together a farflung hierarchy. So the Moguls, on their arrival in India, found well-organized Buddhism a threat and drove it out, yet made peace with the more subserviently minded Hinduism. Just so, centuries before, the powerful bishops trying to establish a single, institutionalized Christianity needed to create a uniform, hierarchically structured religious faith, and a hierarchically structured Church to match.

### The invention of Satan

Elaine Pagels has also pointed to the search for a "devil within" whenever internal differences break out in a society. The Jews had long identified "fallen angels" as troublemakers within the holy community: Belial, Beezlebub, Satan, and others. They were not so much evil as simply obstructors of good human action. But the founders of Orthodox Christianity needed an "enemy of Jesus" with which to castigate doubters. As Pagels points out, this newly forming religion was spread across many nations and faiths, threatening their former integrity. To unify the true believers against this diverse group of ancient attachments – tribe, family, pagan religion, tradition – they needed a single enemy, and Satan was their choice.

*Table VIII.3* Contrasting early Christian assumptions about human nature

| | Orthodox | Gnostic |
|---|---|---|
| *General beliefs about humans* | Pessimistic; lost souls; humans are sinful, in need of redemption | Optimistic, intuitive; of a divine nature, filled with possibilities |
| *Nature and location of God* | External, omnipotent, at a distance; a male deity, "God, the Father" | Immanent in all people; all are part of God. Hence, God is male and female, "Father" and "Mother" |
| *Route to God* | Belief in Jesus as redeemer, the Son of God | Dispel illusions about reality through seeking enlightenment |
| *Appropriate human action* | Repentance and faith; follow dictates of sacred texts, as explicated by clergy | Lead a solitary life, devoted to self-reflection and self-knowledge. Truth is to be found only in one's own immediate experience of God |
| *Role of Jesus* | Savior of the damned, through his bodily resurrection; born of a virgin. (Later he becomes part of the Trinity, as God incarnate*) | Not God, but a teacher, a prophet (as Buddha); anyone can become like Jesus. There was no virgin birth; the resurrection is to be understood symbolically |

*Note*: *This final step in the formal raising of Jesus from the honorary title of Son of God (to which all could accede) to actually God incarnate did not take place until the time of the Emperor Constantine. A theological battle was waged between Arius, an outspoken priest in Alexandria, and that city's Bishop, Athanius. The latter, with overwhelming support from the Emperor, who by then had converted the entire Roman Empire to Christianity, won out when the Nicene Creed declared the Holy Trinity as part of sacred doctrine. For the story of this conflict, see Richard Rubenstein (1999). For a novel set in the time of Justinian, over 200 years later, when the theological battle was still raging over the meaning of the Trinity, see Robert Graves (1975). Chapter 4 of his text explains the battle between the Blues and the Greens, played out in the chariot races at Constantinople – one side believing there was only one nature to the Son, the other, that there were two, Father and Son.

Thus did the hierarchical, male-dominated religion that became Orthodox Christianity overcome all its enemies, including the egalitarian, nondogmatic, female-accepting Jesus of the Gnostics, not to mention a host of pagan deities and ancient heroes. It became rigid, ordered, absolute. It rejected the Gospel of Philip, which too much resembled Taoism in that it refused to choose between opposites, seeing them rather as necessary complements of each other. By employing Satan, the Orthodox Church was to triumph over independent thought once and for all: "You may be good, but you may *not* question." As the good Bishop Irenaeus has written:

> Let those persons ... who blaspheme the creator [in any way] ... be recognized as agents of Satan by all who worship God. Through their agency Satan ... has been seen to speak against God ... the same God who has prepared eternal fire for every kind of apostasy.[88]

And so the stage was set for the next fifteen centuries. Whoever opposed the Church was an enemy of Christ and a friend of Satan, deserving of torture and death. If women gained power, a voice, they became witches, Satan's hand-maidens. Questioners of doctrine were burned at the stake. Wars were fought with infidels, dissenters, and unbelievers. This defense of a single, unquestioned, rigid meaning system would envelope Europe for many centuries.

### Europe: fast-forward

Perhaps the best way to capture the essence of history (in Europe and elsewhere also) over the past few millennia is as a slow-motion battle between the advantages and disadvantages of hierarchical societies. The advantages are material and political. Centralized organization allows increasing efficiency in the production of subsistence needs, freeing up labor for new, communal industries: metal smelting, transportation and irrigation projects, and manufacturing centers. By making social production more efficient, hierarchical ordering promised more for all. But the ideal condition seldom arose, with only a few exceptions, such as early medieval Europe and the Incas of Peru.[89] Most often, however, the rewards went mainly to those at the top of the social ladder.

This added to the disadvantages already present, namely that hierarchical societies deprive most members of fulfillment of their basic human needs for bonding, autonomy, and significant meaning (though the hierarchical religions tried hard to find a substitute for the latter). The result is that hierarchies are intrinsically unstable and require either religious promises or fear of coercion (sometimes both occur together) to keep order. The overheads of coercion become extremely costly, as every large hierarchy in history has discovered.

This intrinsic internal instability of hierarchies makes them vulnerable from two directions. First, they must maintain internal order, using either persuasion or fear. And, as they grow in size, so they attract envy and fear from neighboring peoples: the god-king next door; the infidels with a different set of religious justifications; the barbarian hordes still in need of being converted to the true faith of *our God*, of *our people*. A powerful hierarchy, being a potential threat to others, must be able to defend itself – another expense.

The other huge disadvantage of hierarchies is that because they rely on such a small circle of people for major decision-making (in the United States, for example, the 535 members of Congress make decisions on behalf of 260 million people), they are prone to making self-destructive decisions. Those in power too often presume (as did the Roman Emperors) that they are all-knowing, and hence infallible, a problem recently exhibited by Hitler and Stalin. Moreover, heads of State who are insecure, unable to take criticism or listen to suggestions, become dismissive of the obvious. The historian Barbara Tuchman has recounted several such significant instances in Western history.[90]

In summary, the inability to adapt to changing circumstances is by no means limited to such small, isolated cultures as described earlier. History is full of fallen empires: some brought down by droughts or plagues; some by being overrun by more powerful neighbors; but also some who through their own rigidity failed to adapt. Ancient Rome is a case in point; so too is the Catholic Church that, blind to its own greed and corruption, lost moral control over the faithful middle classes in Renaissance Europe. (Something similar may be happening today).

The Protestant revolution, that lasted a century and a half, shifted political power from the sacred authority of the Church to the secular authority of Commerce, now the West's *new* "sacred authority" ("It's the economy, stupid!"). The new philosophical image of human society that emerged led to enormous institutional changes – the Industrial Revolution, science, republican government, capitalism and competitive individualism – without relinquishing the pessimistic image of human nature as being naturally self-centered and in need of strong elitist control.[91] This "new religion" of the last two centuries or so, however, despite its advertised "freedoms," still has a hierarchical structure. In this instance, however, it is a mobile hierarchy, far more likely to induce stress among people expecting to be "equal," and who soon discover they are not. The balance between cooperation and competition has swung sharply toward the latter. The new "religion" has shifted from Christianity to free-enterprise capitalism and republican "democracy." The powerful arm of this new commercial hierarchy now has a global reach that is fast growing beyond the control of any group of people or any State.

In Chapter IX I turn to an examination of the severe shortcomings of this latest hierarchy, not only in terms of its well-advertised impacts on the environment, but especially its deficiencies in regard to satisfying the deepest needs of human nature, for belonging, for autonomy, and for sacred meaning. The violent history of the twentieth century makes these deficiencies very clear.

# IX

# HUMANKIND CROSSES THE RUBICON, 1900–2000

[A]fter reading several file cabinets' worth of documents on Japanese war crimes as well as accounts of ancient atrocities from the pantheon of world history, I would have to conclude that Japan's behavior during World War II was less a product of dangerous people than of a dangerous government, in a vulnerable culture, in dangerous times, able to sell dangerous rationalizations to those whose human instincts told them otherwise.

Iris Chang (1997: 220)

In the twentieth century:

Henry Ford began mass-producing automobiles
Airplanes were invented
Nerve gases were perfected and used in warfare
Infectious diseases became pandemic
Electricity became virtually ubiquitous in urban areas
Hundreds of giant bridges, thousands of dams, and millions of miles of roads were built; skyscrapers reached over a quarter of a mile in height
Atomic bombs were built and dropped on cities
Television and transistor chips revolutionized communication
Rockets carried men to the moon and back
Genes were isolated and transplanted between species
The protective ozone layer in the stratosphere was damaged
More people died from human violence than in any other century
About one-third of the Earth's forests and fossil fuels were consumed
The global population doubled twice, surpassing six billion
More wealth was expended on weapons and wars than on the education and health of the world's people
More species of life became extinct than ever before
Global warming began occurring far faster than anyone predicted.

These are only a few of the human-driven events that occurred during the twentieth century – the mere wink of an eye, just five-hundredths of one percent (0.05%) of all *Homo sapiens* history. The speed and magnitude of these impacts, their colossal effects on the health of both the planet *and* the human psyche, have not yet sunk into general consciousness. Their probable consequences for the environment and for human disease in the twenty-first century have been well researched,[1] though not yet assimilated into public and political dialogues. My task in this chapter is to focus on how the meaning system that prevailed in the globally dominant West throughout the twentieth century – and which continues unabated today – has grown inimical to our basic human needs for unconditional acceptance, for respectful autonomy (also called "freedom"), and for a shared and sacred social purpose.

In my view, the twentieth century comprised a watershed in human history – a Rubicon – an irrevocable change that places our species in a terribly vulnerable position. The West technologized the megamachine. It followed unquestioningly the logic of the meaning system it inherited in 1900: a combination of beliefs in the great benefits of scientific knowledge; in humans' unlimited capacity for finding technological solutions to all problems; and in the linearity of human "progress." Add to these, three further Western assumptions: (1) of unlimited adaptability of human nature (we can adjust to all demands whatever these may be); (2) of self-interest as the biological basis of human nature, that constrains the kinds of social institutions that can be built; and following from this, (3) of an obvious need for strong societal controls over human behavior.

The above comprise the underlying assumptions of "modernity," the beliefs on which the West's world view is constructed. We use them to justify our present institutions, pointing to the great advances in medicine, labor-saving devices, mobility, levels of consumption and so forth, while shrugging off the growing inequalities, dissatisfactions, and social unease – not to mention ecosystem destruction and global warming. In the Introduction some of these things were cited: the natural crises that face our species as a whole (climate change, energy shortages, pandemic diseases) and the social crises that are rapidly surfacing even in rich, advanced societies such as the United States (disaffection, anger, stress). By now it should be clear to the reader (if not yet the whole society) that it will not be possible to solve our *environmental* problems without also addressing our *human* problems. New technologies do not supply any kind of an answer to widespread and growing psychic dissatisfaction. Having crossed the technological Rubicon, there is no alternative to making some major changes in how Western (and some other) societies think. In an electronic and nuclear age, massive social anger can no longer be suppressed at home by threatening to incarcerate disaffected citizens, nor abroad by threatening to annihilate "rogue states" with massive military attacks.

That is the message of the twentieth century. In this chapter I address how the technologized megamachine of modernity has been rationalized in recent history; how the focus on efficiency, the "bottom line" and personal power in a competitive hierarchy have infiltrated all of Western cultural ideas; and how those ideas were played out globally during the twentieth century.

## The technologized megamachine

Chapter VIII recounted the late Bronze Age replacement of egalitarian agriculturally supported settlements that had existed in the river valleys of temperate Eurasia for several thousand years, by increasingly hierarchical, stratified civilizations that Lewis Mumford dubbed "megamachines." Egypt and Mesopotamia were among the first in a long history of social systems in which ordinary people were made subservient to the control of a powerful elite. The egalitarian societies of the Mother Goddess had given way to vertical hierarchies composed of god-kings, priests and military, artisans, and peasant-slaves.

Except for the relatively brief period of the Greek city-states and the pre-empire Roman republic, the history of civilization has been one of stratified hierarchies, with a few in power, some hangers-on, and a multitude of laborers, servants, serfs, and slaves. According to Mumford, civilizations often began as enlightened, communal hierarchies, such as the Inca of Peru where the lowest peasants had first, not last, call upon subsistence rations. But sooner or later rigid inequalities and harsh treatment of workers and slaves took over. Ancient friezes depict soldiers not as warriors but (as they are in too many countries today) a militia for controlling the peasants and overseeing the slaves. They kept the social machine functioning, providing coordinated labor for construction of monumental public works: giant statues, palaces and pyramids (see Figure IX.1).[2]

Modern industrialized megamachines (we now call them "national economies") are structured in essentially the same way. A few very powerful people make most of the decisions about what the economic machine will produce and the rest are organized into ranked classes, according to an arbitrary "value" assigned to their contributions to the output of the machine. Aside from the greatly increased productivity of industrial megamachines, they differ from the ancient god-king societies in only two ways: the nature of the social authority legitimizing their structure, and the potential for individuals to move between classes. It took about four centuries for these changes to occur in Europe, where the industrial revolution began.

In the sixteenth century, the universal hegemony of the Catholic church on social life was breached by Martin Luther and John Calvin, at the same time that Copernicus and Galileo were arguing that Earth was not the center of the universe. Meanwhile, adventurous traders on worldwide explorations were increasing Europe's wealth and global status. Colonizing abroad began seriously in the seventeenth century, while at home in Europe's metropolitan countries, a new crop of social philosophers were reinventing "human nature." Hobbes's theory of the contract-making individual as the unit of society, and

*Figure IX.1* A "megamachine" in operation
Sketch plus detail of an ancient, incomplete frieze showing a monumental stone bull being hauled on a sledge by slaves to the ancient Assyrian capital of Ninevah *c*.3000 ya. Note how taskmasters or soldiers were essential to the "machine's" operation

*Source*: From Austen Henry Layard (1853) *The Monuments of Nineveh*, 2 vols; redrawn here, with added inset by Michele Lukowski

Locke's claim that all men have the right to own property were moral correctives to the rigid church and state hierarchies that had become both corrupt and abusive.[3]

During the eighteenth century, civil law, meaning law agreed to by the "citizens" (however narrowly defined), evolved as the new basis of social authority, replacing kings and popes. Economic activity was wrenched free from arbitrary monarchical control. The American and French revolutions promised a new order in the world, based on "liberty, equality, brotherhood." The American constitution (however hierarchical in fact) offered the illusion of equal citizens controlling the conditions of social life: "In America, anyone can grow up to be President."[4]

By the end of the eighteenth century, however, the widespread adoption of power-driven machines for all sorts of manufacturing began a process of centralization of economic activity that ultimately replaced the old politico-military hierarchy with an equally steeply structured management hierarchy. Under the legitimizing fig-leaf of the rights of all to accumulate property and to succeed to the top of the economic ladder through "fair competition," the self-rewarding institution of monopoly capitalism was born. By the end of the nineteenth century, it was all too clear that the private ownership of wealth, as exemplified by the wealthy American magnates (later dubbed the "robber barons"), was antithetic to the Enlightenment dream of equal rights and an equal say by all in the construction of social life. Those who owned the wealth called the shots, whatever the popular sentiments might be, and it remains very much that way today (it is now called "free enterprise" and is treated as congruent to political freedom, which of course it is not).[5]

This inequality of economic power was buttressed in two ways. First there was the tight grip of the wealthy elite on economic institutions. When once-autonomous small farmers were forced into cities to join with formerly independent craftsmen as wage-earning employees totally dependent on the factory owner for their survival, they lost their social voices. It was a new form of feudalism, but without the Church's moral teachings (such as it being easier for camels to squeeze through the eyes of needles than for rich men to get into Heaven) to ameliorate its excesses. Second, a new, "scientific" morality was conveniently invented to justify human inequality. Darwin's theory of evolution as a process of selection of the most fit individuals in each generation was eagerly commandeered by the social Darwinists as "proof" of the superior fitness of the winners in the economic competition for power. By this legerdemain of logic, the wealthy promoted themselves as creators of jobs, and thus as social benefactors, while stigmatizing the poor and homeless as unfit, shiftless, and deserving of their fate. The habit of blaming the victim was thoroughly vindicated by calling their fate biologically inevitable. The fact of victimhood "proved" a lack of fitness and hence of a right to live with dignity.

These two factors – the massive dependency of society as a whole on the institutions controlled by monopoly capital and the justification of social hierarchy as "natural" and therefore inevitable – insured that moderate to extreme economic inequality characterized the twentieth century. Indeed, they have been endowed with an aura of inevitability, of being "scientifically true," by both professional economists and evolutionary psychologists, as discussed earlier.

This mindset, this belief system, this new religion, is today more firmly entrenched than ever in the dominant social institutions of not only the industrialized world but also the now-global compass of transnational corporate capitalism. The drive for ever-more efficiency in production, for ever-more competition in the accumulation of wealth and the power it holds, and for ever more rapid technological change is beyond the control of any single government, whether elected or not. Instead, as everyone knows because it is so blatantly obvious, governments are controlled on all sides by an economic system which purchases legislators or supports dictators and their militaries, and which cannot be allowed to fail for fear of triggering economic collapse and social chaos.[6]

This chapter addresses the social impacts that modernity has wrought during the twentieth century as it developed an increasingly strong technological grip on social institutions over time, and spread that grip spatially into the heart of every continent, affecting virtually every living person. For a few, there have been untold benefits. For some there has been a significant increase in physical/material security, traded at the expense of spiritual meaning (many writers have pointed out that Western society as a whole has no spiritual content, being dedicated solely to materialistic exploitation).[7]

By the end of the twentieth century, the benefits of technology were being over-shadowed by enormous physical and psychological costs, the causes of which are still largely unrecognized. The multiple stresses, though different from one culture or class to the next, have been taking their toll on humans everywhere. From the demoralizing loss of independence of subsistence farmers and the destruction of social traditions and trusted relationships among less industrialized people, to the increasing daily stress and speeding up of life in the so-called post-industrial societies, life is less psychologically secure. For many, it is also physically more dangerous.

The massive violence, in terms of outright wars, of internal military coercion of populations and arbitrary state terrorism; of instigated genocides among neighboring communities; of clandestine foreign destabilization of national governments; of the imposed exploitation of human labor and the coerced appropriation of others' resources – all these have made the twentieth century the worst ever in the history of overt violence, and it would have been much worse without nonviolent leaders such as Mahatma Gandhi.[8]

Other kinds of violence are less identifiable in terms of specific perpetrators, but in terms of damaging stress, they can be at least as severe. I refer to the violence inflicted by the institutions of modernity: its claims of inevitable progress, of ever-more rapid change, and of increasing competition with its built-in demand for self-advancement that seriously strains interpersonal and community bonds. The psychic insecurities of *having* to compete throughout life; of perhaps becoming a "loser" in the eyes of others; of having no stable future, no trusted, supportive community to contribute to and be accepted by; of being deprived of any familiar social story that gives one a meaningful identity and a realistic social goal to strive toward – all these wreak enormous psychic stress on people around the planet, stress that is individually transmitted to the next generation.

In this chapter I argue that the institutions of the industrialized megamachine are pathological for human beings. Not only do they fail to make us psychologically more content with our lives; they place us under levels of stress that can cause us to act in inhumane ways. The damage being done to humanity, however, is not intrinsic to technology *per se*, but to the kinds of social institutions and particular technologies the West has chosen to develop, and the uses to which they are put.[9] In the West, most technologies have been developed to control Nature or groups of people. Giant dams, machines to tear up the soil and cut down forests, chemicals to wipe out pests and compensate for depleted soils, all control Nature; and weapons at one extreme and massive propaganda technologies at the other control people. It is now clear that Nature cannot tolerate much more and still support us. It is also critical that we realize that the limit of human tolerance is being reached. People need social environments that foster genuine satisfaction of their intrinsic psychological needs for bonding, autonomy and meaning.

In the latter part of this chapter I offer selected examples of how human societies react when they experience such denial, starting with the evils committed by insecure societies that experienced feelings of national shame within the global community: Japan and Germany, before and during World War II. Next I look at the destructiveness of Western colonialism that, despite façades of political autonomy acquired by former chattel cultures, still persists in the form of economic hegemony. Last, I summarize the ways more and more children and youth around the world are growing up under increasingly stressful psychological conditions.

It is my contention that the evil in each of these examples arises from the misfit between the cosmology of "modernity" and the natural psychic needs of human beings. Our problems lie not in some intrinsic "badness" of human nature, but in creating impossible social conditions for human nature to try to adapt to, and then using coercive force to control the antisocial behaviors that result, including terrorism. "Modernity" itself creates most of the evil in today's world, and then tries to correct it by punitive means – what I call "legalized evil." Thus, before discussing the above examples, I need to clarify the fallacious assumptions underlying modernity, or what I call the "culture of the bottom line."

## The nature of bottom-line mentality

For most Westerners, the words "bottom line" immediately bring to mind the final entry on a corporation's balance sheet – its profit margin. In America, the whole nation is reminded many times a day of its importance. Among the first items on the morning news (barring a school shooting or plane crash) are yesterday's closing figures for the stock markets. These are almost always followed by speculation as to whether or not the director of the Federal Reserve Bank, Alan Greenspan, will play god and manipulate the interest rate. In Great Britain, it is the Chancellor of the Exchequer who is the "high priest" over-seeing the health of the nation's economy. Men like these from all of the "technologized megamachines" form a clan which controls the global economy, to the extent it is controlled by anyone.

Yet the mentality of the bottom line extends far beyond the world of big financiers and corporate boardrooms. It seeps deep into the daily thinking of citizens in the so-called "developed" nations (the technologized megamachines) and in many "developing" nations as well. The "bottom line" takes on a broader context; it becomes a national quantity, the Gross Domestic Product, the total wealth being produced and consumed. It measures the relative economic rank of a society among the global family of nations. It allocates *real* power at global councils, and more tacitly, it defines which are the more "successful" societies, the more "valued" examples of human social life.

In fact, twentieth-century neoclassical economic theory bears major responsibility for the growing social, environmental, and political crises facing the human species as it begins a new millennium. Devised by a group of academics who were determined to turn the study of economics into a value-neutral, quantitative science, it has become nothing less than "the word of God" for governments, bankers, investors, corporate heads – indeed for society at large, as suggested in Figure IX.2.

By "scientifically" defining human values in purely quantifiable, economic terms, Western neoclassical experts have excluded from public and international debate all those human acts and all those benefits of Nature that no one pays money for. Mothers caring for their children, community volunteers, neighbors who help each other, carefree leisure time, or in Nature, forested hillsides that hold water and prevent landslides and floods, insects and birds that pollinate crops, soils that purify water and recycle nutrients. None of these "counts." They are given exactly *zero* value in economic accounting systems.

Meantime, what economists do count as valuable, among other things, are every crime, every divorce, every new health problem, every car accident, because these all create jobs: judges, lawyers, doctors, prisons, hospitals, car repairs. While real, but unpaid-for social benefits are being ignored, social *costs* that someone pays for fixing are treated as social *benefits* – they increase that magic number, the GDP! The economists' curve of economic growth gives an entirely false sense of social progress. In fact, as Clifford Cobb and his associates at Redefining Progress have shown, most real growth in the United States GDP ceased around 1970. "Growth" since then has come mainly from two sources: increased social costs, treated as benefits, and paying people for child-care, food preparation, psychological comfort, and leisure entertainment. These were all things people used to do freely for each other. Now they are paid for, so now they "count."

Finally, economists have utterly ignored the using up of natural capital (the nonrenewable services of the environment) and of social capital (the stable relations among people), both of which are being sorely eroded by the chase after increased "growth." As Cobb and his associates point out:

> It is as if a business kept a balance sheet by merely adding up all "transactions" without distinguishing between income and expenses or between assets and liabilities.[10]

They conclude:

*Figure IX.2* The global economic high priest

Located "somewhere on Wall Street" we can imagine the inner sanctum where the gospel of the "bottom line" and all its sacred dogma are worshipped with the full trappings of any other major religion. The November 15, 1998 issue of the *Guardian Weekly* highlighted the social focus of this bottom-line mentality when it contrasted the funds Western nations raised for two simultaneous crises: $3.5 billion to bale out a tottering global stockmarket, and $200 million for aid to flood victims in Central America, where storms left over 10,000 dead, millions homeless, and a clean-up tab of $2 billion.

*Source*: Original artwork by Michele Lukowski

The GDP is such a crazy mismeasure of the economy that it portrays disaster as a gain.[11]

The magnitude of this "noble lie" is seen in Figure IX.3, which shows not only the economists' curve of "growth" in per capita GDP in the United States over the past few decades, but also what the curve would look like when corrected for "unpaid" work (added on) and for social and environmental costs (subtracted out).[12] It is obvious that economic growth has become a national liability. It is beginning to take the shape of Tainter's curve for the collapse of an overly complex society (see Figure 0.7).

Neoclassical economic theory, says the maverick ecological economist Peter Söderbaum, is "a form of 'institutionalized social irresponsibility'."[13] Unfortunately, both liberal and conservative politicians prefer to go along with the idea of more "growth," the former because a sizable fraction of the new income comes to the government in taxes, and the latter because profits go to private investors. Both therefore "benefit," and so both remain determinedly blind to the real damage it does to their respective *other* main concerns, the liberals' environment and the conservatives' family values. So deeply ingrained has this neoclassical world view become that by the end of the twentieth century it had set in concrete the terms of trade relations globally, defining the rules of the World Trade Organization (WTO) and dictating, via the International Monetary Fund (IMF) and the World Bank, to leaders of developing countries how they must do away with their traditions, commoditize their social relations, and allow outside capital access to their resources.

The ongoing consequences globally are visible everywhere. In the supposedly "rich" industrial nations, stress and youthful disaffection are on the increase. In the "poorer" nations, suffering and unrest are spreading as old social patterns are disrupted and extended families are torn apart.

### *Wrong assumptions have evil consequences*

The public would not so readily trust economists, I think, had they not been raised to believe some of the same underlying assumptions about human nature that are implicit in twentieth-century neoclassical theory. I mention here three such assumptions, which Western societies need badly to re-examine.

(1) *Progress.* The notion of linear progress, upward and onward, the present always an improvement on the past, permeates Western thought. Past or present "undeveloped" cultures are "backward," "ignorant" and so forth. I suggest that we conflate *complexity* with *superiority*: more complex is assumed to be "higher" and "better." But is it? What are we progressing toward? What is the social goal? Perhaps we are simply floundering around, stubbornly maintaining institutions that are no longer adaptive, unable or unwilling to entertain alternative life-styles.

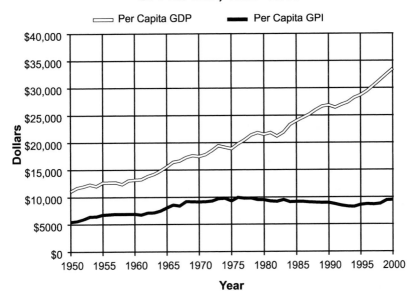

**GPI vs. GDP, 1950–2000**

*Figure IX.3* Alternative measures of economic welfare

The upper curve represents the growth in per capita Gross Domestic Product (GDP) from 1950 to 2000 (corrected for inflation to constant 1996 dollars). This is the government's perception of welfare. The lower curve, or per capita Genuine Progress Indicator (GPI), corrects the welfare expressed in the GDP in two ways.

First, it subtracts both paid-for and unpaid-for economic, social and environmental costs. Economic costs include unequal income distribution, negative balance of trade (owing more than the country lends or pays for), and the cost of consumer durables. Social costs include family breakdown, crime, loss of leisure time, auto accidents, commuting, and under-employment. Environmental costs are pollution of air and water, noise pollution, loss of wetlands, farmlands, and old growth forests, depletion of non-renewable resources, ozone depletion, and so forth.

Second, it adds non-monetized benefits such as the value of parenting and housework, volunteering, services of streets and highways, services of durables, and net capital investment.

As the graph shows, despite the highly touted economic growth suggested by the GDP, the American people in fact are scarcely better off today than they were fifty years ago. It seems the United States may be beginning the decline due to excess complexity, as shown in Figure 0.7.

*Source*: Data courtesy of Clifford Cobb, who prepared them for Redefining Progress, 1904 Franklin St., 6th Floor, Oakland CA, 94612

Two facts might help here. First, precolonial skeletal remains and non-Westernized extant tribal peoples demonstrate over and over again that they were/are healthier than modern Western peoples. Nor were the so-called Dark Ages that bad. Historian Leften Stavrianos calls that time "an age of epochal creativity," when "[b]y the tenth century the West European serf was enjoying a level of living significantly better than that of the proletarian during the height of Augustan Rome." Skeletons from tenth-century London show people were much healthier then than in Victorian times, and experienced less violence.[14] And then there is our common assumption that income parallels longevity, which is just not true. When people are *healthy* they usually live longer and are able to earn more: this was the conclusion of a recent analysis of worldwide data relating longevity to income. When the purchasing power per capita reaches the equivalent of $4000 per year, life expectancy is virtually the same as among the richest people; higher incomes have very little effect on longevity. Yet a family of four in the United States living on $16,000 is in poverty, and usually not faring well healthwise.[15] Obviously Americans (and other Westerners) need to redefine "progress."

(2) *Competition is efficient.* Almost all Western institutions are premised on the notion of scarcity: there is never enough to "satisfy" all. Hence more efficient use of resources is a constant goal, and competition is the best way to improve efficiency.

In Nature there certainly can be competition for food and sometimes mates, but there is also cooperation and interdependence, and much other supposedly "wasteful" behavior that does not seem directly to aid individual survival. Yet as shown earlier, cooperation and interdependence in fact have been profoundly adaptive throughout evolution, *especially* for humans (see Figure II.1) Our brains are designed to work both cognitively and emotionally in cooperation with others. When we create competitive social institutions in schools and workplaces that deny us meaningful cooperative interactions we unleash boundless antisocial pathologies.[16]

As the examples presented in Chapter VI showed, cultures which believe it is natural for a human being to participate spontaneously in the good of the whole because that is what is psychologically most rewarding tend to develop low-violence, uncoerced societies where everyone benefits from the overall cooperative process.

(3) *Human nature is infinitely adaptable.* The Western cultural narrative tacitly assumes all human adults should be able to tolerate the uncertainties of personal psychological security created by modernity, along with the increasing competition and constant need to upgrade one's skills to meet the ever higher demands of productivity. It is wholly the individual's responsibility to make the necessary effort needed to adapt to whatever demands are made and to exercise self-restraint in face of every frustration, while having no meaningful control over the changes being imposed.

316

This may seem an odd claim to make in "free Western democracies," since people supposedly have the choice to utilize a new technology or not. No one has to drive a car; no one has to be computer literate. I submit, only if one joins a low-tech, already existing, highly organized, supportive community such as the Amish is one able to exercise such a choice. Otherwise you will likely find yourself jobless, homeless, and hopeless if you reject training in modern society's imposed technological skills.

We scarcely notice that every industrialized nation *by law* demands children to attend a biologically most unnatural institution, "school," in order to learn the skills of technological complexity (or they must learn them at home). In either case, they must be prepared for survival in a complex society increasingly beyond their personal control. The student dropouts during America's 1960s college revolts against this regimentation of the human spirit, the participants in the sit-ins at Berkeley and elsewhere, seldom ended up as members of successful communes, but as what I call "wilted flower children" living homeless on city streets. After a decade or so, many reluctantly "turned straight" and learned to conform; others still remain adrift. In a technologically hyperdependent culture, opting out is not a real choice, unless one is prepared to become a pilgrim in an Indian ashram or Buddhist monastery, or live in one of the small, struggling "life-simplification" communes that have sprung up. If not, one must try to accept the stress and deal with alienation. Most are finding this increasingly difficult.[17]

An alternative cultural assumption is that there really are limits to the kinds of stress, particularly psychological stress, that a society can impose on human beings. If true, then peoples everywhere need to reassess the wisdom of imposing a "bottom-line," high-efficiency economic system on themselves, especially where the benefits are purely material and essentially devoid of any kind of transcendent meaning.

With that, I turn to some specific examples of twentieth-century "evil" created by the psychological cruelties imposed by implementing the power-driven logic of competing technological megamachine societies. In each case, I focus on how the denial of basic human psychic needs was central to the evil that occurred.

## Reactions of nation-states to global rejection

Every human being experiences a powerful emotional reaction to being rejected by society. Ostracism is the most powerful punishment any group can exert on one of its own. The step just before it, is public shaming; it tends to create anger and resentment in the one who is singled out. Now since personal identities derive from the society in which one lives, this very same emotion can be elicited among a whole culture that feels itself rejected by the global family of nations. On a smaller scale, an "out group" (within a nonhomogeneous larger community) such as one race, caste, or ethnic or religious group, may feel shunned and rejected.[18]

During the sixteenth to nineteenth centuries, Europe's feudal princedoms were coalescing (usually along linguistic lines) into nation-states far more powerful politically than their predecessors. They soon began to expand their new-found power outside Europe, to the Americas, Africa and southeast Asia. By the second half of the nineteenth century, two important cultures were struggling to find their own identity within this growing global family of nations, and both were to develop feelings of inferiority and potential shame. They were the German-speaking peoples of north-central Europe, and the peoples of the islands of Japan. Their histories and the threats they perceived were different, but both experienced a sense of cultural inferiority imposed on them by the global community (then focussed in Europe). By early in the twentieth century, both possessed the military potential to "fight back," to assert their own status as valid members of the world's leading nations, deserving of a piece of the expansionary "pie" being gobbled up by other colonial powers. History records that their efforts ended in defeat, but only after the commission of unbelievably evil acts.

From the point of view of human psychological needs, a sense of inferiority that implies rejection can, and often does, result in the self-delusion of superiority, a psychologically necessary compensation for feelings of inadequacy. Thus is the bully born. Compelled to demonstrate their status, bullies set about dismantling the humanity of others. The contest is no longer to settle a disputed issue, whether over rights to real objects (such as water, a piece of land, or the use of a road or the payment of tribute), or over beliefs (such as religious dogmas or social ideologies). The bully becomes a fanatic about his or her own honor. "I am superior in all things." And when a whole society is affected, this becomes, "We are the master race." It is a calculatedly controlled berserk state, but a form of madness nonetheless.

### The history of Germany

The nation-state now called Germany was the last to coalesce out of the feudal kingdoms of medieval Europe. Elsewhere, various empires had come and gone and by the sixteenth and seventeenth centuries, fairly stable, aristocratically managed kingdoms had formed in England, France, and Iberia, and began establishing a "national identity" for themselves. Later, in the southeast, the remainder of the Hapsburg empire in the shape of Austria-Hungary presented a significant political force, and by the time of Peter the Great's death in 1725, the Russian empire in the East had become another budding power. The diverse kingdoms in north-central Europe bordering on the Baltic Sea, and comprising many of the cities of the old Hanseatic League, found themselves surrounded by increasingly powerful neighbors, with armies equipped with ever-more powerful weapons.

Prussia, the German-speaking state that bordered the eastern half of the Baltic, took upon itself, under its astute Prince, Otto von Bismarck, the unification of the whole of north-central Europe, excepting only Jutland. Only in 1871 did Bismarck succeed, becoming the first Chancellor of the new German Empire. He called it the "Second Reich," the first having been the Holy Roman Empire. For most Europeans, the latter began in AD 800, with the crowning of Charlemagne in Rome, but the new German nation recognized a later date, with the crowning of German-speaking Otto the First in AD 936. The Empire ended in 1806 with the death of another German-speaking emperor, the Austrian Francis II, after which Austria became an empire of its own. Thus did Bismarck cleverly call forth a long prior "history" for his new nation. He was crafting a unifying *identity* for it, and hence for the peoples who would comprise it.

This kind of self-invention of a national identity was necessary to unite the French-speaking province of Alsace-Lorraine in the west with the Polish-speaking peoples in the east, and a disparate assemblage of German-speaking peoples in between into a single nation. As Lionel Rothkrug has pointed out, the new Germany was scarcely a homogeneous people; it had to be based on an invented identity.[19]

Unlike other European nations that claimed legitimacy through a long sequence of aristocratic families, the new German state grasped the eighteenth-century feudal notion of historical Aryanism, a race of "special peoples." As Hannah Arendt observed:

> The organic doctrine of a history for which "every race is a separate, complete whole" was invented by men who needed ideological defini-
> tions of national unity as a substitute for political nationhood....
> Organic naturalistic definitions of peoples are an outstanding charac-
> teristic of German ideologies and German isolation.[20]

Even before Bismarck, the defeat of the Prussian army by Napoleon had cemented among this most dominant tribe of German-speaking people a growing sense of nationalism. During subsequent decades, the other European powers were busy expanding their existing empires outwards – Russia eastward across Siberia, the French, Dutch, English and Portuguese into Africa and south Asia. Prussia's only option, however, was to expand within Europe, to bring all German-speaking people under her control, even though there was no extra economic booty to be had from this local expansion. As Arendt explained, "continental imperialism had nothing to offer except an ideology and a movement."[21]

Bismarck marshaled to his use the productivity of the new industrial machines for making war, outpacing his neighbors. He forced a weakened Austria to withdraw its opposition to the new German state in 1866, and then, in a rapid and decisive attack on the French army in September 1870, he brought Napoleon III's forces to their knees. Alsace-Lorraine became part of the new Second German Reich. Says historian Paul Kennedy:

> Under Bismarck's astonishingly adroit handling, the Great Power
> system was going to be dominated by Germany for two whole decades
> after 1870.[22]

Not only were its industry and educational system and science important, however. So was the sense of being German, or as Jesse Jackson put it for oppressed Black Americans, of being "somebody." The Germans had created out of thin air a new self-identity as a supposedly genetically unique people. Unlike Jackson, however, the nascent Nazis, turned into bullies by the insecurity of their newly defined identity, made highly belligerent claims about their superiority. The emerging social Darwinists were coopting Darwin's ideas to their own purposes, claiming science "proved" that the winner in any struggle is *ipso facto* a superior being and thus, according to the nature of life, deserves to win. By 1900, military and industrial power had made a mockery of national sovereignty for any except the (then) superpowers. The implications of this were not over-looked by the Nazis, who had led the newly birthed Germanic People. Their embryonic intimations of God-given superiority were abundantly watered and able to sprout under the glow of their recent successes and continued obvious industrial and military power in a world where these now counted most.

World War I, however, cannot be blamed on Germany alone, though afterwards that country was made to pay as if it were. Kennedy (quoting Gilbert Murray in 1900) says, "each country seemed to be asserting, 'We are the pick and flower of nations ... above all things, qualified for governing others'."[23] There was a European momentum of leap-frog competition for total hegemony through industrial might. War was inevitable. Its industrially manufactured evils (and there were plenty) were shared by all the belligerents. Everyone was guilty of atrocities.

Perhaps because it was such a psychologically horrible war, for all sides, as well as for innocent civilians, at its termination the victors (if they can be called that) felt justified in punishing the losers in an extreme way, as though vengeance, if harsh enough, could preclude such trauma from ever recurring. The penalties imposed on Germany by the Treaty of Versailles in June 1919 were to have long-term repercussions. Only a relatively small amount of land was taken from Germany, mostly to create the new Polish state and give it a port city, Danzig. Alsace-Lorraine went back to France. And the few overseas German colonies were given to the winning powers. But the Germans were required to almost totally demilitarize and to pay an enormous, highly punitive reparations bill to the victorious nations. It was an ignominious penalty, one that labeled the Germans as the evil cause of all the suffering and death.

Had the global (i.e. Western-controlled) economy proved stable in the decades after the war, the reparations might eventually have been paid and the German economy restored, perhaps followed by the acceptance of Germany into the family of nations. Unfortunately the opposite happened. The capitalist economic bubble broke – twice. A depression in 1922 sent weak economies into a tailspin; and in 1929, a major depression affected all the main trading nations. Says Arendt:

The first World War exploded the European comity beyond repair, something which no other war had ever done. Inflation destroyed the whole class of small property owners beyond hope for recovery.[24]

Germany, with its huge reparations, was hit hardest of all. People's savings were gone; jobs were gone; it took a wheelbarrow full of Deutschmarks to buy a loaf of bread, so bad was the inflation. From being a people invited by their previous leaders to see themselves as a chosen people, they saw around them only unrelieved despair. The elected government of the Weimar Republic, unaided from the outside, collapsed totally when hit by the 1929 crash. It was at this time that Adolf Hitler, son of an Austrian customs official, gradually formed his National Socialist German Workers' party (what eventually was to become the modern Nazis) and began his march to total power. As historian Leften Stavrianos notes, the terrible depression "provided him with an eager audience that greeted him as a Führer who supplied scapegoats for misery [the Jews] and a program for individual and national fulfillment."[25]

A people persuaded half a century earlier to consider themselves a superior race found it easy to blame Jews and other "less fit" peoples for their own present suffering. The humiliation and pain they experienced from the twin calamities of defeat and extreme economic depression produced a level of psychic stress from which Hitler offered relief. His rhetoric (see Table VIII.1) held out hope, moral justification in the eyes of Providence, and empowerment. He promised to redress the wrongs of the past and present, and recreate the global leadership status Germany seemed to hold in 1900. In January 1933 he was duly elected Chancellor of Germany and, on the death of Hindenburg in 1934, became the President as well. In the next few years he created a new German war machine, a modern, highly equipped and trained Wehrmacht. During the period of his greatest popular support in the early 1930s he established both military might with youth raised to believe in their natural superiority as Germans, and, much more insidiously, a secret police that repressed not only the "less-than-human" Jews, but any group that tried to question his ambitions for the German people.

Was the resultant Holocaust that exterminated some six million Jews along with other "undesirables" – some 10 million in total – either in their villages in Poland or later in the infamous gas chambers of the death camps, a *necessary* part of Hitler's strategy to restore self-esteem to the German people? Did they need such vengeance against this scapegoat? How could an ordinary, albeit a physically and psychologically suffering, people become complicit in such a horror? Several historic threads suggest how it could have happened.

Anti-semitism was by no means restricted to Germans; it was widespread among the bourgeois and right-wing elements of Europe and North America. (As a nominal Christian child in San Francisco in the 1930s, I was well aware of it.) Discrimination, special taxes, and segregation (ghettos) had been common-place in Europe for centuries. After World War I almost every country had unwanted refugees of all sorts who were held in concentration camps until they could be deported across borders, whether openly or in secret, and dumped on someone else. The later concentration camps only became death camps when hostilities closed the borders and there was nowhere to send their inmates.[26] Having pronounced the Jews "evil," the Nazis left themselves no choice but to use the physically able as slave labor in their war effort and to exterminate the rest. In the last years of the war there was no spare food nor space in which to house them. The Holocaust became the "final solution."

Hitler used two psychological tactics in his hold over the German people. He legitimized his policies toward Jews by expounding the belief in "natural law," that might makes right. Weakness is a dehumanizing condition; victims are not deserving of compassion. And, through his youth programs, he systematically trained his soldiers, and especially the SS special police, to absolute obedience to authority. Indeed, the German army in World War II executed its own soldiers at a rate 1000 times higher than in World War I.[27] This skillful combination of adoration for a leader who restored their self-identity as a superior race with a fear of disobedience or dissonance insured enthusiastic support among the military and the general populace. Ordinary people were carefully kept in ignorance of the gruesome details by a sophisticated propaganda machine that subtly equated too much concern for the disappearing Jews with a lack of true patriotism for the German nation.

Everyone was bound up into a single collective idea: a state of nationalistic fanaticism. It took a remarkably strong individual citizen in Nazi Germany to hide Jews, though not a few surreptitiously did so.[28] Nor were the atrocities always carried out without compunction. Soldiers oftentimes "missed" when shooting at captured civilians (as did American soldiers in Vietnam). In the death camps, no one person was responsible for the killings. Each had his or her separate task to perform as part of a legal machine; they were just carrying out the orders of a distant leader.[29] Even so, alcoholism was rampant among both the military who were executing civilians and the death camp personnel. Says Roy Baumeister:

> Although alcohol has brought much pleasure to human beings, it is a useful tool for escaping from unwanted emotional states. That makes it a useful tool for performing evil.... Alcohol played a central role in the Holocaust. The guards and officers at concentration camps were very often drunk.[30]

Would the Holocaust have happened without Hitler? Possibly not, though some other rhetorically gifted figure could well have come along to whip up the humiliated and suffering German people. They needed a psychological "healer." Would Hitler have succeeded in his evil acts had not the German people felt humiliated and unjustly punished? I think it highly unlikely. The window through which a people perceives its past can have a powerful influence on subsequent communal acts, a subject I return to in Chapter X, on reconciliation.

### The history of Japan

Although the histories of early twentieth-century Germany and Japan were very different in detail, the psychological impacts of those histories are remarkably similar: a people uncertain of their identity within the family of nations and attempting to restore their self esteem by believing in the natural superiority of their long culture of military honor. The atrocities committed by the armies of Japan are less familiar than those of the Germans' against the Jews, but in terms of sheer numbers killed they were parallel. In China alone, from 1937 to 1945, between 15 and 20 million perished, many of them civilians, in uncontrolled acts of terror or deliberate acts of biological warfare. During the rape of Nanking after its fall to the invading Japanese, December 13, 1937, between a quarter and a third of a million were slain (more than later died in Hiroshima and Nagasaki together, though that by no means justifies or excuses the latter incidents). The slaughter took a mere six weeks. Rape, pillage and wanton killing followed the progress of the Japanese armies westward across northern China. An estimated four million died from cholera, dysentery, typhoid and other diseases caused by germs placed by the Japanese into food and water sources of towns and villages.[31]

Japan was one of the last pre-World War II industrial nations to modernize. For nearly a thousand years it had remained an isolated society, busying itself under the shogun war-lords with the perfection of a highly patriarchal feudal culture based on formalized martial competition. For the elite class of samurai warriors, death in battle was the greatest honor one could experience, and failure to fight to the end was the greatest shame. That demanded self-disembowelment – the commission of hara-kiri, or *seppuko*. Indeed, the whole meaning of society at all levels revolved around these customs of pride and shame.

Isolated as it was from the industrializing world, Japanese society was no match for the metal-clad warships of Commodore Matthew Perry, the American who sailed into Tokyo Bay in July 1852, determined to open up the nation to trade. After the Americans' display of weapons that were unprecedented in shogun experience, the Tokugawa aristocracy was forced to sign treaties allowing outside trade. The nation's isolation ended in cultural humiliation, an ignominious, bloodless defeat. The shogunate disappeared when a dissident group of samurai revolted; but its honor-based culture remained. Defeat only heightened peoples' xenophobic feelings.

In 1868, the rebels replaced the old regime with the Shinto emperor, formerly a person of little power. They reunited the nation by elevating the "ancient sun cult of Shinto into a state religion and used the emperor as a national symbol."[32] The Japanese then began their own path toward modernity, borrowing and copying all possible technologies from the West while retaining their internal cultural patterns. This strategy allowed them decisively to defeat the Chinese in a struggle for suzerainty over Korea in 1894, and then Russia in the war of 1905. Japan continued to industrialize and develop, so that by the end of World War I, it was achieving par with the West in terms of commerce and technology.

The West, however, shunned, indeed isolated, the increasingly competitive Japan both commercially and politically before and during the Great Depression. Meantime, their population having doubled in just sixty years, the Japanese, mimicking the Americans, decided to pursue their own "Manifest Destiny" by expanding into then under-populated China. In the 1930s, Japan abandoned its seat in the League of Nations (which America had never joined) and began militarizing. War toys were pervasive. Schools incorporated military discipline – physical fitness and obedience to authority – into children's daily lives: regimentation, hazing, conformity. Each child was not an autonomous being, but should think like a "cog" in a machine, fully inculcated with a fear of failing to support the group. The expectation of fighting a war was intrinsic to the curriculum, instilling "hatred and contempt for the Chinese people, preparing them psychologically for a future invasion of the Chinese mainland."[33]

When youths were recruited into the army, they received incredibly brutal treatment from their superior officers, treatment designed to totally humiliate them. Writes Iris Chang:

> Japanese soldiers were forced to wash the underwear of officers or stand meekly while superiors slapped them until they streamed with blood ... [This] routine striking of Japanese soldiers, or *bentatsu*, was termed an "act of love" by the officers.[34]

This oppressive militaristic national hierarchy, based on a power-status with the sacred Emperor at the top, led to an enormous potential for brutality among the Japanese army. In war, those who had been humiliated themselves suddenly had the power to vent their rage on others whom they had been taught to view as subhuman. The Chinese, often referred to as pigs, were treated with contempt, or even as evil. All was done in the name of the Emperor, "imbuing violence with holy meaning."[35]

We see in this constellation of three factors – humiliation and absolute obedience to authority, dehumanization of others who are "not us," and a shared religious fanaticism – a profound distortion of all three basic needs of human nature. Humiliation of the self and demand for obedience demolish the exercise of one's autonomy (military training wherever it occurs undertakes this dehumanizing of soldiers, though the Japanese seem to have gone to extremes.[36] It is presumed necessary for creating an effective "fighting machine"). Dehumanizing the enemy is a way of suppressing the spontaneous compassion human beings have for each other, which evolved in human nature to ensure one's acceptance and bonding within a social group. This innate tendency to bond and to feel compassion for others, however, extends to *all* humans. One has to learn whom *not* to trust. This tendency, I believe, is the deepest of all our primate needs, and thus is very hard to repress. (As noted in Chapter VIII, the culturally peaceful Semai, when conscripted into an outside war, could only bring themselves to kill the enemy after seeing their own friends die in battle.) Finally, the whole meaning and purpose of life had been redirected toward serving the Emperor, and the greatest honor was to die in his service.

Millions of Chinese civilians were murdered, some because they aided the Chinese military and later the American forces, but many were wantonly killed for no reason. Women, in particular, were gang-raped, then killed, often by disembowelment (one can hardly explain this kind of behavior in terms of some male "reproductive urge"). But as Chang notes, "rape remained so deeply embedded in Japanese military culture and superstition that no one took the [army's rule outlawing it] seriously." They always killed their victims afterward, "[b]ecause dead bodies don't talk."[37]

These twentieth-century examples of Germany and Japan are recent and well-documented instances of the kind of reactions many cultures have surely experienced throughout the ages when their inner sense of coherence and meaning have been brought into question, whether by internal collapse or external humiliation. Psychological stress placed on a society tends to drive it toward hierarchic order, usually grounded in a fanatical delusion of group superiority, while simultaneously constraining the spontaneous autonomy of individuals. These I believe are natural responses of human societies to extreme pathological conditions. Given the enormous technological changes of the twentieth century, however, particularly in the potential for one society (or even one small terrorist group) to inflict incredible harm on another, it is clear that humankind can no longer ignore the consequences of placing *any* human society in a position of excessive humiliation. "Secret weapons" are never secret very long. (The events of September 11, 2001, have under-scored this point in a terrible way. See my "Postscript" at the end of the book for summary comments.)

This lesson, that humiliating punishment after defeat in war inflicts a terrible psychological wound on a nation's people, was learned, albeit briefly, by America after World War II. The Marshall Plan was instituted in Europe to help the war-torn nations of both sides rebuild, and, in Japan, the United States left the Emperor as nominal head of state while instituting a democratic government and supplying both economic aid and military protection. Both belligerent nations have become accepted members of the global community of Western-style democracies.[38]

Unfortunately, this lesson – that humiliation after defeat is unwise – has been increasingly forgotten in recent years. And it has not been applied at all in the realm of economic warfare, which because it is supposedly nonviolent seems to escape widespread condemnation. This has been especially true in relation to the ex-colonial countries to which I now turn. During the second half of the twentieth century, the promise at independence of autonomous development and nation-building has been thwarted in country after country. "Development" has failed to materialize, owing to a combination of the after-effects of colonial cultural destruction and the predatory economic instincts embedded in the Western meaning system which is spreading its economic hegemony around the globe. The old colonialism has now been replaced by neocolonialism, and extrapolation of the old hierarchical power-control of the military by economic means, and it is having very similar consequences. Economic "defeat" through exploitation is no less humiliating than military defeat, and promises the same psychological backlash, backed by physically harmful technologies when intercultural justice fails to occur.

## Colonialism and after

When I was a child, one-fourth of the global map was colored pink for land belonging to the British; a lesser green area belonged to France, and so on. As historian Leften Stavrianos put it, by 1900 "the greatest land grab in history ended with the extraordinary spectacle of one Eurasian peninsula dominating the rest of the world!"[39] The Europeans did not need colonies to feed themselves, nor were they conquering in the name of religion. It was the pursuit of sheer economic power, and that remains the goal today in the form of neocolonialism. Sometimes religion has been imposed too, to control and subdue, so exploitation might proceed unimpeded.

Colonial exploitation – of resources and people, whether as local labor or transported slaves – extended over 500 years, reaching its peak in 1939, and then rapidly collapsing after World War II. Today, though the political empires are virtually gone, replaced by scores of newly independent nation-states, the struggles to heal from past oppression and to be free of ongoing economic exploitation continue. For too many peoples, independence meant trading one brand of oppression for another, whether local dictators or foreign multinationals, often a combination of both.

As a specific example, I have chosen as a case history the Congo, the name given to the large area lying on the left (south-eastern) bank of the Congo River. Though no two colonial histories are identical, all share much in common with what happened to the peoples living in this large, diverse, and mineral-rich region. Their story reveals the essence of what the majority of the world's people have experienced in the past century or two: social disruption, exploitation, humiliation, and suffering when they made attempts to resist and to regain their selfhood as a people. It explains the deep anger and hatred that is growing against the West, and particularly the United States, in the hearts of the great majority of the world's people, that is mingled with envy for the riches they now see regularly on the village TV screen.

### Disillusion in the Heart of Africa

Long before the Europeans colonized the continent there were African states and kingdoms with trade routes connecting them, especially across the Sahara and down the east coast. Extensive civilizations existed in West Africa from 800 to 1600AD: Ghana first, then Mali and Songhai. It was not an ideal world, however, as a major trading item was human slaves, captured in raids or battles and made to work at home or sold to Arabs or to Europeans.[40]

Movement among the dense jungles further south in west-central Africa was more restricted, so empires were limited. The region that would become the Belgian Congo had in one small corner its own kingdom, the Kongo. Like most other African states, it was not highly centralized politically. Tribes throughout the region asserted their independence and (as noted in Chapter VII) "chiefs and elders were leaders and not rulers."[41] Despotism, so commonly seen after colonial Africa's recent independence, was rare. The customs of the Congo tribes, like African tribes generally, included autonomy, consensual decision-making, and principles of free markets and free trade within and between tribes. These were accompanied by a nature-based world view that required humans to ritually mediate between their domestic world and the spirits in the world around them, the source of both medicines and misfortunes.[42]

Such was the precolonial culture of the dozens of tribes, speaking disparate languages, yet communicating vital information through their drums, and sharing similar, flexible approaches to resolving conflict at all levels, within and between tribes (though the latter were less well developed). As African scholar George Ayittey points out, tragically the new postcolonial native leaders failed to build upon these ancient indigenous institutions.[43] They and their societies, I suspect, were often too disrupted by the colonial experience for that to happen spontaneously.

### The impact of colonialism

By all reports, colonial atrocities were worst in the Belgian Congo. King Leopold of Belgium, trying to make the colony pay, gave free license to concessionary companies and a handful of colonial administrators to collect taxes, impose fines and inflict punishments without any legal oversight. In the areas of the plantations and mines, local people were coopted as slave labor. Any who resisted were killed; violent resistance brought the destruction of whole villages. The left hands of those executed were presented as evidence to superiors; among them were hands of many women and children. "Everywhere rubber and murder, slavery in its worst form," wrote an Englishman in 1884.[44]

The impact was culturally calamitous. After a massacre, survivors would flee to more distant places. African soldiers in the Belgian forces were turned into petty tyrants against their own people, with the right to punish and destroy a whole district. While the British began systematically preparing most of their African colonies for eventual independence by training natives as administrators, the Belgians governed the Congo by a combination of Crown, Roman Catholic Church, and large private companies. After direct control from Brussels was imposed in 1908, the atmosphere in the colony became one of extreme paternalism and racist contempt for African people. Humiliated, treated as children, made to carry passes, they were forbidden to pursue any form of political life that might have prepared them for one day forming a nation, though in their isolated villages the old customs still survived in local governance.[45]

In her best-selling novel, *The Poisonwood Bible*, Barbara Kingsolver vividly paints an image of this sort of paternalistic arrogance in such a village at the time of independence.[46] It is embodied in the person of a psychologically damaged American southern Baptist minister, the Reverend Nathan Price, who takes his family to a mission deep in the interior. Preaching Jesus' love to people whom he judges to be ignorant children, he tries to convert them by threats of eternal damnation if they refuse to believe. He also supposes Western gardening methods and Western ways of settling disputes are superior to theirs. And he presumes to use their language without bothering with its subtleties. His garden ends in catastrophe because he refuses the advice of a village woman. He laboriously explains the Western process of voting to the tribal leaders who are puzzled as they use consensus for making decisions. Voting, they say, means someone remains dissatisfied; it makes enemies. But the Reverend is horrified when the village later takes a vote to reject Jesus Christ as the personal God of their community. Finally, the benighted man has no idea that the word *bangala* means something precious when pronounced one way, but is the name for the poisonwood tree, an extremely noxious plant of the region, when pronounced another. As luck would have it, when he shouts out "Tata Jesus is *bangala*," he is saying "Jesus will make you itch like nobody's business."[47] Yet despite his obnoxious ways the villagers remain willing to listen to him and his ideas with respect, in case they might indeed learn something.

In a way, the behavior of the Reverend Price is a metaphor for Western colonialism in general: not understanding the peoples nor the place, but always assuming *it* has the "real truth," which must be imposed at all costs.

### Independence and its aftermath

The Belgians were among the last to grant independence to their colonies, refusing to do so until 1960. Virtually no goundwork had been laid prior to holding elections. The story of the first year in the life of the new Democratic Republic of the Congo is chilling.

A glance at a map of Africa explains the size of the task that faced the new nation. Many former African colonies are huge in area, encompassing the lands of many, often diverse, tribes. The new Congo comprises an area equal to that of France, Portugal, Spain, Germany and the three low countries (the Netherlands, Luxembourg and Belgium) combined. In its borders live dozens of different tribes all speaking different languages. There was, and still is, almost no infrastructure. Paved roads and electricity exist mainly in major cities and Western-owned mining operations. The elite travel by air, the others by dubious truck-buses or on riverboats. The only schools and medical care for the then population of around 15 million were those provided by missionaries. Says

African scholar Jonathan Kwitny, "At best, missionary work was a haphazard way for a government to provide social services. Often it was an unfair and unacceptable way."[48]

The election of a popular government was held in May 1960. Any number of independence-minded groups put up candidates for parliament. Two were well known in the West: that of Patrice Lumumba, popular for being an independence-activist who was critical of exploitation by the Belgian corporations; and that of Joseph Mobutu, previously a sergeant in the Belgian army who managed to gain promotion to the rank of colonel. Both were young; both sought help abroad wherever they could find it; and neither had any experience at governing anything, though Lumumba, a former postal worker, had studied the political ideas of Kwame Nkrumah, the first prime minister of newly independent Ghana.

Lumumba's party won by far the biggest number of seats, 35 of the total 137 in parliament, but it took much negotiation with other factions before he could form a cabinet. He promptly declared his country "neutral" in respect to the Cold War. He was duly inaugurated as prime minister on Independence Day, in June 1960, but crisis struck immediately. His soldiers, drawn from the old Belgian army, were from rival tribes. Finding themselves suddenly face to face, skirmishes broke out. "Within a week, under the guise of restoring peace, Belgian soldiers were back killing Congolese."[49] Then another rival, Moise Tshombe, leader of the dominant tribe in the mineral-rich Katanga province, declared its independence. Tshombe was backed immediately by remaining Belgian troops and mercenaries, including former Belgian paratroopers, German SS personnel and Italian fascist soldiers.

Lumumba, with no real troops to prevent secession, called on the United Nations for aid, but the U.S. official in charge dragged his feet. By mid-July, despite his parliament's distaste for either Belgian or Russian troops, he turned to the USSR for help. On July 21, the UN Security Council demanded Belgium troop withdrawal, which partially took place. Lumumba promptly withdrew his request to the Soviets, reasserted his government's neutrality, and signed a trade deal with United States businessmen.

Tragically, leadership in the United States was so wrapped up in Senator Joseph McCarthy's Cold-War angst that the CIA dubbed Lumumba a socialist-camp threat, and with President Eisenhower's blessing (he believed the National Security Council's claim that Lumumba was an "impossible person to deal with and was dangerous to [the] peace and safety of the world"), they set about eliminating him.[50]

Once the wheels were set in motion, Lumumba's assassination was inevitable. Only in 1999, however, did the full details become known. Apparently the CIA, which had little power to act inside the Congo, turned to the Belgian minister for Africa, who in October 1960 signed a directive ordering "the final elimination of Lumumba." For several months, Mobutu and others used $1 million of UN development funds to pay the back wages of

Lumumba's troops in an attempt to change their loyalty, thus weakening Lumumba's power. A UN force, headed by an Indian diplomat, was able to stave off Mobutu's activities, however, and undertook to protect Lumumba.

Fearing the UN forces might be defeated, however, Lumumba evaded those protecting him but was soon captured by Mobutu's forces. Mobutu himself was worried that American sentiment might turn against him and toward Lumumba when the newly elected liberal president John F. Kennedy was inaugurated. He had his prisoner flown to Katanga on a Belgian Sabena plane on January 17, 1961. On direct orders of the Belgian foreign minister, Lumumba was tortured and then shot by a Belgian-led execution squad. Later, his body was exhumed and dissolved in acid.[51]

At that point Mobutu, now in charge of the army, became the *de facto* head of state. In fact, he was a military dictator, whose primary virtue seems to be that he had no socialist tendencies whatsoever. Life for the average villager became, if anything, even harder under his rule. His army and hangers-on extracted fees for every transaction and demanded bribes for the right to use the roads to carry produce to market or to send a letter. Unlike taxes, however, none of these payments were invested in infrastructure or public services. A few got rich, either smuggling diamonds or taking big bribes from corporations, or cheating on foreign money exchanges. When Mobutu ran into arrears with his foreign loans (having sequestered much of the country's export profits in foreign banks or squandered them on huge monuments), the IMF ordered the purchase of all foreign goods to cease, leaving struggling entrepreneurs with no access to tools, fertilizers, or machinery with which to improve productivity. What development money there was went for the needs of the big extractive corporations, Mobutu's showpieces.[52]

And so it continued, this Western-imposed corruption of a newly born nation struggling to become a democracy. For thirty-five years the country was called Zaire, the name Mobutu chose, until his replacement by another dubious leader, Laurent Kabila, when it reverted to its original name, Democratic Republic of the Congo. The degree of democracy, beyond that traditionally practiced within villages, remains marginal to this day, and the country continues in violent turmoil, especially in the east where militant refugees from Uganda and Rwanda battle local forces. Kabila himself was assassinated in 2000, and today his youthful son Joseph, as the nation's new, albeit unelected, president, is struggling to unite the various factions and gradually introduce political and social reforms – hopeful signs.[53]

Whether Patrice Lumumba, charismatic though he is said to have been, would have been able to generate a more stable outcome, no one can say. Given the obstacles to creating a national identity virtually overnight for a multitude of distinct tribes living within arbitrarily drawn "national borders" and whose mutual relations with each other ranged from friends, to rivals, to total unknowns, it would have been a very steep uphill task. Few of the recently independent colonial nations have found a smooth path in moving from arbitrarily constructed colonies to integrated cultures with a shared purpose, ancient or newly invented, that gives meaningful identity to their new citizens.

If there is one lesson to be learned from the history and aftermath of colonialism it is that nonviolent social change is a complex and delicate process. It cannot be imposed, from either outside or inside. It seldom succeeds in the absence of meaningful participation by all members of society. A whole people must autonomously choose the direction of change, and become personally involved both in the decision-making and in the implementation of those decisions. Without universal, face-to-face discourse and hands-on engagement in the processes of change, old, nonadaptive social patterns disintegrate and disorder fills the vacuum. The loss of meaning that ensues is the worst possible stress human beings can experience, and the loss can readily turn to violence. As journalist Polly Toynbee has observed, the twentieth century ended with globalwide genocide and ethnic cleansing in more than thirty civil wars, most of them barbaric.[54] The legacy of this is seldom addressed.

The continuing social memory during coming decades, indeed over many future generations, of group traumas experienced in the twentieth century is being ignored in the thinking of world leaders and in most of the research of social theorists. Planning concentrates on food, health, infrastructure, and economic growth (whatever that really means). Almost no attention is given to the need for healing of past traumas and for then building new ties among peoples and new meaning-systems that are owned by the citizens of the emerging new societies, not imposed from outside. I turn next to the extent of the globalwide need for healing, especially among the world's children, the next generation. The last two chapters of the book will then address, respectively, the processes of healing and reconciliation after social trauma, and some living examples of places where people are employing age-old social processes of successful – and peaceful – adaptation and change.

## Damaged youth: a twentieth-century legacy

The opening months of the year 2000 witnessed in the United States the fatal shooting of a little girl by a 6-year-old classmate with whom she had had a fight the previous day. They also saw the jailing of America's two millionth prison inmate. The first event was but one in a spate of school shootings in recent years. The second underscored the fact that though the United States comprises some 5 percent of the global population, it houses 25 percent of the world's prisoners, most of whom are youths and young men. Though some are there for violent crimes, a great many, mainly drug users, are in for victimless crimes that hurt no one directly but themselves. It costs over $100 billion a year to maintain this penal system, approaching expenditures on national defense. More is spent on building new prisons than new university facilities, monies that, by and large, are targeted at the same age group, the nation's most recent generation of adult citizens. Even so, America's prisons are grossly overcrowded and have an abysmal record of rehabilitation; they seem to harm society more than they help it. Meanwhile, performance in schools of even the youngest Americans is declining; more children, at ever-younger ages, are being treated for "restlessness" and "aggressiveness" (now labeled ADHD, or attention deficit with hyperactivity disorder).[55]

What's going on? Why are youth in the United States, the world's greatest nation and its self-proclaimed leader, so problematic for society? Why are they, the next Americans, not more secure, more psychologically mature? Why aren't they flourishing? My answer is: they have become "cultural orphans" in a society too busy creating the illusory American dream to notice it is breaking its own children's hearts. Having been immersed since birth in this "bottom line" *milieu*, children of course have no conscious understanding about *why* they feel and act as they do. In his book, *The Sibling Society*, Robert Bly observed that children today no longer grow up in the vertically oriented world of past societies, where cultural time extends from before one was born and continues into the future long after one dies (the seventh-generation understanding of Native Americans, for example). Instead, children are growing up in an isolated, horizontally oriented subculture of their peers, living for the moment, oblivious of past and future. Far too many Americans have never matured beyond that point, remaining restless and ungrounded, always searching for an identity that forever escapes them.[56]

In the Introduction to this book I listed some of the causes of growing ennui and stress in American society (and to a lesser degree in other Western societies): decreasing family and community bonds; the isolating from society of children in schools, where they are increasingly taught to competitively master academic skills at the expense of meaningful social and participatory learning; and lifelong insecurity in an impersonal work environment. All these causes are themselves consequences of the single-minded national goal of ever-increasing economic efficiency and power. The social price has been decreasing feelings of mutual trust, a further increase in the sense of personal helplessness, and a loss of both self and national identity: in other words, a failure to satisfy all three of the deep-rooted human needs for bonding, autonomy, and meaning.[57] Said some parents in Detroit about the social causes of their children's problems:

> In our pursuit of individual freedom we have come to value convenience over tradition, speed over taking time, getting there over appreciating what's in between, and independence over interconnectedness. Instead of taking a walk to the corner store and stopping to chat with neighbors, we pile into the car and go to a shopping mall full of strangers.
>
> [Q]uality and security cannot be purchased like commodities, bestowed like educational degrees, or stolen by hustling on the streets or speculating in financial markets. *There is a fervent desire for meaning and order, for a life that is more than producing and buying things.*[58]

America's children, and more and more adult Americans also, are not blind to how society fails to value them as people rather than as cogs in the megamachine. But they feel helpless, unable to effect any change in the direction of this headlong rush of "progress." Though similar trends among youth are found in other highly industrialized nations, their responses have been more ameliorative, less punishing. Taxes are much higher, but social help is far more available: paid parental leave after childbirth, generous unemployment support, universal health care, and for those in trouble, less imprisonment and more rehabilitation. On paper, they are economically weaker; in reality, they are socially stronger. They have understood the meaning of Figure IX.3 far better than Americans. Yet they too face future unrest.

Children are our weathervanes; their experiences today are a harbinger of the social climate that is to come. If so many children in America, the world's richest nation, are increasingly disaffected, what have children been experiencing elsewhere in the world?

### When war becomes a child's way of life

The stress experienced by American children – the incessant demand to do more, faster and more efficiently, to unthinkingly produce and consume as a way of life – surely has untoward effects on their brains, but the damage is not nearly as profound as that experienced by children in countries torn by internal wars. Misnamed by military people as "low intensity conflicts," these civil and ethnic battles, which have been spreading globally since the end of World War II, directly affect a whole society, especially its children.

Only in the twentieth century did wars begin to kill more civilians than soldiers. In feudal times, wars were fought by paid armies raised by noblemen. Only with the advent of nation-states were standing armies maintained, but they mainly fought each other on open battlefields. Not until mechanized warfare became possible, with its highly mobile artillery, tanks and aircraft, did the wholesale leveling of cities regularly take place. Since 1900, in almost every armed conflict more noncombatants were killed than soldiers.

Still, wars were costly to fight. It took huge sums to acquire these gigantic weapons. But around 1960, new kinds of lightweight, yet highly lethal weapons were developed, adding to the already available hand-guns, rifles, and grenades. These include assault rifles that fire more than 500 rounds a minute, lightweight machine guns, grenade launchers and small mortars that one or two men can carry. They are cheap, deadly, easy to use, and easy to transport. And they are now widely obtainable. Several European countries, the United States, Russia, China, Israel, and South Africa are the world's leading suppliers. Though sales are supposedly controlled, oversight is poor and few insurgents, if they have the cash, are unable to acquire such weapons.

With a few hundred machine guns and mortars, a small army can take over an entire country, killing and wounding hundreds of thousands.[59]

Guerrilla warfare (as it first was called in South America, guerrilla being Spanish for "little war"), was essentially what was fought in Vietnam. It has characterized virtually all armed conflict since World War II (the Falklands conflict and the Gulf War and Bush's hybrid war on terrorism in Afghanistan being notable exceptions). The end of the Cold War, heralded as the beginning of global peace, instead brought a renewed spate of violence. It deluged the planet with a huge surplus of small weapons, making the world far less stable. As Jeffrey Boutwell and Michael Klare, two arms control experts, report:

> More than 100 conflicts have erupted since 1990, about twice the number for previous decades. These wars have killed more than five million people, devastated entire geographic regions, and left tens of millions of refugees and orphans.[60]

No continent except Australia has been free of such conflict, and the impact on civilians, families, villages, cities – indeed, whole nations – has been enormous. No person is left untouched.

Children in these areas undergo not simply the terror of destruction that is going on around them. They are often witnesses to atrocities, even seeing their family murdered before their eyes. They become refugees, fleeing through jungles or across open fields looking for safety. They are often either induced or forced to join one side or the other as child soldiers. A friend, on reading an earlier draft of this chapter, said it was too depressing. Yet I believe it is necessary for all human beings to imagine themselves, when they were small children, experiencing what such a large number of the youngest generation, with whom they share the planet, have already endured. Without that depth of awareness, the rest of us may expect levels of behavior from them which they are simply unable to perform. They are far too damaged to heal as soon as the fighting stops and simply enter into a "normal life." Americans, in particular, having never known this sort of civilian trauma personally, tend to dismiss its psychic severity out of hand, or worse, refuse to believe that the horrors ever took place (see the Postscript to this book for how this is now changing)

Imagine, for example, this child in Cambodia, where millions died in a prolonged, bloody civil war: "The Khmer Rouge had executed her whole family. Their beatings left her unconscious, lying on the bodies of her loved ones."[61] Or imagine an 8-year-old Cambodian boy fleeing across the killing fields with his grandmother. At one point soldiers find him and chain him overnight to a tree. He is so terrified he messes his pants. When they release him, he goes on alone, surviving on insects.[62]

Finally, imagine being abducted as a child by guerrillas and turned into a willing soldier. Just like the Japanese youth in the 1930s, you are hardened emotionally by being humiliated, beaten, even forced to abuse your own comrades in front of others. Next you are made to kill captives, or even to murder members of your own family or commit atrocities in your home village, so you can never go back. If you spent more than a year with such guerrillas, you likely will never unlearn the automatic use of violent behavior toward those who frustrate you, even though you still understand the difference between right and wrong. In many countries children as young as age 6 are abducted, often after witnessing their abductors kill their families. Some 300,000 child soldiers, both boys and girls, some as young as age 7 or 8, were participating in thirty-six ongoing conflicts around the world as of 2000.[63]

In these accounts I have used the term "guerrilla" to describe these irregular armies. In newspapers, usually that term stands for those fighting whatever government is in power, and the more respectable terms "army" or "militia" are used for government forces; more decentralized armed resistors are often labeled "terrorists." In fact, there is little difference in their tactics or their impacts. "Low intensity wars" are characterized by brutality on all sides, and everyone in society becomes a victim of the prevailing violence.

### The depth of trauma

Human beings don't want to know about things that make them psychologically uncomfortable. They especially don't like facing up to bad situations for which they may bear some moral responsibility. When they hear about human cruelty and emotional suffering, they often refuse to believe it. Novelist Herman Wouk called this "the will not to believe." The West conveniently invented a theory about the human mind that has allowed politicians, the public and, until recently, even psychiatrists to assume that stress is something one can recover from as soon as conditions change. Whether flood, earthquake, famine or war, once the crisis is past people's minds will "snap back to normal." In the past decade, however, it has become crystal clear that this is not the case. As the data discussed in Chapter VI reveal, severe psychic trauma can literally change the structure of the brain, and it takes a great deal of patient, ongoing social support to repair (or at least ameliorate) the damage.

Richard Mollica, the psychiatrist who co-founded the Harvard Program in Refugee Trauma, offers some major insights discovered in the past two decades regarding recovery from violent experiences.

1  The prevalence of trauma: in war-torn countries, hardly anyone remains unscathed. Over three-fourths are demoralized and physically and mentally exhausted; half are also clinically depressed or suffer from post-traumatic stress disorder (PTSD); and one-fourth also are mentally incapacitated. They cannot function in society.

2    The nature of one's trauma can now be measured: new, nonstressful, culturally tailored psychiatric questionnaires allow patients to report the nature of their feelings without having to verbalize the details of their experiences.

3    The folk psychologies in all societies (once one understands the cultural "terms") seem to be describing very similar psychologically abnormal states. What is being studied is therefore universal to all human nature, not just to this or that culture.

4    Some kinds of experience are more traumatic than others: blows to the head, torture, prison, watching children be abused or killed, all tend to produce the most trauma.

5    The most potent events cause changes in the brain (see Chapter VI for details).

6    Mental distress creates social dysfunction: one-quarter of Bosnian refugees in Croatia, for example, could not work, care for their families, or otherwise contribute to society.

Mollica sums up the findings thus:

> [A]lthough only a small percentage of survivors of mass violence suffer serious mental illness requiring acute psychiatric care, the vast majority experience low-grade but long-lasting mental health problems.... For a society to recover effectively, this majority cannot be overlooked. Pervasive physical exhaustion, hatred, and lack of trust can persist long after the war ends. Like chronic diseases such as malaria, mental illness can weigh down the economic development of a country.[64]

Even the World Bank, he notes, "has acknowledged that old development models are not working for war devastated nations, and that new approaches are needed." Among them, he suggests establishing "microenterprise projects to ease depressed people back into productive work."[65] (See also the discussion of work with Cambodian women suffering severe depression at the end of Chapter VI.)

## Lessons learned

What are the take-away lessons of the events of the twentieth century? I offer three, each of which requires some deep rethinking of Western assumptions about human nature and human society.

*Lesson 1: Change cannot be imposed*   Imposing change on a society does not work, either politically or economically. Russia learned this when it imposed communism on the diverse Soviet States in its "Union." Today, the replacement by the Group of 7 (or now, the Group of 8) of Europe's *old*, colonial imperialism with a *new* economic form based on Western "free market capitalism" can lead only to the same stresses globally that it has already produced in the

United States and, to only a slightly lesser extent, in Europe and Japan. Postcommunist Russia is floundering badly as it tries to "follow the rules."[66]

And in modernizing India, the world's largest democracy, where about 20 percent now belong to the "well-to-do" middle class, the same signs of cultural decay are setting in. Writes an old friend who, since retiring from the Indian Forest Service, has lived in the United States to be near his children but who still returns to India for several months each year:

> I am worried about corruption eroding the long cherished values and degenerating the society. Because of terrorism, life is becoming uncertain. Innocent people are being killed! What a tragedy and perversion of human nature!
>
> Though there is perceptible growth and increase in personal spending, there is perceptible absence of humanness, compassion, and tolerance! This is not a good sign! Perhaps things may get worse before they get better![67]

*Lesson 2: Residual traumas must be addressed*  Walking away from past mistakes is not a solution. The colonial era, during which most indigenous societies were seriously traumatized and lost their cultural coherence, by and large ended ungracefully. Few colonial powers adequately prepared subject peoples for independence. Even when they tried, they mostly got it wrong. Rather than facilitating the revival of traditional beliefs about governance, justice, and social meaning that better suited local cultural groups, they insisted on the adoption of inappropriate Western institutions, being keen to insure that former colonies came to look like new, European-style nation-states. What they in fact created was a vacuum of cultural meaning that is still present in all too many of those countries.

One instance where a nation did not walk away from a potentially tragic situation was what the United States did in Western Europe after World War II. When President Harry Truman realized how seriously traumatized and unstable all those countries were, winners and losers alike, he set up the Marshall Plan, by which Europe was able to set about rebuilding. Without it, the second half of the twentieth century could have been far, far worse than it was. Today, two-thirds of the world is in need of a twenty-first-century Marshall Plan. Instead, however, they are experiencing a new form of economic imperialism whose latest institution is the World Trade Organization.

*Lesson 3: Societal healing is a psychological, not an economic, process*  Traumatic healing requires time and social support. Stopping the physical violence, ending the carnage, does not automatically bring a healthy society into being. It should be obvious by now that bringing new stress into the lives of mentally damaged people is the last thing they need if their brains are to heal. They need, instead, to feel secure, to begin to be able to trust others, to begin to feel valued and useful.

The sledge-hammer approach used until now by the World Bank, IMF and the rest of the international investment community has only made things worse nearly everywhere. By assuming the basic problem was a lack of economic growth, which they in turn assumed required investment in industries and infrastructure, not in people's well-being and psychological needs, they eliminated the provision of social services that were needed to begin healing the deep-seated traumas which were the real cause of economic suffering. Cut-throat economic competition and divisive party politics are about as helpful to people trying to repair broken lives as providing stagnant pools of water for mosquitoes to breed in is to controlling an epidemic of malaria.

The children of the world everywhere – from America to Europe, to Africa and Asia – are being traumatized by stresses that are the accumulated legacy of what is sometimes called "the American century," though more than just the United States are to blame. It is time for me now to turn away from this *Night on Bald Mountain*, this world of darkness painted by Moussorgsky's music, and move on to the exhilarating yet calming tones of Schubert's *Ave Maria* (for readers too young to remember, these were the last two pieces in Walt Disney's animated 1940 film, *Fantasia*). Chapter X examines the processes human nature seems to demand to achieve social harmony after violence has been done: the processes of conflict resolution and reconciliation.

# X

# CONFLICT: CONTROL OR RECONCILIATION?

The more the basic physical and psychological needs of groups of people are satisfied by constructive means, the less likely it is that psychological and social processes that lead to group violence arise.

Ervin Staub (1999: 331)

*The human dimension of conflict must become central to peace-making and building peaceful societies. Only governments can write peace treaties, but only human beings – citizens outside government – can transform conflictual relationships between people into peaceful relationships.*

Unless citizens engage in this work, peace will have little chance. Human beings the world over cry out to end violent conflict and to build the practices, processes and structures of peace so they can live in safety, overcome poverty, bury discrimination and find dignity. Their starting point must be the formation of peaceful relationships among citizens who have to work together if they are to achieve those ends.

Harold H. Saunders (1999: xvii, 3)

Shortly after a recent visit to South Africa to see how people there were moving forward with healing their country after the trauma of apartheid, I found myself telling a class of fourth-graders about that experience. After recounting some of the recent history of how Nelson Mandela and others, after much suffering and sacrifice, eventually brought about a peaceful change in society, I got on to the problem of healing the terrible memories. I wrote the African word *ubuntu* on the blackboard and told them that while some translate it as "forgiveness," the Africans understand it as something like "to be sorry *and* to forgive." You can't have one without the other. They cannot happen alone.

To illustrate this, I asked them, "Is it easy to forgive someone who has hurt you?" And in a chorus they instantly answered "No!" (Plenty of "good cops/bad robbers" TV justice here, I thought.) But instead of asking them

"Why is it so hard?" I asked, "And when you have hurt someone else, is it easy to say you are sorry?" This time they had to think longer before slowly shaking their heads. (Not so much help from TV or elsewhere for that one.) Being sorry can be just as hard as forgiving – maybe harder.

This chapter is about this simple-to-state, but oh-so-difficult-to-solve conundrum in human relations. How a society defines and implements something called "justice" determines whether it will rely more on punishment or on reconciliation in attempting to restore order and prevent renewed disorder.[1] Though societies vary greatly in their tendency toward disorder, the very nature of human beings (like other primates) is internally conflictual for each one of us: a tension exists between one's social needs for bonding and shared meaning and one's need for autonomy. Hence, no real society ever permanently solves the ongoing potential for social conflict, but some are much better than others at managing it without overly restricting individual behavior.

It was the late twentieth-century economist/philosopher Kenneth Boulding who identified the three major means human societies have used to enforce social control on less-than-perfect human nature: he called them the *Three Faces of Power*.[2] These are *legalized violence* (military, police, and physical punishment); *economic power*, where the control of resources in the hands of a few channels the behavior of the rest of society; and *love*, the power that mutual trust and compassion exert over behavior. The ratio of how these three are employed in a given society depends on a culture's narrative story, especially its assumptions about human nature.

The more a society's world view expects people to be selfish, scheming, and anti-social *by nature*, the more likely it is (1) to maximize those very qualities in its citizens, and (2) to employ physical coercion to control them. Highly individualistic societies such as the United States tend toward high internal violence and employ violent legalistic methods of social control, of a retributive sort. Punishment, it is argued, is both a way to obtain justice (essentially defined as "getting even") and to prevent and/or cure antisocial behavior.

Twentieth-century socialist dictatorships took the same approach, only more so, as they tried to impose their vision of social justice onto people whose traditional world views and institutions were very different. Coercive social control, as suggested in the previous chapter, whether by hyperindividualistic Western democracies, or by socialist dictatorships, is counterproductive and never produces long-term social stability. To cohere, such cultures often find it necessary to develop outside "enemies" and (as did twentieth-century Germany and Japan) can become a military threat to their neighbors. As ever-more wealth is devoted to prisons, the police and the military, the overhead costs eventually topple the whole structure. Moreover, in this age of modern destructive technology, physical force as a "solution" to social disorder becomes an increasing liability for the whole species.

340

Today economic power is being promoted by the West as the global alternative to military power, and our best hope for a nonviolent future. Indeed, there have been societies (the early Inca in Peru and early medieval Europe) where such economic hierarchies worked reasonably well because (1) the way wealth was distributed among social classes really *was* acceptable to all, and (2) the cultural narrative provided meaningful identity to all. But once the cultural argument gives the "right" to some individuals and groups to accumulate unlimited wealth without regard for the well-being of others, its validity as a social guideline collapses; unrest develops, and physical controls are needed to maintain order. Like centralized military power, centralized economic power becomes increasingly threatening to ordinary human beings in whatever sovereign state they dwell. Modern technology only exacerbates the situation. In an age of globally transmitted television, even the most remote peoples of the planet are aware of the great gap that separates rich and poor, and watch the rapid increase in that gap with dismay.

Interestingly, the United States, with its momentary overwhelming dominance in both military and economic power, drags its feet in supporting any United Nations resolutions passed by the majority of sovereign states that would in any way *restrain* its military dominance, while simultaneously supporting the WTO, controlled by only a few of the wealthiest nations, which gives them a huge advantage in the economic realm.[3] Clearly, America's decision-makers are aware that her economic hegemony may need to be backed up by military force,[4] which brings us back to the dangers of a world order maintained by extremely violent technologies. (These words, I should tell the reader, were written many months before the events of September 11, 2001.)

This leaves us with the third of Boulding's faces of power, the natural power inherent in what he called "love." Boulding defines the term in a rather diffuse way. He chooses, as the nearest explanatory synonym, feelings of benevolence toward someone or something, from concrete items such as one's spouse or a brand of ice cream to abstractions such as a sport or one's country. Yet in its application, he narrows the objects of love to two broad categories: other living creatures, especially humans, and significant beliefs. In fact, he uses "love" to stand for two of the three basic human propensities: our need for bonding and our need for a shared, meaningful world view.

For me, lumping these together is confusing for an understanding of human conflict and how it can best be addressed. The feelings of *love* we have for people are based on our mutual need to belong, to accept, and to be accepted by others. We depend emotionally on them. This elicits feelings of tenderness, of caring, of compassion, of personal loyalty. Of these, the most universal is compassion: we can feel a powerful empathy with utter strangers, living in distant lands, who may hold views about the world quite different from our own. Often we are ignorant of the beliefs held by starving Ethiopians, an orphaned child in East Timor or Kosovo, or an AIDS victim in Kenya. Yet we feel compassion for their suffering as human beings; we identify with their plights.

This, to me, is the *primary characteristic* of human kind. Compassion, the desire to reach out and help even total strangers who are in need, is the most powerful human force there is. And it is the fundamental basis of all human social life. It is also the inner power we all have access to for resolving conflict. The secret lies in reawakening feelings of compassion in those who have lost them and entered into states of mutual anger, distrust, and hate.

In fact there are recent examples of forgiveness by two American couples who lost their children to violence in foreign countries: the Greens, who lost their son Nicholas, killed by would-be carjackers in Italy in 1994, and who donated his organs to Italian children; and the Bealls, who lost their daughter Amy to violently anti-white children in a South African black village where she had gone to help. The parents went on to establish schools and scholarships and other benefits for the villagers in her name, forgiving her young killers.[5]

It is not necessary that two former enemies come to share the *same* sacred meaning in order to live amicably together. Meanings are certainly critical – and differences in beliefs can and do generate terrible conflict. But conflicts can be resolved without any participant group relinquishing its beliefs. The only compromise (if we must call it that) is to accept the possibility of – and then give respect to – beliefs different from one's own. True compassion consists in respecting the need of others for the integrity of *their* beliefs, without feeling one's own are thereby threatened. Finally, imposing one's own beliefs and institutions on others is *never* acceptable; true peace requires complete tolerance of profound difference *on all sides.*

Only in the last few decades of the twentieth century has the amazing power of compassion found its way into general academic thought in the West, escaping finally from the narrow confines of comparative religion into the precincts of philosophy, psychology, and political science. By the end of the 1990s, it finally reached the newly emerging field of conflict resolution. The West, especially Western science, has been determinedly blind in seeing the obvious. Developmental psychology has long insisted that children are born self-centered and must go through a series of learned states of moral development. Only a few adults, so the theory goes, ever achieve the highest levels of true altruism.[6] I long ago dismissed this theory as simply wrong when I watched a 3-year-old boy, sitting on the lap of his recently widowed grandfather, gently offer to wipe away the tears from his eyes. One only has consciously to "see" in order to discover empathy in very young children (see Figure X.1). It is evident everywhere. Embarrassing though it may be to Westerners, who tend to suppose they are at the cutting edge of all knowledge, this important role of reciprocal compassion that pervades human action, and the special human qualities that go with it, have been known and promoted in countless cultures. Here I mention only two important examples.

I introduced the southern African word *ubuntu* at the start of this chapter. According to Archbishop Desmond Tutu, himself of African descent, the concept of *ubuntu* (or, in another African language group, *botho*) is central to

*Figure X.1* Childhood empathy
"A Kosovan refugee is comforted by her daughter." Even without the caption, it is evident that this young child is expressing empathy toward a grieving adult.

*Source*: Courtesy of Andrew Testa and Panos Pictures, London

the historical African world view. Tutu agrees that there is no single Western word that expresses its whole essence. It comprises a whole bundle of virtuous qualities: generosity, hospitality, friendliness, compassion, caring. It means, says Tutu, "My humanity is caught up, is inextricably bound up, in yours ... A person is a person through other persons ... I am human because I **belong**. I participate, I share."[7] It also includes, therefore, ideas of both remorse and apology, as well as forgiveness, as part of maintaining the overall harmony – the "right way for people to be."

> A person with *ubuntu* is open and available to others, affirming of others, does not feel threatened that others are able and good, for he or she has a proper self-assurance that comes from knowing that he or she belongs in a greater whole and is diminished when others are humiliated or diminished, when others are tortured or oppressed, or treated as if they were less than who they are.[8]

To me, *ubuntu* is best described in English by its opposite, the qualities comprising a bully: egoistic aggression. In African culture, where social harmony is the greatest good, anything that subverts this "is to be avoided like the plague. Anger, resentment, lust for revenge, even success through aggressive competitiveness, are corrosive of this good." Adds Tutu:

> To forgive is not just to be altruistic. It is the best form of self-interest. What dehumanizes you inexorably dehumanizes me. It [forgiveness] gives people resilience, enabling them to survive and emerge still human despite all efforts to dehumanize them.[9]

To briefly summarize, *ubuntu* morally outlaws feelings of retribution, of vengeance, of winning at the expense of others, of behaving confrontationally – in short, many of the habits of behavior that characterize highly individualistic Western cultures.

My other example of non-Western peoples' awareness of the importance of compassion is the Sanskrit term *ahimsa*. It means the absence of *himsa*, or violence. It captures in a single word the ideal universe where all nature is connected into one cooperating whole, permeated by mutual support, after the fashion of Indra's Net described in the Introduction. It is the model of humankind to work toward, that of living a life free of violence because one is filled with compassion for all that exists. It is what both Buddha and Jesus taught people to seek.

Indeed, it was when the young Mohandas Gandhi came across the Sermon on the Mount and recognized affiliations between the teachings of Jesus and those in the ancient Sanskrit text, the *Bhagavad Gita*, that he began his path of discovery of *ahimsa*, which became the basis of his program for nonviolent social change in twentieth-century India. He taught, first himself, then millions of followers, the inner skills needed to physically protest injustice without succumbing to feelings of anger or hatred. "'Hate the sin, not the sinner,' is a precept," he said, "which, though easy enough to understand, is rarely prac-tised, and that is why the poison of hatred spreads in the world."[10] For him, *ahimsa* was the basis of truth.

> It is quite proper to resist and attack a system, but to resist and attack its author is tantamount to resisting and attacking oneself. For we are all tarred with the same brush, and are children of one and the same Creator, and as such the divine powers within us are infinite. To slight a single human being is to slight those divine powers, and thus to harm not only that being but with him the whole world.[11]

(This notion, that a single divine essence (God, Creator, or Universal Spirit) is found everywhere, is widespread in India. When I was visiting among a newly inspired religious sect in Bombay, people greeted me or each other by touching their breasts lightly, murmuring "*Jai Yogeshwar*," meaning "God is here," before placing their palms together and bowing in the usual manner. They were confirming the shared presence of the sacred in each of them.[12])

The nonviolent technique of *Satyagraha* ("truth-firmness") that Gandhi taught his followers has become the universal pattern for nonviolent social change in place after place. Danilo Dolci employed it in Sicily on behalf of peasants terrorized by the mafiosi and robbed by corrupt officials. Martin Luther King used it during the civil rights movement in the 1960s in the United States. The people of the Philippines used it in 1986 against the faction of the army that tried to prevent the duly-elected president, Corazon Aquino, from taking office. And it is employed today around the globe by citizens protesting against social injustice and environmental destruction. Refusing nonviolently to comply with unjust or injurious rules can be a powerful political force.

Theories for applying civilian-based nonviolence against invading armies have been developed by Gene Sharp, President of the Albert Einstein Institution in Cambridge, Massachusetts, and former Director of the Program on Nonviolent Sanctions in the Center for International Affairs at Harvard University. Sharp provides multiple examples of the successful use of social nonviolent resistance to invaders.[13] He tends to use military metaphors (such as "transarmament") for the processes described rather than the more spiritually based metaphors of Gandhi and others. This may be necessary in the early stages, where the ears one wants to influence are also being bombarded by Pentagon or War Ministry spokespersons. Ultimately, however, nonviolent action will need to move beyond just ending outright violence, and incorporate techniques for long-term healing and reconciliation.

This is the central question addressed here. When the violence has stopped, how do you fix the residual pain? Once the armistice is signed, what comes next? As the quote from Hal Saunders at the start of this chapter suggests, governments do not make "peace"; ordinary people do. The work of nonviolent change must continue – not anymore as resistance against the other, but as finding a means of reconciling with the other. Without this, the original problem underlying the violence remains ready to flare up again. The Civil Rights movement, for example, made many political changes but it did not, of itself, end racism. This is a much longer, slower process, building trust between former adversaries. It is this non-governmental, non-leader-controlled, people-to-people process that ultimately brings about true peace. And it is *exactly the same process that societies need for continuously adapting their shared world views over time.* It is the ultimate way of doing "politics." It is the process necessary for nonviolent human social and cultural innovation and evolution.

Though it takes a lot of time and requires patience and dedication, it is not costly in other ways. All that is needed are people, *all* the people, participating in that most human of all human activities, talking. Dialogue, discourse, conversation: people telling their stories *and* listening to those of others, as they work out a common future together. This is true participatory democracy. I have chosen to use the recent events in South Africa as a concrete example of the gigantic hurdles a society faces in trying to heal itself after violent conflict.

## South Africa's story

In 1990 Nelson Mandela, the charismatic leader of the banned African National Congress (ANC) party, was released from prison after twenty-seven years by the white racist regime which had sent him there. At the same time, the ban on the party's activities was lifted and the stage set for framing a new constitution for the Union of South Africa, one that would make every citizen a political equal in the voting booth. Part of the bargain, however, was that approval of the new Constitution be given solely to the old white electorate. Without their unco-erced consent, peaceful change would have been out of the question. By 1994, the new Constitution was agreed upon and elections duly scheduled. On April 27, the entire nation – black, white, "colored," Indian, male, female – waited in long, snaking queues at thousands of polling stations to choose their new government. Thirteen days later, on May 10, Mandela was sworn in as the nation's new President.

The particulars of the factors leading up to this remarkable event are fasci-nating – international disapproval and boycotting of economic interaction by foreign citizens and investors had taken their toll. Yet as Archbishop Tutu observed, that this unlikely event came off so amazingly smoothly after so many years of horrendous violence, bloodshed, and aggression was indeed a miracle. Details of the events leading up to this miracle fill volumes and make fascinating reading. Here, however, I focus mainly on the next steps needed in order to deal with the still unresolved pain and suffering of the past. South Africa's constitutional change was much like a "peace" treaty, a "cease fire" signed by the top leadership and momentarily welcomed by the exhausted citizenry on both sides. But such an armistice is merely an enabling device. To make true peace requires mutual understanding in dealing with the past and learning how to live harmoniously together in the future. The signing of pieces of paper and the casting of votes do not suddenly change the conditions of peoples' daily lives nor erase their memories of terrible suffering.

### A very brief history

Originally, southern Africa was inhabited by several tribal groups of which the most dominant were the Xhosa and the Zulu, each comprising numerous subgroups who had not always coexisted peacefully. Among the first Europeans to colonize sub-Saharan Africa was a small Dutch community who settled in 1692 on the Cape of Good Hope as provisioners for ships plying to and from the Indies. Though the numbers of these Boers (today known as Afrikaners) increased, by 1814 new British colonists had overrun the Cape and the Boers trekked northwards to establish an independent state, the Transvaal. When diamonds and gold were found there, however, thousands flocked from everywhere. Increasingly, black laborers were forced to work in the newly opened mines, virtually as slave labor. Tensions grew between the two main groups of whites, and the Boer War left the British in control in 1902, with the indigenous black majority becoming even more marginalized.

During the Boer War "the British incarcerated more than 200,000 people, including Boer women and children and black workers on Boer farms, in what was a new British invention at the time – concentration camps."[14] Almost a quarter of them died as a result of the inhumane conditions, and their grandchildren, even today, deeply resent what happened to their forebears at the hands of the British. Old accounts demand reconciliation if they are not to fester and resurface in twisted new forms.

Gradually the Afrikaners became the dominant political power. With the acquiescence of other whites they introduced the virtually total separation of races known as *apartheid*. Eighty-five percent of the people of South Africa, the entire black and colored population, were denied political rights except in the small reserves known as "homelands" or Bantustans, which were quite insufficient to support them. Consequently, black men were forced to work in white-owned mines and city factories, leaving behind beleaguered women and children. Disruption of family and community life was all-pervasive.

While most of sub-Saharan Africa gained independence from colonial rule in the decades after World War II, acquiring black-majority rule, South Africa, already independent from Britain but governed by a white minority, was forced out of the British Commonwealth because of its racist policies. As black resistance to *apartheid* grew the white minority increased its oppressive military and police violence. The once nonviolent African National Congress, the major black political party, abandoned its Gandhian approach and turned to guerrilla action, training recruits in neighboring Angola and Mozambique. Tensions increased but so did mounting external pressure on the newly elected president, F.W. De Klerk. World opprobrium showed itself in several forms of economic pressure, stirred up by ANC members invited to the United States and other nations. Students at European and American universities formed campus movements that urged financiers to disinvest in South Africa and boycott its currency, the Krugerrand. The Chase-Manhattan Bank recalled a $7 billion loan. Ultimately, De Klerk had to change course, a change that would lead to the freeing of Mandela, to the new Constitution, and to the election of 1994.[15]

A crucial step in De Klerk's negotiations with the ANC was to insure that when black majority rule came into being – as it surely would under the new constitution – there would not be an uncontrolled bloodbath against the old white minority. How could the pent-up resentment be prevented from turning into vitriolic vengeance? The answer was amnesty for one's past oppression. Otherwise the transition to majority rule would have been like asking nineteenth-century southern slaveholders in America not only to free their slaves but also to empower them to vote in retroactive laws declaring slavery a crime and their former masters criminals. If South Africa was to avoid civil war, provision for amnesty for past acts had to be made possible. Thus, the black ANC leaders and the white government agreed that whoever had committed criminal acts for *political purposes* be granted amnesty from future prosecution *if they admitted their acts* and, by acknowledging the inhumanity of them, *exhibited remorse for the harm they had done*. Psychologically, of course, this is an enormously difficult task (as the fourth graders I met with recognized). It requires a public admission of one's inhuman acts, agreement that they were wrong, and a request for forgiveness. In the process, one's own identity suffers feelings of shame and humiliation in a very public way. It is like opening the Christian confessional to the view of everyone.

To insure equality before the new law, the same rules would apply to prior acts committed by overzealous black activists as well, whether against whites or each other. Finally, those violent acts that had no political validity – wanton killings, rape, personal vendettas – would not be granted amnesty. Perpetrators of these would still be subject to prosecution and punishment under the new constitution, just as under the old.

These were the conditions for establishing a "clean slate" for the newly born South African nation. As much of the past as possible would be left, once and for all, *in the past*. There would be a new beginning, a fresh sheet upon which to write a brand new chapter in South Africa's history.

Erasing the past, however, is not a simple task. Murder, torture, violence, humiliation, terror, guilt, and shame do not go away overnight. Memories of these things pass from one generation to the next, achieving a kind of immortality as they are woven into the whole remembered tapestry of a society's history. The Truth and Reconciliation Commission, or TRC, created as a condition of the new South African constitution, could not be the magic eraser of the past that some persons had hoped for. Rather, it would set the stage for a long, ongoing dialogue of national healing. The commission began hearings in December 1995 and completed its final report in mid-1998. It covered abuses occurring between March 1960 and May 1994; over seven thousand requests for amnesty were received, nearly a hundred times what had been expected. Archbishop Desmond Tutu served as its chair.

The following vignettes paint a picture of the total scene: all the crosscurrents of human feelings that together form the memories of the past that South Africa as a whole must explain and move beyond. Here is the whole spectrum of categories of suffering and pain. No one – not *anyone* – escapes her or his share of the torments of their country's violent, inhumane past. All are deeply scarred, even to the very structure of their brains.[16]

### The victims' stories

In a sense, *everyone* is a victim of a society of horror. But for the TRC, victims were the nameless little people who suffered terrible experiences without understanding why, and mostly they suffered unnoticed by society at large. *Apartheid* demanded fear among the oppressed majority: thousands of random acts of violence that would prevent resistance from building.[17] The TRC's task was to give voices to those voiceless victims. Let the widows, the mothers of murdered children, the terrorized survivors of torture be heard by the whole world. For some, it actually did help promote their healing.

Perhaps the most puzzling question for many ordinary black victims was "Why"? For Elsie Gishi, she never knew why men with white scarves came to her house, kicked in the door, and started shooting at her and her children. Her husband was axed to death; a son, wounded, died later in hospital. She still has bullets in her body. Bonisile, 15, and several other children survived. But it made no sense:

> My son, Bonisile, who was smeared with his father's blood on him, was never well again after that, he was psychologically disturbed.[18]

The permanent psychic damage to children who witnessed violence was an oft-repeated story. No matter who was harmed, black or Afrikaner, the hurt was the same. Johannes Roos, an Afrikaner farmer whose wife and three children were in a car that ran over a landmine buried in their driveway one Sunday morning while they were at church, described the horror. The blast severed his wife's legs and injured her arms and throat; she died three days later, without speaking again. His son, part of whose skull and brain were blown off in the blast, suffered convulsions in hospital. Though he partially learned to speak again, he died a few months later. The 5-year-old daughter and baby son survived, but the daughter was never the same.

> That child never cried. The child still does not cry [from 1986 to 1994]. The world can go to pieces around her, but it wouldn't matter...[19]

Nor was it only children who lost the ability to express emotion after inde-scribable trauma. Anna Mtimkulu, whose husband was attacked and "necklaced"*, remained emotionless while describing the details of his murder at the hands of a gang of black vigilantes. Said one observer of her testimony:

> And did you see she never cries ... she just stares at the table in front of her ... as if these stories are not the beginning or the end of some-thing, but part of the ongoing horror of her life. How do people ever live together in the same neighborhood after such a thing has happened? Everytime the comrades see her walking – and she's so tall and so dignified – something must stir inside them.[20]

---

* "necklacing" was a form of execution practiced by black vigilante gangs against supposed informers or other blacks thought to be associated with whites. A tire filled with gasoline was placed around a person's neck and set alight.

The conditions in prisons created victims also. Of his twenty-seven years in prison, Mandela spent many on Robben Island at hard labor in a rock quarry, but he claimed it kept him fit. Torture and beatings in urban prisons were commonplace however. Steve Biko is only the best-known name among the 120 people who died in police custody. And then there was solitary confinement: the rats, the cold, the silence.

> Isolation for seven months taught me something. No human being can live alone. I felt I was going deeper and deeper into the ground. It felt as if all the cells were like coffins full of dead people.
> I had to accept that I was damaged. That part of my soul was eaten away by maggots and I will never be whole again.[21]

Thus spoke Greta Appelgren, involved in the ANC-sponsored bombing of Magoo's Bar.

Women prisoners had the added threats of rape and sexual torture facing them constantly. Sexual humiliation is psychologically hardest of all to speak about. It is too personal, too private. Journalist Antjie Krog describes it thus:

> There seems to be a bizarre collusion between the rapist and the raped. Though rumors abound about rape, all these mutterings are trapped behind closed doors. Apparently [even] high-profile women ... were raped and sexually abused under the previous dispensation – and not only by the regime, but by their own comrades in the townships and liberation camps. But no one will utter an audible word about it.[22]

Rape adds one more cross-cutting dimension to the complex pattern of human bonds being ruptured in a society permeated by violence.

Finally, acts of violence can become psychological boomerangs, damaging the mental health of perpetrators, who thus join the ranks of victims. The following observations were made about two *apartheid* "hit-men" by a woman intimately associated with them. The horrors they secretly committed in order to "let me and the old South Africa sleep peacefully" took a heavy toll:

> I can't explain the pain and bitterness in me when I saw what was left of that beautiful, big strong person. Years had dug deep spoors in his face, robbed of all dignity, no one and nothing to live for. He had only one desire – that the truth [about what he did] must come out. Amnesty didn't matter. It was only a means to the truth. A need to clean up.[23]

> I end with a few lines that my wasted vulture said to me one night when I came upon him, turning his gun over and over in his lap: "They can give me amnesty a thousand times. Even if God and everyone else forgives me a thousand times – I have to live with this hell. The

problem is in my head, my conscience. There is only one way to be free of it. Blow my own brains out. Because that's where my hell is."[24]

Some perpetrators truly become victims, suffering an irreversible moral death. The nature of at least some human beings simply refuses to accommodate evil acts – even when one's society approves them! For me, this is a profoundly hopeful insight into "Who We Are."

These were the extremely devastating emotional responses among some of the perpetrators of violence. Others experienced less pitiable yet still horrendous emotional impacts from their inhumane behavior.

### The perpetrators' stories

Those who wielded physical and psychological power to intimidate or terrorize others experienced a wide range of untoward emotional consequences. In South Africa most of this dirty work was carried out by the "troops," the underlings: noncommissioned military, local police, gangs of youths, hired hands, paid snitches, blackmailed fall guys. Persuaded by money, ideology, or personal loyalty, they carried out acts of unspeakable violence to further the goals of political leaders. And almost all of these women and men suffered in one way or another.

The first line of moral defense for the torturer is the fact that when his victim gives in, the information gained justifies the practice, and, even more insidiously, the victim loses moral standing by capitulating. So if the victim asks, "What kind of man *are* you to inflict such pain on a helpless person?" the successful torturer has only to ask in response, "What kind of man are *you* that you gave in and betrayed your comrades?"[25] The shame of betrayal is stronger than the shame of blatant bullying – something we should not forget as we try to unravel the intricacies of the human heart.

Some torturers, however, seem to suffer from what South African psychologist Ria Kotze calls "a severe form of self-loathing." In particular, she refers to one, Captain Jeffrey Benzien, whom she has been counseling since he had a nervous breakdown in 1994. As Antjie Krog reports it:

> She says Benzien was sitting on his veranda one evening, smoking a cigarette, and then he had a flashback – so intense and real that he burst into tears. His wife called Kotze and told her that when she asked Benzien what was wrong, he kept saying: "I cannot tell you – I'm too ashamed."[26]

Apparently torturers as well as victims can suffer the symptoms of PTSD – just as do both soldiers who kill villagers and survivors of those they murder (see Chapter VI). Again, there seem to be barriers in the human psyche – or at least in those of many human beings – to the commission of blatant evil.

Another psychological casualty is the patriot-perpetrator after his political – and psychological – backing is gone. How does he face the whole of South Africa as he publicly sits before the TRC? How can he compensate? How can he reconnect with humanity in this changed world, when the arguments that once justified his actions are no longer seen as valid? Says Warrant Officer Paul van Vuuren, one of the notorious Vlakplas Five, a group of policemen coopted to murder:

> It is not easy to sit in this chair.... You expose your soul to the nation of South Africa, white and black. And they look at me and they think I am a monster for sure. I can feel it – I can actually say that I see the fear in their eyes as well as the hatred.[27]

For such a person to simply say "I am sorry" to a victim unable to accept mere words is not a solution to the need for forgiveness and a move into the future. Reconciliation is like the "bluebird of happiness" – as you try to grasp it, pin it down, it flies away farther into the distance. When put into the cage, the words, "I am sorry," or the payment of money as restitution merely turn into a black-feathered spirit of emptiness. The hoped-for relief remains elusive. (Perhaps the best "solution" I saw while visiting South Africa was on Robben Island, now a National Park. The Rangers working side-by-side comprised both former prisoners and their former guards, engaged together in a project of national healing.) Healing, however, is often elusive.

Not every perpetrator experienced remorse or depression or self-loathing. The human brain has other routes of escape from the unthinkable, for both victim and perpetrator. One of these is the condition known to psychiatrists as "multiple personality disorder." To me, it is a moot point whether it should be classified as a "disorder" or as a perfectly reasonable neurological adaptation of a human brain that has experienced overwhelming events, and would otherwise be forced to undergo post-traumatic stress symptoms. (Indeed, I think of PTSD less as a "disorder" than as an adaptive response to horrendous threats. As shown in Chapter VI, the brain does its best to respond to a crisis, however bizarre its responses appear to observers outside the crisis situation.) Switching one's personality, then, becomes a way of blocking out unthinkable memories.

In South Africa, one such example was Captain Jacques Hechter, a policeman accused of multiple crimes against other human beings. Explains Krog:

> He has developed two personalities that do not associate with each other and alternate autonomously in the dominant position.... By day Hechter had the personality of a cop, a just man working in an office. By night he became a hangman. In his own words: "a white Afrikaner terrorist."

Strangely enough, the two personas prevent Hechter from suffering any posttraumatic stress symptoms. The moment he becomes uncomfortable and tense in one persona, he switches to the other.[28]

So powerful is this ability to shift that Hechter can totally suppress spontaneous memories of past atrocities, such as the day in 1987 when he electrocuted three people. Asked by Judge Bernard Ngoepe what he remembered, he replied:

> I can ... the electrocution.... I can remember after it was told to me. But it was completely out of my thoughts.... I haven't thought about it for ten years.[29]

Edgar Allan Poe's Dr. Jekyll and Mr. Hyde were not unrealistic personas at all.

Other perpetrators found other means of protecting themselves from the psychic self-destruction that admission of such terrible acts exposed them to. Some Afrikaners never lost the identity bestowed on them by their cultural narrative. They remain totally patriotic (to the Afrikaans language and culture): father-worshipping, God-fearing, a superior race of hunters.[30] Such a self-view is reminiscent of the Nazis in Hitler's Germany and of today's militant white hate groups in Europe and North America. It is, I believe, the self-justifying view of the bully, one who in fact is highly insecure in the legitimacy of his or her own identity.

Some perpetrators, such as Joe Mamasela, a black infiltrator of the ANC who became a cold-blooded murderer, used humor to laugh off fear and remorse. He protected himself from white hatred by making fun of his kaffer (black African) qualities; he and his fellow turncoats joked about who would be the next one of them to be murdered by their own side. By debasing their own dignity with a kind of sick humor, they protected their own sanity.[31]

Others found strength in bolstering their insecure sense of power by bullying those least able to fight back or to even make them feel ashamed; they dehumanized women. Explained the chairperson of the Gender Commission, Thenjiwe Mthintso, addressing the TRC at its special women's hearings:

> Because always, always in anger and frustration men use women's bodies as a terrain of struggle, as a battle ground.[32]

Female captives were treated as whores, unworthy of respect or human treatment. This could be as true for black males as whites. Women were raped and tortured. If they did not succumb to torture, unlike male victims who earned respect for their bravery, women were recipients of increased anger and abuse. Among Afrikaners, in particular, "a black *meid*, a *kaffermeid* at that, had no right to have the strength to withstand them."[33] How close to mental collapse

is the bully who cannot even morally overpower the least of all two-legged creatures? His identity, his whole sense of being, is on the edge of a fatal mental
precipice.

In a violent society, the workaday perpetrators, the insecure humans seeking
praise from someone "important," are as much throwaway persons as are their
victims.

### *The leaders' stories*

So far I have considered the ordinary people, mostly nameless in the everyday
world: the victims of violence and the hatchet men (and occasionally women)
who committed that violence. But in modern societies everywhere (with the
minor exceptions of recluse cultures in the Amazon or enclaves such as the
American Amish) there are leaders who, for better or for worse, capture the
loyalty of a large number of followers. They may be inspirational prophets (a
Gandhi or a Dalai Lama); ideologically inspired orators (an Ayatollah Khomeini
or a Chairman Mao); or smooth-tongued, self-inflated orators. Among the
latter, Hitler has no peers, but Julius Caesar, Winston Churchill and Ronald
Reagan come a close second. All too many, however, are third rate as persons,
and they are everywhere. Modern democracies have had their fair share.
Ordinary people can neither ignore nor wholeheartedly support them, except in
times of deep social uncertainty. Then, flamboyant, charismatic, idealistic
leaders appeal, whatever their message. They simplify; they offer easy solutions,
something that people can act upon. This, I believe, is what happened in the
self-created crisis of South Africa in the second half of the twentieth century.

Once a leader appears with a simplified, usually one-sided "solution" to a
society's problems, it is but a short step for that society to divide into increasingly bellicose camps with opposing leaders whose own simplified "solutions"
are incompatible. Community dialogue evaporates and factional competition
fragments relationships beyond hope of peaceful repair.

The greatest problem factional political leaders create for themselves is the
easy "identity" they offer constituents. "Buy me, and I'll shore up your belief in
yourself. I'll give you the psychological security you've been aching for." The
leader guarantees a new self-respect. The actions of various South African
leaders confirm this diagnosis. All sides, Afrikaner, Zulu, and ANC, shared guilt
in using confrontational political rhetoric. It was the sort citizens in Western
democracies regularly hear before every election (which is creating increasing
cynicism), only in South Africa the words carried inflamed violence in their
wake. During the period of peacemaking, the following are some of the accusa-
tions against the Truth and Reconciliation process made by leaders who were
afraid it might cause them to lose their own supporters.

The Zulu Chief, Mangosuthei Buthelezi, refused a public hearing before the
TRC, comparing it "to the McCarthy Commission [in the United States in the
1950s] and the Spanish Inquisition."[34]

ANC leaders defended their killing of "suspect" blacks, but denied any responsibility for the "necklacing" of supposed black traitors, and denied terrorist bombings of Afrikaners and death squads used against their black archrivals in KwaZulu-Natal.[35]

The Afrikaner leader, F.W. De Klerk, admits state emergency abuses but denies personal responsibility, blaming lower-ranking officers who lied to him or were "bad apple" soldiers.[36]

The male leaders of all three of the above factions profoundly disappointed the TRC's Chairperson, Archbishop Tutu. While all of them agreed bad things had happened on all sides, none expressed personal remorse for the pain inflicted. In his disappointment, Tutu underscored the ultimate interrelatedness of *all* human beings:

> You see, we can't go to heaven alone. If I arrive there, God will ask me: "Where is De Klerk? His path crossed yours." And he also – God will ask him: "Where is Tutu?" So I cried for De Klerk – because he spurned the opportunity to become human.[37]

(The second half of this chapter addresses the truth of the Archbishop's words – whatever religious view one may take, reconciliation ultimately requires both total admission of past horrors and absolute forgiveness.)

Then the commission came to Winnie Madikizela-Mandela, former wife of Nelson Mandela and the idolized leader of the poor, the nameless people in the squalid homelands. She had kept up their hopes during her husband's long imprisonment. Yet she, too, was directly responsible for atrocities committed by those close to her. Her hearings in front of the TRC went as follows:

MADIKIZELA-MANDELA: denies all allegations of human rights abuses, saying they are "ludicrous" and "ridiculous." All the "victims" have lied. She claims she and her aides were fighting a just war.

TUTU: pleads with her. Acknowledges her great role, the love she has earned from the common people. But that the country – all its people – need for her to admit things went wrong, and that she is sorry. "I beg you, please.... You are a great person. And you don't know how your greatness would be enhanced if you were to say, 'I'm sorry ... things went wrong. Forgive me,' ... I beg you."

MADIKIZELA-MANDELA: (after a pause) "I am saying it is true: things went horribly wrong and we were aware that there were factors that led to that. For that I am deeply sorry."[38]

Is it "real"? Does she *mean* it? No one can ever know. But the world heard her say those words publicly, and no matter what happens, they cannot be unsaid. Denied, retracted, dismissed, yes, but never unsaid. *They were said and heard before the whole nation.*

The question arises: Can a political leader who still has followers who need to continue believing in their collective cause, admit to wrongdoing? Doesn't such an admission, asks Krog, dishonor the collective cause? "She [Winnie] personifies their aspirations and their right to status.... If she admits to wrongdoing, she dishonors them all."[39] But surely the oppressed as well as the oppressor have to seek forgiveness for their collective sins. In a culture of violence, no one is lily-white. And, as Tutu argues, even a simple public admission of "being sorry" by a leader is an amazing, wonderful thing.[40]

### The "innocent" beneficiaries' stories

In a great many violent societies, the actual violence is carried out by a tiny fraction of the people, while those who benefit from their acts can hide behind the cloak of ignorance: "We just didn't know ..." about all those horrible things that made their lives comfortable and safe. It was, says Krog (as a sensitive Afrikaner beneficiary of the evils of apartheid), all too easy to claim innocence.

This latent guilt felt by passive beneficiaries of social violence can be a major part of the process of truth-telling and reconciliation. (A similar question plagued Europeans following the fall of the Nazi regime and the revelation of its atrocities. Why did some people risk their lives to protect Jewish neighbors and others turn their backs? It also took nearly half a century after World War II for the Danes and Norwegians to absolve the "betrayal" of the Swedes who, by declaring their neutrality, had avoided occupation by Hitler's troops.[41]) The guilt felt by those in South Africa who benefited from but did not commit any of the atrocities ranges from none to profound. Once the horrors of the past are exposed to view, most human beings actually *do* feel a sense of responsibility; for some, this guilt is strong enough to demand positive action. Among South African black youths who had "neglected to do anything" in the human rights struggle while their activist friends were jailed or killed, some were so overcome with guilt and remorse that they applied to the TRC for amnesty: "[H]ere we stand as a small group representative of millions of apathetic people who didn't do the right thing."[42] Almost no whites did this.

### A summing-up

The TRC labored nearly three years, from December 1995 until its final report in late 1998, to set the stage for moving South Africa and her people from the violent past into a peaceful future. It accomplished an enormously important task: it revealed a large part of the Truth of the past in all its horrible detail. It offered amnesty – relief from retributive punishment – to those who admitted responsibility for their role in that past and made at least some gesture of contrition. It offered a different form of relief to some of the victims of unspeakable violence – just having their stories known, their suffering acknowledged. It was an amazing first step down the long road of healing.

Did the hearings produce "reconciliation"? Did they achieve nationwide "forgiveness"? No. Perhaps a better name for the process would have been the Truth and Amnesty Commission. At least, unlike in Chile where the brutal dictator, General Augusto Pinochet, awarded himself and all his henchmen amnesty for life before stepping down from power, the South African process of granting amnesty was overseen by a cross-section of highly respected citizens from all groups in society and diverse fields of knowledge and wisdom.[43] Nor was amnesty granted to everyone who applied.

Could the TRC have done more? Probably not. Should Mandela's new government have chosen instead a more aggressive approach to past violence, such as the Nuremberg trials held after World War II? It would have meant tracking down, trying and punishing all suspected human rights violators. While the fact that the International Court of Justice in The Hague may soon be given powers to track down and try violent leaders who oppress their own people may well deter future tyrants, for the new government in South Africa to carry out such justice on its own was out of the question. As Desmond Tutu points out in his recent book on the subject, the costs to the already financially weak nation were prohibitive. There were (and still are) more important things to do with the nation's resources.[44]

But there were other, even more powerful considerations. First, there is no evidence that retributive justice helps victims to heal. There is perhaps a temporary sense of satisfaction at "getting even," but the anger and hatred do not end with the executioner's ax or administration of the lethal drug, as the case may be. Even more critical is the fact that it is simply not possible to unscramble the demographic omelet that is South Africa. Since groups on all sides were guilty of inhumanities, the only way of living together after retributive justice, with all its bitterness, was carried out, would be to separate the various factions. But the Afrikaners' past attempts to do this – to separate blacks from whites by forcibly uprooting the former from their tribal lands and consigning them to the Bantustans – was in Tutu's words "a heartless piece of social engineering" that failed horribly and completely.[45] For better or worse, the peoples living in South Africa have to discover how they can create a peaceful life *together*.

## From control to reconciliation

Once violence stops, when one or other side has "won" or a cease-fire agreement has been negotiated, all too often societies newly "at peace" fall back on past institutions of governing, of keeping order; they return to the same social patterns that failed them before. And when unrest starts, they resort to coercive controls, exercised by whoever is newly empowered, to re-establish social order without regard for the *healing processes* needed to make the new conditions of order an inclusive process. It should be clear by now that laws, such as the United States' civil rights laws, and edicts, such as those of Marshall Tito in the former Yugoslavia, do not change how people *feel* toward each other; they only change how they *behave* toward one another by suppressing violence through the threat of physical force. As history repeatedly shows, sooner or later such a threat fails to work.

### Why coercive power never heals

Let's take a moment to consider again the kinds of assumptions that Western societies (and especially the United States) make about human nature. All human societies cohere by a system of laws that must be enforced if they are to be obeyed. (In general people agree to this because representative democracy gives them a small sense of control over the rules.) The implicit assumption in law-based societies, however, is that people are essentially immoral, and need to be made to fear brute power if they are to live in a society. Or as a political scientist friend used to put it: we humans need the club of the caveman to keep us in line. The only fundamental human need being recognized here is the drive for autonomy. The innate compassion that our need for bonding engenders has been seriously discounted.

The social narrative reflects this: morality or goodness or right behavior requires fear as its motivator. No better expression of this exists than in the plethora of American television shows devoted to confrontations between "bad guys" and the "enforcers of law and order." From rustlers in the Wild West, to serial killers or spies. Whether on horseback, in high-speed freeway chases, or in vitriolic battles in a well-policed courtroom, the same cultural message is reiterated – power is needed to maintain social harmony. This is central to the Western meaning system, and so people tend to defend it, not noticing how it creates an essentially authoritarian society. In fact, a frequent consequence of a strictly enforced "rule of law" where punishment is the "solution" to antisocial behavior is a rise in internal violence. It is no accident that the United States has the highest incarceration rate in the world and was recently voted out of its seat on the UN Commission for Human Rights, or that its "enforcers" have been guilty of tragic blunders against its own citizens in their single-minded zeal to impose "order."[46]

Whenever two or more groups with different identities have been in serious conflict anywhere in the world, if the more powerful uses this same authoritarian logic to impose its own world view on the other, peace will remain elusive. From the point of view of both sides, the other constitutes the "bad guys" in need of control. Whenever the more powerful attempt coercion, it almost always fails, often after terrible bloodshed. The only solution is for all parties to mutually work toward revising their assumptions about each other, recognizing their common humanity, and so to recognize the possibility of a universally shared morality that comes out of our human need to belong and the powerful capacity for compassion which that need engenders. Long-lasting peace demands mutual revision and the reconstruction of social narratives by all parties: the process of lasting reconciliation. But I jump ahead.

The dangers of failing to create long-lasting peace are too horrible to contemplate in a world of increasingly murderous technologies. When victims, finally given recognition for their suffering, fail to forgive but continue to feel resentment, they risk becoming the next bully. If they never feel their suffering has been fully noted, or prior oppressive conditions linger on, their unresolved anger may be passed on for generations. The same is true for perpetrators and their descendants, who still feel themselves treated as pariahs because they have either not acknowledged their guilt, or worse, never received forgiveness afterward, even after correcting for previously unjust institutions. Sometimes it takes what seems but a small "cause" to inflame long-suppressed resentments.

Examples exist today that go back at least several generations. Serbs were ruled by the Turks for five centuries and subjected to slaughter by Croats and Muslims during World War II. Though during Tito's regime they were beneficiaries, receiving wealth from Croatia, when the latter declared independence, the Serbs attacked. They lost that confrontation, and 200,000 Serbs living in Croatia either fled or were killed. Not long after, in Bosnia, their retaliation against Muslims who had helped the Croats was brutal, as was their subsequent attack on disaffected Albanians in Kosovo. The punitive bombing of Belgrade by United States-led NATO forces can have done nothing to erase the Serbs' own sense of persecution, even though it caused them to reject the man who had been leading them.

Likewise, in Rwanda the world holds the Hutu people responsible for the 1994 bloodbath, but its cause has a long history. The recent analysis by Mahmood Mamdani shows that far from being either an ethnic or racial conflict, the Tutsi/Hutu enmity is essentially political. Though the two groups may have had separate origins, they have lived together and intermarried for 500 years and speak the same language. Their political identities, however, became distinct when the state of Rwanda began emerging in the 1500s through formalized fusion of "Hutu supernatural powers with Tutsi military powers."

Social polarization, however, began only in the late 1700s as the nation's conquests increased political centralization of growing military power. A hundred years later, the former reciprocity up and down the social hierarchy was now flowing mainly upward to the Tutsi military, yet even so, that power was partially shared with Hutu subchiefs. It was the distant Belgian colonial rulers, with help from the Catholic Church, who would finally turn these political distinctions into racially rigid castes by employing the "superior" Tutsi minority to enforce extremely harsh, exploitative rules against the Hutu majority. These included co-option of both their crops and their unpaid labor. In 1959, the overly stressed Hutus overthrew the Belgian-controlled Tutsi monarch and rioting crowds killed 20,000 Tutsis while 150,000 more fled abroad. Independence in 1962 left the Hutu majority in power. There was relative calm, at least on the surface, though propaganda against Tutsis persisted.

But the new nation's wealth declined when global prices for its exports fell. By then, the better educated Tutsis held all the best jobs, causing resentment. In 1990, and again in 1992, a Tutsi army, the Rwandan Patriotic Front, which had built up in neighboring Uganda, went on the offensive. A "peace" agreement signed in 1993 lasted less than a year, when the Tutsis attacked again. In 1994, the dam of pent-up Hutu resentment burst and unbelievable violence erupted. Some 800,000 Tutsis were killed, at least half their population. The Hutus also killed 50,000 of their own as well, whom they believed were Tutsi sympathizers. Eventually, the Tutsi army brought the killings to an end and over 1.8 million Hutu refugees fled across the border into Congo. Some continue to attack Tutsis, and vice versa.[47]

In these two cases – Yugoslavia and Rwanda – of long-smoldering, *unhealed conflict*, relatively small stresses set off incredible levels of violence against an entire population, not just another army. Ultimately, both sides felt like victims. The world also turned the Palestinians into victims when, after World War II, it created Israel as a Jewish homeland. When Israel's Muslim neighbors, Egypt and Syria, refused to acknowledge the new state, the Palestinians found themselves targets of further Israeli incursions on the lands left to them; they became the victims of other former victims, the survivors of the Holocaust. In Germany, even today, there never has been an attempt to address publicly the past traumas of being perpetrators of that Holocaust and victims themselves of a traumatic war experience. The silence of the postwar years has given rise to "Naziskins" – a growing number of racist adolescent extremists.[48] In South Africa also, there are victims of the past in every ethnic community, and perpetrators as well. In history, every society has been both a "good guy" and a "bad guy." Each retains, often for many generations, its own selected memories of past events.

In these examples (only a few of dozens more around the world) the potential for future violence still exists because of the failure to heal past wounds and deal with present inequities. In fact, the cultural narratives of peoples, from tribes to nation-states, tend to recount the injustices done them in the past and how *their* heroic ancestors overcame them. "Never forget who you are and where you came from," children everywhere are taught. The memory of past wrongs can be kept alive, even for millennia. Jews annually recall their slavery in Egypt; and some Christians even today blame Jews for killing Jesus. The identity of a group, that which helps it cohere – indeed is necessary for that coherence – depends on a shared story. Nor can we expect it ever to be otherwise; human beings, as I have tried to show, have brains that require such shared meaningful stories.

So how is a community of people that is trying to heal after experiencing violence among its own groups ever to move beyond their individual histories and begin to form a new sense of shared identity? How does, say, twenty-first-century South Africa begin to heal itself? How does it begin to create a *new, common* history that belongs to all those long-standing groups? How does a society move beyond order established by coercive force, to order based on

genuinely shared identity and meaning? The answer has to be true reconciliation – far beyond "peace" treaties or even a new national constitution, with its
imposed laws. First, there must be a holistic sense of justice.

### Perceptions of justice

There are two distinct approaches to "justice" that differ in their underlying
beliefs about human nature and how particular networks of relationships should
be maintained. One, a law-based, contractual view of society as an assembly of
individuals, sees justice as adversarial, and punishment of lawbreakers as the
corrective. Courtroom procedures are confrontational: "the people" *versus* the
accused. Those found guilty must pay a "debt to society," not to the victim *per
se*. It is *retributive* in nature, a form of group vengeance against miscreants who
must be made to suffer, to "pay back" for the wrongs they have committed. It
fits rather well within the Billiard Ball Gestalt of a self-centered, individualistic
human nature and the necessity for an authoritarian social order.

The other approach to justice is restorative in its goals, viewing the process as
a means of healing broken community relationships and bringing back
harmony. It tends toward an egalitarian and communal idealism, more in tune
with the Indra's Net Gestalt, with restitution and forgiveness as processes for
mending the past (repairing the net) (see Figure X.2).

As Hugo van der Merwe, whom I knew as a former student from South
Africa, points out, in no cultural subgroup, and certainly not among those in
multicultural, post-*apartheid* South Africa, is one or the other of these views of
justice held uniformly by all members of a group, nor consistently across all
contexts. Some acts really must be punished, while others definitely cry out for
forgiveness. As I have already suggested, black African cultures tend toward the
latter, Western cultures toward the former. Yet many black and colored victims
resent the extent of amnesty awarded by the TRC, and that resentment is
growing as the years go by and the restorative processes seem bogged down in a
quagmire of insoluble problems.[49] This situation is by no means unique to
South Africa. Similar problems that militate against justice and permanent peace
arise in every contemporary society struggling to heal after recent violent
turmoil. Achieving widespread reconciliation in these places will be a slow
process and require substantive support from the global community.

Let me explain. Those most able to give substantive help – matériel, loans,
investments – are the Westernized industrial nations and the international financial system which have yet to acknowledge that global peace does not come out
of economic growth but *just the opposite*. Peace, real peace, and the beginnings
of real economic justice *must come first*; only then is overall economic improvement possible.[50] The West's collective habit of seeking global justice through
trying and punishing former state leaders for war crimes leaves untouched the
causes of the prior violence. As I tried to show in Chapter IX, leaders such as

# Routes to Peace

## End of Hostilities

Coercion and
Retributive Justice   **or**   Reconciliation and
Restorative Justice

suppresses
violence

appropriate for
very particular
acts only

never achieves
true healing

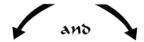

**and**

need for
physical
well-being
(health,
economic
security)

need for
psychological
well-being
(trust, moral
healing)

*Figure X.2* Routes to peace: coercion or reconciliation?
Once hostilities have ceased, how will a new social order be established? The above figure summarizes arguments outlined in the text that contrast the effectiveness of *coercion* – force and the threat of punishment – with *reconciliation* – through healing of past traumas – to both physical and mental security. It is argued that without a major effort toward restorative justice, true peace will remain elusive, since retributive justice itself is simply one more form of violence.

*Source:* Author's idea rendered by Michele Lukowski

Hitler do not *create* violent societies; unresolved past and current events do, in which such leaders, too, are caught-up. In such cases, retributive justice falls far short of the healing needed to break a cycle of ongoing violence. Without both *restoring the physical well-being* of people who are still suffering and *creating a social atmosphere where the ability to trust other groups becomes fully possible,* economic growth remains out of reach, society becomes increasingly unstable, and a coercive form of policing soon returns.

362

These two basic components of restorative justice – restoring physical well-being and the ability to trust – are complementary aspects of reconciliation and social healing. Both are far from adequate in South Africa. Restoring physical well-being requires some top-down assistance to beleaguered communities from the government. Forty percent of people have no jobs; housing is extremely inadequate for the great majority; and there is little health care. Children who become prostitutes to earn money for supper are being infected by HIV, the virus that now affects some 20 percent of the population in southern Africa, either as patients or care-takers of patients. The number of orphans is growing.[51]

During a recent visit I heard the same message over and over again. Opening up the economy to globalization has virtually stopped government support for all social welfare projects: building affordable housing, creating jobs, hiring health care workers and school teachers. Everywhere there is growing hardship and unemployment – and restlessness, as the glow of the political victory wears off. Our group was told that Mandela had forbidden his new government to challenge the neoliberal economic policies of the World Bank and IMF, thus ruling out deficit funding, as used by Roosevelt to restore the American economy after the Great Depression.[52] Whatever is being done in the social sphere is primarily done by local volunteers or members of foreign NGOs, many from Holland and Sweden. The dedication of these ordinary men and women, of thousands of youths, of school teachers everywhere, who are trying to fill the yawning needs of their country, is unbelievably inspiring. Despite the huge odds, their hopes are high. Yet it was clear to me that many whom I met were on the edge of exhaustion.

Thus, while untold numbers of ordinary South Africans of all races are working among the communities of former victims, valiantly struggling to overcome the physical barriers to their recovery, they really need a level of material resources beyond their grasp. There is growing resentment about the government's unresponsiveness, and it was all too evident to us visitors that the white private sector which controls most of the nation's wealth was refusing to make loans to the government for housing projects or to invest in the poverty-stricken communities. One such couple I visited were planning to send their son to the United States for college, and eventually to relocate there themselves. It was all too reminiscent of the "white flight" from American inner cities after the civil rights laws were passed and housing desegregation began, only on a much starker scale.

Meantime, the levels of violence within the black and colored communities have scarcely subsided. A great many youths who grew up as resistance fighters possess no job skills (even if jobs were available), and do not see themselves going back to school like children. Instead, they find a kind of meaning in forming street gangs, modeled after those in the United States that they have seen on TV, and steal valuable goods to make a living. These are their "default communities." Some volunteer workers are listening to them, to how they feel and why they are violent (about which they seem to have great insight), in an effort to help them rehabilitate. On the other hand, police forces, being composed largely of the same (both white and black) abusive, social-control-minded personnel from the *apartheid* era, treat them brutally, as hardened criminals. There has been no time nor funds to train police replacements, and keeping the old force on for several years was also part of the "deal" between Mandela and the former leaders.[53]

Given all these circumstances, the second component of restorative justice, the task of building trust in the new South Africa, becomes even more difficult. Even if the government, in its top-down role of re-allocating resources for righting physical injustices, were to institute that process, it could play only a much smaller, even negligible role in re-establishing social trust. As Hugo van der Merwe makes clear in his analysis of South Africa's situation, government actions in this sphere are mainly symbolic: courts, public hearings, imprisoning or reprimanding perpetrators of abuse, sending checks as reparations to former victims, erecting monuments to martyrs. None of these impersonal things changes how individual people feel toward each other. You may enforce a kind of tolerance, but you cannot legislate respect, much less compassion or love. Violence, van der Merwe reminds us, is something real people do to other real people, *face to face* – and so is trust!

Thus, only face to face, in some sort of human interaction, can trust in former perpetrators be restored. Trust is not created by signing a contract or even making sworn pledges. It is earned through a sequence of personal acts: of apology, remorse, and restitution, on the one side, and by positive forgiveness on the other.[54] Flashing briefly back to our primate cousins, recall Frans de Waal's comments about reconciliation (see Chapter II). When a fight has been healed, the former combatants groom one another *more* than they groom others. Primates have to work at "making up," and that holds true for human beings, too.[55] Interpersonal contacts are needed to heal the traumatized brains and restore trust. It is during this period of personal reconciliation that moral rehabilitation occurs, and both victim and perpetrator feel relief from their respective psychic pains.

## The road to peace

How is peace, real, lasting peace, to be brought about? How do societies such as Rwanda or South Africa ever work through the horrors of their past and heal themselves? How does *ubuntu* or *ahimsa* come into actual being? How do perpetrators find the courage to apologize and regain moral standing and an untainted identity? How do victims get past their anger and resentment to give the gift of forgiveness? How do mutual respect and compassion come about? If my thesis (which is shared by many others[56]) is correct, the goal of a society truly at peace will be reached when all involved have understood that fulfillment of our three basic human needs – for belonging, for autonomy and for purposeful meaning – must be *universally experienced*.

Where does such understanding come from? It cannot be taught out of books; it cannot be imposed by edict; it must be discovered by people themselves. Said President Eisenhower:

> I like to believe that people, in the long run, are going to do more to promote peace than our governments. Indeed, I think that people want peace so much that one of these days governments had better get out of their way and let them have it.[57]

Four decades later, former United States diplomat and long-time peacemaker, Harold Saunders, couldn't agree more with these prophetic words. Power-based diplomacy, the tool of the past, has not brought us permanent peace nor a less violent world. In his latest book *A Public Peace Process*, he states that even voting in a democratic government is not enough. For democracy to work, more than the election of representatives to "look after my interests" is necessary. "[A] working democracy depends on an active citizenry."[58] Both peacemaking and social change have identical requirements. People, *all* the people, must be active participants, talking and listening. *This is the process by which human beings revise and adapt their shared world views.*

This is also how we make peace: there is no other way. Diplomacy and negotiations "at the top" may succeed in ending bloodshed, but they cannot build peaceful societies; they cannot heal; they cannot restore trust; and they cannot create the needed new bridge between past histories of violence and future common purposes of former enemies. They cannot help individual people from all sides discover how to think a little differently about the world around them, to adjust their world views. That takes face-to-face dialogue between people, from all groups and at all levels.

### Rediscovering the biological necessity for dialogue

Once, at a conference of futurists, one of our group, a Navajo who also happened to be a physicist at the Los Alamos Laboratories, was asked how his tribe solved its problems. Well, he told us, we talk, all of us together, men, women, kids, everybody. How long does it take, we asked? As long as it takes; up to nine days, I've experienced. How long each day? Oh, we don't stop. You mean you go nonstop, for nine days and nights? Yes. The children snooze; people leave briefly to prepare food or relieve themselves; but the talking continues until everyone has had her or his say, in full, and the whole group is now thinking with "one mind" (see Chapter VII, pp. 251–2).

The Western mouths of the rest of us gaped open. We certainly believed in participatory democracy, but this – why it was beyond belief.[59] On later reflection, I realized we impatient, hyper-efficient Westerners were the ones who were "out-of-step." For us, talking and listening took up too much of our valuable time. Little did I – or the others – realize at that moment, that it was us, our "advanced culture," which was at odds with human nature. We have tried to short-cut the most central needs of our beings and, in the process, lost our ability to communicate deeply with each other. Western culture, and its system of confrontational politics, is an invitation to misunderstanding and conflict, creating a kind of shared psychic instability that requires legal systems, police, and other threats by the State to contain.

Before the advent of megamachine societies with their hierarchical structures and powerful centralized governments, cultures routinely depended upon local community dialogue, not only to resolve conflicts among members, but to make decisions affecting the whole group. For tens of thousands of years, that is how our ancestors adapted their communities to new circumstances; that's how they "evolved," perhaps aided in their dialogue by the visions of a youth or the wise words of a shaman or elder. Those are the benefits of collective decision-making; a wide variety of ideas are contemplated.

Even now, at the beginning of the twenty-first century, local dialogue within traditional communities is the way that people still make their political and economic decisions and settle their conflicts. These are still the habitual practices of villagers in India, throughout most of Africa, and among Native American tribes. Despite, for most of them, the "overlay" of a centralized representative democracy imposed on these excolonial nations, where communication occurs mainly unidirectionally via mass media, these peoples resist its absolute control.[60]

In fact, in terms of human nature, "democracy" as practiced in the West means a *loss* of personal political control over our individual lives, when compared to these ancient traditional practices. It cannot hurt to repeat again that big, centralized societies are, essentially, anti-human, denying true autonomy to ordinary people. To Westerners, reversing this centralization seems unthinkable because they see only totalitarianism filling the supposed political void of an absence of central power. For local peoples to choose their own rules and settle their own conflicts – at least until recently – has seemed impossible, chaotic, an invitation to disorder. What I believe the West has forgotten is how to talk and listen, to dialogue.

Recently, a diverse group of Western peacemakers, ex-diplomats, social psychologists, conflict resolvers, and anthropologists have *rediscovered* the necessity of face-to-face dialogue, which tribal peoples long understood intuitively, as part of their culture. Using the jargon of their various disciplines, they have managed to show "scientifically" the need for the process of dialogue to effect deep social change. Western "free speech" where anyone may mount a soap-box or rent air-time and speak his or her mind to whatever public will bother to listen is a poor substitute for community "listening" and face-to-face exchange of feelings and the opening up of our inner selves to each other. Indeed, cynicism about "free speech" in an age of costly media is growing; to be meaningfully heard, a citizen must be wealthy – which means speech is not at all "free." What is heard on American airwaves are ideas that those with money wish the rest of society to hear. There is little dialogue, or discourse. Even when "balanced" talk shows offer equal time to "both sides" they usually choose contending elites, often labeled "experts," and seldom present discussants who frame the issue at hand in a quite different way altogether. Confrontational shouting is not even debate, much less dialogue. It is certainly *not* a model for resolving conflict or for public deliberations.

There is simply no substitute for face-to-face dialogue in groups to resolve human conflict and adapt cultural beliefs to changing circumstances. This is what a growing number of peacemakers and others convergently have agreed upon. Dialogue must occur at *many levels* between participants; they must meet *in small groups* who get to know each other, and continue meeting over a *long period of time*.

### The need for "intervenors"

When most people see the word "intervene" in relation to conflicts, they tend to think of neutral peacekeeping forces sent in to stop the fighting or maintain a cease-fire. Or they may think of outside negotiators such as former Senator George Mitchell, trying to broker a peace treaty between leaders of long-term enemies in, say, northern Ireland or the Middle East. Such negotiators, however, often shuttle back and forth between the parties, searching for terms of agreement. A third sort of intervenor is a mediator, whose task has more to do with solving the conflict and bringing healing after the violence has ceased (or in some cases preventing the violence from erupting in the first place). The role of this kind of neutral intervenor is more like that of a marriage counselor rather than a policeman (peacekeeper) or a go-between neighbor (negotiator). They teach people how to talk to each other, how to restore respect and trust.

A mediator's task is to facilitate the learning of the steps that lead to reconciliation, to rebuilding the community or the nation; to help parties discover the process to follow, but not to tell them where to go. Mediators teach skills; they do not manufacture outcomes. They help people learn *how* to dialogue, to hear each other's stories in full, to listen without interruption, and to acknowledge their anger, their hurt, the *reality of their experience*. In short, they help people rediscover compassion for each other.

Once such a stage is reached, the mediator begins to tackle the problems that remain between them, offering possible solutions that might meet the needs of both parties. The purpose is to start a period of brainstorming. If the people who are in dialogue are representing a larger constituency, they will need to test these possibilities with their own "side." So there will likely be many meetings, extending over many months, even years, until mutually acceptable "solutions" are found.

In most cases, that is where the process ends. Yet too often, once an agreement has been reached, the parties still lack the skills for implementing it, of turning their words into actions. In the past decade, some mediators have begun to expand the scope of their task, bringing a far broader spectrum of the diverse interest groups within each party into the dialogue. In large, complex societies the dialogue needs to occur across as many levels of the community as possible, so *all* feel they are owners of the overall process. Widely known as "track-two diplomacy" ("track-one" being the formal diplomacy between governments), it has been given various names by peace-making practitioners: interactive problem-solving workshops, psychopolitical workshops, multi-track diplomacy, interactive conflict resolution, post-conflict peace-building, and a public peace process.[61] Though their emphasis varies (based as each is on real-world experiences) the basic principles are similar.

In addition to expanding the spectrum of groups on each side that are involved in the dialogues, peace practitioners also help their clients (if that is the right word) begin to implement the goals they have agreed upon, to make real the solutions reached on paper. It is part of a permanent institution-building process: helping people discover how to solve the practical, physical, economic and other barriers to implementing their "solution." How do you start a community center? Or build a common school? Or institute a farmers' cooperative? The mediators facilitate the experience of accomplishing something together, as a new "group."

### Steps toward reconciliation

The processes used in facilitating reconciliation vary somewhat according to the particular context, but the stages are similar: first, to address the past as seen by each side; second, to identify common goals for the future; third, to develop concrete projects to meet these goals and begin together to implement them. These have been well elaborated by Vamik Volkan, Director of the Center for the Study of Mind and Human Interaction in Virginia, and I employ his descriptive terms.[62]

The intervenor's first task is to assemble several representative groups of citizens from both sides – citizens from different walks of life: academics, teachers, business persons, mayors or other civil officers, health workers, labor leaders, and so forth, according to the nature of the societies involved. In small groups, the two sides begin meeting for several days at a time, preferably in a neutral place. During this time, they live together, eat together and, most importantly, *talk and listen together*. Repeats of these meetings are held two or three times a year for several years.[63]

*Step 1: Addressing the history*   At the start, these people, though well-meaning volunteers anxious to bring about reconciliation, carry with them a cross-section of the recent violent histories experienced by both sides. The intervenors begin with an airing of past histories as each side describes them. In a way, each is exploring its own identity as well as learning about the other's. Volkan calls these histories the chosen traumas and chosen glories of each

368

side.[64] These comprise the shared remembered past. "Chosen glories" are the stories of past victories and triumphs that are celebrated in songs, plays, novels, and holidays. (In the United States, for example, the War of Independence, the "Founding Fathers," and the "winning of the West" by brave pioneers, and today the claim to lead the world in knowledge, technology, and military might, as well as to be champion of human rights and political wisdom, are some shared national glories.) "Chosen traumas" are the humiliations a people has suffered: defeats, shameful acts, oppression, invasion, betrayals, injustices – all that is painful to recall. (In the American South, humiliation at losing the Civil War, and later at having civil rights laws imposed by the Federal government, still smolders. Shameful acts, such as slavery, the genocide of indigenous peoples, the bombings of civilians in World War II, the napalming and defoliation in Vietnam, are either suppressed or else justified as "necessary" or "inevitable." Other countries and peoples, with their much longer collective histories, have far lengthier lists of both glories and traumas to recite.) In times of stress, both "glories" and "traumas" tend to be exaggerated in the telling.

The intervenors' goal is to uncover and diagnose these perceived highlights on both sides. Sometimes visits to "hot spots" are helpful to bring feelings to the surface: sites of massacres, national cemeteries, memorials to victims. The visions and fears of each group are brought into view – both the obvious pragmatic issues, such as jobs and health care and education, along with the hidden "identity" issues: the collective "meaning" of each group.

During the sessions, facilitators encourage participants from both sides to tell their own personal histories. Naturally, each reflects something of the collective identity of his or her group and its image of the other side. Yet it is the personalized perspective that humanizes the telling and invites empathy in ways that reciting the national history cannot. Says Volkan:

> When participants speak about themselves, facilitators help show how these personal stories reflect the history of the individual's large group and help illuminate members' emotional investment in events and mental representations. When large-group history is thus taken to a personal level, it can be much more intimately shared, which in turn helps loosen the rigidified positions of each party. Work in these small groups enables opposing parties to find a new way of looking at the problems, which they eventually acknowledge as shared.[65]

As one might predict, this process is likely to lead to self-justifying exaggerations on both sides, followed by many emotional outbursts: sometimes of grief, sometimes anger, sometimes extreme guilt and shame. Typically, traditional adjudicators working with disputing parties have instinctively tried to suppress such outbursts, regarding them as detrimental to peacemaking. On the contrary, they can be *essential* to it. In conversation once with John Burton, the father of modern conflict resolution, he told me he had always found such outbursts necessary to the reconciliation process, a prelude to building up trust. He expressed past frustration with well-meaning colleagues who did not understand this.[66] Trust is based on feelings, not on rational calculation, which in fact invites mistrust (this is why game theory is of no use in peacemaking). This is the first lesson of reconciliation. Addressing the emotional residue also enables insights into how to change one's own identity and to modify it, opening the door to social change.

*Step 2: Brainstorming shared new goals* Once trust begins to be established, the group dialogue begins to explore future needs identified as important to both sides. They may address allocation of political power, or rebuilding damaged facilities, or the need for cross-cultural education, or strengthening local economies. Though vague at first, once the group members have returned to their home communities and talked to others, new ideas and new responses emerge. This helps prepare the communities for change, for being less rigid, and to feel they too are participating. Hidden aspects of the relationship may come to the surface also, where they can be dealt with.

*Step 3: Establishing concrete projects* Once the "psychological poisons" as Volkan calls them are removed, dialogue groups can settle on positive projects and begin to identify "Contact Groups" in the locales where these projects will take place. The Contact Groups – usually with the assistance of the facilitators – start making detailed plans for the project, seeking funds, involving any appropriate authorities, and ultimately carrying them out.[67]

Once this stage is reached (which may take several years and tends to proceed in fits and starts, not at all like some orderly corporate process) the groundwork has been laid for ongoing collaboration as the former enemies commence building a shared new history together. The need for the public as a whole on both sides to be increasingly drawn into the process is essential, whether this occurs from grassroots, local communities upward, or with the help of political leaders, from the top down. All segments of both sides need to feel they are both participants and beneficiaries in some aspect of the constructive process. Everyone has to "own" and identify with what is happening.

Each post-conflict situation is unique, so the kinds of projects likely to be proposed during the reconciliation process will vary accordingly, even from one local community to the next. A glance back at Figure X.2 recalls for us that restorative justice has two major requirements: the needs for physical well-being (health, education, economic security) and for psychological well-being (trust, forgiveness, closure, meaning). In South Africa, both are going to be needed, but the urgency for physical security is so great that until it begins to improve for the vast majority there, the building up of trust between the several communities is likely to be gravely hindered. To give the reader an actual example of how such dialogue groups have already been shown to make great progress in social healing, I turn to Estonia, one of the three small Baltic countries in northeast Europe.

In 1944, the Russian armies overran the Baltic states, placed them under strict Soviet control and forced the people to speak Russian. By the time the occupation ended with the collapse of the Soviet Union in 1991, one-third of the population living in Estonia were Russians, many born and raised there, and with no homes in Russia to return to. Suddenly the situation was completely reversed. The once-oppressed Estonian majority reinstituted Estonian as the national language, one which the Russian inhabitants did not know. They now became the underdogs, and tensions began to rise. Volkan and his interdisciplinary team of colleagues were brought in to help heal this rift. After several years, they were able to establish collaborative public projects in three important communities.

One town formed an NGO (nongovernmental, nonprofit organization) to build a Community Center, where classes in both languages could be held, as well as other useful classes; children could gather there after school; and holidays of both groups could be celebrated there. In another town, a pre-school and kindergarten program was instituted so Russian-speaking children could meet with their Estonian peers and learn the language, and share puppet shows and summer camps. At a third site, a farming community with few Russians, the loss of access to the old Soviet markets threatened economic ruin. The group decided that tourism was a good alternative, started an NGO, and researched what was needed to get visitors to come, including plans for a sports center.[68]

The first two projects addressed mainly the need for psychological healing, whereas the third addressed an economic issue arising from independence. But that, itself, could help prevent long-lasting bitterness against citizens who were former occupiers who might well be blamed for the economic distress.

Without healing, people remain in perennial mourning. That message comes through loud and clear.[69] It is a state of permanent paranoia, of never being reconciled. It also requires but a small trigger to set off violence. This is a state of affairs the human species can no longer afford. It is possible, as this chapter has shown, for people to reconcile. But it takes dedicated, persistent work and considerable resources. The latter, however, would be just a small fraction of the current global defense budget. Imagine training a "peace army," equipped not with weapons but with skills as intervenors, ready to go wherever necessary. Instead of coercing people to "behave," they would show people processes for healing and for discovering for themselves what they need to do to rebuild a trusting and just society. Even the costs of the projects they might propose would be trivial compared to what is being spent today on arms, intelligence, surveillance, police – all those costly overheads of refusing to invest even minimally in peace, and in meeting the needs of human nature. As Elise Boulding has amply shown, there is an enormous global peace subculture ready and anxious to undertake these activities as soon as political pathways open up.[70]

This is not a fairytale Utopia. It is quite doable. In the final chapter, I consider how an appropriate educational system could create a whole new generation of adults with the necessary skills of group dialogue and problem-solving, and I finish with glimpses of several places on the planet where whole communities, on their own, have managed to change their world view and create for themselves more humane, just, and peacefully flourishing societies.

# XI

# THE SEARCH FOR AUTONOMY WITHIN COMMUNITY

There is no doubt that, at this time in history, Western Civilization is suffering from a great sickness of the soul. The West's progressive turning away from functioning spiritual values; its total disregard for the environment and the protection of natural resources; the violence of inner cities with their problems of poverty, drugs, and crime; spiraling unemployment and economic disarray; and growing intolerance toward people of color and the values of other cultures – all of these trends, if unchecked, will eventually bring about a terrible self-destruction. In the face of all this global chaos, the only possible hope is self-transformation. Unless we as individuals find new ways of understanding between people, ways that can touch and transform the heart and soul deeply, both indigenous cultures and those in the West will continue to fade away, dismayed that all the wonders of technology, all the many philosophical "isms," and all the planning of the global corporations will be helpless to reverse this trend.

Malidoma Somé (1994: 1–2)

The experience of democracy is not ultimately about winning but about deliberating and acting together. Clearly, democracy cannot be experienced directly at the remote political reaches represented by state and national institutions. But the possibility of the states becoming more independent of federal control could mean that they would come to reflect the culture of local democracy, provided people are willing to do the work of nurturing that culture. Democracy is not about ideological purity, nor is it simply the recognition of differences of race, gender and ethnicity. It is about how we equalize politically in acting together for shared purposes.

Sheldon Wolin (1996: 24)

And so I arrive at the capstone – the final summing up of these thoughts on human nature. I begin with an anecdote repeated many times by my English father-in-law, who kept a pub in rural Hampshire and was a great story-teller. One day, he would say, a chap came in asking how to get to Ipswich (which is about 150 miles to the northeast, the other side of London). The local farmhands at the bar all scratched their heads, most having never been much farther than Basingstoke, the nearest market town. Finally, one of them turned to the traveler and said, "Well, if I wanted to get to Ipswich, I wouldn't start from here."

That's the sort of response I have had from a great many friends about the ideas in this book: you can't get there from here. The future I argue for, like Ipswich, is so far outside their experience of the world they cannot imagine how anyone could possibly get there. The task is too big, too daunting. The story my father-in-law told, however, took place fifty years ago in an England where few farmhands had much schooling or owned cars, and there were few direct motorways. If I walked into the old Queen's Head today, the grandsons of those same fellows could give me directions to Ipswich with no problem. The horizon of feasible possibilities in their lives is greatly expanded compared to that of their forebears.

My point is, the conditions of what is possible are not static. They change. Furthermore, they change because of things real people do, real decisions that are consciously taken by somebody. The decision to build motorways across Europe, for example, was not made because of some inevitable drive toward progress lodged in our genes, but because the horizon of the Western world view at that time offered a possibility of expanded trade and consumption of creature comforts by a continent full of people who had suffered through a half century of brutal wars and deprivation. The technology that brought such terrible violence would be harnessed now for human benefit. The material blessings of a fridge, a vacuum cleaner, and a car for every family would at last bring happiness. Hadn't America lighted the way?

Today, with two TVs, two cars, and three computers per family, a Westerner's life is in some ways more convenient, but it is also more stressful. Furthermore, the strains on the planet of all this production and consumption are showing: there is planetary warming; fossil fuels are becoming scarce; and habitat destruction is spreading. Even worse, human beings are becoming increasingly *dissatisfied*. These things were all pointed out in the Introduction. The world view that still seems to compel us to seek technological fixes for our growing problems has become a soul-destroying social trap. Like the Easter Islanders, we are busily competing with each other to build ever bigger monuments to our god-of-infinite-consumerism, all the while studiously avoiding the loss of both social and environmental capital going on around us. Yet even my good friends, intelligent, well-educated people, who themselves *do* see these problems, are saying with resignation that they cannot be avoided. Your ideas will never work, they say. No one will pay attention until the sky is falling in – and by then it will be too late.

Well, the sky *is* falling in, and people *are* noticing, and grumbling, too. (Surely, after the terrorist attacks in America on September 11, no one can have failed to notice that something very definitely is wrong.) But there seems nowhere to start. We have no map to get us from here to Ipswich. So instead of talking in our daily lives about change, because we have no specific starting points or models to follow – no map – we tend to apply band aids to ease our social pain. More police and prisons to control social violence; more antidepressants for adults and behavior-controlling drugs for restless kids; more drilling for oil when energy grows scarce; and all laced with repeats of the old promises about everyone achieving the American Dream (which like McDonald's golden arches is now a global symbol). As I argued in Chapter IX, when we get the algebraic signs right in measuring our economic well-being, it turns out that we are *not* growing better off; we are making things *worse*. People's intuitive sense of *dissatisfaction* has a very legitimate basis. So the first thing to do is to expose the falsehoods and stop trying to paper over things.

Let me illustrate with a parable:

---

Schubert's productivity

A company chairman was given a ticket for a performance of Schubert's *Unfinished Symphony*. Since he was unable to go, he passed the invitation to the company's Quality Assurance Manager. The next morning, the chairman asked him how he enjoyed it, and instead of a few plausible observations, he was handed a memorandum which read as follows:

1 For a considerable period, the oboe players had nothing to do. Their number should be reduced, and their work spread over the whole orchestra, thus avoiding peaks of inactivity.

2 All twelve violins were playing identical notes. This seems unnecessary duplication, and the staff of this section should be cut drastically. If a large volume of sound is really required, this could be obtained through the use of an amplifier.

3 Much effort was involved in playing the demi-semiquavers. This seems an excessive refinement, and it is recommended that all notes should be rounded up to the nearest semiquaver. If this were done, it would be possible to use trainees instead of craftsmen.

4 No useful purpose is served by repeating with horns the passage that has already been handled by the strings. If all such redundant passages were eliminated, the concert could be reduced from two hours to twenty minutes.

In light of the above, one can only conclude that had Schubert given attention to these matters, he probably would have had the time to finish his symphony.[1]

---

Schubert's symphony – though "unfinished" – fulfills humankind's most basic needs: a group of skilled players treating an audience to a moving evening of Schubert's inspired sounds. It is a celebration of meaning. The Quality Assurance Manager, steeped in modern economic theories of "efficiency," is blind to all this, seeing only one goal: get the completed "product" out as efficiently and quickly as possible, for the least cost in time, effort and wages. In doing so, he is oblivious of destroying the so-called "product," whose value does not lie in getting to the end, but in being immersed *in* the experience itself.

This recalls to mind an awareness I first experienced about age 20. My life was so filled with tasks to be accomplished that there seemed no end to them; one was always rushing to finish this so one could move on to the next. Life was a treadmill running full speed: finish college so you could get started with life; get a job to save for a house; get married; have a career; keep advancing; raise children at the same time. Rush! Rush! Rush! I remember saying to someone, I feel I am rushing through life just to get to the end of it. That's how our generation was raised. Life had "goals," stepping-stones, a "plan" – later called a "career" – to be lived. We lived by the world view of the twentieth century, and left our children a legacy of an even more stressful lifestyle than we knew, as the demands of "efficiency" placed on them kept on growing greater and greater.

I suggest that the social theories on which the Western world view and its institutions are currently based are being driven to pathological extremes and demand revision. Both modern industrial society and so-called postindustrial, information-based society, like the Quality Assurance Manager, are guilty of totally missing the point of human existence. "Productivity" is not the goal of life, nor are saving time and effort. Amassing wealth is not the goal either; nor is efficiency for its own sake; and certainly not that of consuming more and more. None of these provides the depth of meaning needed, nor the sense of communal life that humans crave. Yet we are told that without further growth in consumption, the whole economic enterprise will come tumbling down.

Nor does modern society, even in so-called democracies, offer real autonomy. Our social institutions of "private property" (most of which is not the property of individual people, but is in the hands of competitive giant corporations), and of a distant, centralized political body far removed from the day-to-day participatory control of ordinary citizens, do not provide any sense of personal empowerment. Finally, the stressful pace of life, together with the socially isolating effects of computers and television sets, is weakening any sense of community bonding. Our relationships tend to be temporary. In my judgment, modern industrial society is increasingly failing to meet human needs, and is racing ever faster toward civilizational collapse.

How should we set about changing our collective lives to improve the conditions of our existence and cope effectively with crises? How do we discover the "road to Ipswich"? Where do we start? This is not an easy task, and understanding it requires awareness of the paradox involved in social change.

## Rigidity and flexibility

> What I do know ... is that as a Mormon woman of the fifth generation
> of Latter-day Saints, I must question everything, even if it means losing
> my faith, even if it means becoming a member of a border tribe among
> my own people. Tolerating blind obedience in the name of patriotism
> or religion ultimately takes our lives.[2]

With these words, new-age thinker Terry Tempest Williams eloquently
expresses, from a very personal vantage point, the psychological distress human
beings experience when they face psychic dissonance in their lives. Suddenly
they are aware they must question and perhaps modify their deepest beliefs. For
most humans, the moment anyone suggests changing our assumptions about
the world, the reflex is to resist, to negate. The need for meaning is so
profound, our identity is so wrapped up in that meaning, that we defend our
deepest beliefs and assumptions with enormous emotional force – sometimes
with ferocity! (Recall Figure 0.2.) It is painful to doubt our fundamental
perceptions of the world.

Just like individuals, whole societies retain coherence through maintaining a
common identity, a shared world view, that is also sacred, and is equally
defended by the whole. It is the platform on which it builds its institutions and
organizes itself. This shared meaning, however, must be capable of modification
over time if a society is to adapt to changing circumstances. Otherwise it will
become extinct, either slowly like the Easter Islanders or (as has happened all
too often) in a frenzy of self-inflicted violence. Whatever social remnant arises
out of the ashes (should there be any survivors) will be scarred deeply.

We cannot be pushed to change too fast, however. We cannot live with
constant uncertainty (something that today is increasingly being experienced).
Our lives lose coherence. Our ability to coordinate with each other and form
supportive communities disappears. Change for its *own* sake is just as dangerous
as the inability to change at all. Yet Western culture has institutionalized a *rigid
belief* in the benefits of rapid technological change. "Progress cannot be
stopped." This mental outlook the perceptive British economist-philosopher,
E.F. Schumacher, dubbed "the Forward Stampede."[3]

This paradox in the contemporary Western world view – that of rigid adher-
ence to the idea of a linear progress that demands infinite flexibility from human
beings, who are expected to continuously adapt – is the key to our present crises.
It is in the United States that this thinking is most firmly embedded. To criticize
the basic assumption of "progress," to offer alternative political or economic
possibilities, is to be unpatriotic, unscientific, and backward – a trouble-maker, a
Luddite, a communist, an unrealistic dreamer. (As the reader may imagine, I have
been called all of these.) I believe that foremost American scholar of religion,
Martin E. Marty, who has made a study of fundamentalisms and fanaticisms,
would take this as a sign that American patriotism is verging on fanaticism. He

reminds us of Jacques Ellul's observation: "It is because the modern state has become sacred that once again forces like fascism [are] made possible."[4]

And as the political philosopher, John Gray, notes, the major contending ideologies of the twentieth century, *laissez-faire* capitalism and Marxist socialism were both spawned by the same passion-free, cold reason of the Enlightenment; both were purely intellectual experiments in utopian social engineering. Both ignored what human beings *feel*.

Each was convinced that human progress must have a single civilization as its goal. Each denied that a modern economy can come in many varieties. Each was ready to exact a large price in suffering from humanity in order to impose its single vision on the world. Each has run aground on vital human needs.[5]

The suffering imposed by most rigid Marxist regimes is by now well known. The working masses could easily see the disparity between the equality promised them "one day" and the actuality of bureaucratic corruption and ineptness. They lost faith in the utopian ideal. All their sacrifices and suffering went for naught as societal inefficiencies led ultimately to economic and finally political collapse.[6]

The suffering imposed by *laissez-faire* capitalism, on the other hand, has been more subtle during the latter half of the twentieth century, more psychologically than physically damaging. Whereas Marxism claimed it was promoting the common good and obviously failing, America in particular has claimed that by protecting the rights (especially the *property* rights) of individuals, and their opportunity to freely compete over wealth and status, that it was automatically maximizing the common good. This sleight-of-hand logic places the onus for failure in capitalist societies not on the society's institutions as a whole, but strictly on each individual. If I do not achieve the American dream, if I do not succeed in school, if I do not overcome the barriers of my surroundings, if I am not good at competing, I am told it is my fault. Furthermore, if I succumb to the stress of failure and become angry or try to escape my depression with drugs, I am punished – severely. There are few social safety nets for non-adapters. Whatever the problems of society, they are always the fault of individuals; they are never *collective problems*, arising out of the whole cultural environment.

So far, the success of the American ideology at maintaining its sacred character by putting blame for its failures onto individuals has headed off any concerted public questioning of its underlying premises. Meantime, the crises continue to build – and to be ignored. With the tenacity of scientists still clinging to clearly incorrect theories, both the major political parties and the mainstream media in the United States cling to their rigid beliefs in "progress" and the necessity of "economic growth." Their cognitive dissonance makes them totally blind to the growing crises everywhere around them. Psychologist Leon Festinger explains why:

> When dissonance is present, in addition to reducing it, the person will actively avoid situations and information which would likely increase the dissonance.[7]

The West today, particularly the United States, seems to be suffering from an extreme case of such dissonance-avoiding blindness (or at least it was until September 11). Maverick economist Richard Norgaard argues that public dialogue in the West is being hog-tied by the beliefs and assumptions underlying the accepted world view. Recent generations have been taught that economic efficiency, achieved through unbridled competition, is the prime national "good"; that only "scientific" data about even the most complex issues should be used by decision-makers; and that technological "solutions" exist for every problem. Says Norgaard:

> [T]hese [modernist] suppositions are the only ones which are *publicly* held acceptable for use in *public* discourse in decision-making.[8]

In other words, the theories of Western political economists about human nature, human behavior, and the "ideal" society have become sacred ideas – beyond discussion, beyond question. They are the "Holy of Holies," the national religion, and no one dares to question them (recall Figure IX.2).

In a doctoral thesis on the impossibility of any true discourse being held between the Western world view and those of any others in the world – Native Americans, Muslims, Hindus, Africans – Peter Raine had these things to say:

> The main obstacle to a meaningful dialogue ... lies ... within the scientific secular worldview which, founded on rationality, confuses faith with belief.

Only science has "objective truth" and is therefore universally applicable.

> Universalism ... has become a fundamental characteristic of the Western worldview.... Truth, in Western terms, is subject to the inviolable principle of non-contradiction.... For the Western worldview, rationality, as expressed by the triad of technology, economics and scientific objectivism, is actively promoted as a globalising force. It becomes very difficult for "others" to reject any or all of these main principles without situating themselves outside the mainstream drive of "development" which forces such unifying assumptions and values upon peoples and cultures. To reject technology, economics, or objective rationalism is to open one's worldview to ridicule and denigration.

> The influence of technology and economics must be recognised as a coercive force which undermines the basis of many people's worldviews.[9]

These limitations on public discourse in the major industrial nations, and especially in the United States, underscore the strength of the social controls over public dialogue, despite the ballyhoo about "free speech." In a publicly pronounced "rosy world," any open recognition of the crises that afflict many peoples' daily lives is dismissed or ignored. Cases in point are the recent global demonstrations against the WTO in Seattle in 1999 and against the World Bank and IMF in Prague in 2000, and others since. While vividly reported by presses overseas and the small, environmental and other "dissonant" organs in the United States, the *New York Times*, America's leading paper, printed these condescending remarks:

> Seattle was "a Noah's ark of flat-earth advocates, protectionist trade unions, and yuppies looking for their 1960s fix."
> Prague was "a rogue's gallery of Communists, anarchists, protectionist unions and over-fed Yuppies out for their 1960s fix."[10]

Note that neither environmentalists nor those concerned with social justice are identified as such. Instead, demonization and dismissal are used to effectively close off dialogue with the protesters. The controls held by the monied corporations and financial interests over both the political discourse (via unlimited campaign contributions and lobbying) and the mainstream media in the United States have attracted the attention of a number of insightful critics, including Kenneth Boulding, Herbert Schiller, and David Korten, to mention only a few.[11] At times it seems that the collective American mind is under the spell of an invisible but all-pervasive sorcerer. One despairs of any change occurring until it is too late, and the ax of catastrophe falls somewhere, creating uncontrollable unrest. (As my Postscript to this book suggests, the events of September 11 may prove to have been the initiating catastrophe.)

## The coming revolution against megamachines

Americans may be the last of the world's many peoples to figure out that they have sold their souls to the belief that unregulated free markets are the ideal way of ordering all human affairs. The Europeans, generally more politically astute and socially concerned, are coming to realize the predicament into which they are sinking. Whatever autonomy they once had to exercise control over their lives through elected governments is disappearing altogether. Their distant, representative form of democracy – never affording much decision-making power to individuals – is becoming meaningless as global free trade agreements, designed in secret by powerful commercial interests, are being ratified by politicians too busy to read the intricate details to realize they are signing away the sovereign control of their citizens over their own communities and their own lives. Indeed, Americans subconsciously intuit this too, and like citizens of all the industrialized democracies, they are turning out in fewer numbers than ever to vote in elections.

People have lost faith in politics, because they no longer know what governments are good for. Thanks to the steady withdrawal of the state over the past 20 years from the public sphere, it is corporations that increasingly define the public realm.[12]

These are the comments of Noreena Hertz, who, in her book *The Silent Takeover*, further documents how corporate power has become so great it can dictate policy to national governments. They either threaten to pick up and relocate in more "friendly" places where taxes and wages are lower and environmental constraints fewer, or, if governments refuse to allow them the "rights" embedded in the fine print of the WTO and similar agreements to be free of social concerns or pollution controls, they take them to court.

Yet more and more, ordinary people are waking up to how much they disapprove of the conditions being imposed on their government by such agreements, and how little power they now have over their lives. When polled by MORI, a British opinion research company, the vast majority in the United Kingdom were strongly *against* the trade rules their government had agreed to. "Free Trade" made them feel *less* free, *less* in control than ever. Freedom went instead to the multinationals. As Zac Goldsmith, editor of *The Ecologist*, puts it:

When the political class is so out of step with the wishes of the people it supposedly represents, it is time to pull back and start asking questions. It is time for some real, open, public debate on global economic issues.... It is time to rethink the political love affair with economic growth and unfettered trade. It is time to examine the Western economic worldview. It is time for some honest discussion about where we are going, who is taking us – and what happens when we get there.[13]

As an example, he cites Prime Minister Tony Blair's outspoken political belief: "Globalization is an irresistible and irreversible trend."

In short, the logic imbedded in the Western world view has been driven past the tolerance level of human nature. In the rest of the world, too, discontent is mounting. Russia has dissolved into an almost chaotic internal state, where people increasingly turn to alcohol for relief. The people of rural India – still most of that billion-plus population – are increasing their resistance to "modernity." People in Mexico are discovering their powerlessness. Psychic distress at their condition grows among the Japanese, as reflected in the enormous rise in suicides during the late 1990s. People everywhere are responding to mounting stress (and distress) with one or other of our species' two adaptive psychological responses: anger, that threatens to break out into violence, or withdrawal leading to depression and violence against the self.[14]

In terms of fulfilling the intrinsic needs of human nature – belonging to a community, having individual autonomy, and experiencing transcendent meaning in our lives – the ideals of "liberal democracy" on which the Western world view is grounded are today failing miserably. As Benjamin Barber explains, by pitting individual liberty *against* community, the institutions of the West have aimed at satisfying only our need for personal autonomy, leaving in limbo our need to be accepted, participating members in a supportive and meaningful community.[15] After pursuing the internal logic of this atomistic, mechanistic, Billiard Ball argument for 200 years, the West has now created a world where the only "autonomous individuals" are the giant, faceless multinational corporations, whose freedom is being protected by rules arrived at in private and ratified by unwary, even hoodwinked (sometimes corrupt?), politicians. Ordinary human beings, now wholly without mean-ingful control over this state of affairs ("voting with your dollars" hardly counts as "meaningful control"), are reduced to seeking their psychological satisfaction as mechanized producers and consumers in a context where even their emotions are commoditized. We have all become cogs in a global machine so big even George Orwell could not have imagined it. The world described in his *1984* seems pale by comparison; today's "Big Brother" is far more subtle and has found his way inside our own heads.

A similar mistake regarding the search for utopia was made by Karl Marx and his followers when they left individual autonomy (the West calls it "freedom") out of their logistical calculations, assuming people could be physically coerced into forming meaningful, sharing and just communities. The dehumanizing brutality they imposed on their own peoples to conform to the "ideal" was, I believe, far more to blame for their abundant problems and ultimate collapse than their economic system *per se*. The people never had a real chance to "own" the new society they were trying to create. Thus, *neither one* of these two twentieth-century rival systems (that led to fifty costly years of Cold War) has turned out to be sufficiently satisfactory. To assume that they are the only two ways to organize a global family of interacting peoples, nations, and cultures was the gigantic fallacy of the last century. The task of the twenty-first century is to move beyond such limited visions. Not to do so denies out-of-hand the extraordinary creativity our ancestors exhibited for 200,000 years in inventing workable societies adapted to new conditions, some of which survived incred-ible stresses.

I turn now to consideration of how to begin that task.

## The search for autonomy within community

The title of this chapter, and this section, underlines the fact that any society seeking internal harmony must find a balance between our human needs for individual autonomy and for unconditional acceptance within a community. Such a balance surely can be created in multiple forms, based on how a partic-ular group "sees" the world and humans' role in it: what its past experiences have taught its people. I believe that successful world views have been, and will be more complex, less simplistic than the two "scientifically" based world views that dominated the twentieth century. If a culture is to achieve harmony, I suspect its narrative will look much more inclusive, more like Indra's Net in the intricate gestalt it creates, and it will have incorporated into its "story" the shared myths, however homespun they may seem, that give an emotionally satisfying meaning to the lives of its people. Social harmony comes about when all members of a society *want* to participate in achieving a *commonly shared* "good life," and when they all have a voice in adapting and changing their common vision and devising the institutions by which it is to be achieved. That is *real* democracy!

Before suggesting some of the processes by which building social harmony and achieving adaptive change can come about, I offer three observations that summarize what I have concluded from the prior material in this book.

My first point is that there is no *one* universal solution to building human societies. By now it should be abundantly clear that no economic theory, no science, no religion, no mystical insight nor mythical story, has a *complete* answer, appropriate to all times and places, though some components of one or other of them may guide a community in its future search. *Lesson one*: Do not throw away the messages and wisdom of the past, but do not rigidly adhere to them either.

My second point is that the only way a group of people – be it neighborhood, town, tribe, or state – can usefully generate a new world view, a new way of living together, is *not* to lean heavily on "expert" theorists housed in ivory towers, but to attend to the ideas and desires of those within the group. And by "paying attention," I mean utilizing the age-old human practice of actually talking and listening to each other: to discourse, to dialogue. Each community will have to take into account the past histories of *all* its members and the environmental and social context of the present time in its search for answers. *Lesson two*: Listen to the voices of local, *ordinary* people.

My third point is that this process of inclusive dialogue, so common throughout most of humankind's past, requires social skills now largely missing in Western (and Westernizing) societies. In particular, I refer to the *practice* of dialogue in daily life, for both the resolving of inevitable (often necessary) conflicts, and the political activity of adaptive social change. *Lesson three*: The skills of *active* citizenship must permeate human societies if they are to remain capable of nonviolent, adaptive change.

The rest of this chapter is devoted to exploring ways to develop skills in flexible social change: how to teach the next generation to become participants, and how to create real "communities." To demonstrate that this is not just one more impossible utopian "dream" I also offer three examples of places where people – whole communities – have already taken charge of creating new, more inclusive societies using what are known as the techniques of "strong democracy." These are the behavioral skills needed for a flexible society, for adaptive cultural change.

## Behavior settings for building strong democracy

Most Western social philosophers, whatever their political leanings, tend to break out in goose-bumps whenever anyone suggests basing a governance system on popular discourse at the lowest community levels. "Anarchy" is one cry; "mob rule" another; "tyranny of the majority" is very popular – as though "tyranny of the *minority*" (the present system, where unelected corporate heads have a tight grip on political parties and the media) were somehow better. As Benjamin Barber points out, this elitist point of view has a long history, from Plato, Aristotle, Cicero, Machiavelli and Madison to such modern thinkers as Mary Douglas and many others.[16]

There is also great fear among pundits of "consensual decision-making among equals," the assumption being that there is a tendency for powerful members of a group to intimidate others into agreeing with them. Both Douglas and Barber see strongly held shared values, whether ethnic or religious, as dangerous, assuming they necessarily lead to elimination of dissent and so have totalitarian tendencies. Of course, examples of both fanaticisms have occurred in history, but as Martin Marty pointed out, this usually occurs when a society feels under threat from the outside. Yet there have been, and are today, many, many societies with strongly held shared values or ones that use consensus in decision-making, where open discussion is routine, and "dissent" listened to with respect. I feel great dismay at how little knowledge of such real world societies exists among Western scholars (one more example of the narrowness of modern academic disciplines). As discussed in earlier chapters, the goal of decision-making discussion among most tribal peoples is not to "preserve" a rigid myth, but to use wisdom in finding a common solution to a problem, one that is inclusive, not exclusive. In such societies, "winning an argument" is unthinkable, since that destroys the self-esteem of the "loser." When there is injustice, the goal is to heal the rift, not to allocate blame. When there is difference of opinion, the goal is to take every side into account. That so many Western thinkers have not understood this and dismiss community dialogue as an effective means of politics is an indication of their limited conceptualization of the possibilities of human nature.

There is also among Western political philosophers a shocking ignorance about all kinds of common property management systems, both traditional and modern, that exist around the world. These are communities of people who self-regulate their individual uses of a commonly owned resource – an irrigation system, a forest, a fishery, a grazing site, even a whole ecosystem – in order to preserve its benefits for all. Millions upon millions of people in thousands of towns and villages carry on this way, and today are using this kind of group decision-making to agree on how best to adapt their collective activities to a changing world around them.[17]

Yet another difficulty with Western political theorists is their assumption that, in societies where cultural meaning systems are the basis of coherence, people will *necessarily* be antipathetic to strangers with different beliefs. Therefore, it is essential in a multicultural society to eliminate discussion of ethnic or religious values in political dialogue. Tolerance and harmony are best advanced by avoiding discussion of such identity-forming differences, as though silence about differences makes them disappear. Once again, the "experts", taking the Taliban as their example, seem unaware of some facts: they assume that any religiously or ethnically based society will automatically see others as enemies. Most native cultures in the past, however, when first encountered by Europeans, treated them hospitably, offering help. This was the well-known experience of the Pilgrims in New England. And it happened elsewhere also. Only when violence was used against them did the natives become unfriendly. It is of course the case that some "cult" societies have come into existence by seeing themselves as "good" and everyone else as "bad," as Mary Douglas argues. They, however, formed precisely because their recruits already felt themselves to be outcasts from the mainstream. But these fanatical, often paranoid sects (who under pressure are apt to undertake mass suicide) bear little resemblance to the egalitarian tribal societies discussed in Chapter VII.

In short, participatory dialogue of some form has been the surest means of adapting successfully and without violence throughout human existence. Sometimes it has meant agreeing to try out and adopt the tools or customs of others. Sometimes it meant migrating. Sometimes it meant finding peaceful answers to long-term disputes with neighbors. The latter was the basis of the confederations of independent tribes across North America before the Europeans came. One of these, the Iroquois Confederacy, inspired Jefferson, Franklin and other Founding Fathers as they sought to unite thirteen highly independent colonies into a larger "dialogic community."[18]

The trouble is that America's revolutionary founding myth – that an ordinary citizen's voice could really influence her or his social surroundings, and, as with the native confederacies, would be passed *up* the layers of command to a loosely organized central governing body whose primary functions were to adjudicate differences at lower levels and negotiate treaties with foreign states – that myth disappeared even as the Constitution was being written. The philosophical differences between Jefferson and Madison were settled in Madison's favor. The Bill of Rights was an attempt to redress slightly the loss of a political voice for ordinary citizens.

Today, however, that voice seems so powerless that half the citizens do not bother to vote at all. Most, if strong democracy were suddenly introduced, would have little skill in dialogue, in the processes of listening thoughtfully to each other. Even the Green Parties in Europe and America, with their philosophical goal of grassroots political dialogue, have a long history of serious internal conflicts that have repeatedly split their followers into angry factions. It is the members' cultural lack of practice in the art of serious dialogue and their lifelong experience with confrontational politics that has made their progress difficult.

In recent years, some activist grassroots organizations have begun to incorporate training in the multiple skills of social dialogue, collaborative problem-solving, and nonviolent action as they organize to resist the massive economic and political infrastructures that increasingly restrict their autonomy. This training seems to be making a difference. Reports from participants in the massive demonstrations in Seattle against the WTO in November 1999 described how smoothly the various groups of demonstrators – union members, environmentalists, Greens – were able to coordinate their efforts and respond effectively whenever the dynamics of the situation changed.[19] Their collaboration is not unlike what Edwin Hutchins described among the crew aboard the disabled naval vessel entering San Diego Bay (see Chapter V). An entire group of interacting human minds trained in group coordination is extraordinarily adaptive. The operative word here is "trained." How can the opportunities for learning the necessary skills to do strong democracy be enhanced in society, thus returning power and autonomy to ordinary people? How can we make societies more flexible, more able to adapt their institutions to new circumstances? *How can a whole people come to experience autonomy within community?*

There are many settings where people come together and discuss things of mutual concern. Yet even when they share the same goal, they may find themselves unable to agree on how to tackle it; they lack the skills for collaborative problem-solving. I turn here to two very important settings: schools and local neighborhoods. Both possess important opportunities for inaugurating strong democracy in a society. I begin with schools. With really minor changes, in terms of effort and costs, changes in the physical and cultural aspects of schools could create in just two decades a new generation of citizens comfortable with the skills needed for actively entering into the political life of their world.

### Schools are for becoming participants in society

America's national anxiety about whether its children are lagging behind those in other countries in reading and math skills is founded on the absurd idea that the earlier you attain these mechanical skills the more valuable a human being you will become. Here, "value" is obviously being measured as future contributions to the GNP. Almost everything is wrong with this assumption.

Information is not the same as education. Filling kids with facts and teaching them the mechanical skills of the "three-Rs" produces neither happy children nor creative adults. Turning schools into places of compulsory socialization in conformity with predetermined national goals was an idea proferred by Plato and later adopted in early nineteenth-century Prussia, and most recently promoted by B.F. Skinner, the behavioral psychologist. If one wants to raise engaged, thinking, participating citizens – people flexible and creative enough to help society adapt to new situations – one does not begin by "denying ... children the tools of critical thinking," says critic John Gatto. Nor do you destroy their curiosity, their spontaneity, their attempts to contribute to and be recognized by society at an early age, by consigning them to regimented, ranked holding-tanks called schools, separated from the world around them.

> When you want to teach children to think, you begin by treating them seriously when they are little, giving them responsibilities, talking to them candidly, providing privacy and solitude for them, and making them readers and thinkers of significant thoughts from the beginning. That's if you want to teach them to think.[20]

Ideally, children should be raised in villages, free to apprentice themselves to whichever adult interests them at the moment. In our complex, modern societies, such freedom is not practical. For the time, the best we can do is to modify the schools we have to meet the needs of our children's (and our societies') future.

What needs to be done is to make schools meaningful in the sense we have been discussing in this book, as places for discovering oneself in relation to the whole society in which one lives. Mary Catherine Bateson once said "Boredom has to be taught," and that's exactly what most contemporary schools end up doing.[21] They do it not because teachers want to bore children, but because most of society (parents, school-boards, and politicians, collectively) demands that children meet rigid competency levels in skills that have little to do with what engages them or what society, in fact, really needs. Says Wes Jackson, a humanist philosopher, "Children need reality, not virtual reality."[22] A face-to-face world, not a second-hand textbook/TV world.

### The physical structure of schools

In Chapter VI I described how small schools make every student feel needed within the school community, and thus develop a sense of participatory citizenship, of being a *valued member* of the school community, whether as an elected class officer, a drummer in the band, a member of the debating team, a participant in the Christmas play, or a member of the soccer team. In an "under-populated society," everyone is needed, everyone is important to the success of the whole. Small physical size of a school can greatly enhance the self-confidence of every child that graduates from it, better preparing her or him to cope in a more impersonal world.

It is now clear that small school communities, where every person's contribution is acknowledged, are much happier places than huge impersonal schools. Some of the latter, though hampered by enormous sites, have begun to solve the problem by creating several discrete, smaller schools within a single monstrous building.[23] Yet, while size is important, even *more* important are changes in the meaning of education, which requires changing both goals and curriculum.

## Changing the goals of education

In the United States, the first name that comes to mind when rethinking what schools are "for" is John Dewey. Like that other great believer in participatory democracy, Thomas Jefferson (and, like the author of this book), John Dewey had great "faith in the ability of human nature to achieve freedom for individuals accompanied with respect and regard for other persons, with social stability built on cohesion instead of coercion."[24] He firmly believed in what he called "social intelligence," the collective wisdom of an entire community whose members are in continuous dialogue with each other, and he vehemently resisted the exclusivist elitists who proclaimed the inevitability of representative (weak) democracy in modern, technologically complex societies. A society's greatest danger, said Dewey, lies in becoming blind to the shortcomings of its own "working theories" – its own beliefs and assumptions – and those are exactly what the elitist experts are often busiest promoting, as I have pointed out repeatedly in this text (at times I have referred to this all-too-common failing as "falling into a social trap"). Over three-quarters of a century ago, Dewey was already warning of the social dangers of modern economic theory and its alienation of workers, and anticipating present social problems.[25]

The proper social goal of education, in Dewey's view, was not to prepare trained workers to "keep the economy growing" but to empower future citizens. Using the Dudley Street Neighborhood Initiative (described at the end of this chapter) as one example, Bill Caspary explains how citizens become creative participants in their own lives. "Citizen participants are involved at every level.... [They] learn skills on the job [e.g. their volunteer tasks in rebuilding the community], apprentice themselves informally to professional staff, and then go on to formal academic training."[26] If this learning process is to begin in childhood, where it *should* begin, it necessitates a school curriculum that has citizenship as its central goal.

To actually create a curriculum with citizenship as its central goal would be truly revolutionary. Throughout the entire history of public education in America (and of most other modern industrial nations) its unspoken purpose has been, as it remains today, to turn out the most efficient workforce possible for powering the national economy. The brutal coldness of this goal is glossed over by syrupy phrases such as "helping each child become all he or she can be."

But a phrase like that cannot hide the reality, which all children intuitively sense. Schools are where you learn to compete with one another for scarce places on the socio-economic ladder. The present "crisis" in education is not new. As the inspired modern educator Deborah Meier points out, it's always been around because the goal of Western education has always been to shape the child to "fit" society, not to become a creator of it.[27] This is a social prescription for falling into a fatal cultural trap.

In her groundbreaking book, *The Power of Their Ideas*, Meier shows how the supposedly least fertile educational soil, the public schools of East Harlem on Manhattan, can in fact produce intellectually competent and deeply engaged citizens in large numbers, and at no extra cost! She and her colleagues took the idea of small schools (described earlier) to heart. The small staff and student-body, given autonomy by the local superintendent, were all able to assemble in one auditorium. Teachers could easily meet together to develop guidelines and address crises as they arose. Every child was well known in the school community. It was possible for the whole school to re-create itself as a social institution.

An early task for Meier and her colleagues was to decide, what is education *for*? They threw out the empty snobbery of "academic excellence" as a meaningless term. They would not rely on standardized tests that measure class-background or "socially meaningful" intelligence. Their definition of purpose was "putting all our young people in a position to explore and act upon the fundamental intellectual and social issues of their times." They would accomplish this by encouraging *imagination* and *skepticism* (both laced with humor and fun); *empathy* for how others think and feel; *respect* for evidence; the *ability to communicate* well; a *caring engagement with the world*; and a sense of one's own social reliability, or "*trustworthiness.*"[28] In short, they were setting the stage for children to truly experience "autonomy within community."

The hardest task of all, Meier claimed, *was changing the habitual beliefs and behaviors*, first of teachers, then of students and their parents. It was, and continues to be, a monumental challenge, but it is a rewarding one.[29] Not only are Meier's and her colleagues' goals in educating children highly effective in graduating more intelligent persons for the workforce, as well as better prepared citizens for a strong democracy; they also actually save taxpayers money that would otherwise have been spent on drop-outs and delinquent youth. Imagine how much easier it will be for society, once these former children become teachers and parents themselves, to provide a similar liberating education to the *next* generation!

### Changing the curriculum

Several innovative ways of modifying pedagogy to enhance the democratic effectiveness of schools will round out the picture. I include reinstatement of the arts; community based engagement in learning; utilizing cooperative learning; and teaching children how to resolve conflict through dialogue. The latter two modifications are aimed at what is often called the "hidden curriculum," the unspoken messages about individualism and competition that current school curricula embody. I begin with the arts.

I was stunned a few years ago when I heard the famed violinist Yehudi Menuhin describe the incredible impact his recent reintroduction of the arts had had on the behavior of rebellious British schoolchildren, even those in the most disadvantaged inner city areas. Acting as adviser, he helped to put music, art, and mime back into elementary schools and, for older students, drama and martial arts as well. Not only did discipline problems drop precipitously; performance in academic subjects shot up.[30]

Long considered an unnecessary frill by American taxpayers' associations and their constituents, the much-maligned "useless" arts are finding their way back into schools as more and more data pour in from studies on how arts involvement improves scores on academic tests, decreases delinquent behavior, and improves youths' attitudes about themselves and their future in society. It seems (as aboriginal peoples intuitively sensed) that the arts increase insight learning and problem-solving, and provide social meaning to and emotional expression in the use of our cognitive skills.[31]

Superintendents of Public Instruction in some American states have become enthusiastic sponsors of the arts in pre-schools and schools as ways of stimulating brain development, cognitive skills, and creative thinking, all increasingly valued by the U.S. Department of Labor as "good for the economy" – especially for the computer, graphic arts, and entertainment sectors (such as the Disney Corporation).[32] The suggestion that art may well bring a sense of meaningfulness back into peoples' lives tends to be ignored by officials as a legitimate reason for including them in the curriculum. Meaningfulness, after all, has no immediate commercial value!

Another important curricular innovation that is overlooked for the same reason, but which also gives meaning to students' lives because it actively engages them with other human beings, is involvement with the local community. Not in the familiar "job-apprenticeship" manner now used in some higher schools to teach students what it takes to hold a job, but in a far more integrated way. An excellent example is the El Puente Academy for Peace and Justice in the Williamsburg quarter of Brooklyn, New York. Its Latino name means "The Bridge" and it is an alternative high school located in an Hispanic community characterized by poverty and pollution. In their first year students are helped to find a positive cultural identity in a study called "Who Am I?" They investigate their individual identities and histories, writing an extended essay in English and personal poetry in Spanish.

The next year, "I" becomes "We" as they focus on their local community, its history and current social problems. They address racism and violence (both declining since the program began) and the health impacts of local environmental pollution – a formidable task. As of the year 2000, El Puente school students had amassed enough data on the latter for a report to be published in the *American Journal of Public Health*.[33] Not only does this kind of activity engage youths with their own community as they make valuable contributions to it, thus giving them a meaningful identity; it also requires them simultaneously to practice a whole host of disparate skills: science, math, sociology, history, geography, politics, and of course, reading, writing and speaking. Skills are learned by employing all of them in socially meaningful ways, abandoning rote learning and testing.

Other kinds of "real-world" school projects one could mention are Eliot Wigginton's "Foxfire" program where 9th and 10th graders from rural Appalachia interview the elders in their neighboring communities, recording oral histories and other information from older generations. This work has been published regularly, as the students' and locals' joint effort, in the *Foxfire* magazine. It has survived three decades, giving meaning to the lives of students and communities alike.[34]

Tuscaloosa, Alabama, is the headquarters of yet another organization, the "Pacers," dedicated to schools-in-the-community. As part of The Small Schools Cooperative, U.S.A., it introduces into school curricula the collecting of music, folklore, and oral histories of local people. Other projects under their sponsorship involve schools engaged in local environmental monitoring, such as along the upper McKenzie River Valley in Oregon.[35] All these are but a few examples of still small but growing experiments in engaging children as participating members in their local communities, rather than as merely citizens-in-waiting, closed off from the "real world."

Perhaps the most critical curricular issue of all, however, is the patterns of the daily social interactions in the school itself, including those used in the basic teaching/learning process. If you want to create obedient citizens who will live according to the pre-set rules of a competitive, hierarchically managed society, you give teachers all the authority in the classroom, the school board or the State the ultimate say over what is to be learned and why, and you rank students individually according to their ability to assimilate what is put before them. Are they efficient sponges, or not? Education becomes a social sorting process that values a single kind of ability, a single kind of child.

If we look around us in the world, we discover that there exists a unique "hidden curriculum" in the rearing practices specific to each of the world's cultures. Every society teaches its youth by using the same social patterns it expects them to adopt as adults. In Western industrial societies, the historically dominant pattern of education has been psychologically destructive. It tries to turn children into automatic competitors; it promotes lifelong "winners" and "losers"; it frustrates imagination and creativity; and its extreme individualism destroys the opportunity to develop skills at teamwork and collaborative problem-solving. Maybe I have put it too bluntly, yet this picture is close to the truth, despite the intrepid teachers who try to resist it. Too many modern schools are forced to systematically deprive children of their natural needs to be accepted, to belong; to be spontaneous and curious; to possess autonomy and to feel that their lives matter and have meaning. Why are we so surprised when children's enthusiasm for school so quickly withers and dies?[36] What is seldom mentioned is that too often enthusiasm for joining the adult society – except possibly as unbridled consumers – also shrivels.

One solution is to use pedagogy aimed at creating collaboration, discussion, and mutual help among groups of students. It's hardly a new idea. John Dewey proposed it as early as 1916.[37] While some of the community-based projects described above entail groups of students working together, the use of collaborative learning strategies within the classroom has been much slower in spreading. Two pioneers from Minneapolis, David and Roger Johnson, have argued – and demonstrated with nearly three decades of research – that not only does group learning facilitate social skills, it also enhances the quality of the learning process. Everything, being more "fun," becomes more "meaningful," and hence is understood and retained better. Indeed, collaborative learning, through the verbal sharing of the "special" knowledge researched and contributed by each student member of a group, allows all the others in that group to grasp complex subjects far more efficiently than they could on their own by reading texts or listening to lectures. Each student becomes a teacher for the others. Group learning in fact is more effective![38]

Interestingly, it is often difficult for teachers who intellectually understand the desirability of collaborative learning, even enthusiastically promote it, to shed the old habit of expecting students to "do their own work." During a class at San Diego State University which was specifically designed to encourage group discussion, I found myself with a "problem" when eight or ten students came up with almost identical answers for the final exam essay questions (these had been distributed ahead of time and the students were invited to "study together"). Yet it was only when my faculty colleague reminded me, "But Mary, that's what we *told* them to do," that I discovered the depth of my own old habits of thinking and reacting!

Another positive aspect of group learning is the sense of collective responsibility that it generates. In the anecdotal case of our class at San Diego State, for example, a whole group that chose to write a superficial or poorly argued essay would all be penalized, so there was still individual responsibility involved. No one had to conform to a poor quality group effort. But in cases where the whole group suffers because one person has failed in her or his special contribution to a project, the stakes are much higher. That person risks losing some of the trust of her or his peers; bonds are threatened; shame is involved. Correctly carried out, however, group work is not an opportunity for free-riders to slack off, nor for inept individuals to be inordinately penalized. On the contrary, it can be highly motivating.[39]

An even more powerful sense of responsibility and a recognition of the reality of social interdependence is fostered when a whole group takes responsibility for all of its members meeting minimum standards, as happens in some classes in Japanese schools. This, of course, still places self-interest on an equal plane with altruism. In some schools (at least in socialist countries) an older class may be given the responsibility of tutoring and mentoring a class of younger children, helping them with school work and even organizing extracurricular activities for them. It is not unlike the days of the one-room schoolhouse in rural America, where older children had to help the younger. Says educator Greg Smith, "Such experiences reinforce the recognition of interdependence for both younger and older children."[40]

A natural next step to the above group- and community-promoting curricular changes has been the introduction of formal dialogue skills for use in daily social intercourse. Often packaged under the rubric of "conflict resolution," these are the skills needed for any serious communication between people who hold different views on a particular situation of compelling interest to both. Those skills, described in Chapter X, need to be taught early to children if a whole society is to participate successfully in responding adaptively to a rapidly changing world. All aspects of the curriculum should emphasize not only what being in a community means, but how to peacefully bring about desired changes. How does a group of individuals come to a workable group decision and then start to implement it?

Gradually schools in the United States and elsewhere (including especially the newly liberated South Africa) are recognizing that children facing – or soon likely to face – a chaotic social *milieu* need to learn alternatives to the use of force in the resolution of their differences and the making of mutually acceptable agreements. For more and more children in today's world, school is the safest place in their lives (see Figure XI.1).[41] Skills in how to turn arguments into dialogues are desperately needed everywhere, and schools are a great place to learn.

*Figure XI.1* A school in South Africa
These South African children, at a township school in Cape Town, waved loving good-byes to us visitors as our buses drove off. The barbed wire-topped fence is what keeps them safe from the violent world outside. In a way, it also encloses them in a cultural prison they did not create

*Source*: Photo by author, Cape Town, August 2000

The Johnson brothers, cited above, have been studying for over a decade the consequences of introducing conflict resolution and mediation skills into grammar and middle schools in the United States and Canada. They conclude that not only do students retain these skills, they transfer them to the school-yard and out into their family and community settings. Furthermore, children prefer these solutions to outright fights or even settlements imposed by authorities. The Johnsons also found that children with these social skills do better academically.[42]

The well-recognized social psychologist, Elliot Aronson, writing in the aftermath of the recent series of bloody (and overly publicized) student shootings in middle-class American schools, pleads for the introduction into all schools of processes for building empathy through cooperative learning, the teaching of conflict resolution, the recognition by teachers and fellow students of the worth of each student (to put an end to taunting and bullying), and the creation for all youth of a sense of being equal participants in a shared community. No one should feel "left out."[43] Meeting these goals will, of course, help eliminate the factors that cause bullying in the first place, since bullies themselves are products of personal insecurity.

Though these may seem like impossible ideals to many readers, they are far closer to the reality of many past and present cultures than are those of most Western societies today, especially the United States, the self-proclaimed model for the future.

### Turning neighborhoods into communities

On a brilliantly sunny morning in San Diego, there was a sudden jolt, like an earthquake. I ran outside, saw a plume of black smoke slowly rising, heard a radio blaring something. A Pacific Southwest Airways plane with over a hundred commuters had crashed into a residential neighborhood. The horror was unbelievable. The city rushed to help the expected dozens of injured. News in the affected neighborhood spread by word of mouth. Whose houses were hit? Was anyone home? The hub was the local mom-and-pop corner store, where people went to exchange information. Unfortunately, there were no survivors; all aboard the plane were instantly killed and amazingly the toll on the ground was less than half a dozen people. No others were harmed.

That was nearly twenty years ago. The store probably isn't there now. Neighborhoods in most big cities don't have meeting places like they used to. Yet people still *need* communities; they *like* them, are *happier* in them, and, if given a choice, will often choose poor villages over rich cities. Writes political scientist Jonathan Barker, "[W]hen I travel to Africa, Asia, and Latin America and visit villages and neighborhoods that everyone would classify as poor, I feel my spirits rise. The evidence of difficulty and injustice is palpable, but something makes the experience positive."[44] Anthropologist Patrick Tierney makes the same observation with respect to people abducted as children from one culture to another. Those removed from traditional villages to Western societies have almost always tried to go back, whereas Westerners stolen by tribal peoples have tended to "go native," preferring to stay. This fact, observes Tierney, was also noted by Benjamin Franklin. "There must be something very superior in the nature of their social bond, was Franklin's conclusion."[45]

In her very first book about cities, Jane Jacobs vividly described how it was the structure of their urban neighborhoods that made big, modern cities livable, friendly, safe places: their numerous, small street-level shops; their second-storey apartments where grandmothers kept a sharp eye on goings-on below; stoops where adults sat in the evenings; sidewalks where kids played together. People lived openly *on* the streets *in* their neighborhoods: shopped there, went to school there, knew the familiar places and familiar faces. When those qualities are destroyed – cut through by freeways or bulldozed for "urban renewal" – cities cease to be places where communities can exist.[46]

People *need* interactive communities, and the physical layout of their surroundings is a major prerequisite. (Even early farmers tended to cluster their houses together. The English word "town" comes from Anglo-Saxon *tun*, a fenced living area or village, and people were identified by the town/*tun* they came from.) "Community" means, first and foremost, belonging in a physical place, shared by known others. From them, we acquire our language, our customs, our manners, our beliefs. The advent of the motorized, electronic age in the twentieth century has distracted Westerners from this grounding in their physical surroundings, to the detriment of both local environments and peoples' own sense of identity. Apathy has been our social harvest, especially in the political arena where decisions are made.

No one I know of writes more clearly and more cogently about how community must be anchored in a place of shared meaning, identity and mutual knowledge than Daniel Kemmis, long-time mayor of Missoula, Montana. In his books he argues for a resurrection of the Jeffersonian belief that the anonymity of self in a giant market economy destroys morality, especially one's sense of personal responsibility for the common good. In the United States, the central-ized "weak" democracy that the Federalists put in place – with the professed intention of discouraging ordinary people from serious political engagement – needs to be turned into highly participatory, "strong," *community* democracies that give people back a sense of control over their own lives. The contemporary West's national "confrontational politics" needs to be replaced by collaborative problem-solving, focused on the local community, if environments and societies are to be restored to health.[47]

Being "in control," however, means more than just living in a local commu-nity where people know each other and talk a lot. "Gossip," in its best sense of sharing information and opinions about what is happening locally, has an important role in a community, but by itself does not bring empowerment.[48] That requires dedicated organizations and often, in today's world, specialized knowledge as well. Local city governments usually have some limited powers of their own, though sometimes even these have to be wrested by public initiatives from state governments.[49] Yet even the ordinances of an enlightened city council cannot create community without the constructive inputs of local grass-roots groups.

Such groups – be they churches, service organizations, the local newspaper, the PTA; or special interest groups, such as unions or the chamber of commerce; or branches of larger NGOs, such as (in the US) Public Citizen, the Sierra Club, or the national Civic League; or *ad hoc* groups of knowledgeable citizens that form in response to a particular critical issue such as a local pollution problem or a threatened hospital closure – such groups are essential to the empowerment of a community. They need places to meet – libraries, coffee-shops, church halls; they need funds for covering costs of communicating; and they need good working relations with elected officials. Citizen groups provide the research effort and popular support needed to elected city councils to enable meaningful civic changes to take place. In an empowered democracy, those elected to office are not so much "leaders" at the forefront of policy-making for a passive populace, but "facilitating servants" of an active citizenry, carrying out the formal legislation that it requests.

Finally, Kemmis argues, in today's capital-based economies, people's power can exist only if cities and towns have far more control than most now hold over local economic activity. Like E.F. Schumacher before him,[50] Kemmis says cities plus their "hinterland" (the surrounding natural resource area from which they make their livelihood) must be under the control of local people, not distant, national governments or multinational corporations. The globalization of the world's many economies that is being pushed for today is shockingly undemocratic. It can only do damage to peoples everywhere unless local "city-states" (as Kemmis calls them) regain the right of *their* citizens to control *their* resources and the sources of capital being invested in *their* community and the purposes for which that capital is used. He does not say there would be no global trade; far from it. Rather, such trade should be negotiated and overseen by an interactive network of biogeographically-structured, independent political entities, the city-states, and not by distant national capitals or, worse, politically uncontrolled international bureaus such as the IMF and WTO, and the multi-national corporations they serve.[51]

Reversing the current trend toward uncontrolled globalization of all invest-ment capital is the subject of numerous books. British political philosopher John Gray lashes out at this globalizing trend.

Global capital markets make social democracy unviable.

[D]emocracy and the free market are competitors rather than partners. The normal concomitant of free markets is not stable democratic government. It is the volatile politics of economic insecurity.[52]

Of course, there must be "capital" to initiate new, adaptive enterprises, but every society must be free to regulate how and where it is to be invested. There must be many "capitalisms," each under the local control of local communities.

For that large fraction of humanity existing at the margins of global power, already cut off from access to global capital, Jonathan Barker and his colleagues have documented a myriad of creative solutions: a broad spectrum of micro-political settings that people have generated to pursue independent local socio-economic goals while retaining community stability and autonomy. Such groups have constantly to adapt themselves to manage two critical social tasks – coherence and change – *simultaneously*. They learn to go around the usual resistance to change by skillfully weaving together existing traditions, including religious and/or democratic practices (which helps maintain trust), with innovative ideas based on local, national, or even international sources of research and information.[53]

For more economically sophisticated communities, consultant economist Jeff Gates has described innovative ways to restore economic health without bowing to the demands of outside investors and global capital. He identifies these as "capital without capitalism." For example, when *all* citizens become owners of the capital invested in their workplaces and communities, there exists a true sense of social control over one's life; all people share in the economic benefits of the social whole, as well as taking responsibility for its overall health.[54]

## Places where people are taking charge

As promised at the start of this chapter, I conclude with snapshots of three real-world places where people are successfully taking control over their lives through strong democratic processes of participatory dialogue and decision-making. I have visited each of them, albeit briefly. They are but three of literally dozens of equally inspirational cases (several of which I hope to consider in detail in a later book). These living experiments put an end to Western theorists' claims that communities are no more than "interest groups" competing over scarce resources, and that cooperation is nothing but "mutual self-interest" explainable by mathematical (and therefore "scientific") game-theory models. What follows are the stories of real people in particular places redefining their lives in their own creative ways.

### *Mondragon cooperatives*

The city of Mondragon lies in the heart of Basque country, in the Pyrenees mountains of northern Spain. The Basque are, both genetically and linguistically, among the most ancient, pre-Aryan peoples in Europe, with a distinct culture and unique language. Their long history of equality among themselves put them on the losing side in Spain's civil war, and they suffered greatly as "conquered people" under the fascist regime. For most, it was a time of hopelessness and poverty, controlled by a small clique of elitist families.

In 1941, a young Basque priest named Father José Maria Arizmendiaretta (Arizmendi, for short) was assigned to Mondragon. Equipped with a passion for his people and steeped in the teachings of Catholic social doctrine that weaves social justice with private property, he would profoundly change the Basque economy and social structure. When put in charge of the youth, he soon abandoned the apprentice school and found grassroots funding to start a technical school. Next he arranged for several of its first graduates to study for university degrees while at the same time being employed as supervisors in local factories. Dissatisfied with the treatment of the workers, five of these young men, with their newly acquired skills in engineering and management, found enough financial backing to establish a cooperative, ULGOR. They began building household appliances – paraffin heaters and cookers. In four years they had 100 employees, but no formal company organization. They went back to Arizmendi for help.

The priest had detailed knowledge of Robert Owen, a nineteenth-century English mill owner who had established worker-owned cooperatives. Together, he and the five owners set up a democratic management system, with elected board members from among all the groups of workers (draftsmen, line-workers, office staff and so forth). These were to appoint a General Manager to carry out their agreed policies. The board members were not paid for these duties. They met before work, at 7 a.m., to discuss all aspects of company policy and oversee the manager's effectiveness at carrying them out. The cooperative thus became simultaneously democratic *and* efficient.

Financially, each worker makes a capital investment in the company when hired that grows while she or he remains employed, but is only distributed on leaving or retiring. Of the company's profits, 20 percent is reinvested, 10 percent is given to the community, and the rest goes into workers' accounts. In hard times, both company reserves and worker-owners' capital are tapped to insure minimum incomes to the unemployed. During the recession of the 1980s, Mondragon cooperative workers used this support to go back to school and improve their skills.[55]

Since that first cooperative more than forty years ago, over 200 have sprung up throughout the Basque countryside, spanning manufacturing, banking, research, food distribution and marketing, and health and child care services. They have also strengthened the schools and built new housing. Two essential services for the entire region have been a cooperative bank, the Caja Laboral Popular, which carefully audits and assists both its regular client co-ops and any petitioning new start-ups; and the Technical College and its associated research and development cooperative, Ikerlan, which together maintain the flow of trained workers and innovative ideas into the local economy.

So far, these cooperatives have managed to interface successfully with the wider competitive-capitalist system around them without benefit of political protection from tariffs or quotas. Whether they will survive globalization remains to be seen. Not only have they brought great economic benefits to the region; they have greatly strengthened the integrity and general health of the surrounding communities, *and* they have retained a degree of economic equality unheard of in the outside capitalist world. The income disparities, top to bottom, are less than 10 to 1, as compared to North America where the ratio can easily exceed 100 to 1!

In a meeting in 1992 with Jesús Larrañaga, one of the founders of ULGOR, the original cooperative, I was impressed with the great community building power of the movement as it penetrates via work, schools, and the marketplace, into the daily lives of local people. "More and more, Basques are learning the importance of commitment to community," he observed.[56] Strong feelings of belonging, of autonomy, and of shared meaning were all being forged. It would be a terrible loss if these human benefits were to disappear in some future race for centralization of control of the entire planet by a small cluster of transnational corporations.

### Kerala: India's singular state

When I flew one November day in 1995 from the semi-arid state of Gujarat to Kerala on India's southwest coast, I was not prepared for the tropical lushness. From the air, it looked like an impenetrable jungle below; in reality, it was miles and miles of coconut palms and rubber trees. Nor were the streets of the towns and villages at all like those I'd seen elsewhere. In place of the burlap hovels, piles of steaming rubbish where cows "grazed" at the sides of the roads, and children of all ages running about barefoot, here there were small, tidy houses with neat piles of potentially useful scrap materials stacked beside them, no garbage, and uniformed children – both boys and girls – lined up waiting for the school bus. I had heard a lot about the high "quality of life" in Kerala, but I had no idea it would be so immediately visible. After all, these people had *per capita* incomes the same as the rest of India. How had they managed, in just a few decades, to increase life expectancy at birth to over 70 years, to achieve literacy rates for both men and women of over 90 percent, and to reduce their birth rate to less than two per woman, below ZPG (zero population growth)? It's a story with many threads. I offer but a brief summary here.

Kerala is a "new" state, created in 1956, several years after India's independence, but behind it lies an ancient history. Geographically, it is a narrow strip of land sandwiched between the Arabian Sea and the 3000-foot crest of the Western Ghats. One-tenth the size of California, it has, today, about the same number of inhabitants, some 30 million. Its tropical climate made it the native habitat of an amazing range of spices that have attracted traders from near and far for thousands of years, leading to today's mixed population. The aboriginal Dravidians first faced invading Aryans from the north, and later the Moguls. The famed Malabar Coast was where many peoples from overseas landed and settled: pre-Christian Jews, then early Christians, today called Syrian Christians (St. Thomas reputedly arrived in AD 52), and later, Arabs and European missionaries (first Portuguese Catholics, then Dutch and English Protestants). The result was a heterogeneous population, with three main religions, Hindu, Christian and Muslim, all united by a common language, Malayalam. Like Basque, it is an ancient indigenous language.

Before British rule, the ancient princedoms that now form today's Kerala were at least as caste-ridden as the rest of India. Yet the habit of foreign contact and assimilation of new ideas meant that some of those princes were educated abroad. In Britain they picked up enlightened social world views. By the mid-1800s, local Protestant missionaries, under the auspices of these monarchs, had established many schools and colleges. Their "feminist" wives insisted girls, too, should be educated.[57] In 1888, the *Malayala Manorama* newspaper was founded "for the upliftment of the depressed classes ... and political justice for all." Its very first editorial pushed for abolition of the caste system! With support from the liberal ruling Maharaja of Travancore, the paper flourished; today it is the most widely read paper in all of India (because of Kerala's high literacy rate!) and still politically outspoken.[58]

When the Maharaja died, a socially enlightened princess of the royal house became regent for his underage heir, and instituted a long list of liberal changes, from increased access for the poor to farm lands, local self-government, and infrastructure building, to establishment of the Boy Scouts, a Women's College, and health care, especially for mothers and children. "She influenced and enforced schemes that became catalysts for vast changes in social structure in succeeding generations."[59]

By the time of Indian independence and the establishment of the state of modern Kerala, all these influences – widespread literacy, women's participation in political life, the spread by the *Malayala Manorama* of liberal ideas such as social equality, land reform, and democratic rule – were well in place. Despite the dominance elsewhere in India of the highly centralized, powerful Congress Party, led by Nehru and later his daughter, Indira Gandhi, Kerala's first elected government was Communist – of a very home-grown type. Because its proposed reforms were too decentralizing for the all-powerful Congress Party, both Nehru and his daughter, while prime minister, did all in their power to unseat them. Twice elected, the Communists were also twice thrown out – peacefully. Nevertheless they cemented earlier institutions and pushed through new reforms. They laid the groundwork for the Land Reform Act of 1964, whereby large ex-colonial land holders were obliged to sell off their acreage in small plots to peasants at state-set prices. It was one of the first states where Mohandas Gandhi's "land to the tiller" reform was implemented seriously.[60]

Like the situation in Mondragon, Spain, the future of the peoples of the state of Kerala is by no means certain; they face major new problems as "globalization" presses in upon them, uninvited.

## DSNI: an American neighborhood's story

Dudley Street runs through an area of several dozen city blocks in south Boston, straddling the historic old districts of Roxbury and Dorchester. It is within a short two-mile commute of downtown Boston – potentially desirable real estate! The area has long been abandoned by capital investors, however, leaving its 25,000 mostly poor and racially diverse population an easy target for foreclosures, arson, and exploitation by would-be developers. Bereft of services, it became peppered with empty lots full of garbage and junked cars, and abandoned toxic-factory buildings. The chroniclers of its story, Peter Medoff and Holly Sklar, sum it up thus:

> [I]n a pattern repeated nationally, a thriving urban community was trashed and burned. It was redlined by banks, government mortgage programs and insurance companies in a self-fulfilling prophecy of White flight, devaluation and decline. While tax money subsidized the building of segregated suburbia and upscale "urban renewal," inner city neighborhoods like Dudley were stripped of jobs, homes and government services.[61]

Ignored by all the usual sources of help, the people had no choice but to help themselves, and so they formed the Dudley Street Neighborhood Initiative, DSNI.

When citizens first began informal meetings, they asked the city to "form a partnership," but were met with derision. "This city don't make partnerships with nobody." In the 1980s they realized they needed a strong grassroots organization and managed to get a small, start-up grant from a local foundation. After deciding on the area to be included, they sought input from knowledgeable community members and advisers from nonprofit agencies. These, however, were not to act as their "leaders," but as listeners and facilitators, helping the group define its goals and develop decision-making processes grounded in the community. From the start, it was to be a participatory, self-governing organization with all racial groups represented: Black, Hispanic, Cape Verdean and White (headphones with translations for Portuguese and Spanish speakers were always available at meetings). Thus was DSNI born.

After a carefully run election, the members of the first Board hired an experienced professional director to help them carry out their goals. (Note the parallel here with the "hired managers" of the Mondragon cooperatives and with the appointed "chiefs" of many African and Native American tribes. In each case the skilled professionals do not "run" the community, but are its servants.) The Board chose as its first task a cleanup of the streets and numerous empty lots. Equipped with rakes borrowed from (and returned to) the city's public works, and with some aid from the latter, hundreds of people turned out for the cleanup. When no one came to remove abandoned cars, however, they plastered "FLYNN FOR MAYOR" bumper stickers on them and sent photos to the

*Boston Globe* (Boston's Mayor Flynn was up for re-election at the time). Soon the cars disappeared, the garbage "transfer stations" (where private refuse collectors sorted garbage) were cleaned up, and the empty lots were turned into parks, playgrounds, and food-producing gardens by the local residents. Lively murals were painted on walls of neighboring buildings. Commuter trains into Boston began stopping again at the Dudley Street Station.

The next stage involved making long-term plans for the community. A consultant known for seeking out community input was hired and innumerable planning meetings were held. High-school students were involved in the design and model-building stages. Finally, the city's approval was sought and given. But that was of little use unless DSNI had control over the development of the empty lots. The city agreed to give them control over the lots it owned, and ultimately it also gave them, under Massachusetts law, the right of eminent domain over privately owned lots as well. Low-interest loans were obtained from benevolent foundations and by 1990, fifty parcels had been put into the DSNI Community Land Trust.

By the time of my visit in May, 1997, the upbeat life of the new Dudley Village was abundantly evident. I felt incredibly safe walking in what once had been a dangerous, crime-ridden neighborhood. The first thing one notices is the marvelous Community Town Common that spans both sides of a major intersection. Its giant, stepped plaza, with a bandstand at the back; its clock-bearing wrought-iron arch; and the brightly-painted cut-out silhouettes of people give it a welcoming, parklike atmosphere. There are dozens of brand new, handsome two-storey homes, many built with low-interest loans and sweat equity. Older homes were usually spruced up, too. Less easy to recognize were the new day-care centers and the youth groups' work (mostly done during summer holidays) in landscaping, clean-ups, and so on (see Figure XI.2).

A major problem still is the "brownfields," the abandoned toxic sites that need cleaning up before they can be made useful. I attended a meeting addressing this topic and was truly amazed at the knowledge and interactive skills displayed by all the attendees; they were at home with the complex details. To the uninformed observer (me), the most "unlikely" citizens – aged old men in well-worn clothes, "hippie" youths – made astute, creative contributions. All listened respectfully, whoever was speaking. They had mastered participatory democracy to a degree that I would not have believed (shame on me!).

It is neighborhood groups such as this one – and many others at DSNI – composed of ordinary people, which will continue to see that houses are built and businesses come, and that the streets are safe, and lined by trees, and lighted at night. They plan to introduce urban agriculture into the community, for both local food and for profitable "exports" to downtown Boston restaurants. I know these people will continue to create a thriving, vibrant, and people-friendly neighborhood because they truly enjoyed the empowerment of active citizenship; they liked being together.[62]

*Figure XI.2* Two views of the Dudley Street neighborhood in 1997

These scenes characterize the resurgence of a once seemingly hopeless neighborhood in south Boston's Roxbury district after a decade of community activism and the formation of the Dudley Street Neighborhood Initiative.

*above*: The plaza, clock archway, and bandstand, decorated with colorful silhouettes of community folk. There are thriving shops on the streets around this intersection.

*below*: A nearby park, formerly an old dump-site, now surrounded by bright new, family-owned homes.

*Source*: Photos by author, spring, 1997

## Conclusion: we will discover "the roads to Ipswich" as we go

These three cases – Mondragon, Kerala, and Dudley Street – have much in common despite their very different histories and cultural environments. What they all share, I suggest, is a tacit accommodation in their newly created social institutions of that most profound and general of all human needs, a balance between belonging and shared meaning on the one hand, and individual autonomy and participation on the other.

Whether or not each of them continues in the future to adapt successfully (or even to resist successfully, where appropriate) the stresses they will face from the pincers of Western-driven "globalization" on one side and Mother Nature's inexorable changes from global warming on the other, remains to be seen. I suspect any future societies that do succeed in adapting to and/or resisting both these coming stresses will have the qualities stated above as minimal characteristics. They most certainly will learn to be *flexible* in their cultural meanings, adapting them to new circumstances without losing their ability to preserve a deep purpose in life. Successful societies will continuously build *new traditions* and *new meanings* as part of their processes of adaptation.

Finally, I have not tried in this book to address the future impact of the so-called electronic age on human adaptiveness. It is too soon to tell whether that "age" will even survive the next century. Even if it should still be around, it may be hard to assess, after the fact, whether humankind survived *with the help of*, or *in spite of*, this new technology. I can say with confidence that, like nuclear energy before it, it will not be *the* answer to our future. Of far greater importance to our survival will be avoiding the social trap of supposing that pseudo-communities – whether gangs on the streets, encounter groups, or "virtual communities" on the Internet – are adequate substitutes for real people in real places sharing meaningful lives. In whatever forms the commoditization of human caring comes, be it through centralized welfare systems or payment for personal services, it tends to be destructive of real community – and hence of real human beings.[63]

In the coming century we humans would do well to keep the following thoughts in mind:

## Regarding Human Nature

It does not have unlimited adaptability.

Self-interest is not its fundamental basis.

A healthy society meets basic human needs in a balanced way,
and therefore coercive controls are unnecessary

## Regarding the Future

Evolution is never finished; there is no "final answer."

Like all evolution, cultural evolution is seldom linear.

Human adaptation depends on cultural flexibility,
which in turn means balancing bonding and autonomy
while carefully adjusting "meaning" and "purpose"
and applying the best tools available at the moment
– knowledge, wisdom, resources, dialogue, respect –
to meet the perceived demands of the moment.

There are many "Roads to Ipswich," depending on where
you start, and the path that seems most feasible to you.
The more experiments in cultural adaptation there are,
the richer will our whole species be.

## This Is How We Will Survive

# POSTSCRIPT

Morning, September 11, 2001. The unthinkable happens. Terrorists hijack four scheduled airline flights simultaneously, using them – and their passengers and themselves – as flying bombs. Two take out the huge towers of the World Trade Center in downtown Manhattan; a third dives into the Pentagon; the fourth, apparently deflected by heroic passengers, crashes into open farmland in southern Pennsylvania. The destruction is unbelievable. Dust and smoke obscure and poison the air. Burning buildings collapse onto rescue workers. Two hundred-sixty million Americans watch and listen in disbelief as the details unfold. It can't be real. It can't be happening here. Not *here*! Not to *us*!!

Within an hour, the United States – the nation that claims to be the most powerful in all of human history – is brought to a standstill. All air travel is shut down. Planes in the air head for the nearest airport. People become speechless, whether with rage, fear, disbelief, or simple numbness – a failure to comprehend. What does it mean? "Why?" young students ask professors; "Why would anyone hate us so much?"

"Western civilization," said a thoughtful friend of mine, "is coming to an end." I agreed. It has fallen into a cultural trap. Its rigid, uncritical belief in its own institutions and values has blinded it to their growing maladaptiveness, especially in the eyes of much of the rest of the world. And now that the insulation that protected that belief has been so violently torn away, people, too long bereft of the dialogue skills needed for healthy responses to impending crises, are left with nowhere to turn for answers to their questions. The only framework available is to defend the old ways – to respond in kind. By using its enormous power, America will search out the guilty and everyone and everything associated with them, punishing them a thousand-fold.

This is the path of blind folly. It is like the Easter Islanders who, when their environment began to collapse around them, redoubled their competitive race to build increasingly more impressive statues to their gods. To ignore the obvious fact that massive retaliation will only breed more terrorists capable, given the multiplicity of destructive technologies available in the modern world, of an infinite variety of attacks – on people in subways, via ventilation systems in buildings, through toxins in water supplies – and on and on and on. Today's

406

world is as porous as Swiss cheese. To protect every possible route of entry would demand most of the gross national income, and *still* would not guarantee national security. The consequence could only be total bankruptcy and social collapse, or an all-out global melee – or both. At the end of it, lands will be destitute and surviving peoples utterly traumatized, and nothing at all will have been solved. Retribution is not an option any more.

The other path is one of learning to see the world and Western civilization's shortcomings through the eyes of those who feel threatened by it, indeed often have a history of suffering *because* of it. The arrogant Western – especially American – belief in its own righteousness as the one force of progress and moral goodness in a sea of backward or misguided cultures has led to exactly the kind of narrow vision associated with religious fanatics. "We are doing exactly what God would do if He were in possession of all the facts."

It is the absolute faith in this dominant vision that has already threatened so many outside the West. Its "globalization" program is perceived for very good reasons as a repeat of colonialism, with all the suffering that that episode in history brought. The dismal consequences of "development" for most of the world's peoples has cost them their traditional livelihoods, disrupted their social institutions and provided neither economic nor psychic security. For them, the West has been a massive juggernaut rolling over their lives, depriving them of their autonomy and identity at one fell swoop.

The targets of the September 11 terrorism were the two symbols of this threatening double-barreled power: the World Trade Center and the Pentagon. To terrorists, those working in them were not innocent bystanders but accomplices in the growing global threat from the West. The United States claims to be "leader of the world" and proves it by housing the biggest military and financial engines that serve the wealthiest members of the global community. This same "leader" further displayed its disdain for world opinion – so secure was it in its own power and virtue – when its President (supposedly speaking for all of its citizens) dismissed the Kyoto protocols on global warming, decided to abrogate the Anti-Ballistic Missile Treaty in order to build a costly "shield" (an unlikely protection against anything), and, finally, refused to attend a UN conference in South Africa on racism, complaining huffily that it disagreed with proposed wording in the agenda.

For a nation promoting "democracy," which surely demands not only the right to speak freely, but the obligation to listen, the United States has turned its back on its own principles when they are put to the test in an international forum. The message coming through, loud and clear, is that the United States presumes it is so powerful it does not need to even extend the courtesy of a hearing to others who might disagree with it. This is a message that has resounded around the world, and the anger it engenders is real and understandable. If this book has shown anything, I believe it is this: the demeaning of one human being – or group – by another, the destruction of another's right to an identity as a valued person or culture or of another's right to an equal and respectful hearing that is taken seriously, is such a profound threat to one's psychological well-being that it leads to traumatic responses: either inward withdrawal or outward violence. The world has just seen the consequences of such long-felt, pent-up anger.

To those American students and all others who do not understand "Why anyone could hate us so much," I say leave your insulated mental cocoon; it is not really secure at all. Learn, enquire, find out about the world "outside," and how other people see us. Listen to global radio, use the Internet, make contacts, begin dialogues – engage with the whole human race. Begin to do the listening the government, the media, and the schools have either refused or neglected to do. And as we begin to listen and hear, we will modify Western civilization in ways that make it a more fit member of a diverse global community of peoples, not simply a self-proclaimed, arrogantly threatening and unwelcome "leader."

What emerges, of course, will not be the same Western civilization we have now. Today's will, blessedly, be gone, one more addition to the "ash-heap of history." But what emerges, instead of a remnant of tattered and traumatized peoples and cultures, survivors of a global self-inflicted bloodbath, could well be a vibrant, dynamically dialoguing global community of diverse peoples who at last understand that no single community or nation can peacefully evolve without a worldwide, shared realization that the human needs for bonding, for autonomy, and for meaning must be satisfied for all persons and all societies. There can never be a Utopia in an uncertain world, but there can be an evolution of human self-awareness to the point where extremes of violence of human against human, as happened on September 11, will be forever part of humankind's past. We will have evolved social ideas that take full account of the universal psychological needs of human nature, and thus make such violence unthinkable. That is the only route to true global security.

Cottage Grove, OR
September, 2001

# NOTES

## Introduction

1 Much of the material in this Introduction was presented in an essay, "Life: What Is It?," at the Sixth Conference of the International Society for Philosophy and Psychotherapy, which had the theme "Life, Love, and Death," Oct. 13–15, 1998, FuKuang University, Elan, Taiwan.

2 Karl Popper (1959: 5).

3 William Hazlitt, quoted by W.H. Auden in A. Freemantle (ed.) (1964: 13).

4 Edwin Hutchins (1996).

5 For an excellent yet brief discussion of the Laplacean fallacy, see Michael Polanyi (1962: 139–42).

6 To date, I have not been able to locate the original print from which I made this remembered drawing. At the time when I saw it, hanging on a faculty member's office wall, it caught my eye and I studied it for many minutes, even though, at the time, I had no knowledge of the myth of Indra's Net. When, many years later, that myth came to my attention, this image immediately came back to me. Thus, while I cannot vouch for its "authenticity" as a representation of Indra and his net, it seems to me to conform to what such an image might well have been in an artist/believer's mind.

7 Thomas Cleary (trans.) (1984: 21).

8 *Ibid*, p.19.

9 *Ibid*, pp.20–1. The reader may find some parallels here with the nature of a hologram.

10 David M. Standlea (1998). Quote is from p.96.

11 Mary Catherine Bateson (1990).

12 Murray Gell-Mann (1994: 303). See also Alan Lightman and Owen Gingerich (1991) for an analysis of when scientific theories can no longer absorb "peculiar facts" and a discipline begins to change its viewpoint about the working "truth" it describes. They explore the human psychology involved in changes in world view.

13 At the turn of the millennium the British Government's Natural Environmental Research Council reported that although some of the countryside is beginning slowly to recover from devastation during the past half century, other parts continue to decline. See John Vidal (2000).

14 For how unpaid interactions lie outside the social accounting system, see Jeremy Rifkin (2000). For how helping others is highly emotionally rewarding, see Robert E. Lane (2000).

15 Robert E. Lane (2000: 26ff). See also Michael Ellison (2001).

16 While I was living in England in the 1950s, the resettlement of nuclear working-class families to new "family housing" tracts in London's East End destroyed extended

family relationships. Parents with small children found themselves physically separated from the grandparents who helped to look after the children on a day-to-day
basis, but who now could not afford the bus fare to travel each day to their children's
new homes.

17  See, for example, Harvey Jackins and others (1999). Jackins founded "Re-evaluation
Counseling" in the 1970s. Although not a trained psychologist (and perhaps for this
very reason), he has developed powerful insights into human psychological repression and methods for dealing with it. See also his *The Benign Reality* (1981).

18  See Harvey Wallace (1999) for excellent discussion of this still understudied topic.
Domestic violence affects far too many people in Western countries, especially the
United States. There is some question as to whether the incidence of domestic
violence has been increasing or is simply more frequently reported in recent decades
owing to changes in overall cultural attitudes that permit victims and outsiders more
freedom to speak out and obtain social backing for intervention. Whole societies in
the past have exercised "macro-denial" of common violent behaviors that occur in
private. See Stanley Cohen (2001).

19  Catherine Cameron (2000). Although Elizabeth Loftus and others have argued that
most memories are unsubstantiated, many others, such as Cameron, have files of
corroborated cases that cannot be dismissed. See Elizabeth Loftus (1994) and E.F.
Loftus, S. Polensky, and M.T. Fullilove (1994). Alexander McFarlane and Bessel A.
van der Kolk (1996) counter Loftus' arguments in detail, explaining the complexity
of memory formation at different ages and of conditions of recall; they also note that
perpetrators as well as victims are subject to amnesiac, dissociative repression of traumatic occurrences (see especially pp. 564–71).

20  Bridget F. Grant (2000). On page 112, she writes: "Approximately 1 in 4 children
younger than 18 in the United States is exposed to alcohol abuse or alcohol dependence in the family."

21  See Rodger Doyle (2000) and Sissela Bok (1998) for insightful descriptions of
American attitudes toward violence.

22  Aaron Kipnis (1999: 4) reports how this happened to him after he was beaten as a
child by his stepfather.

23  Psychiatrist James Gilligan, M.D., former director of mental health for the
Massachusetts prison system, states: "America has for many years had the highest
per capita imprisonment rate in the world," higher even than the Soviet Union or
South Africa in their most repressive heydays (Gilligan, 1996: 23). By the turn of
the millennium, two million people were incarcerated in the United States, 10 to
50 times the rate in all other industrialized nations. Interestingly, U.S. presidential
candidate Al Gore lost thousands of votes in Florida, enough to have made him
president, had not the Clinton administration disenfranchised so many black ex-
felons who had served sentences for merely using drugs (see Duncan Campbell,
2000b).

24  Kipnis (1999: Ch. 6, "Drugs and Criminalization"). Many European countries,
particularly Holland, have had considerable success decriminalizing drugs, thus
removing organized crime and all its money from the equation. Not only has drug
use dropped, so have crime, AIDS, and other socially costly diseases, not to mention
prison costs (see Kipnis, 1999: 137–8). And on July 1, 2001, Portugal, a socially
conservative country, enacted a law that totally decriminalizes drug use, treating it as
a social and health problem instead. (Holland and other liberal countries simply
ignore their laws against drug use; Portugal is the first to legally treat it as an illness.)
See Giles Tremlett (2001).

25  Anecdote is by personal communication with David Groves, 1998. Other data are
from the Henry J. Kaiser Foundation's 1999 survey, "Kids and Media at the New
Millennium," reported in John Leland (2000).

26 Herbert I. Schiller (1973); Jerry Mander (1978); Michael N. Nagler (1982). For the effects of media violence on society see Thomas Robinson *et al.* (2001), Craig Anderson and Brad Bushman (2002), and Jeffrey G. Johnson *et al.* (2002).

27 Eliot Marshall (2000d). For manmade environmental pollutants as a cause of ADHD, see Theo Colborn *et al.* (1997), especially Chapters 10 and 11.

28 See Leland (2000), cited in n.25 above.

29 Linda Holler (2002).

30 Lucinda Franks (2000). See also the interview on NPR's Merrow Report, November 29, 2000.

31 P.C. Violas (1978: 13).

32 The political hue-and-cry of presidential candidates campaigning during the 2000 election about keeping America's future economy competitive by pushing schoolchildren to meet ever-higher academic standards is a case in point. No one seemed to notice, during the month-long post-election battle over "validly marked ballots," that had children in earlier decades been trained in citizenship as well as academics, today's voters would have been as skilled in the voting booth as they are in the workplace.

33 Elliot Aronson (2000: 13 and 15).

34 *Ibid*, p.19. Elliot Aronson (2000, ch. 6).

35 See also Ron Powers (2002) for an insightful look at the causes of increasingly violent acts among American teenagers from middle-class homes. He repeatedly demonstrates the absence of meaningful community and feelings of significance in their lives.

36 Nathalie Guibert and Marie-Pierre Subtil (2000: 33).

37 Alice Miller (1980).

38 The November 2000 issue of *Multinational Monitor*, and many other issues as well, document ongoing corporate and regulatory failures to protect workers' physical health. Mental stresses on workers are also the subject of numerous monographs, including such classics as John Kenneth Galbraith (1978) and Paul Wachtel (1983). More recently, see Eileen Applebaum and Rosemary Batt (1993), John Kotter (1995), Anthony Sampson (1995), and Richard Sennett (1998).

39 Wachtel (1983: 120).

40 Sennett (1998: 22).

41 Lewis Carroll (1883/1960: 209–10).

42 See Brayton Bowden, and Public Radio Partnership (1999).

43 See Vern Baxter (1994) and Vern Baxter and Anthony Margavio (1996). See also Tom Brown interviewed by Bowden (1999) for the Public Radio Partnership, Tape #5, and Brown's own book, *The Anatomy of Fire* (1999).

44 Two recent books making this point are: John Gray (1998) and Peter Söderbaum (2000). The first is more polemic, the second more measured in its arguments, with suggestions for modifying our definitions of "economic values."

45 The historic search over several centuries by the Russian people for their own identity – and their failure to find it as they looked outside themselves for "models" to follow – has been well documented by Esther Kingston-Mann (1999). This sad story is being replicated today by any number of societies trying to "modernize" by copying the West, especially the United States.

46 Alan Briskin (1999a, 1999b).

47 Urie Bronfenbrenner *et al.* (1996: Ch.3). For the situation in Great Britain see Richard G. Wilkinson (1994).

48 Tom Brown in Bowden (1999), Tape #5.

49 Rodger Doyle (2000: 22).

50 Bronfenbrenner *et al.* (1996: Ch.21).

51 Kipnis (1999), various places.

52 *Ibid*, pp.173–4.

53 Data cited by Alan Briskin (1999a), Tape #5. See also Shankar Vedantam (2002).

54 James Garbarino (1996).

55 Curtis Gans (2000).

56 Joseph Tainter (1988). Today the impact on our natural support systems is also being ignored, as pointed out recently by a panel of thirty-three scientists (see Pimm *et al.*, 2001).

57 For M. King Hubbert's data see Hubbert (1969, 1971, 1973). His predictions have been confirmed recently by Kenneth Deffeyes (2002).

58 Two well-known leaders in the development of innovative yet sensible designs for energy-efficient systems, from transportation, to building, to industrial processing are Amory and Hunter Lovins of the Rocky Mountain Institute, Aspen, Colorado. A major source of information on energy and other global issues is the Worldwatch Institute, 1776 Massachusetts Ave., NW, Washington, DC, 20036.

59 There are two disparate explanations for the crisis, and how it should be resolved. On the one hand, professional business persons and academic economists see too much regulation and the lack of a competitive free market as the problem, and recommend removing all regulations of utilities and encouraging the building of new generating plants to meet "demand." (See *Manifesto on the California Electricity Crisis*, endorsed by thirty-one such professionals and academics, released under the auspices of the University of California Berkeley, Haas School of Business, January 26, 2001, *http://haas.berkeley.edu/news/california_electricity_crisis.html*. Accessed Jan. 10, 2002.) The other point of view is held by critics of energy corporations. Harvey Wasserman, a senior adviser to Greenpeace USA, blames corporations for their past investment mistakes in energy generation, particularly in costly nuclear power plants, and their big corporate customers who threatened to start generating their own energy more cheaply. He points out that two smaller, publicly owned utilities in California which long ago began to diversify and turn more to renewable energy, were unaffected by the "crisis" as they had enough local energy sources to supply their customers. He argues for publicly owned and controlled local utility systems. (See Harvey Wasserman, "California's Deregulation Disaster," *The Nation*, February 12, 2001; available at *http://www.thenation.com/doc.mhtml?I=20020212&c-3&s=wasserman*. Available Jan. 10, 2001.) Jess Fammarlund, at the Mark Hatfield School of Government at Portland State University, wrote "California's energy crisis hits Northwest like a tidal Wave," in *The San Francisco Chronicle*, June 20, 2001: A-19, in which he describes the long-distance ripples (or tsunamis!) that can occur in highly complex networks; four other states were significantly affected – Washington, Oregon, Idaho, and Montana. I, of course, am far more in agreement with the latter two authors cited. (It now appears the newly defunct energy company, Enron, was also to blame.)

60 Ross Gelbspan (1998).

61 One who argues that today's global warming is being forced by human-produced greenhouse gases is Thomas J. Crowley (2000). One who believes that the human contribution is only marginal is Harm J. de Blij (2000).

62 S.A. Changnon and D.R. Easterling (2000); D.R. Easterling *et al.* (2000).

63 Dennis Normile (2000).

64 Kathryn Brown (2000); Bruce P. Finney *et al.* (2000).

65 Thomas Kocherry and Thankappan Achary (1989). When I visited Kerala in November, 1995, I saw the multicolored and multi-meshed nets hand-tied by local fishermen, and heard their laments about the encroachment of the "big boats."

66 For a general summary on climate and disease see Paul R. Epstein (1999, 2000). For a more detailed analysis of climate change on crops, see C. Rosensweig and D. Hillel (1998), especially pp.101–22.

67 Kader Asmal (2000). Asmal received the 2000 Annual Award at the Stockholm Water Symposium, where such issues as water governance, water supply and pollu-

tion abatement, and water for food security were discussed. The conference concluded that a radical shift in thinking about water availability and management is needed, one that abandons the dominant, economically based approach for a completely different, ecologically based one.

68 Michael A. Mallin (2000).
69 See de Blij (1993: Ch.5); Paul R. Epstein (2000). See also Anthony J. McMichael *et al.* (eds.) (1996).
70 Eliot Marshall (2000a, 2000b).
71 Peter Gill (2000); Robin McKie (2000).
72 See de Blij (2000).
73 Gary Gardner and Brian Halweil (2000). Quote is from p.55.
74 For urban smog effects, see Paul R. Epstein (2000). Comments on asthma and allergies on p. 50. For effects of dust (as well as saline drinking water) due to drying of Aral Sea, see Amelia Gentleman (2000).
75 Jocelyn Kaiser (2000).
76 Constance Holden (2000).
77 Theo Colborn *et al.* (1997).
78 Michael D. Lemonick (2000).
79 National Research Council, Committee on Hormonally Active Agents in the Environment (1999). See also the press release, August 3, 1999, in *The National Academies News*, National Academy of Sciences. Comments are those of endocrinologist Howard A. Bern, a committee member and member of the National Academy of Sciences, in personal communication with the author, November, 1999.
80 I have obviously ignored the possibility of future widespread political violence, either as an outcome of coming crises or in resentment against undue American hegemony. The current American fear of terrorism is not misplaced, but it fails to see that military protection of its privileged position will never resolve its causes. Enemies do not exist without good reason.
81 See editorial from *Le Monde*, reprinted in the *Guardian Weekly*, May 24, 2000: 25, for French motorways story.
82 Personal letter from S.A. Shah, January, 2000. The full quote can be found at the end of Chapter IX.
83 For Japan, see Darius Mehri (2000); for China, see Robin Tudge (2001).
84 C.J.L. Murray and A.D. Lopez (1996).
85 His Holiness the Dalai Lama and Howard C. Cutler, M.D. (1998). Quote is from p.56.

## I Questioning the "scientized" image

1 Edward O. Wilson (1998).
2 For an excellent explanation of the Laplacean fallacy, see Michael Polanyi (1962: 134–42). For limits to chaos theory, which arose as an antidote to a highly predictable, clock-like Newtonian universe, as a "final" model for reality, see Robert Pool (1989) and Stephen H. Kellert (1993). For a more comprehensive synthesis of order in "far-from-equilibrium" systems (like a living organism) see Mae-Wan Ho (1998).
3 Barry Schwartz (1986: 312).
4 Jerome Kagan (1998).
5 Sigmund Koch (1999: 16).
6 Rom Harré (2000), a review of Karl E. Scheibe (2000).
7 Charles Taylor (1985: 92).
8 Randy Thornhill and Craig Palmer (2000).
9 Charles Darwin (1871).

10 Irenäus Eibl-Eibesfeldt (1989: 204–24); also, Robert Hinde (1974: 180–9); Jonathan Cole (1998). H. Haynes, B.L. White, and R. Held (1965) noted in an article that the distance between the face of a suckling infant and its mother's face is the distance at which a newborn's eyes focus most clearly.

11 David Maybury-Lewis (1992: 92–119).

12 For a comprehensive critique of the "evo-psycho" set's just-so stories about male/female sexuality, see Natalie Angier (1999: Ch.18). Crucial "set" members include psychologist David M. Buss (1994), who claims genetically-wired mate "preferences" exist; Randy Thornhill and Craig T. Palmer (2000), who insist rape is a natural male mating strategy, not misogynist violence; Steven Pinker (1997, 1998), who argues that the human brain is hard-wired for male promiscuity; R.V. Short and E. Balaban (1994), biologists who claim universal promiscuity among human males; Robert Wright (1994), who does likewise; Helena Cronin (1991), a biologist who argues males of all animal species are promiscuous and females select the "fittest" mates; and Napoleon Chagnon, the anthropologist who felt compelled to explain Yanomami warfare in evolutionary terms, first as competition over scarce game (protein) and later as reproductive competition for females. (See discussion by Patrick Tierney, 2000: Ch.10.)

13 The diorama of an Australopithecine couple crossing the savanna occurs in the American Museum of Natural History in New York City (see Figure I.2). For insights into how artists' imagined constructions of our fossil ancestors influence deeply our beliefs about human nature see Stephanie Moser (1998).

14 George W. Barlow and J. Silverberg (1980: 15). This book was compiled from papers given at an AAAS annual meeting in 1978, on the subject of sociobiology. The symposium, which as then Chair of the Biology Section, I had helped to get onto the program, lasted two whole days, and attracted enormous public attention because of the racist and sexist implications being read by some into the propositions propounded by the sociobiologists. During the last half-day session, there was a near-riot when E.O. Wilson, author of the controversial book *Sociobiology*, and nominal "father" of the field, was about to speak. Protesters along the standing-room-only sidelines suddenly ran onto the stage and one poured a glass of ice water onto Wilson's head. The session chair averted a riot by allowing the protesters five minutes of mike-time to make their points.

15 It seems it was F.A. von Hayek (1955) who brought the term "scientism" to prominence.

16 It is always dangerous when scientists start proclaiming their pet theories as dogmatic truths, since most theories get modified with time and many are totally wrong. Examples from the past include the following: In the eighteenth century, the prestigious French Academy of Sciences proclaimed the remnants of meteorites in various museums as fakes, since meteorites did not exist but were merely superstitious visions of religious hysterics (Michael Polanyi, 1962: 138). Thomas Huxley, in the nineteenth century, anxious to support Darwin's evolutionary theories, mistakenly skewed data on brain sizes among human races to support the idea of human evolution from apes, claiming some (the white race) as more advanced (cited by Stephen Jay Gould, 1998: 139). In the twentieth century, Barbara McClintock's discovery that genes in maize actually move about on the chromosomes when the plant is stressed was treated as heresy and denied legitimacy for nearly four decades by other geneticists who believed genes were fixed in place. It took twenty years for her ideas to be accepted, and she finally won a Nobel Prize shortly before she died (Evelyn Fox Keller, 1983). More recently, in the 1990s it has been discovered that the cause of Type 2 diabetes, an increasingly prevalent disease, is not a deficiency in insulin receptors at all, as had been the belief for decades. Says Morris White, "Nearly every major feature of this disease that we thought was true 10 years ago turned out to be

wrong." "If we're right ... then the treatment of type 2 diabetes should be completely different in 5 years," says Domenico Accili (quoted by Joe Alper, 2000: 37, 39). Finally, on a lighter note, the universal belief that flocks of chickens are genetically programmed to form pecking orders is not universal, according to Alison Johnson (1994: 97–8). Her free-ranging birds did not do this. Says Johnson, "I cannot believe that after watching our hens for eight years I have missed what Konrad Lorenz ... calls 'a very definite order, in which each bird is afraid of those that are above her in rank.' If our birds are not so orderly, perhaps it is because they are not Teutonic."

17  Daniel Dennett (1995).

18  Paul R. Gross, Norman Levitt, and Martin W. Lewis (1996).

19  Ian Hacking (1999). Quotes can be found on pp.94 and 95; emphasis added. I strongly recommend this elegantly argued and clearly written analysis to all who want to understand this particular battlefield better. It is a good antidote to the polemical writings of the scientists who feel threatened. Among those who have criticized absolutist science, Hacking cites Paul Feyerabend, who argued that the methods of science did not justify the claims of absolute knowledge often made for it (see Feyerabend 1993). Others he cites went further, suggesting the constructionist position noted in the text: that theories are more often shaped by the social world in which the scientists live and work, rather than by the intrinsic properties of reality itself (see Thomas Kuhn, 1970; Bruno Latour and Steve Woolgar, 1986; and Andrew Pickering, 1984).

20  The author worked for two decades on questions of the structure of liquid water inside living cells and its role in facilitating and/or stabilizing the folding of large, biologically functional molecules such as proteins and nucleic acids when in the presence of other small molecules and ions also found inside cells.

21  See Mary Midgley (1978, 1981, 1985, and 1992). The latter two books deal with other issues discussed in this and later chapters as well.

22  See, for example, Susan Blackmore (1999).

23  Midgley (1999).

24  Michael Polanyi (1962: 139); emphasis added.

25  E.F. Schumacher (1977); emphases in original. Internal quotes are of the psychiatrist, Viktor E. Frankl (1969). Quotes are on pp.4, 5, and 5–6, respectively.

26  Peter Alpert, "The Boulder and the Sphere." My quote is from an early, unpublished draft. Other quotes from this work elsewhere in the chapter are in the published paper, Alpert (1995).

27  Alfred North Whitehead (1946: 85–6); second emphasis added.

28  B.F. Skinner (1972).

29  Evelyn Fox Keller (1983). The terms for McClintock's findings, "jumping genes" or "transposons," were first described by her in the 1950s. See pp.10, 11, 187, and 190.

30  Chimpanzees do seem to experience meanings and exhibit weak forms of culture, but the extent to which these are critical for group survival is not clear. Surely, they can perceive "moods" in each other through displays and body language. But planned coordination of behaviors is less obvious. The seemingly dedicated tracking and killing of the remnant males of a fissioned group in the Gombe Game Reserve reported by Jane Goodall (1986: 503–17) does suggest the possibility of communicated moods in a broad sense.

31  Throughout the book I have used a variety of terms more or less interchangeably, to express the concept of "shared meaning." Among these are: world view; world frame; world picture; meaning system; cultural narrative; cultural meaning. The German phrase, *Weltanschauung*, has the same meaning.

32  See F.B.M. de Waal (1982, 1989), and Filippo Aureli and F.B.M. de Waal (2000).

33 Many Native American cultures have oral histories implying that their ancestors moved through various "worlds" during their early wanderings on their new continent, changing their adaptations as they moved about.

34 Signe Howell and Roy Willis (1989: 20). See also Ron Powers (2002) for an insightful look at the causes of increasingly violent acts among American teenagers from middle-class homes. He repeatedly demonstrates the absence of meaningful community and any feelings of significance in the lives of most adolescents.

35 Currently there is a growing body of evidence suggesting that violent behaviors have social causes, whether at the personal or cultural level. See Eliot Marshall's (2000c) news article, "The Shots Heard 'Round the World', " in a special issue on "Violence" in *Science*. Also, comments by Debra L. Niehoff (2000) and by Richard Rhodes (2000), both in "Letters" in *Science*.

36 For Jared Diamond (1997), culture and history are shaped mainly by the environment. Meaning, when considered at all, is seen as a product, never a cause.

## II Why we primates are not "game theorists"

1 Charlie Russell and Maureen Enns (1999).

2 Vernon Reynolds (1976: 158ff). For an analysis of data on feral children, see Douglas K. Candland (1993); and for a catalogue of recorded cases, ancient and recent, see J.A.L. Singh and R.M. Zingg (1939).

3 Cited by Morton Hunt (1982: 228).

4 H.F. Harlow (1959) and H.F. Harlow and M.K. Harlow (1962). Reynolds (1976: 58ff) reports two more cases of children raised with little social contact earlier this century. One, kept in total isolation for six years, developed only partially, and died before age 10; the other, kept with a deaf-mute mother until age 7, was speechless and fearful, but eventually developed normal behavior. As Reynolds observes, sheer physical contact with another human being makes an enormous difference during early development, a point that is dwelt on in Chapter VI.

5 Killer whales and some other marine mammals seem to form lineage groups and engage in considerable within-group interactions, but it is not clear to what extent their normal development depends on this. The same may perhaps be true for elephant families; see Karen McComb *et al.* (2001) who point out the "civilizing" effect of adult females on juveniles, as they teach them both social and survival skills. Thus, heavy poaching of adults causes young males to run amok.

This need for adults as behavioral models is also true for condors. Chicks reared by humans (even though gloves shaped like adult condor heads were used when feeding them) cannot hunt for themselves on being released into the wild. Evidently they must learn from adult birds. Thus, the elaborate efforts at "saving" this endangered species by hatching and rearing them in nurseries has been a failure (see de Waal, 2001a: 27–8).

6 Ruth Bennett (1999).

7 The leaders of this group are, among others, John Tooby and Leda Cosmides, who propose that specific areas of the brain evolved to deal with Pleistocene "problems" such as mate selection, sexual infidelity, language acquisition, and so forth. A general outline of their ideas can be found in Jerome H. Barkow, Leda Cosmides and John Tooby (1992). The vagueness of their arguments decided me against trying to include them here.

8 Only recently has a whole group of genes, known as the homeobox or Hox genes, been identified that seem to direct the three-dimensional anatomical development of organs and appendages in many different kinds of animals. These genes code for proteins which in turn activate the products of other genes, yielding the working proteins that act during embryonic development to control shapes of body compo-

nents: limbs, nervous system, gut and so forth. The Hox genes are very similar in a wide diversity of living animals. For a popular discussion, see Sean B. Carroll, Jennifer K. Greiner, and Scott D. Weatherbee (2001). For a more scientific analysis, see Eric H. Davidson (2001).

Regarding heritable behavioral diseases there is mid-age-onset dementia known as Huntington's chorea. It is now known to be caused by a mutated gene that produces an abnormal form of the protein, huntingtin, that is needed to trigger production of another protein (brain-derived neurotrophic factor) necessary for continued survival of brain cells in the striatum, a critical region of the brain (see Yvon Tottier and Jean Louis Mandel, 2001, for comments and the research article by Chiara Zuaccato and 12 others). Other brain deficiencies such as agenesis of the corpus callosum (which connects the two cerebral hemispheres) may be gene-based, but a specific gene and how it works have yet to be discovered.

9  Richard Dawkins (1998: 90).

10 Richard Strohman (1997: 194). For information on the human genome compared to the genome of other, "simpler" species, see Jean-Michel Caverie (2001). For an in-depth analysis of the human genome to date, see J. Craig Venter and 273 others (2001). The latter conclude there are 26,588 known protein-coding genes and esti-mate a possible 12,000 more, so it is possible there may be nearly 40,000-protein coding genes finally identified, but this is far short of the expected 100,000 such genes.

11 Charles Darwin (1860/1962: 175–6). The term species, used by Darwin here and in his seminal book, *The Origin of Species*, has proven problematic for evolutionary theory, for it puts sharp boundaries between "species" that no longer exist, since living forms are in constant flux. Jody Hey (2001) points out that the term species is more a mental convenience for human thought than an aspect of reality

I strongly recommend Darwin's diaries, as well as his major work, *The Origin of Species*, to those wishing to get inside his mind and grasp the way he thought about the processes of evolution. They offer a good antidote to those "ultra-Darwinists" who use his name to support their own favored interpretations of his theory.

12 J. von Neumann and O. Morgenstern (1947).

13 For the theory of kin selection see W.D. Hamilton (1963, 1975). In the latter, he somewhat modifies his original stark theory. For reciprocal altruism, see R.L. Trivers (1971). And for a highly mathematical analysis of egalitarian cooperation see Robert Axelrod and W.D. Hamilton (1981), and Axelrod (1984). See also Henry C. Plotkin's excellent comments (Plotkin, 1982a) regarding the epistemological errors introduced when linear causality is invoked to explain the evolutionary process; it altogether ignores the fact of responsive adaptations by all organisms that in turn modify their surroundings, and so effect their own evolution. "Hence a complete evolutionary theory must be one which invokes multiple units of selection, and multiple storage sites" (1982a: 11).

14 See Jane Goodall (1986) and Shirley Strum (1987).

15 Dorothy L. Cheney and Robert M. Seyfarth (1990: 71, 79); emphasis added.

16 We Europeans and Americans who have been raised in a world of social contracts, do tend to be social bookkeepers, storing reciprocal debts in our heads. In the Cameroons, for example, it is quite different. According to anthropologist colleagues, Kent Maynard and Susan Diduk at Denison University who have done research there, it is friendship that allows people to make requests of one another. If I need help, I expect you to come if you are free. But if my request is a burden, and you refuse or make only a token effort, no offense is taken. If a favor is given, there is no expectation by either party of an obligation to pay it back. There is no accounting system. Obligations and commitments are not commoditized, even in one's head.

17 See Cheney and Seyfarth (1990: 71).

18  See Richard Dawkins (1976) for the explication of this argument.

19  This was what the maize geneticist Barbara McClintock discovered; DNA did not stay put, but transposed, or "jumped," from one place to another in response to environmental signals. In its new location, it behaved very differently. It was many decades before this "heresy" was accepted; it goes against the hierarchic dogma of a linear process controlled only by genes. For discussion, see Evelyn Fox Keller (1983, 1985). A recent book on the interactions between developing organisms and their environment is J. Gerhart and M. Kirschner (1997). In his review of this book John Tyler Bonner (1998) notes that "A ... major theme that runs through the book is the interplay between rigid hard-wiring of genetic information and exploratory plastic behavior of molecules and cells."

20  See references cited in n.8 and n.10 of this chapter. Also, for coordinated groups of genes acting together see Gehring (1999) and Robert Riddle and Clifford Tabin (1999). It is now becoming clear that genes are few in number and variable in action. Small changes within a gene, or even in its position on the chromosomes, can cause different phenotypes.

21  Barbara McClintock (1984: 801). Since her discovery of jumping genes in maize, they have been found in numerous other organisms.

22  Richard Strohman (1997: 195, 196, 199); emphasis added.

23  Known as alleles, the competing genes offer variations among offspring. An example is the three alternative antigen-coding genes that determine human blood types: A, B, and O. Since we get one gene from each parent, we can have the genotypes AA, AB, AO, BB, BO, and OO. Since "O" means "no antigen," there are just four blood types for transfusions: "A," "B," "AB," and "O."

24  Sometimes alternatives to "cooperate" are given as "defect" or "cheat," behavioral options cited in the Prisoner's Dilemma, another favorite of game theorists. For a full explanation, see Axelrod (1984).

25  The improbability of these assumptions is greatly underscored by the recent revelations about the human genome. Given the number of proteins coded by genes, and the number of controlling functions of other genes in turning coding genes on and off, researchers predicted there would be around 300,000 different genes in humans. The actual number is only 30,000. The same pieces of genetic code turn up over and over again in many different places on the chromosomes, presumably having multiple functions. Genes, it turns out, are not the whole story. Their surroundings in the chromosomes makes a big difference. It becomes more and more likely that many "traits" known to be inherited are not due to genes, *per se*, but to where a gene is located. For all but the simplest of traits, it may be mainly the genes' context that is changing, rather than the genes themselves, and behaviors are seldom simple.

26  Aubrey Gorbman *et al.* (1983: 139ff).

27  Details of the brain's functions are considered in Chapter IV.

28  Elliott Sober and David Sloan Wilson (1998: 97). This book is, for theoretical geneticists, a seriously argued explanation of how group selection could evolve among nonrelated individuals. It opens the floodgates to a lot more useful theory-building than allowed by the old theory about the limited levels at which natural selection can occur.

29  David Sloan Wilson (1975, 1977). For a detailed elaboration of the entire theory of group selection, see Sober and Wilson (1998).

30  For the research on hens, see W.M. Muir (1995).

31  See William Swenson, David Sloan Wilson, and Roberta Elias (2000) for soil ecosystem experiments. For Thompson's overall generalization, see John N. Thompson (1999) (the quote can be found on p.2116). My colleague, John Todd, of Ocean Arks International, has made practical use of readymade associations of

soil decomposers to clean up streams polluted by chemicals related to the old wood preservatives. He inoculated the stream with bits of decaying railroad ties, where natural selection had already done its work assembling a functional decomposer community able to break down these pollutants (personal communication). This work has been written up in a pamphlet titled *Living Machines*, published by Organica, a nonprofit organization located in Budapest; Organica is the Central European Partner of Dr. Todd's non-profit, Ocean Arks International.

32 To my mind, the detailed arguments put forth by Sober and Wilson (1998) completely bring group selection (and also community selection) into respectable Darwinian thinking without resorting to "selfish, competitive" genes. I urge all dedicated skeptics to read it.

33 See Niles Eldredge and Stephen J. Gould (1972). Also, Niles Eldredge (1999). Finally, Stephen J. Gould (1989: 53–64) has a discussion of the conditions under which outbursts of evolutionary activity have occurred in the history of life.

34 Evidence that a meteorite extinguished the dinosaurs is cited in Richard A. Kerr (1992) and in Carl C. Swisher, III *et al.* (1992). There is some dispute, however, as to whether the meteorite caused the extinction. Vincent Courtillot and his colleagues in Paris believe the Deccan Traps, a huge volcanic outpouring in India that occurred around the same time, were the cause of extinctions (see V. Courtillot, 1999). For a comparison of the theories, see W. Alvarez and Frank Alaro (1992: 28–56).

35 Niles Eldredge (1999) p.10. This book is strongly recommended for those who wish to ponder how best to think about the evolutionary process.

36 See Richard W. Byrne and Andrew Whiten (1997). Most of the other chapters in this book are variations supporting this theme. A striking exception is the chapter by Shirley C. Strum, Deborah Forster, and Edwin Hutchins, "Why Machiavellian Intelligence May Not Be Machiavellian," pp.50–85. Strum's work on baboons comes up later in this chapter, and Edwin Hutchins' work on shared (group) cognition in Chapter V.

37 Behaviors of this type have been attributed to humans too, where males supposedly are genetically primed to choose females with waist:hip ratios of 0.7, and to mate as often as possible, while females look for the "best provider," with whom they will trade "sex for meat" in expectation he will support their children. For details, see David M. Buss (1992).

38 See discussion and references cited in Dorothy Cheney and Robert Seyfarth (1990) and also references to social cheats and free-riders in Robin Dunbar (1996).

39 Solly Zuckerman (1932).

40 Shirley Strum and William Mitchell (1987: 88, 89, emphases in original; 90). A decade earlier, British anthropologist Vernon Reynolds had already contrasted baboon and chimpanzee models of the evolution of human social structure, heavily favoring the latter (1976: 50–6).

41 Shirley Strum (1987: 69); emphasis in original.

42 *Ibid*, p.160ff.

43 See Richard Potts (1987: 45–6).

44 Frans de Waal (1989) Chs.3 and 4, and especially pp.154–62.

45 de Waal and Frans Lanting (1997: 20).

46 de Waal (1996: 178ff).

47 Phyllis C. Jay (1965); Yukimaru Sugiyama (1967). Sugiyama did the field work in south India cited by Jay.

48 Reynolds (1976: 54). Reynolds and his wife studied chimpanzees in the Budongo forest of Uganda in the early 1960s. During this same period Jane Goodall, watching chimpanzees in the Gombe Stream Reserve in Tanzania, found similar peaceable, nonaggressive behavior. Her work in this respect has been painstakingly reanalyzed

by Margaret Power (1991), who reports a change between this early behavior and that observed later at Gombe.

49  Goodall (1986: 49).

50  *Ibid*, p.495ff.

51  See *ibid*, pp. 503–34, for a detailed account, and citation of similar observations by others in a nearby reserve. Although Goodall believes that this is "natural" behavior for all chimpanzees, a prelude to human warlikeness, Margaret Power (1991) believes it is a response to excessive stress.

52  Dian Fossey (1983). For further research on gorillas, see George B. Schaller (1964).

53  Frans de Waal (1989: 211).

54  de Waal *et al.* (2000).

55  Power (1991: 33). Goodall, too, recognized this as a potential problem in need of further analysis (see Goodall, 1986: 52). Unlike the secure food supplied to animals in captivity, that used in the wild came at unknown intervals and changed the social dynamic.

56  Douglas Candland (1994), primatologist at Bucknell University, personal communication. Clearly, conditions in captivity vary widely from place to place. de Waal *et al.* (2000) observed high stress with crowding but less aggression among captive animals at the Yerkes Regional Primate Research Center in Atlanta where they made their observations.

57  de Waal (1989: 61–9).

58  See, for example, Francis Fukuyama (1998). Fukuyama reported only on Luit's wounds and subsequent death, calling the other males cold-blooded murderers, and quite ignoring the effort of the three to make-up, a totally distorting omission.

59  de Waal (1982, 1996). Goodall (1986) suggests that such behavior is more likely to occur among captive primates who cannot flee from violent antagonists, and so learn to avert conflict or repair its effects in order to reduce overall social tension. de Waal and his colleagues (2000) agree with this assessment.

60  Frans de Waal and Frans Lanting (1997: Ch.4); quote can be found on p.110. Also see de Waal (1989: Ch.4), for sexuality and placidity in stumptails. More recently, Craig B. Stanford (2000) criticizes the large distinction de Waal seems to make between chimpanzee and bonobo behaviors, claiming that in the "wild" bonobo females are far less sexually receptive, sex is used in the way he describes far less often, and the apes are more aggressive than he pictures them. Unfortunately, Stanford overdraws his case, using exaggerated claims for both species. Furthermore, the fact that under stress in captivity, bonobos do seem to use sex, suggests it is an adaptation to highly stressful situations, which is of interest for human societies also.

61  Frans de Waal and Frans Lanting (1997: 2). For the most recent summary of prima-tologists' varied views on primates as models of human social evolution see de Waal (2001b).

62  See Cheney and Seafarth (1990); Strum (1987); Goodall (1986); and de Waal and Lanting (1997).

63  Goodall (1986: 452).

64  de Waal and Lanting (1997: 133–40).

65  de Waal (1996: 89).

66  These examples appear in de Waal (1996: 78–83).

67  See de Waal and Lanting (1997: Ch.6).

68  de Waal (1996: 177); emphasis in original.

69  See de Waal *et al.* (2000: 81).

70  Christopher Boehm (1999: 154). Like others before him (and no doubt those who will come after him), Boehm has fashioned his thinking after the ideas about human nature he has acquired as a Western political anthropologist. Hobbes' ideas about human nature are intrinsic to his argument.

## III  The selecting of *Homo sapiens*

1  Excellent monographs that argue, with different emphases, for learning from our past adaptations, are: Margaret Power (1991) (emphasis on cooperation in groups and spontaneous empathy); Daniel Goleman (1995) (emphasis on paying attention to our emotional guidelines in understanding human behavior); Debra Niehof (1999) (emphasis on underlying causes of violence).

2  For the first recognition of the role of climate change in evolutionary bursts of species formation, see Niles Eldredge and Stephen J. Gould (1972), and further data in Eldredge (1999). Very recently, the earliest hominid yet found, a 6 to 7 million year-old very ape-like skull (surely quite close to the "common ancestor") turned up in the middle of the Sahara (Gibbons 2002b). In the Pliocene, ancient Lake Chad, on whose shore the fossil appeared, was an enormous lake surrounded by lush forest.

3  It is not certain what should be called a different "genus" and what merely a different "species." Jared Diamond (1992) insists that because the DNA differences between humans and modern chimpanzees are less than between two species of birds currently placed in the same genus, then by rights, chimpanzees should also belong to the genus Homo, and those of our ancestors that we label under the genus Australopithecus should also be called Homo. For our purposes, we are less concerned with the fine points of naming different species than with their probable evolutionary sequencing.

4  See Sarah Blaffer Hrdy (1999).

5  Richard Potts (1996a: 10).

6  Bruce Winterhalder (1995: 182); emphasis added.

7  See Charles K. Brain (1972, 1981).

8  See R.B. Lee and I. DeVore (1968).

9  The famous skeleton, "Lucy," a member of *A. afarensis*, was discovered by Donald Johanson in East Africa, as was an earlier bipedal form, *A. anamensis*, while Dart's *A. africanus* came from South Africa, and another species, *A. bahrelghazalia*, has been discovered way up north in Chad. Variations in the arm and hand bones of these fossils, as well as in the type of plant and animal remains found nearby, suggest some but not all these groups were living both in trees and walking bipedally. See Glenn C. Conroy (1997: 213ff).

10  See Richard (Rick) Potts (1996a: 215–16, 1996b). Only with the advent of *Homo sapiens* did truly organized hunting capable of bringing down larger game develop. Even Neanderthals, who surely ate meat, did not tackle big game often, if at all. It was the Cro-Magnons, or *Homo sapiens sapiens*, who eventually colonized every continent, that often seems to have driven the local megafauna to extinction.

For evidence of later extinctions, see Paul S. Martin (1984); R.N. Holdaway and C. Jacomb (2000); Tim Flannery (2001); Richard G. Roberts and ten others (2001); and John Alroy (2001). Ross D.E. MacPhee, of the American Museum of Natural History, disagrees, arguing lack of evidence for hunting-caused extinctions (carcasses with arrow points) and blames diseases introduced by humans; Russell W. Graham, however, thinks it was climate change that mainly caused the extinctions. See Kate Wong (2001). No one, though, disputes that *Homo sapiens* did hunt big game; the question is, were they responsible for megafaunal extinctions?

Regarding the increase in brain size in *H. erectus* over time, see Milford H. Wolpoff and Rachel Caspari (1997).

11  See Robert J. Blumenschine and John A. Cavallo (1992) and Marvin Harris (1978) for discussions of women's role in obtaining meat.

12  There is now physical evidence that fishing and hunting nets attached to bow frames, as well as bows and arrows, were common 30,000 ya. Stone arrowheads provide evidence for the latter. Evidence of net-hunting dated to 29,000 ya has now been

found in Gravettian settlements in Southern Europe, from Spain to Eastern Russia. These findings explain the prevalence of small animal bones from this time, unearthed in Eastern Europe. People were not getting their protein from clubbing and spearing bigger game, such as mammoths. Similar net-hunting was mastered by Australian aborigines, by Mbuti in Africa, and by North American great basin peoples. See also Sasha Nemecek (2000) for reference to Tom Dillehay's finds of knotted cords and hide tents at a 14,700 ya site in Chile.

Chinese scholar Ma Guang Yan (1995), however, thinks these implements evolved much earlier, the first arrows being pointed sticks. Since most tools made of organic matter rapidly decay, leaving no trace, Ma proposes the global ubiquity of arrow-heads as evidence of a much older, widespread knowledge of bows and nets. As Heather Pringle (1997b) comments, "communal net hunting – capable of reaping huge windfalls of food regularly at very low risk of injury to human participants – may have been the key to development."

See also Sasha Nemecek (2000) for reference to Tom Dillehay's finds of knotted cords and hide tents at a 14,700-year-old site at Monte Verde in southern Chile.

13 Richard B. Lee (1969) notes the suppression of competition for status among the !Kung, an extant group of hunter-gatherers.

14 Paul Shepard (1998: 75). As discussed later, in Chapter VIII, this seems to be the case for the supposedly "warlike" Yanomami Indians in the Venezuelan Amazonian highlands. See Patrick Tierney (2000).

15 At the same time that these tools made hunting more proficient, they also made combat potentially more deadly. But so far as I know, the deadliest weapons of modern war – high explosives, napalm, and nuclear warheads – have never been employed in any activity one might truly call hunting, though some social groups have been known to detonate modern explosives underwater to kill and harvest fish.

16 Konrad Lorenz (1960).

17 This practice led to transmission of a deadly unconventional virus that caused motor nerve damage and death. The cause of the disease was uncovered by D.C. Gajdusek, who subsequently received a Nobel Prize (see D.C. Gajdusek, 1977).

18 It is seldom possible to know the purposes behind archeological evidence of occasional instances of human cannibalism. When human bones have been cleaned prior to burial, one cannot assume the flesh was consumed, or if so, that it was not done ritually, as a sacrament. When scarred human bones have also been fractured (to obtain brains or marrow) and discarded in the middens with animal bones, they may well have served as a dietary resource. See, for example, Alban Defleur et al. (1999) and David DeGusta (1999).

For discussions of causes of infanticide see Mark Nathan Cohen (1977: 42–5) and Patrick Tierney (2000: 265–74, 377) (the last item is a note arguing that the claim that most infanticides were of female newborns is a gross exaggeration; both sexes were almost equally likely to be killed). For natural constraints on female fertility, see R.V. Short (1976). Few anthropologists realize that ovulation is suppressed not only by prolonged lactation, but also by low-quality diet and excess physical exercise or other stress, all of which were common during periods of resource scarcity or other severe natural cataclysms during human evolution. (Only recently has the rapidity of climate swings in the Pleistocene been recognized, for instance.) Finally, infanticide is seldom easy and is usually carried out immediately after birth, before a mother–infant bond develops. In many traditional societies, a newborn is not considered truly human until welcoming ceremonies are performed. See Susan C.M. Scrimshaw (1984: 439–62, especially 449, 460–1).

19 Paul Shepard (1998: 68). See also Robert B. Edgerton (1992) for a comprehensive argument for a naturally troubled and violent human nature. Like Shepard, however,

I question his examples and remain optimistic about human compassion and peacefulness.

20 See H.J. de Blij (2000). World-famous geographer, de Blij argues the present
warming merely replicates, in both magnitude and speed, previous ones that were
not human-driven. We should nevertheless cut back on $CO_2$ emissions, not only to
ameliorate the outcome, but to learn to adapt to further coming crises, as when fossil
fuels and other resources are depleted.

21 This information comes mainly from Thomas Levenson (1989). The quote is from
p.24. For more on climate change, see articles on "Earth's Variable Climatic Past,"
section in *Science* 292: 657–93 (April 27, 2001).

22 See Thomas Blunier and Edward J. Brook (2001); Eric Monnin *et al.* (2001).

23 Laurent Labeyrie (2000); Nicholas Shackleton (2001).

24 See H.J. de Blij (1993: Chs.4–7, 2000).

25 H.J. de Blij (2000).

26 See Michael Balter and Ann Gibbons (2000). See also the detailed report by Leo
Gabunia *et al.* (2000). Pat Shipman (2000) summarizes the significance of this find.
For maps of earliest *Homo erectus* sites, see Kate Wong (2000) and Michael Balter
(2001a). Recently, Wong (2002) pointed out the value of coastal food supplies for
the early evolution of enlarging *Homo* brains, noting the value of shellfish for nour-
ishing brain tissue. This would make coastal migrations more probable than
cross-continental ones. For a history of *H. erectus* finds see Roger Lewin, Garniss
Curtis, and Carl Swisher (2000).

27 See, for examples, articles implying that advances in technology by *H. erectus* in
China and in the Near East paralleled those going on simultaneously in Africa: Ann
Gibbons (2000a); Hou Yamei, Richard Potts and others (2000); Michael Balter
(2000b). (This last article says stone tools at a 780,000-year-old site in Gesher,
Israel, were similar to those found at contemporary sites in Africa.)

28 The dispute is between the "replacement theorists" (sequential waves of humans
emerging as separate species from Africa) and the "multiregional theorists" (a single
species in sufficient contact over time globally that new waves of immigrants could
mate with any or at least some remnants of earlier populations). The replacement folk
rely on statistical data from modern distributions of genetic traits, languages, and
cultures for "proof," while multiregionalists rely mainly on regional differences in
anatomical traits in a long sequence of fossils that suggest local continuity for longer
than the 200,000 years since *Homo sapiens sapiens* supposedly "arose" in Africa. The
major replacement theorists include Allan Wilson, Rebecca Cann, Svante Pääbo, and
Chris Stringer; multiregionalists include Milford Wolpoff, Alan Thorne, John
Relethford, and Erik Trinkhaus (who believes that "modern humans were able to,
and did, reproduce with Neanderthals"; see Cidália Duarte *et al.*, 1999). A 4-year-
old child's fossil skeleton found in Portugal is described as a hybrid of Neanderthal
and modern human features, evidence of interbreeding. Some dispute this interpretation.
      Further citations of some of these researchers' work appear below.

29 Pat Shipman (2000: 492–3).

30 Luigi Luca Cavalli-Sforza (2000: 58ff). There are dozens of resources on the dates of
early human migrations and many disputes. I have chosen to cite Cavalli-Sforza as
both recent and reasoned. Like all histories, his may not be the "final word." For his
treatment of the evolution of full language competency, see p.60.

31 For the Virginia site, see Erik Stokstad (2000). For the Amazon, see Anna C.
Roosevelt (1992, 1994). See also Patrick Tierney (2000) for an evaluation of
Roosevelt's work, which is too little acknowledged in standard texts.

32 The origins of early South Americans are not straightforward. Whereas the modern
languages spoken by tribal peoples of the Americas seem to suggest three waves of

immigration across the Bering land bridge and southward (Cavalli-Sforza, 2000: 134–42, *passim*), detailed studies of numerous skeletons, 11,000 to 11,500 years old, suggest they have an African and Australian morphological affinity, not a resemblance to Asian mongoloids or American Indians (see Walter Neves, 2000, and references therein). However, as Cavalli-Sforza makes clear in his book, languages and genes do not always coincide; a particular language may become dominant in an area that is genetically distinct from the original speakers of that language.

Similarly, the recent dispute over the genetic and morphological affinities of the 9000-year-old fossil found at Kennewick, Washington (known as Kennewick Man) have raised the possibility that its ancestors were of European, not Asiatic, origin. Unfortunately, the battle between scientists and native Americans over possession of the bones has left the DNA studies that might have resolved this in limbo.

33  See Sasha Nemecek (2000) for the contributions of Jodrey, Dillehay, and Adovasio. The latter's quote is on p.84. There is an excellent map in Nemecek's article showing the various possible migration routes of humans to the Americas and the extent of exposed coastal margins. Note that coastlines offer abundant fish, an important nutrient for the developing human brain (Gibbons, 2002).

34  See de Blij (2000). He suggests this single event caused the loss of a score of human genetic subgroups or "races," leaving us today with only four major groups: African, Caucasian, Mongolian/Native American, and Australian Aborigine. Other researchers might include a few others. But surely the genetic loss after that eruption was enormous.

35  For data that foraging societies marry over very long distances, unlike later agriculturalists with which most anthropologists are familiar, see Alan Fix (1999).

36  See Allan C. Wilson and Rebecca L. Cann (1992) as well as the report of the debate it set off in *Science*, 14 August 1992: 873. For the date of 143,000 ya, see H. Horai *et al.* (1996). See also Rebecca L. Cann (2001). Here she notes the tendency for a coincidence among genetic profiles, languages, and cultural knowledges, but Cavalli-Sforza (2000) does a more in-depth analysis of this observation.

37  See Svante Pääbo (1995); Robert L. Dorit *et al.* (1995); and Ann Gibbons (1997b).

38  Cavalli-Sforza (2000: 79).

39  Francisco Ayala (1995).

40  Cavalli-Sforza (2000: 79).

41  *Ibid*, p.81.

42  Alan G. Thorne and Milford H. Wolpoff (1992); Wolpoff (1996).

43  Wolpoff and Rachel Caspari (1997: 23–6).

44  Wolpoff *et al.* (2001).

45  Gregory J. Adcock *et al.* (includes Alan Thorne) (2001). See also Constance Holden (2001) and John H. Relethford (2001a) for succinct summaries of this research.

46  Francisco Ayala (1995: 1936). For a recent analysis of genetic and fossil evidence, see Relethford (2001b).

47  Richard Potts (1996b). For a more recent argument along these same lines see William H. Calvin (2002).

48  Potts (1996a: 121ff).

49  Quoted by Joshua Fischman (1994). For a comprehensive analysis of this subject, see Sarah Blaffer Hrdy (1999).

50  Virginia Morell (1996).

51  See Robert M. Sapolsky (1996).

52  Margaret Power (1991).

53  See Francis L. Black (1992).

54  For conditions of varying human fertility, see R.V. Short (1976). Note that at these high reproductive rates, populations double in around 25 to 30 years if infant

mortality remains low, and can thus grow 8 to 10 times larger in a century. Such explosive growth cannot continue indefinitely.

55 Jerome Kagan (1998: 59). (This issue is discussed in more detail in Chapters IV and VI.)

56 The famous female Japanese macaque, Imo, who discovered how to wash sand from provisioned sweet potatoes, was imitated by her age-mates, then by their mothers, but only a few adult males ever took this up. She later discovered how to separate wheat, scattered on the beach by researchers, from sand by throwing a handful into the ocean and scooping up the floating grains a few moments later, an invention that also spread first among the younger juveniles, and then to adults. These studies are summarized by E.O. Wilson (1975: 170–1). See also T. Nishida (1987).

The use of stones to break open coula nuts by some populations of African chimpanzees but not by others is a second example. See also Gretchen Vogel (1999), and see Andrew Whiten and Christophe Boesch (2001). In the latter article, the results of seven different chimpanzee populations show distinct differences in thirty-nine learned cultural traits in using tools and communicating. It now seems that chimpanzees accidentally flaked stones while using them, creating the possibility of intentional hominid flaking. See Julio Mercador *et al.* (2002).

57 David Sloan Wilson and Elliott Sober (1994: 585). See also Sober and Wilson (1998).

# IV Brain matters

1 For example, Dorothy Cheney and Robert Seyfarth, using recorded sounds of other adults in a fight, observed the behavior of two, noncaptive female baboons. Fights between unrelated kin caused no reaction in either. If the cries were from relatives of one female, the other looked at her; if from relatives of both, they stared at each other until the dominant female physically displaced the other (reported by Elizabeth Pennisi, 1999). Previously Cheney and Seafarth, using the same technique with a troop of vervet monkeys, showed troop-wide knowledge of the cries of different infants, turning the hearers' attention toward the appropriate mother (Cheney and Seyfarth, 1990: 72–80.)

Evidence of memories of past encounters include the retributive chasing and beating of a chimpanzee who kept the group from its dinner at Arnhem Zoo for two hours the previous evening (reported in Ch.III) and the dedicated pursuit over many days and the ultimate killing of a fissioned troop of chimpanzees at the Gombe Stream Reserve, by the stronger faction of the original troop (see Jane Goodall, 1986: 503–14).

2 For examples, see Pennisi (1999) cited above.

3 See Michael Gazzaniga (1998a) and Antonio Damasio (1999).

4 Harry Heft (2001: xxi).

5 For examples, see Ralph Whitlock's columns in *Guardian Weekly.*

6 Michael N. Nagler, personal communication.

7 These capacities, no doubt understood by many past cultures and modern pet owners, may sometimes be induced through human contact. Nevertheless, they show the great potential of many animals for supposedly uniquely human behaviors. Today, they are being rediscovered by Westerners who learn to live peaceably among wild bears or to tame horses using affection and kindness (see Charlie Russell and Maureen Enns, 1999; Monty Roberts, 1996).

See also Mary Midgley (1983), especially Chapter 12. For a general overview of animal consciousness, see Donald R. Griffin (1992), and especially Chapter 11, "Apes and Dolphins," for examples of awareness and subjectivity in two different but highly social groups of mammals. See also M. Roberts (1996).

8 A. Damasio (1999) emphasizes this critical dual role of the brain throughout his book, and, from a somewhat different point of view, the psychologist Daniel Goleman (1995) does likewise.

9 See news article by Marcia Barinaga (1996) and references therein, and also Ingrid Wickelgren (1998).

10 See Frank Sulloway (1979).

11 See Paul D. MacLean (1973). A renamed second edition appeared [MacLean (1990)] by which time, however, his ideas were largely discounted. See also Carl Sagan (1977).

12 Stephen J. Gould (1977: 164).

13 R. Glenn Northcutt (1981).

14 See R. Glenn Northcutt and J. Kaas (1995). It was R. Lande (1979) who first observed that when an evolutionary lineage was being selected for total body size rather than for "intelligence" (the former being most often the case) then the increase in brain size with increasing body size was modest. But when an evolutionary lineage was being selected for some beneficial properties of the brain, then brain size increased relatively more rapidly than body size.

15 This work, by Linda and Nicholas Holland at Scripps Institution of Oceanography in La Jolla, CA, is reported in Carl Zimmer (2000).

16 R. Glenn Northcutt (2001: 669, 670).

17 See, for example, D. Bakan (1966); M.D.S. Ainsworth *et al.* (1978); J.S. Wiggins (1991); and Shmuel Shulman (1995).

18 We have already noted the virtual absence of any discussion of emotions in Gazzaniga (1998a). Merlin Donald (1991) scarcely refers to emotions at all, and Barry Schwartz (1986) and Christopher Wills (1993) ignore them entirely.

19 Barbara L. Finlay and Richard B. Darlington (1995: 1583). A recent conference on brain evolution suggests however that there were dietary limits on the size of the human brain (Gibbons, 2002a).

20 D'Arcy Wentworth Thompson (1917).

21 Walter J. Gehring (1999) gives a summary of the discovery of homeobox gene segments and their role in embryonic organization and differentiation of organ systems. See also Ch.II, n.8.

22 B. Finlay and R. Darlington (1995: 1583). In line with this idea is the fact, discovered by Katerina Senendeferi and Hanna Damasio, that brain *proportions* in our ape cousins are virtually the same as in our own. Thus, the frontal lobes of the cortex account for around 36 percent of the whole cortex in humans, bonobos, chimpanzees, and orangutans. When the human brain increased in size relative to body size, it did so without relative distortion (see Ann Gibbons, 2000b).

23 See citations in Ch.III, n.27.

24 See Stephen J. Gould and Richard C. Lewontin (1979). This kind of evolutionary event was later named "exaptation" by Gould and Elizabeth S. Vrba (1982).

25 William James (1890/1983: 178–9).

26 Recent examples include: David Bohm (1980); B.J. Baars (1988); David Hodgson (1991); Gerald M. Edelman (1992); Henry P. Stapp (1993); Daniel Dennett (1991); A.G. Cairns-Smith (1996); and A. Damasio (1999) cited above.

27 Reza Shadmehr and Henry H. Holcomb (1997).

28 See Tor Nørretranders (1998: 164–5); Alex Martin *et al.* (1994).

29 Joseph Weiss (1990: 81).

30 See Nørretranders (1998: 169).

31 J.J. Hopfield (1994).

32 See "Sleep, Dreams, and Memory," *Science* (2001) 294: 1047–63. Though the need for dreaming in memory formation is not clear, the need for sleep is not in doubt.

33 G. William Domhoff (2000); emphasis added.

34 Damasio (1999). It is impossible to cite specific pages, as this information is developed in multiple ways throughout the book.
35 *Ibid*, p.106.
36 *Ibid*, pp.108, 185.
37 *Ibid*, p.188.
38 See George Mandler (1997: Ch.V) and A.G. Cairns-Smith (1996: 245–9). See also, Raja Parasuraman (1998).
39 Parasuraman (1998: 6–7).
40 Cited by Nørretranders (1998: 199).
41 See Diane Swick and Robert T. Knight (1998).
42 Nørretranders (1998: 235); emphasis in original. For a recent analysis of "free will" see Daniel M. Wegner (2002).
43 *Ibid*, pp.255, 254.
44 G. Mandler (1997).
45 *Ibid*, p.38. The inheritance of schizophrenia appears to be much more complicated than originally assumed. The propensity to develop this affliction is likely due to changes in up to ten genes. But whether or not it actually develops many years later seems to be triggered by a virus acquired during the pre- or perinatal period, passed perhaps from mother to offspring. Stress is known to increase the incidence. That single-placenta twins have a much higher concordance suggests that infection may be more easily transferred from one to the other via back-and-forth cross-placental infection (see J.O. Davis *et al.*, 1995).
46 See Giulio Tononi and Gerald M. Edelman (1998).
47 See Edward E. Smith and John Jonides (1999).
48 See Michael Gazzaniga (1998a); also Gazzaniga (1998b).
49 W. Penfield (1966). Quoted by Cairns-Smith (1996: 174). See also similar comments in Damasio (1999: Ch.6).
50 Cairns-Smith (1996: 154); emphasis in original.
51 *Ibid*, p.201
52 Damasio (1999: 30–1).
53 This argument about the role of feelings and emotions as "guides" to and thus "causes" of behavior was proposed by William James (1890/1983) and further elaborated throughout several chapters of Cairns-Smith (1996). Contemporary psychologists are beginning to recognize the important role of social context in the satisfaction of such intrinsic human psychological needs. See Richard M. Ryan and Edward L. Deci (2000).

## V A thirst for meaning

1 Julian Jaynes (1976: 70).
2 Morris Berman (2000: 1–18).
3 Merlin Donald (1991), especially Chapter 6. For supporting evidence for the early emergence of human symbolic communication, see Henshilwood *et al.* (2002).
4 See A.G. Cairns-Smith (1996: 154).
5 Gregory Bateson (1972).
6 *Ibid*, p.459. (See also p.318.)
7 Among Dewey's many writings, see especially his critique of stimulus/response psychology (Dewey, 1896).
8 See Harry Heft (1996).
9 J.J. Gibson (1979: 198–9). Quoted by H. Heft (1996: 124).
10 For the original theory see D. Rumelhart *et al.* (1986), and J. McClelland *et al.* (1986). For an interpretation of this theory as it applies to the socialized human mind see James Paul Gee (1992).

11 J.P. Gee (1992: 42ff). Note also that although the original Greek plural for *schema* is *schemata*, neuroscientists have repeatedly used *schemas*, and I continue their usage.

12 There are apparently limits to the ability of apes to think and mentally manipulate concepts. They can, for instance, see how to solve the problem of getting bananas that are hung above their reach by stacking up boxes to climb upon. But when taught to use symbols, such as colored shapes or sign language to re-enact relationships, they are highly limited in the ideas they can communicate. For an analysis of symbolic communication between apes and researchers, see Donald R. Griffin (1992: 218–32).

13 See W.C. McGrew (1992: Chs.8 and 9). See also Andrew Whiten and Christophe Boesch (2001) for a recent review.

14 H.C. Plotkin (1986). Plotkin describes four evolutionary levels of the ability to acquire knowledge: genetic (slowest); developmental (environmental shaping); individual learning (experience); and sociocultural (conspecific). Chimpanzees are mostly limited to the first three. The quote is from p.86.

15 See Elliott Sober and David Sloan Wilson (1998).

16 Merlin Donald (1991: Chs.6 and 7).

17 George Lakoff (1987: Ch.4).

18 See Robert Hinde (1974), and Irenäus Eibl-Eibesfeldt (1989), various places in text.

19 See Eibl-Eibesfeldt (1989: 275ff), for discussion of these metaphoric uses of facial and bodily expressions.

20 Robert R. Provine (2000: 79).

21 *Ibid*, p.88ff.

22 *Ibid*, p.92.

23 *Ibid*, pp.110–14.

24 *Ibid*, Ch.7.

25 Merlin Donald (1991: 182). See also pp.37–41 and 182–4.

26 Patricia M. Gray *et al.* (2001). They also discuss the vocal communication skills of birds and of whales, noting that the Tlingit, Inuit and other seafaring peoples long knew the latter' sounds, picking them up through the hulls of their boats for millennia. Quote is from p.52.

27 *Ibid*, p.53.

28 "Brochan Lom, Tana Lom" and "Bodachan A' Mhirein," sung by Jimmie MacGregor and Robin Hall on a Decca Ace of Clubs record, *Scottish Choice*, 1961, London, England.

29 Bruce Chatwin (1987), several places, particularly pp.13, 15, and the closing pages, 322–5.

30 Mark Jude Tramo (2001).

31 E. Hadingham (1979: 28–9).

32 See Ellen Dissanayake (1992). Quotes are from pp.42 and 46; emphasis in original. This wonderfully illuminating book should be read by everyone in charge of education, mental health, and public policy in general.

33 Margaret Power (1991: 132–5, 224–32).

34 Megan Biesele (1983: 58).

35 See the description of how the San people think about equality in R.B. Lee (1969).

36 George Mandler (1997, 28–9).

37 Noam Chomsky (1980).

38 Margaret Donaldson (1978); Lois Bloom (1993).

39 See Merlin Donald (1991: 82–9) and Laura Helmuth (2001).

40 George Lakoff (1987), especially Chapters 1–13. Lakoff continues his arguments that cultural meaning creates symbols in his explanation of "gender" in various grammars. He notes that in a given language, the assignment of gender to words implies some overall mythic relationship or "similarity" among the words sharing the same

gender. In the (nearly extinct) Dyirbal language of a group of Australian Aborigines, there are four genders. In I, human males are the central member, and included are most animals, boomerangs, spears, storms and rainbows (the latter two are mythical men); in II, human females are central, with water, fire, fighting and dangerous things included (women are linked to the sun, hence with sunburn and fire, and hence other dangerous things); in III are edible plants and their products; and in IV, "everything else." Lakoff's point is that mythic, and "chaining" relations (like "trains-of-thought") supersede any supposedly "natural" categories that some modernists assume must exist in nature. Cultural ideas take precedence over what "objectivist" science might claim as "logical" relationships based on "reality." See Chapter 11 for a discussion; for Lakoff, languages are culturally embedded and hence not readily translatable; the meanings are in the world view more than in any "natural reality." In other languages, both plurals and repeats of a sound are used in very different ways grammatically (Gibbs, 2002: 84).

41 *Ibid*, p.58. For a recent elaboration on this dispute see Ray Jackendoff (2002).
42 George Lakoff and Mark Johnson (1980: 57–61).
43 Professor Edward Warren, Philosophy Department, San Diego State University, personal communication.
44 David Bohm and Mark Edwards (1991: Ch.6, "On Meaning"). Quote is on p.201.
45 Clifford Geertz (2000: 16). See also Geertz (1995). Over the years, he has become one of my heroes. When I try to think about culture as a scientist, I find him frustrating; I want anthropological generalizations – rules. These, however, he steadfastly refuses to give. At long last, he has convinced me that "Yes," there are significant differences in cultural meanings, but "No," there are no simple rules by which to describe or classify them. And furthermore, cultures are never static: the world frame that existed in the past generation is now, thirty years later, in need of redescription.
46 Huston Smith (1958: 126).
47 A conversation I witnessed between my nephew, Bill McConnell, and an old woman in a Malian village in 1984. When she complimented his progress in Bambara, he recited this local saying to her, suggesting that he would never really be a "native," which elicited uproarious pleasure from her.
48 Edwin Hutchins (1996: 4, 5–6); emphasis added.
49 *Ibid*, p.72. Note: the Micronesians' linear constellations are unrelated to the common "constellations" of the West, such as Orion or the Big Dipper. They are lines of stars that lie one above the other, rising over the same point on the horizon as the Earth rotates.
50 Ruth Benedict (1946: 14).
51 J.Z. Young (1978: 38); emphasis in original.
52 See Eugene d'Aquili and Andrew Newberg (1999) and Andrew Newberg *et al.* (2001).

## VI How experience shapes the brain

1 Alison Gopnik *et al.* (1999: 186).
2 *Ibid*, p.186.
3 Gerald M. Edelman (1992: 83).
4 See Shannon Brownlee (1999: 44–52). See also Craig F. Ferris (1996) and Michael Sapir (1998).
5 Carolyn Rovee-Collier (1999: 80). See also Gabrielle Simcock and Harlene Haynes (2002) for the role of language in verbalising very early memories. Prelinguistic remembered events may not be retrievable verbally.
6 Madeline J. Eacott (1999).
7 Darlene Francis *et al.* (1999). Quote is from p.1158.

8 Marian C. Diamond *et al.* (1964). Professor Diamond agrees that "wild" environments are even more enriched than the cages she used. She has more recently suggested that mothers (in some societies) who intentionally cut back on food intake, especially protein, during pregnancy in order to have a smaller baby, and hence an easier birth, may be decreasing their baby's intellectual capacities. She has found this to be true for offspring of nutritionally deprived pregnant rats (personal communication).

9 Gopnik *et al.* (1999: 182).

10 Paul Shepard (1998: 158–9).

11 Kenneth Blum *et al.* (1996). Quotes are from caption to Figure 14, p.143.

12 Howard Gardner *et al.* (1996). According to the authors, "intelligence" is whatever a society/culture needs from human behavior. It ranges from inherited (kings, royalty) to meritocratic (elders, wise persons). Today, attributes include the ability to work under stress, to organize others, general knowledge, practical problem-solving. It is becoming clearer, they state, that there are multiple facets to the needed "intelligence" in today's world: linguistic, musical, logical-mathematical, spatial, bodily-kinesthetic, intrapersonal, interpersonal, and naturalists' intelligence of the environment.

13 S.A. Shah (1994).

14 Howard M. Lenhoff *et al.* (1997).

15 Uta Frith (1992, 1993) and Darold Treffert and Gregory Wallace (2002) and references therein.

16 This point has already been made in Chapter IV, n.45, Davis *et al.* (1995).

17 George Mandler (1997: 145). For a thorough discussion of the ethics of both genetic screening and gene therapy as they relate to human reproduction, see Rosemarie Tong (1997).

18 It is now clear that genetic differences within supposedly distinct, homogeneous human populations are far greater than the differences in genes between so-called races and ethnic groups (see Cavalli-Sforza, 2000: 27–31).

19 Irenäus Eibl-Eibesfeldt (1942: 143–4).

20 John Irwin (n.d.: 8).

21 Jean Liedloff (1977: 34).

22 Quoted by Meredith F. Small (1998: 35).

23 Liedloff (1977: 60ff).

24 Small (1998: 131–7).

25 Liedloff (1977: 71, 80ff, 117, 158–9).

26 Jerome Kagan (1998: 149–50).

27 For a description of these stages, see Paul Shepard (1998: 42–7).

28 Liedloff (1977: 108); emphasis added.

29 *Ibid*, p.108.

30 Edward S. Reed (1996).

31 Jerome Bruner (1990: 73).

32 Barbara Rogoff (1995). For a delightful entrée into this whole field, see Rogoff (1990).

33 Barbara Ehrenreich (1989). She gives an excellent analysis of this Western psychological crisis.

34 Rogoff *et al.* (1993).

35 Robert Bly (1996).

36 See Phil Schoggen (1989), especially p.245. This is an update of Barker's original book (see Barker, 1968). Schoggen was also a long-term collaborator with Barker.

37 C.J.L. Murray and A.D. Lopez (1996: 740).

38 J. Larry Brown and Ernesto Pollitt (1996).

39 Theo Colborn *et al.* (1997), especially pp.188–91, 206–9, 250–8. See also Christopher Williams (1997) for a comprehensive list of toxic substances affecting human brains.
40 For a history of alcohol use, see Bert L. Vallee (1998).
41 K.L. Jones *et al.* (1973). This was one of the earliest medical descriptions of this sad malady.
42 National Public Radio, *Morning Edition*, August 14, 1998.
43 Helen Cordes (1998).
44 Liedloff (1977: 72).
45 See John Bowlby (1951) for the original report.
46 Bruce D. Perry *et al.* (1995).
47 See Aubrey Gorbman *et al.* (1983: 446ff), and E. Ronald de Kloet (1992). For the story of the child in a spacesuit see Mary E. Clark (1979), caption to photograph (by NASA) in Figure 10a.3, p.248. The child later died from multiple cancers which his deficient immune system had failed to destroy.
48 Robert M. Sapolsky (1996).
49 Bessel A. van der Kolk (1996). See p.230 for amygdala; quote is on p.234. See also Christine Mlot (1998).
50 Frank W. Putnam (1992, 1989).
51 See Charles B. Nemeroff (1998).
52 For an explanation, see especially Craig F. Ferris (1996); see also Michael Sapir (1998).
53 See Ferris (1996). The information contained in this entire section comes from a variety of sources: A.G. Cairns-Smith (1996); Amy F.T. Arnsten (1998); Karen Wright (1997); Christine Mlot (1998); Robert M. Sapolsky (1996); Charles B. Nemeroff (1998); Craig F. Ferris (1996); Michael Sapir (1998); Frank W. Putnam (1992); Bruce D. Perry *et al.* (1995); Bruce D. Perry (1997); Bruce D. Perry and Ronnie Pollard (1998); and Bruce D. Perry and Jennifer E. Pate (1994).
    Recently Martin H. Teicher at the McLean Hospital Research Center in Belmont, MA, has confirmed these brain changes in seriously abused children. In particular there is damage to the part of the cerebellum that sends suppressive signals to the brainstem and limbic system, resulting in sudden "irrational" shifts in behavior following a change in input signals (see Teicher, 2002).
54 Richard Hellie (1982, 1989). In the latter article, Hellie points out that even up to the present day there has not been a period of stable, non-oppressive history in Russia during which peoples' lives could be relatively free of stress.
55 Hellie (1996).
56 National Public Radio, *Talk of the Nation*, 6 December, 1996.
57 William P. Mahedy (1986).
58 Jonathan Shay (1994). Quote is on p.98; emphasis in original.
59 Perry *et al.* (1995); Perry (1997).
60 Rosalie Bertell (1997).
61 Rachel Brett and Margaret McCalin (1998). See also Center for Defense Information (1997) (Rear Admiral Eugene Carroll, U.S. Navy (Ret.), Director of the Center, was interviewed on this issue by NPR's *Weekend Edition*, November 2, 1996); Mike Wessells (1997); and Dyan Mazurana and Susan McKay (2001).
62 See Nils Johan Lavik *et al.* (1994).
63 See Perry and Pate (1994); Perry and Pollard (1998); and Perry (2001a, 2001b).
64 Alexander C. McFarlane and Bessel A. van der Kolk (1996). Quote is on p.573.
65 Perry (1997: 139); emphasis added.
66 According to retired neurologist Fred A. Baughman, Jr. (2001), "No proof exists that ADHD is a disease with a validating abnormality. Yet the public is told it is a 'disease', that it is 'neurobiologic' or 'neurobehavioral'." (On the same journal page

as this citation is a letter from Dr. Peter R. Breggin, whose other work is cited below.) According to an NIH Consensus Conference on ADHD, in a report of Nov. 18, 1998, there was a five-fold increase in diagnosis of ADHD and in Ritalin use in the United States between 1990 and 1995. The NIH panel suggested that in children under 4 years, it is not clear that ADHD exists and drugs are in any case useless for them. As Baughman states, "In that children who would be the research subjects in the PATS study [Preschool ADHD Treatment Study] have no demonstrable disease, there is no justification for giving them Schedule II stimulant medications."

For a scathing critique of this all-too-common practice in American psychiatry of giving drugs and other invasive treatments to "mental patients" see Breggin (1991, 1998). Because Breggin is very hard on his fellow psychiatrists, his ideas tend to be dismissed out of hand. In fact, he is one of the few professionals who has consistently pushed for the kinds of human interactions necessary to rebuild psychic security – the central argument of this entire chapter.

67 Bruce D. Perry (1994); Bruce D. Perry and Jennifer E. Pate (1994).
68 Herbert Benson (1996).
69 See Benson (1996: 40ff). Benson's and others' work on the placebo effect has been confirmed by brain imaging studies showing that drugs and placebos act on the same areas of the brain (see Holden, 2002).
70 See Mary Beth Kirschner (2000). For the benefits of combining traditional healing and modern medicine, see Lori Alvord and Elizabeth Van Pelt (1999).
71 Roger S. Ulrich (1984).
72 David Brown (1999).
73 This idea runs through the whole of a book on serene living, written by His Holiness the Dalai Lama and Howard C. Cutler, M.D. (1998). Cutler synthesizes this relationship between compassion and both mental and physical health on pp.126–7.
74 Harvey Jackins (n.d.).
75 See Roger Mills (1995) for an explication of the methodology for healing trauma victims developed by him and his daughter, Ami Chin Mills. See also Roger Mills and Elsie Spittle (2001) for an analysis of their methods.
76 This was aired on National Public Radio in 2001, but I did not get a reference. However, a large body of work on healing and human resilience can be found at ResilienceNet online: www.resilnet.uiuc.edu/library.html. Among their publications are several from the international arena by Edith Grotberg, an important researcher in this field.
77 Andrew Newberg and Eugene d'Aquili (1999) and Andrew Newberg et al. (2001: 222–3).
78 Bruce Wilshire (2001: 222–3).
79 Herman T. Blumenthal (1997). Quote is from p.B7. For references on new cell recruitment, see: Elizabeth Gould et al. (1999), and Gerd Kempermann and Fred H. Gage (1999). And for brain plasticity after damage, see Nina P. Azari and Rüdiger J. Seitz (2000).

## VII "Who am I?" – where biology and culture meet

1 Alan Fogel (1993: 160–1).
2 Ibid, p.160.
3 Paul Bohannan (1995: 151).
4 Fogel (1993: 104).
5 Ibid, p.162.
6 See Rom Harré (1981: 84). Nor do the Ica in Colombia seem to have a concept of pronouns (Gibbs, 2002: 85).
7 Fogel (1993: 162).

8 Bohannan (1995: 151). See also Clifford Geertz (2000) for a beautiful exposition of the ephemeral, non-rule-based nature of meaning systems.
9 Richard A. Shweder (1991: 254ff).
10 See Chinua Achebe (1959) for a description of this in precolonial Africa. A man who illegitimately kills a younger boy is banished from his tribe for several years. Fortunately, he has distant relatives with whom he can live during his exile (see p.116ff).
11 Bruce D. Bonta (1993: 2).
12 Karl Deutsch (1966).
13 Lionel Rothkrug (1987: 286).
14 Both quotes are in Dave Hill (2000: 22–3). See also Hilary and Steven Rose (2000).
15 Natalie Angier (1999: 340, 338–9). Her entire Chapter 18, "Of Hoggamus and Hogwash: Putting Evolutionary Psychology on the Couch," offers an excellent, nontechnical critique of the flimsiness of this current scientific fad.
16 *Ibid*, p.198ff.
17 Robert M. Sapolsky (1997: 151ff).
18 Angier (1999: 201ff).
19 For a lively debate between Katha Pollitt, a feminist journalist, and Robert Reich, a dedicated evolutionary psychologist, moderated by Robert Krulwich, listen to the tape of "Are Men & Women Different?" *Bridges*, New York: The Radio Foundation, Inc. (first aired November 1995). They cover virtually all the important issues.
20 Robin Baker and Mark A. Bellis (1996).
21 For women, the average time turns out to be twenty seconds, about twice what the women themselves had guessed (see Angier, 1999: 76).
22 See Riane Eisler (1996); Humberto Maturana (1990: xv).
23 K.G. Heider (1976).
24 Luigi Luca Cavalli-Sforza (2000: 181).
25 See Michael Hagemann (1999).
26 See Sita Venkateswar (1999).
27 David Maybury-Lewis (1992: 92).
28 *Ibid*, p.94.
29 *Ibid*, p.101ff.
30 Sobonfu Somé (1997, 2000).
31 Maybury-Lewis (1992: 117).
32 Peggy Reeves Sanday (1981: 78).
33 Sanday (1981: 165ff). See also Carol Rogers (1975). Also see Maybury-Lewis (1992: 130) where he describes ceremonial male acts of aggressivity against females, while in fact respect for women pervades daily life. Western feminists, of course, tend to disagree on what is "equal" and what is "male dominance" in such societies.
34 These ideas are discussed in great detail in Sanday (1981: Chs.8 and 9), where she reviews various theories of the origins of male dominance: hunting, warlikeness, danger, etc. See especially pp.172ff.
35 See Sanday (1981: 186ff).
36 J. Z. Young (1978: 171); emphasis in original.
37 See Frans de Waal (1992). I realize that both de Waal and I are running against both contemporary ideological currents regarding physical aggression, which form two rigidly opposing camps: the conservative camp which sees it as the only way to "teach" recalcitrant children and citizens alike to behave according to the rules ("spare the rod and spoil the child") and the liberal camp which believes that any physical violence used against another merely teaches that person to use violence back (spanking is never appropriate and demeans the parent). Both de Waal and I think this dichotomy oversimplifies the issue, and prevents deeper insights into all the factors involved during the establishment of stable primate relationships.

38  Lt. Col. Dave Grossman (1995/1996: 31), quoting the first Israeli military psychologist, Ben Shalit (emphasis in original); and p.29, quoting the United States' World War II general, S.L.A. Marshall.

39  Grossman (1995/1996: 190ff). See also Joanne Bourke (1999).

40  See Gene Sharp (1973, 1979) for analysis. Also the recent comprehensive review of nonviolence in the twentieth century by Michael Nagler (2001).

41  Grossman (1995/1996: 191–2).

42  For excellent analyses of human aggression as a communicative behavior, not a biological drive in humans and other primates, see J.Z. Young (1978: Ch.15, "Fearing, Hating, and Fighting"), and Frans de Waal (1992).

43  Dorothy Lee (1959).

44  *Ibid*, p.7ff, and Jean Liedloff (1977: 56, 98).

45  Lee (1959: 9).

46  Fred Begay, Navajo medicine man and physicist at Los Alamos National Laboratory, speaking at Holis Meeting, Commonweal, Bolinas, CA, March 19–21, 1993.

47  Lee (1959: 24).

48  See Peggy Reeves Sanday (1981), especially Chapter 1, "Scripts for Female Power." Also George B.N Ayittey (1991) for citations to the "Queen Mother," especially pp.128, 204, 221; and Paula Gunn Allen (1986: 31–42; 201–3) for Native American gender relations. Prior to AD 750, all North American tribes were acephalous, egalitarian societies (Bruce D. Smith, 1990).

49  Sanday (1981: 177), and M. Kay Martin and Barbara Voorhies (1975).

50  Lee (1959: 11).

51  See Robert Graves (1954).

52  See Max Fauconnet (1968: 442–4).

53  P. Masson-Oursel and Louise Morin (1968: 326).

54  From Pandurangshastri Athavale (1987); Dwayne R. Copp and Alma M. Copp (1991); Pramilla Jayapal (2001); also, author's unpublished notes from personal visit with Athavale in 1992.

55  See Barbara Ehrenreich (1989). Also Brayton Bowden (1999), a five-part series produced by Louisville's Public Radio Partnership exploring workplace issues relating to anger and its impact on personal and organizational effectiveness.

56  Friedrich Engels (1902).

57  For an excellent elaboration of this point see Rupert Ross (1992), especially Chapter 10, "The Doctrine of Original Sanctity," which addresses cultural differences in the meaning of justice between Native Americans and Canadian officials.

58  Stanley Diamond (1971).

59  *Ibid*, p.135.

60  *Ibid*, p.141.

61  Bertram Raven (1999: 163).

62  *Ibid*, p.161.

63  Christopher Boehm (1999).

64  Matt Hern (1996).

65  Wanda C. McCarthy and Irene Hanson Frieze (1999).

66  Wolfgang Scholl (1999). See also Francis Fukuyama, where the author notes sprouting trends in the Western bureaucratic hierarchies to devolve power to lower levels "and rely on the people over whom they have nominal authority to be self-organizing" (1999: 56; emphasis in original).

67  Paul Bohannon (1995); Jared Diamond (1997); Marc Howard Ross (1993a, 1993b); Rupert Ross (1992); Peggy Reeves Sanday (1981).

## VIII History, the story of meanings through time

1 Recall evidence in Chapter VI documenting transgenerational behavior transmission in rats and humans. See also Ch.VI, n.7.

2 Since the Holocaust of the twentieth century, the ancient story of what happened to a group of Jewish families who had taken refuge on the fortress rock of Masada beside the Dead Sea at the time of the second rebellion of the Israelites against their Roman conquerors in AD 73 has been resurrected and turned into a myth taught to all schoolchildren in Israel. It tells how a group of resistance fighters, the Zealots, had fled to the fortress with their families, nearly a thousand persons in all. Despite prolonged brave resistance against incredible odds, when they finally realized their walls would be breached the following day, they agreed upon mass suicide rather than surrendering their wives and children to lifelong slavery. They drew lots as to who would kill the others; when the Romans broke through, they found everyone dead. That is the myth. (See Moshe Pearlman, 1967.) Nachman Ben-Yehuda (1995) plays down the heroic aspects of the story as recently invented. In fact, he says, the revolt was doomed from the start and the refugees were not nearly as "heroic" as pictured, being rather unsavory characters.

With regard to the Iran–Iraq war, which was really fought over control of the Persian Gulf by two competing leaders, casualties were extremely high on both sides of this largely ground-fought struggle. In seven years, 8.5 percent of Iraqi citizens were killed or wounded in battle and 3.5 percent of Iranians, some 2.5 million young men in total. Increasingly, younger youths were employed on both sides, with promises of eternal Paradise should they perish in battle (see James A. Bill, 1984, 1988: 304–6). His 1984 article explains the nature of the differences between Sunni and Shi'ite factions of Islam and how respective politicians have made use of these to gain power.

3 Paul Bohannan (1995). Part II, especially Chapters 6–9, are most helpful. The quote is from p.61. On cultural changes over time see Clifford Geertz (1995).

4 Quoted by Martin E. Marty (1994).

5 *Ibid*, various places.

6 Quoted by Marty (1994).

7 "Identity" and "identity group" are terms that repeatedly come up in the theoretical writings of John W. Burton, a successful international negotiator and one of the founders of the burgeoning field of conflict resolution. Unfortunately, because he could never articulate the psychological underpinnings of "identity," his thinking was not as well accepted as it should have been. He has proved a great inspiration to me and opened many insightful doors in my thinking. Some of his best works are Burton (1979, 1982, 1987, 1990, and 1997).

8 Marty (1994: [p.6 of my own transcript of this tape]).

9 *Ibid* [p.10].

10 *Ibid* [p.4].

11 Stephen J. Gould. (2000: 261). Note that Marty cites the religious fanaticism toward "Reason" indulged in during the French Revolution by Robespierre when he held a "festival of the Supreme Being" (i.e. Reason) (Marty, 1994: [p.4]).

12 Marty (1994: [p.6]).

13 For a succinct account, along with references, of the role of the Iroquois in shaping the thinking of the Founding Fathers, see Christa Daryl Slaton (1992).

14 J. David Lewis-Williams (1983: 4).

15 *Ibid*, p.7. This particular cave-art is only several hundred years old, and so cultural memory of its meaning is still possible. See also Lewis-Williams (1981, 1997) and Jean Clottes and Lewis-Williams (1996) for roles of shamanism and trance states in prehistoric cosmologies.

16 Clottes (1995, 1996), who has excavated the splendid Grotte Chauvet in southern France, points out that most of the animals, so beautifully depicted, were not hunted at all. When humans appear they are stick figures of indeterminant sex or, where sex is distinguishable, females are twice as common as males. Furthermore, ancient footprints on the floor included those of women and children. As Joshua Fischman (1995) quotes anthropologist Randall White as observing about the Grotte Chauvet animals, which did not include reindeer: "They were eating reindeer, but painting rhinos." Evidently this was not a cave for male hunting rituals. The point that certain animals were thought to possess crucial powers is made by Anne Solomon (1996).

Recently, the self-styled "innovative cultural historian and social critic," Morris Berman (2000) dismissed all attempts to interpret the symbolism of prehistoric art, by both Lewis-Williams and Clottes, of cave paintings and by Marija Gimbutas of the earliest European figurines and settlements in Europe (see below), as being "without substantial data." We can know nothing about the human mind prior to written history, he insists. However, he is either unaware of a great deal of firm data that support, in particular, Gimbutas' work (which I reference below) or he refuses to address it. Furthermore, he insists that despite good evidence that prehistoric modern humans had brains indistinguishable from our own, there is no good evidence they had consciousness like ours, and therefore we cannot assume they did. To me, this is an illegitimate way of dismissing theories one prefers not to take seriously. His only interpretations of cave-art are basically without symbolic meaning, as far as I can tell.

I believe the current presumption of cave-art as representations of "hunting magic" is one more symptom of social scientists trying to "explain" human behavior according to overly simplified neo-Darwinian principles of "adaptiveness." They ignore the published evidence that the "weapons" depicted are neither arrows nor spears; see Alexander Marshack (1970: 332), who used microphotography to show that the lines on the tips of the "weapons" were pointing the wrong way, and must represent reeds or the branches of plants. His interpretations of early art are summed up in Marshack (1972). For a comprehensive, heavily documented (albeit unconventional) critique of the whole tendency of modern anthropology to explain preliterate world views in purely adaptationist terms rather than as a search for the *meaning* of the mysteries of life and humans' early feelings of active participation in the ongoing cycles of life and death, see Hans Peter Duerr (1985).

17 See Ellen Dissanayake (1988, 1992).

18 Recently there has been a spate of books re-instituting the belief that human nature, especially human male nature, is incorrigibly violent, and societies have always been violent, warlike, or "sick." Here are some recent examples. Richard Wrangham and Dale Peterson (1996) look at male violence as endemic in both apes and humans. To them, violence is an automatic male response to all "competing" males. Lawrence H. Keeley (1996) is really discussing intra-tribal vendettas in various foraging, egalitarian cultures. By arguing that centralized "civilizations" reduced these vendettas and thus created a more peaceful world, he ignores the internal violence imposed by civilizations on their own peoples, often deemed necessary to maintain "order." Robert B. Edgerton (1992) is the most critical of all about the possibility of peaceful foraging cultures. In his opening chapter he cites those colleagues whom he identifies as Rousseauian idealists; the reader is referred to that chapter for his "hit list." I would add Ashley Montagu as perhaps another. Most, if not all, of Edgerton's examples of extant "warlike" peoples have, in fact, felt the recent impact of outside stresses on their cultural integrity.

19 For references on the human impact on Nature's ecosystems, see Edward Hyams (1952, 1976); W.C. Lowdermilk (1975, revised); W.L. Thomas, Jr. (1956); and for changes in the past 300 years, B.L. Turner II *et al.* (1990).

20 Jared Diamond (1995).

21 Heather Pringle (1997a). The Norse apparently had depended on sporadic visits from Norway for supplies, dying out when the boats failed to come.

22 Ernest Becker (1971: 86).

23 Luigi Luca Cavalli-Sforza *et al.* (1982).

24 For the concept of "cultural traps" (i.e. societies unable to change their ways despite obvious warnings around them) see Robert Costanza (1990), Barbara Tuchman (1984), and Paul Bohannan (1995: Ch.10).

25 These are two of the many oversimplified attempts to explain human nature in stark, Darwinian terms: Robert Ardrey (1966) and Richard Dawkins (1976).

26 Payment by offenders of some form of material wealth to the victims or their families is still a common form of restitutional justice in much of the non-urbanized world. Among India's tribal peoples (some 140 million persons), headmen of the villages of two disputants act as elders who authorize the agreed amount (author's personal study in Gujarat, November–December, 1995).

   Small societies without rulers have many local mechanisms for adjudicating internal conflict. Usually these utilize wise elders. For instance, in native North American cultures, "the elders" are powerfully respected. Their word is "law." In all of India's villages, the panchayet system pertains. Panch (= "five") is the number of wise elders entrusted to sit as a tribunal to settle local disputes. When a dispute occurs between members of two villages, ideally their two "panches" seek a solution. These somewhat "toothless" agents may be ineffectual in the face of a major violent dispute or prolonged external stress.

27 George B.N. Ayittey (1991: 63). Ayittey is writing about precolonial tribal African justice, but its precepts are surely much older, still turning up today in a great many indigenous societies.

28 Chinua Achebe (1959). Achebe describes how, in precolonial Africa, causing the death of another, even accidentally, resulted in banishment for several years to a distant village. Separation or "fission" was the "solution" to wrongdoing – a separation of the perpetrator and victim until time can resolve the pain and permit renewed interaction.

29 Napoleon Chagnon (1968); see also later editions (1977, 1983, 1992, 1997).

30 Chagnon (1987: 358).

31 Chagnon (1988).

32 Marvin Harris (1974, 1979, 1984).

33 R. Brian Ferguson (1995: 19).

34 Clayton A. Robarchek and Carole J. Robarchek (1992: 207).

35 See, respectively, Ferguson (1995) and Robarchek and Robarchek (1992).

36 R. Brian Ferguson and Neil L. Whitehead (1992).

37 Patrick Tierney (2000). An experienced archeologist who has specialized in Latin America, Tierney spent many months of his eleven years of research among the local people, and his criticism of the research methods of prior ethologists is severe. Not surprisingly, it has cast a shadow on the whole field of cultural anthropology.

38 Examples are the Yir Yoront of the York Peninsula in Australia and the Siane of the Eastern Highlands of New Guinea. See, respectively, Lauriston Sharp (1952) and R.F. Salisbury (1962).

39 R. Brian Ferguson (1995). See also Patrick Tierney (2000) who alleges that Chagnon even staged some of the "wars" he recorded on film, whether intentionally or not.

40 Robarchek and Robarchek (1992: 206).

41 *Ibid*, p.207. See also Peter Broennimann (1981). Auca, as he calls them, is another name the Waorani use for themselves. Broennimann and his wife studied the peoples still living in the jungle outside the mission a few years after the mission became fully

established. Their account gives a lively view of what the lives of foraging peoples are like, accompanied by incredible photographs.

42 Brian Ferguson thinks the Yanomami suffered from a fatal attraction to Western goods (Ferguson, 1995: 364ff). It is an idea to which Patrick Tierney (2000) also subscribes.

43 See Brian Ferguson (1992) and references therein. Quote is from p.224; emphasis is added.

44 See Ferguson (1995: Ch.15) for an exhaustive discussion of the ways in which to interpret Yanomami warfare. His idea, that once wars have begun, whether within or between cultures, they become a self-propagating institution is the central point made also by Andrew Bard Schmookler (1984). Schmookler's single-minded argument is that war becomes institutionalized as soon as one faction or party decides to use physical force over another to gain power for itself – what I call the "one rotten apple in the barrel" theory. Unfortunately he ignores any serious discussion of cultural meaning systems, leaving the reader without any useful insights into human nature. "Power" is not just a single entity, wielded for a single purpose everywhere it occurs, as Kenneth Boulding well knew (see his *Three Faces of Power*, 1989/1990).

45 Robarchek and Robarchek (1992: 196ff).

46 *Ibid*, p.205.

47 *Ibid*, p.203; emphasis added.

48 Robert Knox Dentan (1968). Cited by Bruce D. Bonta (1993: 2ff). See also Clayton A.Robarchek and Robert Knox Dentan (1987).

49 Robarchek and Robarchek (1992: 206).

50 Clayton A. Robarchek (1989), especially, p.38ff.

51 Harm J. de Blij (2000). See also Mark N. Cohen (1977). The American agronomist, Jack R. Harlan, agrees with Cohen's analysis. Agriculture was not a sudden, insightful, "civilizing" invention, but a lifestyle forced on foragers. "Hunter-gatherers are real professional botanists ... They knew all they needed to take up agriculture at any place." Quoted by Philip and Phylis Morrison (2000: 106).

52 Peggy Reeves Sanday (1981: 68); emphasis added.

53 *Ibid*, Ch.6.

54 In n.48, Ch.VII, I noted the studies by George B.N. Ayittey (1991) on African cultures, and by Paula Gunn Allen (1986) on Native American cultures regarding women's political power. Sanday (1981) in her Chapter 1, also cites the overall principle and gives various specific references. See also the interesting case of the Fipa in Tanzania where (at least before colonization overtook them) men held biddable governing posts, while women controlled the judicial and punitive system (see Roy Willis, 1989).

55 Lewis Mumford (1961: 6ff). Some examples of such sites include the large burial area in Australia's New South Wales at Lake Victoria, near the convergence of the Murray and Darling Rivers. Only discovered in 1994, this area appears to have been permanently inhabited by a fairly large settled population for over 7000 years. These people lived relatively sedentary lives in an area comprising around 150 square miles, without agriculture, *and* without exhausting the local food supplies. Other, smaller necropoli were found along the nearby rivers in this fertile area of an otherwise arid continent (see Graeme O'Neill, 1994).

Other examples are the well-known mound complexes of the American midwest, the most recently found of which date back to 5400 ya (see Joe W. Saunders and fourteen others, 1997). In the mid-East, sacred sites coopted by the early Hebrews from earlier animistic societies include the oracular "oak of Moreh" (Genesis xii,6), and "En-mishpat," an oracular spring (Genesis xiv,7). See also the classic work by Sir James George Frazer (1922, 1929) especially Volume 1. In Neolithic Europe, the worship of trees was especially prevalent, but was replaced by variations of a "triple-goddess" figure, as poetically explored by Robert Graves (1948). I would hasten to add here that I am not claiming that either Frazer or Graves had a complete grasp of the meaning of these early religious belief systems, though they were generally on the right track regarding the significance of myth and ritual.

56  Mumford (1961: 8).

57  This history is constructed on accumulated data from three main fields of study. First is archeology, the discovery of sites, including animal bones and seeds, that tell much about the economy, as does the garbage. Once-living objects, including charcoal, can be carbon-dated, yielding a time-scale. Other artifacts include art, ceramics, tools, grave-sites, remnants of buildings, streets, etc. Similar cultures leave behind similar clues. Second is genetics. The new DNA techniques allow modern populations to be analyzed for dozens of genetic markers which, with the aid of computers, can be made to reveal the past history of human migrations. Recently, Y-chromosomes of men have been used to explore in depth the genetic past of European peoples. Third is linguistics. The distribution of and detailed differences between extant languages also reveals how cultures have interacted in the past. By "triangulating" information from these three sources, we can begin to build a good general outline of Western history. Add to this new climatic data (as discussed in Chapter III) and the almost serendipitous recent discovery of the flooding of the Black Sea some 7500 ya, and the picture becomes even clearer.

The primary references on which my account is based are as follows:

For *Archeology*: Anne Baring and Jules Cashford (1993); Marija Gimbutas (1980, 1982); and Joan Marler (1997). An earlier pathbreaking predecessor was Merlin Stone (1976). Also see Michael Balter (2000a), an article dealing with finds in an 8000 ya village in Israel with paved streets, monumental buildings and Gravettian-like "Venus" figurines.

For *Genetics*: Luigi Luca Cavalli-Sforza (1997) in Joan Marler (ed.) (1997); Cavalli-Sforza (2000); Ann Gibbons (2000c); Ornella Semino *et al.* (2000). (Among the *et al.* list of 16 authors that I did not name is Cavalli-Sforza.)

For *Linguistics*: Cavalli-Sforza (2000); also the update of interpretations showing that languages and genes are not as closely allied as Cavalli-Sforza originally thought, with languages changing faster than genes, in Michael Balter (2001b). See also Ben Shouse (2001).

For others: for early information on the Black Sea Flood, see Richard A. Kerr (2000). For climate drying around 5500 ya, see Tim Redford (2001). For how earthquake-generated tsunamis could have destroyed past civilizations, see Robert Koenig (2001), especially the inset on the possible cause of the disappearance of the Minoan Civilization on Crete 3600 ya, p.1252.

58  See Cavalli-Sforza (1997, 2000). His substantiation of Gimbutas' theories about the "downfall" of the Goddess culture of Old Europe as the result of incursions by nomadic herdsmen from the steppe gives factual support of "hard science" to her interpretations of the excavations of the early agriculturalists.

59  Marija Gimbutas (1980, 1982). Donna Wilshire (1994) provides a beautifully illustrated account of this theory of the meaning of Goddess symbolism through time. See also papers in Marler (1997).

60  See Barbara Ehrenreich (1997: 102). In this book, Ehrenreich seems set on pursuing the single-minded idea that fear of blood explains the history of violence.

61  Baring and Cashford (1993: 114).

62  For references on Old Europe, see Marija Gimbutas (1982, 1989, 1991); on Crete, Sir Arthur J. Evans (1936) and Martin P. Nilsson (1950); on Mycenae, William Taylour (1970); on Anatolia, James Melaart (1967, 1970). For recent modification to Melaart's interpretations, see Michael Balter (1999). And on the pre-Aryan Indus cities, see Mircea Eliade (1978: s.38 and s.39 plus references on pp.412–13).

63 See Gimbutas (1982: 18) for evidence of trade and sailing. Regarding the peaceful-ness of these societies, writer after writer notes the absence of either depictions of violence or physical fortifications around the early cities. See, for example, Baring and Cashford (1993: 55); Lewis Mumford (1961: 120).

64 Mircea Eliade (1978: 125).

65 Gimbutas (1982: 238).

66 In his review of recent interpretations of the Çatalhöyük site, Michael Balter (1999) notes that 10,000 people were living crowded together so closely that houses were entered from the roof. There was no evidence of warfare, nor of ranking among the buildings, nor signs of hierarchy. In the November 20, 1998 issue of *Science* (282:1441–58) several summary articles on the earliest settlements suggest change in viewpoint old beliefs about the first settlements; they were not necessarily agriculture-driven. It now appears that both the origin of art and of language and symbolic thought began *long before* 40,000 ya; sophisticated tools dating from 90,000 to 130,000 ya suggest symbolic communication was already present at that time.

67 See Cavalli-Sforza (1997, 2000) for recent genetic studies supporting Gimbutas' suggestions. See also references cited in Ch.VIII n.57.

68 Baring and Cashford (1993: 82). Internal quotes are from Marija Gimbutas (1982: Preface).

69 See Baring and Cashford (1993) throughout. Also see discussion in Charlene Spretnak (1984).

70 Baring and Cashford (1993: Ch.7).

71 Leften Stavrianos (1999: 69).

72 Sandra A. Wawrytko (2000). Cavalli-Sforza (2000: 146–7) confirms the genetic differences between northern and southern contemporary Chinese populations.

73 Michiko Yusa (1994).

74 See Jared Diamond (1997) for a comprehensive analysis of how purely ecological factors – horses, metal ores, particular wild grains, and latitudinal considerations – influenced human prehistory. He discusses the military advantage of horse domesti-cation on p.77.

75 Marcel Gauchet (1997: 9).

76 Historian Lewis Mumford (1967) used this term for "civilization" in his monu-mental work *The Myth of the Machine*.

77 Stanley Diamond (1971).

78 Marcel Gauchet (1997: 9–10).

79 Charles Taylor (1998: xiv).

80 For a short summary of this aspect of the world's religions, see Paul Gordon Lauren (1998: 5–9). Quote is from p.5. The prophets or founders of the major religions are: Confucianism: K'ung Fu-tzū; Taoism: Lao Tzū; Buddhism: Siddhartha Gautama; Hinduism: author(s) of *Bhagavad-Gita*; Judaism: Moses and subsequent prophets; Christianity: Jesus and his disciples; Islam: Muhammed.

81 Stanley Diamond (1971: 118).

82 See Huston Smith (1958: 123). Also, Michael N. Nagler (2001), various citations (see his Index).

83 Huston Smith (1958: 225).

84 Elaine Pagels (1979: xv). See also, Elaine Pagels (1995) for further discussion of these Gospels.

85 Pagels (1979: xxxv).

86 This Table is my own interpretation of Pagels' (1979, 1995) descriptions, and is not directly attributable to her.

87 Huston Smith (1958). References to *atman* are in the chapter on Hinduism, espe-cially p.70.

88 Elaine Pagels (1995: 177–8).

89 See Lewis Mumford (1967: 181). He likens Inca society to an authoritarian, yet beneficent communism, "state-controlled, but benignly reproducing for the larger community the common sharing of labor and the products of labor as in a village."

90 The historian, Barbara Tuchman (1984) has elaborated several cogent cases in history, from the fall of Troy to America in Vietnam, where rigidity and blindness among decision-makers led to unnecessary political disasters.

91 For a more extended, yet succinct, description of the historical changes in Europe, see Mary E. Clark (1989: Chs.IX–XII and references therein).

## IX Humankind crosses the Rubicon, 1900–2000

1 A number of references cited in the opening pages of this chapter cover global crises. See, for example, Ross Gelbspan (1998) concerning the impacts of global warming; and Theo Colborn et al. (1997), who reveal data indicting environmental chemicals for multiple physiological pathologies. See also the annual State of the World reports from Worldwatch Institute: Washington D.C.

2 See Lewis Mumford (1967), Chapter Eight, "Kings as Prime Movers," especially p.180ff, and Figures 16 and 17.

3 The changes of the prior four centuries in Western thought are described in more detail in Mary E. Clark (1989: Ch.9, "From God to Man").

4 Two important works on the illusion of American democracy are Creel Froman (1984) and Michael Parenti (1983). Their arguments are analyzed in Clark (1989: Ch.14, "Politics: Worldviews in Action").

5 For a discussion of the philosophical origins of these ideas see Peter Söderbaum (2000), especially Chapter 5, "Political Ideologies, Democracy and Decision-Making." The concept of Billiard Ball, highly individualistic thinking about human rights as being "freedom" from constraints by a group clearly underlies the historical philosophical argument of the Enlightenment. It is part of the ongoing tension, especially in the West, between bonding and autonomy, with autonomy almost always taking precedence.

6 The repeated bailouts of the big, speculative financial institutions – the savings & loans, banks and major investment funds – by national governments and the IMF and World Bank to prevent a global depression like that in the 1980s were all too familiar during the second half of the twentieth century. They were "repaid" by the process of "belt-tightening": shifting public funds from shared social services such as education, health care, and the welfare system that somewhat offset the worst inequalities of capitalism, to pay the debts incurred by those individuals who most profit from it.

7 See, for example, Joseph Campbell (1968: 387–91); Malidoma Patrice Somé (1994: 1–2, 1997); and Marcel Gauchet (1997: 200–7).

8 There are untold references on these imposed "modernizations." I list only a small sample of those dealing with the United States. Noam Chomsky and Edward S. Herman (1979); Jerry W. Sanders (1983); Jonathan Marshall et al. (1987); Holly Sklar (1988). (It is no accident that most books on this subject are published by one or two so-called "left-wing" presses.)

9 For example, the Chinese invented what we call gunpowder in the seventh or eighth century AD, for celebratory fireworks, especially for welcoming in the New Year, and not for propelling bullets and other missiles in war. That first took place in the twelfth century, though whether in Europe, Arabia, or China is not known (see L.S. Stavrianos, 1999: 170).

10 Clifford Cobb et al. (1995: 65).

11 Ibid, quote is from the issue cover.

12 Herman E. Daly and John B. Cobb, Jr. (1989); Cobb *et al.* (1995); Söderbaum (2000).

13 Söderbaum (2000: 74).

14 On the health and vitality of pre-Columbian peoples in the New World see Charles C. Mann (2002). For data on other tribal peoples see Sally Fallon (1999). "Progress" as a belief has also led us to label the period in Europe from the fall of Rome to AD 1000 the Dark Ages, as though people living in those times were somehow benighted, backward, and barely eking out an existence. In fact, "it was an age of epochal creativity." Slaves became serfs with rights as well as duties; changes in farming practices and new inventions increased health and prosperity. "By the tenth century the West European serf was enjoying a level of living significantly better than that of the proletarian during the height of Augustan Rome," says Stavrianos (1975: 2 and 5, respectively). This has been recently substantiated by examination of skeletal remains in London from late Roman to Victorian times. Throughout the Dark Ages, the skeletons revealed that people were much healthier than the periods both before and after. They were taller, had healthier teeth, suffered less rheumatoid arthritis and experienced less violence than in later times. (Reported on National Public Radio *Morning Edition*, January 11, 1999.)

15 David E. Bloom and David Canning (2000). The authors recommend that if "poor" countries are to make economic improvement, the place to start is by improving their health care systems, not by "creating more jobs" through investment. Healthy people create their own economic activities. See also Clyde Hertzman (2001), who argues that social equality and low levels of stress are more important to human health than total national wealth.

16 See Richard Sennett (1998), especially p.22. This social scientist from the London School of Economics analyzes the psychic impact of growing job uncertainty and the likely need to change jobs every few years and of "re-skilling" oneself at least three times in one's lifetime. Constant stress is leaching away people's sense of self-worth, of commitment, of loyalty and trust – all that makes life secure and fulfilling.

17 *Ibid.* In Chapter VII, Sennett shows how the majority feel they are "failures," but are really "victims."

18 Ervin Staub (2000).

19 See Lionel Rothkrug (1987).

20 Hannah Arendt (1968: 46).

21 *Ibid*, p.105.

22 Paul Kennedy (1989: 187).

23 *Ibid*, p.211.

24 Arendt (1968: 147).

25 Stavrianos (1999: 581).

26 Roy F. Baumeister (1999).

27 *Ibid*, p.325.

28 Kristen Renwick Monroe, with the assistance of Connie Epperson (1994), shows how both those who aided the Jews in Nazi Germany, and those who did not, held vastly different perceptions of themselves *vis-à-vis* other persons. Those who helped said: "But what else could I do? They were human beings like you and me." Those who did not said: "But what could I do? I was one person alone against the Nazis." Neither felt they had a choice to make.

The well-publicized case of the village of LeChambon in Vichy France, where the villagers defied orders to turn in refugees, especially Jews, has been analyzed and contrasted with Stanley Milgram's experiments. The authors suggest that far from being unusual, resistance to "evil" is ordinary, and evil not as banal as thought. See François Rochat and Andre Modigliani (1995).

29 Baumeister (1999: 324).

30  *Ibid*, p.340.
31  See Iris Chang (1997). Her record of the history of Nanking's fall has been my main source of information. Other useful sources include Ruth Benedict (1946), which is her interpretation of Japanese character as prepared for the U.S. Army during the war, and John W. Dower (1986, 1999).
32  Chang (1997: 22); Dower (1999: 21–2).
33  Chang (1997: 30).
34  *Ibid*, p.217.
35  *Ibid*, p.218.
36  Lt. Col. Dave Grossman (1995/1996). See also Jonathan Shay (1994).
37  Chang (1997: 49).
38  The German people have made some effort at restitution for the harm caused to Jews and others, and now teach about the Holocaust in their schools. In Japan, the process of admission of the atrocities has been much slower. The Japanese, as a nation, have yet to apologize or offer restitution, though there are vocal minorities, such as the Japanese Fellowship of Reconciliation, that do acknowledge what happened (see Chang, 1997: 224). See also Dower (1999), especially Chapters 15 and 16, for the ambivalence of Japanese toward dealing with their past history. It should be added that the United States and its allies were also guilty of major atrocities in World War II, especially the fire-bombing and nuclear bombing of cities; little public acknowledgment of these is made today, and American schoolchildren grow up largely ignorant of them.
    As Chapter X will show, the process of healing after all these atrocities will take many years, even generations, of hard work on all sides to overcome past pain and hurt.
39  Leften S. Stavrianos (1981: 256).
40  See J.F. Ade Ajayi and Ian Espie (eds.) (1972).
41  George B.N. Ayittey (1991: 251). I have drawn much on this reference, and also on an interview of Ayittey, *c.*1992, on National Public Radio with Michael Phillips in his series on Social Thought.
42  *Ibid*, p.13. The description is of the Bashu people of Congo/Zaire.
43  *Ibid*, p.68.
44  *Ibid*, pp.385, 386.
45  *Ibid*, p.276.
46  Barbara Kingsolver (1998). This novel insightfully juxtaposes various shades of both Western and African cultures with one another, illuminating points of both misunderstanding and understanding among them.
47  *Ibid*, p.55.
48  Jonathan Kwitny (1984: 52).
49  *Ibid*, p.55.
50  *Ibid*, p.57.
51  Much of this description comes from Kwitny (1984: 58–69). The recent details are in Ludo deWitte (2000). The latter was reviewed by Ian Black in the *Guardian Weekly*, January 26, 2000: 7.
52  Kwitny (1984: 38–48).
53  David Gough (2000); Chris McGreal (2001). See also James Astill (2002).
54  Polly Toynbee (1999).
55  Ed Vulliamy (2000); Duncan Campbell (2000a). For costs of maintaining the prison system, see Aaron Kipnis (1999: 173ff). ADD (Attention Deficit Disorder) and ADHD (Attention Deficit with Hyperactivity Disorder) as dubious mental health labels are discussed in Kipnis (1999: 60–6) and in Peter Breggin (1998).
56  Robert Bly (1996: xii).

57 Documentation of Americans', and especially children's, loss of trust and meaning is found in Urie Bronfenbrenner *et al.* (1996).

58 Richard Feldman and Michael Betzold (1988: 290); emphasis added. These quotes are the authors' synopses of the parents' opinions and conclusions.

59 This and most of the other data cited in this section comes from a special report on late twentieth-century war put together by George Musser and Sasha Nemecek (2000). Articles include: "A Scourge of Small Arms"; "Invisible Arms"; "The Human Cost of War: A Historical Perspective"; and "Children of the Gun." Citations are made to individual authors' articles. For details of small arms, see J. Boutwell and M.T. Klare (2000). Quote is from p.48.

60 J. Boutwell and M.T. Klare (2000: 48).

61 R.F. Mollica (2000: 54).

62 The story was told by a (then) 10-year-old survivor, one of a group from "Children of War" which was touring America in the mid-1980s, and who visited my class at San Diego State University.

63 See N.G. Boothby and C.M. Knudsen (2000). See also Mike Wessells (1997). Wessells, a psychologist who has worked helping rehabilitate child soldiers in Sierra Leone and Angola, reports on the details of not only their trauma but on their healing. Like others, he emphasizes "rebuilding the fabric of trust" in minds of traumatized persons, whether "perpetrator/bully" or "victim/target."

64 R.F. Mollica (2000). Quote from p.57.

65 *Ibid.*

66 For a clear description of the causes of the disorder in Russia see Stephen F. Cohen (2001).

67 Letter from Sri S.A. Shah to author, January 10, 2000. Professor Shah was formerly Director of the Gujarat Division of the Indian Forest Service and taught also at the National Forestry University at Dehra Dun. I have visited with him both in India and in the United States. We share professional interests in the question of common property use of basic survival resources such as forests and watersheds.

## X Conflict: control or reconciliation?

1 I have deliberately used "quotes" around certain words to indicate that their meanings vary with world view assumptions. Social "order" can mean many things: social conformity, a ranked society, a rigid society, a smoothly functioning society, and so forth. I intend "order" simply to mean a society relatively free of both violence and coercion, which coheres and functions more or less spontaneously. "Disorder" describes a society prone to disruption and violence – which are avoided via excessive physical or psychological controls. When people "behave" under coercion, they are acting according to the will of others. "Justice" in many Western countries almost always means "getting even" by punishing, in the belief that this both deters and cures "bad" behavior. The victim of injustice too often gains little compensation from this type of "justice"; even the punishment imposed on the perpetrator fails to heal the victim's trauma.

"Democracies" today are scarcely that; rather they merely transfer the personal powers of citizens to a select few who act – at a great distance. In terms of the human need for political autonomy, they scarcely scratch the surface. "Enemies" are more often invented by charismatic leaders to maintain social cohesion among their followers in an unstable society, than they are a group against whom the present society has a legitimate grievance. The Cold War was a case in point.

"Solutions" to conflict are often assumed to take place when agreement to end a dispute is reached, for example, an armistice or other contract agreement. However, as the opening quote argues, such "solutions" are only the very first step in *resolving* a conflict and eliminating its causes. Likewise, "peaceful" is put in quotes because too often people believe a peaceful world is one without active wars. Yet the absence of armed conflict can scarcely be called "peace" if in fact coercion and inequity are still rampant, and potentially violent uprisings are held in check only by ongoing threats of massive retaliation or by spreading fear throughout society.

Finally, the "right" of some to accumulate wealth at the expense of others is often confused with the "moral rights" of all humans – as pronounced in Les Droits de L'Homme and the UN Charter – to be free from certain kinds of threats and deprivation (fear and want) and free to enjoy certain activities (religious or other beliefs, and associations with others). The specification of the moral rights of all human beings is, in fact, an evolving process as our entire species attempts to establish some universal human rights that all future societies will be expected to promote, though the institutions utilized for this may vary widely among them.

2 Kenneth Boulding (1989/1990).

3 The WTO is controlled by "the world's most powerful countries and commercial interests." It was not created by the UN but by select governments and corporations that established their own international governance system, replete with rules and a court to enforce them. Anyone wanting to trade in *their* global market had to follow *their* regulations. Interestingly, a recent poll in Great Britain showed that the vast majority of the public, who had no say in those rules, opposes the control they will have over citizens' lives. See "Who Cares about Global Trade?" *The Ecologist*, May, 2000: 16–19.

4 The Center for Defense Information, an organization of retired military leaders who believe real security requires a balance between defense preparedness, diplomacy and international cooperation, has long criticized excessive US military build-up. Since the end of the Cold War, it has castigated the "military overkill" that claims "preparedness" means being able simultaneously to fight two major wars, alone, arguing that this is nothing but "gunboat diplomacy." See articles appearing in its publication, *The Defense Monitor*: 1994, XXIII(7); 1995, XXIV(1) and (3); 1997, XXVI(3); 1998, XXVII(3) and (5); 1999, XXVIII(3). The last of these focuses especially on the futility and dangers involved in relying on confrontational power strategies for building world peace.

5 One of the most powerful books on compassion is the recent text by Michael N. Nagler (2001). Nagler makes a compelling argument for the intrinsic force present in the psyche of every human being for compassion toward other humans – as well as other living beings. So powerful is this force, he argues, that if fearlessly deployed it can quell the violence swelling in the heart of a fellow human being. He offers well-documented support for this claim.

For the Greens, see Alan Cowell (1994) and the film *Nicholas's Gift*, aired on Columbia Broadcasting System May 26, 2002, in the United States. For the Bealls, see *60 Minutes*, CBS, January 17, 1999, and a follow-up report *60 Minutes II*, February 29, 2000.

6 The most well-known theory of moral development is that of Lawrence Kohlberg, who set forth seven sequential "steps" to full morality. While Kohlberg is surely right that children pick up the moral values of those around them, and hence develop knowledge of their culture's expectations as they grow older, his claims that children are "naturally" selfish and must be "taught" to be loving and empathetic are clearly mistaken (see L. Kohlberg, 1970, 1981).

7 Desmond Mpilo Tutu (1999: 31; boldface added). See also George B.N. Ayittey (1991), Chapter 6. "The Native System of Government: A Summary and an Assessment," which describes the applications of *ubuntu* (although Ayittey does not use that term specifically) in resolving social conflicts in various tribes. He also contrasts the flexibility of tribal traditional law and justice with the rigidity of

Western law. For Africans, the goal is not to punish but to heal in the least painful way possible. "Justice" serves the people, not vice versa, where people "serve" an abstract set of rules. While visiting the Center for the Study of Violence and Reconciliation in Johannesburg I had an opportunity to interview Ms. Pumeza Mafani, who explained the reciprocal meanings of remorse/apology and forgiveness in the term *ubuntu*.

8  Tutu (1999: 31).

9  *Ibid.*

10  Mohandas K. Gandhi (1957: 276).

11  *Ibid.*

12  The sect called Swadhyahya was founded by Pandurangshastri Athavale's father in 1926, and the son has been its leader since the 1940s. I visited several villages and Vidyapeeths (schools) that followed his teachings of compassion and sharing through the belief that God is immanent in every person. Each able-bodied person gives one day's work a week to support the poor or helpless among them. The movement, last I heard, had tens of millions of followers. See Athavale (1987) and Sat Vichar Darshan Trust (1994). See also Pramila Jayapal (2001).

13  See Gene Sharp (1990). See also Sharp (1973, 1980). Resistance includes passively refusing to play by the new rules: striking (refusing to work, or boycotting, such as the Montgomery bus boycott, where one refuses to utilize the oppressor's goods or services); playing "dumb" or "clumsy" (slaves in the U.S. South; Danes all wearing the yellow Star-of-David during the Nazi occupation). For more examples see Leo Kuper (1957) (Kuper records the details of apartheid and the history of the resistance movement). Also see Eva Fogelman (1994). The daughter of Polish survivors, Fogelman describes the variety of motives of those who were "rescuers.") More direct, yet still nonviolent, action occurs during civil disobedience or the active breaking of laws, such as sit-ins and similar demonstrations. See Michael N. Nagler (2001) for an overall analysis of nonviolence. See Mary E. Clark (1989: 465ff and cited references) for more on Gandhi, Dolci, King, and Aquino.

14  Tutu (1999: 28).

15  Personal communication from Jerold Starr, Department of Sociology and Anthropology, West Virginia University, Morgantown, WV, 26506.

16  These vignettes are taken from the powerful account of the TRC hearings by Antjie Krog, an Afrikaner journalist for the South African Broadcasting Corporation. In her (1999) book she vividly describes not only the hearings, but her own and others' reactions to them. What I report here is a minute fraction of the whole picture she so skillfully reveals. To truly grasp the underpinnings of the "evil" side of human nature, one should read this book. For impact on brain structure, Krog makes reference to post-traumatic stress disorder (PTSD) throughout the text. See Chapter VI for a review of brain pathologies caused by prolonged stress.

17  Like other kinds of dictatorships, *apartheid* maintained power by its random use of violence, making life constantly unpredictable. See Nils Johan Lavik (1994: 85–115; comments on South Africa are on pp.96–7). (This entire volume is an excellent, comprehensive analysis of the psychological consequences for the human psyche of violence in all its many forms, and of the processes of healing.)

   Two other reports specifically on the psychological consequences of apartheid are AAAS (1990) and UNICEF (1987).

18  Krog (1999: 12). Testimony of Elsie Gishi.

19  Krog (1999: 101).

20  *Ibid*, p.189.

21  *Ibid*, p.239.

22  *Ibid.*

23  *Ibid*, p.193; letter to TRC by "call me Helena."

24  *Ibid*, p.195; letter to TRC by "call me Helena."
25  *Ibid*, p.93.
26  *Ibid*, p.98.
27  *Ibid*, p.117.
28  *Ibid*, p.119.
29  *Ibid*, p.119; ellipses in original.
30  *Ibid*, p.120.
31  *Ibid*, p.231.
32  *Ibid*, p.235.
33  *Ibid*, p.236.
34  *Ibid*, p.137.
35  *Ibid*, pp.136–7, 163.
36  *Ibid*, pp.136, 165.
37  *Ibid*, p.210.
38  *Ibid*, pp.338–9. There was a moving televised account of this encounter between Tutu and Winnie Mandela on American Broadcasting Association's *Nightline*, October 29, 1998, "Tutu: Healing a Broken Nation."
39  *Ibid*, p.339.
40  *Ibid*, p.139.
41  "Collective guilt" is probably seldom if ever wholly acknowledged by nations whose leaders have engaged in mass violence against a subordinate group. Thus, collective admission of national responsibility for the Holocaust by contemporary German leaders has been less than whole-hearted, though token recognition has been made. Likewise, contemporary Americans have not collectively admitted "guilt" for past atrocities against Native Americans or black African slaves or for the ensuing oppression still faced by many of their descendents.

On the other hand, much has been accomplished at an interpersonal, noncollective level, where individual Germans who grew up in and participated in Hitler's war have individually explained to victims or their relatives their gradual recognition of the horrors of the Holocaust and their sense of often unwitting responsibility for what happened. Michael Henderson (1996) explains how people-to-people interaction (particularly that at the Caux Center in Switzerland) helps former perpetrators and victims find the path to reconciliation on a personal basis. In his book, Henderson recounts multiple incidents of personal acts of reconciliation by victims toward former perpetrators that promoted healing between former enemies.
42  Krog (1999: 159). During my visit to South Africa in August 2000, I was struck by how many of the well-to-do in the white community are not acting in ways that might make up for the past; rather, they seem to be barricading themselves behind the wealth they still control. They are becoming increasing targets of violence by black gangs.
43  Tutu (1999: 27).
44  *Ibid*, pp.19ff. All of Chapter II, "Nuremberg or National Amnesia? A Third Way," explains the advantages of the TRC hearings over divisive as well as costly trials.
45  *Ibid*, p.15.
46  See Jayne Seminare Docherty (2001) for analysis of this confrontation. America's rigid view of how to enforce law and order has become notorious. In the 1980s and 1990s, the FBI, the nation's police force, committed numerous tragic blunders against American citizens in their single-minded pursuit of imposed order. At Ruby Ridge, Montana, the unarmed wife of Randy Wheeler and the baby she held in her arms were killed by FBI agents. In 1993, at Waco, Texas, David Koresh and nearly all the other members of his Branch Davidian religious sect were killed in an almost military-type assault on their compound, Mount Carmel, by FBI agents following fifty-one days of failed negotiations. Whether the FBI or the Branch Davidians

themselves were responsible for the fire in which twenty-one children, along with adults, perished, is still not clear. Dr. Docherty's analysis of the latter tragedy exposes the failure of a law-based enforcement system to comprehend the totally different worlds in which the agents and the Branch Davidians thought and lived. This book is recommended highly for its lucid explication of the profound nature of conflicts between sacred meaning systems.

47 For an excellent historical analysis, see Mahmood Mamdani (2001), especially Chapters 2–4. Quote is from p.62. (The rest of this book is devoted to the genocide itself and the healing that must take place, where justice and truth must be histori-cally contextualized and not limited to the recent massacres.) Other sources include several articles from 1994 in the *Guardian Weekly*, and two feature stories in the *New York Times*: Paul Lewis (1994) and Raymond Bonner (1994). For analysis of both Rwanda and Yugoslavia see Ervin Staub (1999); for Yugoslavia, p.319; for Uganda, pp.310–13. See also Desmond Tutu's comments on Rwanda: Tutu (1999: 257–60).

Finally, Jack David Ellers (1999) makes the important point that neither cultural differences, nor even historic enmities, in and of themselves, cause violent conflict to erupt; that depends on local contexts and recent stressful events. This insightful book is a "must-read" for those studying or mediating ethnic conflicts. The past does not *cause* present violence, but it can significantly lower the threshold.

48 See Desmond Tutu's analysis of the Israeli/Palestinian situation, and the Jews' inability to forgive the Holocaust (Tutu, 1999: 267–8), also Annette Streeck-Fischer (1999) and Jason Cowley (2002).

49 Hugo van der Merwe (1999). A Quaker-raised native Afrikaner, Hugo was in classes of mine during his first years at George Mason's Institute for Conflict Analysis and Resolution. He is now employed by the Center for the Study of Violence and Reconciliation in South Africa. In August 2000, I visited there with a group of People-to-People Ambassadors studying conflict resolution. My personal observa-tions from that visit are included in this section.

50 Numerous authors have pointed this out. See, for example, John Gray (1998) and Peter Söderbaum (2000).

51 Data come from author's personal notes, taken from officers of national agencies and spokespersons for nonprofit NGOs. For the impact of HIV/AIDS on the neighboring country of Botswana where the disease is also rampant refer to Figure 0.9.

52 Kevin Lancaster, CEO, Community Dispute Resolution Trust, Braamfontein, Z.A.; Mark Turpin, Associate Director, Independent Mediation Services of South Africa, Richmond, Z.A.; Dr. Barney Pityana, Director, South African Human Rights Commission (a constitutionally mandated agency), Parktown, Z.A. Among rich nations giving support as aid (gifts) rather than loans to developing countries, the amounts are niggardly. Britain, the best, gives 0.7 percent of GNP. See Larry Elliott (2001).

53 Comments are those of Graeme Simpson, the highly perceptive Director of the Center for the Study of Violence and Reconciliation, Braamfontein, Z.A.

54 Hugo van der Merwe (1999: Ch.12), especially Table 12.1, where he contrasts the top-down, legalistic view of the nature of conflict and the meaning of justice with bottom-up, individual participant's point of view. His analysis of the whole question of what justice means is very helpful.

55 Frans de Waal (1982, 1989); de Waal *et al.* (2000).

56 The notion of non-negotiable human needs as the cause of intractable conflict was first widely promoted by the Australian diplomat turned academic educator, John W. Burton. The best-known exposition of his ideas is found in Burton (1990). Since then (often in parallel with Burton) the varied group of peacemakers cited in n.61, below, have all accepted his theory and elaborated it in various ways. Burton

was one of the first to talk about deep-rooted conflict and non-negotiable needs, and the usefulness of unfettered dialogue in collaborative "problem-solving workshops." Although Burton was somewhat vague about these needs – speaking in general about "identity" and "identity groups" – others have identified a handful of "needs," using different terms, that seem to me equivalent to the three I have identified in this book: security in belonging, feelings of autonomy within one's society, and a shared belief system that gives meaning to group as well as individual life.

57  Dwight D. Eisenhower (1959: 625) (from a speech on British television; quoted by Harold H. Saunders, 1999: 10).

58  Saunders (1999: 11). Enormous numbers of monographs and articles exist regarding traditional forms of community dialogue and local politics. For Africa, see George B.N. Ayittey (1991). For Native Americans, see Paula Gunn Allen (1986) and Rupert Ross (1992). For India, see Ashis Nandy (2000). Other articles in this same issue of *Interculture* further address the inhumane nature of centralized nation-states and the persistence of far more autonomous, loosely constructed and in many ways less rigid local social orders.

59  The occasion was a Holis Meeting (a group of planetary futurists) at "Commonweal," near Bolinas, California, 1993. The Navajo scientist was Dr. Fred Begay.

60  There are hundreds of works analyzing the antidemocratic nature of mass media. Some important American examples are Michael Parenti (1986); Herbert I. Schiller (1989, 1996); Noam Chomsky (1989); and Ian I. Mitroff and Warren Bennis (1993).

61  John Burton (1990) used the term "problem-solving workshops"; Vamik Volkan (2000) and his colleagues at the Center for the Study of Mind and Human Interaction at the University of Virginia call their process "psychopolitical workshops"; Louise Diamond and John McDonald (1996) call it "multi-track diplomacy"; Ronald J. Fisher (1997, 1999) calls it "interactive conflict resolution"; former UN Secretary General Boutros-Ghali (1992) referred to it as "post-conflict peace building"; Harold Saunders (1999) uses the term a "public peace process." The ideas in the pages that follow are drawn from one or more of these sources. Often, the writers use terms from their specialist disciplines that, for the sake of clarity, I have taken the liberty to "translate" into the terms used throughout this book. Although the disciplines do seem to be converging on a consistent picture of human nature, their languages still seem far apart until one makes such translations.

62  Vamik Volkan (2000).

63  The reader should be aware that this process of reconciliation after trauma did not take place with either Germany or Japan for the former victims of the atrocities committed. The Nuremburg Trials did not allow ordinary survivors of the Holocaust to confront the actual individuals who were overseeing them, nor any of the rest of the German public who "just didn't know." (Archbishop Tutu, 1999, makes this point in Chapter 2 of his book. Hence, the Jews have never really been offered the opportunity to forgive.) And with Japan, the treatment of 200,000 "comfort women," kept as sex slaves by the Japanese army during the war and used in unbelievably brutal ways, has never been officially admitted. Though the Japanese government set up a fund for private contributions toward compensation, few of the women will touch such money. They first require an apology. See Doug Struck (2000). Today there are dozens of places around the world where violence has died down but where reconciliation has never occurred: most recent are the Hutus and Tutsis in Rwanda, and the factions in former Yugoslavia and the rest of the Balkans. But many examples go back centuries. In the United States, neither the blacks nor the Native Americans have had real dialogue with the dominant whites, have never

had their own feelings heard face to face. Under a veneer of civility, a great deal of hate and resentment remain unresolved in one nation after another, leading to the tenuous state of global peace today.

64  Volkan (2000: 153–5).

65  *Ibid*, p.164.

66  This conversation took place during a visit to Burton at his home near Canberra, Australia, in 1995.

67  Volkan (2000: 206).

68  *Ibid*, pp.189–96. For more on this process see Saunders (1999: Ch.6).

69  Failure within a community to properly mourn its own lost past due to unresolved trauma can be ritually passed down over many generations. In a recent issue of *Mind and Human Interaction* several articles appeared dealing with this failure to heal. Ilany Kogan (2000) reports on the exaggerated paranoia felt by the children of Holocaust survivors, born and raised in Israel; K. Michelle Scott (2000) discusses the "persistent transmission" of an identity anchored in the self-perception of victimhood among American blacks; and John Hartman (2000) shows how in Poland both sides can be paranoid, seeing themselves as victims: the Jews, of the Nazis, the Christians, of the Soviet communists. In each of these cases, group identity is being formed around the *negative* idea of being persecuted by an "other" rather than the *positive* idea of a satisfying way of "being-in-my-group."

70  Elise Boulding (2000).

## XI  The search for autonomy within community

1  From my friend, Robert Gault's friend, Julie Arrington, who tells me she found it, unattributed, on the Internet.

2  Terry Tempest Williams (1991: 286).

3  E.F. Schumacher, Lindesfarne Tape Series, K3. (*c*.1972).

4  Martin E. Marty (1994).

5  John Gray (1998: 235).

6  Even today there are, however, active communist parties in several countries that have undertaken a different evolutionary route. Several cities in north-central Italy have thrived under elected local communist governments. And the Indian state of Kerala, which is discussed at the end of this chapter, has several times democratically elected – and later defeated – communist governments. But these are examples where people have freely chosen to try out Marxian programs rather than being forced to accept them.

7  Leon Festinger (1957: 3).

8  Richard B. Norgaard (1994: 70); emphasis in original. See also Peter Söderbaum (2000), especially Chapter 1. Both these two and dozens of other "dissident" economists have been denied academic promotions on time and had their work belittled by colleagues. It is the same problem as reported for other maverick scientists, such as Barbara McClintock, whose ideas are discussed in Chapter I.

9  Peter Raine (2001). Quotes are on pp.21, 31, and 43. His doctoral thesis, from Massey University in New Zealand (1998), was entitled "Who Guards the Guardians: The Practical and Theoretical Criteria for Environmental Guardianship." See my Postscript for how some Islamic fundamentalists may have become terrorists because of their fear regarding the absolutist nature of Western claims to a final "truth" about human social orders.

10  Both editorials are by Thomas Friedman and appear in the *New York Times*, quoted by Merrill Goozner (2000: 24). European papers took a very different slant, noting that the Prague protests were "just one of 37 protests around the world against the World Bank and the IMF," and it was but the "first attempt to organise European-

wide coordinated protests against global institutions, with more than 20 nationalities taking part. 'Make protest as global as capitalism,' read one of the banners" (see *Guardian Weekly*, October 4, 2000: 2).

11 Kenneth E. Boulding (1989/1990) gives an overview of various forms of power. All the writings of Herbert I. Schiller address this issue. My favorites are Schiller (1989, 1996). See also the classic by Joe McGinniss (1969). Also, David Korten (2001); Naomi Klein (2000); and Thomas Frank (2000).

12 Noreena Hertz (2001a: 23–4). See also Hertz (2001b).

13 Zac Goldsmith (2000). See also poll results by MORI, a British polling firm, on preceding pages of this same issue. More recently, other authors have pointed to public skepticism: see Thomas Beamish (2002), and Susanna M. Hoffman and Anthony Oliver-Smith (eds.) (2002).

14 For examples from Russia, see Daniel Williams (2000). In India, resistance to globalization has come mainly from women, as recorded by Vandana Shiva (1988). For women's responses to development elsewhere, see Sinith Sittirak (1998); Susan Diduk (1989); and V. Shiva (ed.) (1994). For Mexico, see Naomi Klein (2001, 2000). For growing stress in Japan, see Darius Mehri (2000). Recently, a Japanese mother, a nurse and wife of a Buddhist priest, murdered a neighbor's 2-year-old daughter who was accepted into a prestigious kindergarten that had rejected her own daughter (see Kathryn Tolbert, 1999; Jonathan Watts, 1999). "Some [Japanese] women feel that a mother's identity can be gained only from the educational attainment of her children," say Kenji Kameguchi and Stephen Murphy-Shigematsu (2001).

15 Benjamin Barber (1990).

16 *Ibid*, p.81ff.

17 Classics in this new field are Fikret Berkes (ed.) (1989) and Bonnie J. McCay and James M. Acheson (eds.) (1990). For quarterly updates on publications in this field, see *The Common Property Resource Digest*, published by International Association for the Study of Common Property, P.O. Box 2355, Gary IN, 46409.

An example of how small communities in developing countries are being helped to make grassroots decisions about how best to modify their group livelihoods to accommodate multiple objectives, such as sustainability of local environment, total income, and number of jobs resulting, is a methodology developed by T.K. Moulik and P.R. Shuckla (1992). There are many more examples of similar approaches, each crafted for a particular ecological, cultural, and historical context.

18 See Bruce E. Johansen (1982: 32ff).

19 Paul Hawken (2000), and in the same issue, Jonathan Rowe (2000).

20 John Taylor Gatto (1996: 45).

21 Quoted by Wes Jackson (2000).

22 *Ibid*, p.18.

23 Deborah Meier (1995); Phil Schoggen (1989) Chapter 9, "Behavior Setting Theory Applied to Underpopulated Settings."

24 See William R. Caspary (2000: 84). Quote is from Dewey's *Freedom and Culture*. Caspary's book is a valuable analysis of the applicability of Dewey's thinking to the social needs of the twenty-first century.

25 *Ibid*, various places, including pp.70, 89–91, and 138.

26 *Ibid*, p.189.

27 Deborah Meier (1995: 69–75). In *Ariadne's Thread* (Clark, 1989), I contrasted this rigid "mold-to-fit" approach to education with the more flexible "critique/create" approach that innovative new schools are taking (see Ch.8).

28 Meier (1995: 159–70). Similar results of engaging students in socially meaningful education have been obtained by the Seattle Social Development Project, which focused on high crime areas. Outcomes included raising academic performance and

decreasing drug use and sexual activity, even though these latter were not explicit in the curriculum. See R.D. Abbott *et al.* (1998) and Heather S. Lonezak *et al.* (2002).

29 *Ibid*, pp.155–7.

30 Yehudi Menuhin (1996). Not many months later, I heard of similar results from Itzhak Perlman's introductions of music programs into some American schools.

31 For data and further information contact Americans for the Arts, 1000 Vermont Ave., NW, 12th Floor, Washington D.C., 20005, Tel: (202)-371-2810.

32 Portland City Club (2000).

33 *Weekend Edition* (2000). See Mary E. Northridge (and seven other scholar-authors plus "the Earth Crew" of 27 trained high school students from West Harlem Environmental Action's Earth Crew Youth Leadership Program) (1999). The Crew administered the background surveys to the 7th-grade students being studied at Thurgood Marshall Academy in Harlem for body burden or air pollutants and impact on lung function.

34 Eliot Wigginton (1985, 1991).

35 Pacers, PRSR, Box 870372, Tuscaloosa, AL 37487-0372, Tel: (205) 348-6432.

36 See not only Matt Hern (1996) but earlier classics that criticized standard education: Paul Goodman (1960, 1962); Paolo Freire (1970/1992); and Robert Welker (1992).

37 See John Dewey (1916/1966, 1927). In the mid-1930s, I was in a 3rd-grade class taught by Marian H. Dunbar, a Deweyite teacher *par excellence* in the San Francisco public schools. During those years, the two great bridges were being built under our very noses. I have vivid recollections of many hours spent in collaborative groups, first designing on butcher paper, then measuring, sawing, and hammering together lengths of polished lathes to make models of five different types of bridges. There were five or six in each group, and we had to do a lot of talking and thinking and planning *together*. We had to share knowledge about our community and about bridge architecture. We had to *draw* a design; we had to *calculate* and *measure*; we had to *saw* and *hammer*. We had, most of all, to communicate and *negotiate* to make group decisions. There was no "grade" that I recall. We (and all our parents) admired every group's bridge.

38 David W. Johnson and Roger T. Johnson (1974, 1989, 1994). See also Ron Brandt (1987).

39 In our class at San Diego State University, we did not do a controlled study to see if collaborative study produced "better essays." The goal of the class was to encourage collaborative thinking about civic issues; the subject matter did not lend itself to evaluation about correctness of facts nor, particularly, the art of writing essays. Instead, we tried to stimulate class discussion and group thinking about extremely difficult questions, which incorporated all kinds of information to be evaluated and fitted together. The essays, written during the final exam period, could only be a few paragraphs long. Five of the many essay-type questions out of a list of thirty or more submitted as part of each week's assignment by the students themselves were chosen by faculty to be answered. But students did not know in advance which five it would be, so they needed to have prepared ahead to answer some thirty very hard questions.

40 Gregory A. Smith (1992: 108). He also cites other important contributors to these ideas: Urie Bronfenbrenner (1970) and Elizabeth Cagan (1978). See also his more recent 1993 book.

It may be, however, that when responsibility for others' learning is placed on children, in a school where enormous pressure to "succeed" rests on the entire population of children, as happens in Japan, it can lead to undue stress. In Japan there is a growing epidemic of "school refusal" among youth, where children simply stay at home. Though there is evidence that this is due to excessive pressure on "groups" to succeed, and that it ignores individual learning needs, the literature in

Japan tends to blame the homes for this problem (see Kenji Kameguchi and Stephen Murphy-Shigematsu , 2001). Lack of a "father's discipline" is the reason most often cited, since fathers spend so little time at home.

41 This I have personally observed in the inner city schools of central and south San Diego in the 1980s and in South African townships in 2000.

42 David W. Johnson and Roger T. Johnson (2000). At the conference at which this work was reported, 9- and 10-year-olds from local schools role-played a schoolyard mediation for the audience. In South Africa's "Safer Schools" program, we saw similar activities in a middle school where more than half the students wear armbands indicating they can act as mediators if requested by their peers (visit, August, 2000).

43 Elliott Aronson (2000). Making every child feel like a valued participant in society further requires expanding the concept of "intelligence" from purely academic skills to *all* the multiple skills a society requires. Howard Gardner and his colleagues have incorporated cross-cultural studies of "intelligence" to reveal the multiple facets of thinking that human beings adaptively perform. See Howard Gardner, Mindy L. Kornhaber, and Warren K. Wake (1996) for arguments for changing school curricula to maximize the development of the diverse intelligences that exist among the members of any society. Not everyone has the same strengths, or learns in the same manner. These authors would promote new kinds of schools with new views of "intelligence."

44 Jonathan Barker (1999: 1).

45 Patrick Tierney (2000: 255–6).

46 Jane Jacobs (1961).

47 Daniel Kemmis (1990). See also Kemmis (1995) for building economic contacts between individual cities around the world through sister-city programs.

48 I am always dismayed when "self-help" writers claim that, after a long weekend retreat during which strangers in a group have been baring their souls to one another, there suddenly emerges late on Sunday afternoon, just before everyone disperses, a surge of fellow feeling that they call "community." See for example M. Scott Peck (1987: Chs.5 and 6). The notion that a group learning for the first time to dialogue openly with each other is a "community" rather than people who are simply learning the skills of dialogue and conflict resolution – both, of course essential for permanent community-building – is a common error. It trivializes the quality of the bonds and the coming to share of similar meanings and goals that characterize true human "communities."

49 Kemmis (1990: 92–9).

50 E.F. Schumacher (1974).

51 See Kemmis (1995: Ch.6, "A Sisterhood of City-States"). On the problems of unregulated transnational corporations, see David Korten (2001).

52 John Gray (1998: 88, 213). See also John Gray (2000) wherein he reanalyzes "liberalism," pointing out the failure of all absolutist theories of human nature, human rights, and the "ideal" human society. He especially objects to any possibility of "absolute freedom" in human life. As my friend, the philosopher Mary Midgley, once observed, who would want to be "free" of all commitments to others, all feelings of attachment, all sense of belonging. The last thing the young man wants to hear from his loved one is that he is "free" from his promise to marry her. Absolute freedom is absolute loneliness.

53 Jonathan Barker (1999: Ch.19, "Local Action and Global Power: Shifting the Balance").

54 Jeff Gates (1998).

55 Note how the Mondragon cooperatives have built in their own "Keynesian" mechanism for dealing with the boom/bust cycles of capitalist markets. Elsewhere,

governments are looked to, to soften the blow, as in the 1930s depression, and again in the 1990s and in 2001.

56 Personal interview with Jesús Larrañaga, Mondragon, July 22, 1992. Other information is taken from Roy Morrison (1991) and William F. Whyte and Kathleen K. Whyte (1991).

57 See, for example, Eira Dalton (1963). This is a history of one missionary family from 1800 to 1960.

58 Information on *Malayala Manorama* (as well as much else in this section) comes from an interview, November 25, 1995, with Lt. Col. Jose Vallikappen, General Manager, Corporate Policy and Electronic Media, Malayama Manorama, P.O. Box No.26, Kottayam 868 001, Kerala, from whom I also obtained a small informational centenary pamphlet "One Bright Morning in 1888," about the origins of the newspaper. The liberal Maharaja was His Highness Sri Mulam Thirunal.

59 Konniyoor Narendranath (1995). The regent's name was Maharani Sethu Lakshmi Bayi; she ruled after Thirunal's death, from 1924 to 1931. Despite her power and wealth, she lived a simple, unassuming life.

60 Information from an interview with Sri P.M. Kurian, Kottyam, November 25, 1995; also from A. Gangadharan (1974). Kurian, as overseer of a British owner's estate, presided over the sale of its parcels prior to the actual passage of the law. For further information, see Richard W. Franke and Barbara H. Chasin (1994). (A summary is given in *Multinational Monitor*, July/August, 1995: pp.25–8.)

61 Peter Medoff and Holly Sklar (1994: 1).

62 I want to register my gratitude to Greg Watson, the DSNI Director when I visited, and the many volunteers I met there for their courtesy and help. Pamphlets and further information are available from DSNI, 513 Dudley Street, Roxbury, MA, 02119, Tel: (617)-442-9670.

63 John McKnight (1995). McKnight argues bureaucracies cannot heal poverty, trauma, or crime; only living communities can do those things. Both he and Jeremy Rifkin (2000) rail against the socially destructive effects of commoditizing every aspect of human life.

# BIBLIOGRAPHY

AAAS (1990) *Apartheid and Medicine*, AAAS Publication 90–095, Washington D.C.: American Association for the Advancement of Science.

Abbott, R.D., J. O'Donnell, J.D. Hawkins, K.G. Hill, R. Kosterman, and R.F. Catalano 1998) "Changing Teaching Practices to Promote Achievement and Bonding to School," *American Journal of Orthopsychiatry* 68: 542–52.

Achebe, Chinua (1959) *Things Fall Apart*, New York: Fawcett.

Adcock, Gregory J., Elizabeth S. Dennis, Simon Easteal, Gavin A. Hultley, Lars S. Jermiin, W. James Peacock, and Alan Thorne (2001) "Mitochondrial DNA Sequences in Ancient Australians: Implications for Modern Human Origins," *Proceedings of the National Academy of Sciences* 98: 537–42.

Ainsworth, M.D.S., M.C. Blehar, E. Waters, and S. Wall (1978) *Patterns of Attachment: A Psychological Study of the Strange Situation*, Hillsdale, NJ: Erlbaum.

Ajayi, J.F Ade and Ian Espie (eds.) (1972) *A Thousand Years of West African History*, New York: Humanities Press.

Allen, Paula Gunn (1986) *The Sacred Recovering the Feminine in American Indian Traditions*, Boston: Beacon Press.

Alper, Joe (2000) "New Insights Into Type 2 Diabetes," *Science* 289: 37, 39.

Alpert, Peter (1995) "The Boulder and the Sphere," *Environmental Values* 4: 3–15.

Alroy, John (2001) "A Multispecies Overkill Simulation of the End-Pleistocene Megafaunal Mass Extinction," *Science* 292: 1893–6.

Alvarez, W. and Frank Alaro (1992) "The Extinction of the Dinosaurs," in Janine Bourriau (ed.) (1992).

Alvord, Lori A. and Elizabeth C. Van Pelt (1999) *The Scalpel and the Silver Bear*, New York: Bantam Books.

Anderson, Craig A. and Brad J. Bushman (2002) "The Effects of Media Violence on Society," *Science* 295: 2377.

Angier, Natalie (1999) *Woman: An Intimate Geography*, Boston: Houghton-Mifflin.

Applebaum, Eileen and Rosemary Batt (1993) *The New American Workplace*, Ithaca, NY: Cornell University Press.

Ardrey, Robert (1966) *The Territorial Imperative*, New York: Atheneum.

Arendt, Hannah (1968) *Imperialism: Part Two of The Origins of Totalitarianism*, New York: Harcourt Brace.

Arnsten, Amy F.T. (1998) "The Biology of Being Frazzled," *Science* 280: 1711–12.

Aronson, Elliot (2000) *Nobody Left to Hate: Teaching Compassion After Columbine*, New York: Worth/W.H. Freeman.

Asmal, Kader (2000), in *Stockholm Water Front*, 3, October: 5.

Athavale, Pandurangshastri (1987) *Light That Leads*, Vimal Jyoti, 6/8 Dr. Wilson Street, Bombay 400 004: Sat Vichar Darshan.

Aureli, Filippo and F.B.M. de Waal (eds.) (2000) *Natural Conflict Resolution*, Berkeley: University of California Press.

Axelrod, Robert (1984) *The Evolution of Cooperation*, New York: Basic Books.

Axelrod, Robert, and W.D. Hamilton (1981) "The Evolution of Cooperation," *Science* 211: 1390–6.

Ayala, Francisco (1995) "The Myth of Eve: Molecular Biology and Human Origins," *Science* 267: 1930–6.

Ayittey, George B.N. (1991) *Indigenous African Institutions*, Ardsley-on-Hudson, NY: Transnational Publishing Inc.

Azari, Nina P. and Rüdiger J. Seitz (2000) "Brain Plasticity and Recovery from Stroke," *American Scientist* 88: 426–31.

Baars, B.J. (1988) *A Cognitive Theory of Consciousness*, Cambridge, UK: Cambridge University Press.

Bakan, D. (1966) *The Duality of Human Existence: Isolation and Communion in Western Man*, Boston: Beacon Press.

Baker, Robin and Mark A. Bellis (1996) *Human Sperm Competition: Copulation, Mastur-bation and Infidelity*, New York: Chapman and Hall.

Balter, Michael (1999) "A Long Season Puts Çatalhöyük in Context," *Science* 286: 890–1.

Balter, Michael (2000a) "Unearthing Monuments of the Yarmukians," *Science* 287: 35.

Balter, Michael (2000b) "Dredging at Israeli Site Prompts Mudslinging," *Science* 287: 205–6.

Balter, Michael (2001a) "In Search of the First Europeans," *Science* 291: 1722–5.

Balter, Michael (2001b) "Max Planck's Meeting of the Anthropological Minds," *Science* 293: 1246–9.

Balter, Michael and Ann Gibbons (2000) "A Glimpse of Human's First Journey Out of Africa," *Science* 288: 948–50.

Barber, Benjamin (1990) *Strong Democracy: Participatory Politics for a New Age*, 2nd edn., Berkeley, CA: University of California Press.

Barinaga, Marcia (1996) "The Cerebellum: Movement Coordinator or Much More?," *Science* 272: 482–3.

Baring, Anne and Jules Cashford (1993) *The Myth of the Goddess: Evolution of an Image*, London: Penguin/Arkana.

Barker, Jonathan (1999) *Street-Level Democracy: Political Settings at the Margins of Global Power*, West Hartford, CT: Kumarian Press.

Barker, Roger G. (1968) *Ecological Psychology: Concepts and Methods for Studying the Environment of Human Behavior*, Palo Alto, CA: Stanford University Press.

Barkow, Jerome H., Leda Cosmides, and John Tooby (eds.) (1992) *The Adapted Mind: Evolu-tionary Psychology and the Generation of Culture*, New York: Oxford University Press.

Barlow, George W. and J. Silverberg (eds.) (1980) *Sociobiology: Beyond Nature/Nurture?*, Washington D.C.: American Association for the Advancement of Science.

Bateson, Gregory (1972) *Steps to an Ecology of Mind*, New York: Ballantine.

Bateson, Mary Catherine (1990) "Gaia as Metaphor," Keynote Address, Isthmus Insti-tute 1990 Conference, recorded on audiotape by Silver Mountain Productions, 800/752-4553.

Baughman, Fred A., Jr. (2001) "Letters," *Science* 291: 595.

Baumeister, Roy F. (1999) *Evil: Inside Human Violence and Cruelty*, New York: W.H. Freeman.

Baxter, Vern (1994) *Labor and Politics in the U.S. Postal Service*, New York: Plenum Press.

Baxter, Vern and Anthony Margavio (1996) "Assaultive Violence in the U.S. Post Office," *Work & Occupation* 23: 277–96.

Beamish, Thomas D. (2002) *Silent Spill: The Organization of an Industrial Crisis*, Cambridge, MA: Massachusetts Institute of Technology Press.

Becker, Ernest (1971) *The Birth and Death of Meaning*, 2nd edn., New York: Macmillan/Free Press.

Benedict, Ruth (1946) *The Chrysanthemum and the Sword: Patterns of Japanese Culture*, Boston: Houghton-Mifflin.

Bennett, Ruth (1999) "Jealousy Genes," *Eugene Weekly*, February 11: 10–11.

Benson, Herbert (1996) *Timeless Healing: The Power and Biology of Belief*, New York: Scribner.

Ben-Yehuda, Nachman (1995) *The Masada Myth: Collective Memory and Mythmaking in Israel*, Madison: University of Wisconsin Press.

Berkes, Fikret (ed.) (1989) *Common Property Resources: Ecology and Community-based Sustainable Development*, London: Belhaven Press.

Berman, Morris (2000) *Wandering God: A Study in Nomadic Spirituality*, Albany, NY: SUNY Press.

Bertell, Rosalie (1997) "The Bhopal Legacy: An Interview with Dr. Rosalie Bertell," *Multinational Monitor*, March: 26–8.

Biesele, Megan (1983) "Interpretation in Rock Art and Folklore: Communication Systems in Evolutionary Perspective," in J.D. Lewis-Williams (ed.), *New Approaches to Southern African Rock Art*, Cape Town: The South African Archaeological Society, Goodwin Series No. 4, 54–60.

Bill, James A. (1984) "Resurgent Islam in the Persian Gulf," *Foreign Affairs* 63: 108–27.

Bill, James A. (1988) *The Eagle and the Lion: The Tragedy of American–Iranian Relations*, New Haven, CT: Yale University Press.

Black, Francis L. (1992) "Why Did They Die?," *Science* 258: 1739–40.

Blackmore, Susan (1999) *The Meme Machine*, Oxford: Oxford University Press.

Bleier, Ruth (ed.) (1988) *Feminist Approaches to Science*, New York: Pergamon.

Bloom, David E. and David Canning (2000) "The Health and Wealth of Nations," *Science* 287: 1207, 1209.

Bloom, Lois (1993) *The Transition from Infancy to Language: Acquiring the Power of Expression*, New York: Cambridge University Press.

Blum, Kenneth, John G. Cull, Eric E. Braverman, and David E. Comings (1996) "Reward Deficiency Syndrome," *American Scientist* 84(March/April): 132–44.

Blumenschine, Robert J. and Cavallo, John A. (1992) "Scavenging and Human Evolution," *Scientific American*, October: 90–6.

Blumenthal, Herman T. (1997) "Fidelity Assurance Mechanisms of the Brain with Special Reference to Its Immunogenic CNS Compartment: Their Role in Aging and Aging-Associated Neurological Disease," *Journal of Gerontology: Biological Sciences* 52A, No. 1: B1–B9.

Blunier, Thomas and Edward J. Brook (2001) "Timing of Millennial-scale Climate Change in Antarctica and Greenland During the Last Glacial Period," *Science* 291: 109–12.

Bly, Robert (1996) *The Sibling Society*, Reading, MA: Addison Wesley.

Boehm, Christopher (1999) *Hierarchy in the Forest: The Evolution of Egalitarian Behavior*, Cambridge, MA: Harvard University Press.

Bohannan, Paul (1995) *How Culture Works*, New York: Free Press.

Bohm, David (1980) *Wholeness and the Implicate Order*, London: Routledge.

Bohm, David (1999) *The Limits of Thought*, London: Routledge.

Bohm, David and Mark Edwards (1991) *Exploring the Hidden Source of Social, Political and Environmental Crises Facing Our World*, San Francisco: Harper San Francisco.

Bok, Sissela (1998) *Mayhem: Violence as Public Entertainment*, Reading, MA: Perseus Books.

Bonner, John Tyler (1998) "Book Review," *Integrative Biology* 1(2): 73–5.

Bonner, Raymond (1994) "Rwanda Now Faces Painful Ordeal of Rebirth," *New York Times*, December 29: A1, A6.

Bonta, Bruce D. (1993) *Peaceful Peoples: An Annotated Bibliography*, Metuchen, NJ: The Scarecrow Press.

Boothby, Neil G. and Christine M. Knudsen, "Children of the Gun," *Scientific American*, June: 60–5.

Boulding, Elise (2000) *Cultures of Peace: The Hidden Side of History*, Syracuse, NY: Syracuse University Press.

Boulding, Kenneth E. (1989/1990) *Three Faces of Power*, Newbury Park, CA: Sage Publications.

Bourke, Joanne (1999) *An Intimate History of Killing: Face-to-Face Killing in Twentieth-Century Warfare*, London: Granta.

Bourriau, Janine (ed.) (1992) *Understanding Catastrophe*, Cambridge, UK: Cambridge University Press.

Boutros-Ghali, Boutros (1992) *An Agenda for Peace-Keeping*, Report to Summit Meeting of the Security Council, January 31, 1992, New York: United Nations, VI: 32–4.

Boutwell, Jeffrey and Michael T. Klare (2000) "A Scourge of Small Arms," *Scientific American*, June: 48–53.

Bowden, Brayton and Public Radio Partnership (1999) *Anger in the Workplace*, a series of five half-hour audiotapes, Louisville, KY: Public Radio Partnership, John Gregory (502) 814 6551, www.anger.net.

Bowlby, John (1951) *Maternal Care and Mental Health*, Geneva: World Health Organization.

Brain, Charles K. (1972) "An Attempt to Reconstruct the Behavior of Australopithecenes: The Evidence of Interpersonal Violence," *Zool. Afr.* 7: 379–401.

Brain, Charles K. (1981) *The Hunters or the Hunted: An Introduction to African Cave Taphonomy*, Chicago: University of Chicago Press.

Brandt, Ron (1987) "On Cooperation in Schools: A Conversation with David and Roger Johnson," *Educational Leadership*, November: 14–16.

Breggin, Peter R. (1991) *Toxic Psychiatry: Why Therapy, Empathy, and Love Must Replace the Drugs, Electroshock, and Biochemical Therapies of the "New Psychiatry"*, New York: St. Martin's Press.

Breggin, Peter R. (1998) *Talking Back to Ritalin: What Doctors Aren't Telling You About Stimulants for Children*, Monroe, ME: Common Courage Press.

Brett, Rachel and Margaret McCalin (1998) *Children: The Invisible Soldiers*, Sweden: Radda Barnen (Save the Children) Sweden.

Briskin, Alan (1999a) Tape #5 in Brayton Bowden and Public Radio Partnership.

Briskin, Alan (1999b) *The Stirring of Soul in the Workplace*, San Francisco: Jossey-Bass Inc.

Broennimann, Peter (1981) *Auca on the Cononaco*, Basle: Birkhäuser.

Bronfenbrenner, Urie (1970) *Two Worlds of Childhood*, New York: Simon & Schuster.

Bronfenbrenner, Urie, Peter McClelland, Elaine Wethington, Phyllis Moen, and Stephen J. Ceci (1996) *The State of Americans*, New York: The Free Press.

Brown, David (1999) "Army Takes New Track on Gulf War Syndrome," *Guardian Weekly*, January 3:13.

Brown, J. Larry and Ernesto Pollitt (1996) "Malnutrition, Poverty and Intellectual Development," *Scientific American*, February: 38–44.

Brown, Kathryn (2000) "Pacific Salmon Run Hot and Cold," *Science* 290: 685–6.

Brown, Tom (1999) *The Anatomy of Fire: Sparking a New Spirit of Enterprise*, Lavel, KY: Management General. Online. Available http: <http: //www.mgeneral.com. Queries (502) 566 6652. (Accessed December 17, 2001.)

Brownlee, Shannon (1999) "Behavior Can Be Baffling When Young Minds Are Taking Shape," *U.S. News and World Report*, August 9.

Bruner, Jerome (1990) *Acts of Meaning*, Cambridge, MA: Harvard University Press.

Burton, John W. (1979) *Deviance, Terrorism and War*, New York: St. Martin's Press.

Burton, John W. (1982) *Dear Survivors*, London: Frances Pinter.

Burton, John W. (1984) *Global Conflict*, College Park: University of Maryland.

Burton, John W. (1987) *Resolving Deep-Rooted Conflict: A Handbook*, Lanham, MD: University Press of America.

Burton, John W. (1990) *Conflict Resolution and Prevention*, New York: St. Martin's Press.

Burton, John W. (1997) *Violence Explained*, Manchester, UK: Manchester University Press.

Buss, David M. (1992) "Mate Preference Mechanisms: Consequences for Partner Choice and Intrasexual Competition," in J. Barkow *et al.* (eds.), 249–66.

Buss, David M. (1994) *The Evolution of Desire*, New York: Basic Books.

Byrne, Richard W. and Andrew Whiten (1997) "Machiavellian Intelligence," in R.W. Byrne and A. Whiten (eds.), *Machiavellian Intelligence II*, Cambridge, UK: Cambridge University Press.

Cagan, Elizabeth (1978) "Individualism, Collectivism, and Radical Educational Reform," *Harvard Educational Review* 48(2): 227–66.

Cairns-Smith, A.G. (1996) *Evolving the Mind: On the Nature of Matter and the Origin of Consciousness*, Cambridge, UK: Cambridge University Press.

*California Journal* (2000) "Gun Facts by the Numbers: The Guns in our Midst," 31: 16–17.

Cameron, Catherine (2000) *Resolving Childhood Trauma: A Long-term Study of Abuse Survivors*, Thousand Oaks, CA: Sage Publications.

Campbell, Duncan (2000a) "U.S. jails two millionth inmate," *Guardian Weekly*, February 23: 1.

Campbell, Duncan (2000b) "It's divine justice, Gore is told," *Guardian Weekly*, November 22: 1.

Campbell, Joseph (1968) *The Hero with a Thousand Faces*, Princeton, NJ: Princeton University Press.

Candland, Douglas K. (1993) *Feral Children and Clever Animals: Reflections on Human Nature*, New York: Oxford University Press.

Cann, Rebecca L. (2001) "Genetic Clues to Dispersal in Human Populations: Retracing the Past from the Present," *Science* 291: 17, 42–8.

Carroll, Lewis (1883/1960) *Through the Looking Glass* (annotated by Martin Gardner), New York: Bramhall House/Clarkson N. Potter.

Carroll, Sean B., Jennifer K. Greiner, and Scott D. Weatherbee (2001) *From DNA to Diversity: Molecular Genetics and the Evolution of Animal Design*, Malden, MA: Blackwell Science.

Caspary, William R. (2000) *Dewey on Democracy*, Ithaca, NY: Cornell University Press.

Cavalli-Sforza, Luigi Luca (1997) "Genetic Evidence Supporting Marija Gimbutas's Work on the Origins of Indo-European Peoples," in Joan Marler (ed.), 93–101.

Cavalli-Sforza, Luigi Luca (2000) *Genes, Peoples and Languages*, New York: North Point Press/Farrar, Straus & Giroux.

Cavalli-Sforza, Luigi Luca, M.W. Feldman, K.H. Chen, and S.M. Dornbusch (1982) "Theory and Observation in Cultural Transmission," *Science* 218: 19–27.

Caverie, Jean-Michel (2001) "What If There Are Only 30,000 Human Genes?," *Science* 291: 1255–7.

Center for Defense Information (1997) "The Invisible Soldiers: Child Combatants," *Defense Monitor* 26(4): entire issue.

Chagnon, Napoleon (1968) *Yanomamö: The Fierce People*, New York: Holt, Rinehart & Winston.

Chagnon, Napoleon (1987) "Male Yanomamö: Manipulations of Kinship Classifications of Female Kin for Reproductive Advantage," in L.L. Betzig, M. Borgerhoff Mulder, and P.W. Turke (eds.), *Human Reproductive Behavior: A Darwinian Perspective*, Cambridge, UK: Cambridge University Press.

Chagnon, Napoleon (1988) "Life Histories, Blood Revenge, and Warfare in a Tribal Population," *Science* 238: 985–92.

Chang, Iris (1997) *The Rape of Nanking*, New York: Basic Books.

Changnon, S.A. and D.R. Easterling (2000) "U.S. Policies Pertaining to Weather and Climate Extremes," *Science* 289: 2053, 2055.

Chatwin, Bruce (1987) *The Songlines*, New York: Viking.

Cheney, Dorothy L. and Robert M. Seyfarth (1990) *How Monkeys See the World: Inside the Mind of Another Species*, Chicago: University of Chicago Press.

Chomsky, Noam (1980) *Rules and Representations*, New York: Columbia University Press.

Chomsky, Noam (1989) *Necessary Illusions: Thought Control in Democratic Societies*, Boston: South End Press.

Chomsky, Noam and Edward S. Herman (1979) *The Washington Connection and Third World Fascism*, Boston: South End Press.

Clark, Mary E. (1979) *Contemporary Biology*, 2nd edn., Philadelphia: W.B. Saunders.

Clark, Mary E. (1989) *Ariadne's Thread: The Search for New Modes of Thinking*, New York: St. Martin's Press.

Clark, Mary E. (1995) "Changes in Euro-American Values Needed for Sustainability," *Journal of Social Issues* 51(4): 63–82.

Cleary, Thomas (trans.) (1984) *The Flower Ornament Scripture: A Translation of the Avatamsala Sūtra*, London, Boulder: Shambala.

Clements, Walter C., Jr. and J. David Singer (2000) "The Human Cost of War: A Historical Perspective," *Scientific American*, June: 56–7.

Clottes, Jean (1995) "Rhinos and Lions and Bears, Oh My!," *Natural History*, May: 30–5.

Clottes, Jean (1996) "Prehistoric Cave Art at Vallon," lecture sponsored by the Institute for Science, Engineering, and Public Policy, Eugene, OR, May 13.

Clottes, Jean and J. David Lewis-Williams (1996) *Les Chamanes de la préhistoire: transe et magie dans les grottes ornées*, Paris: Le Seuil.

Cobb, Clifford, Ted Halstead, and Jonathan Rowe (1995) "If the Economy Is Up, Why Is America Down?," *Atlantic Monthly*, October: 59–76.

Cohen, Mark Nathan (1977) *The Food Crisis in Prehistory: Overpopulation and the Origins of Agriculture*, New Haven, CT: Yale University Press.

Cohen, Stanley (2001) *States of Denial: Knowing about Atrocities and Suffering*, Cambridge, UK: Polity Press.

Colborn, Theo, Dianne Dumanoski, and John Peterson (1997) *Our Stolen Future*, New York: Plume/Penguin.

Cole, Jonathan (1998) *About Face*, Cambridge, MA: Massachusetts Institute of Technology Press.

Conroy, Glenn C. (1997) *Reconstructing Human Origins: A Modern Synthesis*, New York: W.W. Norton.

Copp, Dwayne R. and Alma M. Copp (1991) "India's Silent Revolution: The Swadhyaya Phenomenon," *New Realities*, March/April: 9–15.

Cordes, Helen (1998) "Generation Wired," *The Nation*, April 27: 11–16.

Costanza, Robert (1990) "Escaping the Oversimplification Trap," in Mary E. Clark and S.A. Wawrytko (eds.) *Rethinking the Curriculum: Towards an Integrated, Interdisciplinary College Education*, Westbury, CT: Greenwood Press, Chapter 8.

Courtillot, V. (1999) *Evolutionary Catastrophes*. Cambridge, UK: Cambridge University Press.

Cowell, Alan (1994) "Italy Moved by Boy's Killing and the Grace of His Parents," *New York Times*, October 4: A-1, A-6.

Cowley, Jason (2002) "Forgotten Victims," *Guardian Weekly*, April 10: 22.

Cronin, Helena (1991) *The Ant and the Peacock: Altruism and Sexual Selection from Darwin to Today*, Cambridge, UK: Cambridge University Press.

Crowley, Thomas J. (2000) "Causes of Climate Change Over the Past 1000 Years," *Science* 289: 270–7.

Dalai Lama, His Holiness and Howard C. Cutler, M.D. (1998) *The Art of Happiness – A Handbook for Living*, New York: Riverhead Books/Penguin Putnam.

Dalton, Eira (1963) *The Baker Family in India (Kottayam)*, Kottayam: CMS Press.

Daly, Herman E. and John B. Cobb, Jr. (1989) *For the Common Good: Redirecting the Economy Toward Community, the Environment, and a Sustainable Future*, Boston: Beacon Press.

Damasio, Antonio (1999) *The Feeling of What Happens: Body and Emotion in the Making of Consciousness*, New York: Harcourt Brace & Co.

d'Aquili, Eugene and Andrew Newberg (1999) *The Mystical Mind: Probing the Biology of Religious Experience*, Chicago: Fortress Press.

461

Darwin, Charles (1860/1962) *The Voyage of the Beagle* (Leonard Engel, ed.), Garden City, NY: Doubleday.

Darwin, Charles (1871) *The Descent of Man and Selection in Relation to Sex*, 2 vols., London: John Murray; 2nd edn., 1974.

Davidson, Eric H. (2001) *Genomic Regulatory Systems: Development and Evolution*, San Diego: Academic Press.

Davis, J.O., J.A. Phelps, and H.S. Bracha (1995) "Prenatal Development of Monozygotic Twins and Concordance for Schizophrenia," *Schizophrenia Bulletin* 21: 357–66.

Dawkins, Richard (1976) *The Selfish Gene*, New York and Oxford: Oxford University Press.

Dawkins, Richard (1998) *Unweaving the Rainbow: Science, Delusion, and the Appetite for Wonder*, Boston: Houghton Mifflin.

de Blij, Harm J. (1993) *Human Geography: Culture, Society, and Space*, 4th edn., New York: John Wiley & Sons.

de Blij, Harm J. (2000) "Changing Climate, Growing Population, Merging Cultures in a Shrinking World," Chautauqua Lecture, Tape 20–31, Chautauqua, NY: Chautauqua Institution.

de Castro, J.M. Bermúdex, J.L. Arsuaga, E. Carbonell, A. Rosas, I. Martínez, and M. Mosquera (1997) "A Hominid from the Lower Pleistocene of Atapuerca, Spain: Possible Ancestor to Neandertals and Modern Humans," *Science* 276: 1392–5.

de Kloet, E. Ronald (1992) "Corticosteroids, Stress, and Aging," in Claudio Francheschi, Gaetano Crepaldi, and Vincent J. Cristofalo (eds.), *Aging and Cellular Defense Mechanisms, Annals of the New York Academy of Sciences*, New York: New York Academy of Sciences, vol. 663, 357–71.

de Waal, F.B.M. (1982) *Chimpanzee Politics*, London: Jonathan Cape.

de Waal, F.B.M. (1989) *Peacemaking among Primates*, Cambridge, MA: Harvard University Press.

de Waal, F.B.M. (1992) "Aggression as a Well-integrated Part of Primate Social Relationships: A Critique of the Seville Statement on Violence," in James Silverberg and J. Patrick Gray (eds.), *Aggression and Peacefulness in Humans and Other Primates*, New York: Oxford University Press, 37–56.

de Waal, F.B.M. (1995) "Bonobo Sex and Society," *Scientific American*, March: 82–8.

de Waal, F.B.M. (1996) *Good Natured: The Origins of Right and Wrong in Humans and Other Animals*, Cambridge, MA: Harvard University Press.

de Waal, F.B.M. (2001a) *The Ape and the Sushi Master: Cultural Reflections by a Primatologist*, New York: Basic Books.

de Waal, F.B.M. (ed.) (2001b) *Tree of Origin: What Primate Behavior Can Tell Us About Human Social Evolution*, Cambridge, MA: Harvard University Press.

de Waal, F.B.M. and Frans Lanting (1997) *Bonobo: The Forgotten Ape*, Berkeley, CA: University of California Press.

de Waal, F.B.M., Filippo Aureli, and Peter G. Judge (2000) "Coping with Crowding," *Scientific American*, May: 76–81.

Deffeyes, Kenneth S. (2002) *Hubbert's Peak: The Impending World Oil Shortage*, Princeton, NJ: Princeton University Press.

Defleur, Alban, Tim White, Patricia Valensi, Ludovic Slimak, and Evelyne Crégut-Bonnoure (1999) "Neanderthal Cannibalism at Moula-Guercy, Ardèche, France," *Science* 286: 128–31.

DeGusta, David (1999) "Fijian Cannabalism: Evidence from Navatu," *American Journal of Physical Anthropology* 110: 215–41.

DeMenocal, Peter B. (1995) "Plio-Pleistocene African Climate," *Science* 270: 53–9.

Dennett, Daniel (1991) *Consciousness Explained*, Boston: Little, Brown.

Dennett, Daniel (1995) *Darwin's Dangerous Idea: Evolution and the Meanings of Life*, New York: Simon & Schuster.

Dentan, Robert Knox (1968) "Semai Response to Mental Aberration," *Bij dragen tot de Taal-, Land-en Volkenkunde*, 124: 135–58.

Deutsch, Karl (1966) *Nationalism and Social Communication*, Cambridge, MA: Massachusetts Institute of Technology Press.

Dewey, John (1896) "The Reflex Arc Concept in Psychology," *Psychological Review* 3: 357–70.

Dewey, John (1916/1966) *Democracy and Education*, New York: Free Press.

Dewey, John (1927) *The Public and Its Problems*, New York: Holt & Co.

deWitte, Ludo (2000) *L'Assassinat de Lumumba*, Paris: Karthala.

Diamond, Jared (1992) *The Third Chimpanzee*, New York: HarperCollins.

Diamond, Jared (1995) "Easter's End," *Discover*, August: 62–9.

Diamond, Jared (1997) *Guns, Germs and Steel: A Short History of Everybody for the Last 13,000 Years*, London: Jonathan Cape.

Diamond, Louise and John McDonald (1996) *Multi-track Diplomacy: A Systems Approach to Peace*, West Hartford, CT: Kumarian Press.

Diamond, Marian C. (1988) *Enriching Heredity: The Impact of the Environment on the Anatomy of the Brain*, New York: Free Press/Macmillan.

Diamond, Marian C., D. Krech, and M.R. Rosensweig (1964) "The Effects of an Enriched Environment on the Histology of the Rat Cerebral Cortex," *Journal of Comparative Neurology* 123: 111–20.

Diamond, Stanley (1971) "The Rule of Law and the Order of Custom," in Robert Paul Wolff (ed.), *The Rule of Law*, New York: Simon & Schuster.

Diduk, Susan (1989) "Women's Agricultural Production and Political Action in the Cameroon Grassfields," *Africa* 59(3): 338–55.

Dissanayake, Ellen (1988) *What Is Art For?*, Seattle: University of Washington Press.

Dissanayake, Ellen (1992) *Homo Aestheticus: Where Art Comes from and Why*, New York: Macmillan/The Free Press.

Docherty, Jayne Seminare (2001) *Learning Lessons from Waco: When Parties Bring Their Gods to the Negotiation Table*, Syracuse, NY: Syracuse University Press.

Domhoff, G. William (2000) "The Misinterpretation of Dreams," *American Scientist* 88(March/April): 175–8.

Donald, Merlin (1991) *Origins of the Human Mind: Three Stages in the Evolution of Culture and Cognition*, Cambridge, MA: Harvard University Press.

Donaldson, Margaret (1978) *Children's Minds*, New York: W.W. Norton.

Dorit, Robert L., Hiroshi Adakshi, and Walter Gilbert (1995) "Absence of Polymorphism at the ZFY Locus on the Human Y Chromosome," *Science* 268: 1183–5.

Dower, John W. (1986) *War Without Mercy: Race and Power in the Pacific War*, New York: Pantheon.

Dower, John W. (1999) *Embracing Defeat: Japan in the Wake of World War II*, New York: W.W. Norton/New Press.

Doyle, Rodger (2000) "The Roots of Homicide," *Scientific American*, October.

Duarte, Cidália, João Mauricio, Paul B. Pettitt, Pedro Soalo, Erik Trinkaus, Hans ven der Plicht, and João Zilhão (1999) "The Early Upper Paleolithic Human Skeleton from the Abrigo do Lagar Velho (Portugal) and Modern Human Emergence in Iberia," *Proceedings of the National Academy of Sciences* 96: 7604–9.

Duerr, Hans Peter (1985) *Dreamtime: Concerning the Boundary between Wilderness and Civilization* (Felicitas Goodman, trans.), Oxford/New York: Basil Blackwell.

Dunbar, Robin (1996) *Grooming, Gossip, and the Evolution of Language*, Cambridge, MA: Harvard University Press.

Eacott, Madeline J. (1999) "Memory for the Events of Early Childhood," *Current Directions in Psychological Science* 8(2): 46–9.

Easterling, D.R., G.A. Meehl, C. Parmesan, S.A. Changnon, T.R. Karl, and L.O. Mearns (2000) "Climate Extremes: Observations, Modeling and Impacts," *Science* 289: 2068–74.

Edelman, Gerald M. (1992) *Bright Air, Brilliant Fire*, London: Allen Lane, The Penguin Press.

Edgerton, Robert B. (1992) *Sick Societies: Challenging the Myth of Primitive Harmony*, New York: Free Press.

Ehrenreich, Barbara (1989) *Fear of Falling: The Inner Life of the Middle Class*, New York: Pantheon.

Ehrenreich, Barbara (1997) *Blood Rites: Origins and History of the Passions of War*, New York: Henry Holt.

Eibl-Eibesfeldt, Irenäus (1942) *Love and Hate*, New York: Rinehart & Winston.

Eibl-Eibesfeldt, Irenäus (1989) *Human Ethology*, New York: Aldine de Gruyter.

Eisenhower, Dwight D. (1959) *Public Papers of the Presidents: 1959*, Washington D.C.: Government Printing Office.

Eisler, Riane (1996) *Sacred Pleasure: Sex, Myth, and the Politics of the Body*, San Francisco: Harper San Francisco.

Eldredge, Niles (1999) *The Pattern of Evolution*, New York: W.H. Freeman.

Eldredge, Niles and Stephen J. Gould (1972) "Punctuated Equilibria: An Alternative to Physletic Gradualism," in T.J.M. Schopf (ed.), *Models in Paleobiology*, San Francisco: Freeman, Cooper: 82–115.

Eliade, Mircea (1978) *A History of Religious Ideas. I. From the Stone Age to the Eleusian Mysteries*, Chicago: University of Chicago Press.

Ellers, Jack David (1999) *From Culture to Ethnicity to Conflict: An Anthropological Perspective on International Ethnic Conflict*, Ann Arbor: University of Michigan Press.

Elliott, Larry (2001) "World Bank's dream may come true,"*Guardian Weekly*, May 9: 14.

Ellison, Michael (2001) "US workers suffer labour pains as they put in record hours at work," *Guardian Weekly*, September 13: 3.

Engels, Friedrich (1902) *Origin of the Family, Private Property and the State*, Chicago: C.H. Kerr & Co.

Epstein, Paul R. (1999) "Climate and Health," *Science* 285: 347–8.

Epstein, Paul R. (2000) "Is Global Warming Harmful to Health?," *Scientific American*, August: 50–7.

Evans, Sir Arthur J. (1936) *The Palace of Minos at Knossos*, London: Macmillan.

Fallon, Sally (1999) "Nasty, Brutish and Short?" *The Ecologist* 29(1) January/February: 20–7.

Fauconnet, Max (chapter ed.) (1968) "Mythology of the Two Americas," in *New Larousse Encyclopedia of Mythology*, London: Prometheus/Hamlyn, 423–48; cited material pp. 442.

Feldman, Richard and Michael Betzold (1988) *End of the Line: Autoworkers and the American Dream*, New York: Weidenfeld & Nicolson.

Ferguson, R. Brian (1992) "A Savage Encounter: Western Contact and the Yanomami War Complex," in Ferguson, R. Brian and Neil L. Whitehead (eds.), 199–227.

Ferguson, R. Brian (1995) *Yanomami Warfare*, Santa Fe, NM: School of American Research Press.

Ferguson, R. Brian and Neil L. Whitehead (1992) "The Violent Edge of Empire," in R. Brian Ferguson and Neil L. Whitehead (eds.), *War in the Tribal Zone*, Santa Fe, NM: School of American Research Press, Chapter 1, 1–30.

Ferris, Craig F. (1996) "The Rage of Innocents," *The Sciences*, March/April: 22–6.

Festinger, Leon (1957) *A Theory of Cognitive Dissonance*, Stanford, CA: Stanford University Press.

Feyerabend, Paul (1993) *Against Method*, 3rd edn., London: Verso.

Finlay, Barbara L. and Richard B. Darlington (1995) "Linked Regularities in the Development and Evolution of Mammalian Brains," *Science* 268: 1578–84.

Finney, Bruce P., Irene Gregory-Eaves, Jon Sweetman, Marianne S.V. Douglas, and John P. Smol (2000) "Impacts of Climatic Change and Fishing on Pacific Salmon Abundance over the Past 300 Years," *Science* 290: 795–9.

Fischman, Joshua (1994) "Putting a New Spin on the Birth of Human Birth," *Science* 264: 1082–3.

Fischman, Joshua (1995) "Painted Puzzles Line the Walls of an Ancient Cave," *Science* 267: 614.

Fisher, Ronald J. (1997) *Interactive Conflict Resolution*, Syracuse: Syracuse University Press.

Fisher, Ronald J. (1999) "Social–Psychological Processes in Interactive Conflict Analysis and Reconciliation," in Ho-Won Jeong (ed.), *Conflict Resolution: Dynamics, Process and Structure*, Aldershot, UK: Ashgate Press, Chapter 4.

Fix, Alan (1999) *Migration and Colonization in Human Microevolution*, New York: Cambridge University Press.

Flannery, Tim (2001) *The Eternal Frontier: An Ecological History of North America and Its Peoples*, New York: Atlantic Monthly Press.

Fogel, Alan (1993) *Developing through Relationships: Origins of Communication, Self, and Culture*, Chicago: University of Chicago Press.

Fogelman, Eva (1994) *Conscience and Courage: Rescuers of Jews During the Holocaust*, New York: Anchor Doubleday.

Fossey, Dian (1983) *Gorillas in the Mist*, Boston: Houghton Mifflin.

Fox, Robin (ed.) (1975) *Biosocial Anthropology*, New York: John Wiley & Sons.

Francis, Darlene, Josie Diorio, Dong Liu, and Michael J. Meaney (1999) "Nongenomic Transmission across Generations of Maternal Behavior and Stress Responses in the Rat," *Science* 286: 1155–8.

Frank, Thomas (2000) *One Market Under God: Extreme Capitalism, Market Populism and the End of Economic 'Democracy'*, London: Secker & Warburg.

Franke, Richard W. and Barbara H. Chasin (1994) *Radical Reform as Development in an Indian State*, Oakland, CA: Food First.

Frankl, Viktor E. (1969) "Reductionism and Nihilism," in Arthur Koestler and J.R. Smythies (eds.).

Franks, Lucinda (2000) "The Sex Lives of Your Children," *Talk*, February: 102, 107, 157.

Frazer, Sir James George (1922/1929) *The Golden Bough: A Study in Magic and Religion*, New York: The Book League of America.

Freemantle, A. (ed.) (1964) *The Protestant Mystics*, New York: New American Library/Mentor.

Freire, Paolo (1970) *Pedagogy of the Oppressed*, New York: Continuum; 2nd edn., 1992.

Frith, Uta (1992) *Autism and Asperger Syndrome*, Cambridge, UK: Cambridge University Press.

Frith, Uta (1993) "Autism," *Scientific American*, June: 108–14.

Froman, Creel (1984) *The Two American Political Systems*, Englewood Cliffs, NJ: Prentice Hall.

Fukuyama, Francis (1998) "Women and the Evolution of World Politics," *Foreign Affairs*, October: 24–40.

Fukuyama, Francis (1999) "The Great Disruption: Human Nature and the Reconstitution of Social Order," *The Atlantic Monthly*, May: 55–80.

Gabunia, Leo and 13 others (2000) "Earliest Pleistocene Hominid Cranial Remains from Dmanisi, Republic of Georgia: Taxonomy, Geological Setting, and Age," *Science* 288: 1019–24.

Gajdusek, D.C. (1977) "Unconventional Viruses and the Origin and Disappearance of Kuru," *Science* 197: 943–60.

Galbraith, John Kenneth (1978) *The New Industrial State*, 3rd edn., revised, Boston: Houghton Mifflin.

Gandhi, Mohandas K. (1957) *An Autobiography: The Story of My Experiments With Truth*, Boston: Beacon Press, 276.

Gangadharan, A. (1974) *Law of Land Reforms in Kerala*, 2nd edn., Kaloo-Cochin-17: The K.V. Krishnan Memorial Press.

Gans, Curtis (2000) Interviewed on *Weekend Edition*, Washington D.C.: National Public Radio, November 12.

Garbarino, James (1996) *Raising Children in a Socially Toxic Environment*, San Francisco: Jossey-Bass Inc.

Gardner, Gary and Brian Halweil (2000) *Underfed and Overfed: The Global Epidemic of Malnutrition*, Washington D.C.: Worldwatch Institute, Paper 150.

Gardner, Howard, Mindy L. Kornhaber, and Warren K. Wake (1996) *Intelligence: Multiple Perspectives*, Fort Worth, TX: Harcourt Brace.

Gates, Jeff (1998) *The Ownership Solution: Toward a Shared Capitalism for the Twenty-First Century*, Reading, MA: Perseus Books.

Gatto, John Taylor (1996) "The Public School Nightmare: Why Fix a System Designed to Destroy Individual Thought?," in Matt Hearn (ed.), 39–47.

Gauchet, Marcel (1997) *The Disenchantment of the World*, Princeton, NJ: Princeton University Press.

Gazzaniga, Michael (1998a) *The Mind's Past*, Berkeley: University of California Press.

Gazzaniga, Michael (1998b) "The Split Brain Revisited," *Scientific American*, July: 51–5.

Gee, James Paul (1992) *The Social Mind: Language, Ideology, and Social Practice*, New York: Bergin Garvey.

Geertz, Clifford (1995) *After the Fact: Two Countries, Four Decades, One Anthropologist*, Cambridge, MA: Harvard University Press.

Geertz, Clifford (2000) *Available Light: Anthropological Reflections on Philosophical Topics*, Princeton, NJ: Princeton University Press.

Gehring, Walter J. (1999) *Master Control Genes in Development and Evolution: The Homeobox Story*, New Haven, CT: Yale University Press.

Gelbspan, Ross (1998) *The Heat Is On: The Climate Crisis, the Cover-Up, the Prescription*, updated edn., Reading, MA: Perseus Books.

Gell-Mann, Murray (1994) *The Quark and the Jaguar: Adventures in the Simple and the Complex*, New York: W.R. Freeman.

Gerhart, J. and M. Kirschner (1997) *Cells, Embryos and Evolution: Toward a Cellular and Developmental Understanding of Phenotypic Variation and Evolutionary Adaptability*, Oxford: Blackwell Science.

Gibbons, Ann (1997a) "A New Face for Human Ancestors," *Science* 276: 1331–3.

Gibbons, Ann (1997b) "Y Chromosome Shows that Adam Was an African," *Science* 278: 804–5.

Gibbons, Ann (2000a) "Chinese Stone Tools Reveal High-Tech *Homo erectus*," *Science* 287: 1566.

Gibbons, Ann (2000b) "Human Frontal Lobes Sized Right," *Science* 288: 799–800.

Gibbons, Ann (2000c) "Europeans Trace Ancestry to Paleolithic People," *Science* 290: 1080–1.

Gibbons, Ann (2002) "Human Head Start: New Views of Brain Evolution," *Science* 296: 835–7.

Gibson, J.J. (1979) *The Ecological Approach to Visual Perception*, Boston: Houghton Mifflin.

Gill, Peter (2000) "Leprosy: a fight for bodies and minds," *Guardian Weekly*, March 15: 28.

Gilligan, James (1996) *Violence: Our Deadly Epidemic and Its Causes*, New York: Grosset/Putnam.

Gimbutas, Marija (1980) *The Early Civilizations of Europe*, Monograph for Indo-European Studies 131, Los Angeles: University of California Press.

Gimbutas, Marija (1982) *The Goddesses and Gods of Old Europe: Myth and Cult Images, 6500–3500 B.C.*, Berkeley: University of California Press.

Gimbutas, Marija (1989) *The Language of the Goddess*, San Francisco: Harper & Row.

Gimbutas, Marija (1991) *The Civilization of the Goddess: The World of Old Europe*, San Francisco: Harper San Francisco.

Goldsmith, Zac (2000) "The Great Divide," *The Ecologist*, May: 18–19.

Goleman, Daniel (1995) *Emotional Intelligence*, New York: Bantam Books.

Goodall, Jane (1986) *The Chimpanzees of Gombe: Patterns of Behavior*. Cambridge, MA: Belknap/Harvard University Press.

Goodman, Paul (1960) *Growing Up Absurd*, New York: Vintage Books.

Goodman, Paul (1962) *Compulsory Mis-education* and *The Community of Scholars* (published as one volume), New York: Vintage/Random House.

Goozner, Merrill (2000) "Blinded by the Boom: What's Missing in the Coverage of the New Economy," *Columbia Journalism Review*, November/December: 23–4.

Gopnik, Alison, Andrew N. Meltzoff, and Patricia K. Kuhl (1999) *The Scientist in the Crib: Minds, Brains, and How Children Learn*, New York: William Morrow.

Gorbman, Aubrey, Walton Dickhoff, Steven Vigna, Nancy Clark, and Charles Ralph (1983) *Comparative Endocrinology*, New York: Wiley-Interscience.

Gough, David (2000) "Ethnic rivalry sparks Congo killing spree," *Guardian Weekly*, February 23: 7.

Gould, Elizabeth, Allison J. Reeves, Michael S.A. Graziano, and Charles G. Gross (1999) "Neurogenesis in the Neocortex of Adult Primates," *Science* 286: 548–52.

Gould, Stephen J. (1977) *Ontogeny and Phylogeny*, Cambridge, MA: Belknap/Harvard University Press.

Gould, Stephen J. (1989) *Wonderful Life*, New York: W.W. Norton.

Gould, Stephen J. (1998) *Leonardo's Mountain of Clams and the Diet of Worms*, New York: Harmony Books.

Gould, Stephen J. (2000) "Deconstructing the 'Science Wars' by Reconstructing an Old Mold," *Science* 287: 256–61.

Gould, Stephen J. and Elizabeth S. Vrba (1982) "Exaptation – A Missing Term in the Science of Form," *Paleobiology* 8: 4–15.

Gould, Stephen J. and Richard C. Lewontin (1979) "The Spandrels of San Marco and the Panglossian Paradigm: A Critique of the Adaptationist Programme," *Proceedings of the Royal Society*, Series B, 205: 581–98.

Grant, Bridget F. (2000) "Estimates of US Children Exposed to Alcohol Abuse and Dependence," *American Journal of Public Health*, 90: 112–15.

Graves, Robert (1948) *The White Goddess: A Historical Grammar of Poetic Myth*, London: Faber & Faber.

Graves, Robert (1954) *I, Claudius* and *Claudius the God*, Harmondsworth, UK: Penguin.

Graves, Robert (1975) *Count Belisarius*, Harmondsworth, UK: Penguin.

Gray, John (1998) *False Dawn: The Delusions of Global Capitalism*, New York: The New Press.

Gray, John (2000) *Two Faces of Liberalism*, New York: The New Press.

Gray, Patricia M., Bernie Krause, Jelle Atema, Roger Payne, Carol Krumhansi, and Luis Baptista (2001) "The Music of Nature and the Nature of Music," *Science* 291: 52–4.

Griffin, Donald R. (1992) *Animal Minds*, Chicago: University of Chicago Press.

Gross, Paul R., Norman Levitt, and Martin W. Lewis (eds.) (1996) *The Flight from Science and Reason*, Annals of the New York Academy of Sciences, vol. 775.

Grossman, Lt. Col. Dave (1995/1996) *On Killing: The Psychological Cost of Learning to Kill in War and Society*, Boston: Little, Brown.

Grotberg, Edith (1998) *The International Resilience Project*. www.resilnet.uiuc.edu/library.html (04/22/02).

Guibert, Nathalie and Marie-Pierre Subtil (2000) "Why Schools Fall Prey to Violence," first published in *Le Monde*, January 27, reprinted in *Guardian Weekly*, February 9: 33.

Hacking, Ian (1999) *The Social Construction of What?*, Cambridge, MA: Harvard University Press.

Hadingham. E. (1979) *Secrets of the Ice Age: The World of Cave Artists*, New York: Walker.

Hagemann, Michael (1999) "More Questions About the Provider's Role," *Science* 238: 777.

Hailman, Jack P. (1982) "Evolution and Behavior: An Iconoclastic View," in Henry C. Plotkin (ed.), 205–54.

Hamilton, W.D. (1963) "The Evolution of Altruistic Behavior," *American Naturalist* 97: 354–6.

Hamilton, W.D. (1975) "Innate Social Aptitudes of Man: An Approach from Evolutionary Genetics," in Robin Fox (ed.), *Biosocial Anthropology*, New York: John Wiley & Sons, 133–55.

Haraway, Donna (1988) "Primatology Is Politics by Other Means," in Ruth Bleier (ed.).

Harlow, H.F. (1959) "Love in Infant Monkeys," *Scientific American*, July.

Harlow, H.F. and M.K. Harlow (1962) "Social Deprivation in Monkeys," *Scientific American*, November.

Harré, Rom (1981) "Psychological Variety," in P. Heelas and A. Lock (eds.), *Indigenous Psychologies: The Anthropology of the Self*, New York: Academic Press, 79–103.

Harré, Rom (2000) "Acts of Living," *Science* 289: 1303.

Harris, Marvin (1974) *Cows, Pigs, Wars and Witches*, New York: Random House

Harris, Marvin (1978) *Cannibals and Kings*, New York: Vintage.

Harris, Marvin (1979) "The Yanomamo and the Cause of War in Band and Village Societies," in M. Margolis and W. Carter (eds.), *Brazil: Anthropological Perspectives. Essays in Honor of Charles Wagley*, New York: Columbia University Press, 121–32.

Harris, Marvin (1984) "A Cultural Materialist Theory of Band and Village Warfare: The Yanomamo Test," in R. Brian Ferguson (ed.), *Warfare, Culture, and Environment*, Orlando: Academic Press: 111–40.

Hartman, John (2000) "Polish–Jewish Ethnic Conflict: Threats to Identity and the Failure to Mourn," *Mind and Human Interaction*, 11(1): 27–41.

Hausheer, Roger (1980) "Introduction" to Isaiah Berlin, *Against the Current: Essays in the History of Ideas*, New York: Viking.

Hawken, Paul (2000) "N30: WTO Showdown," *YES! a journal of positive futures*, Spring: 45–53.

Hayek, F.A. von (1955) *The Counter Revolution of Science: Studies on the Abuse of Reason*, London: Free Press of Glencoe.

Haynes, H., B.L. White, and R. Held (1965) "Visual Accommodation in Human Infants," *Science* 148: 528–30.

Hearn, Matt (ed.) (1996) *Deschooling Our Lives*, Gabriola Island, BC: New Society Publishers.

Heft, Harry (1996) "The Ecological Approach to Navigation: A Gibsonian Perspective," in J. Portugali (ed.), *The Construction of Cognitive Maps*, Dordrecht, The Netherlands: Kluwer Academic Publishers, 105–32.

Heft, Harry (2001) *Ecological Psychology in Context: James Gibson, Roger Barker, and the Legacy of William James's Radical Empiricism*, Mahwah, NJ: Lawrence Erlbaum.

Heider, K.G. (1976) "Dani Sexuality: A Low Energy System," *Man* 11: 188–201.

Hellie, Richard (1982) *Slavery in Russia, 1450–1725*, Chicago: University of Chicago Press.

Hellie, Richard (1989) "Patterns of Instability in Russian and Soviet History," *The Chicago Review of International Affairs* 1(3) (August): 3–34.

Hellie, Richard (1996) "Interpreting Violence in Late Muscovy from the Perspectives of Modern Neuroscience," a paper presented at the 28th National Convention of the AAAS in Boston, November 15, Session 7–24.

Helmuth, Laura (2001) "From the Mouths (and Hands) of Babes," *Science* 293: 1758–9.

Henderson, Michael (1996) *The Forgiveness Factor: Stories of Hope in a World of Conflict*, Salem, OR: Grosvenor Books.

Henry J. Kaiser Foundation (1999) "Kids and Media at the New Millennium," in John Leland, "America's families man the trenches of a media war," *Register Guard*, Eugene, OR, 25 September 2000 (from the *New York Times*).

Henshilwood, Christopher S. and 10 others (2002) "Emergence of Modern Human Behaviour: Middle Stone Age Engravings from South Africa," *Science* 295: 1278.

Hern, Matt (ed.) (1996) *Deschooling Our Lives*, Gabriola Is., BC: New Society Publishers.

Hertz, Noreena (2001a) "We Must Stay Silent No Longer," *Guardian Weekly*, May 16: 23, 24.

Hertz, Noreena (2001b) *The Silent Takeover: Global Capitalism and The Death of Democracy*, London: Heinemann.

Hertzman, Clyde (2001) "Health and Human Society," *American Scientist*, November/December: 538–45.

Hey, Jody (2001) *Genes, Categories, and Species: The Evolutionary and Cognitive Causes of the Species Problem*, New York: Oxford University Press.

Hill, Dave (2000) "Let's go back to Stone Age sex?," *Guardian Weekly*, April 12: 22–3.

Hinde, Robert (1974) *Biological Bases of Human Social Behaviour*, New York: McGraw Hill.

Hinde, Robert (1990) "Human Aggression: Biological Propensities and Social Forces," in Paul Smoker, Ruther Davies, and Barbara Munske (eds.), *A Reader in Peace Studies*, Oxford, UK: Pergamon Press, 172–81.

Ho, Mae-Wan (1998) *The Rainbow and the Worm: The Physics of Organisms*, 2nd edn., Singapore: World Scientific Publishing Co.

Ho, Mae-Wan (2000) "The Entangled Universe," *YES! a journal of positive futures*, Spring: 20–3.

Hodgson, David (1991) *The Mind Matters: Consciousness and Choice in a Quantum World*, Oxford: Clarendon Press.

Hoffman, Susanna M. and Anthony Oliver-Smith (eds.) (2002) *Catastrophe and Culture: The Anthropology of Disaster*, Santa Fe, NM: School of American Research Press, and Oxford: James Currey.

Holdaway, R.N. and C. Jacomb (2000) "Rapid Extinction of the Moas (Aves: Dinornithiformes): Model, Test, and Implications," *Science* 287: 2250–4.

Holden, Constance (2000) "Random Samples: Dioxin Routes Mapped," *Science* 290: 201.

Holden, Constance (2001) "Oldest Human DNA Reveals Aussie Oddity," *Science* 291: 230–1.

Holden, Constance (2002) "Drugs and Placebos Look Alike in the Brain," *Science* 295: 947, 949.

Holler, Linda (2002) *Erotic Morality: The Role of Touch in Moral Agency*, New Brunswick, NJ: Rutgers University Press.

Hopfield, J.J. (1994) "An Envisioning of Consciousness," *Science* 263: 696.

Horai, H., K. Hayasabe, R. Kondo, K. Tsugane, and N. Takakata (1996) "Recent African Origin of Modern Humans Revealed by Complete Sequences of Hominoid Mitochondrial DNAs," *Proceedings of the National Academy of Sciences*, 92: 523–6.

Hou Yamei, Richard Potts, Yuan Baoyin, Guo Zhengtang, Alan Deino, Wang Wei, Jennifer Clark, Xie Guangmao, and Huang Weiwen (2000) "Mid-Pleistocene Acheulean-like Stone Technology of the Bose Basin, South China," *Science* 287: 1622–6.

Howell, Signe and Roy Willis (eds.) (1989) *Societies at Peace*, London: Routledge.

Hrdy, Sarah Blaffer (1999) *Mother Nature: A History of Mothers, Infants, and Natural Selection*, New York: Pantheon.

Hubbert, M. King (1969) Chapter 8 in "Energy Resources," National Research Council (U.S.) Committee on Resources and Man, *Resources and Man*, San Francisco: W.H. Freeman, 157–242.

Hubbert, M. King (1971) *Energy Resources of the Earth*, San Francisco: W.H. Freeman.

Hubbert, M. King (1973) *A National Fuels and Energy Policy Study*, Serial 93–40 (92–75) Part I, Washington D.C.: U.S. Government Printing Office.

Hunt, Morton (1982) *The Universe Within*, New York: Simon & Schuster.

Hutchins, Edwin (1996) *Cognition in the Wild*, Cambridge, MA: Massachusetts Institute of Technology Press.

Hyams, Edward (1952) *Soil and Civilization*, New York: Harper & Row; 2nd edn., 1976.

Irwin, John (n.d.) *The Liberation of Men*, Seattle, WA: Rational Island Publishers.

Jackins, Harvey (n.d.) *How 'Re-evaluation Counseling' Began*: PO Box 2081, Seattle WA, 98111: Rational Island Publishers.

Jackins, Harvey (1981) *The Benign Reality*, PO Box 2081, Seattle, WA 98111: Rational Island Publishers.

Jackins, Harvey and others (1999) *The Human Male: A Men's Liberation Draft Policy*, PO Box 2081, Seattle, WA 98111: Rational Island Publishers.

Jackson, Wes (2000) "What Can a Suburbanite Do?," *Timeline*, March/April: 15–18.

Jacobs, Jane (1961) *The Death and Life of Great American Cities*, New York: Vintage.

James, William (1890) *The Principles of Psychology*, New York: Holt; reprinted, Cambridge, MA: Harvard University Press, 1983.

Jay, Phyllis C. (1965) "The Common Langur of North India," in Irven DeVore (ed.), *Primate Behavior: Field Studies of Monkeys and Apes*, New York: Holt, Rinehart & Winston.

Jayapal, Pramila (2001) "India's Silent but Singing Revolution," *YES! a journal of positive futures*, Winter: 33–7.

Jaynes, Julian (1976) *The Origin of Consciousness in the Breakdown of the Bicameral Mind*, Boston: Houghton Mifflin.

Johansen, Bruce E. (1982) *Forgotten Founders: How the American Indians Helped Shape Democracy*, Boston: Beacon Press.

Johnson, Alison (1994) *A House by the Shore: Twelve Years in the Hebrides*, London: Warner (Little, Brown).

Johnson, David W. and Roger T. Johnson (1974) "Instructional Goal Structure: Cooperative, Competitive, or Individualistic," *Review of Educational Research* 16(2): 105–23.

Johnson, David W. and Roger T. Johnson (1989) *Cooperation and Competition: Theory and Research*, Edina, MN: Interaction Book Company.

Johnson, David W. and Roger T. Johnson (1994) *Leading the Cooperative School*, 2nd edn., Edina, MN: Interaction Book Company.

Johnson, David W. and Roger T. Johnson (2000) "Teaching Students to Be Peacemakers: Results of Twelve Years of Research," paper presented at the conference of the Society for the Psychological Study of Social Issues, Minneapolis, June.

Johnson, Jeffrey G., Patricia Cohen, Elizabeth M. Smailes, Stephanie Kasen, and Judith S. Brook (2002) "Television Viewing and Aggressive Behavior During Adolescence and Adulthood," *Science* 295: 2468–71.

Jolly, Alison (1985) "The Evolution of Primate Behavior," *American Scientist* 73: 230–9.

Jones, K.L., K.W. Smith, C.N. Ulleland, and A.P. Streissguth (1973) "Pattern of Malformation in Offspring of Chronic Alcoholic Mothers," *Lancet* 1: 1267–71.

Kagan, Jerome (1998) *Three Seductive Ideas*, Cambridge, MA: Harvard University Press.

Kaiser, Jocelyn (2000) "Evidence Mounts That Tiny Particles Can Kill," *Science* 289: 22–3.

Kameguchi, Kenji and Stephen Murphy-Shigematsu (2001) "Family Psychology and Family Therapy in Japan," *American Psychologist* 56: 65–70.

Keeley, Lawrence H. (1996) *War Before Civilization: The Myth of the Peaceful Savage*, New York: Oxford University Press.

Keller, Evelyn Fox (1983) *A Feeling for the Organism: The Life and Work of Barbara McClintock*, New York: Freeman.

Keller, Evelyn Fox (1985) *Reflections on Gender and Science*, New Haven: Yale University Press.

Kellert, Stephen H. (1993) *In the Wake of Chaos: Unpredictable Order in Dynamical Systems*, Chicago: University of Chicago Press.

Kemmis, Daniel (1990) *Community and the Politics of Place*, Norman: University of Oklahoma Press.

Kemmis, Daniel (1995) *The Good City and the Good Life*, Boston: Houghton Mifflin.

Kempermann, Gerd and Fred H. Gage (1999) "New Nerve Cells for the Adult Brain," *Scientific American*, May: 48–53.

Kennedy, Paul (1989) *The Rise and Fall of the Great Powers*, New York: Vintage Books/Random House.

Kerr, Richard A. (1992) "Huge Impact Tied to Mass Extinction," *Science* 267: 1421–2.

Kerr, Richard A. (2000) "A Victim of the Black Sea Flood Found," *Science* 289: 2021.

Kingsolver, Barbara (1998) *The Poisonwood Bible*, New York: HarperCollins.

Kingston-Mann, Esther (1999) *In Search of the True West: Culture, Economics, and Problems of Russian Development*, Princeton, NJ: Princeton University Press.

Kinzey, Warren G. (ed.) (1987) *The Evolution of Human Behavior: Primate Models*, Albany, NY: SUNY Press.

Kipnis, Aaron (1999) *Angry Young Men*, San Francisco: Jossey-Bass, Inc.

Kirschner, Mary Beth (2000) "Grey Matters: Stress and the Brain," Washington D.C.: National Public Radio Series, November 28.

Klein, Naomi (2000) *No Logo*, New York: Picador USA.

Klein, Naomi (2001) "Time to fight free-trade laws that benefit multinationals," *Guardian Weekly*, March 21: 27.

Koch, Sigmund (1999) *Psychology in Human Context: Essays in Dissidence and Reconstruction*, Chicago: University of Chicago Press.

Kocherry, Thomas and Thankappan Achary (1989) "Fishing for Resources: Indian Fisheries in Danger," *Cultural Survival Quarterly* 13(2): 31–4.

Koenig, Robert (2001) "Researchers Target Deadly Tsunamis," *Science* 293: 1251–3.

Koestler, Arthur and J.R. Smythies (eds.) (1969) *Beyond Reductionism*, London/New York: Macmillan.

Kogan, Ilany (2000) "Breaking the Cycle of Trauma: From the Individual to Society," *Mind and Human Interaction* 11(1): 2–10.

Kohlberg, L. (1970) "The Moral Atmosphere of the School," in N. Overley (ed.), *The Unstudied Curriculum: Its Impact on Children*, Washington D.C.: Association for Supervision and Curriculum Development, ASCD Elementary Council, National Education Association.

Kohlberg, L. (1981) *Essays on Moral Development, Vol. I. The Philosophy of Moral Development: Moral States and the Idea of Justice*, San Francisco: Harper & Row.

Korten, David (2001) *When Corporations Rule the World*, 2nd edn., Berkeley, CA: Berrett-Koehler.

Korten, David and Ruth van Gelder (2001) "What to Do When Corporations Rule the World: An Interview with David C. Korten," *YES! a journal of positive futures*, Summer: 48–51.

Kotter, John (1995) *The New Rules*, New York: Dutton.

Krog, Antjie (1999) *Country of My Skull*, New York: Times Books/Random House.

Kuhn, Thomas (1970) *The Structure of Scientific Revolutions*, 2nd edn., Chicago: University of Chicago Press.

Kuper, Leo (1957) *Passive Resistance in South Africa*, New Haven, CT: Yale University Press.

Kwitny, Jonathan (1984) *Endless Enemies: The Making of an Unfriendly World*, New York: Congdon & Weed.

Labeyrie, Laurent (2000) "Glacial Climate Instability," *Science* 290: 1905–7.

Lakoff, George (1987) *Women, Fire and Dangerous Things: What Categories Reveal about the Mind*, Chicago: Chicago University Press.

Lakoff, George and Mark Johnson (1980) *Metaphors We Live By*, Chicago: University of Chicago Press.

Lande, R. (1979) "Quantitative Genetic Analysis of Multivariate Evolution, Applied to Brain Body Size Allometry," *Evolution* 33: 402–16.

Lane, Robert E. (2000) *The Loss of Happiness in Market Democracies*, New Haven, CT: Yale University Press.

Latour, Bruno and Steve Woolgar (1986) *Laboratory Life: The Construction of Scientific Facts*, 2nd edn., Princeton, NJ: Princeton University Press.

Lauren, Paul Gordon (1998) *The Evolution of International Human Rights: Visions Seen*, Philadelphia: University of Pennsylvania Press.

Lavik, Nils Johan (1994) "Organized Violence and Mental Health – Historical and Psychological Perspectives on the 20th Century," in Nils J. Lavik *et al.* (eds.), 85–115.

Lavik, Nils Johan, Mette Nygård, Nora Sveaass, and Eva Fannemel (eds.) (1994) *Pain and Survival: Human Rights Violations and Mental Health*, Oslo/Boston: Scandinavian University Press.

Leakey, Meave and Alan Walker (1997) "Early Hominid Fossils from Africa," *Scientific American*, June: 74–9.

Lee, Dorothy (1959) *Freedom and Culture*, New York: Prentice Hall.

Lee, Richard B. (1969) "Eating Christmas in the Kalahari," *Natural History*, December: 14–22, 60–3.

Lee, Richard B. and I. DeVore (eds.) (1968) *Man the Hunter*, New York: Aldine.

Lemonick, Michael D. (2000) "Teens before Their Time," *Time*, October 30: 65–74.

Lenhoff, Howard M., Paul P. Wang, Frank Greenberg, and Ursula Bellugi (1997) "Williams Syndrome and the Brain," *Scientific American*, December: 68–73.

Levenson, Thomas (1989) *Ice Time: Climate, Science, and Life on Earth*, New York: Harper & Row.

Lewin, Roger, Garniss Curtis, and Carl Swisher (2000) *Java Man: How Two Geologists' Dramatic Discoveries Changed Our Understanding of the Evolutionary Path to Modern Humans*, New York: Scribner.

Lewis, Paul (1994) "U.S. Forces U.N. to Put Off Plan to Send 5,500 Troops to Rwanda," *New York Times*, May 17: A2, A4.

Lewis-Williams, J. David (1981) *Believing and Seeing: Symbolic Meaning in Southern San Rock Paintings*, London: Academic Press, 103–16.

Lewis-Williams, J. David (1983) "Introductory Essay: Science and Rock Art," in J. David Lewis-Williams (ed.), *New Approaches to Southern African Rock Art*, Cape Town: The South African Archeological Society, Goodwin Series No.4: 3–13.

Lewis-Williams, J. David (1997) "Agency, art and altered consciousness: a motif in French (Quercy) Upper Paleolithic parietal art," *Antiquity* 71: 810–30.

Liedloff, Jean (1977) *The Continuum Concept: In Search of Happiness Lost*, Reading, MA: Addison Wesley.

Lightman, Alan and Owen Gingerich (1991) "When Do Anomalies Begin?," *Science* 255: 690–4.

Loftus, Elizabeth F. (1994) *The Myth of Repressed Memory*, New York: St. Martin's Press.

Loftus, Elizabeth F., S. Polensky, and M.T. Fullilove (1994) "Memories of Childhood Sexual Abuse: Remembering and Repressing," *Psychology of Women Quarterly* 18: 67–84.

Lonezak, Heather S., Robert D. Abbott, J. David Hawkins, Rick Kosterman, and Richard Catalano (2002) "Effects of the Seattle Social Development Project on Sexual Behavior, Pregnancy, Birth and Sexually Transmitted Disease Outcomes by Age 21 Years," *Archives of Pediatrics and Adolescent Medicine* 156: 438–47.

Lorenz, Konrad (1960) *On Aggression*, London: Methuen.

Lowdermilk, W.C. (1975) *Conquest of the Land through Seven Thousand Years*, revised edn., Washington D.C.: U.S. Department of Agriculture Soil Conservation Service, Agricultural Information Bulletin no.99 (GPO #001–000–03446).

Ma Guang Yan (1995) "How Was the Bow and Arrow Invented: An Investigation of Its Origin," *Issues in Integrative Studies: An Interdisciplinary Journal*, 13.

MacLean, Paul D. (1973) *A Triune Concept of the Brain and Behaviour*, Toronto: University of Toronto Press.

MacLean, Paul D. (1990) *The Triune Brain in Evolution. Role in Paleocerebral Functions*, New York: Plenum Press.

Mahedy, William P. (1986) *Out of the Night: The Spiritual Journey of Vietnam Vets*, New York: Ballantine/Epiphany.

Mallin, Michael A. (2000) "Impacts of Industrial Animal Production on Rivers and Estuaries," *American Scientist* 88 (January/February): 26–37.

Malotki, E. (1978) *Hopitutuwutsi: Hopi Tales. A Bilingual Collection of Hopi Indian Stories*, Flagstaff: Museum of Northern Arizona Press.

Mamdani, Mahmood (2001) *When Victims Become Killers: Colonialism, Nativism, and the Genocide in Rwanda*, Princeton, NJ: Princeton University Press.

Mander, Jerry (1978) *Four Arguments for the Elimination of Television*, New York: William Morrow.

Mandler, George (1997) *Human Nature Explored*, New York: Oxford University Press.

Mann, Charles C. (2002) "1491," *Atlantic Monthly*, March: 41–53.

Marler, Joan (ed.) (1997) *From the Realm of the Ancestors: An Anthology in Honor of Marija Gimbutas*, Manchester, CT: Knowledge, Ideas and Trends.

Marshack, Alexander (1970) "Le bâton de commandement de Montgaudier," *L'Anthropologie*: 332.

Marshack, Alexander (1972) *The Roots of Civilization: The Cognitive Beginnings of Man's First Art, Symbol, and Notation*, New York: McGraw Hill.

Marshall, Eliot (2000a) "A Renewed Assault on an Old and Deadly Foe," *Science* 290: 428–30.

Marshall, Eliot (2000b) "Reinventing an Ancient Cure for Malaria," *Science* 290: 437, 439.

Marshall, Eliot (2000c) "The Shots Heard 'Round the World'," *Science* 290: 570.

Marshall, Eliot (2000d) "Planned Ritalin Trial for Tots Heads into Uncharted Waters," *Science* 290: 1280–2.

Marshall, Jonathan, Peter Dale Scott, and Jane Hunter (1987) *The Iran Contra Connection: Secret Teams and Covert Operations in the Reagan Era*, Boston: South End Press.

Martin, Alex, James V. Haxby, Francois M. Lalonde, Cheri L. Wiggs, and Leslie G. Ungerleider (1994) "Discrete Cortical Regions Associated with Knowledge of Color and Knowledge of Action," *Science* 270: 102–5.

Martin, M. Kay and Barbara Voorhies (1975) *Female of the Species*, New York: Columbia University Press.

Martin, Paul S. (1984) "Prehistoric Overkill: The Global Model," in Paul S. Martin and Richard G. Klein (eds.), *Quaternary Extinctions: A Prehistoric Revolution*, Tucson: University of Arizona Press.

Marty, Martin E. (1994) "Fanaticism: A World of Upheavals," Chautauqua Lecture, Tape 94–11, Chautauqua, NY: Chautauqua Institution.

Maturana, Humberto (1990) Preface to *El Calix y La Espada* (Spanish edition of *The Chalice and the Blade*) by Riane Eisler, Santiago, Chile: Editorial Cuatro Vientos.

Maybury-Lewis, David (1992) *Millennium: Tribal Wisdom and the Modern World*, New York: Viking Penguin.

Mazurana, Dyan and Susan McKay (2001) "Child Soldiers: What about the Girls?," *Bulletin of the Atomic Scientists*, September/October: 30–5.

McCarthy, Wanda C. and Irene Hanson Frieze (1999) "Negative Aspects of Therapy: Client Perceptions of Therapists' Social Influence, Burnout, and Quality of Care," *Journal of Social Issues*, 55(1): 33–50.

McCay, Bonnie J. and James M. Acheson (eds.) (1990) *The Question of the Commons: The Culture and Ecology of Communal Resources*, Tucson: University of Arizona Press.

McClelland, J., D. Rumelhart, and the PDP Research Group (1986) *Parallel Distributed Processing: Explorations in the Microstructure of Cognition*, Vol. II, Cambridge, MA: Harvard University Press.

McClintock, Barbara (1984) "Significance of Responses of the Genome to Challenge," *Science* 226: 792–801.

McComb, Karen, C. Moss, S.M. Durant, L. Baker, and S. Sayialei (2001) "Matriarchs as Repositories of Social Knowledge in African Elephants," *Science* 292: 491–4.

McFarlane, A.C. and B.A. van der Kolk (1996) "Conclusions and Future Directions," in B.A. van der Kolk, A.C. McFarlane, and L. Weisaeth (eds.), *Traumatic Stress: The Effects of Overwhelming Experience on Mind, Body, and Society*, New York: Guilford Press.

McGinniss, Joe (1969) *The Selling of the President 1968*, New York: Trident Press.

McGreal, Chris (2001) "Congo villagers tell of a life plagued by killers on all sides," *Guardian Weekly*, August 15: 3.

McGrew, W.C. (1992) *Chimpanzee Material Culture: Implications for Human Evolution*, Cambridge, UK: Cambridge University Press.

McKie, Robin (2000) "Despite years of success, eradication [of leprosy] may be impossible, scientists warn," *Guardian Weekly*, March 15: 28.

McKnight, John (1995) *The Careless Society: Community and Its Counterfeits*, New York: Basic Books.

McMichael, Anthony J., Andrew Haines, Rudolf Slooff, and Sari Kovats (eds.) (1996) *Climate Change and Human Health*, Geneva: World Health Organization, World Meteorological Organization and UN Environment Program.

Medoff, Peter and Holly Sklar (1994) *Streets of Hope: The Fall and Rise of an Urban Neighborhood*, Boston: South End Press.

Mehri, Darius (2000) "Death by Overwork: Corporate Pressure on Employees Takes a Fatal Toll in Japan," *Multinational Monitor*, June: 26–8.

Meier, Deborah (1995) *The Power of Their Ideas*, Boston: Beacon Press.

Melaart, James (1967) *Çatal Hüyük: A Neolithic Town in Anatolia*, London: Thames & Hudson.

Melaart, James (1970) *Excavations at Haçilar, I and II*, Edinburgh: Published for British Institute of Archeology at Ankara by Edinburgh University Press.

Menhuin, Yehudi (1996) Interview on *Performance Today*, Washington D.C.: National Public Radio, April 22.

Mercador, Julio, Melissa Panger, and Christophe Boesch (2002) "Excavation of a Chimpanzee Stone Tool Site in the African Rainforest," *Science* 296: 1452–5.

Midgley, Mary (1978) *Beast and Man*, Ithaca, NY: Cornell University Press.

Midgley, Mary (1981) *Heart and Mind: The Varieties of Moral Experience*, New York: St. Martin's Press.

Midgley, Mary (1983) *Animals and Why They Matter: A Journey around the Species Barrier*, Harmondsworth, UK: Penguin Books.

Midgley, Mary (1985) *Evolution as a Religion: Strange Hopes and Stranger Fears*, London: Methuen.

Midgley, Mary (1990) "Why Smartness Is Not Enough," in Mary E. Clark and Sandra A. Wawrytko (eds.), *Rethinking the Curriculum: Toward an Integrated, Interdisciplinary Education*, Westport, CT: Greenwood Press.

Midgley, Mary (1992) *Science as Salvation: A Modern Myth and Its Meaning*, London: Routledge.

Midgley, Mary (1999) "Being Scientific about Ourselves," *Journal of Consciousness Studies* 6(4): 85–98.

Miller, Alice (1980) *Am Anfang war Erziehung*, trans. 1983, 1990, *For Your Own Good*, New York: Farrar, Straus, & Giroux.

Mills, Roger (1995) *Realizing Mental Health*, New York: Salzburger and Graham Publishers.

Mills, Roger and Elsie Spittle (2001) *The Wisdom Within*, Renton, WA: Lone Pine Publishing.

Mitroff, Ian I. and Warren Bennis (1993) *The Unreality Industry: The Deliberate Manufacturing of Falsehood and What It Is Doing to Our Lives*, New York and Oxford, UK: Oxford University Press.

Mlot, Christine (1998) "Probing the Biology of Emotion," *Science* 280: 1005–7.

Mollica, Richard F. (2000) "Invisible Arms," *Scientific American*, June: 54–7.

Monnin, Eric, Andreas Indermühle, Andre Dällenbach, Jacqueline Flückiger, Bernhard Stauffer, Thomas F. Stocker, Dominique Raynaud, and Jean-Marc Barnola (2001) "Atmospheric $CO_2$ Concentrations over the Last Glacial Termination," *Science* 291: 112–14.

Monroe, Kristen Renwick (with the assistance of Connie Epperson) (1994) " 'But What Else Could I Do?' Choice, Identity and a Cognitive-Perceptual Theory of Ethical Political Behavior," *Political Psychology* 15: 201–26.

Morell, Virginia (1996) "Life at the Top: Animals Pay the High Price of Dominance," *Science* 271: 292.

Morrison, Philip and Phylis Morrison (2000) "Time Travelers in the Field," *Scientific American*, February: 105–6.

Morrison, Roy (1991) *We Build the Road as We Travel*, Philadelphia: New Society Publishers.

Moser, Stephanie (1998) *Ancestral Images: The Iconography of Human Origins*, Ithaca, NY: Cornell University Press.

Moulik, T.K. and P.R. Shuckla (1992) "Sustainable Development in Micro-Watershed: The Planning Model," pre-print of Working Paper from the Indian Institute of Management, Vastrapur, Ahmedabad 380 015, Gujarat, India.

Muir, W.M. (1995) "Group Selection for Adaptation to Multiple-Hen Cages: Selection Program and Direct Responses," *Poultry Science* 75: 447–58.

Mumford, Lewis (1961) *The City in History*, New York: Harcourt, Brace & World.

Mumford, Lewis (1967) *The Myth of the Machine: Techniques and Human Development*, New York: Harcourt, Brace & World.

Murray, C.J.L. and A.D. Lopez (1996) "World Health Organization–World Bank Global Burden of Disease Study," Policy Forum, November 1: 740. Reported in "Letters," *Science*, 274, December 6.

Musser, George and Sasha Nemecek (2000) "Waging a New Kind of War," *Scientific American*, June: 46–65.

Nagler, Michael N. (1982) *America without Violence*, Covelo, CA: Island Press.

Nagler, Michael N. (2001) *Is There No Other Way?*, Berkeley, CA: Berkeley Hills Press.

Nandy, Ashis (2000) "The Illegitimacy of Nationalism: Rabindranath Tagore and the Politics of Self," *Interculture*, April, Issue 138: 5–20.

Narendranath, Konniyoor (1995) "She Was a Ruler of Great Foresight," *Expressweek* (Kochin/Cochin), November 25: 4.

National Research Council, Committee on Hormonally Active Agents in the Environment (1999) "Hormonally Active Agents in the Environment," Washington D.C.: National Academy Press.

Nemecek, Sasha (2000) "Who Were the First Americans?," *Scientific American*, September: 80–6.

Nemeroff, Charles B. (1998) "The Neurobiology of Depression," *Scientific American*, June: 42–9.

Neumann, J. von and O. Morgenstern (1947) *Theory of Games and Economic Behavior*, Princeton, NJ: Princeton University Press.

Neves, Walter (2000) "Luiza Is Not Alone," Letters, *Science* 287: 974–5.

Newberg, Andrew and Eugene d'Aquili (1999) *The Mystical Mind: Probing the Biology of Religious Experience*, Augsburg, Germany: Fortress Press.

Newberg, Andrew, Eugene d'Aquili, and Vince Rause (2001) *Why God Won't Go Away: Brain Science and the Biology of Belief*, New York: Ballantine.

Niehof, Debra (1999) *The Biology of Violence*, New York: Free Press.

Niehoff, Debra L. (2000) "Letters," *Science* 290: 1093, 1094, 1096.

Nilsson, Martin P. (1950) *The Minoan Mycenean Religion and Its Survival in Greek Legend*, Lund: Lund University Press.

Nishida, T. (1987) "Local Traditions and Cultural Transmission," in B.B. Smuts, D.L. Cheney, R.M. Seyfarth, R.W. Wrangham, and T.T. Struhsaker (eds.), *Primate Societies*, Chicago: University of Chicago Press.

Norgaard, Richard B. (1994) *Development Betrayed: The End of Progress and a Co-evolutionary Revisioning of the Future*, London: Routledge.

Normile, Dennis (2000) "Warmer Waters More Deadly to Coral Reefs Than Pollution," *Science* 290: 682–3.

Nørretranders, Tor (1998) *The User Illusion: Cutting Consciousness Down to Size*, New York: Viking Penguin.

Northcutt, R. Glenn (1981) "Evolution of the Telencephalon in Nonmammals," *Annual Review of Neurosciences* 4: 301–50.

Northcutt, R. Glenn (2001) "Changing View of Brain Evolution," *Brain Research Bulletin* 55(6): 663–74.

Northcutt, R. Glenn and J. Kaas (1995) "The Emergence and Evolution of Mammalian Neocortex," *Trends in Neurosciences* 18: 373–9.

Northridge, Mary E. and 7 others (1999) "Diesel Exhaust Exposure Among Adolescents in Harlem: A Community-Driven Study," *American Journal of Public Health* 89: 998–1002.

O'Neill, Graeme (1994) "Cemetery Reveals Complex Aboriginal Society," *Science* 264: 1403.

Pääbo, Svante (1995) "The Y Chromosome and the Origin of All of Us (Men)," *Science* 268: 1141–2.

Pacey, A. (1983) *The Culture of Technology*, Cambridge, MA: Massachusetts Institute of Technology Press.

Pagels, Elaine (1979) *The Gnostic Gospels*, New York: Random House.

Pagels, Elaine (1995) *The Origin of Satan*, London: Penguin.

Parasuraman, Raja (1998) "The Attentive Brain: Issues and Prospects," in Raja Parasuraman (ed.), Chapter I.

Parasuraman, Raja (ed.) (1998b) *The Attentive Brain*, Cambridge, MA: Massachusetts Institute of Technology Press.

Parenti, Michael (1983) *Democracy for the Few*, New York: St. Martin's Press.

Parenti, Michael (1986) *Inventing Reality*, New York: St. Martin's Press.

Pearlman, Moshe (1967) *Zealots of Masada*, New York: Scribner.

Peck, M. Scott (1987) *The Different Drum: Community-Making and Peace*, New York: Simon & Schuster.

Penfield, W. (1966) "Speech, Perception, and the Uncommitted Cortex," in J.C. Eccles (ed.), *Brain and Conscious Experience*, Berlin: Springer-Verlag, 217–37.

Pennisi, Elizabeth (1999) "Are Our Primate Cousins 'Conscious'?," *Science* 284: 2073–6.

Perry, Bruce D. (1994) "Neurobiological Sequelae of Childhood Trauma: PTSD in Children," in M. Michelle Murburg (ed.), *Catecholamine Function in Posttraumatic Stress Disorder: Emerging Concepts*, Washington D.C.: American Psychiatric Press, 233–54.

Perry, Bruce D. (1997) "Memories of Fear," in J. Goodwin and R. Attias (eds.), *Images of the Body in Trauma*, New York: Basic Books.

Perry, Bruce D. (2001a) "The Neurodevelopmental Impact of Violence in Childhood," in D. Schetky and E.P. Benedek (eds.), *Textbook of Child and Adolescent Forensic Psychiatry*, Washington D.C.: American Psychiatric Press, 221–38.

Perry, Bruce D. (2001b) "The Neuroarcheology of Childhood Maltreatment: The Neurodevelopmental Costs of Adverse Childhood Events," in K. Franey, R. Geffner, and R. Falconer (eds.), *The Cost of Maltreatment: Who Pays? We All Do*, San Diego: Family Violence and Sexual Assault Institute, 15–37.

Perry, Bruce D. and Jennifer E. Pate (1994) "Neurodevelopment and the Psychobiological Roots of Post-traumatic Stress Disorder," in L.F. Koziol and C.E. Stout (eds.), *The Neurophysiology of Mental Disorders: A Practical Guide*, Springfield, IL: Charles C. Thomas, 129–46.

Perry, Bruce D. and Ronnie Pollard (1998) "Homeostasis, Stress, Trauma and Adaptation: A Neurodevelopmental View of Childhood Trauma," *Child and Adolescent Psychiatric Clinics of North America* 7(1): 33–51.

Perry, Bruce D., Ronnie A. Pollard, Toi L. Blakley, William L. Baker, and Dominico Vigilante (1995) "Childhood Trauma, the Neurobiology of Adaptation, and 'Use-dependent' Development of the Brain: How 'States' Become 'Traits'," *Infant Mental Health Journal* 16: 271–91.

Pickering, Andrew (1984) *Constructing Quarks: A Sociological History of Particle Physics*, Edinburgh: Edinburgh University Press.

Pimm, Stuart L. and 32 others (2001) "Can We Defy Nature's End," *Science* 293: 2207–8.

Pinker, Steven (1997) *How the Mind Works*, New York: W.W. Norton.

Pinker, Steven (1998) "Boys Will Be Boys," *The New Yorker*, February 9.

Plotkin, Henry C. (1982a) "Evolutionary Epistemology and Evolutionary Theory," in H.C. Plotkin (ed.), Chapter I.

Plotkin, Henry C. (ed.) (1982b) *Learning, Development and Culture*, New York: Wiley.

Plotkin, Henry C. (1986) "An Evolutionary Epistemological Approach to the Evolution of Intelligence," in H.J. Jerison and I. Jerison (eds.), *Intelligence and Evolutionary Biology*, Berlin/New York: Springer Verlag, pp.73–92.

Polanyi, Michael (1962) *Personal Knowledge: Towards a Post-Critical Philosophy*, Chicago: University of Chicago Press.

Pool, Robert (1989) "Is Something Strange about the Weather?," *Science* 243: 1290–3.

Popper, Karl (1959) *The Logic of Scientific Discovery*, New York: Harper & Row.

Portland City Club (2000) "Discussion: The Role of Arts Education in Schools," March 31; broadcast on Oregon Public Broadcasting, April 4.

Potts, Richard (Rick) (1987) "Reconstruction of Early Hominid Socioecology: A Critique of Primate Models," in Warren G. Kinzey (ed.), 28–47.

Potts, Richard (Rick) (1996a) *Humanity's Descent: The Consequences of Ecological Instability*, New York: Morrow.

Potts, Richard (Rick) (1996b) "Evolution and Climate Variability," *Science* 273: 926.

Power, Margaret (1991) *The Egalitarians: Human and Chimpanzee*, Cambridge, UK: Cambridge University Press.

Powers, Ron (2002) "The Apocalypse of Adolescence," *Atlantic Monthly*, March: 58–74.

Pringle, Heather (1997a) "Research News: Death in Norse Greenland," *Science* 275: 924–6.

Pringle, Heather (1997b) "Ice Age Communities May Be Earliest Known Net Hunters," *Science* 277: 1203–4.

Provine, Robert R. (2000) *Laughter: A Scientific Investigation*, New York: Viking Penguin.

Putnam, Frank W. (1989) *Diagnosis and Treatment of Multiple Personality Disorder*, New York: Guilford Press.

Putnam, Frank W. (1992) "Altered States: Peeling Away the Layers of a Multiple Personality," *The Sciences*, November/December: 30–6.

Rahnema, Majid (1990) "Swadhyaya: The Unknown, the Peaceful, the Silent Yet Singing Revolution of India," *IFDA Dossier*, 73 (April): 19–34.

Raine, Peter (2001) "Beyond Universalism: The Shaman and the Ecologist: An Ever Open Horizon," *Interculture*, Issue No. 140.

Raven, Bertram (1999) "Kurt Lewin Address: Influence, Power, Religion, and the Mechanisms of Social Control," *Journal of Social Issues* 55(1): 161–86.

Redford, Tim (2001) "Desert expedition unearths spectacular clues to the origins of Egyptian civilisation," *Guardian Weekly*, January 10: 21.

Reed, Edward S. (1996) *The Necessity of Experience*, New Haven, CT: Yale University Press.

Relethford, John H. (2001a) "Ancient DNA and the Origin of Modern Humans," *Proceedings of the National Academy of Sciences* 98: 390–1.

Relethford, John H. (2001b) *Genetics and the Search for Modern Human Origins*, New York: John Wiley.

Reynolds, Vernon (1976) *The Biology of Human Action*, San Francisco: W.H. Freeman.

Rhodes, Richard (2000) "Letters," *Science* 290: 1093, 1094, 1096.

Riddle, Robert D. and Clifford J. Tabin (1999) "How Limbs Develop," *Scientific American*, February: 74–9.

Rifkin, Jeremy (2000) *The Age of Access: The New Culture of Hypercapitalism Where All of Life Is a Paid-for Experience*, New York: Tarcher/Putnam.

Robarchek, Clayton A. (1989) "Hobbesian and Rousseauian Images of Man: Autonomy and Individualism in a Peaceful Society," in Signe Howell and Roy Willis (eds.), 31–44.

Robarchek, Clayton A. and Carole J. Robarchek (1992) "Cultures of War and Peace: A Comparative Study of Waorani and Semai," in James Silverberg and Patrick Gray (eds.), *Aggression and Peacefulness in Humans and Other Primates*, New York: Oxford University Press, Chapter 9, 189–213.

Robarchek, Clayton A. and Robert Knox Dentan (1987) "Blood Drunkenness and the Bloodthirsty Semai: Unmaking Another Anthropological Myth," *American Anthropologist* 89: 356–65.

Roberts, Monty (1996) *The Man Who Listens to Horses*, New York: Random House.

Roberts, Richard G. and 10 others (2001) "New Ages for the Last Australian Megafauna: Continent-Wide Extinction About 46,000 Years Ago," *Science* 292: 1888–92.

Robinson, Thomas N., Marta L. Wilde, Lisa C. Navracruz, K. Farish Haydel, and Ann Varady (2001) "Effects of Reducing Children's Television and Video Game Use on Aggressive Behavior," *Archives of Pediatrics and Adolescent Medicine* 155: 17–23.

Rochat, François and Andre Modigliani (1995) "The Ordinary Quality of Resistance: From Milgram's Laboratory to the Village of LeChambon," *Journal of Social Issues* 51: 195–213.

Rogers, Carol (1975) "Female Forms of Power and the Myth of Male Dominance: A Model of Female/Male Interaction in Peasant Society," *American Ethnology* 2: 727–56.

Rogoff, Barbara (1982) "Integrating Context and Cognitive Development," in M.E. Lamb and A.L. Brown (eds.), *Advances in Developmental Psychology*, Vol. 2, Hillsdale, NJ: Erlbaum.

Rogoff, Barbara (1990) *Apprenticeship in Thinking*, Oxford: Oxford University Press.

Rogoff, Barbara (1995) "Observing Sociocultural Activity on Three Planes: Participatory Appropriation, Guided Participation, Apprenticeship," in A. Alvarez, P. del Rio, and J.V. Wertsch (eds.), *Perspectives on Sociocultural Research*, Cambridge, UK: Cambridge University Press, 139–64.

Rogoff, Barbara, Christine Mosier, Jayanthi Mistry, and Artin Göncü (1993) "Toddlers' Guided Participation with Their Caregivers in Cultural Activity," in Ellice A. Forman, Norris Minick, and C. Addison Stone (eds.), *Contexts for Learning: Sociocultural Dynamics in Children's Development*, New York: Oxford University Press, 230–53.

Roosevelt, Anna C. (1992) "Secrets of the Forest: An Archaeologist Reappraises the Past – and Future – of Amazonia," *The Sciences*, November/December: 22–8.

Roosevelt, Anna C. (1994) "Strategy for a New Synthesis," in Anna C. Roosevelt (ed.), *Amazonian Indians*, Tucson: University of Arizona Press, 4–15.

Rose, Hilary and Steven Rose (eds.) (2000) *Alas, Poor Darwin: Arguments against Evolutionary Psychology*, London: Jonathan Cape.

Rosensweig, C. and D. Hillel (1998) *Climate Change and the Global Harvest*, New York: Oxford University Press.

Ross, Marc Howard (1993a) *The Culture of Conflict: Interpretations and Interests in Comparative Perspective*, New Haven, CT: Yale University Press.

Ross, Marc Howard (1993b) *The Management of Conflict: Interpretations and Interests in Comparative Perspective*, New Haven, CT: Yale University Press.

Ross, Rupert (1992) *Dancing with a Ghost: Exploring Indian Reality*, Markham, Ont., Canada: Reed Books.

Rothkrug, Lionel (1987) "Holy Shrines, Religious Dissonance and Satan in the Origins of the German Reformation," *Historical Reflections* 14(2): 143–286.

Rovee-Collier, Carolyn (1999) "The Development of Infant Memory," *Current Directions in Psychological Science* 8(3): 80–5.

Rowe, Jonathan (2000) "Clueless In Seattle," *YES! a journal of positive futures*, Spring: 54–5.

Rubenstein, Richard (1999) *When Jesus Became God*, San Diego: Harcourt Brace.

Rumelhart, D., J. McClelland, and the PDP Research Group (1986) *Parallel Distributed Processing: Explorations in the Microstructure of Cognition*, Vol. I, Cambridge, MA: Harvard University Press.

Russell, Charlie and Maureen Enns (1999) "Walking with Giants: The Grizzlies of Siberia," *Nature*, Public Broadcasting System, February 14.

Ryan, Richard M. and Edward L. Deci (2000) "Self-Determination Theory and the Facilitation of Intrinsic Motivation, Social Development, and Well Being," *American Psychologist* 55(1): 68–78.

Sagan, Carl (1977) *The Dragons of Eden*, New York: Ballantine.

Salisbury, R.F. (1962) *From Stone to Steel: Economic Consequences of a Technological Change in New Guinea*, Melbourne: Melbourne University Press, and London: London University Press.

Sampson, Anthony (1995) *Company Man*, New York: Random House.

481

Sanday, Peggy Reeves (1981) *Female Power and Male Dominance: On the Origins of Sexual Inequality*, Cambridge, UK: Cambridge University Press.

Sanders, Jerry W. (1983) *Peddlers of Crisis*, Boston: South End Press.

Sapir, Michael (1998) "Angry Adolescent Brains," *American Scientist* 86: 331–2.

Sapolsky, Robert M. (1996) "Why Stress Is Bad for Your Brain," *Science* 273: 749–50.

Sapolsky, Robert M. (1997) *The Trouble with Testosterone*, New York: Scribner.

Sat Vichar Darshan Trust (1994) *The Systems (The Way and the Work)*, Vimal Jyoti, 6/8, Dr. Wilson Street, Bombay 400 004: Vallabhdas J. Jhaveri, for Sat Vichar Darshan Trust.

Saunders, Harold H. (1999) *A Public Peace Process: Sustained Dialogue to Transform Racial and Ethnic Conflicts*, New York: St. Martin's Press.

Saunders, Joe W. and 14 others (1997) "A Mound Complex in Louisiana at 5400–5000 Years before the Present," *Science* 277: 1796–9.

Schaller, George B. (1964) *The Year of the Gorilla*, Chicago: University of Chicago Press.

Scheibe, Karl E. (2000) *The Drama of Everyday Life*, Cambridge, MA: Harvard University Press.

Schiller, Herbert I. (1973) *The Mind Managers*, Boston: Beacon Press.

Schiller, Herbert I. (1989) *Culture Inc: The Corporate Takeover of Public Expression*, New York and Oxford, UK: Oxford University Press.

Schiller, Herbert I. (1996) *Information Inequality: The Deepening Social Crisis in America*, New York and London: Routledge.

Schmookler, Andrew Bard (1984) *The Parable of the Tribes: The Problem of Power in Social Behavior*, Boston: Houghton Mifflin.

Schoggen, Phil (1989) *Behavior Settings: A Revision and Extension of Roger G. Barker's Ecological Psychology*, Palo Alto, CA: Stanford University Press.

Scholl, Wolfgang (1999) "Restrictive Control and Information Pathologies in Organizations," *Journal of Social Issues* 55(1): 101–18.

Schopf, T.J.M. (ed.) (1972) *Models in Paleobiology*, San Francisco: Freeman, Cooper.

Schumacher, E.F. (*c*.1972) Lindesfarne Tape Series, K3.

Schumacher, E.F. (1974) *Small Is Beautiful: Economics As If People Mattered*, London: Abacus, Sphere Books.

Schumacher, E.F. (1977) *A Guide for the Perplexed*, New York: Harper & Row.

Schwartländer, Bernhard, Geoff Farnett, Neff Walker, and Roy Anderson (2000) "AIDS in a New Millennium," *Science* 289: 64–7.

Schwartz, Barry (1986) *The Battle for Human Nature: Science, Morality and Modern Life*, New York: W.W. Norton.

Scott, K. Michelle (2000) "A Perennial Mourning: Identity Conflict and the Transgenerational Transmission of Trauma within the African American Community," *Mind and Human Interaction* 11(1): 11–26.

Scrimshaw, Susan C.M. (1984) "Infanticide in Human Populations: Societal and Individual Concerns," in Glenn Hausfater and S.B. Hrdy (eds.), *Infanticide: Comparative and Evolutionary Perspectives*, New York: Aldine.

Semino, Ornella and 16 other authors from 9 different countries and 13 different institutions (2000) "The Genetic Legacy of Paleolithic *Homo sapiens sapiens* in Extant Europeans: A Y Chromosome Perspective," *Science* 290: 1155–9.

Sennett, Richard (1998) *The Corrosion of Character: The Personal Consequences of Work in the New Capitalism*, New York: W.W. Norton.

Shackleton, Nicholas (2001) "Climate Change Across the Hemispheres," *Science* 291: 58–60.

Shadmehr, Reza and Henry H. Holcomb (1997) "Neural Correlates of Motor Memory Consolidation," *Science* 277: 821–5.

Sharp, Gene (1973) *The Politics of Nonviolent Action*, Cambridge, MA: Porter Sargent.

Sharp, Gene (1979) *Gandhi as a Political Strategist, with Essays on Ethics and Politics*, Cambridge, MA: Porter Sargent.

Sharp, Gene (1980) *Social Power and Political Freedom*, Boston: Porter Sargent.

Sharp, Gene (1990) *Civilian-Based Defense: A Post-Military Weapons System*, Princeton, NJ: Princeton University Press.

Sharp, Lauriston (1952) "Steel Axes for Stone Age Australians," in E.H. Spicer (ed.), *Human Problems in Technological Change*, New York: John Wiley & Sons, Case 5.

Shay, Jonathan (1994) *Achilles in Vietnam: Combat Trauma and the Undoing of Character*, New York: Atheneum.

Shepard, Paul (1998) *Coming Home to the Pleistocene*, Washington D.C./Covelo, CA: Island Press.

Shipman, Pat (2000) "Doubting Dmanisi," *American Scientist* 88 (November/ December): 291–4.

Shiva, Vandana (1988) *Staying Alive: Women, Ecology and Survival in India*, New Delhi: Kali Press and London: Zed Books.

Shiva, Vandana (1994) *Close to Home: Women Reconnect Ecology, Health and Development Worldwide*, Philadelphia: New Society Publishers.

Short, R.V. (1976) "The Evolution of Human Reproduction," *Proceedings of the Royal Society*, London B 195: 3–24.

Short, R.V. and E. Balaban (eds.) (1994) *The Difference Between the Sexes*, Cambridge, UK: Cambridge University Press.

Shouse, Ben (2001) "Spreading the Word, Scattering the Seeds," *Science* 294: 988–9.

Shulman, Shmuel (ed.) (1995) *Close Relationships and Socioemotional Development*, Norwood, NJ: Ablex.

Shweder, Richard A. (1991) *Thinking Through Cultures*, Cambridge, MA: Harvard University Press.

Simcock, Gabrielle and Harlene Haynes (2002) "Breaking the Barriers? Children Fail to Translate Their Preverbal Memories into Language," *Psychological Science* 13: 225–31.

Singh, J.A.L. and R.M. Zingg (1939) *Wolf-Children and Feral Man*, New York: Harper.

Sittirak, Sinith (1998) *The Daughters of Development*, London: Zed Books.

Skinner, B.F. (1972) *Beyond Freedom and Dignity*, New York: Bantam.

Sklar, Holly (1988) *Washington's War on Nicaragua*, Boston: South End Press.

Slaton, Christa Daryl (1992) *Televote: Expanding Citizen Participation in the Quantum Age*, New York: Praeger.

Small, Meredith F. (1998) *Our Babies, Ourselves*, New York: Anchor Press.

Smith, Bruce D. (ed.) (1990) *The Mississippian Emergence*, Washington D.C.: Smithsonian Institution Press.

Smith, Edward E. and John Jonides (1999) "Storage and Executive Processes in the Frontal Lobes," *Science* 283: 1657–61.

Smith, Gregory A. (1992) *Education and the Environment: Learning to Live with Limits*, Albany, NY: SUNY Press.

Smith, Gregory A. (1993) *Public Schools That Work: Creating Community*, London/New York: Routledge.

Smith, Huston (1958) *The Religions of Man*, New York: Harper & Row.

Sober, Elliott and David Sloan Wilson (1998) *Unto Others: The Evolution and Psychology of Unselfish Behavior*, Cambridge, MA: Harvard University Press.

Söderbaum, Peter (2000) *Ecological Economics*, London: Earthscan.

Solomon, Anne (1996) "Rock Art in Southern Africa," *Scientific American*, November: 106–11.

Somé, Malidoma Patrice (1994) *Of Water and the Spirit: Ritual, Magic and Initiation in the Life of an African Shaman*, New York: Tarcher/Putnam.

Somé, Malidoma Patrice (1997) *Ritual: Power, Healing, and Community*, New York: Penguin/Putnam; first published, 1993, Swan Raven.

Somé, Sobonfu (1997) "Wisdom from West Africa," San Francisco: New Dimensions Tape #2674.

Somé, Sobonfu (2000) *The Spirit of Intimacy: Ancient Teachings in the Ways of Relations*, Fairfield, NJ: William Morrow.

Spretnak, Charlene (1984) *Lost Goddesses of Early Greece: A Collection of Pre-Hellenic Myths*, Boston: Beacon Press.

Standlea, David M. (1998) "The Buddhist World View and Environmental Ethics," Master's Thesis, San Diego State University, CA.

Stanford, Craig B. (2000) "The Brutal Ape vs the Sexy Ape?" *American Scientist* 88 (March/April): 110–12.

Stanley, Steven (1996) *Children of the Ice Age*, New York: Harmony Press.

Stapp, Henry P. (1993) *Mind, Matter and Quantum Mechanics*, Berlin: Springer-Verlag.

Staub, Ervin (1999) "The Origins and Prevention of Genocide, Mass Killing and Other Collective Violence," *Peace and Conflict* 5: 303–36.

Staub, Ervin (2000) "Genocide and Mass Killing: Origins, Prevention, Healing and Reconciliation," *Political Psychology* 21(2): 367–82.

Stavrianos, Leften S. (1975) *The Promise of the Coming Dark Ages*, San Francisco: W.H. Freeman.

Stavrianos, Leften S. (1981) *Global Rift: The Third World Comes of Age*, New York: William Morrow.

Stavrianos, Leften S. (1999) *A Global History: From Prehistory to the 21st Century*, 7th edn., Upper Saddle River, NJ: Prentice Hall.

Stokstad, Erik (2000) " 'Pre-Clovis' Site Fights for Recognition," *Science* 288: 247.

Stone, Merlin (1976) *When God Was a Woman*, New York: Barnes & Noble.

Streeck-Fischer, Annette (1999) "Naziskins in Germany: Traumatizations in the Past and Present," *Mind and Human Interaction*, 10(2): 84–97.

Strohman, Richard (1997) "The Coming Kuhnian Revolution in Biology," *Nature Biotechnology* 15: 194–200.

Struck, Doug (2000) "Japanese army's sex slaves vent their anger in Tokyo," *Guardian Weekly*, December 20.

Strum, Shirley (1987) *Almost Human: A Journey into the World of Baboons*, New York: Random House.

Strum, Shirley, Deborah Forster, and Edwin Hutchins (1997) "Why Machiavellian Intelligence May Not Be Machiavellian," in Richard W. Byrne and Andrew Whiten (eds.), *Machiavellian Intelligence II*, Cambridge, UK: Cambridge University Press, 50–85.

Strum, Shirley and William Mitchell (1987) "Baboon Models and Muddles," in Warren G. Kinzey (ed.), 87–104.

Sugiyama, Yukimaru (1967) "Social Organization of Hanuman Langurs," in S.A. Altman (ed.), *Social Communication among Primates*, Chicago: University of Chicago Press.

Sulloway, Frank (1979) *Freud: Biologist of the Mind*, New York: Basic Books.

Swenson, William, David Sloan Wilson, and Roberta Elias (2002) "Artificial Ecosystem Selection," *Proceedings of the National Academy of Sciences* 97: 9110–14.

Swick, Diane and Robert T. Knight (1998) "Cortical Lesions and Attention," in R. Parasuraman (ed.) (1998), *The Attentive Brain*, Cambridge, MA: Massachusetts Institute of Technology, Chapter 8, 143–62.

Swisher, Carl C., III, Jose M. Grajales-Nishimura, A. Montanari, S.V. Margolis, P. Claeys, W. Alvarez, P. Renne, E. Cedilln-Pardo, F.J.-M.R. Maurrasse, G.H. Curtis, J. Smit, and M.O. McWilliams (1992) "Coeval $^{40}$Ar/$^{39}$Ar Ages of 65.0 Million Years Ago from Chicxulub Crater Melt Rock and Cretaceous-Tertiary Boundary Tektites," *Science* 287: 1954–8.

Tainter, Joseph (1988) *The Collapse of Great Civilizations*, Cambridge, UK: Cambridge University Press.

Taylor, Charles (1985) *Philosophy and the Human Sciences*, Cambridge UK: Cambridge University Press.

Taylor, Charles (1998) "Foreword" to Marcel Gauchet. (See entry under Gauchet, 1998).

Taylour, William (1970) "New Light on Mycenaean Religion," *Antiquity* 44: 270–9.

Teicher, Martin H. (2001) "Scars that Won't Heal: The Neurobiology of Child Abuse," *Scientific American*, March: 68–75.

Thomas, W.L., Jr. (ed.) (1956) *Man's Role in Changing the Face of the Earth*, Chicago: University of Chicago Press.

Thompson, D'Arcy Wentworth (1917) *On Growth and Form*, Cambridge, UK: Cambridge University Press.

Thompson, John N. (1999) "The Evolution of Species Interactions," *Science* 284: 2116–18.

Thorne, Alan G. and Milford H. Wolpoff (1992) "The Multiregional Evolution of Humans," *Scientific American*, April: 76–83.

Thorne, Alan G., Rainer Grün, Graham Mortimer, Nigel A. Spooner, John J. Simpson, Malcolm McCulloch, Lois Taylor, and Darren Curnoe (1999) "Australia's oldest human remains: age of Lake Mungo 3 Skeleton," *Journal of Human Evolution* 56: 591–612.

Thornhill, Randy and Craig T. Palmer (2000) *A Natural History of Rape*, Cambridge, MA: Massachusetts Institute of Technology Press.

Tierney, Patrick (2000) *Darkness in El Dorado: How Scientists and Journalists Devastated the Amazon*, New York: W.W. Norton.

Tolbert, Kathryn (1999) "Japanese mother kills toddler over school admission," *Santa Rosa, CA, Press Democrat*, November 27: A4.

Tong, Rosemarie (1997) *Feminist Approaches to Bioethics*, Boulder, CO: Westview Press.

Tononi, Giulio and Gerald M. Edelman (1998) "Consciousness and Complexity," *Science* 282: 1846–51.

Tottier, Yvon and Jean Louis Mandel (2001) "Huntingtin – Profit and Loss," *Science* 293: 445–6.

Toynbee, Polly (1999) "Better luck next century," *Guardian Weekly*, December 22: 11.

Tramo, Mark Jude (2001) "Music of the Hemispheres," *Science* 291: 54–6.

Treffert, Darold A. and Gregory L. Wallace (2002) "Islands of Genius," *Scientific American*, June: 76–85.

Tremlett, Giles (2001) "Lisbon takes drug use off the charge sheet," *Guardian Weekly*, August 1: 5.

Trivers, R.L. (1971) "The Evolution of Reciprocal Altruism," *Quarterly Review of Biology* 46: 35–57.

Tuchman, Barbara (1984) *The March of Folly*, New York: Alfred A. Knopf.

Tudge, Robin (2001) "Grass is greener on other side of the Great Wall," *Guardian Weekly*, February 7: 20.

Turner, B.L., II, W.C. Clark, R.W. Kates, J.F. Richards, J.T. Mathews, and W.B. Meyer (eds.) (1990) *The Earth as Transformed by Human Action*, Cambridge, UK: Cambridge University Press.

Tutu, Desmond Mpilo (1999) *No Future Without Forgiveness*, New York: Doubleday/Random House.

Ulrich, Roger S. (1984) "View Through a Window May Influence Recovery from Surgery," *Science* 224: 420–1.

UNICEF (1987) *Children on the Frontline. The Impact of Apartheid, Destabilization and Warfare on Children in Southern and South Africa*, Geneva: UNICEF.

Vallee, Bert L. (1998) "Alcohol in the Western World," *Scientific American*, June: 80–5.

Van der Kolk, Bessel A. (1996) "The Body Keeps the Score: Approaches to the Psychobiology of Posttraumatic Stress Disorder," in Bessel A. van der Kolk, Alexander C. McFarlane, and Lars Weisaeth (eds.) *Traumatic Stress: The Effects of Overwhelming Experience on Mind, Body, and Society*, New York: Guilford Press, Chapter 10.

Van der Merwe, Hugo (1999) "The Truth and Reconciliation Commission and Community Reconciliation: An Analysis of Competing Strategies and Conceptualizations," Doctoral Thesis in Conflict Resolution, George Mason University, Fairfax, VA.

Vendantam, Shankar (2002) "Pills overtake therapy as favored treatment for depressed," *Guardian Weekly* January 23: 33.

Venkateswar, Sita (1999) "The Adaman Islanders," *Scientific American*, May: 80–8.

Venter, J. Craig and 273 others (2001) "The Sequence of the Human Genome," *Science* 291: 1304–51.

Vidal, John (2000) "Tide may have turned after years of ecological decline," *Guardian Weekly*, December 13: 12.

Violas, P.C. (1978) *The Training of the Urban Working Class: A History of Twentieth Century American Education*, Chicago: Rand McNally.

Vogel, Gretchen (1999) "Chimps in the Wild Show Stirrings of Culture," *Science* 284: 2070–3.

Volkan, Vamik (2000) "The Tree Model: A Comprehensive Psychopolitical Approach to Unofficial Diplomacy and the Reduction of Ethnic Tension," *Mind and Human Interaction*, 10(3): 142–210.

Vulliamy, Ed (2000) "In the dark heart of small town America: a six-year-old boy shoots one of his classmates dead. Who is to blame?," *Guardian Weekly*, March 5: 6.

Wachtel, Paul (1983) *The Poverty of Affluence*, New York: The Free Press.

Wallace, Harvey (1999) *Family Violence: Legal, Medical and Social Perspectives*, Boston: Allyn & Bacon.

Watts, Jonathan (1999) "Girl, 2, strangled by school rival's mother," *Guardian Weekly*, December 8: 3.

Wawrytko, Sandra A. (2000) "Prudery and Prurience: Historical Roots of the Confucian Conundrum Concerning Women, Sexuality, and Power," in Chenyang Li (ed.), *The Sage and the Second Sex: Confucianism, Ethics, and Gender*, Chicago: Open Court Press, 163–97.

*Weekend Edition* (2000) "Reconstructing Minority Youth's Outlook," Washington D.C.: National Public Radio, June 11.

Weiss, Joseph (1990) "Unconscious Mental Functioning," *Scientific American* 262(3): 74–81.

Welker, Robert (1992) *The Teacher as Expert: A Theoretical and Historical Examination*, Albany, NY: SUNY Press.

Wessells, Mike (1997) "Child Soldiers," *The Bulletin of the Atomic Scientists*, November/December: 32–9.

Whitehead, Alfred North (1946) *Science in the Modern World*, New York: Macmillan.

Whiten, Andrew and Christophe Boesch (2001) "The Cultures of Chimpanzees," *Scientific American*, January: 61–7.

Whitlock, Ralph (1993) *Guardian Weekly*, September 19: 30; November 21: 30.

Whyte, William F. and Kathleen K. Whyte (1991) *Making Mondragon*, 2nd edn., Ithaca, NY: ILR Press, Cornell.

Wickelgren, Ingrid (1998) "The Cerebellum: The Brain's Engine of Agility," *Science* 281: 1588–90.

Wiggins, J.S. (1991) "Agency and Communion as Conceptual Coordinates for the Understanding and Measurement of Interpersonal Behavior," in D. Cicchetti and W. Grove (eds.), *Thinking Clearly about Psychology: Essays in Honor of Paul E. Meehl*, Minneapolis: University of Minnesota Press, Vol. 2: 89–113.

Wigginton, Eliot (1985) *Sometimes a Shining Moment*, Garden City, NY: Anchor Press/Doubleday.

Wigginton, Eliot (ed.) (1991) *Foxfire: 25 Years*, Garden City, NY Anchor Press/Doubleday.

Wilkinson, Richard G. (1994) *Unfair Shares: The Effects of Widening Income Differences on the Welfare of the Young*, Ilford, Essex: Barnardo's Publications.

Williams, Christopher (1997) *Terminus Brain: The Environmental Threats to Human Intelligence*, London: Cassell.

Williams, Daniel (2000) "Russian women fill void left by alcoholic men," *Guardian Weekly*, July 5: 33.

Williams, Terry Tempest (1991) *Refuge: An Unnatural History of Family and Place*, New York: Vintage.

Willis, Roy (1989) "The 'Peace Puzzle' in Upifa," in Signe Howell and Roy Willis (eds.), Chapter 7.

Wills, Christopher (1993) *The Runaway Brain: The Evolution of Human Uniqueness*, New York: Basic Books.

Wilshire, Bruce (2001) "Music, the Body, and Healing," in S. Kay Toombs (ed.), *Handbook of Phenomenology and Medicine*, Dordrecht/Boston: Kluwer Academic Publishers pp. 215–25.

Wilshire, Donna (1994) *Virgin, Mother, Crone: Myths and Mysteries of the Triple Goddess*, Rochester, VT: Inner Traditions.

Wilson, Allan C. and Rebecca L. Cann (1992) "The Recent African Genesis of Humans," *Scientific American*, April: 69–73.

Wilson, David Sloan (1975) "A Theory of Group Selection," *Proceedings of the National Academy of Sciences* 72: 143–6.

Wilson, David Sloan (1977) "Structured Demes and the Evolution of Group Advantageous Traits," *American Naturalist* 111: 157–85.

Wilson, David Sloan and Elliott Sober (1994) "Reintroducing Group Selection to the Human Behavioral Sciences," *Behavioral and Brain Sciences* 17: 585–654.

Wilson, Edward O. (1975) *Sociobiology: The New Synthesis*, Cambridge, MA: Belknap/Harvard University Press.

Wilson, Edward O. (1998) *Consilience: The Unity of Knowledge*, New York: Knopf.

Winterhalder, Bruce (1995) "Tracking the Hunting Hypothesis," *American Scientist*, 83(2) (March/April): 181–3.

Wolin, Sheldon (1996) "Democracy & Counterrevolution," *The Nation*, April 22: 22–4.

Wolpoff, Milford H. (1996) *Human Paleontology*, 2nd edn., New York: McGraw Hill.

Wolpoff, Milford H. and Rachel Caspari (1997) *Race and Human Evolution*, New York: Simon & Schuster.

Wolpoff, Milford H., A.G. Thorne, J. Jelinek, and Zhang Yinyun (1993) "The Case for Sinking *Homo erectus*: 100 Years of *Pithecanthropus* is Enough!," in J.L. Franzen (ed.), *100 Years of Pithecanthropus: The Homo erectus Problem*, Courier Forschungsinstitut Senckenberg 171: 341–61.

Wolpoff, Milford H., John Hawks, David W. Frayer, and Keith Humley (2001) "Modern Human Ancestry at the Peripheries: A Test of the Replacement Theory," *Science* 291: 293–7.

Wong, Kate (2000) "Paleoanthropology Migration: Global Positioning," *Scientific American*, August: 23.

Wong, Kate (2001) "Mammoth Kill," *Scientific American*, February: 22.

Wrangham, Richard and Dale Peterson (1996) *Demonic Males: Apes and the Origins of Human Violence*, Boston: Houghton Mifflin.

Wright, Karen (1997) "Babies, Bonds, and Brains," *Discover*, October: 74–8.

Wright, Robert (1994) *The Moral Animal*, New York: Vintage.

Young, J.Z. (1978) *Programs of the Brain*, Oxford: Oxford University Press.

Yusa, Michiko (1994) "Women in Shinto: Images Remembered," in Arvind Sharma (ed.), *Religion and Women*, Albany, NY: SUNY Press, 92–120.

Zimmer, Carl (2000) "In Search of Vertebrate Origins: Beyond Brain and Bone," *Science* 287: 1576–9.

Zuaccato, Chiara and 12 others (2001) "Loss of Huntington–Mediated BDNF Gene Transcription in Huntington's Disease," *Science* 293: 493–8.

Zuckerman, Solly (1932) *The Social Life of Monkeys and Apes*, London: Routledge & Kegan Paul; 2nd edition, 1981.

# INDEX

Note: in the following index, f means figure, t means table, and n means note, when occurring after page number. Also, as Chinese names are normally written with last name first and no comma they are entered in the Index in the same way they appear in the text. (Exception is Ho, Mai-Wan, who has adopted Western usage.)

complexity: confused with superiority 135; diminishing benefits of 27f7

composers, manic-depression in 201

computer-like brain programs, not present at birth 152

concentration camps: Boer war and 347; drunken guards at 322; not originally death camps 322

concrete projects, reconciliation through 370

concrete referents, metaphors as 179

confederations of tribes 385

conflict: addressing history of 368; between belief systems 236; between bonding and autonomy in primates 59; 130; caused by rigid meaning systems 64; cross-cultural misunderstandings in 5; need for new insights into 64; primitive solutions to 278–9; relationships and 278

conflict resolution: among primates 93; compassion and 342; dialogue essential for 367, 383; emotional outbursts and 369; as lengthy process 368; schools and 393, 394 synonyms for process of 449n61; teaching skills for 392; unveiling group identities during 369;

confrontational politics, as problem 395

Confucianism, as nontheistic religion 299

Congo: Belgian colonial atrocities and 327; as example of neocolonialism 326; paternalism toward 327; gorillas in 90; independence and consequences of 327, 328; tribal diversity in 330

Congo, Democratic Republic of: child-rearing in 211; conditions in 328; early history 328; first election in 329; huge size of 328

Congo tribes: egalitarian precolonial nature of 327; nature-based world view of 327

Congress Party, not powerful in Kerala 400

connectedness, as human need 190

Conroy, Glenn C. 421n9

conscience: dependence of on feelings 148; extended consciousness and 146

conscious attention: memory storage and 150; sequencing of 154

conscious awareness: of feelings by humans and 148; half-second lag in 152; hard to define 144; triggered by brain stem 133

conscious control, suppressed during stress 219

conscious meaning, as innate human need 130, 260

conscious memory, prefrontal cortex and 141

conscious self, not always in control 141–2

conscious thought: brainstem/limbic origins of 155; frontal lobe and 150; lags behind emergency action 152; linearity of 154; part of human nature 57

consciousness 144–58; accident or adaptation? 148–9; as awareness of own feelings 158; brain areas involved in 145; critical to all primates 146; diencephalon and loss of 155; emotional modulation of 148; as epiphenomenon 148; evolution of 147f3; hard to define 145; language not necessary for 146; levels of have fuzzy boundaries 144; levels of ignored by behavioral sciences 127; as minor aspect of brain function 62; needs stories 160; not evolutionarily recent 146; not scientific concept 144; physical nature of 140; Pleistocene origins of 161; prelinguistic arts and 174; present among all vertebrates 146; thalamus and 133; theories of 140; world views make sense of 190

consensual decision-making, fear of 384

conservative politicians, mental inflexibility of 314

Consilience 39

Constantine, Emperor 302t3

constraints of social life 231, 234

constructionists, defined 48

contact groups, implement reconciliation projects 370

contact signals used by primates 93

contemporary societies and curtailment of human needs 204

continental drift 81; and climate change 110

continental shelves, exposed during ice ages 114

contrasting visions of order 297t2

contrition, verbal expression of 130

control, strong democracy and 395

conversations without speech, affect signals and 169

cooperating groups: adaptive for sexual reproduction 77; selection for 240

cooperation: adaptiveness of 316; crucial in human evolution 102; essential for infant survival 130; imperative in ice ages 115; mutual self-interest of 397; supposed gene for 74; as un-Darwinian 70

cooperatives, worker-owned (see also worker-owned cooperatives) 398; Mondragon successes of 398–9

fundamental human needs, critical roles throughout life 209
fundamentalisms, as anti-rationality 272
fundamentalists, most not fanatics 270
fungicides, and brain development 215
fusioning of groups during Pleistocene 123
future, adaptation to 404
future societies, characteristics needed for survival 404
fuzzy boundaries of categories 177

Gabunia, Leo 423n26
Gaelic mouth-music 171
Gage, Fred H. 432n79
Gaia hypothesis 12
Gaia, goddess mother of Ouranos 294
Gajdusek, D.C. 422n17
galago, small brain of 136
Galbraith, John Kenneth 411n38
Galileo: quote from 53; world view change and 307
game theorists: humans as 8; primates as 65–97
game theory: applies Western behavior to evolution 70; assumes genes control behavior 72; assumes one-gene-caused traits 75; behavioral evolution and 70–1; fits stereotypical social behavior 71; genetic determinism and 67–80; inappropriateness of 72–6; not applicable to primate behaviors 71; not needed to explain social life 80; useless to peacemaking 370
game-theory models of communities 397
Gandhi, Indira 400
Gandhi, Mohandas K. 61, 445n10–11; on civilization 296; on face-to-face violence 249; "land to the tiller" and 400; as leader 354; pathway to *ahimsa* of 344; *Satyagraha* and 345; twentieth-century role of 310;
Gangadharan, A. 453n60
Gans, Curtis 25, 412n55
Garbarino, James 24–5, 411n54
Gardner, Gary 413n73
Gardner, Howard 429n12, 452n43; on multiple intelligences 201
Gates, Jeff 453n54; on alternatives to capitalism 397
gatherings, nature of early human 174
Gatto, John Taylor 451n20; says schools omit critical thinking 386

Gauchet, Marcel 297, 440n75,78, 441n7; disavowal of major religions by 296; on impact of hierarchies on humans 295
Gault, Robert 450n1
Gazzaniga, Michael 425n3, 426n18, 427n48; on emotions of risk-taking 127
GDP (*see also* Gross Domestic Product) 312; counts disaster as a gain 314
Gee, James Paul 427n10–11
Geertz, Clifford 432n8, 435n3; on cross-cultural understanding 181; wisdom of 429n45
Gehring, Walter J. 418n20, 426n21
Gelbspan, Ross 30, 412n60, 440n1
Gell-Mann, Murray 14, 409n12
Gender Commission of TRC, findings 353
gender and intelligence, MacLean's theories of 135
gender distinctions in herding societies 284
gender identities, cultural differences in 284
gender oppression in India 255
gender relations, in Goddess cultures 292
gene distributions: as keys to human history 116–20
gene function, depends on context 72
gene loss, frequent in small populations 117
gene studies of populations, as uncertain 118
gene theory, not a paradigm of life 68
genes: cooperative as dangerous to survival 70; eliminated by chance during Pleistocene 118; functions vary with location in genome 73; intelligence and 201; levels of fitness of 76, 79; modern human mostly from Africa 118; mental abnormalities and 201; multiple functions of 75; naked as functionless 73; need of for living cell to create organism 73; non-deterministic nature of 72; not always expressed 72; not in control of life 73; Pleistocene migrations and 242; sexual dimorphism and 239; as sole causes of problem behavior 200; structure of 67; as ultimate description of life 68
genes, behavior and intelligence 200–2
genes vs context 87–8
Genesis, and origins of human awareness 144
genetic bottlenecks: caused by catastrophes 115; common in Pleistocene 117; explanation of 117–18
genetic determinism: game theory and 67–80; incorrectness of 74; as linear thinking 68

homicide: as cultural act, not genetically driven 106; high American rates of 17
hominid ancestors: individual intelligence in 167; not killers, but prey 103
hominid behavior, little evidence about 100
hominid brain: evolution of 129–31; flexible behavior and 129; not as unique as thought 129
hominid evolution: food scarcity as driving force 101; early theories 101; inclusive, revised theory 103
hominid extinctions, not caused by modern humans 116
hominid/chimpanzee divergence 101
hominids, continuous female receptivity of 240; definition of 101; evolve group intelligence 167; failure to adapt causes extinctions 101; no paleontological evidence of warlikeness 106; two evolutionary bushes of 101
*Homo* bush 101, 108f2
*Homo erectus*: aesthetic sense in 173; Asian fossils of resemble modern humans 119; capable of mime 161, 168, 174; changes in tools of 139; cortex enlarged in 129; dispersal of soon after evolving 111; facial expressions of 169; followed migrating animals 113; forms of communication in 173; global genetic network of 119; *Homo sapiens* nonviolent toward 116, 123; local traits of passed to modern humans 112; long-term survival of 111; migrations of 111, 112, 113; prolonged survival of 112; schema formation in 167; skulls of similar to Aborigines 119; subject to genetic bottlenecks 118; symbolic communication in 169; tools of 111; widespread distribution of 106
*Homo habilis*, Wernicke's area in 175
*Homo sapiens* (*see also* modern humans) 1, 113; about to experience climate change 107; early social life of 205; female migrations of 242; first big game hunters 104; impact on planet of 14; migrations of 113; multiregional evolution of 112; net-hunting more important than big game 104; nonviolence toward *Homo erectus* of 123; origin of cultural differences in 174; origins of 113; pair bonds and 42; preceded by earlier *Homo* species 99; preceded by *Homo erectus* 106; subject to genetic bottlenecks 118

*Homo* species 108f2; first sign of brain enlargement in 104; only hominid to leave Africa 111; uncertainties about 112
homosexuals: as social threats 200; valued as uniquely gifted 200
honeybees, stereotypical behaviors of 157
Hopfield, J.J. 426n31; "awareness" not a scientific concept 144
Hopi: male shamans in 245; motifs of 183f2; relaxed marriage rules of 244
Horai, H. 424n36
hormonally active agents, cause multiple diseases 35
hormones: binding of in hypothalamus 133; mimic effects of stress 221; release of in response to feelings 156; sexual dimorphism and 239
horses, taming of 288
Hou Yamei 423n27
Howell, Signe 61, 416n34
Hox genes 416n8
HPA-axis: as central endocrine network 217; stress and 218f3; stress response of inhibited by love 221
Hrdy, Sarah Blaffer 421n4, 424n49
Hubbert, M. King 27, 412n57; graph of fossil fuel consumption 29f8
Hughes, Howard, despair caused by separation 233
human acts, not valued unless paid for 312
human ancestors, foraged over large areas 113
human autonomy, over-emphasized in West 283
human baby, atricial state of 194
human behavior: assumed to follow simple rules 66; flexibility of 196; reductionist analysis of 181; shaped by world view 11; speculation about evolution of 47
human beings: adapt by "changing their minds" 54; capable of moral extremes 61; how alike are we? 181; internal conflicts of 340; limited adaptability of 377; most lack power today 382; not born killers 249; predisposition for meaning 61; resist believing others' suffering 335; as servants of Gross National Product 386; technological control of 311
human blood types 418n23
human brain: anatomy of 132f1; built-in problems of 125; conditions for healthy development of 213 emotional and cognitive connections in 155–6, 216;

violent outbursts, in stressed males 246
Virginia, site of 18,000 ya settlement 113
virtual reality 26f6: absence of physical
    contacts in 19; schooling as 387
visions and fears, unveiling of 369
visual lobe of cortex 132f1, 142
Vlakplas Five 352
Vogel, Gretchen 425n56
voice box, evolution of 170
Volkan, Vamik 449n61–2,64–5,67–8;
    Estonian project of 371; post-conflict
    healing and 368
volunteers, over-stressed in South Africa 363
voodoo, power of based on belief 226
Voorhies, Barbara 434n49
Vrba, Elizabeth S. 426n24
Vulliamy, Ed 443n55
Vygotsky, Lev S., on social context of mind
    209

Wachtel, Paul 22, 411n38,39
Waco, Texas 447n46
Wake, Warren K. 452n43
Walker, Alan 109f2
Wallace, Alfred Russel, and theory of
    evolution 46
Wallace, Gregory 430n15
Wallace, Harvey 410n18
Wandering God 161
Waorani 437n41; beliefs of 282; conversion of
    281; defense of lands by 280; extreme
    autonomy of 282; fear of witchcraft among
    283; foreign diseases and 280; "fierceness"
    myth 282; simple world view of 282; slave
    trade and 280; studies of violence in
    279–84 passim; trapped in vengeance 281;
    violence not due to scarcity 280
war: children and 333–5; as intercultural
    phenomenon 293; as stressor 214
war crimes, punishment not effective justice
    361
War of Independence, as United States' glory
    369
War on Terrorism, state army in 334
war-crime tribunals, incomplete healing of
    449n63
warfare, unlikely in mimetic world 174
war-making: assumed relationship to hunting
    105–7; no innate basis of 106, 107
war-torn countries: ubiquity of trauma in
    335
warmer periods, length of most recent 110

warming and cooling cycles, not well
    understood 110
warning calls in birds, gene for 75, 79
Warren, Edward 429n43; on translating
    Greek philosophy 180
wars: as cause of trauma 224; recent changes
    in 333; twentieth century worst for 310
Washburn, Sherwood 84
Washington, George, as sacred symbol 236
Wasserman, Harvey 412n59
water scarcity, as cause of future migrations 31
Watson, Greg 454n62
Watts, Jonathan 451n14
Wawrytko, Sandra 440n72
weak democracy, claimed as inevitable 388
wealthy, as social benefactors 309
Wegner, Daniel M. 427n41
"wee folk", prized as oral historians 201
Weimar Republic, collapse of 321
Weiss, Joseph 426n29; on functions of
    unconscious mind 143
Welker, Robert 451n36
well-being, restoration after injustice 362
Wernicke's area, and symbolic language 175
Wessells, Mike 431n61, 444n63
West Nile virus, transferred to New York 32
Western conflict resolvers, emphasize role of
    dialogue 366
Western culture 16; absence of ubuntu in
    344; assumes universal intolerance of
    "other" 384; confrontational politics of
    366; dangers of too rapid change in 377;
    dismisses other world views 379;
    encourages antisocial behavior 94; giant
    institutions thwart human needs 213;
    ignores needs for bonding and meaning
    382; as imperfect model for humankind
    259; lacks spiritual content 310; loss of
    deep dialogue in 365; politics of
    childhood in 193; post-colonial resistance
    to 326; punishment oriented 361; sees
    communities as interest groups 397;
    social order depends on fear 358;
    weakness of meaning system 236
Western democracies, limited choices in 316
Western navigation 186
Western world view: changing horizons of
    374; held as sacred 379; imposed on
    former colonies 337; inimical to human
    nature 35, 263, 381; minimizes need for
    shared meaning 189, 190; as obstacle to
    dialogue 379; overpragmatized 190;
    pathological nature of 376; pits freedom